HISTORY OF THE LABOR MOVEMENT
IN THE UNITED STATES
VOLUME I

HISTORY OF
THE LABOR MOVEMENT
IN THE UNITED STATES

VOLUME I: *From Colonial Times to the*
Founding of the American Federation of Labor

BY PHILIP S. FONER

INTERNATIONAL PUBLISHERS, NEW YORK

To Roslyn

For this edition, the author has added
notes on pages 142, 432 and 474.

Fourth Printing, 1972
(*See Errata, page 568*)

COPYRIGHT, 1947, BY

INTERNATIONAL PUBLISHERS CO., INC.

Library of Congress Catalogue Card Number: 47–19381

ISBN (cloth) 0–7178–0089–x; (paperback) 0–7178–0376–7

PRINTED IN THE UNITED STATES OF AMERICA

CONTENTS

PREFACE   9

1. LABOR COMES TO AMERICA.   13
Labor Conditions in Europe, 14 ... Getting to America, 17.

2. LABOR IN COLONIAL AMERICA   19
Slaves and Indentured Servants, 19 ... Emergence of Wage Earners,
22 ... Labor Conditions and Organizations, 24 ... Struggles for Democracy, 28.

3. LABOR AND THE AMERICAN REVOLUTION   32
Background for Revolution, 32 ... The Sons of Liberty, 34 ... Po-
litical Action, 37 ... The Road to Independence, 40 ... The War for
Independence, 43 ... Victory, 46.

4. AMERICAN INDUSTRIAL DEVELOPMENT, 1783-1880   48
Obstacles to Industrial Growth, 48 ... Role of Transportation, 52 ...
Rise of the Factory System, 53 ... Industrial Expansion on the Eve
of the Civil War, 55 ... Industrial Growth During the Civil War,
58 ... Industrial Expansion After the Civil War, 60 ... Trends Toward Monopoly, 60 ... Crises, and Labor's Answers, 62.

5. EARLY TRADE UNIONS   65
Labor Conditions in Post-Revolutionary America, 65 ... The Merchant
Capitalist Enters, 67 ... Temporary Labor Associations, 69 ... The
First Trade Unions, 70 ... Union Policies and Practices, 72 ...
Labor and the Courts, 77.

6. LABOR AND JEFFERSONIAN DEMOCRACY   82
Sources of Jeffersonian Democracy, 82 ... The Democratic-Republican
Societies, 85 ... The Federalist Counter-Offensive, 87 ... The Tri-
umph of Jeffersonianism, 89 ... Labor and the Embargo, 91 ...
Labor and the War of 1812, 93 ... Extension of Democracy, 95.

7. TRADE UNIONISM AND LABOR STRUGGLES, 1819-1837   97

Labor Conditions, 97 ... Labor's Awakening, 101 ... City Centrals, 112 ... National Labor Organization, 113 ... The Ten-Hour Day, 115 ... Labor and the Public, 118.

8. EARLY LABOR PARTIES   121

The Political Awakening, 122 ... The Workingmen's Program, 123 ... Philadelphia, 127 ... New York, 130 ... New England, 140 ... Decline and Disappearance, 140 ... Achievements, 141.

9. LABOR AND JACKSONIAN DEMOCRACY   143

Labor's Estimate of Jackson, 143 ... The Bank War, 144 ... Labor's Role in New York, 149 ... Rise of the Loco-Focos, 153 ... Loco-Focoism Spreads, 159 ... Achievements of the Loco-Focos, 162.

10. THE ERA OF UTOPIANISM   167

Decline of the Trade Unions, 167 ... Spread of Machinery, 168 ... Credo of the Utopians, 170 ... Owenism, 173 ... Fourierism, 174 ... Producers' Co-operatives, 178 ... Consumers' Co-operatives, 181 ... Land Reform, 183 ... Utopian Reformers and Trade Unionism, 188.

11. THE TEN-HOUR MOVEMENT, 1840-1860   191

The Revival of Trade Unionism, 192 ... Factory Workers and the Labor Movement, 192 ... The Ten-Hour Philosophy, 199 ... New England Workingmen's Association, 202 ... Ten-Hour Strikes, 207. ... Ten-Hour Laws, 210 ... Decline in New England, 211 ... Upsurge in Pennsylvania, 212 ... Activity in the 'Fifties, 213 ... Political Action in New Jersey, 216 ... Results of the Ten-Hour Movement, 217.

12. TRADE UNIONS AND LABOR STRUGGLES IN THE FIFTIES   219

Labor Conditions, 219 ... Local Trade Unions, 220 ... Immigrant Labor, 224 ... English Influences, 227 ... The German-American Labor Movement, 228 ... National Labor Organization, 234 ... Unemployment Demonstrations, 237 ... Revival of Unionism, 240 ... New England Shoemakers' Strike, 241 ... Labor and Politics, 245.

13. **LABOR IN THE ANTE-BELLUM SOUTH**   249
Slavery, 250 ... Resistance, 252 ... White Workers and Slavery, 258
... Slavery's Dilemma, 264.

14. **NORTHERN LABOR AND SLAVERY**   266
Uncertainties, 267 ... Labor and the Abolitionists, 270 ... Wage
Slavery and Chattel Slavery, 272 ... Impact of Slavery Extension,
276 ... The Slaveholders' Program, 280 ... Emergence of the Republican Party, 282 ... Election of 1856, 286 ... Fighting Republican
Conservatism, 288 ... Lincoln and Labor, 291 ... Election of 1860,
293.

15. **LABOR AND THE CIVIL WAR**   297
Labor and the Secession Crisis, 298 ... To Arms!, 306 ... Fighting
for What?, 310 ... English Workers and the Civil War, 312 ... Contributions of Negro Workers, 317.

16. **LABOR AND THE COPPERHEADS**   321
Labor and the Draft, 321 ... Copperhead Propaganda, 324 ... War-
time Contrasts, 325 ... Wartime strikes, 327 ... Failure of the
Copperhead Campaign, 329 ... Labor Turns to Lincoln, 331 ... Role
of the Labor Press, 333 ... Workingmen's Democratic-Republican
Association, 335 ... Victory, 336.

17. **THE LABOR MOVEMENT 1861-1866**   338
Causes of Trade Union Revival, 338 ... Women Workers, 341 ...
More and Bigger Unions, 344 ... The Molders, 346 ... The Labor
Press, 349 ... The Employers' Counterattack, 352 ... Labor Tightens
Its Ranks, 355 ... Political Action, 357 ... A National Perspective,
359 ... Towards an Eight-Hour Day, 363.

18. **THE LABOR MOVEMENT 1866-1872**   370
Founding the National Labor Union, 370 ... The First Congress, 371
... Strengthening the National Labor Union, 375 ... The Eight-Hour
Day, 377 ... Women Workers and Woman's Rights, 382.

19. **THE LABOR MOVEMENT 1866-1872** (*continued*)   389
Labor and Reconstruction, 389 ... Organization of Negro Workers,

395 ... Negro Labor Conventions of 1869, 402 ... The National Colored Labor Union, 403.

20. **THE LABOR MOVEMENT 1866-1872** (*concluded*) 409
International Labor Unity, 409 ... The First International in America, 413 ... The Co-operative Movement, 417 ... Monetary Reform, 420 ... Political Action, 423 ... Decline of the National Labor Union, 429.

21. **THE BIRTH OF THE KNIGHTS OF LABOR** 433
Rituals of the Knights of Labor, 434 ... Role of Uriah S. Stephens, 435 ... Early Structure of the Knights of Labor, 437.

22. **THE LONG DEPRESSION 1873-1878** 439
Decline in Union Membership, 439 ... Persistence of Unionism, 440 ... Depression Living, 442 ... Unemployed Demonstrations, 445 ... Lassalleans and Marxists, 448 ... The Socialist Movement Unites, 450.

23. **CHALLENGING THE GREAT DEPRESSION** 454
Textile Strikes, 454 ... The Long Strike of 1875, 455 ... The Molly Maguires, 460 ... The Great Strikes of 1877, 464.

24. **INDEPENDENT POLITICAL ACTION, 1873-1878** 475
The Rise of Greenbackism, 475 ... Labor Parties and Greenbackism, 479 ... The National Greenback-Labor Party, 482 ... Chinese Exclusion, 488 ... Demagogy's Brief Sway in California, 489 ... The Socialist Movement, 493.

25. **BEGINNINGS OF THE MODERN LABOR MOVEMENT, 1878-1881** 497
Revival of Trade Unionism, 497 ... The International Labor Union, 500 ... The Knights of Labor, 504 ... The "New Unionism" of the 1870's, 512 ... The Cigar Makers, 514 ... The Federation of Organized Trades and Labor Unions, 518.

REFERENCE NOTES 525
BIOGRAPHICAL SKETCHES 560
INDEX 569

PREFACE

The study of the history of the labor movement in this country did not begin in earnest until the twentieth century. In 1886, when Professor Richard T. Ely, of Johns Hopkins University, later of the University of Wisconsin, published his *Labor Movement in America,* he admitted that he had only scratched the surface of his subject. "I offer this book merely as a sketch," he wrote in the preface, "which will, I trust, some day be followed by a book worthy of the title History of Labor in the New World." A year later, *The Labor Movement—The Problem of To-day,* edited by George E. McNeill, a prominent trade union leader during the post-Civil War era, came off the press. It contained an account of the history of the American labor movement from Colonial times to 1886, as well as special discussions of the histories of a number of trade unions. "The history that we present " wrote McNeill, "is the compilation of such facts as could be gathered from records of labor organizations, newspapers and pamphlets, and from the varied experiences of a large number of thinking men in all parts of the country."

Much more, however, could be gleaned from records of labor organizations, newspapers and pamphlets than appeared in McNeill's valuable volume. But first the formidable task of collecting this material had to be accomplished. A good deal was achieved by Professor Ely himself, who, in the course of two decades, gathered a vast collection of labor literature which was eventually turned over to the John Crerar Library of Chicago. The most significant work in labor research was conducted by Professor John R. Commons of the University of Wisconsin and his collaborators, Dr. John B. Andrews and Dr. Helen L. Sumner. Under the auspices of the American Bureau of Industrial Research, with headquarters in Madison, these scholars began early in the twentieth century, an exhaustive survey of libraries, bookshops, historical societies, and personal collections all over the country, to unearth pamphlets and files of newspapers which would throw light on the development of labor organizations in the United States. The survey produced an enormous collection of hitherto unknown sources of labor material, much of which was deposited in the Wisconsin State Historical Society. In 1910 about one-tenth of the material collected during the survey was published in the ten volumes of the *Documentary History of American Industrial Society,* thus making available for students a vast body of source material on the labor movement from 1820 to 1880.

9

Meanwhile, under the direction of Professor Commons, a number of his students (David J. Saposs, E. B. Mittleman, H. E. Hoagland and Selig Perlman) together with Helen L. Sumner and John B. Andrews, began the preparation of the first truly detailed history of the American labor movement. The first two volumes of the *History of Labor in the United States* by John R. Commons and Associates, covering the period from Colonial beginnings to 1896, appeared in 1918. A third volume by Don D. Lescohier and Elizabeth Brandeis, and a fourth volume by Selig Perlman and Philip Taft, bringing the story of the labor movement down to the 1930's, were published in 1935.

The work of John R. Commons and Associates, especially in the case of the earlier volumes, which broke virgin soil, was so exhaustive that for many years nearly all histories of the American labor movement were little more than generalized summarizations of what had been presented in detailed fashion in the *History of Labor in the United States*. But it has become clear that the time is ripe for a new study of the history of the labor movement in the United States. For one thing, an important body of literature dealing with American labor history, some of it in the form of memoirs penned by trade unionists, and much of it in the form of unpublished theses and dissertations in colleges and universities, has appeared since the publication of the earlier volumes of the *History of Labor in the United States*. This monographic material throws new light on the growth of the labor movement in specific periods and in special areas, and makes necessary a re-evaluation of conclusions reached in all previous writings on the subject. More important, however, is the growing realization that the work of John R. Commons and Associates, though containing much valuable material, suffers from certain distinct limitations. Recent events in the labor movement have only served to accentuate these limitations.

The Commons-Wisconsin school's pragmatic theory of the labor movement pervades every chapter of the volumes of the *History of Labor in the United States*. This school regards the labor movement as an experimental process of building unions and adapting their policy to "environment." Great stress is constantly placed upon the peculiarities of the American environment (absence of feudal restrictions, free land, class fluidity, democratic political institutions, etc.) which, it is argued, has prevented the American worker from becoming class conscious. Thus, whereas class consciousness served as the unifying principle of the labor movements of Europe, "job consciousness," according to the Commons-Wisconsin school, took its place in the labor movement in America. The only labor organizations, according to this school, which could survive in America were those which recognized this basic difference and made their organizations revolve about the individual worker's job. Others which preached principles of labor solidarity and common action, the unity of the skilled and unskilled in industrial unions, of the foreign born and native Americans, of Negro and white, of women and men, and dared to project issues other than the limited objective of wage and job control, went counter to the only acceptable "consciousness" for American labor as a whole and were doomed to failure. Then, too, labor history, said the Commons-Wisconsin school, had proved that the only wise political policy that should be pursued by American labor organizations was that of a non-partisan political policy. Labor's efforts in the past to engage in independent political action, in the eyes of the Commons-Wisconsin school, always ended in failure and always seriously weakened the trade unions. The American Federation of Labor under the leadership of Samuel Gompers became for this school the supreme demonstration of correct policies to be pursued by the American labor movement, and the volumes of the *History of Labor in the United States* became in effect an apologia of Gompersism—craft unionism, no politics in the unions, and community of interest between labor and capital.

Even while this theory of American labor history was being formulated, life itself was demonstrating the divergence of interest in the fundamental relationship between labor and capital and was disproving the thesis set down by the Commons-Wisconsin school. Recent events have completely exploded this analysis of the history of the American labor movement. The rise of the Congress of Industrial Organizations, the organization of the mass production industries through the medium of industrial unionism, the effective unity established in recent struggles between Negro and white workers, and the great influence exerted by the labor movement in the political arena since 1935 and in the world-wide struggle against fascism, not only indicate how the Commons-Wisconsin school miscalculated regarding the policies the labor movement had to adopt to achieve success, but they also show that precisely those policies hailed by this school had to be abandoned if the task of organizing the great mass of American workers was to be accomplished.

A further important shortcoming of the work of John R. Commons and Associates as a history of American labor is that it does not deal with the labor movement in its larger economic, political and social setting. Recent studies have emphasized labor's contributions to the growth of American democracy, have demonstrated the need for qualifying and deepening our understanding of the role played by the frontier in shaping our democratic institutions, and have established that many of the decisive struggles in our history must be studied in terms of a class struggle rather than as a sectional struggle.

This volume undertakes to present a new interpretation of the history of the labor movement in the United States based upon manuscripts, newspapers, pamphlets and the existing monographic material in American history, economics and related subjects. It traces the growth of the labor movement from its origin to the founding of the American Federation of Labor in 1881. A subsequent volume, now in preparation, will carry the story to the recent period in labor history.

This history devotes considerable space to the growth of the trade unions, but it is not intended to be only a history of trade unionism in the United States. Special attention has been and will continue to be paid to the role of the working class in outstanding democratic and social struggles throughout the history of this country. Throughout our history, too, the working class, while concentrating on the struggle for immediate demands, searched for a more basic solution to the problems of poverty and insecurity. Many gravitated towards those who spoke and wrote of the need to abolish the wage system and to replace the present social order with a new and better system of society.

Out of the working class have come great heroes and heroines who have made notable contributions to our democracy. The story of these men and women has been left out of the history that has been handed down to us, but it has been told in detail in the present volume.

The writer has many indebtednesses to acknowledge for help in the preparation of this volume. Numerous libraries and historical societies have made available to me their collections of manuscripts, newspapers, pamphlets and published and unpublished monographic studies. I wish to take this opportunity to thank the staffs of the Wisconsin State Historical Society, the Library of Congress, the American Antiquarian Society, the New York Historical Society, the John Crerar Library of Chicago, the American Philosophical Society, the Library Company of Philadelphia, the Public Libraries of New York, Boston, Chicago, Buffalo, and Detroit, the libraries of the following colleges and universities: Wisconsin, Harvard, Southern California, New York, Tulane, North Carolina, Chicago, Syracuse, Rochester, Buffalo, Western Reserve, Yale, Princeton, Pennsylvania, Michigan, and Columbia. I also wish to thank Florence Thorne for permission to use the Samuel Gompers Letter-Books, and Agnes Inglis of the Labadie Collection of the University of Michigan Library who graciously supplied material from the Collection.

I am indebted to William Olsen of the Department of English of New York University who read the entire manuscript with painstaking care and offered valuable advice for improvement. Dr. Sidney Jackson, Dr. Claire Green, Mr. A. Landy, Mrs. Sophia Tevan and Elizabeth Lawson likewise read the complete manuscript. Their kindly criticism was very helpful. Dr. Henry David of Queens College read sections of the galley proofs, and made suggestions for which I am grateful.

The author, of course, is solely responsible for all errors that may occur in the book and for all opinions expressed in it.

PHILIP S. FONER

CHAPTER I

Labor Comes to America

Captain John Smith once wrote of Colonial America: "Nothing is to be expected thence but by labour." [1] This was by way of advice to English merchant capitalists, who looked forward to America as a source of great profits. They soon learned that Captain Smith was right—that in Virginia, Massachusetts, and Pennsylvania were no fabulous cities ripe for looting like those visited by Marco Polo. Whatever wealth there was in the new world would have to come from the hard labor of mining, cutting down forests, planting and harvesting crops, and constructing buildings, roads, and bridges. America would bring great profits, the Virginia Company wrote, in the winter of 1616-17, in a broadside to prospective investors, as soon as there were "more hands" in the new world to exploit its resources. [2]

But where would these hands come from? In America there were Indians who could be captured and sold as slaves. Unfortunately, the Indians were inclined to escape to their tribes and then return in increased numbers to pay their respects to their former masters by taking their scalps. Hence in New Amsterdam the government ordered all masters to pay Indian workers wages. This action, it assured employers, was necessary "for the timely and possible prevention of all mischief," because the Indians were threatening to "take their pay by resorting to other unbecoming means." Attempts to enslave the Indians proved unsuccessful. [3]

Employers increased their appeals to the colonizing companies in Europe for laborers, carefully specifying, however, that they needed, not gentlemen of taste and refinement who would rather "starve for hunger than lay their hands to labour," [4] but men and women who could build and maintain permanent and profitable settlements. The colonial financiers launched a vast propaganda campaign to induce the poor of Europe to emigrate to America. Leaflets and pamphlets informed laborers that

13

in America they could secure "three times the wages for their Labour they can in England or Wales," and that poor servant girls could obtain rich husbands. Agents traveled throughout poverty-stricken districts and enlarged on the glorious prospects in the New World. The Virginia Company even circulated a coin in 1630 bearing the following terse inscription:

In England land scarce and labour plenty,
In Virginia land free and labour scarce.[5]

To doubters came letters from the first settlers in America—many of them forged—urging relatives and friends to pack up their belongings and begin life anew. "If a workman will only work four or five days a week," wrote one correspondent, "he can live grandly." America was "a plentiful land, plentiful indeed." [6]

LABOR CONDITIONS IN EUROPE

A plentiful land! So too was England, but not for the common people. Feudalism was on its death bed in England. Although now and then it gave spasmodic evidence of vigor, it had been pretty thoroughly replaced by a capitalist economy. As the new economy advanced, it brought both important progressive changes and increased misery. The rapid rise of the woolen industry, for example, caused more and more land to be devoted to sheep-raising rather than to grain-growing. The land was enclosed, tenants were driven off to make room for sheep, and a few herders took the place of many farm laborers. The number of paupers who had neither land nor work increased rapidly, and their plight was aggravated by the dissolution of the monasteries, which deprived the poor of charitable aid.

Prices soared fourfold as a result of the influx of gold and silver from the New World. But wages, in 1600, it has been estimated, had but a fourth of the purchasing power they had had a century before.[7]

Wage rates remained practically stationary, and by the Statute of Apprentices enacted in 1563 anyone receiving wages above the maximum fixed in the law was sentenced to twenty-one days in prison; anyone paying such wages was sentenced to ten days. In the same act justices of the peace were empowered to modify fixed wages according to the time of the year and the price of goods. Since the justices were often employers they set wages at the lowest point, leaving it to the home parish to keep the laborers from starving to death. The parishes, however, contributed so little that many workers starved.[8]

In 1618, although the estimated lowest sum to maintain a family was £20, 11s, per year, wages for workingmen rarely rose above

£8, 8s, 9d. In 1623, the wool workers of Wiltshire complained that they were "not able by their diligent labours to get their livings, by reason that the clothiers at their will made the work extreme hard, and abated wages what they pleased...." About seven years later, textile workers in the eastern counties charged that their wages were lowered to such an extent that they were forced "to sell their beds, wheels, and working tools for want of bread...."[9]

As long as they remained in England the English workmen could do little to improve their living standards. They could not leave their work to seek more profitable employment, for under the Master and Servant Acts, a worker who left his job could be imprisoned for three months. He was haled before a justice of the peace, frequently the employer himself, and was not permitted to give evidence in his own behalf. A prison term, moreover, did not clear the worker of the fine he owed his employer for his absence. Repeated prison terms were sometimes meted out to workmen for the same breach of contract.[10]

Thus, although nominally free, many English workers lived in virtual slavery. And of none was this more true than of the miners in Scotland. In 1606 a Scottish law stated that a runaway coal miner was to be regarded as a common thief. Anyone guilty of harboring or employing him and failing to surrender him within twenty-four hours after notification would be fined one hundred pounds. By the same Act, complete authority was granted to mine owners "to apprehend all vagabonds and sturdy beggars" and force them to work in the mines on terms set by the owners themselves.[11]

To defend themselves, workers frequently tried to organize labor associations and on a number of occasions actually went out on strike. But each time the government moved swiftly to protect the interests of the employers. As early as 1349 a group of bakers' servants were indicted in London "for conspiring among themselves that they would not work for their masters except at double or treble the wages formerly given." In 1360 Parliament declared all alliances and associations of masons and carpenters null and void, stating that every "mason and carpenter of what condition that he be shall be compelled by his master to whom he serveth to do every work that to him pertaineth to do." Again in 1548 Parliament declared that any workmen who joined forces and announced that they would not work "but at a certain price and rate" and "at certain hours and times" would be punished:

"For the first offence ten pounds...or twenty days imprisonment and [he] shall have only bread and water; and for the second offence [he] shall forfeit twenty pounds...or suffer punishment at the pillory, and for the third offence shall forfeit thirty pounds...or shall sit on the pillory and lose one of his ears, and shall at all times after that be taken as a man infamous." [12]

In later years the severity of the punishment was somewhat mitigated, but at no time until the 1820's did the law favor attempts of the worker to improve his status. After an intensive study of six centuries of labor conditions in England, Professor Arnold T. Rogers concluded that from 1563 to 1824, a conspiracy, "concocted by the law and carried out by parties interested in its success," * was organized to "cheat the English workman, to tie him to the soil, to deprive him of hope, and to degrade him to irremediable poverty." [13]

The English ruling class could prevent workmen from organizing, but it could not halt demonstrations of protest. Riots of unemployed workers were so frequent in sixteenth-century England that the Venetian ambassador wrote home: "It is not certain where this disturbance will end, but things can not certainly go on thus." Many wealthy Englishmen shared his fears, and looked to the colonies to "drain from the Mother-Country the disaffected and the vicious." [14]

Elsewhere in Europe, too, the ruling classes were becoming uneasy, and they welcomed agents who came to boost the land of milk and honey across the ocean. Irish peasants and artisans were particularly receptive to this message, for British legislation had placed high tariffs upon Irish linen and cattle entering England, had deprived the entire Scotch-Irish population of self government, and forced them to pay tithes to the established church to which they did not belong. In Germany, too, peasants and artisans eagerly accepted the pamphlets distributed by William Penn who had visited the Rhine region in 1677 to recruit colonists. To read the contemporary accounts of terrific exploitation of German peasants and artisans by brutal landlords and princes, of the slaughter of hundreds of thousands of innocent people in the Thirty Years' War and in subsequent conflicts, is to understand why many were ready to follow Penn's advice.

In short, the poor of Europe came to America because they faced starvation and religious and political oppression at home. The story of the Scotsman, John McBeath, farmer and shoemaker by trade, father of five children, presents the underlying causes for emigration. McBeath told an officer who interviewed him on board ship that:

---

* As early as 1776, Adam Smith, commenting on this conspiracy, declared that whenever the government attempted "to regulate the differences between masters and their workmen, its counsellors are always the masters." "We have no acts of parliament against combining to lower the price of work," Smith added, "but many against combining to raise it." (*An Inquiry into the Nature and Causes of the Wealth of Nations*, London, 1845, p. 27.)

"[He had] left his own country because crops failed, he lost his cattle, the Rent of his Possession was raised, and bread had long been dear; he could get no Employment at home, whereby he could support himself and Family.... That he was encouraged to emigrate by the Accounts received from his own and his Wife's Friends already in America, assuring him that he would procure comfortable subsistence in that country for his Wife and Children, and that the price of labour was very high." [15]

GETTING TO AMERICA

But escape from the misery of Europe was not so simple as the propagandists had pictured it. The voyage from England cost from £6 to £10, an enormous sum for workers. And "our ancestors who migrated here," Thomas Jefferson once remarked, "were laborers not lawyers." [16]

To get to America most of these laborers bound themselves out for a period of years as indentured servants. They signed contracts with merchants and shipmasters in Europe to do "any work in which the employer shall employ them" for two to seven years in return for their passage. Some of these Redemptioners signed no indenture or contract in Europe, but were allowed a certain number of days after arriving in America in which to arrange payment for their passage. Most of them were led to believe that the planters and merchants in America would be only too willing to advance the cost of the passage, and that they could quickly repay them out of their earnings, and then go free. Many of them found their hopes "cruelly blasted" and "involved in all the complicated miseries of a tedious laborious and unprofitable service." [17]

All too often the emigrants were compelled to agree that surviving passengers would be responsible for the fares of those who died in passage. The voyage was so frightful that many did die. "There is on board these ships terrible misery," wrote Gottlieb Mittelberger who spoke from experience, "stench, fumes, horror, vomiting, many kinds of seasickness, fever, dysentery, headache, heat, constipation, boils, scurvy, cancer, mouthrot, and the like, all of which comes from old and sharply salted food and meat, also from very bad and foul water, so that many die miserably." Another survivor tells us: "To keep from starving we had to eat rats and mice. We paid from 8 pence to 2 shillings for a mouse, 4 pence for a quart of water." [18]

In June 1767, the editor of the South Carolina *Gazette* asked the citizens of Charleston to aid three hundred Irish indentured servants who had just arrived. He had visited their lodgings and had found in each room "two and three score at a time, many dying, some deprived of their sense, young children lying entirely naked whose parents had expired a few weeks ago." [19]

In New York, Philadelphia, Boston, and Charleston, the shipmasters or the merchants who were their agents, inserted advertisements in the colonial newspaper to inform customers of their human merchandise: "To be sold on board the 'Snow Henry,' Capt. Stewart, now lying at the new Dock," went a typical notice, "choice Irish butter and potatoes; also the indented time of several servant men."

Another typical advertisement announced: "Just arrived from London ... a parcel of young, likely men-servants, consisting of Weavers, Joyners, Shoemakers, Smiths, Brickmakers, Bricklayers, Sawyers, Taylors, Staymakers, Butchers, Chairmakers, and several other trades, and are to be sold very reasonable either for ready money, Wheat, Bread or Flour by Edward Hoane in Philadelphia." [20]

Not all who were sold at auction had come to America of their own free will. Some were prisoners sentenced to labor in the colonies because of some trivial offense. Others, especially children, had been kidnaped by agents called "men-stealers," "crimps," and "spirrits" in London, Bristol, or Liverpool. Later, more and more of the cargoes were Negroes who had been seized in Africa, chained in pairs by the arms, the ankles, or the necks, crowded into the holds of vessels, and after frightful voyages sold in America.

Probably half the immigrants to Colonial America were indentured servants. By 1770 a quarter of a million had entered America, of whom more than a hundred thousand were victims of kidnaping or prisoners sentenced to service. By this time between three to four thousand Negro slaves were being imported annually into South Carolina alone, and there were about five hundred thousand Negro slaves, approximately 20 per cent of the colonial population. [21]

The great majority of the colonists, then, were working people. In England and on the Continent they and their ancestors had been artisans, day laborers, small tradesmen, and farmers. Though most of them did not find in America the "happy circumstances" and the ample "reward for work" promised them by glib propagandists, it was they and their descendants who were to build a new civilization and a new democracy on this continent.

CHAPTER 2

Labor in Colonial America

Throughout the Colonial period the free workers were the least numerous and the least important section of American labor. In Pennsylvania, Maryland, and Virginia at the time of the Revolution probably three out of four persons were or had been indentured servants, and about one out of six of the three million colonists were Negro slaves. Less than forty thousand Negroes lived in the North. In at least five southern colonies, Negroes equaled or outnumbered the white population.

SLAVES AND INDENTURED SERVANTS

On the tobacco, rice, and indigo plantations of the South (cotton and sugar did not become important until about a half-century later), slavery displaced the indenture system fairly early. Planters discovered that a slave—a worker for life, whose children became the property of the master—was a more profitable investment than a servant who left after his period of indenture was up. Moreover, a master could often hire out idle slaves. Slave maintenance was less than half that of the indentured servant, a fact that made slavery a labor system desirable to both southern planters and northern merchants.

Slavery, however, did not develop at once in Colonial America. The first Negroes came as indentured servants, and as their indentures ended they were freed. Not until the 1660's did enslavement begin. Between 1664 and 1682 slave codes in many colonies transformed the Negro servant into a slave.* Negro children were legally declared the property of the owners of their mothers. Slaves were forbidden to meet together,

*In Colonial New England, however, Negroes occupied a dual status since the law regarded them as both property and persons. (See Lorenzo J. Greene, *The Negro in Colonial New England, 1620 to 1776*, New York, 1943, p. 167.)

to own or bears arms, to leave their master's plantations without written permission, to testify against a white man. If a Negro slave struck a white person, he received forty lashes regardless of whose fault it was, whereas a master's killing a slave was not a crime, it being assumed that no master would kill his slave "except in self-defense." [1] When a Maryland master, in 1656, killed a slave by pouring hot lead over him, he was acquitted on the ground that the slave was "incorrigible"; and when, in 1735, John Van Zandt of New York whipped a slave to death, the coroner's jury concluded that the death was due to the "visitation of God." [2]

The thousands of indentured servants who came to America to escape poverty and persecution at home frequently found "worse plagues than those ... left behind." [3] Their lot was hardly better than that of the Negro slave; indeed, some observers believed it to be worse. For while a master found it necessary to take care of his slaves, who were property for life, he knew that indentured servants would leave in a few years. And he was under no obligation if these servants left his employ crippled and disabled from hard work and brutal punishment.

To be sure, the law sometimes provided that "if any man smite out the eye or tooth of his man servant or maid servant, or otherwise maim or much disfigure him, he shall let them go free from his service." But this was cold comfort, for the servant knew that should he prefer charges he himself was subject to punishment if he failed to prove his case before a court dominated by the masters. In New York, for example, a servant who could not substantiate his complaint was "enjoyned and ordered to serve ... six months time gratis Extraordinary for every such undue Complaint." [4]

Like the indentured servant, apprentices—children and adolescents bound out to virtual slavery for a number of years—also had much to complain of. Although they were supposed to be taught a trade, the frequent complaints registered in court records indicate that only too many masters kept their apprentices ignorant of the trade, at the same time beating them "in a most cruel and immoderate manner without any just reason for the same," fed them on "morsels of coarse bread," and generally "deprived [them] of the common necessaries and conveniences of Life." [5]

Unfree workers in Colonial America groaned "beneath a worse than Egyptian bondage." One contemporary observed that indentured servants and Negro slaves had "neither convenient food to eat or proper raiment to put on, notwithstanding most of the comforts [the wealthy] enjoyed were solely owing to their indefatigable labors." [6] Little wonder so many of them ran away from their masters. Despite the vigorous efforts of planters and merchants to keep them apart, white servants and Negro slaves often fled together from common oppression to seek a common freedom. One notice which appeared in the Pennsylvania *Gazette* of September 10, 1747, read: "Ran away from the Subscriber—A White Man and a Negro, it is supposed they are gone together." Another notice in the issue of October 8, 1747, read: "There went away with Ann Wainwright, White Servant, a Negro slave Woman belonging to June Bailard."

Runaway servants who were captured were severely whipped, often branded with the letter R, and they were always forced to serve extra time—sometimes as much as two years for each offense. The General Assembly of Maryland even passed an act in 1641 making it a felony punishable with death for a servant to run away from his master "with intent to convey himself out of the province." [7]

But severe punishment did not halt the escapes. Court records tell the stories of people like Isaac Robinson of Massachusetts, who was brutally whipped dozens of times "for running away from his master very often and enticing others to run away," * and of Francis Bates, who was severely punished for repeatedly "provoking his fellow servants" to escape. [8]

Instead of running away, unfree workers often rose up in organized revolt. More than forty slave plots were discovered in Colonial America. In some of them Negro slaves and white indentured servants had formed common plans. The Charleston plot of 1730 was so extensive that a contemporary observed: "Had not an over-ruling Providence discovered their Intrigue, we had all been in blood." Nine years later, on the Stone plantation, near Charleston, more than two hundred slaves revolted. Before they were overtaken and massacred, they had burned houses and crops, and killed several slave owners, sparing one who had been good to his slaves. [9]

Not all slave revolts occurred in the South. In New York City, in 1712, twenty-three armed slaves revolted against "hard usage ... received from their masters." The revolt was crushed but a correspondent to the New York *Gazette* of March 18, 1734, warned the slaveowners that "had it not been for His Majesties Garrison, that city in all likelihood had been reduced to ashes, and the greatest part of its inhabitants murdered."

The severe whippings given to the runaways were as nothing com-

* Robinson could be considered as one of the earliest labor organizers in America. Another was Sam, a Negro slave in Maryland, who was convicted in 1688 of having "several times endeavored to promote a Negro insurrection in this colony." (*William and Mary College Quarterly Historical Magazine*, Vol. X, Jan., 1902, p. 177.)

Not only did organized mass desertions of bound servants occur frequently in Colonial America, but there are even numerous records of strikes conducted by these unfree workers in protest against working conditions. (See Richard B. Morris, *Government and Labor in Early America*, New York, 1946, pp. 167-74.)

pared to the savage punishment suffered by those who took part in slave insurrections. A woman slave was burned at the stake in Jamaica, Long Island, in 1708, for plotting a revolt. As the flames slowly consumed her, a horn filled with water was placed within reach of her mouth and then taken away, again and again "as a terror to others." Of the execution of twenty-one slaves captured in the New York uprising of 1712, Governor Hunter wrote: "Some were burnt, others hanged, one broken on the wheels, and one hung alive in chains in the town, so that there has been the most exemplary punishment that could be possibly thought of." [10]

Brutality did not end the dangers of slave insurrections, and some concessions were granted, such as better food, clothes, and treatment for slaves. In the North, where slavery had never been very profitable, fear of Negro slaves mounted, and proposals were made to replace slaves by free workers.

EMERGENCE OF WAGE EARNERS

It was in the seaport towns and the cities that a free laboring class emerged. For a long time the economic life of Boston, Philadelphia, and New York was geared to the shipping industry. At first English and Dutch vessels carried most of the Colonial commerce but it was not long before the colonists were building their own ships. A demand was thus created for carpenters, smiths, joiners, shipwrights, caulkers, ropemakers, sailmakers, and other artisans and laborers. As early as 1685 William Penn observed that in Philadelphia "there inhabits most sorts of useful tradesmen as Carpenters, Joyners, Bricklayers, Masons, Plumbers, Smiths, Glaziers, Taylors, Shoemakers, Butchers, Bakers, Brewers, Glovers, Tanners, Felmongers, Wheelwrights, Millrights, Shiprights, Boatrights, Ropemakers, Saylmakers, Blockmakers, Turners, etc." Two years later a French visitor to Boston noted that "there are here craftsmen of every kind, and particularly carpenters for the building of ships." [11]

As trade and commerce expanded and wealth increased, skilled craftsmen in the luxury field also made their appearance—silversmiths, goldsmiths, watchmakers, and jewelers. In 1720, New York had thirteen silversmiths, four watchmakers, two goldsmiths, and one jeweler.

In the beginning few artisans and craftsmen were wage earners. In the larger towns they produced articles in their own homes which were frequently small shops as well and here their wives and children would sell their goods. Another type of craftsman was the traveling artisan, mason, carpenter, shoemaker, or candle-maker who carried his tools with him and stopped at farmhouses to work up raw material supplied by the farmers. He was paid in money or in corn or wheat. Much of the labor in blacksmithing, carpentry, weaving and shoemaking in the colonies was performed by these itinerant workers.*

As the population grew, many traveling artisans settled down, usually in small villages, rented or built their own home, and opened a workshop in one of the rooms. When the farmer who lived nearby came to town to sell his produce, he would buy articles difficult to manufacture at home.

As the demand for commodities grew, the artisan shopkeeper found that his own labor could not supply the market. For ten or twenty pounds (fifty to a hundred dollars) he could buy an indentured servant, usually a skilled worker, who would work for seven years for food, lodging, and an occasional suit of clothes. Of the 1,838 indentured servants who came to Philadelphia in April, June, and July of 1709, 56 were bakers, 87 masons, 124 carpenters, 68 shoemakers, 99 tailors, 29 butchers, 45 millers, 14 tanners, seven stocking menders, six barbers, four locksmiths, 95 cloth and linen weavers, 82 coopers, 13 saddlers, two glass blowers, three hatters, eight lime-burners, two engravers, three brickmakers, two silversmiths, 48 blacksmiths, three plotters, six turners.[12]

Negro slaves were also used as skilled workers in the Colonial shops, generally hired by the month or the year. But the demand for free workers grew. However valuable the indentured servants and slaves were on plantations and farms where the work was done all the year they were not so profitable as the free worker in the shops and mills where the work was seasonal. A servant or slave had to be clothed, fed, and sheltered during the slack season, but a free worker could simply be given notice that he was no longer needed. When a servant or slave ran away, the master lost a considerable investment. As Adam Smith observed, in his *Wealth of Nations,* "at Boston, New York and Philadelphia ... the work done by freemen comes cheaper in the end than that performed by slaves." [13]

By 1715, Colonial newspapers were carrying want-ads for scores of different types of free workers, ranging from watchmakers to furriers. An employment bureau, set up in New York in 1770, informed master craftsmen "that they may be supplied with journeymen by applying to Mr. Couters at the sign of the Three Lyons near the North Church

---

* Nevertheless, opportunities for itinerant workers remained limited for many years, since each household in the countryside was almost a factory in miniature. Each farmer was his own carpenter, blacksmith, shoemaker, and a dozen other craftsmen rolled into one. Governor Moore of New York reported as late as 1767 that in most farm houses in the colony clothing was "manufactured for the use of the Family, without the least design of sending any of it to market, ... for every home swarms with children who are set to work so soon as they are able to spin and card." (E. B. O'Callaghan, Ed., *Documents Relative to the Colonial History of the State of New York,* Albany, 1856, Vol. VII, p. 888.)

where there is a House of Call opened and all journeymen are desired to call there for work." [14] Thus a wage-earning class came into existence in Colonial America, its numbers increasing through the expiration of the indentures and through the immigration of free workers. The skilled workers were known as journeymen, artificers, handicraftsmen, artisans and mechanics; unskilled workers were common laborers or ditchers and diggers.

Ship-building, brewing, flour milling, cooperage or barrel-making, tanning, saddlery, and iron-making were the chief Colonial industries sufficiently developed to require a number of workers. Each furnace in the New England and the middle colonies employed eight or nine men, besides wood-cutters, coalers, carters, and other common laborers. Ship-building was undoubtedly the most important industry in Boston, New York, Philadelphia, Newport, and Charleston. In 1720 Boston had fourteen shipyards, which produced annually about two hundred ships; in 1712 Newport had more than a dozen, and in 1718 Philadelphia had at least ten. They provided employment for many workers, skilled and unskilled alike. It is estimated, for example, that in 1713, there were at least 3,500 sailors in the port of Boston and Salem alone. By the eve of the Revolution, lumber mills and iron works were employing large groups of workers, and many workers were employed as weavers, shoemakers and cabinet makers in large shops in New York, Boston, and Philadelphia.[15]

The typical Colonial shop, however, did not have many workers, partly because the English government limited the number. In 1750, such a shop would consist of a master craftsman, who was the owner and employer, two or three journeymen, and a similar number of apprentices. The master craftsman still worked side by side with his wage workers. He provided the capital and the raw material and sold the finished articles.

LABOR CONDITIONS AND ORGANIZATIONS

In any analysis of labor conditions in Colonial America one must constantly remember that the scarcity of labor "assured the workman of a higher standard of living than was obtainable by a person of similar employment in England or on the Continent." One student of the subject has estimated that the "colonial workman commanded real wages which exceeded by from 30 to 100 per cent the wages of a contemporary English workman." [16] Skilled craftsmen were imported from Europe throughout the entire Colonial period, and to induce them to emigrate Colonial industrialists were willing to offer extremely attractive conditions.

Available surveys of wages in the various trades in Colonial America are entirely too lacking in comprehensiveness to permit any thorough general conclusions. A few statistics may be cited. In 1630, wages of carpenters in Massachusetts were approximately twenty-three cents a day with board, or thirty-three cents without board, those of laborers with board were as low as eleven cents a day, while those of bricklayers and masons in 1672 were twenty-two cents a day with board. A carpenter in 1770 earned about 50 cents a day; a butcher 30 cents; a shoemaker 70 cents; a laborer 21 cents. The general wage was about two dollars a week. Unquestionably, some of these workers were able to supplement their income through subsistence farming.[17]

However, all was not milk and honey in the life of a Colonial wage-earner. During unemployment periods, the Colonial worker was often unable to keep his children from starving and himself from jail. In 1737, the lieutenant-governor of New York observed that many workers in the colony were "reduced to poverty from want of employ." And in Colonial New Jersey, so many workers were unemployed in 1765 that the Provincial legislature had to appropriate 200 pounds to be used in buying grain for the more distressed families.[18]

High prices and currency fluctuations often reduced real wages. When prices fell the workers did not benefit because many Colonial courts ordered them "to be content to abate their wages according to the fall of the commodities." When prices went up the courts fixed maximum rates and fined workers heavily when they sought or received wages above the rates.* A court record in New England reads: "William Dixie paid 3s fine for taking 3s per day; James Smith fined 2s, John Stone and Jno Sibley 3s each for taking excessive wages." [19] This action, employers argued, was necessary "to save the American Workingman from himself." One American employer remarked in 1769: "It is certain that high wages more frequently make labouring people miserable; they too commonly employ their spare time and cash, in debauching their morals and ruining their health." [20]

In order to keep wages down, manufacturers often employed Negro slaves. Unable to halt this practice, white workers in the South began to emigrate to the northern colonies. But the same competition faced the workers in the North. The free mechanics of Philadelphia in 1707 protested the "Want of Employment and Lowness of wages occasioned by the Number of Negroes ... hired out to work by the day." [21] Thirty years later free workers in New York protested the "pernicious practice of breeding slaves to trade," which forced the free worker to leave for other colonies.[22]

---

* While most wage control legislation in Colonial times failed owing to labor scarcity and inability to get workers to stay on the job, demands for such laws were made throughout the period. In almost all cases where such legislation existed, the worker and not the master was prosecuted.

Another competitor was the half farmer-half artisan who came to the towns during the winter and returned to the farm in time for the spring planting. A mechanic in New York wrote in 1757: "A Farmer ought to employ himself in his proper occupation without meddling with Smiths, Masons, Carpenters, Coopers, or any other mechanical Arts, except making and mending his Plow, Harrow, or any other utensil for farming." [23]

The workers had still to learn that these problems of growing capitalism could only be met by limiting the working day through the power of trade unions, by resolutely fighting for higher wages and better working conditions. Class lines were still fluid in early America. The master craftsman still worked at his bench; often he and his workers co-operated in fighting the big merchants who refused to abide by established standards. Skilled workers could become master craftsmen, and unskilled workers could move to other places or become farmers.

Even so, labor organization did take place in Colonial America.* The Journeymen Caulkers of Boston issued a joint statement in 1741 stating that they would no longer accept payment for their work in notes on shops for money and goods, a practice which had "greatly impoverished themselves and their families." For the future, they continued, they would receive and take "no other pay for their service than good lawful publick bills of credit." [24] "This good and commendable example," the *Boston Weekly News-Letter* of February 12, 1741, remarked, "will soon be follow'd by Numbers of other Artificers and Tradesmen."

The following advertisement in the *New York Weekly Journal* of January 28, 1734, indicates that maid servants were organizing to improve their working conditions:

"Here are many women in this Town that these hard Times intend to go to Service, but as it is proper the World should know our Terms, we think it reasonable we should not be beat by our Mistresses Husband[s], they being too strong, and perhaps may do tender women Mischief. If any Ladies want Servants, and will engage for their Husbands, they shall be soon supplied."

The closest thing to trade unions before the Revolution were the benevolent societies for masters, journeymen and apprentices, formed in

---

* There were even a few guilds in Colonial America, the best known of them being the Carpenters' Company of Philadelphia, founded in 1724. Although these Colonial craft guilds sought to follow the practices of the European guilds by regulating their respective industries, determining wages, hours, and conditions of labor, and inspecting the workmanship and the quality of materials, they were not very successful. Workers in Colonial America were too widely scattered to be regulated and supervised by a guild. Usually, only masters belonged to these guilds.

a few leading towns. Generally their purpose was that of "assisting such of their members as should by accident be in need of support, or the widows and minor children of the members." They paid sick benefits, provided funds for indigent members, occasionally loaned money, and provided "strong boxes" for savings. They did not usually deal with questions of wages, hours, or conditions of labor. But the benevolent society of house painters of New York in 1767 did petition the Board of Councillors to prevent master craftsmen from importing mechanics from neighboring colonies, paying them less money and thereby lowering wages in New York City. Before the benevolent society was formed such petitions were regularly ignored. When the Board of Councillors received this petition a committee was appointed at once and ordered to report "with all possible speed." [25]

A few strikes were called in Colonial times.* In 1684 the truckmen employed by the municipal government of New York refused to move dirt from the streets until the price per load was increased. The strikers were "Suspended and Discharged" "for not obeying the Command and doing their Dutyes as becomes them in their Places." A week later the carters asked to be returned to their jobs. They were ordered to conform to certain "Laws and Orders established," and to pay a fine of six shillings each. About a century later, in 1770, the coopers of New York determined "not to sell casks except in accordance with the rates established." The coopers were tried and convicted of a conspiracy to restrain trade, and ordered to pay fifty shillings "to the church or pious uses." Those who worked for the city were dismissed.[26]

The same city government had been kinder years before in 1758 when the powerful shipping merchants had combined to lower the wage scale for ship carpenters, able seamen, and laborers. Six years later a colony-wide employers' association was set up in New York City. Each member agreed not to "receive in his Service" any workers who could not pro-

* These were not really strikes of workers against employers, but protests of master craftsmen against prices fixed by local authorities. John R. Commons and Associates state that the Philadelphia printers' strike of 1786 was the first authentic labor strike in American history. (*History of Labor in the United States,* New York, 1918, Vol. I, p. 25.) Richard B. Morris indicates, however, that there may even have been a strike of journeymen tailors in New York in 1768. ("Criminal Conspiracy and Early Labor Combinations in New York," *Political Science Quarterly,* Vol. LII, March, 1937, p. 77.) The twenty journeymen tailors announced on March 31, 1768, that they would work in families at "three Shillings and Six Pence per Day" with "Diet." (See *New York Journal,* April 7, 1768.)

An extremely interesting report in the Charleston *Gazette* of October 29, 1763, announced that Negro chimney sweepers "had the insolence, by a combination amongst themselves, to raise the usual prices, and to refuse doing their work, unless their exorbitant demands are complied with."

duce "a Recommendation in writing, from the Master, or Mistress, whom they last served in this Colony." [27] No fines were imposed upon these employers nor were they prosecuted for conspiracy.

In 1746 a number of Savannah carpenters went on strike. Immediately the trustees of the colony invoked a parliamentary statute to suppress the strike. The report of their action, dated December 29, 1746, read in part:

"An Advertisement being read, sign'd by several Carpenters at Savannah and stuck up at several Places in the said Town, whereby they have combin'd and resolved not to work below particular Prices Specified therein

"Ordered

"That the Act of Parliament Intitled. ... be sent over to the President and Assistants, with orders for them to apprize the People of the Consequences of the said Act, and to put the same in force." [28]

STRUGGLES FOR DEMOCRACY

During the seventeenth century in some of the colonies, the common man, slaves and indentured servants excepted, had been able to vote. During the following century, property qualifications for voting were introduced disenfranchising the poor. In Pennsylvania the right to vote in 1750 depended upon the ownership of 50 pounds of "lawful money" or 50 acres of land. As a result, only 8 per cent of the rural population could vote and only 2 per cent of the population of Philadelphia. Suffrage in New Jersey was restricted to freeholders who owned at least 100 acres of land, and in South Carolina to those who owned "a settled plantation" or one hundred acres of unsettled land. Josiah Quincy, the Massachusetts lawyer, said of the South Carolina Assembly: " 'Tis true that they have a house of Assembly: but who do they represent? The laborer, the mechanic, the tradesman, the farmer, husbandman or yeoman? No the representatives are almost if not wholly rich planters." [29]

Resentment grew among the masses who had not come to America to be deprived of their vote, taxed to support an established church in whose doctrines they did not believe, robbed of the chance to buy land by speculators and landed gentry who seized and held vast estates, imprisoned if they fell into debt, forced to dress in common clothes to distinguish them from the upper classes, and in general treated as if they had been destined to live in abject poverty and ignorance. Nor were they loth to express their resentment. Riots often took place on election days, when small shopkeepers, artisans, and laborers would march to the polls armed with sticks and stones and demand the ballot. These demonstrations were supplemented by literary protests in prose and verse, such as:

Now the pleasant time approaches;
Gentlemen do ride in coaches,
But poor men they don't regard,
That to maintain them labour hard.[30]

Two incidents in Massachusetts revealed that the common people were not going to cringe before the ruling classes. In 1667, Emanuel Downing, a ship-carpenter, was arrested in Essex County for having "uttered diverse seditious & dangerous speeches of a Very high nature against the Crown and dignity of our Sovereigns Lord King Charles the Second," such as the statement that "he cared not more for him [the King] than any other man."[31] Also, there is the better known case of Governor Joseph Dudley of Massachusetts who one wintry day in 1705 came upon some carters on the road to Boston. He haughtily ordered them out of the way to permit his carriage to pass. But the carters refused, and one of them told the Governor: "I am as good flesh and blood as you, . . . you may go out of the way."[32] The carters were arrested and later released, but in all aristocratic circles the incident was discussed. The lower classes, went the common lament, were getting out of hand. But this outcry was moderate indeed compared with the shrieks of the aristocrats when the lower classes rose up in revolt with the aim of ending the "insolent domination in a few, a very few, opulent families."

Virginia experienced a revolt in 1646, led by Nathaniel Bacon, against the planter aristocracy. The rebellion, said the report of the King's investigators, sprang "from the poverty and uneasyness of some of the meanest whose discontent renders them easyer to be misled." Bacon's army was described by a contemporary as "Rabble of the basest sort of people, whose condition was such, as by a change could not admit of worse." He was shocked to hear them talk "of sharing men's estates among themselves."

Bacon died suddenly of fever, but before the rebellion was drowned in blood by Governor Berkeley it had gained a number of democratic rights for the people. The statute preventing propertyless freemen from electing members to the House of Burgesses was repealed. Freeholders and freemen of every parish gained the right to elect the vestries of the church.

None of these democratic reforms remained after the revolt was crushed, yet their memories lived on. Bacon was truly the "Torchbearer of the Revolution," and for generations after any leader of the common people was called a "Baconist."[33]

One such Baconist was Jacob Leisler who in 1689 led the people of New York City against the mercantile aristocracy, captured the Fort, and overthrew the government. City artisans and laborers, classified by

Governor Bellomont as "the scum of the people, Taylours and others scandalous persons," formed the majority of Leisler's party. Before the movement was defeated, several important democratic rights were won. A committee of safety was elected by the people, free men who owned no property were given voting rights, and representatives to the Colonial government were elected by all voters.[34]

Although Leisler's regime was overthrown, a number of the democratic advances made during the rebellion continued. Suffrage in New York City remained more liberal than in other colonies before the Revolution. About 10 per cent of the total white population of New York City possessed the right to vote. Although the government was controlled by merchants, crown officers, lawyers and landowners, the opportunity existed for the political movement of the artisans.

This opportunity did come during the aldermanic campaign of 1734, when the Court Party representing Governor Cosby and the merchants was determined to retain control of the city government by re-electing their aldermen and councilmen. Arrayed against them was the Popular Party supported by the artisans and aided by John Peter Zenger's *New York Journal*. In a handbill distributed by the Popular Party during the campaign, the workingmen of New York were urged "to chuse no courtiers or trimmers; or any of that vain tribe that are more fond of a *Feather* in their Hats, than the true interest of the *City*. Nor to chuse any *dependents* on them." It reminded the voters that *"A poor honest man* [is] preferable to a rich knave." Towards the end of the campaign, the workingmen were rallied to the polls by this song:

> *Our Country's Rights we will defend,*
> *Like brave and honest men,*
> *We voted right and there's an end*
> *And so we'll do again.*[35]

The election was a triumph for the Popular Party. John Fred, laborer; Johannes Burger, bricklayer; William Roome, painter; Henry Bogart, baker; and other artisans were elected to the common council, which by 1735 the Popular Party completely controlled. Governor Cosby complained to the Lords of Trade in London of the "misled populace in this city," and another conservative said that the city was "entirely at the Beck of the Faction and for the most part men of the Low Class." [36]

Infuriated by the victory of the people, Governor Cosby took action against John Peter Zenger. The songs, ballads, and several issues of the *Journal* were condemned by the Governor's Council and the Supreme Court. Zenger himself was arrested on a charge of seditious libel. He was defended by the eighty-eight year old prominent lawyer, Andrew Hamilton of Philadelphia, without fee or reward. Stressing the issue of a free press, Hamilton said: "the Question before the Court ... is not of small nor private Concern, it is not the Cause of a poor Printer, nor of *New York* alone. ... It is the Cause of Liberty; and I make no Doubt that your upright Conduct this Day, will not only entitle you to the Love and Esteem of your Fellow-Citizens; but every Man, who prefers Freedom to a Life of Slavery will bless and honor You. ..." [37]

The verdict was "not guilty" and the precedent of a free press had been established in America.

Later the conservatives in New York regained control of the city government, but the rich and the "well-born" in Colonial America never recovered from the panic created by the political upsurge of the people of New York City. Their fright became greater when in 1740 a struggle began between the aristocrats and the people of Massachusetts. The frightening fact was that the farmers and artisans were marching together against the hated creditors who were sending Colonial silver to Europe and refusing to accept payment of debts in paper money. The mercantile aristocrats were denounced as "griping and merciless usurers" who "heaped up Vast Estates" by exploiting the poor. Hard-pressed farmers and town mechanics urged the establishment of a "Land Bank" that would issue paper money.

To the mercantile aristocrats in Boston it was clear that "fundamentally the struggle was to decide whether the common people or wealthy gentry were henceforth to control the public life of the colony." Naturally they fought the Land Bank proposal, and when the bank was agreed to by the Colonial Assembly, they turned to the King and Parliament. The British government dissolved the Land Bank. [38]

In no colony, therefore, were the common people able to limit the power of the upper classes. Every movement to restore the democratic rights of the lower classes and to achieve others had been crushed, some with the timely assistance of the British King and Parliament. Yet the triumph of the landed, professional, and mercantile aristocracy was only temporary. In these struggles urban workers and artisans and country farmers forged a significant alliance. They were to utilize this alliance during the American Revolution, when, by uniting their struggle for greater freedom at home with the movement for independence, they fought for and won a more democratic regime in America.

CHAPTER 3

Labor and the American Revolution

During the era of the American Revolution, workers combined and acted as a class in resistance to the British policy and in advancing their economic and political interests in America.

The American Revolution was the culmination of two great movements operating simultaneously: one, to free the colonies from the repressive imperial control of Britain; the other, to democratize American political, economic, and social institutions. The Revolution was successful because of the unity of the workers, the majority of the small farmers, and sections of the planter-merchant aristocracy who collaborated for the defeat of the common enemy.

BACKGROUND FOR REVOLUTION

The economic weapon of the enemy was the British mercantile policy, according to which the American colonies existed for the sole purpose of increasing the profits of British manufacturers, merchants, and landlords. The colonists were forced to send their commodities only to England, or to England first, if they were destined for a non-British port. They could import only goods produced in England or goods sent to the colonies by way of England. They were not allowed to export wool, yarn, and woolen cloth from one colony to another, "or to any place whatsoever," nor could they export hats and iron products. They could not erect slitting or rolling mills or forges and furnaces. After 1763, they were forbidden to settle west of the Appalachian mountains. By the Currency Act of 1764 they were deprived of the right to use legal tender paper money and to establish colonial mints and land banks.[1]

It is true that the colonists were often able to circumvent these restrictions by illegal production and smuggling. But this became increasingly difficult after 1763, when more rigid inspection and enforcement followed upon complaints of English business men. A Bostonian wailed in 1765: "A colonist cannot make a button, a horseshoe, nor a hobnail, but some sooty iron monger or respectable button-maker of Britain shall bawl and squall that his honor's Worship is most egregiously maltreated, injured, cheated and robbed by the rascally American republicans." [2]

All classes in America—the retainers of the Crown excepted—suffered from these restrictions. The Proclamation of 1763 shattered the prospects of southern planters to recoup their fortunes through speculation in western land. It ended the hopes of land-hungry poor farmers and city mechanics of escaping to the frontier. Restraints on Colonial trade hurt the merchants, lowered the prices of farm products, lowered wages especially among sailors and dockyard laborers, and resulted in unemployment. Workers became alarmed because these restraints stopped them from becoming independent producers. The prohibition of paper money increased the pressure on the debtor and seriously hampered exchange among merchants. In short, "a handful of English capitalists carried more weight at Westminster than the welfare of millions of Americans." [3]

Still these restraints upon American economic liberty would not by themselves have united all colonists in opposition to British Colonial policy, for they affected different classes and sections at different times. Other tyrannical measures adopted after 1763 largely contributed. The Stamp Act of 1765, which placed a tax on every legal document, every newspaper or commercial paper throughout America; the Tea Act of 1774, which gave a monopoly to the East India Company; and the acts that closed the port of Boston as a penalty for dumping British tea— these measures united all sections and classes in angry opposition. Many Americans came to realize that if Parliament could impose a stamp tax, it could levy a poll tax, a land tax, and, a pamphlet issued in 1765 added, a tax "for the light of the sun, for the air we breathe, and for the ground we are buried in." [4]

The colonists fought the repressive measures of the British government by petitions, demonstrations, and non-importation agreements. "Taxation without Representation is Tyranny," "Natural Rights of Man," and "Liberty and Property" were the democratic slogans under which they fought.

The controversies with Great Britain filled the minds of the common people with sentiments of liberty which meant freedom from the oppressions of the Colonial aristocracy as well as from British rule. America should be free from all "Foreign or Domestic Oligarchy." [5]

But to many members of the Colonial ruling class, the "levelling principles" and "democratic notions" of middle-class and lower-class Americans were more menacing than any Stamp Act or Tea Act imposed by British tyranny. Hence throughout the two decades of Colonial opposition to Britain preceding the outbreak of the War for Independence, they sought so to conduct the struggle that it would not be turned against themselves. When their conservative methods were no longer possible they tried to stop the people's movement. Gouverneur Morris spoke for the Colonial aristocracy when he wrote:

"The mob begin to think and to reason.... I see, and I see with fear and trembling, that if the disputes with Britain continue, we shall be under the domination of a riotous mob. It is to the interest of all men, therefore, to seek for reunion with the parent state." [6]

THE SONS OF LIBERTY

By the latter part of 1765 the conduct of the struggle against Great Britain was no longer entirely in the hands of conservative merchants and planters who had hitherto dominated the political life of Colonial America. The mechanics and workingmen of the larger towns had formed their own militant organizations which thrust aside hesitant conservatives, prodded those who wished to move more slowly and in countless ways pushed the Revolution forward until British rule was overthrown in a revolutionary war. Sometimes they called themselves "Regulators"; in Pennsylvania they were known as the "Associators," and in Connecticut, they were referred to as "The United Company." Usually they were known as the "Sons of Liberty." *

These revolutionary bodies mainly consisted of artisan shopkeepers, mechanics, day laborers, carpenters, joiners, printers, shipwrights, smiths, calkers, rope-makers, seamen, masons, and other members of the urban lower classes whose names have rarely been recorded in history books.[7] Mercantile and professional groups supplied the leadership to the Sons of Liberty. Outstanding leaders were Samuel Adams of Massachusetts, Christopher Gadsden of South Carolina, John Lamb of New York, and Stephen Hopkins of Rhode Island. But the laboring class worked closely with the lawyer, planter, and merchant leaders. Thus Ebenezer Mackintosh, a leather worker, and Paul Revere, leader of the North End Caucus, a club composed mainly of craftsmen and workers, consulted frequently with Samuel Adams in Boston, and William Johnson, a mechanic, worked closely with Christopher Gadsden in Charleston.

Under their leadership the Sons of Liberty demonstrated against the

* Sometimes workers in specific trades would operate through separate organizations which were affiliated to the Sons of Liberty. Thus the seamen in New York City carried on much of their revolutionary activity through the Sons of Neptune. (See broadside in New York Historical Society dated December 20, 1773, containing a message from Tom Bowlin, a seaman, "to his worthy mess-mates" calling upon the Sons of Neptune to prevent the landing of British tea in New York which would "put the finishing Stroke to our Liberties.")

oppressive measures of the British ministry, secured the repeal of the Stamp Act, made possible the enforcement of the non-importation agreements and the boycott on English tea. It was they who forced officials appointed to sell stamps to resign, and frightened others out of town; they compelled merchants who refused to abide by non-importation agreements to apologize publicly; they tarred and feathered those who persisted in acts detrimental to the revolutionary cause.[8]

To the enemies of freedom the Sons of Liberty were always "the mob," "the mixed rabble of Scotch, Irish, and foreign vagabonds," "descendants of convicts," "foul-mouthed and inflaming sons of discord and faction." [9] But to Samuel Adams they and their allies, the small farmers,* were the "strength of every community," and it was in the hands of those "two venerable Orders of Men stiled Mechanics and Husbandmen" that he placed the enforcement of the non-importation movement. It was the "firm patriotism" of the town labor and the small farmers, said Adams, "that must finally save this country." Dr. Joseph Warren, another revolutionary leader, expressed the same confidence in the patriotism of the artisans when he wrote in June 1774, concerning the enforcement of the non-importation agreements: "I fear New York will not assist us with good grace, but she may perhaps be ashamed to desert us; at least, if her *merchants* offer to sell us, her *mechanics* will forbid the auction." [10]

Before the hostile eyes of Tories, the Sons of Liberty, armed with a variety of weapons and determined to "fight up to their knees in blood" rather than be ruled by tyrants, paraded to public meetings in military formation, with Liberty Tree medals suspended from their necks. In inns and taverns they held weekly educational meetings where the latest newspapers, pamphlets, and handbills were read aloud for the benefit of the illiterate.[11] And at singing festivals they raised their voices in revolutionary song, warning aristocrats that they dared to be free from domestic as well as British tyranny. One of the songs ran:

Come Rally Sons of Liberty
Come All with hearts United
Our motto is 'We Dare Be Free'
Not easily affrighted!

---

* In some colonies artisans, mechanics, and day laborers, organized in the Sons of Liberty, attempted to forge an alliance with radical farmers in the hinterland. The Liberty Boys in Boston, for example, contacted rural radicals throughout the colony and succeeded in securing the passage of anti-stamp resolutions in many towns and villages. In New York, however, the Sons of Liberty did nothing to form a united front with the farmers, who were eager to co-operate. For an analysis of this problem, see Irving Mark, *Agrarian Conflicts in Colonial New York, 1711-1775*, New York, 1940, pp. 135, 138, 148, 152.

Oppression's Band we must subdue,
Now is the Time, or never;
Let each Man prove this motto True
And Slavery from him sever.[12]

Sometimes the women would join in the chorus, for the Sons of Liberty had the first women's auxiliary in America—the Daughters of Liberty. These women refused to drink tea and made the non-importation agreements effective by boycotting English goods. They popularized their homespun clothing in the slogan, "It is better to wear a Homespun Coat than to lose our Liberty." When a festival of the Daughters of Liberty was interrupted by a man who denounced the Revolution, the women seized the intruder, stripped him to the waist, and in the absence of tar and feathers, covered him with molasses and the downy tops of flowers.[13]

The Daughters of Liberty were accused of acting contrary to the will of God who had decreed that woman's place was in the home. But the Sons of Liberty welcomed their help. "With the Ladies on our side we can make every Tory tremble," they announced joyfully.[14]

After the repeal of the Stamp Act, the Sons of Liberty continued their organization. Delegates from the Sons of Liberty of New York City helped to form societies in other localities. The various organizations were united into an association of Sons of Liberty. Similar activity was carried on in Boston and Charleston.[15]

These radical societies not only marked the first effective intercolonial union, but helped to forge working class solidarity. When the British troops were quartered in Boston in 1768 the authorities issued a call for workers to build barracks. Though the non-importation agreements had caused unemployment among the carpenters and bricklayers, they refused to work. Bonuses and higher wages failed to move them. They proved so "mulish" that General Gage was forced to send to New York for workers. Paul Revere was sent galloping off to New York to get the support of New York carpenters and masons, members of the Son of Liberty. After listening to Paul Revere they instantly resolved not to work for "enemies to this country."[16]

Sons of Liberty came into existence in Dublin, Ireland. They assisted the Americans morally and financially, drank toasts hailing the "Sons of Liberty throughout the World," and recruited Irish liberals and radicals to fight in Washington's army. Even in England a group of mechanics urged on the American Liberty boys: "You have only to persevere, and you will preserve your own liberties and England's too."[17]

The Sons of Liberty welcomed this international solidarity. Their determination was further strengthened by the Constitutional Society of

London which sent money to the widows and children of Americans who had fallen in the Battle of Concord. English weavers, seamen, tailors, and miners encouraged the Sons of Liberty to continue the non-importation agreements even though they endured unemployment and were in a "starving condition" as a result of the loss of the American market. General Gage reported in 1768 that "the News of the Tumults and Insurrections which have happened in London and Dublin ... is received by the Factions in America, as Events favorable to their Designs of Independency." [18]

POLITICAL ACTION

These national and international relationships were later to stand the American workers in good stead. So was the experience they gained in the field of political activity during the Revolutionary era. Having no vote, they had exerted little influence in Colonial governments. But when the legal governments of the Crown started to crumble and the period of control by extra-legal committees and congresses set in, the mechanics forced the conservatives to recognize their power. A Philadelphia mechanic voiced the sentiments of his fellow-workers all over the country when he wrote in the *Pennsylvania Gazette* of September 27, 1770:

"It has been customary for a certain Company of leading Men to nominate Persons, and to settle the Ticket, for Assembly-men, Commissioners, Assessors, etc., without ever permitting the affirmative or negative Voice of a Mechanic to interfere.... This we have tamely submitted to so long, that those Gentlemen make no Scruple to say, that the Mechanics (though by far the most numerous, especially in this County) have no Right to be consulted; that is, in Fact have no Right to *speak* or *think* for themselves. Have we not an equal Right of electing or being elected? ...I think it absolutely necessary that one or two Mechanics be elected to represent so large a Body of the Inhabitants."

When, in 1773, the conservative merchants of New York organized a Committee of Fifty-One to control the course of the revolution, the artisans acted independently by setting up their own organization, the Committee of Mechanics. This committee was the old Sons of Liberty, and like its parent it pressed for the overthrow of "inveterate enemies" at home and abroad. It called meetings to raise money "for the relief of the poor of Boston," whose port had been closed by the British; enforced a rigid non-importation agreement; organized a Committee of Correspondence; influenced the carpenters and masons against going to Boston to fortify Boston Neck, and forced the merchants to refuse the use of their vessels for the transportation of British troops and military stores. It raised again the issues fought for by the Sons of Liberty, "equal right for the classes hitherto excluded from voting," and voting by ballot instead of *viva voce*.[19]

Victories were won. The right to vote was extended to most workers by making residence the only requirement. It was agreed to convene a Continental Congress, a demand raised by the Committee of Mechanics. One last effort to run things was made by the conservative groups when they proposed that the delegates to the Continental Congress be chosen only from the Committee of Fifty-One. The mechanics replied by nominating their own full slate of candidates. Finally representatives of the merchants and mechanics conferred and came to an agreement. To bring about unity the Committee of Mechanics agreed to withdraw its slate while the merchants agreed to unite with the mechanics in a broader Committee of One Hundred.

The same drive toward unity was taking place in the other colonies too. The mechanics of Charleston were dissatisfied with the original non-importation agreement initiated by the merchants for it ignored some of their most serious grievances. One of their demands was for the prohibition of the importation of slaves who were being hired out as craftsmen. Four days after the original agreement had been drawn up the mechanics met under the Liberty Tree and drew up two amendments, one providing that no slaves be brought into the colony, the other that no goods imported from Great Britain be purchased from transient traders. The merchants in Charleston amended the proposals of the mechanics by extending the time of the prohibition of the slave trade. But the mechanics refused the amendment and joining with the small planters put pressure on the merchants. The planters, on their part, gave orders to their agents not to purchase from or sell to any merchants who refused to accept the amendments of the mechanics. The result was that the merchants called for a joint committee to draft a non-importation agreement with equal representation from the mechanics, planters, and merchants. Ultimately, a general committee consisting of 13 merchants, 13 planters, and 13 mechanics drew up and enforced a unity non-importation agreement.[20] *

During this period the mechanics of Charleston elected their own representatives. A dispatch from Charleston to the *Boston Chronicle* of October 1, 1768, reported that "a number of the leading mechanics

---

* In 1770 a New York mechanic wrote: "Nothing can be more flagrantly wrong than the Assertion of some of our mercantile Dons, that the Mechanics have no right to give their Sentiments about the Importation of British Commodities." (Broadside signed *Brutus* and dated after May 10, 1770, in Rare Book Room, New York Public Library.)

of this city assembled under some trees in a field adjacent to the rope-walk in order to select six gentlemen to represent the inhabitants of Charles Town in the ensuing General Assembly." When the mechanics in Boston read this report, they marched to the town meetings, ignored legal restrictions on their right to vote, and took over the real authority of the government. "The Merchants in Boston," one aristocrat wrote in 1770, "are now entirely out of the question in all debates at their Town Meeting which is carried on by a mob of the lowest sort of people." "At these meetings," added the American Board of Customs Commissioners, "the lowest Mechanicks discuss upon the most important points of government with the utmost freedom." [21]

After 1770 craftsmen in other cities and towns followed the lead of Charleston. In 1772 the Patriotic Society was formed in Philadelphia to preserve "our just Rights and Privileges to us and our Posterity against every attempt to violate and infringe same, either here or on the other side of the Atlantic." [22] Two years later it took the name of the Mechanics Association of Philadelphia, and united with the small farmers of the back country.

An extra-legal provincial conference was called in Pennsylvania in 1776 "for the express purpose of forming a new government . . . on the authority of the people alone." All residents of the colony who were twenty-one years of age and had been taxpayers and residents in their city and county for one year had the right to elect delegates to the constitutional convention if they would take an oath to support the revolutionary cause. Out of this convention, in which workers and farmers were well represented, emerged the most democratic constitution of that time. It guaranteed freedom of speech and religion, increased representation for the back country, and allowed all residents who had paid taxes to vote and hold office. Reactionaries called this document a "mobocracy of the most illiterate," and James Allen, Esq. of Philadelphia wailed: "All Power is in the hands of the Associators. . . ." [23]

In every colony conservatives bemoaned the fact that the Revolutionary movement had "brought all the dregs to the top." [24] The Governor of Georgia observed tearfully that in Savannah the "Parochial Committee are a Parcel of the Lowest People, chiefly Carpenters, Shoemakers, Blacksmiths, etc. . . ." [25] Joseph Galloway, a reactionary Pennsylvanian, betrayed his rage in the following couplet:

Down at night a bricklayer or carpenter lies,
Next sun a Lycurgus, a Solon doth rise.[26]

The common people did not take these attacks lightly. A minister in Charleston, South Carolina, was dismissed by his congregation for asserting "that *mechanics* and *country clowns* had no right to dispute about politics, or what King, Lords and Commons had done, or might do." The Newport, Rhode Island, *Mercury* of September 26, 1774, spoke for the people when it informed "All *such* divines ... that mechanics and country clowns (infamously so-called) are the real and absolute masters of King, Lords, Commons and Priests...."

THE ROAD TO INDEPENDENCE

Unlike the conservatives who relied on the moderates in Parliament to prevent the struggle from terminating in blood, the mechanics knew that the British rulers were determined to continue their control over America even if it were necessary, as one member of Parliament threatened, to "burn and set fire to their woods." [27] Workers had already given their lives to the revolutionary cause. Five of them had been shot on Boston Commons on March 2, 1770, by British soldiers. These victims of the Boston massacre were Crispus Attucks, a Negro seaman who had escaped from slavery; Samuel Gray, a ropewalk worker; James Caldwell, a young seaman; Patrick Carr, an artisan, and Sam Maverick, a joiner's apprentice. All five were buried in a common grave.*

After the massacre the mechanics grimly armed themselves for the inevitable conflict. They organized local militia, collected stores of arms and ammunition, and at meetings of the Sons of Liberty trained themselves in the art of war. In Boston, where most of the British troops were quartered, the mechanics organized an amazing espionage system for "watching the movements of British soldiers and gaining every intelligence of the movement of the Tories."

They soon learned of General Gage's intention to move military stores from Portsmouth, and Paul Revere, a member of the intelligence committee, rode all night to inform the Portsmouth Liberty Boys. Assisted by mechanics and small farmers in neighboring towns and villages, they seized the supplies before the British could get to them. Later the Boston artisan rode again, this time to warn Samuel Adams and John Hancock of General Gage's plan to arrest them, and to conduct them to safer quarters. Eventually the espionage committee unearthed information of supreme importance. On the night of April 18, 1775, the spies discovered that eight hundred Redcoats were leaving their barracks in full battle array, moving to seize the Patriots' military stores at Concord, eighteen miles north of Boston. The lantern in Christ's Church flashed the signal to the countryside and Paul Revere started on his epic ride. At Lexington the British troops were fired upon by the Minute Men,

---

* The bitter antagonism of Boston workers to British soldiers who accepted part-time work at low wages was a factor of some importance in the Boston Massacre. (See Richard B. Morris, *Government and Labor in Early America*, pp. 190-91.)

and at Concord they were met by the militia organized by the Sons of Liberty. The troops retreated, leaving behind close to three hundred killed, wounded, or prisoners, while the Americans had lost about ninety men.

Five days later on a Sunday, Israel Bissel, a Boston mechanic, rode his tired horse into New York City to spread the news of Concord and Lexington. Small shopkeepers, mechanics, and workingmen broke open the city arsenal, seized ammunition and about six hundred muskets which they distributed. Thus armed, the Liberty Boys formed a Voluntary Corps and assumed government of the city. They took over the customs house and the public stores and unloaded two vessels of material intended for British troops in Boston. A few weeks later the militia of the Sons of Liberty clashed with British troops embarking for Boston, persuading a number of the soldiers to desert, and detaining the others.

The "shot heard round the world" had the same effect in other colonies. In Savannah, Georgia, the Sons of Liberty broke open a magazine, took six hundred pounds of gun powder, seized guns and powder from a British ship in the harbor, and began to organize a regiment of soldiers. When Ebenezer McCarthy, one of their members, was arrested and imprisoned the Liberty Boys broke into the jail, set him free, and paraded in military formation through the streets. The mechanics and liberal merchants of Philadelphia formed a Military Association. In Newark, New Jersey, the Sons of Liberty met and unanimously resolved that they were "willing at this alarming crisis to risk their lives and fortunes in support of American liberty." [28]

Revolution and war faced the people. For almost a year, however, it took the form of an armed demand for the redress of grievances. The workers knew that they would have to fight for their liberties but conservative groups believed that conciliation was still possible. As the dominant element in the Continental Congress, they soft-pedaled the demand for separation, assuring the King that Americans were not "desirous of independency." The mechanics had instructed their delegates to the provincial and continental congresses to fight for independence, and Christopher Gadsden told the Provincial Congress of South Carolina that he spoke the minds of the mechanics of Charleston when he urged the Congress to declare itself in favor not only of the liberties, but of the independence of America.[29] When elected by the mechanics to the Continental Congress Gadsden read aloud on February 10, 1776, from a pamphlet entitled *Common Sense,* written by a man who had been a cobbler, a staymaker, a civil servant, a laborer in a weaver's shop: "The period of debate is closed. Arms, as the last resort, must decide the contest." Tom Paine's vigorous language and unanswerable arguments proved that the colonists could not remain loyal to George III and preserve their liberties. He expressed the people's hopes when he said that independence would result in a democratic form of government and establish in America "an asylum for mankind," a "haven of refuge for the oppressed peoples of the world." "We have every opportunity and encouragement before us to form the noblest, purest constitution on the face of the earth. We have it in our power to begin the world over again." [30]

But there were many who did not want to begin the world over again. "We do not want to be independent. We want no revolution," said Joseph Hewes, a North Carolina merchant delegate to the Continental Congress. Independence would let in a "republican Tyranny—the worst and most debasing of all possible Tyrannies." [31]

On May 29, 1776, the Committee on Mechanics in New York demanded that New York delegates vote for independence. The Provincial Congress, dominated by conservatives, refused so to instruct their delegates to the Continental Congress, and on June 11 notified the delegates that they were not authorized to speak for the province. But Richard Henry Lee of Virginia had already introduced his famous resolution, "That these United Colonies are, and ought to be, free and independent States." A committee was appointed at once to draft a Declaration of Independence, and in the home of a bricklayer named Graaf, Thomas Jefferson wrote the great revolutionary document.

The news of the Declaration of Independence filled the workers with joy. In some colonies, moreover, they were the only ones to rejoice. Edward McCrady writes: "There was but one party in South Carolina which was heart and soul in the cause, and that was the old Liberty Tree Party under Christopher Gadsden . . . [composed of] the common people." [32]

It is clear, then, that had the mechanics and laborers had their way, the break with England would have come sooner. But after 1770 wealthy planters, lawyers, and merchants assumed leadership of the revolutionary movement and gradually relegated the mechanics to a subordinate place. It was inevitable, of course, that this should happen. In a country predominantly agricultural, the mechanics, artisans, and day laborers were far less numerous than the farmers and less influential than merchants and planters. In the earlier phases of the revolutionary movement, the urban lower classes were able to exert tremendous influence because it was easier to organize in the cities than in the country districts, where roads were wretched and communication difficult. Throughout the remainder of the revolutionary struggle, the mechanics and laborers were able to prod the more conservative elements but they were not yet strong enough to lead the revolutionary movement for any length of time.

Nevertheless, the services rendered by the revolutionary ancestors of the working class of today cannot be underestimated. They served as "the spearhead of the movement to free the colonies from England and to establish greater democracy in America," made up "the bulk and formed the backbone of the great street demonstrations of the day, and in addition, furnished the forces necessary to circulate petitions, distribute handbills, fight British troops, and dump tea into harbors." [33] Had it not been for them, the Revolution would have been stillborn.

THE WAR FOR INDEPENDENCE

Their revolutionary ardor also helped to bring about victory in the War for Independence. From a Boston artillery company headed by Captain Paddock and composed entirely of mechanics came a number of officers for the American forces. Of fifty-seven men in two companies of the 11th Pennsylvania Regiment whose trades have been listed, only seven were the "embattled farmers" of legend and poetry; the rest consisted of workers of all trades and of common laborers. And there were others whose work was vital and whose contribution to victory was important. They supplied the labor force of the Revolution—teamsters, blacksmiths, gunsmiths, artisans of a dozen crafts who, as one order put it, "when occasion requires it, are to act the Part of Soldiers in either attack or defence as well as Artificers." [34]

Indentured servants too enlisted in the Revolutionary army, their masters receiving payment for their unexpired time. In Lancaster County, Pennsylvania, so many enlisted that in 1781 the county treasurer refused to pay their masters "as it will take more state money than we will receive in the taxes." [35] By an act of the Continental Congress, all indentured servants who had enlisted were declared free men.

Negro workers—free and slave—played a part in the Revolutionary war that is not generally appreciated. Not permitted to participate in the upsurge against Great Britain before the outbreak of war, many slaves at first went over to the British, who had promised them freedom in return for military service. To halt this, a number of states offered freedom to slaves who enlisted in the Continental army. Rhode Island, in 1778-1779, offered Washington a regiment of Negroes. From 72 Massachusetts towns and from Pennsylvania Negroes enlisted to fight in mixed battalions. A Hessian officer wrote in his journal, "No regiment is to be seen [among the Americans] in which there are not Negroes in abundance, and among them are able-bodied, strong and brave fellows." [36] Salem Poor, a Negro soldier, was commended by fourteen officers in a special message to the Massachusetts legislature which said that he had "behaved like an experienced officer, as well as an excellent soldier" at the battle of Bunker Hill. "In the person of this said Negro," they continued, "centres a brave and gallant soldier." The state of Massachusetts also paid tribute to a Negro woman, Deborah Gannett, who had served in disguise as a soldier for seventeen months in the Fourth Massachusetts Regiment of the Continental Army. She was granted a reward of 34 pounds by the state for her "extraordinary instance of female heroism." [37]

The army of the American Revolution was a people's army. It was an army that suffered hunger, cold, and defeat, but which fought on to victory. Washington's touching description of the ragged Continentals at Valley Forge reveals the stuff our Revolutionary forefathers were made of:

"To see men without clothes to cover their nakedness, without blankets to lay on, without shoes, by which their marches might be traced by the blood from their feet, and almost as often without provisions as with them, marching through the frost and snow, and at Christmas take up their winter quarters within a day's march of the enemy, without a house or hut to cover them till they could be built, and submitting to it without a murmur, is a mark of patience and obedience which in my opinion can scarce be paralleled." [38]

The plight of Washington's men at Valley Forge was not entirely due to the British blockade. Much of it was due to the "avarice and thirst for gain" of merchants and manufacturers who were supposed to supply the army. "Speculators, various types of money-makers and stock-jobbers," wrote Washington, were the "murderers of our cause." [39] These profiteers stayed at home, hired substitutes to fight for them, and piled up fortunes in government contracts, currency speculation, and land jobbing at a time when mechanics, small farmers, and patriotic members of the upper classes were giving their lives and possessions to their country.

Anger was mounting on the home front too against the "murderers of our cause." Prices had soared 300 per cent. Abigail Adams, the wife of John Adams, wrote in April, 1777, that there was "a great cry against the merchants, against monopolizers, etc., who, 'tis said, have created a partial scarcity." [40] The people were demanding that states and towns should control prices and all distribution of goods. Connecticut led the way. The state government in 1776 passed an act fixing prices and wages, the preamble to which vigorously damned monopolizers.[41] Soon New York, New Jersey, Pennsylvania, and all the New England states had passed laws fixing wages and prices and setting up controls over the distribution of goods.

Legislation could not control prices if no enforcement agencies existed. It was easy for employers to keep wages at the legal level while violating the price level. Workers were furious when they saw themselves victimized by "an insatiable thirst for riches." A strike of sailors for higher wages took place in Philadelphia in January, 1779. The strike was broken by troops and the strikers were jailed. Discontent grew and some workers weakened. They felt that they were shedding their blood "merely in order to exchange the rule of one oligarchy for that of another no less oppressive and self-seeking." [42] Such, however, was not the general mood. The lower classes decided to enforce price control laws in their own way. In Beverly, Massachusetts, working women raided merchants' storerooms and compelled the merchants to sell their goods at legal prices.

The most effective action occurred in Philadelphia. Pennsylvania had passed a price-fixing law in October, 1778, but up to the summer of 1779 it had not been enforced. That summer a mass meeting elected a committee of enforcement, with the general instructions that "we have arms in our hands and know the use of them, nor will we lay them down till this is accomplished." The committee announced a new schedule of prices and warned the merchants that those who violated the schedule would be severely punished. Alarmed, the monopolizers fell in line, and prices took a drop. When Tom Paine and the Committee of Inspection visited Robert Morris and seized a cargo of flour, the wealthy Philadelphia merchant and financier complained that it was "inconsistent with the principles of liberty to prevent a man from the disposal of his property on such terms and for such considerations as he may think fit." [43]

The British and their Tory traitors hoped to turn the resentment of the masses against the Revolution. They assured the workers that desertion of the cause "would bring lasting honor and immediate rewards instead of uncertainty and poverty they had otherwise to face." Only a few workers capitulated. More characteristic was the action of the Baltimore Whig Club consisting of sailors, watchmakers, tailors, and shoemakers. In 1777 they ordered a Tory printer, William Goddard, "to leave town by morning and the country in three days," or else he would be "subject to the resentment of a Legion." [44]

When the British commander, Clinton, heard of the threats of mutiny by the Pennsylvania 11th Regiment because they "had not seen a paper dollar in the way of pay for near twelve months," he sent them enticing messages and also dispatched emissaries to negotiate. But these emissaries fared badly. A few of them were captured by the soldiers and hanged. Their bodies were left to swing in the wind for five days as a lesson to those who questioned the loyalty of Pennsylvania workingmen to the Revolution.[45]

VICTORY

The surrender of Cornwallis in 1781 and the subsequent Treaty of Peace did not usher in the millennium for American labor. But the American Revolution was the first full step that the common people of our country took on their long march toward freedom. There was much left to fight for. Though slavery as an institution continued, abolition had begun. Massachusetts had abolished slavery in 1780, and in the same year Pennsylvania had passed an act of gradual emancipation. Rhode Island stated the principle which would take a second revolution to realize:

"Whereas, the inhabitants of America are generally engaged in the preservation of their own rights and liberties, among which that of personal freedom must be considered as the greatest, and as those who are desirous of enjoying all the advantages of liberty themselves should be willing to extend personal liberty to others...." [46]

The Revolution had broken the back of the indenture system. Thousands of servants had gained their freedom by their enlistment in the army, and importation of new indentured servants had practically ceased. A meeting of New York citizens on January 24, 1784, called for the abolition of the "traffic in White People, heretofore countenanced in this state, while under the arbitrary control of the British government," because such traffic was contrary "to the idea of liberty this country has so happily established." [47]

The Revolution had opened up the vast areas which the Proclamation of 1763 had closed to settlement. Though the speculators were the first to profit, and the great estates of the Penns, the Fairfaxes, the Granvilles, and other loyalists fell into the hands of a few monopolists, the large increase in the population of the frontier communities showed that the common people had also benefited.

The gains of the Revolution were recorded in the state constitutions. Though most of these favored the rich, democratic advances were made the fundamental law in all of them. The doctrines of the right to life, liberty, and the pursuit of happiness were inserted in the Bills of Rights of nearly all state constitutions. In many, churches were disestablished; freedom of worship was guaranteed; *viva voce* voting was prohibited, and feudal practices like primogeniture and entail, which kept vast areas of land in the hands of a few families, were abolished. Finally, the right of the people to elect delegates to a special constitutional convention, and their right to ratify the draft of the constitution, were recognized for the first time in modern history.

The Revolution freed American economic life from the restrictions of British mercantile policy, extending trade and making a national industry possible. This in turn produced the American labor movement which in its future struggles would realize the aspirations of the mechanics, artisans, and day laborers who had died for American freedom. From the Revolution, American labor gained precious experiences. It learned in the Sons of Liberty the value of collective action and militancy. It learned the value of close contact with workers of other cities and countries through its Committees of Correspondence. From its activities in town meetings, provincial and continental congresses, it learned how to collaborate with its allies toward common national objectives. Furthermore, the Revolution was a powerful influence in shaping the ideology of the American labor movement. The following statement is typical. In June, 1836, the Journeymen Cordwainers' Union of Philadelphia replied to the warning of their employers that they would not employ any shoemakers who belonged to a labor organization:

"It is our prerogative to say what institution we will be members of, that being bequeathed to us by our forefathers—the toilworn veterans of '76 who Nobly moistened the Soil with their Blood in defence of equal rights and equal privileges, that we, their descendants, might enjoy the Blood-Bought Legacy free and unmolested." [48]

For many generations July 4 was celebrated in much the same way that May 1 was observed after 1886. It was a day of parades, banquets, festivals, a day for dramatizing the demands of the working class. One factory worker wrote the following song for the celebration in Fall River, July 4, 1844:

> *Again we hail the day's return,*
> *That gave us independence,*
> *And freedom's fires, that warmed our sires,*
> *Still glow in their descendants.*
>
> *Then let us sing till welkin ring,*
> *When freedom's friends assemble,*
> *And deal such blows upon her foes,*
> *As made her foemen tremble.*
>
> *This day we to each other pledge,*
> *To fight for him who labors;*
> *With truth we will our warfare wage,*
> *And save our guns and sabres.* [49]

The great revolutionary expression—life, liberty and the pursuit of happiness—gave backbone to labor's desire for higher wages, shorter hours, and better working conditions. And the sacrifices their Revolutionary fathers had made stimulated the workers of the 'twenties, 'thirties and 'forties in their demands for a greater share of the wealth produced by their labor.

CHAPTER 4

American Industrial Development, 1783-1880

The American labor movement was not the result of chance. Nor was it something imported into this country from Europe, although immigrants experienced in trade unionism hastened its rate of growth. It was the product of social and economic forces engendered by the growth of industry in America. It was indigenous to America, a logical and inevitable concomitant of the industrial development of this country.

OBSTACLES TO INDUSTRIAL GROWTH

The War for Independence burst the shackles imposed upon American trade and industry by the British mercantilist system. But political independence did not all at once bring economic stability. Directly after the Revolution, commerce was seriously interrupted by the restrictions imposed by England, France, and Spain on ships flying the American flag, which were completely excluded, for example, from the lucrative West India trade. At the same time, the growth of promising industries that had emerged during the Revolutionary War was abruptly checked by the dumping of European goods on the American market.[1] The want of a strong central government under the Articles of Confederation only served to make matters worse. Interstate trade wars developed; several states set up free ports for European goods, while some did not even permit traders from other states to sell their wares without paying heavy fees.

Fortunately these conditions did not last long. By 1800 American merchants had not only regained their former position in world trade but had forged rapidly ahead. While France and England were battling in Europe, American merchants took over a considerable portion of the carrying trade. In addition, crop failures in Europe created an immense demand for American foodstuffs. The registered tonnage of the United

States in foreign commerce increased from 157,000 in 1795 to over a million in 1807.

Industrial growth, however, was much slower. The new constitution adopted in 1787 removed the impediments to commercial intercourse among the states but it could not create overnight a new economic life in America. In 1800 the vast majority of Americans were still isolated farmers. Transportation and communication facilities were so limited that a considerable market for industrial products could hardly exist. For the most part, the rural household was self-sufficient. Alexander Hamilton estimated in 1791 that in many districts "two-thirds, three-fourths and even four-fifths of all the clothing of the inhabitants are made by themselves."

Other obstacles impeded the rise of industry. Capitalists were not interested in investing in manufactures. Merchant princes like Elias Hasket Derby of Salem and Stephen Girard of Philadelphia were reaping huge fortunes in foreign commerce. By 1805, profits from the carrying trade ranged from $50,000,000 to $70,000,000 annually. The total failure of many of the industrial enterprises convinced most merchants that surplus funds should be invested in real estate. Robert Lee, a budding industrialist, in a letter to the Newark *Centinel of Freedom* of August 14, 1810, complained of "the scarcity of capital for manufacturing purposes or the diversion of capital into other channels of employment, where there is a greater prospect of gain, or where it can be employed with greater facility and ease to the proprietor."

Another obstacle was the tendency to view the rise of industry with disfavor because of the belief that it would bring in its wake vice, profligacy, and demoralization of the population.[2] Many, no doubt, were influenced by *Notes on Virginia,* published in 1782, in which Thomas Jefferson expressed the hope that America would never see its citizens occupied at a workbench, and that it would be best for the nation if "for the general operations of manufacture ... our workshops remain in Europe." Jefferson later changed his views on this score, and many Jeffersonians became ardent advocates of industrial development. On January 25, 1794, the Columbia *Centinel,* a Jeffersonian paper, urged its readers to give up the use of articles of British manufacture and begin to "Buy American." In that way, it added, American industry could survive and grow strong despite "the oppressive burdens imposed upon it by the European nations." The Philadelphia *Aurora,* another Jeffersonian organ, demanded a protective tariff to assist the rise of industry in America. "Why should not the manufacturers of a Free republic," it asked on January 29, 1802, "have as much protection from the government as the subjects of a despot?"

But many Americans agreed that industry ought to stay in Europe, that great cities were "pestilential to the morals, the health and the liberties of man." The news that came from Manchester, Birmingham, Leeds, and other manufacturing centers in England of mass unemployment, the horrors of child and female labor, and the miserable living conditions of the working class convinced them of the correctness of their stand.

Gradually the situation changed. The demand for foodstuffs in Europe increased the need for transportation facilities. Soon turnpikes and canals were built to fill this need. Better communications resulted in country merchants getting commodities from the East to sell to farmers whose higher prices for wheat and corn enabled them to buy finer clothing and better shoes than could be made at home.

Immigration and natural reproduction, too, increased the market for industrial goods. And transportation made this market available. At first, English manufacturers reaped the fruits of this expanding market. But the embargo, the non-intercourse acts, and the War of 1812 halted the flood of foreign merchandise that swamped American markets.

The events following the embargo gave American manufacturers a temporary monopoly over the home market. The decline in the shipping trade caused capitalists to shift their investments to other fields, and industry absorbed a considerable portion of this capital. Finally, the War of 1812 convinced many Americans that domestic manufactures were necessary for the independence of this country. "We must now place the manufacturer by the side of the agriculturist,'" observed Jefferson in 1816. "Shall we make our own comforts, or go without them, at the will of a foreign nation? . . . Experience has taught me that manufactures are now as necessary to our independence as to our comfort." [3]

Patriotism and industrial development became one and the same. Naturally, manufacturers were not loth to emphasize this theme. At a dinner at Philadelphia in 1808, Colonel David Humphrey, a Connecticut manufacturer, offered the following toast: "The Best Mode of Warfare for our country—the artillery of carding and spinning machinery, and the musketry of shuttles and sledges." [4]

Cotton and woolen factories, flour mills, iron forges, shoe shops, carpet, cotton bagging, calico, earthenware, glassware, soap, sealing wax, and paper mills sprang into existence during the decade 1806-1816. The mills in the area of Providence alone increased from 41 to 169 between 1809 and 1815, and spindles from 20,000 to 135,000. From the beginning of the century to 1810 the number of spindles in the cotton industry had increased about thirty times, and in the following five years it increased again more than six times to reach the astounding figure of about half a million. The total value of the capital invested in the textile industries was estimated as high as fifty million dollars in 1815.

However, not many of these establishments were in existence a few years later. A deluge of supplies began pouring in from Europe as soon as the treaty of peace with England was signed. British manufacturers now deliberately set out to destroy American industry by selling goods in America below the cost of production. Said Henry Brougham, Esq., in Parliament in 1816: "It is well worth while to incur a loss upon the first exportation, in order, by the glut, to stifle in the cradle, those rising manufacturers in the United States, which the war has forced into existence contrary to the natural course of things." [5]

British manufacturers had many advantages which enabled them to carry this policy into effect. English goods were both cheaper and better than those produced in America. In addition, they could be bought on longer credit terms than could American goods, for American manufacturers had little cash.

Importations which totaled only $13,000,000 in 1813 rose to $147,000,000 in 1816, and between 1815 and 1820 each inhabitant of the United States consumed imported goods averaging $13.50 in contrast to $2.50 per capita for the period 1810-14. As a result, many newly arisen industries in America disappeared. In 1815 nearly 150 mills were in operation in Rhode Island; a year later all were closed with the exception of the old Slater mill. By 1819, when a severe panic hit the country, most of the manufacturing establishments in America "were broken up, their owners ruined, and their property sold at enormous sacrifice." Henry Clay told Congress in 1820 that along the highways were to be seen the ghosts of once prosperous factories, "which their proprietors could no longer keep in motion against the overwhelming pressure of foreign competition." [6]

Yet, despite ruthless competition and the effects of economic depression, American industry surged forward again. Old factories revived and new ones equipped with more modern machinery made their appearance.

As long as the southern slave power controlled the national government, it placed important barriers in the way of industrial development by preventing the enactment of tariff laws and other measures necessary to enable American industrialists to overcome "the overbearing pressure of foreign competition." But the market expanded so rapidly and the demand was so great that foreign production alone could not meet it. Between 1820 and 1840, the population of the United States almost doubled. From all parts of the country came the cry for commodities produced in textile factories, shoe shops, hardware plants, iron mills, distilleries, and leather establishments.

"America," observed Frederick Engels in 1844, "with its inexhaustible resources, with its unmeasured coal and iron fields, with its unexampled wealth of water power, but especially with its energetic and active population ... has in less than ten years created a manufacture which already competes with England in the coarser cotton goods, has excluded the English from the markets of North and South America, and holds its own in China, side by side with England. ..." [7]

ROLE OF TRANSPORTATION

Once again, transportation made possible the expansion of the market. In the 1820's, hundreds of steamers plied the rivers and coastways. Nearly every part of the interior, through turnpikes, rivers, lakes, and canals, was connected with cities on the coast. In 1825, the Erie Canal was built. It carried industrial products west of the Appalachians and brought foodstuffs to the East. It reduced the cost of transportation by as much as 85 per cent. Finally, it initiated an era of such a rapid expansion in transportation that according to the *Buffalo Republican* of April 25, 1828, "Even the most attentive find it difficult to obtain the desired information concerning the railroads and canals which are completed or proposed."

A number of these projects, being purely speculative, never materialized. The panic of 1837, resulting in part from over-expansion and undue speculation in canals and railroads, cut short the completion of many other projects. Still, by 1850, the canal system was well developed. Canals carried coal and iron from Pittsburgh to Philadelphia, wheat and corn from the West to New York City, and manufactured goods from New England to Ohio and points west.

Railroads gradually superseded canals because they were faster and cheaper. In addition, they carried goods the year around, whereas water routes were frozen for more than four months during the year.

The New York Central, started in 1832, had by 1850 grown from a little seventeen-mile road between Albany and Schenectady to a huge system stretching from New York to Buffalo. During the 'forties, 6,000 miles of railroad track were laid in the United States, most of them in the East. In the 'fifties, 21,000 miles of railroad were laid, most of them in the West. At the beginning of the decade, Ohio, Indiana, and Illinois had a combined railroad mileage of 913. By 1860, it had increased to 8,000 out of a total of 30,793 miles in the entire country.

The South alone constructed 7,562 miles of new road during this decade. In 1850, Tennessee did not have a single mile of railroad. Ten years later, it had 1,197 miles.

This increase in railroad mileage during the 'fifties brought the entire West within easy reach of the industrialized East. Moreover, it made possible an enormous growth in the population of this very important section. In 1840, Ohio, Indiana, Illinois, Michigan, and Wisconsin had a population of 2,900,000—more than half in Ohio. In 1860, Illinois alone had a population of 1,712,000; Indiana, 1,350,000; Michigan, 749,000; and Wisconsin, 776,000. Ohio's population at this time was 2,339,000.

Transportation was a key industry, and, together with iron, steel, and coal, was basic to America's industrial development. In 1812, it took six days to go from Philadelphia to Pittsburgh by stagecoach. In 1834, it took three days and nineteen hours to travel by canal. In 1854, the railroad took fifteen hours.

Technological advances also played their part in American industrial development. Fitch's and Fulton's steamboats, Whitney's cotton gin and system of interchangeable parts were the products of the minds of what Frederick Engels called America's "energetic, active population." So were the numerous inventions that swamped the patent office in Washington. From 1790 to 1810, an average of 77 patents were issued annually; in 1830, the number had increased to 544; by 1850, it had risen to 993, and in 1860, to 4,778. During most of these years, the United States had actually granted more patents than England and France combined. In 1841, an Englishman, testifying before Parliament, declared: "I apprehend that the chief part, or a majority, at all events, of the really new inventions, that is, of new ideas altogether in the carrying out of a certain process by new machinery, or in a new mode, have originated abroad, especially in America." [8]

RISE OF THE FACTORY SYSTEM

The factory system in America developed first in the textile industry. Britain had tried desperately to hold back this development by prohibiting the exportation of textile machinery, plans, or models, and the emigration of textile workers. But this could not stop Americans from experimenting with textile machines. In Rhode Island, the wealthy Quaker merchants, William Almy and Moses Brown, were investigating the possibilities of establishing the textile industry.

In 1798, Samuel Slater, an English mechanic, came to America. Learning of Brown's efforts, he offered his services as manager of a cotton spinning mill.[9] Brown readily accepted the offer and supplied the capital. Slater drew up the plans of the Arkwright spinning machine from memory and turned them over to David Wilkinson, a Pawtucket blacksmith, who in 1790 built the first Arkwright machinery to be successfully operated in the United States. A year later, several machines, tended by children and operated by water power, were producing satisfactory yarn.[10]

The factory system in America begins with Slater's Pawtucket mill. Yet it was by no means a full-fledged factory. Machinery was used only for turning raw cotton into yarn; weaving was still done by local farmers in their cottages.

In 1815 the first modern factory in America made its appearance. Five years before, Francis C. Lowell had gone to England to study the organization of cotton factories. Returning to America with a host of new ideas, in 1812 he induced a group of New England merchants to invest their fortunes in his factory. These capitalists set up the Boston Manufacturing Company and established a cotton factory in Waltham, Massachusetts. There for the first time all the processes in the manufacture of cotton cloth were brought together under one roof. The first cloth came off the looms on February 2, 1816. Mass production in the textile industry had started.[11]

Soon after, the system spread throughout Massachusetts, New Hampshire, and Maine. Lawrence, Lowell, Dover, Manchester, Holyoke, and Chicopee became industrial centers, owned and dominated by great families of Boston—the Lowells, Abbots, Appletons, and Lawrences. Absentee owners, these capitalists rarely visited the factory towns, where so many workers lived in diseased and squalid surroundings.[12]

The emergence of the factory system in the production of woolens was much slower. As late as 1830, household production for home use and domestic production on a putting-out basis still exceeded factory production. And even in 1860, most of the work in Philadelphia was still being done by hand-loom weavers who owned their own looms and tackle and worked on material furnished by merchant capitalists.

Woolen factories appeared in New England during the 1820's and 1830's. By 1860, 1,700 mills with 640,000 spindles, 16,000 looms, and an annual output of $90,000,000, employed more than 60,000 laborers. The boot and shoe industry also entered slowly into the factory stage of production. Before 1840 the work was divided between in-workers, who labored in a central workroom owned by a merchant capitalist, and out-workers, who labored in their own homes. The out-workers, some of them women, sewed the shoes together, being supplied with leather, binding, and thread by the merchant. Binding was also done by women who worked in their homes and were paid on a piece-work basis.

Specialization and division of labor already existed but machinery was hardly used until the 1840's, when the McKay sewing machine was introduced. By 1855, there were splitting machines, soling machines, buffing machines, and machines for dyeing outsoles and heels. Much of this machinery was driven by steam or water power, although the full application of power to shoe machinery did not occur until the Civil War.

The factory system came into being in the shoe industry around 1855, by which time there were already specialization of function, division of labor, the widespread use of machinery, and mass production. The census of 1860 spoke of the industry as daily assuming the characteristics of the factory system, being conducted in large establishments of several stories, each floor devoted to a separate part of the work, with the aid of steam power and all the labor-saving contrivances of the trade.

The census also reported that fully one-twelfth of all the workers engaged in manufacturing were employed in the shoe industry. In 1860, there were 12,487 establishments, employing 123,029 workers and producing boots and shoes valued at $91,891,490.[13]

INDUSTRIAL EXPANSION ON THE EVE OF THE CIVIL WAR

Iron production was barely developing into a full-grown industry when the Civil War began. This industry was organized on an almost feudal basis. Several individuals owning huge tracts of mineral lands in New Jersey and Pennsylvania, employed workers in their mines and mills whose lives they completely controlled. All houses, stores, churches, and schools were owned by the iron barons and payment was in commodities, the workers constantly in debt to the lords of the mines and mills.

Corporations took over the iron industry in the 'thirties. At that time America was second only to Great Britain in iron production, even though it was a rather poor second. Fifty-five thousand tons of pig iron were produced in America in 1810, 180,000 tons in 1830, and 988,000 tons in 1860.

Pittsburgh developed slowly as an important iron-producing center. In 1826, there were only seven rolling mills in the entire region, and they consumed only 6,000 tons of ore. In 1850, 14 mills consumed 59,000 tons. In 1857, 21 mills consumed 132,600 tons. Prior to the Civil War, its iron industry was geared more to agricultural than industrial needs. In the agricultural era, the manufacturer of wrought iron supplied the "country iron workers, blacksmiths by profession or necessity, with bar iron to be shaped to meet the needs of farmer, wagoner and mill owner." In the industrial era, beginning in 1859, the demand for iron "came increasingly from industries engaged in the production of finished iron goods and the machinery of industry and commerce."[14]

As America's industrial development proceeded, the coal industry rose to a position of prime importance. Before 1825, no appreciable amount of coal was mined in this country—less than 50,000 tons in 1820. Not only were most deposits still inaccessible, but our economic life had, as yet, little use for coal. Steam engines were few, most machinery being operated by water power. Wood was the household fuel, and charcoal was used for smelting iron. Most of the early railroads used wood-burning locomotives, and steamboats on the Ohio River did not abandon the use of wood until the early 'fifties.

The situation soon changed. The building of canals provided an outlet for coal. The market was now no longer purely local, although not until the first railroads entered the coal region in the 'forties was the transportation problem really solved.

In the 'thirties, coal began to supplant wood as household fuel. In 1839, the introduction of the hot blast made possible the use of anthracite coal in iron furnaces. As iron production rose and the number of furnaces, rolling mills, and iron and steel works increased, coal output also soared. By 1860, it was already 14,334,000 tons, of which 8,500,000 tons were anthracite.

This increase in coal production was a certain sign that America was rapidly making the change from an agrarian to an industrial economy. Another sign was the rise of the corporation. Although individual ownership and partnerships were most characteristic before the Civil War, the corporation was advancing rapidly in the textile, iron, and coal industries. In the field of railroad construction no other form but the corporation existed. It cost about $15,000,000 to build the Baltimore & Ohio; $30,000,000 for the New York Central, and about $25,000,000 for the Erie. Granted that much of these huge sums went to fill the purses of wealthy promoters, no one individual or partnership in America would have provided the money necessary to build these roads.

The influence of industrialists over American economic and political life began even before the Civil War. In Boston in 1850, for example, fifteen families, known as the "Boston Associates," controlled 20 per cent of the cotton spindles in the country, 30 per cent of the railroad mileage in Massachusetts, 39 per cent of the insurance capital of that state, and 40 per cent of Boston's banking resources. These families— the Lawrences, Lowells, Appletons, Cabots, Dwights, Eliots, Lymans, Sears, Jacksons—controlled the Bay State, its press, pulpit, schools, factories, legislature—in short, its economic, political, and cultural life.

Business control over American politics did not await the Civil War. Nor did the trend toward monopoly. Referring to such a trend in the iron industry, the Pittsburgh *Morning Post* declared in 1849: "The wealthy monopolists are anxious to crush those who are doing a small business, and get them out of the way, in order that they may fix prices to suit themselves." [15]

In some industries there were actually fewer establishments in 1850 than in 1840, and fewer still in 1860 than in 1850. In cotton manufacture, for example, the number decreased from 1,240 in 1840 to 1,094 in 1850, and to 1,091 in 1860. Yet during these same years, the capital invested had doubled, the amount of raw material used more than trebled, and the number of workers employed increased by almost 70 per cent. A similar development can be observed in the woolen industry, in which the number of establishments decreased between 1850 and 1860 by more than 10 per cent, while the value of output increased.

Although trustification was not yet becoming widespread, in some industries there was a decided trend toward the elimination of small establishments and the creation of larger ones.

America was making the transition from an agricultural to an industrial nation, and even though the domination of the nation's political life by the southern slavocracy limited the speed with which this transformation developed, it could not entirely hold it back. The total value of our manufactures rose during the period 1840-1860 from $483,278,000 to $1,885,861,000, an increase of nearly fourfold. The number of workers in manufacturing establishments having an output valued at $500 or more rose from 791,000 in 1840 to 1,311,000 in 1860. Over 5,235,000 cotton spindles were in operation in 1860 as compared with 2,284,631 in 1840, an increase of more than twofold. In 1860 more than 1,900 woolen mills were putting out products valued at $68,865,000 as compared with $20,696,999 in 1840. Silk manufacture increased during the same period from next to nothing to $6,500,000. From 1850 to 1860 the value of stove manufactures increased from about $6,000,000 to nearly $11,000,000; tools and farm machinery from approximately $10,500,000 to $21,000,000; furniture and upholstery from $7,000,000 to $28,000,000; vehicles from $18,000,000 to $36,000,000.

Between 1820 and 1860 the population of the United States grew from less than 10,000,000 to 31,000,000, increasing each decade about one-third above the previous one. Cities flourished as trade and industry expanded. The percentage of people living in cities was 4.9 in 1820, 8.5 in 1840 and 16.1 in 1860. In 1790, only six cities had a population of over 8,000; in 1860, the number of such cities was 141. In 1810, no city had a population of 100,000; by the year 1860, there were eight cities above that figure—New York, Philadelphia, Baltimore, Boston, New Orleans, Cincinnati, St. Louis, and Chicago. In 1790, New York City had a population of 49,400; it had risen to 1,174,700 in 1860. That same year, Philadelphia had a population of 565,520; Chicago, 109,260; Baltimore, 212,000, and New Orleans, 168,170.

The astonishing growth in urban population reflected the rise of American industry. The following census figures of manufacturing in 1860 provided the background for this growth:

Section	Number of Establishments	Capital Invested	Average Number of Laborers	Annual Value of Products
New England	20,671	$257,477,783	391,836	$468,599,287
Middle states	53,387	435,061,964	546,243	802,338,392
Western states	36,785	194,212,543	209,909	384,606,530
Southern states	20,631	95,975,185	110,721	155,531,281
Pacific states	8,777	23,380,334	50,204	71,229,989
Territories	282	3,747,906	2,333	3,556,197
Total	140,533	$1,009,855,715	1,311,246	$1,885,861,676

Karl Marx correctly predicted in 1858 that "when the inevitable transition to the factory system takes place in [the United States], the ensuing concentration will, compared with Europe and even with England, advance in seven-league boots." In 1860 the United States occupied fourth place in world industry. In 1894 it occupied first place, producing about one-third of the world's manufactured goods. America's production in that year totaled $9,498,000,000; the United Kingdom, $4,263,000,000; Germany, $3,357,000,000; France, $2,900,000,000; Austria, $1,596,000,000; and Europe as a whole $17,352,000,000.[16]

INDUSTRIAL GROWTH DURING THE CIVIL WAR

This remarkable development began with the Civil War. The war years and the years immediately following worked revolutionary changes in American economic life. From 1860 to 1870, the total number of manufacturing establishments increased by 8 per cent and the value of manufactured products by 100 per cent. The number of factory workers went from 1,311,000 to 2,054,000.

The war itself greatly stimulated industrial growth, hastened the rise of large-scale manufacturing, and encouraged the construction of railway and telegraph lines. It boomed the production of agricultural machinery, canned food, ready-made clothing and shoes. The use of the harvester revolutionized agriculture, made possible large-scale production of grain, and pushed the frontiers westward. By the time the war ended, the factory system had been fastened upon many American workers, whose lingering hope of escaping the wages system by becoming small producers was waning fast. Even the mechanic in the smaller towns found it more and more difficult to compete with the mechanized factories in the industrial cities, whose cheap goods were carried everywhere by the railroads.

During the war the shift from workshop to mechanized factories took place with amazing speed, a transformation reflected by the fact that the number of patents for new machines leaped from 3,340 in 1861 to 6,220 in 1865. But most of all it can be seen in the changes of specific trades. In the ship-joining industry the mortising machine, planing machine, and jig-saw were introduced. In the cigar trade the hand-press and the mold were adopted. Machines for planing wood moldings, for cleaning streets, and for fashioning hoops and staves were other innovations. By the end of the war large-scale machine production had become characteristic in the shoe, metal, cigar, printing, textile, and many other industries.[17] Early in 1864, a workingman submitted an analysis to *Fincher's Trades' Review*, the outstanding labor paper of the Civil War era, of the revolution under way in the shoe industry:

"Comparatively few people are aware," he wrote from Lynn, Massachusetts, "of the quiet, steady revolution that is going on in the business of shoemaking, and particularly as that business is conducted in Lynn. ... The rapid progress made during that time [April, 1861], and especially within the past year or two, in the introduction of machinery in shoemaking has been beyond all previous calculation. It may almost be said that handwork has already become the exception, and machinery the rule. The little shoemaker's shop and the shoemaker's bench are passing rapidly away, soon to be known no more among us, and the immense factory, with its laboring steam-engine and its busy hum of whirling wheels, is rising up in their place, to change the whole face of things in the ancient and honored metropolis of the workers in the gentle craft of leather."

By this time the skilled craftsman found that he had little advantage over the "green hands." A foreman of a large shoe manufacturing establishment remarked that he could "take an unskilled laborer from the street and in two days' time teach him to do some portions of the work as well as a man who had spent years in learning the shoemaker's trade." In the coopering industry machine-made staves displaced the most skilled phase of the cooper's art, leaving only the relatively simple task of "settin-up," which any worker could learn in a few days. Similarly, in the cigar making industry molding machines enabled employers to use girls who could be trained in a few days to do work formerly performed by skilled artisans. Thus arose the "partially skilled" workers—young boys and girls who were easily trained and paid half as much as the skilled journeymen used to receive. During the war they flocked into fields before considered the exclusive property of the skilled mechanics.[18]

INDUSTRIAL EXPANSION AFTER THE CIVIL WAR

After the Civil War and the crushing defeat of the slave power, capitalism developed "at a headlong pace." As Marx pointed out, "the handing over of an enormous proportion of the public land to speculative companies for exploitation by means of railways, mines, etc." led to the "creation of a financial aristocracy of the meanest sort," which was eager to invest wherever profits could be rapidly accumulated. Fixed capital in industry rose from $533,245,331 in 1849 to $2,790,272,606 in 1879 and the value of manufactured goods, produced now for a protected home market, rose from $1,885,861,676 in 1859 to $5,369,579,171 in 1879.

The economic expansion of the two decades after the Civil War is reflected in the statistics of industrial production. Between 1860 and 1880 alone, the capital invested in mining increased by more than twenty times, while the total value of the production increased from 90 to 250 million dollars. In 1860, 14,000,000 tons of coal were mined; in 1884, almost 100,000,000 tons. Between 1874 and 1882, the production of Bessemer steel ingots leaped from 191,933 tons to 1,696,450. In 1865 Massachusetts manufactured 718,660 cases of boots and shoes; two decades later, 2,633,075 cases annually. In 1860 there were 30,626 miles of railroad in operation; in 1884, 125,739 miles. Between 1860 and 1870 railroad mileage increased by almost 80 per cent, and during the next decade the same rate of increase was maintained.

According to the United States Census of 1900, manufactures, estimated at $1,885,862,000 for 1860, came to $3,385,860,000 in 1870 and $5,369,579,000 in 1880, almost a four-fold increase. During the same period the capital invested in manufactures jumped from $1,009,856,000 to $2,790,274,000, and the number of workers employed went from 1,311,000 to 2,733,000.

TRENDS TOWARD MONOPOLY

Accompanying the emergence of a highly mechanized industrial system was the trend toward greater concentration. The trend, initiated earlier, went on with amazing speed during the war. Only big industrialists, after all, could afford to introduce machinery, expand their plants, and so compete successfully for lucrative government contracts. The result was a foregone conclusion: many small business enterprises either went out of existence or were taken over bodily by bigger ones.

In 1865 most businesses were still conducted on a small scale, but not many years elapsed before consolidation of small competing firms occurred. By absorbing and crushing small competitors, giant monopolies evolved, capitalized at tens of millions of dollars.

Every industry was influenced by the trend toward centralization, but it was most marked in the telegraph, railroad, salt and pepper, and petroleum industries. At first in the hands of many small competing companies, the telegraph industry soon came under the control of two principal companies, the Western Union and the American. Even these two corporations were in reality one, the same capitalists "owning into each other to such an extent as to make them virtually one." In 1864 a rival group formed the United States Telegraph Company, but two years later the new company, with $6,000,000 worth of shares, was absorbed by the Western Union, which by this time controlled a capital of $40,000,000 and 70,000 miles of wire.

By the end of the war the Pennsylvania Railroad, which had started with one short line from Philadelphia to the Susquehanna River, had absorbed more than 138 small roads representing more than 250 corporations, and by 1871 it controlled more than 3,000 miles of track, with an annual income of over $40,000,000. By the acquisition, during the war, of the Pittsburgh, Fort Wayne, and Chicago Railroad, the Pennsylvania completed the first trunk line between Lake Michigan and the Atlantic coast. Other large railroad consolidations were also accelerated by the war. The Erie took over several small roads. The Chicago and Northwestern absorbed the Peninsular line as well as roads between Boston and Ogdensburg, New York, and four between Quincy, Illinois, and Toledo, Ohio.

The railroads that carried coal foresaw the profits that would come from control of the mining regions, and quickly acquired claims to territory. By 1871 the Reading Railroad had already taken possession of about 70,000 acres of land, and its annual report to stockholders boasted: "The result of this action has been to secure and attach to the company's railroad a body of coal lands capable of supplying all the coal tonnage that can possibly be transported over the road for centuries." The coal subsidiary of the Reading controlled more than 75 per cent of all the collieries in Schuylkill County.[19]

In short, a nation of small enterprises had entered the war and emerged with the factory system dominant and the trend toward concentration in full swing. To be sure, giant trusts did not reach national proportions until the 'eighties, but the Civil War hastened the tendency. During the war, the first combination of petroleum refineries was completed and the Rockefeller empire began to take form. And in 1866 the *Commercial and Financial Chronicle* could say:

"There is an increasing tendency in our capital to move in largei masses than formerly. Small business firms compete at more disadvantage with richer houses, and are gradually being absorbed in them. Thus we have more men worth $100,000 in some of our large commercial cities than were reputed five years ago to be worth fifty thousand dollars. No doubt much of this reputed capital is fictitious. But the power accumulating in the moneyed classes from the concentration of capital in large masses is attracting the attention of those observers of the money market. It is one of the signs of the time and will probably exert no small influence over the future growth of our industrial and commercial enterprise." [20]

It was also to exert "no small influence" over all of American society, including government, schools, press and Church. For the story of this expansion of industry and increasing concentration of wealth is also the story of corruption in one form or another. To secure land grants, loans and subsidies from the government and thereby rob the nation of its richest resources, the railroads engaged in an orgy of fraud. The Union Pacific paid close to a half million dollars in graft to congressmen and state legislators between 1866 and 1872, while the Central Pacific handed out as much as $500,000 annually during the years 1875 to 1885. Senator Hoar said on the occasion of the completion of the first transcontinental railroad:

"When the greatest railroad of the world, binding together the continent and uniting the two great seas which wash our shores was finished, I have seen our national triumph and exaltation turned to bitterness and shame by the unanimous reports of three committees of Congress that every step of that mighty enterprise had been taken in fraud." [21]

One of these committees, the Poland Committee, which investigated the Credit Mobilier fraud, declared in its report delivered in 1873:

"This country is fast becoming filled with gigantic corporations, wielding and controlling immense aggregations of money and thereby commanding great influence and power. It is notorious in many state legislatures that these influences are often controlling, so that in effect they become the ruling power of the state. Within a few years Congress has to some extent been brought within similar influences." [22]

CRISES, AND LABOR'S ANSWER

But the acceleration of American economic life was not constant. Every few years, industry came to a halt: shops and factories closed, workers were discharged, and small business men were swallowed up by bigger ones. The years 1819, 1837, 1854, 1857, 1860, 1873 marked periods of severe economic crisis. During these periods, misery stalked the land.

During each crisis, people began to ask why it was that industry was so suddenly prostrated. And each time the spokesmen for the upper class gave the same answer—overproduction. Too many factories, too many canals, too many railroads, too many banks existed. Too much cotton cloth had been made, too much food had been produced, too many shoes had been fashioned—too much of everything to yield a profitable return. Hence, industry had stopped, and workers were unemployed.

No one said that the people who produced these goods did not earn enough to buy much of what they had made. No one said that New England cotton factories averaged for decades 10 per cent a year on their investments, and that Samuel Slater accumulated a fortune of $700,000 in forty years and the "Boston Associates" made millions at the same time that the textile workers starved. No one said that iron works in the 'fifties declared dividends ranging from 40 to 100 per cent while the iron workers lived under almost feudal conditions. No one said that railroad promoters, iron producers, lumber kings and oil tycoons had amassed huge fortunes by seizing and monopolizing the best natural resources of the land—resources that belonged to the people. No one in power said these things, but Joseph Weydemeyer, an early American Marxist, said in the summer of 1853: "Those stoppages of trade, which precisely in our day have shaken the entire structure of society in revolutionary fashion—they are produced by nothing else but a disparity in the growth of the two (productive capacity and markets). For the increase in the consumptive capacity of the market cannot keep pace with the increase in the productive capacity of the industrial forces." During the terrible years of the depression that began in 1873 and lasted until 1879, a worker wrote:

"What changes in a century! Look at our thousands of miles of railroads, our countless mills and factories, our mines and forges, our vast wealth! All created by labor in one century. And what has labor to show for its share of the good things it has produced? Literally nothing. It has neither railroad, factory, forge or mine. Capital has cunningly appropriated everything." [23]

The remarkable story of a century of American economic development is largely the story of labor. For without labor this industrial development could not have taken place. No one expressed it better than a member of the Miners' Union in Illinois who wrote during the Civil War:

"Without labor where would all our inventions be? Without labor where would all our mineral wealth be? ... Without labor we would be without the power of steam, as it has been developed during the past 75 or 80 years, for without labor this great invention would never have been developed, for who can say that Watt was a capitalist. I think history will prove that he was a working man. Without labor where would our Railroads and our Steamboats be? Without labor our canals would be undug—our rivers nothing but fish ponds; our mineral wealth would be buried in the bowels of the earth. Where would our gold be if we were all capitalists? Where would our millions of tons of iron ore, our lead, our copper, and last, but not least, our millions of tons of coal just here in the wealthy and flourishing State of Illinois? . . .[24]

Abraham Lincoln was President when this union miner wrote these words. Lincoln probably never read this statement, but had he done so, he would have agreed fully with its basic point. For he himself said:

"No good thing has been or can be enjoyed by us without having first cost labour. And inasmuch as most good things are produced by labour, it follows that all such things of right belong to those whose labour has produced them. But it has so happened, in all ages of the world, that some have laboured, and others have without labour enjoyed a large proportion of the fruits. This is wrong and should not continue. To secure to each labourer the whole product of his labour, or as nearly as possible, is a worthy object of any good government." [25]

"Labor is the foundation of the entire political, social and commercial structure," said William H. Sylvis, the outstanding labor leader of the Civil War years. It was "the author of all wealth," he declared, yet capital appropriated to itself the vast bulk of the wealth which labor had created. Of what value, he asked, were "railroad networks, canals, mineral resources, factories, magnificent cities, public buildings, and internal improvements if the wealth is controlled by and for the benefit of a few individuals while the great mass, the 'producing classes' are reduced to poverty?" [26]

America, labor knew, was rich enough to provide everyone with the economic foundation for happiness. But to enjoy this happiness, labor had to unite to wrest from capital a larger share of the national income. Under the leadership of their trade unions and political organizations, the American workers through struggle secured higher wages, shorter working days, better conditions, numerous democratic reforms and an improved status in the community commensurate with their importance to society.

CHAPTER 5

Early Trade Unions

Faced with degrading conditions and a subsistence livelihood, the American worker could do one of three things: one, he could remain at his work and accept the wages and conditions offered him by his employer; second, he could leave his work and seek a better life elsewhere; third, he could unite with his fellow-workers and force the employers to grant the improvements required. Some workers stayed on the job and accepted exploitation without putting up much of a struggle to alter their status. Others tried to escape by moving to other districts or by becoming independent farmers on the frontier or independent producers. But even before the Federal Constitution was adopted American workers were uniting with their fellow workers in trade unions to improve their living conditions.

LABOR CONDITIONS IN POST-REVOLUTIONARY AMERICA

American labor gained little from the expansion in trade and commerce after the War for Independence. In the early factories workers toiled long hours for miserable wages. Young children constituted the principal labor supply in the textile plants. Samuel Slater's first nine operatives were seven boys and two girls under twelve years of age. In 1820 half of the factory workers were boys and girls "of the tender age of nine and ten years," who worked twelve to thirteen hours a day for wages ranging from 33 cents to 67 cents a week.[1] A typical advertisement of the period appeared in the Rhode Island *Manufacturers' and Farmers' Record* of May 4, 1820: "Wanted—a family of from five to eight children capable of working in a cotton mill." When Josiah Quincy, a New England statesman, visited a textile mill in Pawtucket in 1801, the owner pointed with pride to the number of children at work. By keeping out of mischief and not wasting time playing games, he said, these children were serving God as well as aiding their families. Quincy, however, was not impressed by this eloquent defense of child labor:

"But an eloquence was exerted on the other side of the question more eloquent than his, which called us to pity these little creatures, plying in a contracted room, among flyers and coggs, at an age when nature requires for them air, space, and sports. There was a dull dejection in the countenances of all of them." [2]

Most of the other textile workers were daughters of nearby farmers who lived in crowded and badly ventilated company boarding houses. Their hours were long, from five in the morning to seven at night, and their wages were small, averaging little more than $2 to $3 a week.[3] Skilled workers in establishments far removed from factory life fared little better. In the late 1780's, a carpenter, mason, or smith in New York City earned four shillings a day. An unskilled worker, ditch digger, hod carrier, earned two shillings a day. Even so, John Jay, a New York conservative, protested that the "wages of mechanics and labourers ... are very extravagant." The extent of this extravagance is revealed by a report in the *New York Daily Advertiser* of January 13, 1791, that "many of our small tradesmen, cartmen, day laborers and others, dwell upon the borders of poverty and live from hand to mouth." Six hundred New York journeymen appealed for public relief in 1797 because they were "in want of sufficient *fire* and *food*" to maintain themselves and their families. They complained that while prices had risen 50 per cent since the Revolution, wages had remained stationary.[4] * Nine years later a skilled shoe-worker testified, "I could only make eight dollars and a

---

* The following table indicates the relation of wages to the cost of living during the years when the first trade unions were formed: 1900 = 100.

Year	Money Wages	Cost of Living	Real Wages
1791	23	42	55
1792	25	46	54
1793	27	49	55
1794	29	53	55
1795	33	61	54
1796	33	65	51
1797	31	60	52
1798	33	60	55
1799	29	57	51

Sources: Jurgen Kuczynski, *A Short History of Labour Conditions in the United States of America, 1789 to the Present Day*, London, 1943, pp. 20-21; see also Hansen, "Wholesale Prices for the United States," *Publications of the American Statistical Association*, Vol. XIV, p. 804, and *New York Daily Advertiser*, Sept. 7, 1785.

half a week and I worked from five in the morning till twelve or one at night.[5]

Even these wages were not paid regularly, and they were generally paid in scrip which could only be redeemed at stores owned or controlled by the employers. The high prices charged here swallowed up a considerable portion of these meager earnings. The consequent bitterness among workers is revealed by the following account written by an Englishman who came to this country in the post-Revolutionary era:

"All the mechanics with whom I conversed complained of the difficulty which they experienced in getting *paid* for their labour, much of what they did receive being given them in orders upon shops for necessaries and clothing; the extra price charged by the store-keeper, under the circumstances, causing in their judgment a clear loss to them of *three-quarters of a dollar per week.*" [6]

What kind of life could the worker enjoy on twenty-five or fifty cents a day? "The simplest food, drink, and clothing and the meanest hovel were the terms of his existence," a recent study of New York in 1789 points out. "In 1795 it cost ten cents a day to maintain a pauper in the Almshouse, and this sum was naturally based on the wholesale purchase of provisions, clothing, and fuel, and it excluded rent. Yet in that year, as in 1789, a common laborer blessed with a wife and child had less per head with which to provide for the three of them than an inmate of the poorhouse." [7]

Working days were from sunup to sundown. In summer this meant a working day of from fourteen to sixteen hours, with two hours or less off for meals; in winter it meant nine to twelve hours, with one hour or less off for meals. Since wages were usually paid by the day rather than by the number of hours worked, employers were tempted to get their work done during the late spring, the summer and the early fall when they would secure more hours for the same wages.

THE MERCHANT CAPITALIST ENTERS

Nor was this all. Profound changes in American economic life were making the skill of the craftsmen less important. No longer did a master craftsman, who owned a shop, manufacture to order for a few local customers. No longer did he employ only one or two journeymen and apprentices. He was now manufacturing for markets in the South and West, and as the demand increased, he expanded his shop and took on more workers.

But competition was also increasing. Turnpikes and canals made it possible for producers to compete for the same market, and to meet the competition, employers reduced wages and increased working hours. This trend increased after the entrance of the merchant capitalist. One of the great difficulties faced by producers for a distant market was the serious lack of credit and financing facilities. The farmers who bought boots and shoes and other manufactured articles had little cash, and small manufacturers and local retail merchants could not afford to sell on credit. This gave the advantage to the importing merchants in the seaboard cities, who not only possessed considerable capital but also received credit from abroad. The small manufacturers sought desperately to meet the situation by themselves, even organizing associations, one of whose functions was to grant loans to members. But this was a futile makeshift arrangement.

This situation brought the merchant capitalist into being. He did not have to know how to manufacture. He did not even own shops or mills and employ workers. He bought raw materials, found a producer to manufacture them into finished goods, and secured the markets for their sale. He had his own capital or obtained large credit. In either case he could sell on fairly long credit terms.

As the sphere of the merchant capitalist expanded, the master craftsman who owned a shop became little more than a labor contractor. His profit was the difference between the price he received from the merchant capitalist and the wages he paid his workmen. To increase these profits, he divided his workers into teams so that by specialization and division of labor the work would be speeded up, set skilled against unskilled, and hired women and children to do the work of men at one-quarter their wages, and in every way forced greater exertions from the workers. A few employers who wished to pay the usual wages were threatened by the merchant capitalists and forced to capitulate. Keep profits soaring by cutting wages and increasing hours in the sweatshops, became the slogan for employers and capitalists alike.[8]

Relations between workers and employers were profoundly affected by this development. This is not to say that the emergence of trade unionism in America can be explained solely by the extension of the market and the rise of the merchant capitalist. Trade unions were formed because workingmen depended on their wages for their livelihood and because they had learned through experience that individually they could do nothing to maintain or improve their living standards. The entrance of the merchant capitalist hastened a development that was inevitable once a wage earning class had arisen in America.

TEMPORARY LABOR ASSOCIATIONS

It was to bring some concrete meaning to the Declaration of Independence that American workers shortly after the Revolution set up their first trade unions. These unions were organized by skilled craftsmen, not by unskilled factory workers. That the factory workers had reasons for complaint is obvious. But a considerable number of them were children who could not be expected to organize and most of the others were young women who had an alternative to organizing in trade unions and forcing an improvement in their lot—they could leave when conditions became intolerable and return to their farms. The skilled mechanics, however, had no such alternative. Few of them owned farms or gardens from which to supplement their inadequate wages. Without organization they would continue to "dwell upon the borders of poverty and live from hand to mouth."

Prior to and immediately after the Revolution workers and employers had co-operated on a number of issues, and had even formed mutual benefit societies "for the laudable purpose of protecting such of their brethren as by sickness or accident may stand in need of assistance, and for the relief of the widows and orphans of those who may die." [9] Yet during these years the workers complained of inadequate wages and bad working conditions, and a feeling of resentment was emerging among them. As early as 1773, Jonathan Boucher, a Maryland clergyman, observed that "both employers and the employed ... no longer live together with anything like attachment and cordiality on either side: and the labouring classes, instead of regarding the rich as their guardians, patrons, and benefactors, now look on them as so many over-grown colossuses whom it is no demerit in them to wrong." [10] In short, co-operation between workers and employers was breaking down before the appearance of the merchant capitalist. His appearance by intensifying exploitation hastened the process.

The first significant break in this relationship occurred when the journeymen left the mutual aid societies to which employers and workers belonged and formed their own benevolent associations. Mutual aid societies of journeymen, printers, carpenters, shoe workers, hatters, tailors, and bricklayers were quite common in the 1790's. But these mutual aid societies were not enough. Labor came to realize that it was just as important to prevent their employers from thrusting them into need as it was to assist each other when they were in distress. Once this understanding developed, trade unions emerged.

Before the first permanent trade unions were formed, skilled workers united into temporary associations to improve their conditions. In 1778 the journeymen printers in New York combined and demanded an increase in wages. They sent a letter to their employers informing them that "as the necessaries of life are raised to such enormous prices, it cannot be expected that we should continue to work at the wages now given; and therefore request an addition of Three Dollars per week to our present small pittance." [11] Unless the request was granted, they declared, they would not continue to work. After the increase was reluctantly granted the printers saw no reason for continued existence of their organization and abandoned the association.

The first authentic strike took place in America in 1786, six years before the organization of the first permanent American trade union. Determined to secure a wage of a dollar a day, the journeymen printers of Philadelphia met and adopted a resolution in which they announced that in the future they would "not engage to work for any printing establishment in this city and county under the sum of $6 per week." They concluded, "We will support such of our brethren as shall be thrown out of employment on account of their refusing to work for less than $6 per week." When the employers refused to grant the request, the printers struck, or conducted a "turn-out" as it was called, and succeeded in winning their demands.[12]

Other turn-outs soon followed. Philadelphia house carpenters struck for a ten hour day in 1791; Baltimore sailors struck for a higher wage in 1795, and in the same year, New York carpenters and masons struck to raise their wages two shillings a day. So alarmed were the employers that a writer in the *New York Daily Advertiser* for March 30, 1795, warned that "An acquiescence on the part of the citizens on this occasion will in all probability not only excite similar attempts among all other descriptions of persons who live by manual labor but induce reiterated efforts to increase their wages at seasons when they find their services most wanted. . . ."

All of these strikes were led by temporary associations which lasted only while the struggle was on. Experience soon taught the workers that temporary organization would not enable them to maintain their wage rates in face of the permanent pressure of the employer to reduce them. What was needed was a permanent organization that had regular meetings, had a treasury for emergencies, and a plan for the struggles to come.

THE FIRST TRADE UNIONS

Beginning with the 1790's, skilled journeymen in several cities converted their mutual aid societies into trade unions that would conduct struggles for higher wages and shorter hours as well as assist members during periods of sickness. Employers tried to prevent this transition to trade unionism. A few legislatures were influenced to pass laws prohibiting workers from using their benevolent societies to fix wage scales. As an answer to this legislation, groups of workers like the Philadelphia printers dissolved their mutual aid societies and re-established them as trade unions.[13] The purpose of these societies is made clear in the preamble to the constitution of the Journeymen Cordwainers of the City of New York, adopted in 1805:

"We, the Journeymen Cordwainers of the City of New York, impressed with the sense of our just rights, and to guard against the artifices or intrigues that may at any time be used by our employers to reduce our wages lower than what we deem an adequate reward for our labour, have unanimously agreed to the following articles as the Constitution of our society." [14]

Here the New York shoe workers were asserting that labor had to organize a stable, continuous combination so as to be prepared to meet any attempt by employers to reduce wages. The statement also reveals that as early as 1805 American labor was determined to maintain its right to decide what it considered an "adequate reward" for its labor.

The first organization of workers in the United States to maintain a permanent union was formed by the Philadelphia shoemakers in 1792, after previous attempts had failed. In 1794 the Federal Society of Journeymen Cordwainers of Philadelphia was organized and this union continued to exist until 1806. In 1799, the society conducted the first strike of a permanent union. The strike against reduction in wages is also significant because it was the first sympathetic strike on record: the bootmakers turned out to aid the shoemakers secure their demands. The society paid one of its members to picket the master-shoemakers' shops. The strike lasted for about ten weeks but was lost. The twelve years' existence of the Cordwainers Society, however, was marked by a number of successful struggles for higher wages.

A few months after the Philadelphia cordwainers had organized, the Baltimore journeymen tailors and the New York printers set up their unions. The New York Typographical Society, organized in 1794, remained in existence more than ten years. Another New York union, the Journeymen Cabinet and Chair Makers, was formed in 1796 and lasted until 1837. The New York Society of Journeymen Shipwrights came into existence in 1803 and the House Carpenters of the City of New York in 1806. That same year the tailors in New York formed a union. Judging from notices in contemporary newspapers, these last three organizations were still functioning in 1819. The Journeymen Cordwainers Society of New York, organized in 1805, was flourishing forty years later.[15] *

Most early unions, however, did not continue so long. A lost strike often meant the end of a union. Sometimes a victorious strike dissolved a union because the members believed it had accomplished its purpose. Only the printers and shoemakers had enough strength and understanding to remain in existence for many years and in different parts of the country. By 1810 permanent organizations of shoemakers and printers existed in Philadelphia, New York, Baltimore, Pittsburgh, Boston, Washington, and New Orleans.[16]

UNION POLICIES AND PRACTICES

Because of the short lives of the first American unions and the failure of most of them to leave records and proceedings, it is not easy to learn just what these labor organizations were like and how they functioned. Fortunately the records of the printers' and cordwainers' unions have been preserved, making possible a study of early American trade union practice.

Upon becoming a member of the union, a worker usually took an oath to stand by its wage scales, to keep its proceedings secret, and to assist members to get employment "in preference to any other person." He paid an initiation fee, generally about forty or fifty cents, and regular dues from six to ten cents a month. He was required to attend monthly meetings. Since workers traveled about from city to city in search of work, he was usually permitted to be absent for three months. When he returned and proved that he had been out of town, he was still "deemed a lawful member, by paying one month's contribution."[17]

Members were required to conduct themselves in a decent and orderly manner at meetings. Any member who did not keep silent after the president called for order could be fined, usually about six cents. Fines were also imposed for absence without cause from membership meetings, ten or twelve cents for the first offense, twenty to twenty-five cents for the second, and fifty cents for the third. Concerning absences the New York Cordwainers' constitution said: "It is the duty of the private members to attend the meetings and cooperate with its officers in promoting the welfare of the society. In doing this, they will recollect they are promoting their own individual welfare."[18]

---

* Frequently unions of a particular trade in a city dissolved and continued under a new name. The New York Typographical Society reorganized as the Franklin Society in 1799, and continued in existence until 1804. Another or second New York Typographical Society was formed in 1809 and continued until 1818, although a reference in the New York *Daily Plebian* of January 21, 1845, indicates that it may have continued its existence up to 1845.

Members could be expelled if after a trial they had been found guilty of "frequent intoxication," "gross immorality," "giving a brother member any abusive language in the society-room during the hours of meeting," and "frequent neglect of business" that had caused their families to suffer and their employers to lose money. A member of the New York Typographical Society was expelled because he was judged guilty of "turning wrong a half sheet of twenty-fours and without mentioning the circumstances to his employer, leaving the city even neglecting to note down the signature letter in his bill." This was deemed "conduct highly derogatory to the character of the New York Typographical Society and disgraceful to himself as a member." The unions were proud that "all the best workmen" were members of the organization.[19]

The first American trade unions were local craft unions concerned primarily with local craft problems. They had no organic connection with unions in other cities nor did connections exist among unions of different trades in the same locality. Essentially these unions were small groups operating locally within a single industry. The members of these unions were workers in a single craft or skill. In this early period, there was little division of labor in the production of a commodity. Most members of the cordwainers' union made the entire shoe themselves. The union printer not only cut the type but also set and printed it. The skilled wage earners worked in small shops and did not come into contact with workers in other trades. It was natural for these workers to form strictly craft unions.

At first members of the unions fought mainly to preserve their skill protesting against the employment of "learners, runaway apprentices, and half-way journeymen," and all other unskilled workers, who, it was said, "will work for what they can get." [20] But even then the skilled workers were fighting a losing battle. Employers, egged on by merchant capitalists, began to use more and more apprentices at considerably lower wages than those paid skilled journeymen. Division of labor began to make some headway in the handicraft trades. Skilled workers were forced to teach apprentices a particular phase of the work, in which these "green" workers would specialize. Soon the skilled men worked for the same wages as the apprentice. The employers were more interested in quantity and price than in quality, and many quickly trained, specialized workers could produce faster and cheaper.

The skilled journeymen fought this new trend vigorously. Many of them blamed the apprentices instead of the employers. Through their experience the journeymen learned that they could maintain their wage standards only through organizing the apprentices and setting wage scales for skilled and unskilled work. The journeymen cordwainers learned this lesson as early as 1805, and provided in their constitution that apprentices were eligible for membership.

Experience taught them another lesson, that a labor union could not be effective if it allowed employers to be members. Their membership was the result of two factors. First, labor felt that the employer who worked in the shop was a member of the producing class, not of the idle exploiting class of capitalists, the bankers, "and all who now live on, or intend hereafter to live without useful labor." [21] Secondly, in some trades "class commuting" was frequent. In the printing trade a worker who had become an employer could remain in the union if he paid the union scale to his journeymen. In the boot and shoe trade where class commuting was rare, there was no provision for employer membership. This is one reason for the greater militancy of the cordwainers' unions.

One of the first unions to recognize the weakness in employer membership was the New York Typographical Society. The union had approved a resolution in 1809 that said, "between employers and employed there are mutual interests." Eight years later it discovered an employer member conspiring with other employers to break the union. The union expelled him and amended its constitution to exclude employers because:

"Experience teaches us that the actions of men are influenced almost wholly by their interests, and that it is almost impossible [that] a society can be regulated and useful where its members are actuated by opposite motives and separate interests. This society is a society of journeymen printers, and as the interests of the journeymen are separate and in some respects opposite to that of the employers, we deem it improper that they should have any voice or influence in our deliberation." [22]

The emphasis on experience provides us with a key to an understanding of these early American unions. Labor learned from experience which taught it how to proceed in its efforts to secure better conditions and how to improve upon tactics in the struggle to wrest these conditions from the employers.

In the beginning, trade union tactics were fairly simple. The members of the union would meet, draw up a wage scale and pledge not to work for any employer who did not pay the wages demanded. By 1802 some unions would select a committee to present the wage scale to the employers. Those who accepted the proposed list and paid the wages were sometimes honored with a special resolution, while those who refused faced a strike and found their shops picketed by "tramping committees." Strikers received strike benefits; by 1810 the cordwainers and the printers paid benefits regularly to those "brethren who had been thrown out of employ in consequence of their refusing to work for less than the established prices." [23]

The trade agreement was the next step in trade union tactics. As early as 1799 a trade agreement was made between the Philadelphia shoemakers and their employers. Ten years later, the New York Typographical Society appointed a committee of three to confer with a committee of all the employers in the trade for the purpose of establishing a uniform wage scale throughout the city. After several meetings a wage scale was agreed upon. The New York printers tried as early as 1815 to set up a uniform wage scale for the cities of the East in order to stop employers from sending work out of the city. The printers were unsuccessful.[24]

A number of unions appointed "tramping committees" to see that employers lived up to agreements. When it was discovered that it was better to appoint and pay one man to do this, "the walking delegate" came into existence. In most strikes, however, unpaid committees were used.

Another lesson the workers learned very early was the need for a closed shop.* Too often the employers broke an agreement by bringing in non-union workers at less than the scale. Before a month had passed the wages of the union members had been cut to the level of the new workers. No union could be effective so long as its members had to compete in the same shop with unorganized workers, for the latter could take all the advantages secured by the influence and activities of the union and then co-operate with employers against it in case of a strike. The New York Typographical Society put the case concisely in 1809: "We conceive it to be *the duty* and the interest of every journeyman printer in the City to come forward and unite with his fellow-craftsmen in promoting an object which has for its end the benefit of the whole." [25]

But a closed shop could be established only by discipline. Understanding this the New York Journeymen Cordwainers in 1805 made the closed shop part of their constitution: "No member of this society shall work for an employer that has any Journeyman Cordwainer or his apprentice in his employment, that does not belong to this Society, unless the Journeyman come and join the same."

Should any member "work on the seat" with a person or persons that had not joined the society, and failed to report to the president at the very next meeting, he would have to pay a fine of one dollar. Subsequent violation of this rule would lead to expulsion.[26]

Other cordwainers' unions had similar agreements—not always written ones—and in most cases they were strictly enforced. One worker

* The closed shop goes back to 1794 when the shoemakers of Philadelphia compelled employers to hire only union members.

testified in a court case in Philadelphia: "If I did not join the body no man would sit upon the seat where I worked, nor board or lodge in the same house, nor would they work at all for the same employer." [27]

"Traveling cards" were another means of enforcing the closed shop. This system was very effective among the printers. A journeyman appealed to his union in Washington for reinstatement. "I have for a long time past wished to go to New York, but I cannot procure employment there without I take with me a certificate from this society, which, of course, I cannot procure unless the society will reinstate me in my membership, which I now most respectfully and earnestly request them to do." [28]

Workers have always held a deep hatred for scabs. A group of New York seamen who had struck for higher wages in 1800 were so infuriated by the scabs who were working the ships that they marched to the docks "with drums and fife, and colours flying" and engaged in a bloody battle with the gang who were there to protect the "rats." A Philadelphia cordwainer was fined five dollars for contempt of court in 1806 when he arose during a labor trial and shouted, "A scab is a shelter for lice." [29]

Scabbing during a strike was the worst offense a union member could commit and called for immediate expulsion. The New York Typographical Society not only expelled any member found guilty of taking the place of a worker who had been "discharged by an employer in consequence of supporting the rules of this society by refusing to work for less than the established prices," but also provided that his name should be "reported to the different typographical societies in the United States." [30] This exchanging of "scab lists" was one of the many signs of the emergence of labor solidarity at a time when there was no organic connection among the local unions of different cities.*

* At least one effort, however, was made during this period to achieve such unity. Early in 1796 the Federal Society of Philadelphia Cabinet Makers, which was engaged in a strike for higher wages and to defeat the determination of employers "not to employ any journeymen cabinetmakers as society men, but as individuals," issued an address "to their Mechanical Fellow-Citizens" urging the different unions to meet together "to   digest a plan of union, for the protection of their mutual independence." "We hope and intreat," went one of its appeals, "that a union of the respective mechanical branches in this city, and throughout America, will immediately take place, in order to repel any attack that has or may be made on societies of this description. . . . We find ourselves necessitated to call aloud to you for a communication of sentiment and assistance, as we feel that the united efforts of all the societies, must produce a more permanent establishment of the independence of each, than the individual exertion of a single one. Hasten then, fellow citizens, to declare yourselves ready at any time to assist one another, in a cause which will determine the independence of so useful a body as the working citizens of America." (See *Dunlap and Claypoole's American Advertiser*, July 16, 1795, Feb. 18, 1796 and Philadelphia *Aurora*, April 7, 1796.)

In 1810 when the Philadelphia printers went on strike for higher wages, the employers advertised in New York for printers promising them twice the normal wage. The Philadelphia union corresponded with their brothers in New York who promptly supported their "typographical brethren of Philadelphia in the demand for a rise of prices," asserting that "... we pledge ourselves to each other that we will not take any situation vacated by any of our brethren in Philadelphia under the present circumstances." [31] *

This was less than twenty years after the first trade union had come into existence in America. But already some trade unions had established the policies of collective bargaining, demands for a minimum wage, the effort to secure a "closed shop," scab lists, strike funds, unity between skilled and unskilled workers, "traveling cards," and solidarity among different local unions of the same trade.

As a result of these policies, important economic gains were secured. Wages for carpenters in Massachusetts increased from 74 cents a day in 1791 to $1.13 in 1820; and wages of painters from $1.15 a day in 1800 to $1.34 in 1820.[32] Statistics for other trades are not available, but there seems to be no reason to doubt that here too trade union activity brought significant increases in wages.

LABOR AND THE COURTS

These results, moreover, were achieved in spite of bitter opposition of the courts which permitted employers to combine to force down wages and establish blacklists while the combining of workers was judged a conspiracy.† Stephen Simpson, a labor leader, wrote in the *Working Man's Manual* published in 1831:

* When their employers advertised for workers to break a strike in 1803, assuring them that they "will find constant employment and generous wages by application to the Master Curriers of the city and county of Philadelphia," the Journeymen Curriers' Society of Philadelphia inserted the following notice in the press:
    "NOTICE
    "To the Journeymen Curriers of all parts of the Union
    "Your brethren of Philadelphia take this method of informing you that they have turned out unanimously for higher prices—They therefore think that as they ask no more than the prices established in New York, that their brethren of the trade will take no notice of any advertisements of the employers here to allure them to the city; more especially as the master curriers have entered into resolutions to lower the prices that have been current for twenty years past." (Philadelphia *Aurora*, Nov. 9, 1803.)
    † Employers had united even before the appearance of the early trade unions, but now they increased their activity to combat labor's demands and "to break them [the unions] up altogether root and branch." At times employers accepted the

"If mechanics combine to raise their wages, the laws punish them as conspirators against the good of society, and the dungeon awaits them as it does the robber. But the laws have made it a just and meritorious act, that *capitalists* shall *combine* to strip the man of labour of his earnings, and reduce him to a dry crust, and a gourd of water. Thus does power invert justice, and derange the order of nature." [33]

Although no legislation was enacted in the United States similar to the English eighteenth century laws against combinations of workmen, British judicial precedent was followed in charging conspiracy to American workers' organizations. The charge was based upon the doctrine of conspiracy in the English common law—the body of principles and rules of conduct which the court developed from cases between individuals which were brought to the judges to settle—according to which any two or more men who plotted the harm of a third or of the public could be indicted on the criminal charge of conspiracy, and legally punished. In short, workers could not unite to obtain benefits not obtainable by them as individuals. For example, in the Philadelphia cordwainers' case, November, 1805, the prosecution admitted that any of the journeymen "might lawfully ask, whatever wages he thought proper for himself, but that where two or more agreed to ask the same prices, they are guilty of a violation of the law...." [34]

The doctrine struck at the heart of trade unionism, for the only way workers can elevate themselves is through collective bargaining, since individually the vast majority of workers had no bargaining power.*

Space does not permit a detailed account of all these early anti-labor court actions, prosecuted in the name of the state, but instigated and financed by the employers. It is possible, however, by examining one case to understand the basic issues involved in all of them.

Eight shoe workers in November, 1805, were indicted in Philadelphia by a grand jury on charges of forming "a combination and conspiracy to raise wages." This case was of nationwide prominence because it was part of the political struggle between the Federalists who controlled the judiciary and the Jeffersonian Democratic-Republicans who con-

---

terms of the union merely to gain time to recruit strike-breakers and then proceeded to lock-out the union members. (See Commons, *op. cit.*, Vol. I, pp. 132-34; G. A. Stevens, *History of the New York Typographical Union, No. 6*, New York, 1913, p. 134, and Philadelphia *Aurora*, August 1, 1804.)

* In 1937 Chief Justice Charles Evans Hughes of the United States Supreme Court, speaking for the majority in the National Labor Relations Board *vs.* Jones & Laughlin case, declared: "Long ago we stated the reason for labor organizations; we said that they were organized out of the necessities of the situation; that a single employee was helpless in dealing with an employer;... that union was essential for giving laborers opportunity to deal on an equality with their employer."

tended that English common law had been swept away by the Revolution. Counsel for the employers was Jared Ingersoll, son of a prominent Loyalist, ardent Federalist, and champion of the English common law. Counsel for the shoemakers was Caesar A. Rodney, a leading Jeffersonian, soon to become Jefferson's Attorney-General, an uncompromising enemy of the common law which he regarded as a remnant of British tyranny.[35]

Before the trial started, the workers appealed to the public to join with them in opposing the establishment of a precedent dangerous to all progressive movements in America. This appeal was published in the Jeffersonian newspaper, the *Aurora*, of November 28, 1805, and was signed by James Ghegan and George Keamer, president and secretary of the Cordwainers' Society:

"If the association of men to regulate the price of labor," it declared, "is to be converted into a crime, and labeled with the same reproachful terms as a design against the freedom of the nation, the prospect is a very sad one for Pennsylvania ...

"What we have here said," the appeal concluded, "will inform the public of our conduct, and will shew that under whatever pretences the thing is done, the name of freedom is but a shadow, if for doing what the laws of our country authorise, we are to have task masters to measure out our pittance of subsistence—if we are to be torn from our fireside for endeavouring to obtain a fair and just support for our families, and if we are to be treated as felons and murderers only for asserting the right to take or refuse whatever we deem an adequate reward for our labor."

The trial took place in the Mayor's Court before a jury composed of two innkeepers, a merchant, three grocers, a tobacconist, a watchmaker, and a master tailor. Job Harrison, the first witness for the prosecution was a self-confessed scab and labor spy. Another witness, Anthony Bennett, testified that he had been threatened with death by members of the union. When asked how he knew he would be killed if he did not join the union he replied: "They have threatened to do it. Not to my face but according to what I have understood. They have broken my windows with potatoes. They have abused me."

A leading argument of the prosecution was that unless the union was crushed, industry would leave Philadelphia. Could a jury of respectable citizens, asked Ingersoll, permit these labor organizations "composed of men who have been only a little time in your country" to exist when rather than "submit to the laws of the country" they were seeking to "alter them according to their own whim or caprice?"

Caesar Rodney's defense was based on a brilliant attack upon English common law. He argued that American employers were hiding behind a law passed in England in 1349, the Statute of Laborers, which had forced all workers who survived the Black Plague to work at wages fixed by the state in the interest of the employers. Was it for this, asked Rodney, that the American people had sacrificed and struggled through a long and difficult war? He had only contempt for the charge that unions would force businessmen out of Philadelphia. Not only was the charge untrue but it was immaterial.

"The labourer," Rodney insisted, "is surely worthy of sufficient hire to enable him to live comfortably." Furthermore, the society of journeymen cordwainers "had as much right to create itself, as the associations to promote commerce, agriculture, the arts, or any other object."

The prosecution's appeal to patriotism, he continued, was a cloak to hide the fact that it was not the public's welfare but the profits of employers that were at stake in the trial. "When you see a formidable band of masters attending on the trial of this cause, and some of the most eminent counsel in the city employed to prosecute it; and when you see, further, that it is not taken by any of their customers it will require strong arguments to convince you, it is done out of pure patriotic motives." Rodney concluded with an earnest appeal for justice:

"If you are desirous of introducing a spirit of inequality into our government and laws, if you think that the labourer and the journeymen enjoy too great a part of liberty ... such disposition and opinion will lead you to convict the defendants. If, on the other hand, you are satisfied with the wise and liberal principles of our government, ... if you are content with the blessings enjoyed under our Constitution which secures to the citizen an equality of rights which recognize no distinction of classes—I shall look for a verdict of acquittal." [36]

The composition of the jury made the verdict a foregone conclusion. The workers were found "guilty of a combination to raise wages," and were each fined eight dollars.

This decision served as a precedent for future verdicts. In 1809 in New York tailors were found guilty of conspiracy and fined one dollar and costs. In Baltimore and Pittsburgh shoemakers in 1814 and 1815 were found guilty and fined. Of the six recorded cases charging the shoemakers with criminal conspiracy between 1806 and 1815, four cases were decided against the workers. The light fines are a testimonial to the temper of the people, but the decisions show as well that the aim of employer and court was to drive trade unionism out of American life. Thus the Recorder for the 1815 trial of the cordwainers in Pittsburgh wrote: "The verdict of the jury is most important to the manufacturing interests of the community for it puts an end to these associations which have been so prejudicial to the successful enterprize of the capitalist in the western country." [37]

For a time the employers and the courts were successful in hindering the development of trade unionism. When the cordwainers of Philadelphia were outlawed by the courts in 1806, they turned to organizing a producers' co-operative society. But neither court decisions nor employers' coercion could stop the development of the American labor movement. The message of the Philadelphia Typographical Society to their striking brothers in New York is typical of the necessity and the will to go forward: "Persevere in your laudable struggle, and remember that no great struggle was ever yet attained without danger and difficulty." [38]

CHAPTER 6

Labor and Jeffersonian Democracy

Come each true-hearted Whig and each Jolly Mechanic
Who never knew fear or political panic
Come rally your forces and muster your bands
To support the Old Cause with your hearts and your hands.[1]

By the old cause this workers' song of 1785 meant the cause of freedom for which the people had fought during the Revolutionary War. Now there was a need for a new struggle to preserve it. The new struggle was for Jeffersonian democracy.

SOURCES OF JEFFERSONIAN DEMOCRACY

The immediate sources of Jeffersonian democracy go back to the day when the Revolutionary soldiers returned to their homes to find them mortgaged, their families in debt, and their government in the hands of wealthy merchants and landed gentry. These men were piling up their wealth by speculating in land, in soldier certificates, treasury warrants, and continental paper. The common people organized politically to win the peace as they had won the war. Political campaigns were waged in all states to lift the postwar burdens from the small farmers, mechanics, and laborers. In most of these campaigns the working class was handicapped because the right to vote was usually restricted to property-owners.

One of the few states without property qualifications for voting was the state of Pennsylvania. In New York twenty-pound freeholders or occupants of tenements valued at forty shillings a year could vote for members of the assembly.[2] Few mechanics were freeholders but a number of mechanics rented apartments valued at forty shillings a year. More and more mechanics and laborers qualified as the year advanced.

Some workmen thought in terms of independent political action. On

October 9, 1784, a mechanic in Philadelphia urged fellow-workingmen to nominate their own candidates in the coming election:

"All the miseries of mankind," he said, "have arisen from freemen not maintaining and exercising their own sentiments. No reason can be given why a free people should not be equally independent in this, as in other respects, in their political as well as their religious persuasions." [3]

His advice was not followed, but in New York City the following spring the mechanics nominated their own ticket for the State Assembly. The movement started when the mechanics had been defeated in their attempt to incorporate their Mechanics' Society. Aaron Burr had led the opposition to the bill on the ground that it would give the working-men "too much political influence." The Council of Revision vetoed the bill after the legislature had passed it.

After this defeat, the mechanics resolved to gain real representation in the State Legislature. A mechanic on April 14, 1785, stated in the *New York Packet* that "the pedantic lawyer, the wealthy merchant, and the lordly landholder have already had their interests ... attended to." Why then, he asked, should not the "respectable mechanics and cartmen" be represented by men of their own class who could press their claims? He continued: "The great, the mighty and powerful ones are constantly classified together, for what purpose? To prey upon the weak, the poor, the helpless. ... Are there no men worthy of our confidence, but merchants and lawyers?" Remembering the days when they had marched under the banner of the Sons of Liberty, the Mechanics' Society nominated the first mechanics' ticket in post-Revolutionary America. All but one on the ticket were elected, among them two workingmen—a shoemaker and a smith. Most of the others were "friendly to the cause." [4]

In the 1790's similar resentment over the control of the national government by a clique of wealthy men led to the formation of political organizations by mechanics and laborers all over the country.

It is manifestly impossible here to show in detail how the government of the United States was taken over in the 1790's by the mercantile and financial aristocracy and how the usurpation was opposed by the workers. A few facts must serve to suggest the manifold political activities of American labor during the era of Jeffersonian democracy.

Unlike many small farmers opposed to ratification of the new Constitution (fearing that they would never be safe "from the insolence of great men—from the tyranny of the rich—[and] from the unfeeling rapacity of the exciseman and tax-gatherer"), the mechanics and laborers followed the lead of Jefferson in supporting it. They were just as eager as employers to achieve national economic stability and to halt the dumping of British goods in American markets, which was causing considerable unemployment. A Bill of Rights, they believed, would aid in preventing certain evils predicted by those opposed to the Constitution. Early in 1788, Boston mechanics, under the leadership of Paul Revere and Benjamin Russell, voted unanimously in favor of ratification of the Constitution and adopted a resolution expressing an earnest desire that Massachusetts would soon ratify the document. In New York and Philadelphia, too, mechanics and laborers agitated for ratification.[5] A Philadelphia mechanic who heard a foe of ratification protest that he did not like to have the new Constitution "crammed down our throats" replied:

"If Mr. F—— had had no victuals to *cram down his throat* but what he had procured with borrowed money or upon credit, as has been the case for three months past, and solely from the decay of trade occasioned by want of a good federal government, he would not require three or four months to consider the new Constitution." [6]

Eager for a strong central government, the mechanics and laborers joined with others in the community to push Thomas Jefferson's demand for a Bill of Rights. That the first ten amendments were finally included in the Constitution was the result of this pressure. As one student has put it: "They came out of the people and were made directly for their benefit." [7]

But provisions in a written document guaranteeing freedom of religion, press, speech, assembly, and petition to all were not sufficient of themselves. Whether the Bill of Rights was to be meaningful or to become a dead letter depended upon the plain people. The *Newark Gazette* stated the case accurately when it wrote on March 19, 1794: "It must be the mechanics and farmers, or the poorer class of people (as they are generally called) that must support the freedom of America."

For freedom was once again in danger. When Jefferson returned from his mission to France, he was appalled to find that the wealthy merchants and speculators were dominating the country after the adoption of the Constitution. Hamilton and the Federalists were open in their determination to subvert the republic into a monarchy. The Federalists hated democracy, calling it "government of the worst." John Jay summed it up for them when he said, "Those who own the country ought to govern it." The common people were entirely too ignorant to be entrusted with political privileges. The proper place for mechanics and laborers was at the work-bench and for small farmers at the plow. Affairs of state were reserved for "the rich and the well-born." [8]

With the able assistance of Alexander Hamilton, "the rich and the well-born" did nobly by themselves. Hamilton's funding program alone provided enormous profits for Federalist merchants and bankers who were paid by the government the face value of the soldiers' certificates and other securities they had purchased from farmers and laborers at one cent on the dollar. And these same farmers and workers were forced to pay high excise taxes to provide the revenue for the operation of the plan. Finally, James Madison spoke up: "Of all the shameful circumstances of this business, it is among the greatest to see the members of the Legislature who were most active in pushing this job openly grasping its emoluments." [9]

At the moment when the common people were beginning to realize that the future they had won was in danger, news came of great events in France. The French Revolution was now to rekindle revolutionary ardor in the country from which it had drawn its inspiration. There was no joy among the Federalists, but the American people celebrated. New York mechanics in 1794 resolved, "May the light of freedom which was kindled in America and reflected to France in a blaze illuminate the world and lay despotism in ashes." [10]

It was no simple matter, however, to get rid of "all tyrants, plunderers and funding speculators." The Federalists were powerful, well organized, determined. They had money in abundance for bribery, manipulation, and corruption. It was difficult for the widely dispersed people to meet, to act together. They had little money, few newspapers to challenge the Federalist press, and few clergymen to speak for them. But in the cities and large towns lived the artisans, mechanics, and laborers. Men who had belonged to the Sons of Liberty, and were even now forming benevolent associations and trade unions, knew how to organize. By 1792 these labor veterans and militant farmers were out in force to preserve the gains of the Revolution.

THE DEMOCRATIC-REPUBLICAN SOCIETIES

These new organizations were called Democratic Societies or Republican clubs. Their top leadership often came from intellectuals and the well-to-do, but their main membership was made up of urban workers and small farmers. According to a recent study made by Eugene P. Link, of the 206 identified members of the Philadelphia society 103 were craftsmen, and of the 177 identified members of the Charleston club 34 came from the same class.[11]

From the Democratic Societies came frequent expressions of solidarity with the people of France. In an address "To the People of the United States" one of the clubs declared:

"Shall we Americans who have kindled the spark of Liberty, stand aloof and see it extinguished when burning a bright flame in France, which hath caught it from us? Do you not see if despots prevail, you must have a despot like the rest of nations? If all tyrants unite against free people, should not all free people unite against tyrants? Yes, let us unite with France and stand or fall together." [12]

Each meeting of a Democratic Society was devoted to lectures, forums, discussions, and the composing and adopting of resolutions, addresses to the people and remonstrances to the President, Congress, and the state legislatures. The Societies constantly lashed out against secret sessions of Congress and state legislatures. They demanded that legislators, executives, and judges abandon the use of "dark, intricate, antiquated formalities," and "obsolete phraseology" which only lawyers and classical scholars could understand. The plain people had a right to be heard and no fine-spun theories of "monocrats" could keep them silent.

To the Democratic Societies belongs the credit for the post-Revolutionary demand for popular education, and for putting into practice the progressive theories on education advanced by their leader, Thomas Jefferson. As the Democratic Society in Philadelphia put it: "The establishment of public schools upon proper principles will insure the future of independence and republicanism." By means of Correspondence Committees, the Societies made public education a national issue. Even though no state-supported schools were established at that time, the founding of our public school system was the direct result of the work of these societies in which American workers played so important a part. At least ten colleges and academies were begun or aided by members of these popular societies.[13]

Education is not, however, confined to the schools. The press has always been a vital force in spreading or suppressing knowledge. The Democratic Societies felt the need for a press because "the greater part of the American newspaper seemed to be lock, stock and barrel in the hands of the anti-democrats." In the words of William Manning, a poor, untutored farmer, "A labouring man may as well hunt for pins in a hay-mow as to try to collect the knowledge necessary for him to have from such promiscuous piles of contradictions." [14] Manning published in 1797 his *Key of Libberty* which proposed a "labouring society" to which all Americans who worked for a living could belong. The society was to be based on the principle made famous almost a century later by the Knights of Labor. Manning said, "...as Labour is the sole parent of all property by which all are supported, therefore the calling ought to be honorable and the labourer respected." The most important function of the organization would be to furnish the labouring classes "with a monthly magazine [and a] weekly newspaper." [15]

Although no weekly labor press resulted from the activities of the Democratic Societies, they broke into the press on all issues concerning the welfare of the people. The New York Democratic Society paid for a supplement in the *New York Journal* for April 20, 1794, which gave in full the principles and constitution of the Associated Democratic Society of Chittenden, Vermont. Other societies whenever possible had their resolutions, circular letters, patriotic speeches, and proceedings reported in the press. They published numerous pamphlets, one of which was Tom Paine's *Rights of Man*, emphasizing the following paragraph: "Several laws are in existence for regulating and limiting workmen's wages. Why not leave them as free to make their own bargains as the lawmakers are to let their farms and houses? Personal labor is all the property they have. Why is that little and the little freedom they enjoy to be infringed?" [16]

The featuring of this defense of trade unionism is not strange, for the journeymen's associations, organized in the 1790's, co-operated and worked closely with the Democratic-Republican clubs. The membership and leadership of the two often overlapped. On many a July 4, the societies of carpenters, printers, cordwainers, coopers, and cabinet-makers joined officially with the Republican Club in the community and drank toasts to "The Fourth of July, may it ever prove a memento to the oppressed to rise and assert their rights." [17]

THE FEDERALIST COUNTER-OFFENSIVE

The Federalists fought the Democratic Societies and the many Jeffersonian newspapers by an elaborate Red scare. The Societies, the Federalists thundered, were part of a vast, secret and subversive international body known as the Bavarian Illuminati, organized by the "bloody French Jacobins," subsidized by Paris gold. Timothy Dwight, president of Yale College, warned that if the people's movement succeeded holy worship would become "a dance of Jacobin phrenzy," their psalms would be "Marseilles hymns," the Bible would be "cast into a bonfire," and the wives and daughters of Americans would become "the victims of legal prostitution; soberly dishonoured; speciously polluted; the outcasts of delicacy and virtue, and the loathing of God and man." [18]

"Every attempt to restore the liberties of mankind, or to check the progress of arbitrary power," wrote a Jeffersonian in 1797, "is now styled Jacobinism." [19]

Red scares may retard but cannot halt the march of freedom. By 1795, although the Democratic Societies had begun to disintegrate, their work was continued in town meetings and in Orders of St. Tammany. The popular societies had served their purpose. They had helped to crystallize the formation of the Democratic-Republican Party led by Thomas Jefferson.

Although the Republican Party included many manufacturers, merchants, and professional men, the bulk of its membership consisted of working farmers, mechanics, craftsmen, and day-laborers.* Especially active were the maritime workers, who were seriously affected by the British practice of imprisoning American sailors and seizing American ships. These maritime workers were outspoken in their opposition to all anti-democratic elements. In a letter to William Willocks, a columnist for Hamilton's paper and a bitter foe of the people's movement, "A Sailor" wrote, "If your name continues in the papers under such dirty pieces, you will soon be a corpse." [20]

Failing to frighten the people with their lies, the Federalists turned to force and terror, steam-rolling through Congress the Alien, Sedition and Naturalization Acts. Formerly these same men had welcomed European workers because the rapidly growing commerce and industry were demanding an abundant and cheap supply of labor. Hamilton had lauded these immigrants "who by expatriating from Europe, have improved their own condition and added to the industry and wealth of the United States." [21] When the immigrants not only added industry and wealth to their adopted country but liked their new country so well that they demanded more wages and democratic rights, the Federalists sought either to deport them or make citizenship extremely difficult to obtain.

The Naturalization Act calling for five to nineteen years residence was aimed particularly at the Irish workers who had come to the United States in large numbers when the Irish Rebellion of 1798 had been crushed. These workers were active in trade unions, St. Tammany societies, and the Democratic Party. These Irish, one Federalist thought, were "the most God-provoking Democrats this side of Hell," and he urged that they be sent back where they had come from. Harrison Gray Otis wrote to his wife, "If some means are not adopted to prevent the indiscriminate admission of wild Irishmen and others to the right of suffrage, there will soon be an end to liberty and property." [22]

Another step to crush criticism of the Federalists was the Alien Act which empowered the President to deport at his own discretion any alien he might consider dangerous to the "peace and safety of the United States." Edward Livingston, who was leading the fight in Congress against the anti-Alien bills, said that such an attack could easily be extended to citizens. And it was. The Federalists jammed the Sedition Act through Congress. It imposed a fine not exceeding $2,000 and imprisonment not exceeding two years for anyone who should "write, print utter or publish ... any false, scandalous and malicious writing or writ-

* In Boston and New York some workingmen supported the Federalist Party because they were attracted by its demand for protective tariffs.

ings against the government of the United States, or either house of the Congress of the United States or the President of the United States, with intent ... to bring them ... into contempt or disrepute."

David Brown, an itinerant mechanic of Massachusetts labeled by the Federalists the "Wandering Apostle of Sedition," was sentenced to eighteen months in jail and a $400 fine. He was guilty of having erected a liberty pole at Dedham, Massachusetts, on which he had pinned the following leaflet:

"Here is the 1,000 out of 5,000,000 that receive all the benefit of public property and all the rest no share in it. Indeed all our administration is as fast approaching to the Lords and Commons as possible—that a few men should possess the whole Country and the rest be tenants to the others. There [always] has been an actual struggle between the labouring part of the community and those lazy rascals that have invented every means that the Devil has put into their heads to destroy the labouring part of the Community.... I never knew a Government supported long after the confidence of the people was lost, for the people are the Government." [23]

Intimidation, jails, and fines did not prevent the election of Jefferson in 1800 as the third President of the United States. One of his first acts in office was to nullify all the prosecutions and sentences under the Alien and Sedition Acts.

THE TRIUMPH OF JEFFERSONIANISM

Though most workers could not vote, their part in Jefferson's Presidential campaign was crucial. In New York, it will be recalled, many mechanics and laborers could vote for members of the state assembly. Hamilton even admitted in 1796 that elections for the legislature had become a "question between the rich and the poor" of New York City.[24] Since the legislature of New York voted for the presidential electors, a victory in New York City for the Republicans would guarantee twelve electoral votes for Jefferson.* Victory depended on the vote of the artisans,

* "In New York," wrote Jefferson to James Madison on March 4, 1800, "all depends on the success of the city election." He went on to point out the significance of this election in the entire national campaign: "... if the city election of New York is in favour of the republican ticket, the issue will be republican; if the federal ticket for the city of New York prevails, the probabilities will be in favor of a federal issue, because it would then require a republican vote both from Jersey and Pennsylvania to preponderate against New York, on which we could not count with any confidence." (Paul Leicester Ford, ed., *The Writings of Thomas Jefferson*, New York, 1892-1899, Vol. VII, pp. 433-34.)

mechanics, clerks, journeymen, and laborers. In order to win, the Federalists tried to coerce their workers by telling them to choose between Jefferson and their jobs.* The *New York Daily Advertiser* of April 28, 1800, tried to frighten merchant and worker:

"Merchants, your ships will be condemned to *rot* in your harbours, for the *navy* which is their protection Jefferson will destroy. Cartmen, you may *burn* your carts, for the merchants will no longer be able to give you employment. The music of the hammer along our wharves and the hum of busy industry will not be heard. The temple of the most High will be profaned by high impious orgies of the Goddess of Reason, personated as in France by some common prostitute."

"Turn out then," it concluded, "you who are friends to the stability of government—to the security of property—the preservation of religion and the faithful execution of the laws...."

The wealthy merchants, bankers and lawyers did turn out, but so did the mechanics and laborers. It was they who carried the city for Jefferson.

None of the horrors promised by the Federalists came to pass. During Jefferson's administration democracy was extended in several states by the removal of property qualifications for voting. Universal suffrage in the new states on the frontier was almost taken for granted. In 1804 the people of Maryland amended their state constitution, extending suffrage to non-property holders. A few years later South Carolina established universal manhood suffrage for white citizens.

An important battle for trade unionists was the struggle of Jefferson and his party against the use of English common law in America. Common law, the Jeffersonians said, consisted of "unwritten rules, promulgated by judges ... that is to say, by the caprice, or the bigotry, or the enthusiasm of the judge." [25] The prosecution and conviction of the Philadelphia cordwainers in 1805 hastened the process of republicanizing the common law. Professor Walter Nelles of Yale University Law School writes: "Throughout the era before the Civil War the power of Jeffersonianism was tremendous. There would have been more [conspiracy] cases otherwise. And when Toryism pressed and won an occasional case, its moderation in victory was well advised." [26]

On November 22, 1804, three weeks after the re-election of Jefferson,

---

* A journeyman printer summed up the practice of employers in New York in the following bitter observation: "Let all your workmen be of the right, thoroughgoing federal stamp...If any of them presume to speak well of liberty and equality, dismiss them instantly; and if the magistrate of your district is a good federalist, you need not be exact in paying them what may be due." ("A Brother Typo" in *Republican Watch-Tower*, Nov. 11, 1800.)

the *New York Evening Post* called for a nationwide day of mourning in which to recall the good old days when mechanics, laborers, and other plain people did not meddle in politics. "The truth is, Democracy and Jeffersonianism reign triumphant throughout the land, and men of character, of sense, and of property have nothing left but to sit down quietly and let the torrent rage." Instead of sitting down quietly the Federalists concentrated on the state governments and the courts where they believed they could find shelter from the "rage of the Jacobins." They changed their names in some states to Federal Republicans in order to get votes. Hamilton had even proposed a Christian Constitutional Society with branches in all cities which were controlled by the "Jacobins." He suggested that a special appeal be addressed to the "different classes of mechanics" to get them to become members.[27]

These were not the main Federalist devices to halt democracy. As early as 1803 they had worked out a plot for an armed coup d'etat by which they hoped to overthrow Jefferson. Another and more extensive plot aimed to separate the New England states from the union and reunite them with Britain. Anthony Merry, British minister to the United States, so informed his government: "They naturally look forward to Great Britain for support and assistance when the occasion shall arrive." [28]

England was not the only ally on which the anti-Jeffersonians counted. Aaron Burr looked to Spain for assistance. While the Federalists were trying to separate New England from the rest of the union, Aaron Burr was trying to separate the western from the eastern states.

LABOR AND THE EMBARGO

British assistance was not long in coming. England announced her Orders in Council in 1807, forbidding the new world to trade with the European Continent unless Britain gave her approval. British captains continued to seize American vessels and impress American seamen. Napoleon's "Berlin and Milan decrees" dovetailed with British policy when he forbade American trade with the British Isles and began to seize American ships. On December 22, 1807, President Jefferson replied with an embargo on all shipping to and from America until the belligerents would modify their practice. The British Orders in Council received the whole-hearted support of the Federalists. Foster, British minister to America, was present at one of the conferences of the Federalists. He wrote: "The sum of these suggestions was that we should neither revoke our Orders in Council nor modify them in any manner.... In short they seemed to think that Great Britain could by management bring the United States into any connection with her that she pleased." [29]

The success of these treasonable schemes depended largely upon the reactions of the common people. All at once the Federalists became solicitous of the suffering caused by the embargo, exaggerating the economic losses by ignoring the fact that Jefferson's policies were stimulating the growth of American industry. Some Federalists were hopeful that the embargo would turn the unemployed against Jefferson. There were articles in the Federalist press about the "grass growing in the streets and ships rotting at the wharves." "The busy hum of labour," the *New York Commercial Advertiser* of July 12, 1808, editorialized, "once so grateful to the ear, the token of the nation's prosperity, [has been] succeeded by the poor man's groan, the labourer's complaint and the miserable beggar's petition." In Charleston the Federalist employers who were renowned for their callousness toward labor now observed that the "day laborer who lives by the sweat of his brow finds his scanty profit diminished by the operation of this wretched policy." [30]

Although there was much suffering in many seaport towns, few workers were fooled by these lurid tales. They saw it differently: "The *British faction* in Boston having encouraged the depredation of our commerce, and the capture of our seamen, the government is reduced to the necessity to lay an embargo to prevent a continuance of the outrage. If the produce of the farmer is lower, this faction must answer for it. If bankruptcies take place in our seaports, this faction must answer for them. It is *old toryism* that is accountable to the farmer, tradesman, seaman, and merchant, for their present difficulties." [31]

The unemployed did not curse Jefferson and vote Federalist. On January 8, 1808, a notice in the *New York Daily Advertiser* called on all unemployed seamen to join in a mass meeting to demand jobs from the city government. No denunciations of Jefferson were found in the announcement nor in the subsequent meeting. A few days later unemployed journeymen and ship carpenters met and demanded assistance from the city. A program of public works was set up to provide for "those out of employment in consequence of the embargo." [32]

Workers who openly voiced their support of Jefferson's policies were fired by Federalist employers, and others were threatened with loss of jobs if they did not sign petitions protesting the embargo. When intimidation failed, they drew up fake petitions. One such petition forwarded to the Massachusetts state legislature contained the signatures of 110 sailors. The legislature obligingly appointed a committee to meet with the signers. Six signers were finally located. They testified that a man they had never seen before had canvassed the waterfront, stopped seamen and had asked them to sign a paper. [33]

The central issue in the New York City election of 1808 was the embargo. Barent Gardiner, an outspoken enemy of the embargo, was nominated by the Federalists, while the Republicans nominated Congressman G. S. Mumford who had voted for the embargo and still defended it. Mumford was elected by a great majority.[34]

LABOR AND THE WAR OF 1812

"The Federal leaders made no scruples of telling me," wrote the British minister in Washington on December 11, 1811, "that they mean to give their votes for war, although they will remain silent in the debates; they add that they see no end to restrictions and non-importation laws but in war, that war will turn out the Administration, and then they will have their own way, and make a solid peace with Great Britain." [35]

As war approached the Federalists voted against all measures for adequate preparation. Once the War of 1812 had started, they increased their sabotage. Federalist governors in New England refused requests of the national government for militia. Federalist merchants and bankers refused to lend money to their country. Federalist businessmen carried on an extensive trade with the enemy. So extensive was this trade that the British admitted that had it not been for these supplies their forces in Canada would have suffered famine. Recently published documents from the British archives reveal that the Federalists had dispatched an agent to Sir John Sherbrooke, the English Commander in Canada, to seek military support for the separation of New England from the Union. "This step," said the agent," will paralyze the Authority of the United States and crush the baneful democracy of the country."

Sir John wrote to Lord Bathurst on November 20, 1814:

"It is right that your lordship should be informed that there is a very strong democratic Party in each of these Commonwealths And as they will in the event of any attempt being made to separate New England from the Union most probably be assisted by the General Government in resisting this measure, it appears that the Federal party wishes to ascertain at this early period whether Great Britain would under these Circumstances afford them Military Assistance to effect their purpose should they stand in need for it." [36]

When war came, labor responded wholeheartedly to President Madison's call for volunteers. In Norfolk, New York City, Philadelphia, Newark, Charleston, workers were the first to enlist. The New York Typographical Society called upon its members to defend the nation, and established a special fund to assist the wives and children of members in the armed forces. The mechanics of Charleston formed a military company and swore to emulate the courage of their Revolutionary fathers. [37] While Federalists were plotting America's defeat in the summer of 1814, the workers and other citizens of New York City were building fortifications to defend the city from imminent invasion. An appeal on August 27, 1814, to the citizens of New York appeared in the *New York Columbian:* "Arise from your slumber! Let every citizen arise and enroll himself instantly and prepare to defend the city to the last extremity. This is no time to talk! We must act, and act with vigor, or we are lost."

Within a few days 25,000 men had been armed and were in training to defend their city. The workingmen of the New York Manufacturing Company and the Eagle Manufacturing Company volunteered as a group and trained before and after working hours; they spent their working days making arms and ammunition. David H. Reins, secretary of the New York Typographical Society, organized a company composed entirely of union printers.* [38] Other citizens were working on the fortifications of Fort Greene in Brooklyn. Five hundred members of the Journeymen Carpenters' Society worked for two weeks without pay. Members of the curriers', plumbers', cabinet-makers', and chair-makers' unions dug trenches side by side with tradesmen, shopkeepers, women, and city officials. On August 17, several hundred union workers from Paterson, New Jersey, came to help with the digging. Some one hundred and fifty free Negroes joined in the work. [39]

This great effort of the people to defend New York inspired one of the most popular songs of the war, *The Patriotic Diggers:*

To protect our rights
   'Gainst your flints and triggers,
See on Brooklyn Heights
   Our patriotic diggers;
Men of every age,
   Color, rank, profession,
Ardently engage,
   Labor in succession.

Here the mason builds
   Freedom's shrine of glory,
While the painter gilds,
   The immortal story
Blacksmiths catch the flame,
   Grocers feel the spirit,
Printers share the fame,
   And record the merit.

* In September, 1814, the Philadelphia Typographical Society resolved to appropriate one day's labor for each of its members "on the fortification now erecting for the defense of the city." Later, on October 14, 1814, the Society voted to assist "the wives of such members of this society now absent in the service of the country, as may be in the need of assistance...." (George A. Tracy, *History of the Typographical Union*, Indianapolis, 1913, p. 44.)

Scholars leave their schools,
  With their patriotic teachers,
Farmers seize the tools,
  Headed by the preachers,
How they break the soil,
  Brewers, Butchers, Bakers,
Here the doctors toil,
  There the undertakers.

Plumbers, founders, dyers,
  Tinmen, turners, shavers,
Sweepers, clerks and criers,
  Jewellers, engravers,
Clothiers, drapers, players,
  Cartmen, hatters, tailors,
Gaugers, sealers, weighers,
  Carpenters and sailors!

CHORUS

Pick-axe, shovel, spade,
  Crow-bar, hoe and barrow,
Better not invade,
  Yankees have the marrow! [40]

The British flinched before this magnificent defense and abandoned their plan of capturing New York City.

The one hundred and fifty Negroes who joined in the defense of New York City were by no means the only Negro Americans to participate in the War of 1812. One sailor in ten was a Negro in Perry's fleet at the Battle of Lake Erie.[41] A company of Negro soldiers fought under Andrew Jackson at the Battle of New Orleans. Old Hickory paid his tribute to them in a special order, in which he pointed out that their valor had "surpassed" his highest hope.[42]

EXTENSION OF DEMOCRACY

After America's victory in the War of 1812 had secured her independence, the Jeffersonians took up again the struggle to extend democracy. In Connecticut in 1817, the Republicans and the Episcopalians established the coalition American Toleration and Reform Party, and campaigned for religious toleration, a new constitution, and various government reforms, particularly universal manhood suffrage. The party carried the election. In June, 1818, *Niles' Register* joyfully announced the victory: "Emancipation! The legislature of Connecticut has passed a law extending the right of suffrage to all who pay taxes and do militia duty." The Conservative *Connecticut Courant* was in despair. "The fatal instrument is signed, sealed and delivered," it said on October 20, 1818, after the new constitution had been ratified. "Thousands have been blindly led to perform an act, by which they have sealed their own destruction, and fastened their children and posterity in bondage."

A few years later, New York and Massachusetts followed in Connecticut's footsteps and swept away all property qualifications for voting. Other states soon followed suit.

Conservatives grieved over these final triumps of Jeffersonianism. Men of wealth and property were "to be placed in the hands and power of such men as throng the city for day labor." [43] In November, 1821, Peter Jay, a prominent Federalist, noted the fact that "there seems to be a passion for universal suffrage pervading the union." "When those who possess no property," he concluded, "shall be more numerous than those who have it, the consequence will, I fear, be severely felt." [44]

Thomas Jefferson faced the consequence calmly. "I am not among those who fear the people," he wrote in 1816. "They and not the rich are our dependence for continued freedom." [45]

CHAPTER 7

Trade Unionism and Labor Struggles, 1819-1837

The economic depression of 1819-1822 destroyed even those unions that had managed to survive the strikes and the conspiracy charges. Unemployment was general; 20,000 workers in Philadelphia and a like number in New York City were without work.[1] A printer who arrived in New York in 1820 recorded: "I had barely two dollars in my pocket when I got here with my family. We lived eight days without tea, sugar, or meat—on bread and butter only with cold water. It is pinching times."[2]

LABOR CONDITIONS

Nothing was done by public officials to relieve the suffering of the unemployed. Down in far-off Louisiana, Edward Livingston, a Jeffersonian Democrat, proposed a system of public relief to the legislature. "Political society," he argued, "owes perfect protection to all its members in their persons, reputations and property; and it also owes necessary subsistence to those who cannot procure it for themselves." He maintained that unemployment was the result of an unnatural growth of industry which glutted the markets, and that the workers who produced the profits were "left to starve or become objects of public charity." Therefore the community and the employers "ought not to complain that it is forced to give occasional support to the unfortunate instruments of its prosperity." Society should never forget that the "preservation of life is the first object, property is only a secondary one. Can it be supposed that any just contract could stipulate that one of the contracting parties should die of hunger, in order that others might enjoy, without deduction, the whole of their property?"[3] These ideas were too advanced for the legislature of Louisiana.

The prevailing "erroneous opinions" of the upper classes about the

97

poor were listed by Matthew Carey, a rich Philadelphia businessman in his widely circulated pamphlet, *Appeal to the Wealthy of the Land ... on the Character, Conduct, Situation, and Prospects of those whose Sole Dependence for Subsistence is on the Labour of their Hands* (*Essay I*):

"1. That every man, woman, and grown child, able and willing to work, may find employment.

"2. That the poor, by industry, prudence, and economy, may at all times support themselves comfortably, without depending on eleemosynary aid—and, as a corollary from these positions.

"3. That their sufferings and distresses chiefly, if not wholly, arise from their idleness, their dissipation, and their extravagance.

"4. That taxes for the support of the poor, and aid afforded them by charitable individuals, or benevolent societies, are pernicious, as by encouraging the poor to depend on them, they foster their idleness and improvidence, and thus produce, or at least increase, the poverty and distress they are intended to relieve."

But the suffering of the working class and the callousness of the upper classes created what John Quincy Adams called "a general mass of disaffection."[4] This feeling was intensified by the fact that every few years another industrial depression hit the nation and the suffering had to be endured again. Again in 1829 unemployment was general. The editor of the *New York Commercial Advertiser* noted in January of that year: "There is unquestionably more intense suffering at this moment, than there has been for many previous years, if ever." A correspondent for the *New York Times* reported: "Thousands of industrious mechanics who never before solicited alms, were brought to the humiliating condition of applying for assistance, and with tears on their manly cheeks, confessed their inability to provide food or clothing for their families." When prosperity returned, labor had little share in it. The average worker, said a contemporary, lived "on the brink of starvation, has nothing left for his old age, if he lives to attain it; becomes a vagrant supported by charity; and is finally buried at the expense of the parish."[5] A moving "Appeal of the Working People of Manayunk to the Public" describes the conditions among many workers in August, 1833, several years after the depression of 1829:

"We are obliged by our employers to labor at this season of the year, from 5 o'clock in the morning until sunset, being fourteen hours and a half, with an intermission of half an hour for breakfast, and an hour for dinner, leaving thirteen hours of hard labor, at an unhealthy employment, where we never feel a refreshing breeze to cool us, overheated and suffocated as we are, and where we never behold the sun but through a window, and an atmosphere thick with the dust and small particles of cotton, which we are constantly inhaling to the destruction of our health, our appetite, and strength.

"Often do we feel ourselves so weak as to be scarcely able to perform our work, on account of the over-strained time we are obliged to labor through the long and sultry days of summer, in the impure and unwholesome air of the factories, and the little rest we receive during the night not being sufficient to recruit our exhausted physical energies, we return to our labor in the morning, as weary as when we left it; but nevertheless work we must, worn down and debilitated as we are, or our families would soon be in a starving condition, for our wages are barely sufficient to supply us with the necessaries of life. We cannot provide against sickness or difficulties of any kind, by laying by a single dollar, for our present wants consume the little we receive, and when we are confined to bed of sickness any length of time, we are plunged into the deepest distress, which often terminates in total ruin, poverty and pauperism.

"Our expenses are perhaps greater than most other working people, because it requires the wages of all the family who are able to work (save only one small girl to take care of the house and provide meals) to furnish absolute wants, consequently the females have no time either to make their own dresses or those of the children, but have of course to apply to trades for every article that is wanted." [6]

The plight of the unskilled laborers was even more tragic. Many unskilled Irish peasants had come to America when their English landlords had dispossessed them following the drop in the price of grain after the Napoleonic Wars. Thousands of them found no work at all, and those who did worked under killing conditions on canals and turnpikes at wages ranging from 50 to 87 cents a day. Matthew Carey commented on the conditions of the unskilled workers:

"Thousands of our labouring people travel hundreds of miles in quest of employment on canals, at 62, 75, and 87 cents per day, paying a dollar and a half or two dollars a week for their board, leaving families behind, depending on them for support. They labour frequently in marshy grounds which destroys their health, often irrevocably. They return to their poor families—with ruined constitutions, with a sorry pittance, most laboriously earned, and take to their beds sick and unable to work. Hundreds are swept off annually, many of them leaving numerous and helpless families. Notwithstanding their wretched fate, their places are quickly supplied by others, although death stares them in the face." [7]

In 1829 a committee of 90 prominent Philadelphia women and 138 men sent a petition to the War Department protesting the pay received by women homeworkers making shirts for the army. An expert seamstress, they said, by working from morning to night could make no more than 50 cents a day. Moreover, they were frequently out of work. The War Department replied that it could do nothing, since the issue was "so intimately connected with the manufacturing interests and the general prices of this kind of labor in the city of Philadelphia." [8]

Prices for this kind of labor were the same in other cities. In New York women made pantaloons for four cents apiece and cotton shirts for five cents. "With the utmost unremitting industry," a New York physician declared, "they can sew no more than three pair of pantaloons or one shirt a day." The Reverend M. Ely remarked in 1829 that a slave in the states of Kentucky, Virginia, and Tennessee was actually "much better compensated" than were working women in the Empire City. Workers in cotton factories, said Matthew Carey, had not yet reached the level of the slave, but "some of them are fast descending to it." For work that began at sunrise in the summer until ten at night printers, dyers, and mule spinners received from $2.50 to $5.80 a week. Women averaged $2.25 a week; children under twelve earned fifty cents. [9]

Mill workers were often forced to buy at company stores, where prices were exorbitant. In fact, wages were frequently paid in store orders. As a result, these workers lived in abject poverty. "Very few were able to keep out of debt," asserted Carrol D. Wright, the noted nineteenth-century American labor statistician, "The balance of the account was generally against the workmen." [10] When unemployed, these workers were denied relief and ordered back to the towns and villages from which they had come. [11]

At Waltham, Lowell, Lawrence, Dover, and Chicopee, the factory girls lived in boarding-houses leased by the companies. Their lives were carefully regimented. Boarding-house matrons were instructed to report the names of any girls who stayed out late, did not attend church, and discussed grievances. Those reported were promptly discharged.

In the mills, too, the company exercised complete control over the girls. One regulation of most textile factories required the girls to sign a pledge to work for such wages "as the company may see fit to pay and be subject to the fines imposed by the company." Fines were imposed for the least infraction of the rules. One regulation bluntly announced: "The bell to call the people to their work will be rung five minutes and tolled five minutes; at the last stroke, the entrance will be closed and a fee of 12½ cents exacted of anyone for whom it may be opened." Factory workers in Paterson continually complained that the employers "have been uniformly in the practice of deducting one quarter from each day's labor, when we were behind the time but five minutes." [12] It was said to be a common thing in Paterson, as a result of this fine system, "to see little children, and some of very tender years, at daylight in the cold of winter season, running through the snows and storms with a crust in their hands, and lest by being a few minutes too late they should incur the displeasure of their employer and get discharged." [13]

Factory girls were even forced to sign what became later known as a "yellow dog contract" which stated: "We also agree not to be engaged in any combination whereby the work may be impeded or the company's interest in any work injured; if we do, we agree to forfeit to the use of the company the amount due to us at the time." Since wages were often paid twice a year this clause carried considerable weight.* Moreover, the mill owners had an effective blacklist system which made it impossible for any girl to obtain work with a new company who did not bring with her a "regular discharge" from her former employer. A "regular discharge" was given only to those who had worked a full year and were not guilty of "insubordination." [14]

These then were the conditions for American workers in the years following the panic of 1819, and these were the conditions which caused a revival of trade unionism in the 'twenties and 'thirties. More American workers were beginning to understand that, disunited, their wages would remain depressed, hours from "sun to sun," and the harshness of life continue. United, the workers would be able to command decent wages, shorter hours, and better working conditions.

LABOR'S AWAKENING

As early as 1823 signs of labor's awakening made themselves evident. A group of New Orleans printers met in Mechanics' Hall late in March, 1823 and, prompted by the "low ebb to which the fraternity has been reduced by not receiving regular pay from their employers," organized themselves into a trade union. [15] Soon workers in various trades in New York, Philadelphia, Baltimore, Charleston, Wilmington, and other cities were organizing and presenting their demands for increased wages and shorter hours, threatening to strike if their terms were not met.

* In the more adequately financed mills, wages were paid monthly, but in most factories pay day came only every three or every six months. Wages, moreover, were seldom paid in cash; workers were usually required to take payment in tokens redeemable only in goods at the company store. The wages of single workers, compelled to live in the company boarding house, had deductions for room and board, and rarely was there much remaining for the worker to spend. (See Constance M. Green, "Light Manufactures and the Beginnings of Precision Manufacturing Before 1861," in Harold F. Williamson, *The Growth of the American Economy*, New York, 1944, p. 243.)

These new unions had many features of the earlier labor organizations, but they also broke new ground. Earlier labor bodies had called themselves societies and associations, but in the New York celebration of the opening of the Erie Canal, a weavers' union took part. This same year witnessed in New York the first "all women" strike in American history when the women tailors organized and struck for higher wages.

Carpenters, masons, stone-cutters, hatters, tailors, riggers, stevedores, cabinet-makers, cordwainers, and other workers set up fairly stable unions and conducted many successful strikes for higher wages. In 1827 the unions in Philadelphia formed the Mechanics' Union of Trade Associations, the first city-wide federation of American workers, which recognized that all labor, regardless of trades, had common problems that could be solved only by united effort as a class. While it is true that in a sense the political activities of the pre-1820 trade unions in the Democratic Societies and in the Democratic-Republican Party initiated the American labor movement, we can set the date for the origin of the American labor movement, as we understand such a movement today, in 1827 with the organization of the Mechanics' union of Trade Associations of Philadelphia.

The Mechanics' Union of Philadelphia arose out of the ten-hour movement which spread like wildfire through labor's ranks during the decade 1825-1835. The movement itself began even before the first permanent unions were formed, for as far back as 1791 the Philadelphia carpenters had gone on strike for a ten-hour day and additional pay for overtime. We do not know what the outcome of the strike was, but we do know that it was the first step American labor took to secure a shorter working day.

In 1825 Boston carpenters started the first of a number of strikes for shorter hours. The strike itself was a failure, but the character of the opposition to it makes an analysis of the struggle worth while. Here for the first time labor saw the employers and the merchant capitalists join hands and resources in a great offensive against any movement for better conditions and resort to hypocritical moralistic arguments to justify exploitation. A ten-hour day, the carpenters were told, was bad for the workers; it would "exert a very unhappy influence on our apprentices, by seducing them from that course of industry and economy of time, to which we [the employers] are anxious to enure them," and it would "expose the Journeymen themselves to many improvident temptations and improvident practices." Trade unions, said the employers and capitalists, were un-American. They had been brought over from Europe by foreigners who carried with them "a spirit of discontent and insubordination to which our native Mechanics have hitherto been strangers." If allowed to grow, these combinations of labor would injure all classes, inasmuch as they gave an artificial and unnatural turn to business and tended "to convert all its branches into monopolies." [16]

This from the leading monopolists in New England—capitalists who so completely dominated the building trade that they could threaten to stop all construction for the entire season before they would permit carpenters to work ten hours a day.

In the spring of 1827 workers in Philadelphia were stimulated by an anonymous pamphlet addressed to the mechanics and workingmen of the city. It called upon labor to fight to gain "sufficient knowledge" to make the inestimable blessing of universal suffrage worth something, and it specifically recommended a free labor press, libraries, reading rooms, and forums for the workers. For labor to take advantage of these facilities, the pamphlet concluded, it was necessary to establish throughout the city a ten-hour day.[17] One result of this pamphlet was the formation of the Mechanics' Library Company, which published in Philadelphia that year the weekly *Mechanics' Free Press,* the first labor paper in America of which any issues are now in existence. Another was that it inspired the carpenters to turn out for the ten-hour day.

"They believe," said the Philadelphia carpenters, "that all men have a just right, derived from their creator, to have sufficient time in each day for the cultivation of their mind and for self-improvement." Other workers in Philadelphia viewed the strike as their own, saying that "thousands yet unborn" would reap the advantage.[18] The strike failed but it taught the workers that only united action of all workers could win the battle against the employers. Hence, in the fall of 1827, fifteen unions formed the Mechanics' Union of Trade Associations. Their aim, according to the preamble to the union's constitution, was to avert "the desolating evils which must inevitably arise from a depreciation of the intrinsic value of human labor; to raise the mechanical and productive classes to that condition of true independence and inequality [sic] which their practical skill and ingenuity, their immense utility to the nation and their growing intelligence are beginning imperiously to demand."

This preamble is truly a remarkable document, with a surprisingly modern ring. It asserts that a rise in the living standards of the workers would benefit employers, who, in their own interest, ought to grant higher wages, for, says the preamble, high wages spell buying power and general prosperity, whereas, low wages spell general business stagnation and failure: *

---

* Most of the labor literature of the period emphasized this theme. It was also admirably set forth in William M. Gouge's widely circulated booklet, *A Short History of Paper Money and Banking in the United States* (Philadelphia, 1833, pp. 27-28): "If the real wants of the community, and not their ability to pay, be considered, it will not, perhaps, be found that any one useful trade or profession has

"If the mass of the people were enabled by their labour to secure for themselves and their families a full and abundant supply of the comforts and conveniences of life, the consumption of articles, particularly of dwellings, furniture, and clothing, would amount to at least twice the quantity it does at present, and of course the demand, by which alone employers are enabled either to subsist or accumulate, would likewise be increased in equal proportion. . . . It is therefore the real interest (for instance) of the Hatter, that every man in the community should be enabled to clothe his own head and those of his family with an abundant supply of the best articles of that description; because the flourishing demand, thereby created, and which depends altogether on the ability of the multitude to purchase, is that which alone enables him to pay his rent and support his family in comfort. . . ."

On the other hand, if labor was miserably paid, "the demand for their articles must necessarily cease from the forced inability of the people to consume: trade must in consequence languish, and losses and failures become the order of the day." [19]

The Mechanics' Union of Philadelphia which lasted until 1831 devoted most of its energy to political action. Its most important contribution to the rising labor movement was its example of labor solidarity among workers of various trades. The next development of this trend was the organization in 1831 of the New England Association of Farmers, Mechanics, and Other Workingmen.

Like the Mechanics' Union of Philadelphia, the New England Association was a product of the struggle for the shorter workday. Although by this time the ten-hour day had been gained in New York and to some extent in Philadelphia, New Englanders still worked from sunup to sunset. In 1827 the carpenters and masons of Boston had been unsuccessful in securing the shorter workday, but the movement continued, spreading north to New Hampshire and south to Connecticut. "Meetings have been held and resolutions adopted in various parts of New England," said the *Boston Transcript* of February 20, 1832, "recommending ten hours per day, as the amount that ought hereafter to be considered a day's work." Out of one such meeting in Providence, Rhode Island, came the call for the organization of a movement which would unite "the

---

too many members. The number of educated physicians, for example, is not too great for the population. But, not a few physicians remain without employment, while many persons, from inability to pay for medical advice, suffer all the evils of sickness. It cannot be said that we have too many shoemakers, tailors, or cabinetmakers, while multitudes are but indifferently provided with clothing and furniture." Gouge, a progressive Philadelphia editor, was active in the workingmen's movement and may have had a hand in drafting the preamble of the Mechanics' Union of Trade Associations.

cultivators of the soil, and the mechanics and every class of laborers [to overthrow] the oppression of the idle, avaricious, and aristocratic."

The New England Association first convened in Boston, February, 1832, to draw up a constitution. One of its provisions was that all members except practical farmers should pledge themselves to work only ten hours a day with no reduction in wages. It was found impossible to enforce this provision so a war chest was set up to relieve any member thrown out of work for living up to the pledge. But this war chest was puny indeed compared to the $20,000 put up by the employers to break the Boston ship-carpenters' strike for the ten-hour day. Discouraged in its attempt at direct trade union action for the shorter day, the Association turned to political action. Vigilance committees organized in various states collected data on labor conditions and memorialized state legislatures to regulate the "hours of labor, according to the standard adopted by the Association." After four conventions, the Association devoted most of its time to political activity. Its most important contribution to the labor movement in the United States was the fact that it made the first attempt to include all groups of workers in a single organization—factory workers, common laborers, and skilled mechanics. The true union, the founders of the Association believed, should "embrace every citizen whose daily *exertions* from the highest Artist to the lowest Laborer, are his means of subsistence." These men—Dr. Charles Douglas, editor of the *New England Artisan,* a weekly labor paper published in Rhode Island, Seth Luther, the *Artisan's* "Travelling Agent," and John B. Eldredge and Samuel Whitcomb, Jr., trade union leaders—believed strongly in labor solidarity, and when they emphasized the need for "the organization of the Workingmen in every town and county in New England," they meant all types of workers.[20]

Association leaders had expected to recruit many factory workers whose current militancy seemed to promise much in the way of trade union organization. When, in 1828, the mill owners in Paterson, New Jersey, tried to change the dinner hour from 12 to 1, the operatives, mostly children, conducted the first recorded strike of factory workers in America. "The children would not stand for it," said one observer, "for fear if they assented to this, the next thing would be to deprive them of eating at all." [21] The militia was called out to quell this labor disturbance. Later that year four hundred girls in the textile factories at Dover, New Hampshire, went on strike, and as they paraded through the town they asked: Who among the Dover girls could "ever bear the shocking fate of slaves to share?" [22]

Soon after its formation the Association appointed lecturers to spread the doctrines of trade unionism to the factory girls. Their efforts to organize the women were unsuccessful. Though it failed to recruit factory workers in any number, the Association brought the conditions of the factory prisons to public attention and initiated the movement to place the operatives under the supervision and protection of the law of the land. It also denounced the practice of forcing little children to work in factories "without any time for healthy recreation and mental culture." [23]

One of the Association's most important contributions to the labor movement was its publication of an address delivered by one of its leaders, Seth Luther. Luther was the Tom Paine of the first labor movement, and his *Address to the Working Men of New England* was widely read during the 1830's. It was both a call to action and a penetrating analysis of conditions in New England factories which made a mockery of the Declaration of Independence. It was to restore the ideals of the Revolution that Luther wrote his impassioned analysis.

He began by referring to the sufferings and privations of the great patriots of the Revolutionary War. When we read "of their undying zeal and untiring efforts, we feel it incumbent upon us to sound an alarm when our rights are not only endangered, but some of them already wrested from us by the powerful and inhuman grasp of monopolized wealth." These monopolists, he said, were advising the American people to follow the splendid example of England. Luther revealed that beneath the cover of English monarchical brilliance, half the people of England were starving. Child labor, shortened lives of workers, ignorance, vice and universal squalor—is this what the manufacturers wanted in the land of Washington, Revere, and Warren?

"A patriotic cry is kept up by men who are endeavoring by *all the means in their power* to cut down the wages of *our own people,* and who send agents to *Europe,* to induce *foreigners* to come here, to underwork *American* citizens, to support *American* industry and the *American* system." After describing the conditions in the "prisons of New England called cotton mills," Luther said, "We do not believe there can be a single person found east of the mountains who ever thanked God for permission to work in a cotton mill."

The time had come to bring an end to this type of "American system" and replace it with an American system "where education and intelligence are generally diffused, and the enjoyment of life and liberty secured to all." Only through united effort and organization could the workers bring this new system into being. Men of property who maintained organization "to protect their precious persons from danger," ranted and denounced the efforts of the poor to seek justice as a "most *horrible combination*." But these arguments had been used before. "The Declaration of Independence was the work of a combination, and was as hateful to the *traitors and tories* of those days as combinations among working men are now to the *avaricious* monopolist and *purse proud artistocrat*." Luther's address concluded:

"Fellow citizens...farmers, mechanics and laborers, we have borne these evils by far too long; we have been deceived by all parties; we must take our business into our own hands. Let us awake. Our cause is the cause of truth—of justice and humanity. It *must prevail*. Let us be determined no longer to be deceived by the cry of those who produce nothing and who enjoy all, and who insultingly term us—the farmers, the mechanics and the laborers—the lower orders, and exultingly claim our homage for themselves, as the *higher orders*—while the Declaration of Independence asserts that 'All men are created equal.' " [24]

Luther's *Address* quickly ran through three editions and a special edition for European workers was planned. From Maine to Philadelphia, workers were stirred by his call to restore the ideals of the Revolution. He reached them at a time when workingmen were being hard hit by the steeply rising cost of living. The price index rose from 90.1 in 1833 to 115.7 in 1836. Yet skilled mechanics were averaging only $4 to $5 a week, cotton factory operatives from $2.19 to $2.53 a week, seamstresses on home-work $1 to $1.25 a week, and several thousand women in Massachusetts, working in their homes as shoe binders, as little as 25 cents a day. Moreover, most workers were paid in notes issued by state banks and actually worth only 50 cents on the dollar in payment for goods and rents. [25]

Luther's pamphlet strengthened the determination of American workers to unite to solve their problems—a determination fired by the revolutionary European upheavals of the early 'thirties. The Revolution of 1830 in France in particular convinced them that the workers were "the masters of their own liberties, that they have but to will it, and cooperate one with another, and they must be free." [26] A message sent by mechanics and workingmen of New York to the workers of Paris declared: "Fellow Laborers! We owe you our grateful thanks. And not we only, but the industrious classes—the *people* of every nation. In defending your own rights, you have vindicated ours." [27] *

* Another example of the interest of the early labor movement in the international struggle for freedom is the Philadelphia Typographical Society's contribution of $90 in 1827 to assist the Greek people in their battle for independence. (See George A. Tracy, *History of the Typographical Union*, p. 55.)

On September 13, 1834, the *National Trades' Union* (New York) printed the address of the working men of Nantes, France, to the Trades' Union of England which proposed "to unite the working men of several countries." The labor paper hailed the address. "This," it declared, "is now the most important movement that has ever been made in the world. From it will result union and harmony

All of these factors led to a great uprising of the labor movement in the years 1833-1837. During this period labor organization grew with a rapidity hardly matched again during the century. Trade union membership grew from 26,250, to 300,000. In New York City 11,500 workingmen, almost two-thirds of the workers, were organized. More than 150 unions were organized in New York, Philadelphia, and Baltimore. But trade unionism was no longer confined to the Atlantic seaboard. Workers were organizing unions in Buffalo, St. Louis, Pittsburgh, Cleveland, Cincinnati, Louisville, and other regions emerging out of the frontier stage.[28]

Wage earners who had never before been organized, incluaing plasterers, cigarmakers, seamstresses, handloom weavers, and milliners, now formed unions and went on strike. In the four years from 1833 to 1837, in the country as a whole, there were one hundred and sixty-eight strikes. Of these, one hundred and three were for higher wages, twenty-six for a ten-hour day, and four for the closed shop. Unions in the building trades —carpenters, bricklayers, masons, plasterers, and painters—struck thirty-four times; the shoemakers or cordwainers twenty-four times, and the rest of the strikes were scattered among tailors, hatters, bakers, sailors, rope makers, printers, stonecutters, mechanics in government arsenals, leather dressers, glass cutters, railroad laborers, stevedores, and so forth.[29]

Women too "caught the spark of freedom's fire." "Women as well as men have certain inalienable rights," said the Lady Shoe Binders of Lynn, Massachusetts, when they formed their Society, "among which is the right at all times of peaceably assembling together to consult upon the common good." "We know of no method so likely to procure us relief," said another group of women workers, "as that which has of late been successfully practiced by the mechanics of this city."[30] Women tailors and seamstresses, umbrella sewers and bookbinders, shoe binders and cordwainers, in New England, New York, Philadelphia, and Baltimore joined together for protection "against the inevitable consequences of reduced and inadequate wages."

Women in the factories were also on the march. Indeed, the factory girls were among the most courageous fighters of the period, for they

---

between nations that have ever been hostile to each other. The interest of labor is a subject upon which all workmen can agree ... [and] we may expect that it will not be long before the working classes of every part of the civilized world will be united by an indissoluble bond."

Probably the most practical example of international labor solidarity during the 1830's was the action in 1832 of the Typographical Association of New York in sending a delegate to visit the Journeymen Printers Unions of Great Britain to warn their members not to believe advertisements which appeared in the British newspapers announcing that "hundreds of printers could find employment and good wages" in New York City. These printers, the delegate informed the British trade unionists, would be used as strike-breakers. (*Boston Post,* November 17, 1832.)

had to conduct their struggles not only against their employers but against the overwhelming prejudice of the time against public activity of women.

"It required some spirit," one writer states, "for Yankee 'young ladies' to brave public opinion in order to develop strike tactics at this early period.... It was felt that young women should not march about the streets, making a spectacle of themselves. And yet, in spite of disapproval they were prepared to do this in order to protect their standards whether it was conventional or not." [31]

When the factory owners cut wages in 1834, the Dover, New Hampshire, girls were the first to defy convention by turning out seven hundred-strong and marching down to the courthouse where these "daughters of freemen" drew up a statement which declared: "However freely the epithet of 'factory slaves' may be bestowed upon us, we will never deserve it by a base and cringing submission to proud wealth or haughty insolence." The strike was lost, but the girls, refusing to return to the factories, went home. They raised a fund to pay transportation for those who lived some distance from the mills, and sent an appeal to editors "opposed to the system of slavery attempted to be established in our manufacturing establishment," urging them to advise girls against coming to Dover to work.[32]

When the wages at Lowell, Massachusetts, were cut 15 per cent early in 1834, the girls held several protest meetings. A few days later the leader of the movement was fired. As she left the mill, she waved her bonnet in the air as a signal to the others who were watching from the windows. They struck, assembled about her, and eight hundred marched in a procession about the town. After listening to one of their leaders make a "flaming Mary Wollstonecraft speech on the rights of women and the iniquities of the monied aristocracy," they resolved "to have their own way even if they died for it." On the second day of their turn-out the strikers issued a proclamation entitled *Union is Power:*

"We circulate this paper wishing to obtain the names of all who imbibe the spirit of our patriotic ancestors, who preferred privation to bondage and parted with all that renders life desirable—and even life itself—to produce independence for their children."

Twelve hundred more girls responded by joining in a pledge "not [to] go back into the mills to work unless our wages are continued to us as they have been." They also pledged "That none of us will go back unless they receive us all as one." [33]

The strike was broken. Many of the Lowell girls went home to the farms but those who remained in the mills were not discouraged by their failure. When the factory owners cut wages another 12½ per cent in 1836, 1,500 Lowell girls struck again. As they paraded in their strike demonstration they sang:

> Oh! Isn't it a pity that such a pretty girl as I
> Should be sent to the factory to pine away and die?
> Oh! I cannot be a slave;
> I will not be a slave,
> For I'm so fond of liberty
> That I cannot be a slave.[34]

This time the girls formed the "Factory Girls Association" with a membership of 2,500. Their resolutions informed the manufacturers that they would not receive communications except through their officers. They were "daughters of freemen" and would not permit corporation tyrants to dominate their lives. "As our fathers resisted unto blood the lordly avarice of the British ministry," they announced, "so we, their daughters, never will wear the yoke which has been prepared for us." They would rather die in the alms-houses "than to yield to the wicked oppressions attempted to be imposed upon us." The strike lasted a month. Evicted from their boarding houses, and with no funds to sustain them, the girls were starved into submission.[35]

Other factory girls followed "the example of their pretty sisters at Lowell." When the girls of Amesbury were ordered to tend two looms at the same pay, they stopped work, proceeded to the Baptist Vestry, elected officers and adopted resolutions pledging that "under a forfeit of five dollars" they would not go back until the speed-up was abandoned. "The agent," reported the *Boston Evening Transcript* of March 25, 1836, "finding them determined to persevere, sent a written notice that they might come back." The strike was victorious.

These struggles, though militant, were not succeeded by stable labor organizations. Although employers did not greatly fear these activities, they took no chances. Strike leaders were discharged for "mutiny" and their names forwarded to other manufacturers to prevent them from getting jobs elsewhere.

Some workingmen were hostile to the entrance of women into industry and their activities in the labor movement on the ground that women workers lowered men's wages. But many agreed with Seth Luther who pointed out in an *Address:* "It is quite certain that unless we have the female sex on our side, we cannot hope to accomplish any object we have in view."[36] Thus when the Ladies' Shoe Binders of Lynn struck for higher wages in 1834, they were supported by the men's Cordwainers Union, which solicited strike funds and, even more important, resolved that they "would not work for any shoe manufacturer" who refused to meet the women's demands. They even urged all citizens in Lynn and surrounding towns to boycott such manufacturers.[37]

The Philadelphia Journeymen Cigar Makers welcomed the formation of a union of women workers in the trade, and in 1835 resolved, "That the present low wages hitherto received by the females engaged in cigar making, is far below a fair compensation for the labor rendered. Therefore Resolved, That we recommend them in a body to strike with us, and thereby make it a mutual interest with both parties to sustain each other in their rights." [38]

In 1836, in Philadelphia, the men's Cordwainers Union and the Ladies' Shoe Binders Society—though not organically united—struck together. The men announced: "Although they [the employers] may forget that they have mothers, we have resolved to take them under our protection, to flourish or sink with them." Even if they won their demands, they declared, they would not work until the women had won theirs.[39]

Co-operation between factory workers and skilled mechanics occurred frequently during the 1830's. The best example is the great struggle in Paterson during the summer of 1835. On July 3, the children in Paterson's textile mills struck for the reduction of the working day to 11 hours for five days and 9 hours on Saturdays. Other reasons for the strike were: opposition to the store-order system, the vicious fine system, and holding back of full wages. Toward the end of the month, the parents and guardians of the striking children formed the "Paterson Association for the Protection of the Working Classes of Paterson." They called for assistance from the workers in neighboring cities.

Newark workers responded at once by setting up a committee to raise funds and sending another committee to investigate conditions in Paterson. The investigators reported that conditions in the Paterson mills "belong rather to the dark ages than to the present times, and would be more congenial to the climate of his majesty the emperor and autocrat of all of the Russias, than this 'land of the free and the home of the brave,' this boasted asylum for the oppressed of all nations." The mechanics of Newark urged the strikers to stand out until they won, and promised continued financial support. Money and encouragement came from New York workers as well.

Heartened and sustained, the Paterson workers held out until the owners agreed to reduce working time by one and one-half to two hours per day. The working week was to be 69 hours, 12 hours a day for the first five days and nine hours on Saturdays.[40]

This working class solidarity led to organic labor unity. The Mechanics' Union of Trades' Associations had vanished, but its spirit was marching on.

CITY CENTRALS

About the middle of May, 1833, the journeymen carpenters of New York turned out for an increase in pay from $1.37 to $1.50 per day. Within two weeks, several trades passed resolutions of sympathy, and collected about $1,200. With this help the carpenters held out for a month. They won $1.50 a day for a ten-hour day from March to November, and $1.37 for a nine-hour day during the rest of the year. Encouraged by this successful trade union unity, the printers called on the journeymen mechanics and artisans to form a general union. On August 14, 1833, the General Trades' Union of New York was organized.[41]

Three other cities established trades' unions in 1833: Baltimore, Philadelphia and Washington. In the following year a central labor association was formed in Boston and in 1835 and 1836 eight other trades' unions were set up in Albany, Troy, Schenectady, Pittsburgh, Cincinnati, Louisville, New Brunswick, and Newark so that by the end of 1836 there were at least thirteen city trades' unions in the United States. In very few countries at this time were so many trade unions organized around a central labor body as in the United States.

Once organized, they grew rapidly. The Philadelphia Trades' Union * had only three societies with less than 400 members when it started in November, 1833; by April, 1836, it had 50 societies with a membership of 10,000. Among these members were common laborers, factory workers, and skilled mechanics.

"The Union makes no distinction between natives and foreigners," it proclaimed, "All are alike welcome to its benefits. If he is a workingman in favor of the emancipation of all who labor from the thraldom of monied capital, he is welcome to our ranks. We ask no qualification of birth or parentage, no sign or token to gain admission amongst us." [42]

To promote the general welfare of the workers, the trades' unions engaged in numerous activities. Traveling agents helped unorganized workers to set up locals which became members of the central union. The organizer for the Philadelphia union in a general appeal to labor spoke of the union as "a school in which every mechanic has an opportunity of learning how to defend and protect his rights." [43]

Some of the trades' unions started their own newspapers; others supported existing papers friendly to labor. All trades' unions assisted member unions during strikes with boycotts or money and sometimes both. In 1833 the Baltimore Trades' Union boycotted hatters who refused to

* Philadelphia seems to have had two trades' unions, one formed by the factory workers in August, 1833, and the other in November, 1833, by the skilled journeymen.

pay decent wages. These employers, it declared, were displaying the same greed and avarice "which gave birth to the celebrated Stamp and Tea Laws." [44] Frequently a trades' union in one city aided workers from another. The Newark Trades' Union supported a strike in 1835 of Philadelphia handloom weavers.

The New York General Trades' Union was well organized. It had its official organ, the *Union,* a daily newspaper which was launched to answer the charges of reactionaries that trades' unions advocated "acts of riot and violence," that the "leading members of trades' unions are foreigners" and that "personal aggrandizement is the main object of all the leaders—laziness and ease being characteristic of their whole lives." [45] The Union also set up a strike fund committee to assist member unions financially and to institute boycotts, and communicated with trades' unions throughout the country during strikes to prevent workers from coming to take the strikers' jobs. As a result of these activities labor in New York won many victories. Because of the financial assistance it had received from the City Central, the New York Tailors' Union won in October, 1833, a substantial increase in wages. [46] Two years later, a committee of New York employers announced in amazement:

"The different trades are combined in what is called a 'Trades' Union,' and each in its turn is supported by others in striking for higher wages. Within a year or two past, the Journeymen Printers, Journeymen Carpenters, Journeymen Hatters, Journeymen Tailors, and we believe several other trades have successfully 'turned out.'" [47]

The organization in more than a dozen cities of central labor bodies represents an extremely significant advance in the development of the American labor movement. Prior to their formation, workers engaged in strikes had been dependent for financial and moral support upon somewhat sporadic aid voted by other trade unions. Now, however, a group of workers who conducted a sanctioned strike were assured of certain support and financial assistance.

NATIONAL LABOR ORGANIZATIONS

Although the local trades' union remained the chief medium of labor solidarity during the early thirties, some efforts were made toward national organization. Better transportation by canal and railroad made it easier for employers to attack local unions through the blacklist and the shipment of scabs from one industrial section to another. Many workers were convinced that it would be hard to secure higher wages and shorter hours from employers who had to compete with manufacturers in other cities who paid low wages and worked their men 12 to 14 hours a day. They believed that national trade organizations would "equalize wages throughout the country as far as practical, and insure that promptness and concert of action necessary to accomplish our object and maintain justice." [48]

Accordingly five trades—cordwainers, printers, comb makers, carpenters, and hand-loom weavers—set up national organizations between 1835 and 1836. Others tried but failed. One failure worthy of mention was the call in December, 1836, of the Cotton and Woolen Spinners' Society of Philadelphia to "Factory Workers in General Throughout the United States," urging them to unite in a national trade union.[49]

The national labor organizations of the 'thirties did not last very long. The movement was premature for although the market was expanding, it had not as yet become a truly national market. Until it did, no national labor organization could really become stabilized, for unionism could not develop further than the limits imposed by the economy of the country. This is also the story of the first national labor federation of America, the National Trades' Union. It was started in March, 1834, when the New York General Trades' Union invited central labor bodies throughout the nation to send delegates to a national convention to be held in New York City.

Late the following August delegates from Boston, Brooklyn, Poughkeepsie, Newark, Philadelphia, and New York met in City Hall to form the National Trades' Union. They had been convened, in the words of the call to the convention, because the "state of feebleness that in the first case suggested a union of the members of a trade into Societies, suggested also in the second a Union of Trade Societies, which should be carried into effect throughout the United States. The rights of each individual would then be sustained by every workingman in the country, whose aggregate wealth and power would be able to resist the most formidable opposition." [50]

This perspective was never realized because its leadership was mostly drawn from middle class reformers whose panaceas substituted final goals for immediate needs, thus losing touch with reality. Nevertheless its mere existence was a new and important thing in American life, as the delegates to the convention realized. As the delegation from Philadelphia said in its report, "It may be asked, abstract from the discussion and recommendation of measures, 'What good has the convention done?' We can answer: 'It has formed a National Union.' And is there any so unwise as to ask what union can do?" [51]

For the first time American labor had a national voice, and in the three years of its existence the National Union spoke for labor on all such issues as wages and hours, currency reform, public education,* factory legislation, prison labor, and free land. Employers, said the union, would not suffer by agreeing to the ten-hour day. "It is well understood by mechanics and others, who have experience in manual labor operations, that violent and unremitting bodily exertion for 12 or 14 hours a day while it is exceedingly injurious to the health of the employed, is accompanied with no particular advantage to the employer, that is, that as much will be performed by day laborers in the end who work ten hours a day as by those who work twelve." [52] A committee was appointed to collect data on all prevailing hours of labor as evidence from which to argue for the legislative enactment of the ten-hour day. Another committee drew up the first trade union program for women workers. This report called on the men to admit women into their unions or to form separate unions and "make one auxiliary to the other" so that "in case of difficulties they would be governed by their laws and receive their support." It also made a blistering attack upon upper middle class women, who were more concerned with converting Africans to Christianity than with the welfare of "their own oppressed countrywomen." [53]

THE TEN-HOUR DAY

At its convention in 1835, the National Trades' Union proposed that when employers united to resist labor's demands, one general strike should be called by the City Trades' Union. This plan never went beyond the paper stage. But that very year in Philadelphia for the first time an American city experienced a general strike.

The impulse for this strike came from the Boston carpenters who had struck in 1825 and 1832 for the ten-hour day. Both strikes had failed

---

* In 1835 the National Trades' Union urged all affiliated bodies to agitate for the establishment of libraries in cities, towns and villages "for the use and benefits of mechanics and workingmen." This is one of the earliest pleas for public libraries in America.

Labor, however, was not content merely to campaign for public libraries, and in several cities libraries and reading rooms were set up by the workingmen themselves, usually under the sponsorship of the trades' union of the vicinity. In Philadelphia a "Society for the Diffusion of Knowledge among the Working Classes" was established in 1835 "not only to enlighten the mind upon general subjects, but to teach that class, who supply the fountain of existence, whence their evils spring and how to remedy them." In Rochester, New York, a "Mechanics' Literary Association" was formed in 1836 by the trade unions. "We know," said the circular announcing its formation, "that the laboring class has for ages been in the habit of looking up to the learned professions for all the knowledge that is necessary in guiding the affairs of State, or in ruling the affairs of men, and it requires no very discerning eye, to see that all rulers rule for their own benefit, rather than for the benefit of the many." (*National Trades' Union*, January 30, April 16, 1836.)

because in the face of the combined strength of the employers the ranks of the workers had been split by the presence in the unions of small employers who checked the militancy of the workers. With this lesson in mínd, the carpenters, masons and stone-cutters, in their strike for the ten-hour day in 1835, took the conduct of the strike out of the hands of small employers and elected Seth Luther and two other class conscious workers as leaders. They issued a circular at once explaining their demands and asking for assistance, and a traveling committee visited other cities. Despite these new tactics, and despite the assistance from workers in other cities, they were obliged, wrote the president of the carpenters' Union, "to acknowledge the defeat of our fondest wishes and our most ardent desires." [54]

In a larger sense, the strike was not lost, for it had started the struggle that would finally bring the ten-hour day to Boston. American workers had been inspired by the bold and patriotic strike circular, part of which read:

"We have been too long subjected to the odious, cruel, unjust and tyrannical system which compels the operative mechanic to exhaust his physical and mental powers. We have rights and duties to perform as American citizens and members of society, which forbid us to dispose of more than ten hours for a day's work." [55]

Wherever the Boston circular was studied, a strike developed for the ten-hour day.* It led to the great Philadelphia general strike which started when the Irish workers on the Schuylkill River coal wharves turned out for increased wages and the ten-hour day. So militant were these workers that no scabs dared to take their places. "Three hundred of them headed by a man armed with a sword, paraded along the Canal, threatening death to those who unload or transfer the cargoes to the 75 vessels waiting in the river." [56] Reprinted by the Philadelphia Trades' Union as soon as the strike was called, the Boston circular was distributed at various meet-

---

* William Thompson, president of the Carpenters' Society of Philadelphia, told Seth Luther that "the carpenters considered the Boston circular had broken their shackles, loosed their chains, and made them free from the galling yoke of excessive labor." One sentence in the circular especially evoked a response from workingmen: "We claim *by the blood of our Fathers,* shed on our battle fields in the war of the Revolution, the rights of American citizens, and no earthly power shall resist our righteous claim with impunity." (See Seth Luther, *An Address delivered before the Mechanics and Working Men of the City of Brooklyn, on the celebration of the sixtieth anniversary of American Independence,* Brooklyn, 1836, pp. 18-20. Copy in the Library Company of Philadelphia.)

Workingmen everywhere agreed with the Boston worker who said during the ten-hour strike in that city: "By the old system we have no time for mental cultivation—and that is the policy of the big bugs—they endeavor to keep people ignorant by keeping them always at work." (*Boston Post,* April 17, 1835.)

ings of the labor unions. A call to action swept through the city, inspired by the circular:

> *Strike till the last arm'd foe expires,*
> *Strike for your altars and your fires,*
> *Strike for the green graves of your sires,*
> *God and your native land.*[57]

Every day new groups of workers joined the coal heavers for a ten-hour day. The house painters met and denounced the "present system of labor as oppressive and unjust—destructive of social happiness, and degrading to the name of Freemen." [58]

It was not long before every union was out. Leather dressers, printers, carpenters, bricklayers, masons, and city employees; hod-carriers, coal heavers, painters, bakers and dry goods clerks preceded by a fife and drum corps paraded with their banners which read: "From 6 to 6, ten hours work and two hours for meals." We marched, said John Ferral, Philadelphia's leading trade unionist, "to the public works and the workmen joined with us. Employment ceased, business was at a standstill, shirt-sleeves were rolled up, aprons on, working tools in hand were the orders of the day." [59]

On June 6, a great mass meeting was held in the State House courtyard. Here, workers, lawyers, doctors, and some business men joined in approving the demand for the ten-hour day. This meeting unanimously adopted a set of resolutions which praised one business man who had agreed to the ten-hour day; it gave full support to the workers' demand for wage increases; it asked for higher wages for women workers, and encouraged the coal heavers to continue the strike. The meeting also called on all citizens to boycott any coal merchant who worked his men more than ten hours. Before adjourning, the meeting issued this stirring statement: "This meeting is satisfied that the working classes are the bone and sinew of the land; and...upon their health, virtue and happiness depend the security and perpetuity of our glorious and free institutions." [60] Before this united front of the community the employers capitulated. "The blood-sucking aristocracy," wrote John Ferral, "...stood aghast; terror-stricken, they thought the day of retribution had come...." [61]

When the Philadelphia city government learned that the public works employees had joined the general strike, it hurriedly convened and after deliberation announced that the "hours of labour of the working men employed under the authority of the city corporation would be from 'six to six' during the summer season, allowing one hour for breakfast, and one for dinner." The local town government of Southwark, a suburb of Philadelphia, followed, and not only was the working day reduced to ten hours but an increase of 12½ cents a day was granted. On June 22, hardly three weeks after the coal heavers had struck, the general strike had been won. The ten-hour system and a corresponding advance of wages for piece-workers had been adopted throughout the city.[62]

The victory in Philadelphia was bad news to the conservatives, news "full of mischief" according to the New York *Journal of Commerce*. "If such is to be the reward of turn-outs," it correctly predicted on June 8, 1835, "there will be no end to them."

Carried by the labor press to cities in New Jersey, New York, Connecticut, Massachusetts, Maryland, and even to South Carolina, the news everywhere aroused great enthusiasm. A wave of strikes swept the country, most of which were successful. By the end of 1835, with the exception of Boston, the standard day's work for skilled mechanics was ten hours.*

In general, as a result of trade union activity, most skilled mechanics' working day had decreased to ten hours and there was a downward trend in working hours for most workers.

In many trades also, wages reflected the unionizing activity of the 'thirties. Wages for carpenters in Massachusetts rose from $1.07 per day in 1821 to $1.40 per day in the 1830's; for painters from $1.15 to $1.32, for millwrights from $1.13 to $1.39, for metal workers from $1.23 to $1.54, for glass makers from $1.13 to $1.62, for printers from $1.25 to $1.38, for cotton mill operatives from 44 cents to 90 cents, for woolen mill operatives from $1.12 to $1.20, and for laborers from 80 cents to 87 cents.[63]

LABOR AND THE PUBLIC

To no small extent these victories of labor were the result of its ability to win public support. No strike took place in the 'thirties without the union taking measures to bring its problems to the public. The first step in public relations was the issuance of "cards" in the newspapers:

---

* While the following statistics taken from the *Tenth Census* do not give us a complete picture of working hours in American establishments during the 'thirties, they are nevertheless revealing:

Year	Total number re- porting	8 hours to less than 11 (Number	per cent)	11 to less than 13 (Number	per cent)	13 to less than 14 (Number	per cent)
1830	37	18	48.7	14	37.8	5	13.5
1835	48	24	50.0	18	37.5	6	12.5

Tenth Census, Volume XX, p. xxviii.

"TO THE PUBLIC

"The Journeymen Cordwainers of the township of Orange [New Jersey], having made a strike for an advance of wages, which they believe perfectly just and reasonable, embrace this method of laying their case before a discriminating public, in order to counteract unfounded reports or misunderstanding that might arise in regard to their present efforts to obtain an advance of wages. . . .

"That employers, generally, have not a feeling in common with their workmen, is morally certain, unless it be for their personal aggrandizement. Hence the differences between them. This may appear strange to some, still it is no less strange, than true that in our country, famed for the liberality of her institutions, the wisdom of her laws, the equality of her citizens, men should exist who in the very face of their country's Institutions, should endeavor to build up an aristocracy, better befitting the *hot-beds* of Europe than the atmosphere of free America."

Another typical "card" issued by the Journeymen Curriers of Newark stated: "The labor of their hands and intelligence of their minds is their actual property, and they consider it their province to put a fair and just value on their own articles, and not leave the prices to the mercy of those who would grind them and give them just what they pleased." "How can we be free," asked the Journeymen Cordwainers of New York, "while we have no control over the only commodity we have to dispose of—our labor?" And the Piano Forte Makers and Organ Builders of New York made the same point in their card, "As labor is the only merchandise which the journeymen have in the market, they have a right to set a price on it, and those who will not enjoy the privileges are slaves and we recommend them and their masters to the attention of the abolitionists." [64]

Employers generally replied with their own "cards." Usually they claimed that wages were more than adequate, and that they were quite willing to discuss grievances individually with any workman, but they refused to be coerced by labor into sitting down and discussing business matters with radical agitators infected with the "moral gangrene of trade union principles." They asked the public to decide if a group of "lazy, idle mischief makers from abroad should be allowed to threaten the destruction of our prospects as a manufacturing community" by destroying the happy relations that existed between worker and employer. Sometimes labor would reply: "If the employers consider the wages which they have been giving sufficient to support a man, we recommend them to go to work themselves, and test the weight of their theory." Sometimes workers challenged employers to submit their books to an impartial committee to determine whether wages were too low. When the Lady Shoe Binders of Lynn read a "card" inserted in the press denouncing their union as "detrimental to the prosperity of the town," they replied: "We can only say, that we regard the welfare of the town as highly as any one can do; and that we consider it to consist, not in the aggrandizement of a few individuals, but in the general prosperity and welfare of the industrious and laboring classes." [65]

"We are proud to say that we are affected with trade union principles, and hope the symptoms of the disease may never be eradicated," asserted a group of workers, because, they said, only through collective action could they *obtain that which the God of nature intended as their right, but which avarice denies them—a comfortable subsistence.*" [66]

This was the spirit of American labor during the 1820's and 1830's. Determined to secure what all citizens of a democracy should enjoy, workers organized trade unions, city central labor bodies, and national labor federations, and won militant strikes for higher wages and shorter hours.

CHAPTER 8

Early Labor Parties

"The poor have no laws; the laws are made by the rich and of course for the rich." This statement was part of an address by the Association of Working People of New Castle County, Delaware, in 1829, but it expressed a feeling that was shared by the vast majority of American workers.[1]

Several years had passed since the right to vote had been granted to non-property holders in several states. Yet to most workers the privileges of citizenship had brought little but unfulfilled promises. Everywhere the children of workingmen were deprived of education and kept in ignorance. Everywhere the workers themselves were thrown into prison for petty debts, forced to serve at their own expense in the militia, and taxed heavily at the same time that many wealthy property-holders were exempted. It mattered little in most communities by what names the political parties called themselves, for the candidates for public office were "taken entirely from the class of citizens denominated or supposed to be rich."

Trade unions alone could not change these conditions. As long as workers continued to cast their votes for candidates who had taken over the political philosophy and practices of the old Federalist Party and continued to ignore the welfare of the common people, these conditions would remain and so long would the promise of the American Revolution remain unfulfilled. Yet these officials had been elected by the votes of the workers. Of what value, then, was the franchise if the common people permitted the wealthy to dominate their government? A pamphlet circulated among the mechanics and working men of Philadelphia, early in 1827, pointed out that the blessing of universal suffrage was permitted by the workingmen to be directed against their "prosperity and welfare" by individuals whose interest was "at variance" with theirs.[2]

On March 13, 1830, the *Working Man's Advocate* of New York made the same statement:

"Do you not perceive the aristocracy of the nation is leagued against you? And do you not perceive that it is plainly the interest of those who live on your labor to make it as profitable as possible? Why then do you send these very men to your legislature and give them almost every office? ... Think ye they will legislate for you against themselves? Slightly then have you read the human heart. Awake then!"

THE POLITICAL AWAKENING

The awakening began in Philadelphia where, in the summer of 1828, the first labor party in America was formed. This movement spread westward to Pittsburgh, Lancaster, Carlisle, Harrisburg, Cincinnati, and other cities in Pennsylvania and Ohio. It went south to Delaware where in 1830 the workers elected thirteen out of eighteen of the officers of the borough of Wilmington; and north to New York City, Newark, Trenton, Albany, Buffalo, Syracuse, Troy, Utica, Boston, Providence, Portland, Maine, and Burlington, Vermont. All told, independent workers' political parties were organized in 61 cities and towns during the years 1828 to 1834, and in communities where no independent parties were formed this movement stimulated the growth of mechanics' clubs which advocated legislation for the benefit of wage earners.

Along with the rise of the workers' parties went the formation of labor papers. Almost fifty labor weeklies were published in the cities and towns during the years 1827-1832.*

* The *Journeymen Mechanics' Advocate* (Philadelphia, 1827), the first American labor paper, died in its first year. The following year, however, two weeklies—the *Mechanics' Gazette and Free Herald* and the *Mechanics' Free Press*—were established in Philadelphia, the latter by the Mechanics' Library Company. During the next few years many others made their appearance in other cities and states: the *Spirit of the Age* of Tuscaloosa, Alabama; the *Delaware Free Press* of Wilmington; the *Farmers' and Mechanics' Advocate* of Charlestown, Indiana; the *Liberalist* of New Orleans; the *New England Farmer and Mechanic* of Gardner, Maine; the Boston *Working Man's Advocate;* the *Village Chronicle and Farmers' and Mechanics' Advocate* of Newark, New Jersey; the *Mechanics' Press* of Utica, New York; the *Working Men's Advocate* of Albany, New York; the *Independent Politician* of Sandy Hill, Washington County, New York; the *Workingmen's Bulletin* of Buffalo, New York; the *Spirit of the Age* of Rochester, New York; *the Southern Free Press* of Charleston, South Carolina; the *Working Men's Union* of Ravenna, Postage County, Ohio; and several papers in New York City, the outstanding ones being the *Working Man's Advocate,* the *Daily Sentinel,* the *Free Enquirer,* and *The Man.*

THE WORKINGMEN'S PROGRAM

Not all of these papers were official organs of the labor parties, but all of them advanced the movement by popularizing "Working Men's Measures." These measures—denounced in conservative circles as "Workeyism"—were the demands of the newly arisen parties. The demand common to most of the parties was the establishment of a system of public education for the children of the poor as well as the rich. It was not a new demand. In the 1790's, the mechanics and laborers of the Democratic Societies had demanded public education. Since that time, much had happened to convince workingmen that the issue was of the utmost importance. They saw their children growing up in ignorance; it was estimated in 1834 that 1,250,000 children in the United States were illiterate. The few schools that existed for the children of the poor carried the pauper taint, and so few children attended them. Workingmen demanded education for their children not as "a grace and bounty or charity," but as "a matter of right and duty." They were convinced that without education their children would never be able to take their rightful place in American society. For these children as for all poor people, the "land of opportunity" would remain but a meaningless phrase.[3]

Education, said one group of workingmen, was "necessary to enable us to raise us from that state of ignorance and poverty, and consequently of vice and wretchedness and woe, to which we have been degraded by the subtle and deceitful machinations of the crafty and wicked." Newark workers considered "education alone, and that generally diffused the only prop that will support the fabric of Democracy from being crushed beneath the weight of a monopolized and monied aristocracy." And Philadelphia workers declared that only by procuring for all children in the nation free education would workingmen be able to preserve the republic "from the dangers of foreign invasion and domestic infringement."

Much as they feared foreign invasion, the compulsory militia system intensely irritated workers in all parts of the country, and workingmen's parties aimed to secure its abolition. According to this system, all citizens had to turn out at stated periods, usually three times a year, to parade and drill. Failure to report brought a fine of twelve dollars annually, and failure to pay the fine brought a jail sentence. This requirement was no burden to the wealthy who avoided duty by paying the fine, but to workers who could not afford to pay the fine or to be absent from work, it was a heavy burden. They were ready at a moment's notice to defend their country, but they saw little value in the "expensive and useless machinery of pageant and parade."[4]

Abolition of imprisonment for debt was another important demand. It was estimated that in 1829 more than 75,000 persons were in prison in the United States because of debts, more than half of them for sums of less than twenty dollars. In New York City alone, nearly a thousand people were in jail for debts of five dollars or less, and in Concord, Massachusetts, William Cutter, a soldier of the Revolution, was in jail for the crime of a $12 debt. It is little wonder that workers, farmers, and small business men joined in denouncing this "vicious relic of feudal tyranny" which was "inconsistent with the spirit of our republican institutions." [5]

The absence of a mechanics lien law caused "not less than $300,000 to $400,000 [to be] plundered annually from the useful and industrial classes of our citizens." When an employer went bankrupt, the workers usually received no part of the wages due to them, and at a time when wages were often paid on a monthly, or even semi-annual basis, some employers found it profitable to go bankrupt in order to pocket unpaid wages. Petitions to the legislatures over the course of thirty years having brought no redress, workers decided at last to use their power at the polls to obtain this needed legislation. [6]

Opposition to chartered monopolies was another important reason for the formation of workingmen's parties. Profit-making corporations were created individually by special monopoly charters from the state legislatures. Men with small capital and little political influence rarely secured such charters. Many business ventures, therefore, were monopolized by a small group of capitalists who were able to charge high prices. The workingmen of Locust Grove, Pennsylvania, went on record as "opposed to chartered monopolies, as they feel sensibly the effect they produce on the laboring classes.... All competition may be laudable when left free to all persons, as it may have a tendency to prove beneficial to the community at large. But chartered monopolies make a few wealthy to the disadvantage of and misery of the mass of the people. They frequently turn many industrious men out of employment or reduce their wages." [7]

The worst of all monopolies, according to the workingmen, was the banking monopoly. Labor feared that banking monopolies would grow in power and influence until they would control American economic and political life. With unlimited sources of capital in their hands, bankers constituted a small and powerful group. Soon no amount of opposition would succeed in unseating them, hence action was imperative before they could entrench themselves to "perpetuate an aristocracy which eventually may shake the foundations of our liberties and entail slavery upon our posterity." [8]

Also objectionable was the fact that banks restricted competition and often prevented new men from entering business. Bank credits were already playing an important role in business, for the expansion of trade caused frequent delays in collection of debts. Businessmen were consequently becoming very dependent upon credit facilities. Naturally, wealthy merchant capitalists who were also bank directors secured credit more easily than small businessmen or journeymen who wished to set up business. To workingmen, therefore, banks seemed part of a gigantic monopolistic conspiracy to stifle competition, reduce employment, and raise prices.

In addition to this general fear of financial monopolies, workers had specific grievances against the banks. Wages at this time were usually paid in bank notes whose value fluctuated in relation to the solvency of the bank of issue. Whereas merchants took bank notes only at a discount, workers were forced to take them at face value. Hence the workers' purchasing power varied from week to week and from day to day. It was a common practice in New York City for employers to go down to Wall Street Saturday morning and purchase at a discount enough bank notes to meet their payroll. "While our own tables and families are scantily provided," declared a meeting of workers and others in Philadelphia in 1829 "opposed to the chartering of any more new banks in this commonwealth," "they [the banks] enable others to gamble in trade and live in luxury."

Throughout the nation, working men demanded the abolition of bank notes, and the payment of wages in specie. A number of the working men's parties also called for the outright repeal of charters granted to banks. Others demanded the passage of laws limiting the power of these financial institutions. A few even advanced the demand that the government should take over control of banking and issuing of currency, thereby providing a stabilized currency system which would check inflation and at the same time prevent any domination of political life by banking monopolists.[9]

One of the most bitter complaints of the working men was directed against the competition of convict labor. A contractor could hire prisoners at a very low wage: fifteen cents a day for tailors, fifteen to twenty cents a day for coopers, twenty-five cents a day for shoemakers, and ten cents a day for weavers. "By such competition," said a group of stonecutters, "many workmen will soon be thrown out of employment or compelled to work for low wages, and unless they can by other means obtain a livelihood, be reduced to a state of want and misery."[10]

Unequal taxation was another grievance. The labor parties wished to replace poll taxes or taxes on the necessaries of life by a "fair income or property tax [which] would bear much more equally or impartially on all the people." On the other hand, they advocated that bonds and mortgages be taxed and the exemption of church property from taxation be ended, not only because it was a form of special privilege similar to monopolistic charter but because it also represented the dangerous "connection of church and state." [11] This provoked the attack that the workingmen's parties were opposed to God and religion, but the workers were quick to reply that while they took no stand on matters of personal religious belief they were following Thomas Jefferson in their views on the separation of church and state.

Many workingmen's parties called for greater democracy in governmental machinery. They demanded the elimination of property qualifications for holding office, and condemned the caucus system of nominating candidates as a method through which a handful of party leaders controlled the selection of men for public office. They also opposed indirect elections, for "there should be no intermediate body of men between the electors and the candidates [and] that all important officials be elected directly by the people." There was also considerable opposition to the filling of offices by appointment because "it is the nature of man to favor his own interest—and as the interests of the lawyer and speculator are different from those of the Farmer and Mechanic, who are the real producers of wealth and independence, we must expect that in such a state of things, that monied institutions and wealthy men will be favored, our laws made unintelligible, and the interests of the working people neglected." [12]

Hence workers called for the election of all important officials. And at least one labor party, the Association of the Working People of New Castle, Delaware, went even further. In 1831 it demanded the enfranchisement of women.

"We apprehend," it declared, "that it would be no easy task at this more advanced part of the march of the mind, to maintain the ground that was assumed, in excluding females in the right of voting at the polls. This interesting portion of the community comprises a fair moiety of our population. Wherefore should they be denied the immunities of free men? Does anyone deem that their interference in public affairs would be prejudicial to the general interest?" [13]

Workers were also concerned with their economic position as a class. Although most were not yet ready to advocate a thoroughgoing reorganization of society, the growing contrast of wealth and poverty caused many workers to share the sentiments expressed by Stephen Simpson in the *Working Man's Manual*: "Our object ... strikes at a *fundamental principle* in the distribution of wealth—that *labour* shall share with *capital,* in the profits of trade, in a more equitable ratio. And as capital is vested in the *few,* and labour resides in the *many*—it only requires that the latter combine to bring government into their own hands, to secure all they desire." [14]

All in all, workers were bent upon realizing the principles of the Declaration of Independence by changing economic and social conditions. "The objects we have in view," said one labor party, "are hallowed by the sympathy of patriotism—it is the finish of the glorious work of the Revolution." Theirs was a movement which "Jefferson, if he yet lived, would receive and recognize as his own." For he would be the first to recognize "that the cause of the workingmen is the cause of the country." [15]

These were also the sentiments of John Greenleaf Whittier. "The industrious mechanics," he observed early in 1829, "may be ranked among her [republican America's] firmest supporters, and the time is not far distant when he shall be placed upon his just station in the scale of society.... The people—the 'bone and sinew' of the nation are calling forth their giant energies and who shall arrest this progress." [16]

PHILADELPHIA

It was fitting that the first labor party was formed in Philadelphia in which city the first strikes in American history had taken place. It was here that the first labor paper had been published and a city central labor body organized. It was this labor body, the Mechanics' Union of Trades' Associations, which took initial steps to organize the workers of Philadelphia for independent political action.

At a meeting of this body in May 1828, the question of legislation to establish a ten-hour day in the city and to remedy other grievances of the working class was hotly discussed. The Association decided to call on its constituent unions to voice their opinions on the question of nominating candidates to "represent the interest of the working classes" in the coming elections for city council and state legislature. The cordwainers, hatters, and carpenters, the chief unions in the Association, were all for it, the carpenters resolving unanimously that "...we entertain the most heartfelt satisfaction and approbation for the measures in contemplation by the said 'Mechanics' Union of Trade Associations,' and will use every exertion to carry the said measures in effect." [17]

Taking action at once, the Association adopted a by-law, providing for nominations for the fall elections, and called four meetings in Philadelphia to which all were invited "without respect to party or sectional names." At the same time it announced that: "The Mechanics and Working Men of the City and County of Philadelphia are determined to take the management of their own interests, as a class, into their own immediate keeping...." [18]

Out of the district meetings called by the Association came nominating conventions where candidates for city and state offices were chosen. Although most of the delegates to these conventions were workingmen, no wage earners were nominated on the Working Men's Ticket, due largely to the fact that property qualifications existed for all offices. However, those nominated were pledged to uphold the principles of the movement and to "support the interests and claims of the Working Classes." The Working Men's candidates were placed on both the Jackson and the Federalist tickets after they had been nominated by the workingmen.

Most of the support for the Working Men's Ticket came from "Committees of Vigilance" set up by the county nominating convention.

The results of the election revealed that better organization was needed before a workingman's ticket could carry the day. As a consequence, there arose permanent political clubs in and around the city to aid in the election of public officials and help secure "general diffusion of constitutional, legal and political knowledge among the working people." [19] This need for greater organization was met in March, 1829, when the Republican Political Association of the Working Men of the City of Philadelphia was formed. It began at once to organize the workingmen for the fall election of 1829. Nominations for office were left to the city and county conventions. Delegates were chosen democratically at ward meetings to attend city and county nominating conventions.

Efforts to break up these meetings failed, as did the attempts of the local Democratic Party to split the Association by provoking internal dissension through Red baiting. In an effort to avoid commitments to either of the old parties, and in response to the warnings of many ward meetings against fusion with the Federalists or Democrats, the nominating conventions selected candidates before the other parties met. Even so, the Federalists endorsed nine and the Democrats three Working Men's candidates for city offices, and the former also endorsed three assembly and senate candidates.

Despite threats of economic reprisals (no secret ballot existed at this time), the Working Men were able to elect enough candidates to hold the balance of power. Twenty of the 54 workers' candidates, all of whom had received endorsement from either Federalists or Democrats, were elected. The *Mechanics' Free Press* did not receive the victory in a partisan spirit. It said: "The balance of power has at length got into the hands of the working people, where it properly belongs, and it will be used, in the future, for the *general* weal." [20]

Still the movement was not content to rest on its laurels. In Southwark, a suburb of Philadelphia, the local association issued an address to its membership and supporters urging them to "prepare for the coming season." Throughout the winter and spring of 1829-30, organization and education continued. To the City Convention of 1830 delegates came from fifteen wards. By this time political associations had been formed in Lancaster, Phillipsburg, Carlisle, and Pike Township. "For the purpose of watching over the rights and more effectually guarding against all encroachment on the laboring party of the community," went a Proclamation of the Pike Township Association, "we, Farmers, Mechanics and Laborers, inhabitants of Pike Township, Clearfield County, do hereby form ourselves into a society to be called the 'Working Men's Society of Grampion Hills.' " [21]

During the 1830 campaign the question of candidates for public office was widely discussed: should only workingmen be nominated for office or should "tried friends" of the movement be nominated as well? It would seem from the resolutions of the ward clubs and county conventions that a majority favored the nomination of workingmen only. They called for the support of only those men "who are engaged in productive pursuits." The Allegheny County Association expressed the belief that "however patriotic a man may appear to be, it is evident that none can so completely understand our interests, and that none will be so vigilant in protecting them as those, who in promoting the public welfare, most effectually secure their own." [22]

The workingmen's movement faced a well-organized attack from the newspapers during the 1830 campaign. Charges of "anti-religious," "infidelity," and "agrarian" were hurled at the movement, and "workeyism" was played up in all the denunciations. Frances Wright, the militant champion of woman's rights, who advocated the abolition of slavery, the separation of church and state, and the elimination of clerical influence in education, was credited with being the ideological parent of the workingmen's movement. The workers answered that they had no sympathy with the agrarians, were not connected with Miss Wright, and stated that "those who introduce either the subject of Agrarianism or religion into our political proceedings are the avowed enemies of our righteous cause." [23] But the campaign of lies had its effect. The Democrats carried both the city and county elections. However, the Association ticket received approximately 1,000 votes for its candidates, and in Northern Liberties, a suburb of Philadelphia, eight commissioners were elected.

The story of the Philadelphia party after 1830 can be swiftly told. City and county conventions were held in 1831, and a ticket nominated but the movement had lost its vigor. No candidates were elected in 1831, the last election in which the Association participated. The failure to unite the separate political associations into a statewide party contributed greatly to the short life of the movement.

NEW YORK

At the time the workingmen of Philadelphia were organizing for independent political action, a similar movement was developing in New York. Associated with this second American labor party at one time or another were some of the outstanding figures in the labor and intellectual world: Frances Wright; Robert Dale Owen, son of the distinguished English Utopian Socialist Robert Owen; George Henry Evans, editor of the *Working Man's Advocate* and *The Man,* and, later, leader of the land reform movement; Ebenezer Ford, president of the Carpenters' Union; John Commerford, president of the Chairmakers' and Gilders' Union Society; Levi D. Slamm, leader of the Journeymen Locksmiths Union; and Thomas Skidmore, the radical self-educated machinist who was engaged after working hours in writing a book to which he gave the title: *The Rights of Man to Property: Being a Proposition to Make it Equal Among the Adults of the Present Generation; and to Provide for its Equal Transmission to Every Individual of Each Succeeding Generation, on Arriving at the Age of Maturity.*

The Working Men's Party of New York had its origin in a movement to prevent the lengthening of the working day. In 1829, New York City was the only community in which labor had already secured recognition of the ten-hour day. But the employers were attempting to restore the eleven-hour working day. A meeting of leading trade unionists was called for April 23, 1829, to discuss the best ways of countering the employers' offensive. A few days later a mass meeting was called and five thousand workers responded. They resolved not to work for any employer longer than the "just and reasonable time of ten hours a day." All workers who violated this pledge would have their names published in the press as enemies of labor. To prepare for a possible strike the meeting raised a fund of one hundred dollars. A Committee of Fifty was elected to organize the strategy for the preservation of the ten-hour day. The alertness and unity of the workingmen soon forced the employers to give up their scheme to lengthen the working day.[24]

The Committee of Fifty did not disband after this victory. It met regularly and, as the fall elections approached, called another mass meeting of workers to discuss the part labor could play in the campaign. To this meeting the Committee of Fifty submitted a report recommending the nomination of a Working Man's Ticket in order to secure redress for its most pressing grievances. The meeting adopted the report, and the second American labor party was born.

The official title of the new party was the New York Working Men's Party. The slate for the State Assembly, nominated by the Committee of Fifty, included two carpenters, two machinists, a painter, founder, cooper, grocer and physician. For the State Senate the new party had a joint candidate with the Clay, Adams, anti-Tammany forces.[25]

Up to this time the most prominent figure in the Committee of Fifty had been Thomas Skidmore who had formulated most of the resolutions introduced by this body to the various mass meetings. It was his resolution, recommending the formation of a workingman's party, that asserted that even the election of labor candidates would not solve the problems of the working class. Only a revolutionary transformation of existing property relations would bring real relief. Skidmore proposed that every young man, twenty-one years of age, and every unmarried woman should receive a free grant of one hundred and sixty acres of land, to be held in perpetuity so long as the settler tilled his soil. But the right to sell or rent land was to be abolished forever. No one should be permitted by law to own more than one hundred and sixty acres, for no man could by his own labor use more. He did not propose the immediate confiscation of big holdings in the east, but advocated a law whereby the government should claim holdings exceeding one hundred and sixty acres at the owner's death. By such means, he hoped to abolish inequality at the end of one generation.

After the nomination of a Working Man's ticket, Frances Wright and Robert Dale Owen entered the movement. Both had considerable following among the people of New York. For more than a year they had been organizing a liberal movement in the city. By means of their weekly newspaper, the *Free Enquirer,* and their public lectures, they popularized their belief that only through a scientific, rational approach to all issues and by the education of the youth could the problems of the day be met. Both Owen and Miss Wright appealed especially to the workers for support, believing that the working class alone had the strength and organization to carry their theories into practice. In an address entitled "To Young Mechanics," Frances Wright declared:

"If therefore I have addressed myself at all times, more especially to the industrious classes, it has been for two reasons—First, that they comprise the only large mass among the heterogeneous fragments of society; and, secondly, that their interests at the time being are more nearly approached to the great natural interests of man, and incline, therefore, more immediately to wholesale reforms and general union." [26]

In spite of the great prejudice against the participation of women in public affairs, Miss Wright's lectures were well attended by working people. She gave clear expression to labor's desire for free education, higher wages, shorter hours, and a place in the life of society. Moreover, unlike many intellectuals who shrank from the class struggle, Miss Wright recognized that labor was becoming class-conscious, and welcomed this development. She wrote in the *Free Enquirer* for November 27, 1830:

"What distinguished the present from every other struggle in which the human race has been engaged is that the present is, evidently openly and acknowledgedly, a war of class, and that this war is universal ... ; it is now everywhere the oppressed millions who are making common cause against oppression; it is the ridden people of the earth who are struggling to throw from their backs the 'booted and spurred' riders whose legitimate title to starve as well as work them to death will no longer pass current; * it is labour rising up against idleness, industry against money; justice against law and against privilege. And truly the struggle hath not come too soon. Truly there hath been oppression and outrage enough on the one side, and suffering and endurance enough on the other, to render the millions rather chargeable with excess of patience and over abundance than with too eager a spirit for the redress of injury, not to speak of recourse to vengeance."

Owen and Miss Wright hailed the new workingmen's party. Like Skidmore they believed that other reforms were "partial, ineffectual, temporary or trifling," compared with what they regarded as the major reform—the establishment of a national system of education. They recognized that this major reform would be possible as soon as labor had influence in the government. Hence, they co-operated closely with the workingmen's movement, and their own organization, the "Association for the Protection of Industry and the Promotion of National Education," endorsed the Working Man's ticket.[27]

Barely a week remained before election day after the Working Men's ticket was nominated. To this difficulty was added the lack of funds, the treasury having only $75. But, in spite of this, as the campaign drew to a close it became clear that the labor party was a power to reckon with, and the press became hysterical. They begged the voters to defeat the " 'Infidel Ticket,' miscalled the 'Working Men's ticket' ... a ticket got up openly and avowedly in opposition to all banks—in opposition to social order—in opposition to the rights of property."[28] This new party, said the press, was the creature of that insane, atheistical woman, Fanny Wright. The following editorial in the *Commercial Advertiser* of October 31, 1829, is typical:

* Miss Wright was paraphrasing Thomas Jefferson's famous remark in his last letter, June 24, 1826, in which he wrote a few days before his death: "...The general spread of the light of science has already laid open to every view the palpable truth, that the mass of mankind has not been born with saddles on their backs, nor a favored few booted and spurred, ready to ride them legitimately, by the grace of God." (Philip S. Foner, ed., *Basic Writings of Thomas Jefferson*, New York, 1944, p. 807.)

"Lost to society, to earth and to heaven, godless and hopeless, clothed and fed by stealing and blasphemy—such are the apostles who are trying to induce a number of able-bodied men in this city to follow in their course ... to disturb the peace of the community for a time; go to prison and have the mark of Cain imposed upon them; betake themselves to incest, robbery and murder; die like ravenous wild beasts, hunted down without pity; and go to render their account before a God, whose existence they believed in their miserable hearts, even while they were blaspheming him in their ignorant, snivelling and puerile speculations. Such is too true a picture, in all its parts, of some of the leaders of the new political party which is emerging from the slime of this community and which is more beastly and terrible than the Egyptian Typhoon."

To counteract this type of raving, the *Working Man's Advocate* was started on October 31, 1829. Its editor and printer was George Henry Evans, an associate of Robert Dale Owen. Evans had come to this country from England at the age of fourteen and had become apprenticed to a printer at Ithaca, New York. He had formerly been the printer of the *Free Enquirer*. For a time both the *Advocate* and the *Enquirer* were printed from the same press.

This leading labor paper in the United States carried on its masthead the slogan, "Equal Education for All: All Adults to Equal Privileges." Its first editorial announced: "The working classes have taken the field and never will they give up the contest until the power that oppresses them is annihilated."

Its influence was not confined to New York City, for it had subscribers in Albany, Buffalo, Syracuse, New Haven, New London, Hartford, Springfield, Massachusetts; and in New Hampshire.* This important paper remained in existence until 1836 when it suspended publication because of the poor health of its editor. It resumed publication in 1844 when Evans again became active in the labor movement.

In spite of the brief campaign, the lack of resources and the unprincipled opposition of the press, the Working Man's Party won an impressive victory. All but one of its candidates for the Assembly, the physician, received over six thousand of the seventy thousand votes cast. Leading the ticket was Ebenezer Ford, president of the Carpenters' Union. Ford was elected to the Assembly, and became the first labor representative to the New York State Assembly since the victory of the

---

* The size of its circulation is not recorded, and it probably did not total more than a few hundred copies. It must be remembered, however, that the *New York Courier and Enquirer,* with the largest circulation in the country, claimed 4,500 in 1833, and not many other papers reached even half that figure.

Mechanics' ticket in 1785. Moreover, the most successful candidate for the State Senate publicly acknowledged his debt to the Working Men's Party.[29]

The *Working Man's Advocate* had good reason to rejoice. "The result," it observed on November 7, 1829, "has proved beyond our most sanguine expectations favorable to our cause . . . the cause of the people . . . we have done more than could reasonably have been expected at this election. If the Working Men's ticket had been nominated a week sooner, there is very little doubt that it would have succeeded."

The conservative press did not share this elation. The election of Ebenezer Ford, a common carpenter, was called a disgrace to New York City. It would scare away traders and investors from the nation's commercial emporium, for what business men would feel safe in a city whose banks would be destroyed by radical working men led by fanatical agitators from England and Ireland? The *Journal of Commerce* predicted that the worst was yet to come. The fatal mistake, it added, was made when universal suffrage was adopted, for "by throwing open the polls to every man that walks, power was placed in the hands of those who had neither property, talents, nor influence in other circumstances." [30]

Victory was not confined to New York City. Upstate, in Salina, the Farmers and Mechanics' Party elected its entire slate in the spring elections of 1830. In Troy and Albany the farmers and working men won all but one ward.* These victories spread "terror and dismay among the aristocracy of the state of New York." [31]

However, all was not going well within the movement. On December 29, 1829, Thomas Skidmore split the party when he and about forty of his followers organized what they called the Poor Man's Party. On the surface it seemed but a minor issue that had led to the split. After the elections there was much discussion about the form of the permanent organization of the party. The Committee of Fifty called a mass meeting on December 29, at which it presented its plan, drawn up by Skidmore, calling for the continuation of general mass meetings as in the past. Opposed to this vague form of organization was George Evans who proposed instead that the party be based, as in Philadelphia, on local wards or clubs in which the working men could conduct day-to-day activities. Skidmore attacked the ward plan, arguing that this form

---

* The emblem of the Albany party was an arm and hammer superimposed over a plow, "a sort of American precursor of the hammer and sickle." (Jeremiah Ingersoll, *New York City Labor and Jacksonian Democracy,* unpublished Ph.D. dissertation, University of Chicago, 1939, p. 69.) The symbol of the Farmers, Mechanics and Working Men of Kings County was a Hammer and Wheat Sheaves. (*Working Man's Advocate,* July 27, 1830.)

of organization would make it easy for enemies to gain control of the party.

Skidmore was defeated, the meeting voting for the ward plan of organization. Not only did the workers want the ward plan because it was superior but they felt that Skidmore was more interested in putting across his agrarian plans for equal division of property than such immediate demands as education, mechanics lien laws, and abolition of imprisonment for debt. They feared that under the loose type of organization proposed by Skidmore it would be easy for him to incorporate his program in all the statements issued by the party, which was exactly what he had done up to that time. Up to now, the workers had been so concerned either with the struggle to retain the ten-hour day or with the political campaign that they had not paid much attention to the fact that their resolutions also called for the equal division of all property among the present generation. Now that they were considering a permanent organization, most of the members were unwilling to accept Skidmore's program as part of the movement. When Skidmore arose to speak at the December meeting he was greeted by the cry, "No Agrarianism." [32]

Skidmore was a remarkable man. Even his enemies granted that he was an "ardent supporter of the true interests of the working classes and a never-tiring devotee in the worship of human liberty." [33] In the new social order Skidmore was planning he outlawed all discrimination on account of religion, race, or sex. He was thus one of the earliest advocates of full equality, including suffrage, both for women and Negroes. Nevertheless, his doctrinaire approach to working class problems isolated him. He failed to understand that the workers had supported the new party out of their desire to solve immediate needs, and not to establish a new social order. Instead of linking these immediate demands with his program for a basic change in the social system, he argued that such reforms as public education, abolition of imprisonment for debt, etc., were of little or no significance. Moreover, he refused to have anything to do with a movement that had rejected his program. His new party, he maintained, was the only true working class party in the city, and in his newspaper, the *Friend of Equal Rights,* he began a series of bitter attacks on the Working Man's Party.

Skidmore's new role was analyzed by the *Daily Sentinel,* a New York labor paper: "Whatever be his motives, he is doing what in him lies to divide our party.... If he were suborned by the aristocratical party, and kept in their pay for the express purpose of sowing dissension where nothing but dissension can produce defeat... he could not do their bidding more effectively than he does now." [34]

Skidmore's defection did not seriously weaken the party. Only a few workers followed him. The party organized itself on the ward plan and elected a general executive committee of seventy members. Of the seventy, five were grocers; two, merchant tailors; one each a teacher, oil merchant, farmer and broker; the remaining members were workers, mainly skilled mechanics such as carpenters, cabinet makers, masons, blacksmiths, printers, tailors, cartmen, and chair makers. Though there were no unskilled or factory workers, the *Working Man's Advocate* stated there is "but one of the committee who is not a working man." [35] The exception was the broker. The definition of workingman, it is obvious, was quite broad. Evans himself defined "a Working Man" as "one who followed any *useful* occupation, mental or physical, for a livelihood." The Working Men's movement, he added, "cannot in political affairs, act with those who are following occupations that add nothing to the necessaries, comforts, or conveniences of life, nor with those who have never followed a useful occupation for a livelihood." [36]

Even though the movement included small employers and shop-keepers, the names of the labor parties signified a distinction between the common people and the big employers. The latter felt this, too, as we see in the objection of Amos A. Lawrence, a prominent New England factory owner, to the Working Men's Party: "We are literally all work-ingmen; and the attempt to get up a 'workingmen's party' is a libel upon the whole population as it implies that there are among us a large number who are not working men." [37]

In spite of the split in the party, workingmen looked confidently to the fall election of 1830. The *Daily Sentinel* offered a word of warn-ing. "If we were asked," it declared, "whether the people's ticket will succeed at the next election, we should ask in reply, what chance is there of our avoiding dissensions among ourselves." [38] This warning was timely, for a few weeks after the first split the Working Men's Party was again disrupted. The new issue was the education program of Robert Dale Owen and Frances Wright.

Owen and Miss Wright considered the economic demands of the party as secondary to the basic issue of a national, republican education, "free for all and at the expense of all; conducted under the guardianship of the state at the expense of the state, and for the honor, the happiness, the virtue, and salvation of the state." Such a system would bring about a truly democratic society in which there would be no need for me-chanics' lien laws and legislation limiting the power of the banks and abolishing imprisonment for debt.[39]

The outstanding feature of their educational plan was the state guardianship system. Under it, children would be taken from their parents at an early age and placed in state boarding schools until they reached maturity. They would wear the same clothing, experience the same treatment, and be taught in the same branches of learning. There would be no room for religious instruction; only knowledge based on the experience of the senses would be in the curriculum. Parents might visit their children but would not be permitted to interfere with or interrupt their education.[40]

Owen and Miss Wright were convinced that public day school education would be of little value to workingmen's children if parents were not able to feed and clothe their children properly. Why, then, they argued, should one support the demand for a public day school which would mirror all the disadvantages of present-day society? Under the common school system the children would still be under the influence of parents who would instill into their minds their own prejudices and religious superstitions. How then could there be an education which would create equality, bring an end to class divisions, and inaugurate a new social order? Finally, the teachers in the common school would never teach the full truth. "They dare not speak," said Frances Wright, "that which, by endangering their popularity, would endanger their fortunes. They have to discover not what is true, but what is palatable." Palatable, she added, mainly to the wealthy, the politicians, and the clergy.[41]

There were many workers who agreed with much of what Owen and Miss Wright had to say about the common school system. Some even supported the state guardianship plan. Thus the painters' union and a number of journeymen typographers went on record in support of their plan.

But most workers were against the prospect of breaking up homes and removing their children from religious influences. Naturally, the conservative press made much of this point and accused the Working Men's Party of destroying the family, the foundation of society. To be sure, the state guardianship adherents denied these charges, and asserted that "it is not our wish that children should be freed from the control of their parents." Their denials did not carry much weight.[42]

Nevertheless the split in the party over the state guardianship plan did not result from the merits or demerits of the plan. This issue was seized upon by a group of politicians known as the Cook-Guyon faction who had been attracted to the party by its 1829 victories. Anxious either to control or split the party, they picked on the state guardianship issue and denounced it as a "specious attempt to palm upon ... the great body of working classes the doctrine of infidelity," and called upon the workers to "preserve the civil institutions of your country from the baneful, levelling system of a fanatical set of foreigners."[43]

The Owenites played right into their hands by insisting that the state guardianship plan become the "great design of our party." "With this

Great Measure," said Owen, "we will stand or fall." [44] The same doctrinaire approach displayed by Skidmore was now exhibited by Owen who had said, in criticizing and opposing the agrarian reformer, that "reform ought never to travel faster than the public mind."

A serious split took place in the party; pro- and anti-state guardianship factions held meetings in the various wards. Opposition members were expelled from ward committees by one or the other faction, and two general executive committees were formed, the "General Executive Committee opposed to Agrarianism and State Guardianship" and the Owen faction.

The rank-and-file workers attempted in every possible way to heal the split; they knew that unless the movement was united it would have little success in the coming elections.

"I fear," wrote a worker, "that unless the true friends of the party come forth and show their devotion to the common cause, Tammany and Regency will triumph over us. Will the Working Men of this city continue to waste their strength in intestine contentions and nightly brawls, when a higher point is before them? When we have an enemy powerful and cunning, shall we, instead of marching unitedly to the attack, permit ourselves to be divided into two hostile parties? God forbid. Let us stop. Both sides are to blame. Let us put away the bone of contention and turn our efforts to the great political objects of the party." [45]

Judging from the resolutions adopted at various ward meetings, this appeal voiced the sentiments of the party membership. The resolutions called upon both parties, "who claim to be the Executive Committee," to resign their seats in order that a new election might take place throughout the city. Only if the factional disputes ended, these resolutions asserted, would the Working Men's Party be able "to secure to the poor man and his children their rights." [46]

These appeals were ignored. Both factions were too deeply steeped in maneuvers to gain control of the movement to listen to the voice of the rank and file. The worst fears of the workingmen were soon to be realized.

The first workingmen's state convention ever held in New York assembled at Salina on August 25, 1830. Before the convention even got under way, it was confronted by the split that had developed in the New York City movement. Two sets of delegates—one representing the Owen and the other the Cook-Guyon faction—claimed the right to be seated in the name of the Working Men's Party. A member of the Owen delegation proposed that there be a general discussion of the claims of the two groups, but instead the matter was referred to a committee of three, the members of which were friendly to the Cook-Guyon faction. As was to be expected, the committee reported in favor of the anti-state guardianship delegation. Owen's delegates then withdrew, leaving the convention in the hands of the Cook faction.

The convention nominated Generals Erastus Root and Nathaniel Pitcher, two Tammany men, for governor and lieutenant governor. To the *Working Man's Advocate* both were "decidedly party men ... men who had never even advocated our leading measures ... much less pledged themselves to support them." It summed up the convention in four words: "The Working Men Betrayed." [47]

Immediately after the adjournment of this convention, the Owen faction held a mass meeting and voted complete disapproval of the Salina proceedings. On September 14, they held another meeting at which they nominated Ezekiel Williams, a leather manufacturer, and Isaac Smith, a merchant, for governor and lieutenant governor, both known as friends of the workingman.

There were three Working Men's tickets in the campaign of 1830. The Owen faction ran a full city and state ticket and endorsed candidates of other parties for Congress. The Cook-Guyon faction had a complete city and state ticket, except for the gubernatorial positions, their nominees having refused to accept the designation. Quite logically, therefore, this group supported the pro-Henry Clay candidates for these offices. In return, the Clay party supported the Cook-Guyon ticket instead of nominating one of its own. The third workingmen's ticket represented the Skidmore or agrarian faction. It styled itself the original Committee of Fifty Party and nominated local and state candidates. [48]

A week before election day, the *Working Man's Advocate* predicted that the majority of the workingmen who had voted for the new party in 1829, disgusted by the factional fights, would return to Tammany Hall. Tammany swept the city election, and captured a majority of the seats in the State Assembly as well as the governorship. The combined vote for the Working Men's tickets was 2,180. Tammany's gains roughly equaled the decline in the vote for the Working Men's ticket. "Agrarianism in New York is now dead, gone, buried, and transported back to England where it originated," Tammany proclaimed. [49]

The campaign of 1830 was the swan song of the New York Working Men's Party. The three factions continued to function. Each held meetings and adopted resolutions. But the workingmen went their own way back to the old parties.

By the fall of 1831, the Skidmore faction had disappeared, and the Cook-Guyon faction had amalgamated with the Clay or National Republican Party. The Owen faction supported a full ticket for the state legislature which included candidates from both the Tammany and anti-Tammany slates who had expressed agreement with the "Working Men's Measures." A year later, the Owen faction merged with Tammany Hall.

NEW ENGLAND

Following Philadelphia and New York, important steps in political action were taken in New England. Though the New England Association of Farmers, Mechanics and other Workingmen did not itself engage directly in political campaigns, it stimulated its constituent bodies in various cities to put independent tickets into the field. In the Massachusetts state election of 1833 the Working Men's Party of Massachusetts, the political descendant of the Association, polled 3,459 votes and gained control of ten towns. Most of the votes, however, came from the agricultural districts, Boston contributing only 519 votes. Of the ten towns, six of them lay in the western part of the state. Its strength was agrarian with an urban complement of carpenters, masons, and ship caulkers. There could be little electoral strength from the factories where most of the workers were women and children.[50]

DECLINE AND DISAPPEARANCE

There are many reasons for the decline and disappearance of these first labor parties in our history. The most important one can be laid to the state of development of capitalist society in America. A workers' party could not stabilize itself as long as its dominant membership, the skilled journeymen, could still set up their own shops and become employers. Then, most factory workers, being women and children, could as yet play but a small part in the movement, and many of the common laborers were not as yet naturalized citizens. Class lines were still too fluid for a permanent working class political party.

No doubt the violent denunciations heaped upon the early labor parties helped to isolate them from the voters. These intemperate attacks, however, were well answered at the time. Said one paper friendly to the workingmen's movement, "They are called *Radicals, Levellers* and other opprobrious names, in order, if possible to bring them and their efforts into contempt. They are in the same situation that the republicans were in '98 when they were branded as *Jacobins, disorganizers*, etc., by the aristocrats then in power." [51] This forthright stand lent courage to many workers. Yet there is little doubt but that the violent denunciations of the workingmen's movements resulted in the loss of adherents.

Insufficient connection between the trade unions and the political parties weakened both. Political action alone, it was believed, would solve all the problems of the workingmen. Nowhere in the addresses or publications of the movement was there mention of the need to build trade unions, nor did the political parties show much interest in the strikes, wage struggles, or other problems of the unions. George Henry Evans was not even a union member, and Robert Dale Owen and Frances Wright displayed little interest in unionism.

A weakness common to the trade unions as well was lax control over the membership. Dues or other obligations were not considered necessary for party membership; only adherence to general principles was considered necessary.* This limited the possibility of effective party organization, and accelerated disintegration once a defeat had been suffered.

Internal dissension carefully fostered by outside politicians helped weaken the early parties, and where the politicians were unsuccessful, the utopian thinkers succeeded by placing their panaceas for the ills of the world above the immediate reforms. Finally, the established parties weaned away support from the labor parties by championing some of the "Working Men's Measures," and during the Bank war beginning in 1832, the working men rallied to Andrew Jackson's party.

ACHIEVEMENTS

The brief existence and the weaknesses of the early labor parties do not obscure their great accomplishments. They revealed that labor was emerging as an independent force in American life, even though the working class was not numerous enough to make this force powerful in the councils of the nation. These parties revealed that the workers were becoming conscious of themselves as a separate class whose interests were different from those of the capitalists. Their short existence does not mean, as so many have said, that the early working class movements had failed, nor that independent political action by the workers must end in defeat. True, the workingmen's parties disappeared, but not until they had made a great contribution to the advances of American democracy.

On December 11, 1830, barely a year and a half after the first party had been formed, the *Working Man's Advocate* proudly wrote: "Many of the reforms called for by the working men are now acknowledged to be just and reasonable, and even advocated by several of the presses which have hitherto supported the party in power." Thus, the *Advocate* was summing up one of the most important results of the rise of workingmen's

* Article III of the Constitution of the Working Men's Republican Association of Philadelphia read: "The regular monthly contributions shall be half a dime, the payment of which shall be optional with the members." (*Mechanics' Free Press,* April 3, 1830.)

parties. These organizations carried on pioneer activity in behalf of democratic progress in America.

It is true that these reforms were carried out only after the death of the labor parties, but by its very existence this movement had forced the older parties to incorporate into their program the demands of the people. The abolition of imprisonment for debt, the enactment of the mechanics' lien laws, and the abolition of the compulsory militia system came about largely through the efforts of wage earners.[52] Similarly, labor deserves considerable credit for the movement for a more equitable tax system, and the adoption of more democratic methods of nominating public candidates for office. Our public school system, free from the taint of charity, was introduced primarily because of the impetus given to this demand by labor. The "potent push" for the movement for tax-supported schools "came from the firm demand of an aroused and insistent wage-earning class armed with the ballot." [53] The Pennsylvania public school system, for instance, dates from 1834.

To the above achievements must be added the contributions of the workingmen's movement to the national struggle for economic and political democracy led by Andrew Jackson.*

---

* Since the publication of this volume in 1947 the question of whether labor did or did not support Andrew Jackson has become one of the most disputed issues of early American labor history. (For the controversy over this thesis, see W. A. Sullivan, "Did Labor Support Andrew Jackson?" Political Science Quarterly, vol.LXII, 1947, pp.569–60; Edward Pessen, "Did Labor Support Jackson?: The Boston Story," ibid., vol.LXIV, 1949, pp.262–74; R. T. Bower, "Notes on 'Did Labor Support Jackson?: The Boston Story,'" ibid., vol.LXV, 1950, pp.441–44; Walter Huggins, Jacksonian Democracy and the Working Class (Stanford, 1960). The difficulty of reaching a clear conclusion is illustrated in the case of the Boston story. Edward Pessen, examining election returns in Boston during the Jacksonian era, concluded that workingmen more generally voted Whig than Democratic and that they either rejected or ignored so-called workingmen's candidates. But Robert T. Bower, working from the same sources, concluded that "Jackson and his political allies did get their support from working class groups," and so did the workingmen's candidates.

CHAPTER 9

Labor and Jacksonian Democracy

The story of the workingmen's parties of the late 'twenties and early 'thirties is in reality the first stage, in terms of local issues, in the struggles of Jacksonian Democracy. From these parties would now come the forces that would supply the impetus to carry on successfully during the second or national stage of Jacksonian Democracy.

LABOR'S ESTIMATE OF JACKSON

Although the early labor parties emerged during the era of Andrew Jackson, there is little evidence that any of them either looked to Jackson for ideological leadership or believed that his first administration was of real significance. A number of demands raised by the labor parties, such as opposition to party caucuses, had been popularized by "Old Hickory." Most workers hailed his election in 1828 as their own victory, yet his first administration did not convince them that he was following in Jefferson's footsteps. They gave Jackson credit for his honest republicanism, his opposition to the federal subsidizing of private stock companies, and his proposals for the direct election of a President for a single term. They criticized him for his connections with Tammany, his militaristic views, his partisanship in turning opponents out of office, and his contempt for the rights and just claims of the Indians.[1]

It was to Jefferson and not to Jackson that the workingmen turned for inspiration in their political and economic struggles. They were proud that they were of the "Jefferson school to the backbone," and that the "spirit of Jefferson" was manifest in every resolution and address they adopted. When they thought of the approaching Presidential election of 1832 they said, "We want, in fact, another *Jefferson*." As late as the summer of 1830, workingmen in many cities asserted that none of the national political leaders were worthy of consideration as the next president, and that they were reserving their judgment. The working-men of New York stated that they did not consider Jackson or Henry Clay entitled to labor's vote since neither had ever "evinced any par-ticular anxiety or interest in the measures of reform that the working-men are maintaining." [2] Some workers proposed that labor should have its own candidate, and a movement was started to call a national con-vention of the workingmen all over the United States. Considerable senti-ment developed in favor of Colonel Richard M. Johnson of Kentucky who was hailed for his opposition to imprisonment for debt, his advocacy of a national system of education, and his congressional fight against stop-ping Sunday transportation of the mails. The New York Journeymen Bookbinders Association came out for Johnson calling him the "fearless and uncompromising champion of religious freedom." "He is our man for President," editorialized the *Working Man's Advocate*, "and we recommend him to our fellow working men as the most suitable candi-date for office." [3]

THE BANK WAR

But after July 10, 1832, American workers wanted only one man for President—"Old Hickory," for on that day Jackson had vetoed the bill to recharter the Bank of the United States.

"It is to be regretted that the rich and powerful too often bend the acts of government to their selfish purposes," the message of veto said. "In the full enjoyment of the gifts of heaven and the fruits of superior in-dustry, economy, and virtue, every man is entitled to protection by law. But when the laws undertake to add to these natural and just advan-tages, artificial distinctions, . . . to make the rich richer and the potent more powerful, the humble members of society, the farmers, mechanics, and laborers, who have neither the time nor the means of securing like favors to themselves, have a right to complain of the injustice of their govern-ment." [4]

Thus spoke the Andrew Jackson who had led a coalition of small farmers and organized workingmen in the Presidential campaign of 1828.* That the philosophy expounded in this message should appeal to these workingmen is not surprising, for in their own independent political gatherings, they had already formulated most of these views. Jackson's

* One student of the election of 1828 points out that "the working population of the East united with the farmer of the West in the election of Jackson in 1828." (Herman Hailprin, "Pro-Jackson Sentiment in Pennsylvania, 1820-1828," *Pennsyl-vania Magazine of History and Biography*, vol. L, 1926, p. 237.)

message struck the dominant note of working class thought during the 'thirties: the philosophy of equal rights, "a social philosophy," Marquis James correctly emphasizes in his biography of Jackson, "calculated to achieve a better way of life for the common man." [5] As expounded most lucidly by William Leggett, the progressive editor of the *New York Evening Post,* and referred to in working class circles as "the oracle of equal rights," this doctrine demanded that "the property of the rich be placed on the same footing with the labours of the poor," opposed governmental policies which imposed taxes "to burden the poor and let the rich go free," and condemned the granting of special privileges to chartered corporations which in turn strengthened the power of monopoly —a power used by the rich to the injury of the poor.[6] The proper function of the government, according to the equal rights doctrine, had been stated by Jackson in his message: to "confine itself to equal protection, and, as heaven does its rains, shower its favors alike on the high and low, the rich and the poor...."

In vetoing the bill to recharter the Bank, Jackson had struck at the "King Monopoly." To be sure, Nicholas Biddle, the reactionary president of the Bank, viewed Jackson's message as "a manifesto of anarchy." But the common people, whom Biddle called "the merest rabble," regarded it both as a beacon of hope and a call to arms. To them the Bank was a symbol of economic exploitation and political reaction. Operating under an exclusive charter from the government, it had rapidly become the greatest of all monopolies and was already threatening to become more powerful than the government itself. American democracy, many workers and small farmers feared, was endangered by an institution which concentrated "so much power in the hands of so few persons irresponsible to the electorate," and which used its funds—the people's money, for it was a federal depository—to corrupt legislators and to bribe the press. They still remembered the sentiments voiced by Jefferson in 1803 when he pronounced the Bank of the United States to be an institution of the "most deadly hostility existing, against the principles and form of our Constitution." [7] Events had demonstrated to the workingmen that though the body of Federalism was dead, its spirit lived in the men who ran the Bank; they had the same Federalist contempt for democracy and the welfare of the people. As a meeting of several thousand workingmen in New York put it during the Bank controversy:

"We want little more to convince us that the cause of the Bank is aristocratic and unjust than the simple fact that we find the same men arrayed in its favor who have always been opposed to our interest; who endeavored to deprive us of [our] rights of suffrage; who opposed the last war [1812], and almost every other democratic measure that has ever been brought forward in our state or general government." [8]

As early as May 15, 1830, the *Working Man's Advocate* called upon the labor press to oppose the rechartering of the Bank of the United States. "We hope and confidently expect," it said, "that all papers advocating the cause of the working men will promptly and with spirit unite their exertions against this oppressive monopoly." Most of the newly arisen labor papers responded to this call so that by the time Jackson's veto was submitted to Congress, the workingmen were ready to support him. They rallied behind him in the Presidential campaign, the main issue of which, according to the workers, was "whether the Bank or the people shall rule the country." [9] Their support was needed, for Jackson's veto had split the Democratic Party, and many conservative Democrats joined with the former Federalists to form the Whig Party whose candidate, and the Bank's, was Henry Clay.

Workers were warned not to vote for Jackson. A New England factory owner told his workmen, "Elect General Jackson and the grass will grow in your streets, owls will build nests in the mills, and foxes burrow in your highways." [10] The people replied by re-electing Jackson by an even greater majority than they had given him in 1828.

But Biddle was not one to submit to the triumph of a democratic principle. "Who doubts," asked the *Boston Courier,* a pro-Bank newspaper, "that if all who are unable to write and read had been excluded from the polls, Andrew Jackson could not have been elected? Those who turned the scale in his favor were brutally ignorant." [11] Shortly after the election Biddle set about to engineer the passage of a new recharter bill. Enough money was on hand to buy the votes necessary to override a second veto.

To meet this threat Jackson decided to remove the government deposits from the Bank. His order provided that no further government funds were to be deposited and that the withdrawals were to take place in the natural order of government business which meant that the funds would not be exhausted for two years. A mass meeting of New York workingmen stated that the President "is entitled to, and has, our entire approbation and our greatest gratitude." [12]

At the convention of the New England Association of Farmers, Mechanics and Workingmen, delegates spoke out in favor of the course Jackson had taken. Said Samuel C. Allen, leader of the workingmen's movement in New England:

"I am encouraged in my hopes of an economical reform by the course which the President has taken in regard to the United States Bank....

What government in these days has been able to stand against the power of *associated wealth*? It is the real dynasty of modern states, let the forms of their government be what they may. If the great influence and political trepidity and personal firmness of the President shall save the government and the country from its grasp he will be the restorer of freedom to the people." [13]

Biddle's response to Jackson's action proved that the Bank was a menace to American democracy. Just as the Federalists had tried to turn the workers against Jefferson by blaming him for the distress which followed the embargo, so Biddle now sought to turn the country against Jackson by manipulating a financial crisis. Biddle reduced discounts, called in balances against state banks, raised exchange rates, and used other financial tricks to blackmail the American people into another charter. While Biddle was weeping publicly because of that "angry ignoramus" in the White House, he wrote to the head of the Boston bank: "Nothing but the evidence of suffering abroad will produce any effect.... A steady course of firm restriction will lead to ... the re-charter of the Bank." [14]

Biddle's hoped for "evidence of suffering" was not long in coming. A wave of failures swept Philadelphia, New York, and Washington. By May, 1834, the financial distress of the country was acute as business house after business house failed. A few business men put the blame where it belonged and agreed with the *Bankers' Magazine* that the "pressure was wholly owing to the unprincipled action of Mr. Biddle." [15] Most of them, however, agreed with Samuel Slater, a New England factory owner, that the crisis was the result of the "hostile stand that a few prigs of the Government had taken against that respectable Institution, the Bank of the United States." [16] They held mass meetings protesting the removal of federal deposits, and sent delegations to Washington demanding the end of anti-Bank policies. They did their best to turn the workers against Jackson. At first they relied on pathos and personal abuse. "Our mechanics [are] discharged by hundreds for want of employment, and our streets are filled with public beggars who would willingly if they could earn their daily pittance." And all of this was happening because "Andrew Jackson, laboring under the infirmities of age, the decay of his mental faculties and the constant gratifications of unrestrained and uncontrollable passions, has perpetrated a most unconstitutional and tyrannical act." [17]

In desperation, many pro-Bank employers resorted to economic intimidation, slashed wages, and even discharged workers who refused to sign petitions demanding an end of the President's anti-Bank policy. The *New York Courier and Enquirer,* the recipient of a $52,975 loan from the

Bank, publicly boasted that it had dismissed printers who did not agree that Jackson was responsible for the hard times.*

"We wish it to be distinctly understood," it said, "that whenever we are called upon to reduce the number of persons in our employ, that reduction will always fall upon those who differ with us in opinion on great national questions. If there must be suffering let it be, as far as practicable, among those who uphold the measures which produce it; and we hope employers generally, will act upon this principle." [18]

These actions of the pro-Bank employers steeled the workers.† It strengthened their conviction that Biddle's display of power was a danger to the country. "With a Banking system, the evident tendency of which is to make large numbers of men dependent upon a few employers," declared a mass meeting of New York workingmen, "and with employ- ers acting upon the *Courier's* principles, where...would be the liberties of this now boasted republic in a few short years?" [19]

The trade union movement of the early 1830's took a leading part in the battle against the Bank. In New York City, where the movement was strongest, the labor organizations rallied their members behind the President. The cordwainers, printers, stone cutters, cabinet makers, up- holsterers, and other trade societies held special meetings at which they affirmed their support of Jackson and their opposition to banks and all monopolies. Furthermore, they publicly condemned employers who dis- charged workers for refusing to sign petitions denouncing the President. In Philadelphia, the unions took the same steps to endorse Jackson. The Journeyman Hatters Society in that city showed its admiration for the President by presenting him with a fur hat. They had suffered grave persecution from their employers, these workers declared in presenting their gift, but, "true to the principles of '76," they intended to fight until the "bank monster" was slain.[20]

Extremely important in the anti-Bank struggle was the penny labor weekly, *The Man,* edited by George Henry Evans. *The Man* called Jackson the "deliverer of his country and the immortal champion of political justice and equal rights." It nicknamed Biddle "Autocrat Nicholas the First," and charged that he was seeking by means of Her Majesty,

---

* An announcement in the *Newark Daily Advertiser* of November 6, 1834, in- formed the public that the Newark Saddle and Harness Manufacturing Company had been started by a few workers who, "owing to an assertion of political rights [in support of Jackson's policies] during a late contested election, were promptly discharged from employment."

† "Can we give way under a little temporary privation," asked a workingmen's mass meeting held in New York to support Jackson, "when we recollect what the heroes of the Revolution suffered before their objects were achieved? Perish the thought!" (*The Man,* April 4, 1834.)

the Bank, to impose a monarch upon the American people. In issue after issue *The Man* insisted that the Bankites were admirers of English institutions, and desired to duplicate in America a hereditary monarchy, a hereditary, reactionary House of Lords, a House of Commons elected on the basis of a sharply restricted property suffrage, a combination of Church and State, a stratified class society, an educational system confined to the children of the rich, and a system of heavy taxation upon newspapers so that only the rich could afford to buy them.[21]

When a Congressional investigating committee disclosed that many stockholders of the Bank were English noblemen, *The Man* published their names. All told, more than nine million dollars' worth of bank stock was held by foreigners in their own names, not counting that held by foreign princes and dukes in the names of their American agents.

"Is not this fact enough to alarm the American people?" it inquired, "A *Bank* in the heart of the Republic with its branches scattered over the Union; wielding two hundred millions of capital; owning an immense amount of real property; holding at its command a *hundred thousand debtors;* buying up our newspapers, entering the field of politics; attempting to make Presidents and Vice-Presidents for the country; and that Bank owned, to such an extent by the *nobility of Europe."* [22]

Although it attacked the English aristocracy and denounced the Bank for the extent of its foreign control, *The Man,* like the entire labor movement, was not narrowly nationalistic. It carried accounts of all movements in England and other countries which were in the interest of the working class. The Chartist movement in England, the activity of trade unions in France and Germany, the shorter-hours movement in Europe, the plight of the poor in Russia, Denmark, Austria, and Brazil were all fully reported in *The Man.* Editorials pointed out that the struggles of workers in America and those in Europe and Latin America were identical. To lend weight to this contention, *The Man* published a letter from an English trade unionist which discussed the American struggle over the Bank:

"The radical party in England are looking forward with sanguine anticipations of Jackson's success; and thousands of hearty wishes are duly breathed for his prosperity. We look upon the affair in this country, as one big with the fate of Europe. Upon the issue of this contest depends the existence of the cursed Banks in England." [23]

LABOR'S ROLE IN NEW YORK

The most important activity of the trade unions and the labor press in the battle against the Bank was the organizing of political support for Jackson. The Whig Party made special efforts to win over the laboring men, knowing that if it could carry local and Congressional elections it could force Jackson to abandon his campaign against the Bank. In New York City where the split in the Democratic Party was sharpest, the Whigs were confident that they would win. On February 8, 1834, the Whig Party called upon the workers of New York to meet in City Hall Park to protest the removal of the deposits. Among those who co-operated in organizing this meeting were the former leaders of the Cook-Guyon faction which had split the Working Men's Party.

The workers attended the meeting not to hiss but to cheer Jackson. They refused to recognize the sponsors as officers of the meeting and elected their own presiding officers. They then proceeded to adopt a set of resolutions expressing approval of the measures taken against the Bank. When the original sponsors tried to regain control of the meeting, the platform was demolished. The pieces were carried away by the workers who paraded away shouting, "Hurrah for Jackson!" [24]

Following this incident, the workers began to play a more active part within the Democratic Party. Trade union leaders served on ward committees and spoke at Tammany meetings. In the mayoralty election of 1834, the first popular election for mayor in New York City, the trade unionists supported Lawrence, the Democratic candidate who was opposed by Verplanck, the pro-Bank Whig candidate. The President, the workers appealed, had done his part. "Will you be found wanting to yourselves, and your children? If you answer no, then your vote must be for Lawrence-Jackson and the Constitution." [25]

This election had nationwide significance. A victory for the Whigs would be a serious setback for the President. Jackson himself was supremely confident. "You know," he told a worried party leader, "I never despair. I have confidence in the people." [26] The confidence was not misplaced. Labor in New York stood fast. Workers marched to the polls singing:

> *Mechanics, cartmen, laborers*
> *Must form a close connection,*
> *And show the rich Aristocrats,*
> *Their powers at this election. . . .*
>
> *Yankee Doodle, smoke 'em out*
> *The proud, the banking faction*
> *None but such as Hartford Feds*
> *Oppose the poor and Jackson.*[27]

Lawrence carried the day. On April 12, 1834, the *Working Man's Advocate* broke the news of the "Glorious Triumph" with the headline, *THE BANK DEFEATED!*

Although the workers of New York had helped to elect a Tammany candidate, they did not continue to support Tammany uncritically. They knew that many leaders in Tammany opposed the Bank of the United States because it was a rival of the state banks in which they held large shares of stock and wanted the state banks to control the economic and political life of the nation. But to the workingmen as advocates of the hard money policy and as opponents of the control of all banks over the currency, the difference between a national and state bank was only in words. Indeed, they feared that speculative mania introduced by state banks would frustrate their entire campaign to reduce the proportion of paper money in circulation and to arrange the nation's economy to the advantage of the laboring classes rather than the speculators and financiers. The victory over the Bank of the United States would be of slight value if it were replaced by local banking monopolists.

In order to combat the influence of the conservatives in the Democratic Party, the workers formed the Democratic Working Men's General Committee in May 1834. Among the active members were some of the former leaders of the Working Men's Party—George Henry Evans, Ebenezer Ford, Levi D. Slamm, John Commerford; Alexander Ming, Jr., Robert Townsend, Jr., and Ely Moore.

The leaders of Tammany viewed the new committee with hostility, and charged it with conspiring to split the Democratic Party. The committee answered that its only concern was the nomination of genuine opponents of special privilege for state and national offices. It warned Tammany that it would not support any candidate for national or state office who would not make known his opposition to all monopolies and all charters of incorporation granting exclusive privileges.[28]

Tammany was forced to accept these conditions because it needed the votes. It agreed to the General Committee's demands that all Democratic candidates for the fall, 1834, election oppose banks and other monopolies, favor the prohibition of further issuance of bank notes of small denominations, and take a firm stand against all movements to restore imprisonment for debt. Tammany also nominated several workingmen for the state legislature, and Ely Moore, president of the New York General Trades' Union, was named Democratic candidate for Congress.

All the workingmen on the ticket were elected, Ely Moore becoming the first representative of organized labor in Congress. His maiden speech was an answer to Representative Waddy Thompson of South Carolina who had threatened the business men of the north with an insurrection of the hungry unemployed who would "rob by lawless insurrection, or by the equally terrible process of the ballot box." Moore replied that the terms "agrarians, levellers, and anarchists" had been used throughout history by aristocrats and despots who sought an excuse for plundering and oppressing the people. History proved, he argued, that the real danger to social stability, the cause of decay and disintegration of nations, had always been the concentration of wealth and political power in the hands of a small aristocracy. "History, sir, will bear me out in the declaration that the aristocracy of whatever age or country, have at all times, invariably and eternally robbed the people, sacrificed their rights, and warred against liberty, virtue, and humanity." The exponents of equal rights, he went on, were defending the best interests of the country in favoring a "government founded on persons, and not on property; on equal rights and not on exclusive privileges. They were the party whose interest and welfare are identified with the preservation of the Union and with the stability and integrity of the Government." The laboring classes had no intention of denying themselves or any one else the right to accumulate property through industry and frugality. What they opposed was the granting of special privileges to a few individuals which enabled them to monopolize property and capital.

"Where there is one instance where the rights of property have been violated by the people, or popular institutions, there are five thousand instances where the people have been plundered by the heartless cupidity of the privileged few. Sir, there is much greater danger that capital will unjustly appropriate to itself the avails of labor, than that labor will unlawfully seize on capital."

Moore turned next to the defense of trade unionism; the organizations of workingmen were "intended as a counter-poise against capital, whenever it shall attempt to exert an unlawful, or undue influence." As agencies of self defense and of self preservation, they could not be conspiracies, and hence were legal.

"Both the laws of God and man, *justify resistance* to the robber, and the homicide, *even unto death!* They are considered necessary guards against the encroachments of mercenary ambition and tyranny, and the friends of exclusive privileges, therefore, may with propriety dread their power and their influence. The union of the working men is not only a shield of defence against hostile combinations, but also a weapon of attack that will be successfully wielded against the oppressive measures of a corrupt and despotic aristocracy." [29]

Moore's speech was published by the *National Laborer* of Philadelphia and distributed all over the nation. In several cities, moreover, workers held banquets in honor of Ely Moore and resolved to renew political activities in their communities so that soon there would be other labor representatives in Congress and the state legislatures.*

RISE OF THE LOCO-FOCOS

Meanwhile a split was rapidly developing in New York between the state bank Democrats and the anti-monopoly workingmen. To the workers, the accelerated growth of the state banks was but exchanging a "King bank for a lawless aristocracy of banks." The inflationary effects of the state bank notes were drastically reducing real wages. Not a few workers were determined to put an end to the whole system of banking, "to disband entirely this standing army of non-producers called Bankers."[30] Another factor for the cleavage in Tammany was the autocratic manner in which the organization was run. To the workers who advocated greater participation by the people in nominations and elections this situation became intolerable.

Accordingly, in the summer of 1835, they secretly formed the "Equal Rights Democracy" within Tammany for the purpose of restoring the Democratic Party to its "original purity." This group came out openly in the fall and was endorsed by William Leggett of the New York *Evening Post*.[31] In the fall of 1835 Tammany split the Democratic Party by nominating candidates sympathetic to the banks. Included among them was Charles Henry Hall who had repudiated his pre-election pledge by voting in the assembly to extend bank charters. Working class candidates were eliminated from the ticket. Although ratification of candidates by a mass meeting at Tammany Hall was usually a formality, the Equal Rights group was determined to secure the rejection of the pro-Bank nominees. They organized for the ratification meeting of October 29. As the meeting opened, a bank president nominated a prominent bank director as chairman; the working men refused to accept the nomination, took the chair from the bank director and seated instead a trade union leader.

Outnumbered and defeated, the Tammany supporters left the room. Hoping to stop the meeting they turned off the gas, but the workers

---

* Although he was hailed for this speech, Moore was sharply criticized by the labor movement for his stand on prison labor. He had been appointed to a commission to investigate this serious threat to the living standards of workingmen and signed the report practically upholding the system of convict labor. This action was denounced by workers as "a barefaced piece of treachery," and the Democratic Working Men's General Committee on March 5, 1835, officially resolved "that the conduct of Ely Moore in signing that report, has convinced us that he either wants political honesty or moral courage sufficient to advocate those great principles the profession of which led to his political advancement." (See *New York Evening Post*, April 25, 1835; *The Man*, February 21, March 2, 7, 11, 14, 20, 1835.)

produced "loco-foco" matches to light candles and went on to nominate a list of anti-monopoly candidates. Because of the way in which the meeting had been illuminated, Whig and Tammany papers dubbed the ticket the Loco-Foco ticket. The workers assumed the name themselves, taking great pride in it as the symbol of the people's revolt against monopoly.

In the elections, Tammany defeated the Whigs by a narrow majority, whittled down by the more than 3,500 votes cast for the Loco-Foco candidates. Tammany control in the spring of 1836 was prevented by the Loco-Foco votes. Discussing the election results a general meeting of the Equal Rights workingmen resolved:

"That although it is the same to a monopoly-oppressed people, whether the Bank Whigs or Bank Democrats are in power, yet we rejoice over the defeat of the Tammany party because it will have a tendency to break up the evil combination existing between the office holders and the aristocracy of the Democracy." [32]

Events were calling more and more for independent political action but for several months the anti-monopolists tried to "regain possession of Tammany Hall" instead of forming a new party. Then Mayor Lawrence who owed his office to working class support called out the militia during a stevedores' strike. Right after this setback came one of the most shocking and alarming court decisions in American labor history. Although the employers depended upon scabs, blacklists, lock-outs, local police and state militia to fight the unions, their chief reliance was still the judiciary. Thus the cordwainers had been tried on conspiracy charges in Pennsylvania in 1821 and 1829, and in New York in 1835; the tailors of Buffalo in 1824, in Philadelphia in 1827, and in New York in 1836; the hatters in New York in 1823; the spinners of Philadelphia in 1829, and the carpet weavers of Connecticut in 1834.

The trial of the 24 militant journeymen tailors in Philadelphia in 1827 is important because the verdict stressed the "injury to trade" aspect of conspiracy rather than the so-called criminal phase. Labor convictions were to bear this character more and more. In the 1835 trial of the Geneva shoemakers, for instance, unionism was defended on the ground that without it workers were powerless. "You forbid these men that union which alone can enable them to resist the oppressions of avarice. ... You deprive them of the means and opportunity of learning the rights and duties which they are to exercise as citizens." [33]

The jury was not impressed. Within twenty minutes after the hearings were concluded, it found the men guilty. And the verdict was upheld when an appeal was carried to the New York State Supreme Court.

Chief Justice Savage, who delivered the decision, maintained that organized workers forced wages up too high; employers, therefore, could not afford to continue competition. Thus the shoeworkers had obstructed the business of boot and shoe-making and were guilty of "a statutory offence because such practice was injurious to trade and commerce." [34]

Twenty-five members of the Union Society of Journeymen Tailors were brought to trial in New York in 1836 on charges of "conspiracy to injure trade, riot, assault, battery." They were found guilty, and fined a total of $1,150. Henry Faulkner, president of the society, was fined $150, and the others $50 or $100 each. While the defendants were paying their fines, a worker in the courtroom stepped up and handed over his wages to the fund. Later, unions in other cities sent contributions to the tailors.

Judge Edwards in passing sentence on the workers ruled that the "trades of this country...are rapidly passing from the supreme power of the state into the hands of private societies." He continued:

"In this favored land of law and liberty, the road to advancement is open to all.... Every American knows that or ought to know that he has no better friend than the laws and that he needs no artificial combination for his protection. *They are of foreign origin and I am led to believe mainly upheld by—foreigners.*" [35]

A storm of protest greeted this verdict and dictum of Judge Edwards. Answering his charges, the New York *Evening Post* proved that eleven of the indicted members were native-born citizens, and of the other nine, five were naturalized citizens. "At any rate even if the union is so popular among our workingmen from other climes, we have reason to believe it is countenanced and supported by the great majority of our native born." It estimated that two-thirds of the workingmen of New York belonged to labor organizations, refuting the charge that "it is a few foreigners or only foreigners that comprise our Trades' Unions." [36] A complete answer was offered by the Philadelphia *National Laborer:* "It is of little consequence in what country, or by what men Trades' Unions originated, as it is sufficient to know that *oppression* has forced them into existence." [37]

Progressive America lashed out at the doctrine that trade unions were conspiracies and that to organize for a living wage was injurious to trade and commerce. "If this is not *slavery,*" wrote William Cullen Bryant, editor of the New York *Evening Post* and a leading American poet, "we have forgotten its definition. Strike the right of associating for the sale of labour from the privileges of a freeman, and you may as well bind him to a master or ascribe him to the soil." [38] Even more vigorous in his denunciation was John Greenleaf Whittier, the militant liberal poet:

"So then it has come to this, that in a land of equal rights a laborer cannot fix the amount of his wages in connection with his fellow laborer, without being charged as a criminal before our courts of law. The merchants may agree upon their prices; the lawyers upon their fees; the physicians upon their charges; the manufacturers upon the wages given to their operatives, but the *laborer* shall not consult his interest and fix the prices of his toil and skill. If this be the *law*, it is unjust, oppressive and wicked. It ought not to disgrace the statute book of a republican state. . . . The whole doctrine is borrowed from the feudal aristocracy of Europe. If carried into practice generally, as it has been in New York, the condition of the free and happy laborers of our country will be little better than that of the Hungarian Miner, or the Polish serf." [39]

The verdict roused workers all over the country; four labor papers were founded within two weeks to fight the decision,[40] and proposals streamed into the *Union,* organ of the New York General Trades' Union, proposing that a state convention of working men be held to elect a legislature pledged to remove Savage and Edwards from office. The *Union* not only endorsed these proposals but suggested "cutting loose from both political parties, and running a truly working man's ticket." [41]

Anonymous handbills portraying coffins were spread throughout the city, calling for a mass demonstration at the time when Judge Edwards was to pronounce sentence. They read in part:

"THE RICH AGAINST THE POOR!

"Judge Edwards, the tool of the aristocracy, against the people! Mechanics and working men! A deadly blow has been struck at your liberty! The prize for which your fathers fought has been robbed from you! The freemen of the North are now on a level with the slave of the South! with no other privilege than laboring, that drones may fatten on your life-blood! Twenty of your brethren have been found guilty for presuming to resist a reduction of their wages! and Judge Edwards has charged an American jury, and agreeably to that charge, they have established the precedent that workingmen have no right to regulate the price of labor, or, in other words, the rich are the only judges of the wants of the poor man. On Monday, June 6, 1836, at ten o'clock, these freemen are to receive their sentence, to gratify the hellish appetites of the aristocrats!" [42]

Summoned by the coffin handbill, crowds assembled in the City Hall Park on the stated day, but dispersed without taking any action. However, a week later, over twenty-seven thousand people gathered at a great mass meeting in the park. The *Union* called it the "greatest meeting of working men ever held in the United States."[43] The meeting adopted a fighting program, denounced the decision as a "concerted plan of the aristocracy to take from them that *Liberty* which was bequeathed to them as a sacred inheritance by their revolutionary sires." These courts and the aristocracy were trying to degrade workers into "mere tools to build up princely fortunes for men who grasp at all and produce nothing." "We have before us an example worthy of imitation—that *Holy Combination* of that immortal band of *Mechanics,* who despite the injury inflicted upon 'trade and commerce,' *'conspired, confederated and agreed'* and by overt acts did throw into Boston Harbor the tea that had branded upon it 'Taxation without Representation.' "

Taxation without representation, said a resolution, was once again the issue. The common people were taxed, but had no representation as long as judicial and legislative posts were held by men who had no sympathy for the working class. It was time then for "cutting loose from both political parties and running a truly workingmen's ticket." Not content with expressing the need for political action, the meeting issued a call for a state convention to be held at Utica, September 15, 1836, and elected a "Committee of Correspondence" to prepare for the convention. Many of the committee members were leaders of the New York General Trades' Union and the Loco-Foco movement.[44]

Even before the meeting convened, news arrived that eight journeymen shoemakers at Hudson, New York, had been acquitted in a conspiracy trial. A few days later came the news that a jury in Philadelphia had voted "not guilty" in a conspiracy trial. These swift results of the labor protests only served to strengthen labor's determination to wipe out the conspiracy doctrines once and for all.[45]

Within a few weeks, meetings of farmers and working men were held in Poughkeepsie, Troy, Albany, and Hudson, to protest the decision of Judge Edwards and to elect delegates to the convention. On September 15, 1836, this historic convention of Mechanics, Farmers, and Working Men opened in Utica. Ninety-three delegates were seated. One of the most important actions of the convention was its Declaration of Independence which declared the independence of the workers and farmers from the old parties. It expressed opposition to bank notes and paper money, to the arbitrary power of the courts; it demanded legislation to guarantee labor the right to organize to increase wages. To make certain that the courts would no longer be "as aristocratic, arbitrary and oppressive as they were in the dark ages of feudalism," the convention called for the election of judges for a term of three years only.

In keeping with its Declaration, the convention voted to form a political party "separate and distinct from all existing parties or factions" in the state. It chose the name Equal Rights Party, and nominated for governor and for lieutenant governor, Isaac S. Smith of Buffalo who had been a candidate for office on the workingmen's ticket of the Owen faction in 1830 and 1832; and Moses Jaques, a New York trade union leader, respectively. It pledged to support for other offices only those candidates who would sign a pledge to oppose all monopolies.[46]

The *Union* hailed the Utica convention, calling the Declaration the "second declaration of our Independence," and described the coming election as the "first conflict of our second Revolution." "The Revolution of 1776," it said, "was against the monarch and aristocracy of England; this of 1836, is against charters and monopolies." [47]

Soon news arrived that Equal Rights tickets had been nominated in twenty counties and that six or seven newspapers were supporting the movement. One of these papers, the Albany *Microscope,* warned against the tricks of politicians, using the history of the first labor parties as a lesson:

"Remember the regretted fate of the workingmen—they were soon destroyed by hitching teams and rolling with parties. They admitted into their ranks, broken down lawyers and politicians, who had long since ceased to possess the confidence of anybody. They place upon their tickets, men whose very names brought the case of political perdition and death upon them, prematurely. Their principles were *originally* of a similar nature with those which constitute the present Equality; but they became perverted, and were unconsciously drawn into a vortex, from which they never escaped." [48]

In the election of 1836, the regular Democrats nominated Martin Van Buren and Colonel Richard M. Johnson for President and Vice-President. Placing no faith in the "consistency, or the ability, or the democratic faith of the other candidates," [49] the Equal Rights Party sought to obtain from the Democratic candidates an endorsement of their principles and a pledge to maintain a consistent stand against paper money and monopolies. From Johnson they received a thoroughgoing acceptance and a pledge to carry out their principles but Van Buren refused to take a stand on the anti-monopoly issue. The Equal Rights movement therefore refused to endorse Van Buren, even though it knew he was Jackson's choice. It dismissed all Presidential candidates as "four second-rate men" whose election could not aid the working men.[50]

In the congressional and state legislative elections, held that same year, the Equal Rights Party held the balance of power between the Whigs and the Democrats. Three of the four candidates for Congress endorsed by the Equal Rights Party were elected; they admitted after the election that the party of the workingmen had been responsible for their victory. The Equal Rights Party helped also to elect a state senator and two assemblymen. But the outstanding result of the election was that the Equal Rights votes had prevented Tammany control of the congressional and legislative delegations. Tammany received a drubbing in the mayorality and aldermanic contests the following spring when their candidates received about 12 per cent of the total vote. Rebuked by the Democrats for causing the Whig victory, the working men replied that they had nominated separate candidates because they "could see no great difference in principles between national Bank Whigs and State Bank Democrats." [51]

By withdrawing support from the regular Democratic ticket the New York workingmen had done more than insure the election of the Whigs. They had taught both political parties that labor could not be dismissed in political affairs. The conservatives and the machine politicians could nominate their candidates, but without the votes of the working men they could not elect them.

LOCO-FOCOISM SPREADS

The lesson was learned in other states too. In 1834-1835 a split occurred in the Pennsylvania Democratic Party similar to the one that had taken place in New York. The progressive wing of the party, led by the Philadelphia labor movement, supported a separate ticket in the state election of 1835. Henry A. Muhlenberg, staunch opponent of the Banking Monopolists, was nominated for Governor, and William English and Thomas Hogan, Philadelphia trade union leaders, were nominated for the State Senate and Assembly. The Whig ticket won the election, but the workingmen succeeded in teaching the Democratic politicians that their views could not be ignored. [52]

In Massachusetts the left wing of the Democratic Party was led by workingmen's leaders such as Seth Luther, Dr. Charles Douglas, Theophilus Fisk, and Orestes Brownson, and liberal politicians and intellectuals like Frederick Robinson, George Bancroft, and Robert Rantoul, Jr. By 1836 the radical wing, with the support of the national administration, had taken over the control of the Democratic Party in the Bay State. [53]

The Equal Rights political movement or Loco-Focoism, as it was commonly called, attained its greatest influence in New York. One reason was that in several cities outside of New York the trade unions were prohibited by the constitutions from engaging in "party politics." Yet even in most of these communities, events forced the workingmen to take a firm and independent political stand, as decisions such as the one in the New York Journeymen Tailors' case prompted these central labor bodies to petition their state legislatures asking for redress. It soon became clear, however, that as long as labor had no independent voice in political contests such petitions would be ignored. In an appeal to workers in Pennsylvania, New Jersey and Ohio, the *National Laborer* urged: "Up, then, workingmen, away with party attachments, and prove by your suffrages, that your rights shall not be invaded with impunity." [54]

The workingmen of Philadelphia were not slow in responding. An important city and state election was coming up in the fall of 1836. In July of that year, Mayor Swift of Philadelphia had infuriated the working class by his action in forcing the arrest and illegal imprisonment of several laborers who were on strike for higher wages. The workingmen of Philadelphia were determined to prevent the re-election of the anti-union mayor. A mass rally, called by the Philadelphia Trades' Union in Independence Square late in August, voiced fiery opposition to the re-election of Mayor Swift. A committee headed by William English and John Ferral was empowered to confer with the Democratic-Whig and Democratic-Van Buren parties to insist upon the nomination of progressive candidates for mayor and for the city council. The committee was also instructed to petition President Jackson to establish the ten-hour day in the Philadelphia Navy Yard. [55]

A month later an overflowing audience listened to the Committee's report: they had been ignored by the Democratic Whigs but the Van Buren Democrats had responded favorably and had pledged that they would not "place in nomination for council any persons who would in any event vote for *John Swift* for Mayor," that they "deprecate the unconstitutional and oppressive conduct of Mayor Swift in exacting excessive bail and his *illegal imprisonment* of the poor laborers who were merely claiming their undoubted rights." In addition, they agreed to nominate William Edwards, a member of the Philadelphia Trades' Union, as a candidate for the State Assembly. The committee reported that the President had ordered the ten-hour day in the Navy Yard.

The meeting roared its approval of the Committee's report, and in a special resolution praised the President "for the prompt manner in which he has granted the demand of the workingmen of Philadelphia in establishment of the ten-hour system in our navy yard."

"Resolved, That the enemies of the ten-hour system, Trades' Unions, etc., be confounded with their audacity, when even the government has knocked under." [56]

In the following election a Council friendly to labor and hostile to Mayor Swift was swept into office. And William Edwards was sent to the state legislature to represent the working class of Philadelphia. [57]

The Equal Rights movement also played an important part in Dorr's Rebellion, a movement which arose in the early 1840's for a more liberal constitution in Rhode Island, and for the elimination of high property qualifications for suffrage. Seth Luther, prominent New England labor organizer, was one of the leaders of this popular uprising. Many workingmen marched in the great suffrage parades, carrying banners on which were inscribed the slogans: "No taxation without representation," "Suffrage, the inalienable Right of Man," "Liberty or Revolution." At the same time in New York, workingmen resolved, "That we consider the cause of Dorr and Free Suffrage to be peculiarly the cause of workingmen without regard to party, and that we recommend our fellow-workingmen throughout the country, to express their opinions freely on this subject." [58] Although Dorr's Rebellion was put down, it had done its work. Because of it "the constitution which went into effect in May 1843, was liberal." [59]

When the speculative boom in land, canals, turnpikes, and railroads ended in the panic of 1837, the Loco-Foco movement developed rapidly, assuming great significance in all commercial and industrial communities. Unemployed mechanics and laborers marched in parades sponsored by local workingmen's political committees demanding "Bread! Meat! Rent! Fuel! Their prices must come down! * The voice of the people shall be heard and will prevail!" When a mass meeting of New York workers, called by the Equal Rights Party, was broken up by the police, it was resolved, "That we, the Equal Rights Party, free citizens of the Republic, will hold another public meeting of the People in the Park on the first of April in order to ascertain whether or not this community is under civil or martial law." [60]

The suffering and distress of the working classes increased in May, 1837, when the banks in the country suspended specie payment, refusing any longer to redeem their paper bank notes in hard money. Everywhere the workers rallied in mass meetings, demanding that the banks resume specie payments and calling upon the national government to end the power of financial institutions over the nation's economy. Twenty thousand persons attended a meeting in Philadelphia, called together by John Ferral, Thomas Hogan, and other trade union leaders. Henry D. Gilpin, a Philadelphia lawyer active in the Jacksonian movement, attended the meeting and observed that he had "never seen the working classes more deeply agitated and roused."

"This afternoon," he wrote to President Van Buren on May 15, 1837, "the largest public meeting I ever saw assembled in Independence Square.

---

* Prices shot up enormously during the crash. Flour had sold at $5.62 a barrel in March, 1835; it was selling at $7.75 in March, 1836, and $12 in March, 1837. Pork, which had sold at $10 in March, 1835, rose to $16.25 in March, 1836, and $18.25 in March, 1837. The wholesale price of coal climbed from $6 a ton on January, 1835, to $10.50 in January, 1837. (See Congressional Globe, 26th Congress, 1st Session, Appendix, p. 528; A. H. Cole, Wholesale Commodity Prices in the United States, 1780-1861, Cambridge, 1938, pp. 246-49; Arthur M. Schlesinger, Jr., The Age of Jackson, New York, 1945, p. 218.)

It was called by placards posted through the city yesterday and last night. It was projected and carried on *entirely* by the working classes; without consultation or cooperation with any of those who usually take the lead in such matters. The officers and speakers were of those classes.... It was directed against the banks and especially against the issue of small [?] tickets by the Corporation. I could not hear the resolutions distinctly but they were to the effect that the banks must resume specie payments, that they must forthwith redeem their five dollar notes, and that measures must be taken to prevent the export of gold and silver...." [61]

Workingmen's political movements were most active during this turbulent period. They called upon the national government to institute a ten-hour day for government employees, to relieve distress among the unemployed by a public works program; they called for a government banking system to check the tide of speculation fostered by private and state banks. These demands were justified "inasmuch as the burden of military duty in peace and war is always borne by the laboring classes, the laborer has an additional claim to the protection of the government of the United States." [62]

ACHIEVEMENTS OF THE LOCO-FOCOS

President Martin Van Buren responded magnificently to the demands of the workingmen. In a message to Congress on September 4, 1837, Van Buren proposed a treasury system independent of the banking interests. All federal deposits were to be placed in the treasury in Washington or in sub-treasuries in designated cities. The Independent Treasury system aimed to remove the public funds from the banks, reduce the amount of specie on which paper could be issued, end the use of bank notes in the payment of the revenue and require payment in legal tender. Although this plan did not meet all the demands of the workingmen, it was the triumph of a principle which the workers had been fighting for since 1829—the separation of government and banking institutions, the limitation of the power and control of the banks and the adoption of a hard money policy.

A meeting of conservative Democrats and Whigs in New York denounced Van Buren for having "surrendered to the Hideous Monster of Locofocoism." The administration, they said, was applying the "doctrines promulgated in 1829 by a faction of which Robert Dale Owen, a disciple of Fanny Wright, was leader." But on the other hand, Orestes Brownson, a former leader of the New York Workingmen's Party, wrote to Van Buren, "I wish to thank you in the name of liberty and humanity for the firm stand you have taken during the struggle which has been going on for some time between the Democracy and the moneyed power of this country ... you are now indeed with the people and Sir, the people will sustain you." [63]

On March 31, 1840, President Van Buren again endeared himself to the working classes and again aroused the fury of conservatives by issuing an executive order establishing the ten-hour day for federal employees on public works without a reduction in pay. Van Buren publicly announced that the ten-hour system was "originally devised by the mechanics and laborers themselves," and declared in reply to the Whig charge that he was establishing a dangerous precedent by refusing to reduce wages as working hours were reduced:

"The labor of an industrious man is in my judgment only adequately rewarded, when his wages, together with the assistance of those members of his family, from whom assistance may reasonably be required, will enable him to provide comfortably for himself and them, to educate his children and lay up sufficient for the casualties of life and the wants of advanced age.

"To accomplish these objects it is necessary that the pay of the laborer should bear a just proportion to the prices and necessaries and comforts of life; and all attempts to depress them below this equitable standard, are in my opinion at war as well with the dictates of humanity as with a sound and rational policy...." [64]

Such statements caused reactionaries to froth at the mouth, but in labor circles they aroused rejoicing. Years later Michael Shiner, a self-educated free Negro who worked in the Washington Navy Yard, wrote: "... the Working Classes of people of the United States Machanic and labourers ought to never forget the Hon ex president Van Buren for the ten hour sistom.... May the lord Bless Mr Van Buren for the ten hour sistom ... his name ought to be Recorded in evey Working Man heart." [65]

One thing of great significance in American political history emerged during the Jacksonian era. The fact that workingmen refused blindly to follow a political party and used their right to vote to remedy their special grievances forced the politicians to make special efforts and concessions to secure the growing labor vote. In the election of 1840, the Whigs abandoned at least outwardly their appearance of conservatism and presented William Henry Harrison as the "poor man's friend," and featured as a campaign slogan, "Tippecanoe and no reduction of Wages." [66] And in 1842, Chief Justice Shaw of Massachusetts, a Whig, delivered an opinion in the case of *Commonwealth* v. *Hunt* in which for the first time the right of workingmen to organize and bargain collectively was judicially recognized.

This case had grown out of a Boston-wide strike, called in November,

1839, by the Boston Journeymen's Bootmakers' Society to prevent the employment of bootmakers who would not join the society. Seven of the union leaders had been indicted at that time for "unlawfully, perniciously, and deceitfully designing and intending to continue, keep, form and unite themselves into an unlawful club, society and combination, and make unlawful by-laws, rules and orders among themselves and other workmen" in the occupation of bootmakers. No charge of violence had been made, nor had the indictment stated that the strike had been called with the malicious intent of destroying the plaintiff's business. But the Constitution of the Boston Journeymen Bootmakers' Society had been introduced in court as evidence that the regulations provided therein were agreements which constituted a conspiracy even though these regulations had never really been fully enforced. Although the union leaders had been ably defended by Robert Rantoul, Jr., an outstanding New England reformer, the Bootmakers had been found guilty by the Municipal Court in October, 1840.

Two years later the case came on appeal to the Supreme Judicial Court of the State of Massachusetts where the decision of the lower court was reversed with the ruling by Chief Justice Shaw that associations could be entered into, the object of which is to adopt measures "that may have a tendency to impoverish another, that is, to diminish his gains and profits, and yet so far from being criminal and unlawful, the object may be highly meritorious and public spirited."

"The legality of such an association will therefore depend upon the means to be used for its accomplishment. If it is carried into effect by fair or honorable and lawful means, it is to say the least, innocent, if by falsehood or by force, it may be stamped with the character of conspiracy." [67]

In other words, the action of workingmen in seeking to induce all those engaged in the same occupation to become members of a trade union did not in itself constitute a conspiracy and hence was not illegal. The legality of such action depended on the means used to accomplish this end. The last provision, of course, left enough leeway for reactionary judges and later decisions cut out some of the heart of Shaw's reasoning. Nevertheless, the highest court in a state had finally recognized the right of workers to organize.

Was it an accident that this decision came at this particular period in American history? Professor Walter Nelles thinks not. He believes that Chief Justice Shaw was quite aware of labor's strength at the ballot-box and was seeking workers' votes for the Whig Party. "I am convinced," he writes, "that Shaw was subconsciously if not consciously influenced by such a thought when he decided *Commonwealth* v. *Hunt*." [68]

"It seems clear now," writes Arthur M. Schlesinger, Jr. in his study, *The Age of Jackson,* "that more can be understood about Jacksonian democracy if it is regarded as a problem not of sections but of classes." [69] The account of labor's part in progressive movements that characterized Jacksonian democracy definitely substantiates this conclusion. It is clear that the early workingmen's parties had already laid the groundwork. The militant trade union movement of the 1830's had also made a valuable contribution and its expansion had added considerably to labor's influence in politics. Some labor historians mechanically separate trade unionism and independent political action, and try to prove, on the one hand, that labor showed little interest in politics during the years they had strong unions, and, on the other hand, that the turn to trade unionism was induced by labor's failures in political action. This is not so. At no time during this period were the economic and political activities of the workers separate or in opposition. Rather they tended throughout to supplement and to complement each other, depending upon the historical needs of the moment. It is true that some of the leaders of the Workingmen's movement were not much interested in trade unionism, believed that the evils complained of by the laboring classes "having been produced by legislation, will also have to be cured by legislation," and regarded "the ballot box, the modern *panacea* for all grievances." [70] But events themselves showed the mass of the workers that political and trade union struggles had to be united.

In Philadelphia the labor party grew out of the Mechanics' Union of Trade Associations. Political and economic action were combined in the New England Association of Farmers, Mechanics and other Workingmen. The original workingmen's party in New York grew out of the successful struggle to prevent the lengthening of the working day. The shorter work day made their political activity possible and necessary because workers saw themselves as an indispensable part of the national life in which they had a special interest and a special voice. The rise of the General Trades' Union in New York increased the workers' influence in Tammany, as evidenced by the election of the president of the union to Congress. The conspiracy convictions of 1835 and 1836 challenging labor's right to organize brought home again the need for political action as the complement to trade unionism.

Throughout this period a close relationship was established in New York and other cities between the trade union and political movements of labor. That is not to say that political and economic organizations were identical. The more general demands advanced by the early labor parties attracted small shopkeepers, farmers, and intellectuals as well. But the broad base of these parties consisted of organized workers. It was on the initiative of the New York trade unions that the Equal Rights Party was organized. And most important, the unity of trade unionism and political action during this era resulted in legalizing—if even in a limited sense—labor's rights to organize.

The workers of the Jacksonian era were not anti-capitalist minded; they were interested in eliminating the evil influence of the banks over American political life; they wanted an end to the system of privileged monopolies; they demanded a stable currency so that their wages would not be subject to fluctuation. No one expressed these view of labor more cogently that did Andrew Jackson when he said:

"My feeble voice has hitherto but raised its sound in favour of a metallic currency to cover the labour of our country; and as long as pulsation beats, it will continue to support this system. Without labour prospers, commerce and manufacturers must languish and the country be distressed. This is a government of the people, for their happiness and prosperity, and not for that of the few, at the expense of the many...." [71]

Those workers who wanted to do away with banks as an institution were utopian indeed. For they could no more abolish banks than they could prevent the introduction of machinery. The thinking workers were anxious to hasten the expansion of trade and industry; they simply wanted to prevent their growth from being stunted by the blind and short-sighted policy of a few powerful financial groups. Essentially labor believed that a people's government should act on behalf of the people and not for the advantages of the capitalists. As a mass meeting of laborers and mechanics of Rochester, New York, declared in 1844:

"Resolved, we the Laborers and Mechanics of this city, do hereby enter our solemn protest and decided disapprobation against all Legislation of every kind and form, which has for its objects, or the tendency of which is, to aid capitalists to enrich themselves by wrongfully oppressing the Workingmen.

"Resolved, That we are opposed to the principle that it is the duty of the Government to 'take care of the rich, and the rich will take care of the poor'; for it is a self-evident fact, that in wealth there is power; therefore, if a preponderance or a preference is made in favor of either class of the community, it should be in favor of that class which needs the protecting arm of special legislation." [72]

During the age of Jackson, the workers impressed this principle upon the leaders of the government and helped establish the doctrine that economic democracy alone would give political democracy meaning. In later years these principles were to be forgotten by American political leaders, but they remained imbedded in the minds and hearts of the working classes and they were to raise them again and again in their local and national struggles.

CHAPTER 10

The Era of Utopianism

The crisis of 1837 dealt trade unionism a devastating blow. Production almost came to a standstill, and thousands upon thousands of workers were thrown out of employment. As early as January, 1838, 50,000 persons were said to be unemployed in New York City alone, and an additional 200,000 were described as living "in utter and hopeless distress with no means of surviving the winter but those provided by charity." [1]

Everywhere the same story was told; workers were "dying of want" in Philadelphia, Baltimore, Lowell, Boston, and other commercial and industrial cities. Everywhere, too, a cry of despair arose from starving workers—a cry "not for the bread and fuel of charity, but for *work! work!*" Said a group of workingmen in New York: "We do not want alms. We are not beggers. We hate to sit here idle and useless; help us to get work. We want no other help." [2]

DECLINE OF THE TRADE UNIONS

With one-third of the working class unemployed, and most of the others working only part-time, the trade unions of the 1830's found it impossible to keep their heads above water. One after the other, local societies, city trade unions, and the promising National Trades' Union passed out of existence, taking with them the first labor newspapers. The process of disintegration was hastened by the offensive of employers, who saw in the depression their chance to smash the militant labor organizations. One newspaper, the *New Yorker,* urged businessmen to "employ no men who do not forever abjure the unions." It said further, "The rules of the unions as to hours, pay, and everything else, ought to be thoroughly broken up." [3]

A few unions struggled magnificently to keep their organization alive. The Philadelphia Cordwainers announced in May, 1837, that depression or no depression they intended at all hazards to maintain their wage scale. A month later, the New York printers issued an address to their fellow craftsmen, urging them to remain in the union and to combat any effort to lower their wages. Let the employers see, said the organized printers, "that the insignificant and paltry pittance which you now obtain for your support shall not be reduced at their pleasure—that for them to grow richer you will not consent to become poorer." The address concluded, "Without union nothing can be effected—with it everything. Come forward, then, you who are not members of the association; and join in putting a shoulder to the wheel. Support the association, and the association will support you." [4]

The employers' offensive continued; by 1839 wage cuts ranging from 30 per cent to 50 per cent had been forced on the workers. This does not mean that labor activity was entirely absent during the lean years after 1837, or that the working class had ceased all efforts to improve their social and economic conditions. Unemployment demonstrations, support of reading rooms and lecture rooms, rallies of workingmen to demand shorter hours and equal rights before the law are proof that the labor movement was not dead. It had but changed its form.

Seeing their organizations smashed one by one, the workers were, as one contemporary graphically stated it, "ready to explode." [5] For years they had called on the government to curb the insane financial speculation, the blind and wasteful development of internal improvements, the fevered increase in the number of banks and the amount of banknote circulation which had now plunged the nation from prosperity to misery. And now that their fears had come true, the same groups who were responsible for this suffering told their workers to "go home and *plant corn,*" "as if the labourer was responsible for the decrease in business, and his wife and children must be punished and starved so that the employer's account of profits and gain may foot up as they did when business was good." [6]

"How is it that a country as rich as ours is yet pinched for the common necessaries of life?" asked a workingman. "A vigorous, healthy and intellectual population, yet bowed down with gloom and despair ... with ruin and starvation before their eyes." [7]

SPREAD OF MACHINERY

The concentration of industry during the panic of 1837, and the extensive use of machinery immediately after the crisis, threatened, as one worker put it, to "annihilate the last surviving hope of the honest mechanic." [8] Were not the factory owners saying publicly that they regarded their workers as mere cogs and wheels? One mill owner remarked of his workers, "So long as they can do my work for what I choose to pay them I keep them, getting out of them all I can. What they do or how they are outside of my walls I don't know nor do I consider it my business to know. They must look out for themselves as I do for myself. When my machines get old and useless, I reject them and get new ones and these people are part of my machinery." [9]

"Part of my machinery"; these words sent a chill through thousands of skilled workers as they saw the machine threatening to extend itself into all parts of American production. The machine became an occult power. Said Thomas Devyr, a working class leader:

"Machinery has taken almost entire possession of the manufacture of cloth; it is making steady—we might say rapid—advance upon all branches of non manufacture; the newly invented machine saws, working in curves as well as straight lines, the planing and grooving machines, and the tenon and mortise machine, clearly admonish us that its empire is destined to extend itself over all our manufactures of wood; while some of our handicrafts are already extinct, there is not one of them, but has foretasted the overwhelming competition of this occult power." [10]

During the 'twenties and 'thirties, American labor leaders welcomed the introduction of machinery but insisted that it be used for the benefit of society and not for the profits of a few capitalists. As far back as 1829 Thomas Skidmore in his study, the *Right of Man to Property,* said:

"The steam engine is not injurious to the poor, when they can have the benefit of it; and this, on supposition, *always* being the case, instead of being looked upon, as a curse, [it] would be hailed as a blessing. If then, it is seen that the steam engine, for example, is likely to greatly impoverish or destroy the poor, what *have they to do but lay hold of it, and make it their own? Let them appropriate also,* in the same way, *the cotton factories, the iron foundries, the rolling mills,* houses, churches, ships, goods, steam boats, fields of agriculture,... as is their right." [11]

John Commerford, a leading figure in the trade union and Loco-Foco movements, in an address at the second anniversary of the General Trades' Union of New York and vicinity in 1835, argued for the social control and operation of machinery for the benefit of all. The time would come, he predicted, when the power of capital over machinery would be ended, and the machine would work for and not against the laborer. "Machinery will not then be used, as it now is, for the benefit of the few, but for the mass. Governments will become the legitimate guardians of its improvements, and they will be compelled to keep machinery in operation for the comfort and convenience of the people." [12]

As the factory system spread and the prospects of using machinery for the benefit of the mass faded, American workers became more and more alarmed at what they called "growing industrial feudalism." An address in behalf of the workingmen of Charlestown, Massachusetts, early in the 'forties read: "Brethren, put these things together, and tell us, if the natural tendency in this country is not to reduce us, and that at no distant day, to the miserable conditions of the laboring classes in the old world? We stand on the declivity; we have already begun to descend! What is to save us?" [13]

CREDO OF THE UTOPIANS

There were some who said that the only solution lay in prayer and spiritual comfort; others insisted that if the workers would elevate themselves mentally they need have no fear of what the factory system would do to their body and spirit. There were a few who said that the suffering of the people came from the nature of capitalism; a few capitalists, they explained, had gained control of the means of production and used this control not for the welfare of the people, but for their own profits. Whenever these profits stopped, they shut down production, threw thousands out of work, spreading misery throughout the land.

The solution, according to this school of thought, lay in a new social order which would abolish all types of slavery and oppression by restoring to the people control over the productive forces. Only such a society could answer the question asked by the workingmen of Charlestown, for it would usher in an era of universal freedom, peace, and harmony in place of war, discord, and suffering. Finally, this new social order could be built overnight! The plan was already formulated; all that was necessary was that the rich and the powerful endorse the scheme and support it financially. All people could then join in and build the communal co-operative society. The people who held out these glowing visions were the Utopian Socialists, American disciples of two great European thinkers, Robert Owen and Charles Fourier.

Robert Owen was a Welsh factory owner who, early in his life, observed the ills of the new industrialism. Determined to do something to eradicate these evils, he established model textile mills at New Lanarck, Scotland. He paid comparatively good wages, shortened working hours, provided schools and nurseries for the children of his employees, replaced slums with decent housing, and even kept all workers on at full pay when his mills were forced to close during a cotton shortage. During the 1820's Owen began to think in terms that went beyond the sentiments of model factory towns established by benevolent factory owners. What was needed, he said, was a new system of society in which the producers of commodities should own the means of production in common. He proposed the establishment of communities which would be operated by co-operative labor; and in which private property would be abolished as would all distinctions between capitalists and laborers and producers and consumers.[14]

Though none of the Owenite community experiments in England succeeded, Owen exerted a powerful influence on the English workingmen's movement; and the famous Rochdale consumer co-operatives, started by British weavers in 1844, were among the products of this influence. And as Engels says in his masterly study, *Socialism: Utopian and Scientific,* almost every progressive activity in England during the nineteenth century bore the impress of Owen's work.

At the same time that Owen was evolving his plans for a new social order, Charles Fourier was engaged in a similar enterprise in France. Like Owen, Fourier believed that the organization of co-operative communities would eliminate the social evils of capitalism; but his communities, known as phalanxes, were to be joint-stock enterprises and unlike Owen's societies would not be based upon community ownership of property. The profits of the enterprise would be divided into three parts —four-twelfths to be paid as dividends on capital, three-twelfths to individuals of special talent, and five-twelfths to labor.

The basic difference between Owen and Fourier was that the former abolished individual property rights while the latter preserved them. Another major difference was that Owen believed that the industrial development could contribute to human progress if society were better organized, while Fourier regarded industrialism as a great. evil and believed that the salvation of mankind lay in an "agrarian, handicraft economy."

In Owen's society, "Mechanism and science will be extensively introduced to execute all the work that is over-laborious, disagreeable, or in any other way injurious to human nature." Fourier, on the other hand, planned to have this work performed by members of the phalanx. By making these tasks honorable, they would become attractive.[15]

Despite these fundamental differences, Owen and Fourier had much in common. Both believed in a co-operative society which would remove ownership and control of the means of production from a handful of capitalists. Both believed that partial reforms were worthless and that it was necessary to "remodel the world entirely, and abolish all dissension and warfare." No friend of progress can help but admire the strivings of these social reformers for a better society, yet their strivings were never thought out scientifically and were therefore doomed to failure.

Owen and Fourier relied upon the exploiters to end exploitation voluntarily. If only some generous and far-seeing king, prince, or capitalist would contribute part of his wealth to the cause, a small experimental community could be financed. In a year or two the mass of the people would see the contrast between life in a co-operative community and life in a capitalist community. Then the biggest problem would be how to manage the influx of thousands of people anxious to set up similar communities. Among these thousands would be the capitalists themselves, for they too would come to endorse the new society in order to escape the danger of revolution created by an aroused working class. Thus Robert Owen appealed to the capitalists in the United States to realize that the new co-operative communities presented their only avenue of escape from eventual destruction.

"These establishments," he wrote," will enable the capitalists and men of extensive practical experience to solve without difficulty the Great Problem of the Age, that is, how to apply the enormous and ever-growing new scientific powers for producing wealth, beneficially for the entire population, instead of allowing them to continue, as heretofore, most injuriously to create enormous riches for the few and to impoverish the many, driving them toward a desperation that will ultimately, if not timely prevented by this measure, involve the over-wealthy in utter destruction." [16]

The following story told of Charles Fourier is illustrative of the naïveté of the Utopians: "Once he announced publicly that he would be at home at a certain hour to await any philanthropist who felt disposed to give him a million francs for the development of a colony based on Fourieristic principles. For twelve years thereafter he was at home every day, punctually at noon, awaiting the generous stranger, but alas, no millionaire appeared." [17]

For a time the Utopians gained numerous converts, many of whom were intellectuals who, sickened by the growing contrast between wealth and poverty, welcomed a program which by appealing to reason and good will would bring in an era of equality and happiness. They followed up their mistaken theory that a co-operative society could grow up within capitalist society by insisting that the working class should have no part in its own emancipation. Owen bluntly stated that he did not wish to "have the opinions of the ill-trained and uninformed on any of the measures intended for their relief and amelioration. No! On such subjects, until they shall be instructed in better habits, and made rationally intelligent, their advice can be of no value." [18]

OWENISM

Early in 1825 Robert Owen came to America where in the new world of promise people were not controlled by the "dead hand of a feudal past." No venture for the transformation of society had ever before received such a wide and influential hearing in the United States. On two separate occasions, February 25 and March 7, 1825, he addressed the House of Representatives in the presence of James Monroe, the President of the United States, John Quincy Adams, the President-Elect, heads of departments, and members of both houses of Congress. Owen's frequent lectures to audiences ranging from New York to New Orleans were carefully reported in the American press, and models of his proposed community were printed and widely circulated in the newspapers.

The first Owenite community in America was established at New Harmony, Indiana, where Owen had purchased 30,000 acres from the Rappites, a religious sect that had founded a communal group on the Wabash, and had already cultivated the land and built houses, mills, factories. On April 27, 1825, Owen's "Kingdom Come-in-the-Wilderness" invited the "industrious and well-disposed" the world over to join the community. Close to a thousand persons from all parts of America flocked to New Harmony during the summer of 1825. Others arrived later, among them some of the great minds of the day: William Maclure, president of the Philadelphia Academy of Natural Sciences; Josiah Warren, economist, naturalist, and the inventor of a rotary press; Thomas Say, entomologist; Gerard Troost, internationally famous Dutch chemist and geologist; Robert Dale Owen and David Dale Owen, sons of Robert Owen.

The colony failed; lack of planning and the absence of clear and forceful leadership made for repeated quarrels and divisions which helped to wreck the community. After having spent more than $200,000 on the purchase of the property and the debts of the community, Owen withdrew all financial support from it. The adventurers, speculators, and idlers who had attached themselves to the community left as soon as Owen announced that they would have to go to work. But many workers accepted Owen's offer of leasing farms and homes to them at very reasonable rates. As a co-operative community, however, it was finished.

Eighteen other Owenite communities were formed in New York, Ohio, and Indiana during 1826-1827. But they all met the fate of New Harmony. By 1828 Owenism as a movement had practically disappeared. In the 'forties it revived somewhat. Owen returned to America in 1845 and issued a call for a "World Convention" to be held in New York City "for the commencement, in the New World, of a new social order for the benefit of all, upon the principles upon which the American government was based by its far-seeing founders." [19] The convention met for eight days, but its resolutions remained only on paper. Once again, Owen had been unsuccessful.

FOURIERISM

Owen's plans attracted considerable discussion in America, and many of his followers carried forth his ideals years after the model communities had failed. It was Owen who prepared the way for Fourier's popularity. Fourier himself never came to the United States, nor did he live to see the brief period during which his ideas swept the country. He died in Paris on October 10, 1837, three years before Albert Brisbane, his great American disciple, had published the first of several books and many articles in which he introduced Fourier's philosophy to Americans.

Albert Brisbane, father of Arthur Brisbane, Hearst's famous mouthpiece, was the only son of a well-to-do landowner. During a visit to France, Brisbane came upon Fourier's writings. He returned to America in 1834 to devote himself to furthering the cause of the French Utopian. His first book, the *Social Destiny of Man, or Association and Reorganization of Industry,* was published in 1840. Half of the volume was devoted to Fourier's writings, and the rest contained the author's commentaries and illustrations showing how the system could be adapted to American conditions.

The most influential convert to Fourierism in America was Horace Greeley, the distinguished liberal journalist.* Greeley had been a working printer and had participated in the workingmen's movement in New York City. The suffering during the crisis of 1837 and the increased introduction of machinery during the 'forties convinced him that the vaunted advantages enjoyed by the American workers over their European brothers did not really exist.

* There are two opinions of Horace Greeley among present-day historians. One school regards him as a sincere radical reformer who "was to the social revolution of the 'forties what Thomas Jefferson was to the political revolution of 1800." (See John R. Commons, "Horace Greeley and the Working Class Origins of the Republican Party," *Political Science Quarterly,* vol. XXIV, pp. 468-88.) Others grant that Greeley was sincere but point out that he championed those programs that diverted the attention of the working class from the basic struggles to improve their immediate conditions, opposed strikes and was lukewarm to trade unionism. (See Norman J. Ware, *The Industrial Worker, 1840-1860,* pp. 21-22, 167, and Arthur M. Schlesinger, Jr., *The Age of Jackson,* New York, 1945, pp. 294-96, 364, 367.) There is much to be said for the latter viewpoint, but it overlooks the fact that the *New York Tribune* did open its columns (at times for a price) to issues of great significance to labor, did report events in the labor movement much more sympathetically than most newspapers of the period and did give support (frequently in a vacillating manner) to many campaigns waged by the labor movement.

"To talk of Freedom of Labor ... when the fact is that a man who has a family to support and a house hired for the year is told, 'If you will work thirteen hours per day, or as many as we think fit, you can stay, if not, you can have your working papers, and well you know that no one else hereabout will hire you'—is it not the most egregious flummery?" [20]

Greeley thought that the factory system should be "counteracted by some radical change in our social economy." [21] One day on a trip to Boston he read Brisbane's book on Fourierism; he returned to New York City an enthusiastic believer in industrial association, as it was called. When he founded the *New York Tribune* Greeley opened the columns of his newspaper to Brisbane. On March 1, 1842, the paper carried the following headline, "Association or Principles of a True Organization of Society." Then followed the first of many articles which appeared regularly in the columns of the *Tribune* until September 9, 1843. Later the movement established its own newspapers—the *New York Phalanx,* the *Harbinger,* the *Social Reformer,* etc.—but these little magazines with their limited circulations could not be as influential as Brisbane's columns in the widely read *Tribune.* Brisbane analyzed the evils of contemporary society and showed how Fourierism remedied each evil. The following is a typical excerpt:

A general view of the contrasts between the present false Social Order and Association, that one is Hell and the other Heaven upon Earth.

Result of our Present Societies	*Results of Association*
1. Waste	1. Vast economies
2. Indigence	2. General Riches
3. Fraud	3. Practical truth
4. Oppression	4. Real Liberty
5. War	5. Constant Peace
6. Disease uselessly and artificially produced	6. Preventive System of medicine
7. Predominance of all prejudices; and obstacles offered to improvements	7. Progress in all branches and opening offered to improvements

To end this hell and to bring in this heaven all that was needed was to find enough capital to buy 6,000 acres of land; the property would be held in the form of a joint stock association each member of which was to be both partner and stockholder; each worker in the co-operative would receive the necessities of life at cost and receive high wages as well as dividends on the stock. Peace and happiness! Just one Association would be a model for others; it would soon convince all the people in America that the new society was superior to the old, just as it had taken the single steamboat of Robert Fulton to convince the world that it was superior to any ship in creation." [22]

Even more attractive to workingmen was a pamphlet distributed by the Rochester Fourier Society in December, 1843, entitled *Labor's Wrongs and Labor's Remedy*. The pamphlet vigorously attacked the status of the working class in capitalist society. "What are the working classes of every nation considered by the non-producers, the idlers," it declared, "but beasts of burden; without heart and without souls whose doom it is to labour and to die?" What was the cause of labor's poverty and suffering, it asked? "Your labor has too many idlers to support," it answered, "who think it dishonorable to work." * The solution was obvious; workers should become members of a Fourierist phalanx where almost immediately they would receive for their labor "at least one-fourth more than in the best circumstances labour receives at the present time." [23]

These appeals must have been alluring to mechanics who, frightened by the sudden appearance of the factory system, were casting about for some means of returning to the good old days of Jeffersonian democracy, which, in retrospect, seemed days of security and independence. For a time, quite a few of these workers believed that they had found the avenue of escape in the association movement, just as the middle-class social reformers of the day thought that the same movement was the answer to their prayer for a principle by which the forces making for class divisions might be arrested or counterbalanced, and by which the proletarian misery and revolutions in Europe could be kept away from America.

So easy did the road to utopia appear that Fourierism soon numbered its adherents in America in thousands. After a tour of New York State early in 1843, Albert Brisbane reported jubilantly to the *Tribune:* "In all the principal towns and many of the smaller ones the people are taking up the subject with the greatest enthusiasm and energy—forming societies for the dissemination of the doctrines and organizing small associations." [24]

During the next ten years, more than forty Fourierist communities were established in localities as widely separated as Illinois and Massachusetts. They attracted individuals from all classes in society and

---

* In advancing this concept, the pamphlet deviated from Fourier and Brisbane, neither of whom considered fraud or the unequal distribution of wealth as the cause of labor's misery. It was the discordant organization of the social system that caused poverty, they argued, not the greed of the capitalists.

especially gained many recruits from the working classes. Shoemakers, bootmakers, tailors, carpenters, joiners, cabinet-makers, painters, carpet-weavers, blacksmiths, iron molders, machinists, masons, laborers, teamsters, watchmakers, and clerks were among the different categories of workingmen listed as members of various phalanxes in America.[25]

The first phalanx founded in the United States was Sylvania, established in Western Pennsylvania in 1843 by a group of mechanics who had formerly lived and worked in Albany and New York City. On January 17, 1843, the *Tribune* announced: "The Sylvania Association is undertaken by intelligent and energetic working-men, who, despairing of obtaining the aid of men who have capital, have determined upon building up an Association by their own labor."

The capital for Sylvania came from the workingmen themselves and from a few friends who became stockholders by subscribing to not less than one share at twenty-five dollars. Throughout its brief existence, the colony was faced with the difficulty of obtaining capital. "It asks of the opulent and the generous," the executives of the association appealed publicly, "subscriptions to its stocks in order that its lands might be promptly cleared and improved, and its buildings erected."[26] Unfortunately, the opulent were not generous, and the generous were not opulent.

There were other difficulties too. The workers had had no previous training as farmers, and the work was exceedingly difficult. The climate was severe; the buildings were barely more than shanties, and the life in the wilderness of Western Pennsylvania was anything but comfortable. Several branches of industry, including shoemaking, were established, but difficulties in obtaining markets prevented their growth. On August 10, 1844, Brisbane announced the failure of the colony:

"We are requested to state that the Sylvania Association, having become satisfied of its inability to contend successfully against an ungrateful soil and an ungenial climate, which unfortunately characterize the domain on which it settled, has determined on a dissolution."[27]

Most American phalanxes, like Sylvania, failed within a few years after they were founded. The North American Phalanx, on which Fourierism practically staked its all in this country, remained in existence for thirteen years, and Brook Farm in Massachusetts lasted six years.*

---

* Although it did not begin as a Fourieristic community, Brook Farm was the most famous of all the phalanxes founded in America. Associated with it, directly or indirectly, were the intellectual giants of the day: William E. Channing, George Ripley, Ralph Waldo Emerson, Theodore Parker, Nathaniel Hawthorne, John Greenleaf Whittier, Margaret Fuller, and Elizabeth P. Peabody, to mention but a few.

The great majority, however, went under before their first year was over.

The reasons for the failure can be swiftly recounted. In some communities, bitter conflicts over such issues as observance of the Sabbath and the character of the educational program hastened the decline. In others, frequent complaints that the stockholders received a greater reward and had a more important voice in managing affairs than working members speeded up the process of disintegration. Several phalanxes, moreover, found it impossible to continue and do business because of the inability to secure a firm legal title by means of an act of incorporation. But in almost all cases, the chief difficulty arose from the failure to secure sufficient capital. Some capitalists joined the Fourierist movement and even loaned land to a phalanx. But frequently this gesture was simply a shrewd device to get their property improved by the community, for when the phalanx failed, they received arable land in place of wilderness.[28] Most capitalists, however, ignored the appeals of the Utopians, who urged them to support a movement which would eliminate struggles of "class against class, or labor against capital."

Writing to a friend from Brook Farm, Nathaniel Hawthorne, the novelist, predicted that the venture would not succeed. "I form my judgment," he added, "not from anything that has passed within the precincts of Brook Farm but from external circumstances—from the impracticability that adequate funds will be raised or that any feasible plan can be suggested for proceeding without a considerable capital." [29] In 1845, George Ripley, one of the founders, wrote to Brisbane, urging him to help raise $15,000 for Brook Farm. Brisbane's reply revealed the bankruptcy of his principle that support for the association would come from wealthy capitalists. "You want capital," he wrote, "and immediately for Brook Farm. Now it seems to me as a problem as perplexing to get $15,000 for B[rook] F[arm] as it does to raise $100,000. Where can it be had?" [30]

PRODUCERS' CO-OPERATIVES

The failure of the phalanxes did not signify the end of the influence of utopian socialism in America. It did, however, convince many workingmen that it was "impossible to introduce any system of complete cooperation at once." [31] But these workers still believed that a new organization of production and distribution was absolutely essential if labor was to maintain and improve its living standards. The result was a significant trend during the 'forties and 'fifties toward producers' and consumers' co-operatives.

Producers' co-operatives, it will be recalled, had been started in several cities during the 1830's. In 1836, in Philadelphia alone, factories and stores had been opened by cabinet-makers, cordwainers, and hand loom weavers. Other trades were about to follow suit when the panic of 1837 wiped out all of these early efforts.

In the 'forties, the producers' co-operative movement revived and attracted considerable attention. Much of this, of course, was due to the influence of Fourierism in working class circles. But to a considerable extent, it was also the result of the stimulus supplied by the French Revolution of 1848. During this revolution, Louis Blanc's remedies for the evils of capitalist society excited a great deal of attention among the working class of Paris. Blanc proposed that the state should set up social workshops and factories which would then become independent bodies competing against private capitalism. Like Owen and Fourier, Blanc was confident that the result of this competition would be the gradual elimination of capitalist production and the establishment of a new social order.*

Yielding to the demand of an aroused working class, the Provisional Government of France set up a few "national workshops" but confined their functions to the building of roads and digging of ditches. Workingmen in America, however, did not stop to examine the makeshift character of these so-called workshops or pay too much attention to the fact that Blanc himself had denied that the enterprises were based upon his principles. They were interested only in the fact that their brothers in France were making great efforts to change the existing system. Labor papers like the *Voice of Industry,* published in Lowell, Massachusetts, devoted a great deal of space to the course of the workshops set up in France, and called upon American workers to emulate their working class brothers across the ocean. All in all, the advocates of producers' and consumers' co-operatives were greatly spurred by the activities of the French Socialists.[32]

The first important producers' co-operative in America, however, antedated the French Revolution of 1848 by several months. It began in the winter of 1847-48, during a strike of iron molders near Cincinnati. To support themselves during the strike, twenty of these molders established a co-operative stove and hollow foundry. Their total investment was $2,100, but they obtained enough credit from two wealthy philanthropists to continue their venture even after the strike was lost, and secured a

* According to Blanc, the workmen's associations would be collectively owned, the compensation for labor would be based on the amount of time devoted to work and the exchange of goods would be facilitated by the use of paper money representing accumulated labor. The government through its "minister of progress" would finance the early associations and later would supervise the functioning of the entire system. In the transition stage the government would nationalize the railroads, mines, the Bank of France and the storage and marketing facilities of wholesale and retail trade.

charter of incorporation from the State of Ohio under the title of "Journeymen Molders' Union Foundry." Early in 1850, the venture was still going strong. The capital had increased to $7,792 and 47 workers were employed at the union scale of wages. By this time, a store had been established in Cincinnati for the sale of stoves and castings produced at the co-operative foundry. Horace Greeley, who visited the foundry in 1850, described it as "the most commodious on the river." An enthusiastic champion of co-operation as a solution for the problems of the working class, Greeley informed labor of the virtues of the union foundry:

"While other molders have had to work 'off and on,' according to the state of the trade, no member of the Journeymen's Union has stood idle for a day for want of work since the foundry was first started." [33]

However, shortly after Greeley's visit, the co-operative failed, for it was impossible to compete successfully with private enterprises which possessed much more capital and were ready to sell below cost to force the workingmen's venture out of business. But the initial success of the Cincinnati foundry and the news of the workshops established in France stimulated other workingmen to organize similar ventures. When the Boston journeymen tailors failed to win a strike to secure the acceptance of their price scale in the summer of 1849, they, too, decided to set up a co-operative shop. Several mass meetings were held in Boston to raise funds to launch the enterprise and about $500 was collected. Late in September, 1849, the Boston Tailors' Associative Union began to engage in production. This contagion spread to a group of striking printers in Boston who set up a co-operative printing shop called the "Boston Printers' Protective Union." In addition to commercial printing, the association published the *Protective Union,* a weekly paper which urged workingmen to abandon the use of strikes to improve their conditions and to concentrate upon the organization of co-operative shops. These enterprises, the workingmen were assured, would make them "their own masters and not only put the tools into the hands of the workers but ensure them the enjoyment of the full product of their industry instead of diverting the larger part into the pocket of the employer." [34]

To workingmen who were seeking an escape from a rising industrial system and who were trying desperately to preserve their rapidly disappearing status as skilled and independent craftsmen, such appeals hit home. The spring of 1850 saw the establishment of a host of producers' co-operatives all over the country. In Pittsburgh, an iron foundry, two or three glassworks, and a silver-platers' shop were set up. Wheeling, Virginia, boasted a co-operative foundry with a capital of $25,000 and a nail-cutters' association. Co-operative stores of seamstresses were established in Boston, Philadelphia, Providence, and other cities. In New York, the coopers, hat finishers, shade painters, German cabinet-makers, and tailors organized co-operative shops, and it was even reported that the dry goods clerks were making plans to "form a joint stock store for the purpose of freeing themselves from the control of any individual employer." When the tailors established their co-operative clothing store, a mass meeting of New York trade unionists was held to bestow the blessings of the city's entire working class upon the venture. The meeting unanimously resolved to advance "the principle of co-operation as one of the chief means whereby the masses may redeem themselves from a state of degradation." [35]

Invariably, these producers' co-operatives met the same fate as the phalanxes, but their existence is a striking illustration of the influence of the Utopians as well as of the determination of American workers to maintain their independent status in the face of major economic changes.

CONSUMERS' CO-OPERATIVES

The consumer co-operative movement sought to eliminate the profits of the middleman and thereby to reduce the cost of living to workers and farmers. From 1839 to 1843, several "Farmers and Mechanics Stores" were set up in Vermont and New Hampshire by joint stock associations organized by farmers and mechanics. A member of one such store in New Hampshire described the venture as "a scheme by which the Farmer and Mechanic may exchange the products of their labor without: 1st, the risk of unjust price, 2nd, of extortion and imposition." [36]

It was not, however, until 1845 that the consumer co-operative movement really got under way. On October 6, 1845, a group of Boston mechanics set up the first Working Men's Protective Union. This association, soon to become the model for hundreds of similar organizations, had as its main purpose the purchase, at reduced prices, of necessities for its members. It also included mutual benefit features such as provisions for sickness and old-age insurance. For the payment of an initiation fee of $3 and a small monthly assessment, a member of the Protective Union could purchase groceries, fuel, and other goods at the association store. The prices charged at the store, it was estimated, would save him $66.66 a year or in ten years, with interest, $879.62. In addition, a member would receive $3 a week when sick provided the condition was not due to "debauchery or licentiousness," and when he reached the age of 65 and had been on the roll for at least ten years, would receive a weekly pension of $7.50.

The protective union movement was enthusiastically endorsed by working men who lived constantly on the edge of poverty and insecurity. By December, 1847, forty divisions had been set up with a membership of over 3,000, most of them located in eastern Massachusetts. During 1850 alone, the New England Protective Union chartered 101 new divisions and enrolled 5,564 new members. Throughout the decade and a half, from 1845 to 1860, over 800 protective unions were organized in the United States and Canada. The majority were set up in the New England states and New York, but some even appeared in Michigan, Wisconsin, and Illinois.[37]

The spread of the protective union movement was the result of a well organized campaign conducted by labor papers and traveling lecturers. The *Voice of Industry* ran a series of weekly educational articles on the subject of "Protective Unions," and played a big part in the spread of the movement. John Orvis, one of the lecturers sent out by the Boston Working Men's Protective Union, traveled throughout New England and western New York explaining the principles of the movement to audiences composed of workers and farmers. Moreover, even Brisbane and his disciples took to the lecture platform to urge workingmen to join a protective union and set up co-operative stores. The leaders of the Association movement viewed protective unionism as "an entering wedge for Fourierism," and were convinced that through their experience with consumer co-operatives, workers would see the need for a complete reorganization of society.

To a certain extent this feeling was justified. Although the leaders of the protective union movement mainly emphasized the money-saving features of the scheme, they rarely left it at that. They were careful to indicate that the ultimate objective of the movement was a completely reorganized society. Nor were they hesitant in revealing how this new society would come into being. It would start with the combining of stores so that instead of sixty grocery stores in a city there would be about six protective union stores. The elimination of middlemen and the reduction of lighting, heat, and transportation costs would reduce the price of commodities for workers just as the presence of so many empty stores which could be converted into dwellings would reduce their rent. In like manner, factories and transportation facilities would be taken over by the protective unions and combined. The middlemen, traders, and employers would be eliminated and forced to join the ranks of the laboring classes.

Yet even this was only the beginning. As protective unions spread throughout the country, the new society would gradually take form. Divisions in Lowell and Lynn would specialize in manufacturing cloth and boots and shoes; those in the West would raise flour; Vermont would produce butter and cheese; and the South would grow cotton, rice, and sugar. Each division would exchange goods which would be carried from one section to another on protective union ships and railroads. The capitalist wage system would soon be but a sad memory and no real problem would exist for workingmen and women.

It is doubtful, however, whether this dream was shared by the rank and file of the protective union movement. The *Voice of Industry* admitted that many who joined the movement "know but little about it further than there is a saving of dollars and cents." Again, a committee of the New England Protective Union appealed to all members to think beyond the immediate function of the movement:

"Brothers, shall we content ourselves with the miserable idea of merely saving a few dollars, and say we have found enough? Future generations, aye, the uprising generation is looking to us for nobler deeds.... We must proceed from combined shops to combined houses, to joint ownership in God's earth, the foundation that our edifice must stand upon." [38]

In the end, the protective union movement was no more successful than were the phalanxes or the producers' co-operatives. By 1855, its influence had waned and, though the panic of 1857 gave it a temporary lift, the movement was a thing of the past when the Civil War started. The reasons for this rapid decline are not difficult to discover. Merchants lowered prices to undersell the protective union stores and sold their goods on longer credit terms than ever before. The protective unions never had enough capital to engage in price wars with private businessmen or to sell on a credit basis. And very few workers had sufficient means to pay cash. Conflict within the movement over control and resentment at the abandonment of the sick benefit fund contributed to the difficulties. Finally, at the very time that businessmen were denouncing the protective union movement as "socialism" and calling its adherents enemies of private property, the social reformers were criticizing it for not going far enough. The Associationists soon lost all hope of converting the members of the protective unions to socialism. Thus Brisbane said in disgust in 1851: "Do they care about Socialism? No, they don't, but they found out that they get their goods at twenty per cent less than they used to at the grocer's and they care about that." [39]

LAND REFORM

About the same time that Robert Owen and Albert Brisbane were appealing to American workingmen in behalf of their reform programs, another group known as Agrarians or National Reformers were eliciting strong support from the working class. The land reform movement was led by English-born George Henry Evans, formerly the editor of the

Working Man's Advocate and *The Man,* and a leader of the working-men's movement during the Jacksonian era. In 1836, Evans, forced by poor health to abandon his activity as a labor journalist and to sever his connections with the labor movement, had retired to a farm in upstate New York to recuperate. In the early 'forties he returned to activity to lead the crusade for free public land. His interest in agrarian reform had been evident during the 'thirties, but not until 1841 did he present a specific plan for land reform. Evans advanced the thesis that land monopoly was the "king monopoly, the cause of the greatest evils," and that the only way to solve the problems facing American workers was to restore their rights to ownership of the land. "If a man has a right on the earth, he has a right to land enough to raise a habitation. If he has a *right to live,* he has a right to land enough to till for his subsistence." [40]

Control of large tracts of land by a few individuals, Evans believed, placed the landless workers completely at the mercy of the employers. "The poor," he argued, "must *work* or *starve* in the manufactories as in England, unless they can cultivate the land." In America, the debasement of the working class, which had already taken place in Europe, could still be prevented if a law were passed granting every citizen his rightful heritage—a portion of the public lands. Enough workers, Evans contended, "would avail themselves of such a law to prevent such a surplus of work in the factories as would place the whole body (as now) at the mercy of the factory owners."

Not only would land reform free workers from dependence on capital, but as workers moved west to establish their homes on the public land, the employers would be forced to advance the wages of those who still remained in the East and landlords would be compelled to reduce their rents. Labor scarcity alone, Evans contended, would bring about better conditions for the workers in the factories and shops. Hence, through this program, "those who remain, as well as those who emigrate, will have the opportunity of realizing a comfortable living." [41]

But land reform would also "undo the work of the Industrial Revolution," and restore economic independence to workers who were being crushed by technological improvements. The triumph of machine labor and ultimate prostration of human labor could not be averted under existing conditions. It was useless to fight it; one had to "escape from an evil which it is impossible to avert." In Europe, there was little hope of getting the laboring population out of the difficulties and distress caused by the Industrial Revolution, for there, every parcel of land, "God's inheritance to man," was fenced in and appropriated by the aristocracy. Hence, the European working class had no other alternative, as long as it remained in the Old World, "except to sell the labor of their bodies for whatever price it will bring, live upon that pittance as long as it will sustain them alive, and when it fails sink into their last earthly refuge—the grave."

In America, however, the land and its resources belonged to the people or were held by the government in trust for them. Let the workers, then, redeem their right, go to the land in the West and live in Rural Republican Townships created out of the public domain. There, any landless man would have the right to settle on a quarter section farm or village lot—he could have no more than that, and his farm or lot was to be inalienable—and everyone coming of age was to have the same right. Here in the Rural Republican Townships, the mechanic would be a farmer-artisan, working part of the time on the land and part of the time making commodities with his own tools. The shoemaker artisan-farmer would exchange the shoes he made with his tools for a suit of clothing fashioned by the tailor artisan-farmer. They could also sell their products directly to local traders in the village square.[42]

Thus, according to the land reformers, the time would soon come—once the public land was made available to all—when the industrial cities would fall to pieces. All the inhabitants would leave for the happy life in the townships, leaving behind nothing but "warehouses, shipyards, and foundries to accommodate international commerce at the great sea and the river ports of the earth." Gone would be the old social order in which workers labored in poverty and misery at soulless machines. In its place would be a new society of prosperity, peace, dignity, and security.

Evans went so far as to provide a specific timetable, indicating the exact course that the peaceful revolution would pursue, once the free land program was enacted. The imaginary schedule appeared in Evans' paper, *Young America,* on February 8, 1851, and predicted that if Congress passed a land reform law in 1851, the following events would soon occur:

"1855—General prosperity such as was never known before civilization. Free trade is established. . . . Emigration is all the rage in Europe. British Statesmen become alarmed and concede 'The Charter.' . . .

"1860—Labor for wages now being voluntary is about the same price as it was in Oregon and California in 1850, ranging from three to eight dollars a day. Rents in the cities now are merely nominal. . . .

"1870—No man or woman in the United States begs 'leave to toil.' . . .

"1880—Free Soil Republics are now springing up all over South America and Europe. . . .

"1890—Almost every family in the Union is now in possession of a Home, and there is no want of employment. . . . Machinery now works for the laborers not against them. . . .

"1900—The United States is now a Nation of Freeholders. The doctrine of the Declaration of 1776 is fully recognized and practiced....Men wonder why their fathers tolerated Land Monopoly...and debating whether the Millennium has arrived."

"And all this," concluded Evans, "can be obtained by a simple *vote*, if the workingmen throughout the country will unite." [43]

Evans' program, it is obvious, contained aspects of Utopianism. But land reform, unlike the program of the Associationists, was an integral part of the labor movement, even if the workers did not fully accept Evans' theory that it would solve all of their problems.

In several other respects the land reformers differed from the utopians. For one thing, they did not appeal to the capitalists for support, nor even include them in their plans; in fact, they boasted that they did not enroll in their ranks "a single man of wealth." [44] For another, they differed with the Fourierites over the issue of political action. Brisbane and his leading disciples were unalterably opposed to political and administrative reforms, regarding them as useless and a waste of time and energy. Evans disagreed, for his experience in the early workingmen's parties had convinced him that political action by labor was of great value and could accomplish miracles. He made political action the cornerstone of his entire program. To render the public lands available to all citizens, a Congressional law would have to be passed. This could only be accomplished by mass pressure and political action. To bring his program to the people Evans formed the National Reform Association, called public meetings, organized ladies' auxiliaries, and distributed throwaways and memorials. In addition, he revived the *Working Man's Advocate,* which was changed later to *Young America,** and he also utilized the columns of Greeley's *Tribune* to urge the workers to organize politically for land reform. Working closely with him were men who had had years of experience in the labor movement—Seth Luther, John Ferral, John Commerford, and others. [45]

In 1845, the walls of New York were plastered with circulars bearing the title, "Vote Yourself a Farm." Thousands of copies of this handbill were distributed throughout the country by Evans and his followers. It asked:

"Are you tired of slavery, of drudging for others—of poverty and its attendant miseries? Then, Vote Yourself a Farm." [46]

* Evans adopted this title from the movement in the Old World known as Young Europe, and said that it meant "the great army of progress." (See *Young America,* March 25, April 15, 1845; also Saul F. Riepma, *Young America: A Study in American Nationalism before the Civil War,* unpublished Ph.D. thesis, Western Reserve University, 1940. For an interesting account of the activities of the National Reformers in the anti-rent movements of up-state farmers in New York, see Henry Christman, *Tin Horns & Calico,* New York, 1945, pp. 71-2, 121-23, 219, 233.)

The response to this appeal startled conservatives. Workingmen throughout the North and West and even in a few areas of the South joined the National Reform Association, organized ward clubs, and signed a pledge to vote for no man for any legislative office who would not agree in writing "to use all the influence of his station, if elected, to prevent all further traffic in the Public Lands of the States of the United States, and to cause them to be laid out in farms and lots for the full and exclusive use of actual settlers." Some communities even witnessed the launching of independent workingmen's tickets to advance the principles of land reform along with other progressive reforms such as full right of suffrage, election of all officers by the people, direct taxation of property, and reform of the legal system. In Pittsburgh, where John Ferral was championing the cause of land reform, the movement held the balance of power for a time.[47] All in all, it seemed as if the millennium sought by the National Reformers was close at hand. As one of Evans' disciples put it:

> *See the Agrarian Ball a rolling,*
> *Hark, the Knell of Avarice tolling,*
> *Roll the ball to every station,*
> *In our own great Yankee nation,*
> *Push along and keep it moving,*
> *The People's cause is still improving.*[48]

It is doubtful, however, whether any considerable number of working-men regarded land reform as the program which would elevate the working class. Very few workers could move to the West even if they wanted to. The costs of migrating and of outfitting a farm were far greater than the average worker could afford, even if he possessed knowledge of farming methods and was willing to leave familiar surroundings in eastern cities. To most urban factory workers, farm life on the frontier was both unfamiliar and unattractive. When asked by an English traveler in 1843 why they submitted to exploitation at the hands of capitalists and why they did not "leave ... and go to the land," a group of factory workers replied:

"We could not travel to the West without money, and we cannot save money; it is as much as we can do to provide our families with necessaries. We should want money to travel, then money would be wanted to buy the land, to buy agricultural implements, to buy seed, and then we should want more to support us till we could dispose of part of our crops, and then we have no money at all. But, suppose we had all these means, we know nothing about the cultivation of land—we have all our lives worked in a factory, and know no other employment, and how is it likely that we should succeed? Besides which, we have always been used to live in a town, where we can get what little things we want if we have money, and it is only those who have lived in the wilderness, who know what the horrors of a wilderness-life are." [49]

Nevertheless, the fact that few laborers actually did leave the industrial and commercial centers of the East and turn westward did not completely stifle the influence of the land reform movement in working class circles. The speeches of labor leaders and editorials in the labor press continually emphasized the fact that the struggle for free land was necessary, even if no workers went west, for the very presence of free land and the existence of the possibility of moving westward would stay the hands of capitalist oppressors in the East.[50]

Another belief widely held by workingmen was that free land would prevent the piling up of great numbers of immigrants in the industrial cities, thereby preventing the decline in wages which inevitably follows such a concentration of workers. In addition, during periods of depression, the presence of free land would drain off unemployed workers from the "overcrowded cities to the Great West." Labor scarcity would give those workers who remained "a better chance" to obtain employment, and would soon result in higher wages and shorter hours. Not all workingmen agreed on this point. During a mass meeting of unemployed workers in 1857, workingmen hissed the proposal that they should concentrate upon moving to the West. "One man has told us to go West," said a worker. "Why if we should, our places would have been filled with other laborers from abroad!" [51]

While the evidence offered by recent researchers into the question indicates that there were few movements of workingmen to the West, it does not in any sense negate the fact that the existence of the frontier exercised a real and important influence on the development of the labor movement, and influenced to a marked degree the conditions and the ideology of the working class. Furthermore, the struggle against land speculators and slaveowners for free land attracted the support of many workingmen who correctly regarded it as one of the most important aspects of the movement for greater democracy in America.

UTOPIAN REFORMERS AND TRADE UNIONISM

If Owenites, Associationists, and Land Reformers differed in many ways, they did agree on one point: Unless their specific program was adopted, the workers could not really solve their problems. The Owenites and Associationists even publicly condemned the efforts of workers to secure shorter hours, arguing that "a mere shortening of hours of labor" would only convert them "from twelve and fourteen to ten hour slaves." [52] Nor for that matter would increased wages help the working class. An Associationist told a convention of New England workingmen in 1847: "No. None of these expedients will avail you. The whole system of labor for wages is wrong, an accursed system. The blackness of death is in its train. It has no sympathy with light. It is not laden and productive of life. Like the poisonous fire-lamp, it destroys all that comes within its fatal embrace. As the fearful maelstrom swallows up whatever ill-fated object comes within its reach, so are you under the present system absorbed by the unsatiated maw of capital." [53]

The language is striking, but its aim was to convince workingmen that anything short of the abolition of capitalism was useless. Evans shared this view—in a somewhat different form. He supported the ten-hour movement and the demands for higher wages and even called upon New England workingmen to agitate for a shorter working day. At the same time he tried to convince the workers that such agitation for shorter hours and higher wages was bound to fail unless land reform was first achieved. "This," he declared, "is the first measure to be accomplished, and it is as idle to attempt any great reform without that as it is to go to work without tools." The struggle for immediate demands was useless, since it could not "elevate them to the true dignity of independence." [54]

Evans and the Associationists, in various degrees, shared the same outlook on trade unionism. To the Associationists, trade unions were bad not only because they concerned themselves primarily with the immediate demands of the workers, but because they conducted strikes which stirred class antagonisms at a time when it was necessary for all classes to unite in building a new social order. Evans, although never a class harmonizer, believed during the land reform period of his life that trade unions were of little value to landless workers. "Not only do I think that trade associations are not the *only* remedy for the oppressions of the working men," he wrote in the *Working Man's Advocate*, "but I doubt whether they would be a remedy at all. They have been tried repeatedly and almost universally failed,* except when they have degenerated into mere partnership. And why? Simply because *associations* of landless men can no more keep up the price of their labor than can individuals." Nor could strikes accomplish anything for labor since they could not get at "the root of the evil"—surplus labor—which "frequently compels the employer to reduce wages." [55]

The utopian reformers not only pronounced these views. They entered labor organizations and attended working class meetings for

---

* This attitude was not confined to Evans. At a meeting of reformers in 1847, several people "spoke of the inutility of the Trades' Unions that had existed in the United States." (See *Proceedings of the Industrial Congress of 1847*, Lowell, June 18, 1847.)

the sole purpose of convincing the working class that they were wasting their time and energy fighting for better conditions within their present society. If they would but devote themselves to co-operatives or to voting themselves farms, all their grievances would be remedied. Being persuasive speakers and excellent parliamentarians, the social reformers were often able to convince workers' organizations to abandon trade union struggles for immediate demands and to convert their movement into a co-operative or a land reform institution. In fact even when workers were indifferent or hostile, the utopians were able to capture the loosely organized working class meetings and to push through resolutions endorsing Associations or land reform as "the only means by which the industrious millions can be rendered permanently prosperous." As a result a movement initiated by workingmen to secure shorter hours and higher wages would often be transformed into one which devoted itself to the establishment of a phalanx in a wilderness in Pennsylvania, Indiana, or Illinois, or a Rural Republican Township in the West.

The era of utopianism did not end the evils of capitalism in America any more than it did in the European countries, but it did call attention to the need to remedy a situation in which millions starved in the midst of plenty, and hundreds lived in luxury on the wealth produced by tens of thousands of workers. For every one that benefited by technological advancements, why did tens of thousands have to be destroyed? "Must labor," the Utopians asked, "the creator of wealth, lose from age to age, and from century to century, one portion after another of its just and fitting reward?" [56]

The utopians found no remedy for the ills of industrial society. Their philosophy could not discover the relation between the immediate needs and the ultimate emancipation of the working class. By ignoring political action they took from the worker his key to freedom. By ignoring the immediate needs of the working class, the utopians weakened the trade union and political movements of the working class—the only movements which educate and train the workers for the socialist transformation of society. Finally, they did not understand that the development of capitalism was a precondition for socialism. As Karl Marx said in criticizing the land reform movement, the "capitalist evil" they were vainly trying to avert was "historically good, for it will frightfully accelerate social development and bring ever so much nearer new and higher forms of the communist movement." [57] And as Joseph Weydemeyer, an early American Marxist, emphasized in the New York *Turn-Zeitung* of August 1, 1852: "The accumulation of capital is not harmful to society; the harm lies rather in the fact that capital serves the interests of a few. If the bourgeoisie has fulfilled the first task, it is the task of the proletariat to put an end to this state of affairs which has ended in chaos."

CHAPTER 11

The Ten-Hour Movement, 1840-1860

While utopian reformers were whipping up feeling about the evils of industrial development, the industrialization of the nation's economy was drawing sharper lines of demarcation between workers and employers. Between 1840 and 1860 the number of men engaged in manufacturing establishments having an output of $500 a year or more increased from 791,000 to 1,311,000. According to the Census of 1840, the total value of manufactured products was $483,278,000; in 1850 it was $1,019,-106,000; and in 1860, 1,885,861,000. The railroad mileage of the country increased from 2,800 in 1840 to 30,600 in 1860. Along with the industrialization of the country went ever-increasing urbanization; the percentage of the total population living in communities of 8,000 or more inhabitants increased from 8.5 in 1840 to 12.5 in 1850 and 16.1 in 1860.

American workers learned soon enough that it was useless to strive to stop capitalist development, and that economic security could not be achieved through the simple solutions offered by the Owenites, the Fourierites or the Land Reformers. It would take continuous day-to-day economic and political struggles and united action of the workers to bring the benefits of industrial advances to the mass of the American people. This realization was best expressed in the poem which heads the constitution of the American Miners' Association, formed in 1861:

> *Step by step, the longest march*
> *Can be won, can be won,*
> *Single stones will form an arch,*
> *One by one, one by one.*
>
> *And by union, what we will*
> *Can be all accomplished still,*
> *Drops of water turn a mill,*
> *Singly none, singly none.*

REVIVAL OF TRADE UNIONISM

The trade union movement revived slowly from the ravages of the crisis of 1837. It was only a matter of time before most workers would reject the utopian belief that the capitalists would help them solve their problems. Early in the 'forties, a group of workers in New England appealed to their fellow-laborers throughout the country to abandon any such illusions:

"Brethren, we conjure you ... not to believe a word of what is said about your interests and those of your employers being the same. Your interests and theirs are in a nature of things, hostile and irreconcilable. Then do not look to them for relief.... Our salvation must, through the blessing of God, come from ourselves. It is useless to expect it from those whom our labors enrich." [1]

These words stirred the workers of America. After years of depression, they leaped at the opportunity to secure a better way of life through organization. Nowhere was this more evident than in New England, where, in the early 'forties, mechanics' and laborers' associations sprang up like mushrooms. *"Organize," "Union Is Strength"* became the watchwords of the hour. Veteran trade unionists, forced by blacklists to abandon their organizations during the worst years of the depression, took on new life and called upon their fellow-workers to form unions and prove to the capitalists that they were "true representatives of those noble spirits that so fearlessly denounced the usurpations and tyranny of a British King." [2]

Vigorous and militant labor newspapers carried this message into New England cities and towns. The Boston *Laborer*; the Lynn *Awl* and *True Workingman*; the Lowell *Working Man's Advocate* and *Voice of Industry*; the Fall River *Mechanic* were but a few of the new labor papers which contributed to the revival of trade unionism in New England. For the first time New England factory workers set up a militant labor press.

FACTORY WORKERS AND THE LABOR MOVEMENT

Prior to the 1840's, it will be recalled, factory workers had not played an important part in the labor movement. True, the Dover and Lowell girls had conducted militant strikes during the 'twenties and 'thirties, but rarely had they combined to continue the struggle for better conditions, nor had they joined the skilled workingmen in their organized movements. Instead, most of them had returned to their farm homes, cursing the factory owners who were trying to reduce them to the status of slaves, and warning others to stay away from the "factory prisons."

As long as the majority of the factory girls came from nearby farms and their earnings in the factories were not their sole means of support, the appeals of trade unionists urging them to organize had little effect. But in the 1840's, the situation was drastically altered. Gradually a permanent working class began to emerge in the factories. During the crisis of 1837, a good many farmers in New England had lost their farms. "As the New England farms disappeared," writes Norman J. Ware, the outstanding authority on labor conditions between 1840 and the Civil War, "the freedom of the mill operatives contracted. They could no longer escape... a permanent factory population became a reality." [3] As one factory girl explained in 1845, the workers in the mills were composed "of a large share of poverty's daughters whose fathers do not possess one foot of land, but work day by day for the bread that feeds their families. Many are foreigners free to work... according to the mandates of heartless power, or go to the poor house, beg or do worse." [4]

These factory girls were actually responsible for the beginnings of a labor press representing the factory workers. It came into being as a result of an earnest effort made by the girls themselves to demolish a gigantic conspiracy organized by the mill owners. [5] European travelers to this country were wined and dined by New England manufacturers, were persuaded to record in the journals of their travels that Lowell, Waltham, Lawrence, and Chicopee were truly industrial utopias, and that the girls were cared for more as pupils "at a great seminary than as hands by whose industry profit is to be made out of capital." Even poets were paid to write verses in praise of the factory system. A typical poem was entitled "Song of the Factory Girls," and went, in part:

> Oh, sing me the song of the Factory Girl!
> So merry and glad and free!
> The bloom in her cheeks, of health how it speaks.
> Oh, happy a creature is she!
> She tends the loom, she watches the spindle,
> And cheerfully toileth away,
> Amid the din of wheels, how her bright eyes kindle,
> And her bosom is ever gay. [6]

In 1841, a widely publicized magazine, the *Lowell Offering,* came into existence. It helped continue the myth of New England's factory paradise and became a powerful weapon for the mill owners. On its title page, it carried the words: "A Repository of Original Articles Written by Females Employed in the Mills." As a result, for several years it was accepted as the voice of the mill workers. Since it studiously avoided publishing any complaints against conditions in the factories, it helped to establish the tradition of a benevolent mill system.

The *Lowell Offering* achieved international fame. Charles Dickens in his *American Notes* referred to it as the "first clear notes of real life in America." An American returning from England reported: "The *Lowell Offering* is probably exciting more attention in England, than *any* other American publication. It is talked of in the political as well as literary world." And in France, Thiers * arose in the Chamber of Deputies, waved a copy of the *Lowell Offering* in the air, and solemnly proclaimed that the magazine proved that in a democracy, labor could possess a mind and soul as well as a body.[7]

It is hardly surprising that the *Lowell Offering* was welcomed by factory owners, and that they sent a written tribute to the editors, praising "the worthy enterprise in which they are engaged." † [8] For the editors of the *Lowell Offering* were not in the least concerned with wages and hours. "We could do nothing to regulate the price of wages of the world," wrote one of the editors. "We would not if we could, at least we would not make that a prominent subject in our pages, for we believe there are things of even greater importance." As for hours and working conditions—these were matters over which workers "have no control." They would come as a result of the kind-heartedness of the factory owners. The corporations would "in their own good time introduce the ten-hour system, and will not this be a noble deed?" [9]

What, then, were the "things of even greater importance"? The only thing that really mattered, said the magazine's editor, was to "elevate, instruct and purify the mind and soul of the workers; to give them an outlet for the spiritual and emotional needs of the soul; to provide them with sweetness and light." Let the factory girls, therefore, meet in improvement circles where they would read and study. Armed with learning and culture, they could protect themselves from the crushing power of the machine which dehumanized the worker and robbed him of dignity and self-assurance. At the same time, they would prove to the world that there was "Mind among the Spindles." As long as the mind and the soul were free, what did it matter what happened to the body? The philosophy of the factory girls should be that of the Apostles: "Having food and raiment, let us be therewith content." [10]

The *Lowell Offering* was popular everywhere but among the factory girls. True, they wrote poems and stories for the magazine, believing

* In 1871, Thiers played a conspicuous role in the brutal suppression of the Paris Commune and in the wholesale slaughter of the Paris proletariat during the "Bloody Week" when reaction triumphed.

† In January, 1843, the *Offering* was purchased by William Schouler from its former proprietors. Schouler was an agent of the mill owners, a bitter foe of the ten-hour day, and was intensely hated by almost all factory girls. In a signed statement, Schouler called upon all "who feel an interest in the progress and good name of the factory system" to support the *Offering*.

that it was important to prove that a factory worker was an individual with a mind and emotions and not merely a part of the machinery. But they also submitted articles which showed the true conditions in the factories, and stressed the need for shorter hours, higher wages, and better working conditions. When the editors of the magazine refused to publish these articles, the girls denounced it as a company organ which soothed the consciences of the rich Boston and New York capitalists who were "enjoying the luxuries purchased by their large dividends wrung from the sufferings of the factory girls." [11]

Disgusted by the treachery of the *Lowell Offering,* the New England factory girls set up their own magazines and journals. In 1842, a fortnightly periodical, *The Factory Girl,* saw the light of day in New Hampshire. This magazine was edited by a man, assisted "by several operatives of undoubted ability," and announced that it would speak out in defense of "a half-helpless army of laborers." Three years later, the *Voice of Industry,* a weekly labor paper, made its appearance in Lowell, Massachusetts. It devoted considerable space to the plight of the factory girls, even establishing a regular column edited by one of the leaders of the working women. In May, 1846, the paper was taken over entirely by the girls themselves. In the same year, the *Factory Girl's Album and Operative's Advocate* began its career in Exeter, New Hampshire. Although published by a man, it was edited by "an association of females who are operatives in the factories, and consequently well qualified to judge the wants of those whose cause they will advocate." "It will speak fearlessly," it announced, "advocating a ten-hour system and a general reform among the many abuses now practiced upon the Factory Operatives." [12]

These new periodicals at once demolished the myth concerning the so-called "Beauties of Factory Life." Letters from the factory girls themselves were featured in each issue. One girl complained in a letter to *The Factory Girl* of March 1, 1843, that she and her friends were forced to work from six in the morning until ten o'clock at night, for which they received $1.56 per week:

"What a glorious privilege we enjoy in this boasted republican land, don't we? Here am I, a healthy New England girl, quite well behaved, bestowing just half of all my hours, including Sundays, upon a company for less than two cents an hour." [13]

Other letters told of girls who, being "scarcely paid sufficient to board themselves," were forced to abandon their virtue to obtain favors. They told of managers who found the girls "languorous" in the morning and who conceived the "brilliant" plan of forcing them to work on empty stomachs. They told of wage reductions of 40 per cent in mills that were earning enormous profits; of workers forced to accept their wages in store orders, which meant a loss of about 50 per cent in the value of these wages. Many letters complained of the unbearable speed-up, and pointed out that, whereas ten years ago the girls had tended two looms making from 216 to 324 picks a minute, they were now forced to tend four looms making 480 picks a minute, "the increased work being done by labor and the profit going to capital." The letters also protested vehemently against the blacklist system employed by all corporations to terrorize the factory workers. Under this system, a worker had to bring an honorable discharge from his former employer before he could obtain a new position.[14]

In every issue, the new factory magazines emphasized the fact that it was impossible to take a neutral position "while manufacturers and operatives were diametrically opposed in their pecuniary interests."[15] This note of class struggle was sounded in poems, stories, articles—even in definitions such as the following, which appeared in *The Factory Girl* of January 15, 1843:

"*Overseer*—a servile tool in the hands of an agent; one who will resort to the lowest, meanest, most groveling measures to please his master and to fill the coffers of a soulless corporation."

"*Operative*—a person who is employed in a factory and who generally earns three times as much as she receives."

"*Contemptible*—for an overseer to ask a girl what her religious sentiments are when she applies to him for employment."

The importance of the factory magazines cannot be overemphasized. Workers smuggled them into the mills and they were eagerly read and passed along. These magazines stimulated and helped build the Female Labor Reform Associations of the 'forties.

The first and most important Female Labor Reform Association, organized in Lowell, Massachusetts by twelve factory girls, all of them workers in the cotton mills, began its career in January, 1845. Six months later, its membership had grown to five hundred, and it was growing steadily. "Our numbers have been daily increasing," said its president, Sarah G. Bagley, in May, 1845, "our meetings generally well attended, and the real zeal of the friends of equal rights and justice has kindled anew."[16]

The constitution of the Lowell Female Labor Reform Association provided that every member should pledge herself "to labor actively for reform in the present system of labor."* The Association conducted a

* Article 9 of the constitution declared: "The members of this association disapprove of all hostile measures, strikes, and turn-outs until all pacific measures prove abortive, and then that it is the imperative duty of everyone to assert and

tireless campaign to convince the public of the need for reform in the mills. A committee was appointed to expose and counteract the false impression created by the newspapers and corporation apologists. A regular "Female Department" was conducted in the *Voice of Industry*, and, in 1846, the Association was able to buy this labor journal. At the same time, it organized fairs, May parties, and social gatherings at which copies of *The Valentine Offering*, a collection of articles and poems written by the factory girls, were sold. It established an "Industrial Reform Lyceum," at which outstanding lecturers spoke to the factory girls on the need for the ten-hour day. The Association also published and distributed famous "factory tracts," which contained stirring poetry written by the factory girls.[17]

The Lowell Association did not, however, confine itself to "Valentine Offerings" and poetry. When the Massachusetts Corporation in Lowell ordered weavers to tend four instead of three looms, and at the same time reduced wages one cent a piece, the Association called a meeting of the factory girls to protest this order. At the meeting, the women workers drew up a pledge and resolved that they would not tend a fourth loom unless they received a wage increase in ratio to the increased work. They further resolved that any worker who signed the pledge and then violated it should have her name published in the *Voice of Industry* as a traitor to the working class. Every weaver who worked for the corporation signed the pledge, and not a single girl violated the agreement. The company was forced to rescind its order.

The Association exerted its influence in the political field as well. When a committee of the Massachusetts state legislature reported adversely on the demand for a ten-hour law, it attacked William Schouler, its chairman, as "a corporation machine or tool," and announced that it would campaign to defeat him for re-election. The campaign was successful, and after the election, the Association published a resolution expressing their "grateful acknowledgements to the voters of Lowell" for "consigning William Schouler to the obscurity he so justly deserves." [18]

Representatives of the Lowell Association attended mass meetings of factory girls in Manchester and Dover, New Hampshire, and in Fall River, Massachusetts and in each of these cities, Female Labor Reform Associations were organized.*

By means of the "factory tracts," the Lowell union also contacted

maintain that independence which our brave ancestors bequeathed us and sealed with their blood." (*Voice of Industry*, Feb. 27, 1846).

* In New York City, a Female Industrial Association was formed in March, 1845. Delegates from the following trades were represented in the organization: tailoresses, plain and coarse sewing, shirt makers, book folders and stitchers, cap makers, straw workers, dressmakers, crimpers, fringe and lace makers. Elizabeth Gray was the president. (*Working Man's Advocate*, March 8, 1945.)

factory girls in Western Pennsylvania and they, too, soon formed an association in their area. An appeal from the Lowell Association to all working women in America, urged them to organize for the struggle for a better life. It was necessary, said the appeal, to have "a complete union among the worthy toilers and spinners of our nation": "by organizing associations and keeping up a correspondence throughout the country, and arousing the public mind to a just sense of the claims of humanity we hope to roll on the great tide of reformation until from every fertile vale and towering hill the response shall be echoed and reechoed: Freedom—Freedom for all!" [19]

No study of this interesting labor organization would be complete without some reference to its tireless president, Sarah G. Bagley, an early pioneer among American working women. At the time the Lowell union was formed, Miss Bagley had been a weaver for more than eight years. For four of these years, she had, after working hours, conducted a free evening school for the factory girls who were so eager to acquire an education that they were called the "culture-crazy girls." [20]

Sarah Bagley had been a member of the famous Lowell Improvement Circles, where the girls had met and discussed the latest writings of leading authors and out of which had emerged the *Lowell Offering*. But Sarah Bagley soon discovered that it was futile to attempt to improve the mind after thirteen hours of speed-up in the mills; hence she became the most outspoken opponent of the *Offering*. She denounced it publicly as a corporation tool, and declared that it gave a completely false picture of conditions in the mills and the workers' reaction to these conditions. When the *Offering* finally expired in 1845, due to lack of support from the factory girls, Miss Bagley wrote: "Peace to its slumbers, and if it should ever witness a morn of resurrection, may it be prepared to take a high stand among the redeemed as the bold defender of the rights of the people." [21]

Miss Bagley constantly emphasized the need for labor newspapers. "The Press," she declared, "takes every effort to slander our efforts and ridicule our operations." It is not surprising, then, that she became one of the first woman labor editors in America. In May, 1846, Sarah Bagley took over the editorship of the *Voice of Industry*. She pledged her readers a heart "wrapped up in the cause of the oppressed," and her editorials proved that she kept her pledge. In one editorial, for example, she vigorously denounced corporation agents who threatened to blacklist all girls who joined the Lowell union: "Deprive us, after working thirteen hours, of saying our lot is a hard one! We will make the name of him who dares the act stink with every wind." [22]

Sarah Bagley contributed a large part to the labor movement of the 'forties. In March, 1845, she represented the Female Labor Reform

Association of Lowell at the convention of the New England Working-men's Association. She was not a silent delegate but eloquently appealed to the workingmen to help their sisters win the ten-hour day. Since working women could not vote, they appealed "in vain to legislators," so it remained for the men to answer the question of whether or not their sisters and daughters should also enjoy the blessings of shorter hours. The factory girls, said Miss Bagley, claimed "no exalted place" in the labor movement, but wished "like the heroines of the Revolution ...to furnish the soldiers with a blanket or replenish their knapsacks from our pantries." [23]

In behalf of the factory girls, she presented the Association with a silk banner on which was inscribed the motto: "Union for Power—Power to bless humanity."

THE TEN-HOUR PHILOSOPHY

The issue which led to the formation of the New England Working-men's Association and which united laboring men and women in the 'forties was the struggle for the ten-hour day. The New England workers had not shared the gains of the ten-hour movement of the 'twenties and 'thirties, and the vast majority of workers, mechanics, and operatives alike still worked twelve to fourteen hours each day.* In other sections, too, factory workers experienced the same oppression and some mechanics had been forced during the depression years to return to the "sun-up to sun-down" system familiar to the agricultural areas around the mill towns.

The ten-hour movement of the 'forties and 'fifties developed a philosophy of its own to justify its demand and to win public support. In order to benefit both the laborer and the community the worker needed more time for mental cultivation and bodily rest. The physical and mental effects of sunrise-to-sunset labor were so demoralizing that the average worker could never hope to devote his energies to anything but unceasing toil. "We hold the doctrine that masses were created to toil and the few to think in abhorrence," declared a meeting of workingmen in New Jersey. "All have minds to think as well as physical powers to labor, all should have time for the cultivation and enjoyment of the one as well as the exercise of the other." [24] And a group of journeymen house carpenters in Nashville, Tennessee, spoke their mind in 1847:

---

* A distinction should be made between the hours spent in the mills and the actual working time. A fourteen-hour day was in many cases a twelve-and-a-half hour working day when mealtime was deducted. Nevertheless there were operatives who worked fourteen or fifteen hours a day. (See Norman F. Ware, *The Industrial Worker, 1840-1860,* Boston and New York, 1924, pp. 129-30.)

"We are flesh and blood, we need hours of recreation. It is estimated by political economists that five hours labor per day by each individual would be sufficient for the support of the human race. Surely then we do our share when we labor ten. We have social feelings which must be gratified. We have minds and they must be improved. We are lovers of our country and must have time and opportunity to study its interests. Shall we live and die knowing nothing but the rudiments of our trade? Would the community of which we are members suffer loss because we are enlightened?" [25]

The community would definitely stand to gain if the working class was enlightened. Said the ten-hour advocates: The prosperity and welfare of the nation depended "mainly on the intelligence, virtue and energy of the working classes," for it was in proportion to the degree that their interests were promoted, their energies awakened, and their intellectual and physical faculties developed "that a nation becomes truly great and prosperous." [26]

A number of ten-hour advocates regarded the lessening of the hours of labor as "the primary social step" towards the achievement of a new social order. As the workers became more enlightened they would grasp more clearly the necessity for putting an end to the present economic system and join eagerly in the crusade for a co-operative society. "Let this [ten-hour] system be generally established," said the Fall River *Mechanic,* "and every reform which tends to the elevation of the laboring classes will meet with far better success than it will at the present time." [27]

And the possibilities for the enlightenment of the working masses, said the ten-hour proponents, were limitless. After all, one of the outstanding scholars in America, the man who knew all the languages of Europe and several of Asia, including Hebrew, Chaldaic, Samarian and Ethiopic, was Elihu Burritt, "the learned blacksmith." * Given the time for in-

---

* Burritt lectured to workers throughout New England on the value of intellectual training and other subjects. Especially was he anxious to eradicate the impression that lingered among some workers that the wealthier classes were superior beings. "Don't take off your hat in obsequious reverence to the Girards, Astors, or any speculating capitalists of the country," he said in lecture after lecture. "Who were they or who are the men that have succeeded them in the ranks of wealth? They are the oligarchy, are they, that own all the banks, warehouses, factories and shipping of the nation? Grant that! But why should this show of wealth impress you with a sense of inferiority as a class?" (Merle Curti, *The Learned Blacksmith,* pp. 3, 23, 34-35.)

Burritt's lectures to workers must be distinguished from the efforts of apologists for the capitalists to reach the laboring classes through the medium of lectures and impress upon them the thought that the poor were really the fortunate ones in American society. With great wealth in one's possession, said these spokesmen for

tellectual and moral culture other workers too could become "learned" and like Burritt contribute to the advancement of American civilization. Indeed, "let the mechanics have all but ten hours per day for rest and mental culture and they will soon be the predominant, the most influential class." [28]

These arguments the employers combatted in their own inimitable way. "Yes, I verily believe," said one mill owner, "there are a large number of operatives in our cotton mills who have too much spare time now." To reduce the working hours "would increase crime, suffering, wickedness and pauperism." The manager of a mill in Chicopee, Massachusetts, added: "It is not the hours per day that a person works that breaks him down, but the hours spent in dissipation. . . . The effect of the dimunition of the hours of labor would be to reduce wages, and in our opinion increase dissipation." * [29]

The contention that a reduction in working hours would result in a reduction in wages was discussed at considerable length by the ten-hour advocates. One group among them, led in the main by the intellectuals, felt that a shorter working day could be achieved only if the workers were willing to accept a corresponding reduction in daily pay. They argued, however, that such a reduction would only be temporary and that when the ten-hour system became universal, wages would again rise. Another group of ten-hour advocates—and by far the more influential one—held that a reduction in hours would not necessarily bring a reduction in daily wages. On the contrary, a dimunition in the number of hours worked would lead to an increase in wages. A shortening of the working week, they argued, was identical with a shortening of the supply of labor, and since wages were "governed by the great law of trade—the law of supply and demand," a shortening of the supply of labor would mean an increase in wages.[30]

There was also a difference of opinion among the ten-hour advocates as to the methods employed to secure the shorter working day. Some

the employers, one could still suffer the evils of poverty, by indulging wants which even ample means could not gratify. On the other hand, the poor worker could feel comparatively rich by indulging no wants which his means would not permit him to gratify. William Ellery Channing, the Unitarian preacher, was fond of reminding the workers that they had "the easiest lot" in life compared to the trials and tribulations of the wealthy who were always suffering "from eating too much." (See Catharine M. Sedgwick, *The Poor Rich Man, and the Rich Poor Man*, New York, 1836; and Elizabeth P. Peabody, *Reminiscences of Rev. Wm. Ellery Channing*, Boston, 1880, p. 415.)

* To meet the charge that shorter hours would only demoralize the workers, the Fall River *Mechanic* urged those who gained the ten-hour day to show its true effects by studying and learning. In addition, it advocated that the workingmen of Fall River "open and sustain an economical and useful Evening School." (Fall River *Mechanic*, May 18, Nov. 30, 1844.)

advocated legislative enactments only and called for the launching of a huge campaign to convince legislators that incessant toil was inconsistent with the health, happiness, and liberty of the laborer and with the welfare of the community. In accordance with this principle laws must be passed restraining employers from hiring workers for more than ten hours a day. Others believed that groups of workers should concentrate upon achieving an agreement with their employer and establishing the ten-hour day in their own shop or factory. Still others favored the adoption of methods used successfully by workers in England in their struggle for shorter hours. This plan of action was popularized in America by John C. Cluer, an English labor organizer who had come to this country early in the 'forties. It included three points: first, a convention be called of workers and manufacturers to discuss and agree on a program for the reduction of working hours; if the convention failed, a petition campaign to the legislatures should be instituted, and, finally, if that method also failed to bring results, a general strike or, as it was popularly called, a Second Independence Day be initiated. This general strike would take place on July Fourth on which day all New England workers would "declare their independence of the oppressive manufacturing power." [31] The selection of the Fourth of July for the beginning of this great upheaval, said the ten-hour advocates, was quite logical, for the movement was in keeping with the basic principle of the Declaration of Independence. "The all day system," declared the Fall River *Mechanic* of July 13, 1844, "does not allow the pursuit of happiness, and hence there is propriety in connecting with the Fourth your effort to reduce the hours of labor from an indefinite number to ten."

NEW ENGLAND WORKINGMEN'S ASSOCIATION

Throughout most of the period under discussion, this movement sought to attain the shorter working day by legislative enactment. In 1840 the ten-hour system had been established for Federal government employees by the executive order of President Van Buren. To do the same thing for employees of private concerns involved the state legislatures which had chartered them. The problem was to organize enough mass pressure to overcome the control exercised by the corporations over the legislatures.

The first important steps for the attainment of the ten-hour day by legislative enactment occurred in 1842 when the Ten-Hour Republican Association was formed by a group of New England mechanics. The organization immediately started a petition campaign to force the Massachusetts legislature to limit the working hours in the state. Most of the petitions did not refer specifically to the ten-hour day, but the Lowell petition which contained almost 1,600 signatures called definitely for a law which would require that manufacturing corporations "shall not employ persons to work more than ten hours a day." [32]

The Ten-Hour Republican Association initiated the campaign for the ten-hour day but it was too vague and local an organization to carry the movement to a successful conclusion. In the fall of 1844, however, a new labor organization, the New England Association of Working-men, came into being, which gave vigorous support to the shorter work-day crusade.

The Association was largely the product of the activities of the me-chanics of Fall River, Massachusetts. Early in 1844 these men organized a Mechanics' Association to further the ten-hour cause in their commu-nity. The Association distributed pledge cards binding the signers not to work for more than ten hours and conducted a number of strikes for the shorter working day. It was assisted in these activities by its auxiliary, the Ladies Mechanic Association of Fall River, in May 1844. The auxiliary conducted regular fairs, raising large funds to support the ten-hour movement.* The work of the ladies, wrote a workingman, reminded him of the Daughters of Liberty of revolutionary days. "We think," he went on, "that if our employers had seen the ladies, they would have said it is time to yield the question." [33] The Mechanics' Association itself paid a great tribute to the woman's auxiliary:

"We owe much of our success to their efforts in our behalf. Without their timely encouragement and assistance, many of our members would have given up the contest as hopeless. But when the opposition was arrayed against us, with all their unholy weapons, when defeat seemed to stare us in the face, the wives, and mothers and daughters of the mechanics have come forward to our aid, and bid us persevere in our work of reform. Mechanics, may we never forget their works of benefi-cence." [34]

In April, 1844, the Fall River Mechanics' Association set up a publish-ing committee to print a weekly paper, *The Mechanic,* "to advocate the cause of the oppressed Mechanic and Laborer in all its bearings." A few weeks later these militant mechanics released a circular to mechanics all over New England denouncing the long hours and consequent degra-dation of New England workingmen, and calling for united action to secure the ten-hour day and equal rights. Specifically, it issued a resound-ing summons for a general convention of New England workingmen to be held in the fall of 1844. No place or date for the convention was

* The following "card" appeared in the *Fall River Mechanic* of July 13, 1844: "The Fall River Mechanics' Association most gratefully acknowledge the reception of Three Hundred Dollars from the Ladies' Mechanic Association, the proceeds of their Fair. In behalf of the Association, Wilbur Read, President."

specified, however. But on July 20, the shoemakers of Lynn endorsed the call and suggested that the convention be held at Boston, August 21, 1844, and proposed that in addition to the ten-hour day the convention should take into consideration "the inadequate compensation of labor and to devise means whereby it can be improved." Owing to requests for further delay, the date for the convention was finally set for October 16, 1844.

The Fall River Mechanics' Association was not content merely to issue a call. As many communities in New England had no newspapers friendly to labor, it was necessary to bring the message of trade unionism to the workers of these communities and to make certain that representatives would attend the convention in the fall. Thus, the Association sent S. C. Hewitt, a mechanic, into the field as a lecturer. "The object of the Association in sending out a Lecturer at this time," it announced, "is to arouse the people in other places to the necessity of *organizing* and preparing to represent themselves in convention next September." [35]

Hewitt began his organizing tour on July 25 in Pawtucket, Rhode Island, and concluded it on August 24 in Taunton, Massachusetts. In one month he visited cities and towns in Massachusetts, Rhode Island, and Connecticut, and attended a convention of the Journeymen Cordwainers Association in Lynn where his lecture resulted in a vote of support for the convention and a promise to send delegates. Usually Hewitt's procedure was to enter a town in the morning, distribute handbills urging workers * to attend the evening's mass meeting, and then at night to lecture on the need for the laborer "to take the business of *reform* in his own hands and show himself a *man.*" Only by organizing into associations could they hope to gain the ten-hour day and remedy "the general evils of social life *as it is.*" After the lecture, the floor was always thrown open for discussion. On one occasion (in Providence, Rhode Island), Hewitt was surprised to find himself supported by a leading employer of the community, who told the meeting that he had already established the ten-hour system in his shops "and found it to work admirably" since the men did "full as much work as before, and operated much more cheerfully." In several towns, moreover, clergymen would take the platform and join Hewitt in urging the workers to organize to battle for shorter hours.

Following the lecture, steps would be taken to form an association so

---

* At first Hewitt called upon all workingmen to attend the meeting—expecting that working women would understand that they were included in the term. He discovered, however, that it was necessary to mention women specifically in the call. Working women, Hewitt believed, belonged in every labor movement being organized, "for females, in general, work harder than males, and hence should feel interested in any movement which aims at the amelioration of the working classes." (*Fall River Mechanic*, August 31, 1844.)

that delegates could be elected to the convention in the fall. In Milford, Connecticut, the audience was totally unreceptive and nothing could move them. "Such coldness in every place would have a tendency to discourage me in my labors," wrote Hewitt from Milford, "but I am truly thankful that such is not the fact—this is the only instance of the kind."

But there was plenty of coldness displayed by the employers and the authorities. Hewitt's handbills were confiscated and in more than one town he found all halls closed to him. In Worcester, Massachusetts, the chairman of the committee in charge of the Town Hall took one look at Hewitt's handbill in which the word "oppression" appeared and said that he could not allow the hall to be used to spread falsehood since he did not "see any oppression among the laborers of New England." In Rhode Island, Hewitt was refused halls on the ground that he was starting an "insurrection" and was guilty of "treason."

But Hewitt was not intimidated. In Norwich, Connecticut, he spoke in a hall used by a phrenologist and his audience was larger than usual. In Stonington, Connecticut, however, he could not even find a friendly phrenologist. "So I concluded," he writes in his *Journal*, "to call a meeting in the street." The following night the meeting was again held in the street.

"Several houses were applied for today, in which to hold our meeting, and every one *refused!* So we had to meet again in the *street!!* The audience was much larger to-night than the first. We organized the meeting as well we could *in the dark!* and took the necessary steps to the formation of an Association here." [36]

Thus in 1844—as at all other times in the history of the American labor movement—the organization of workers was the result of the tireless, unselfish activities of brave men and women who faced ostracism, rebuffs, and other forms of opposition to carry their message to the working class.

While Hewitt was holding forth in halls and streets, the labor press in Massachusetts and New Hampshire was spreading the news of the convention to other workers. And in the towns and cities of New England, mechanics' associations were enthusiastically endorsing the proposed convention. At the same time, utopian reformers, chief among whom were the Associationists (advocates of Fourierism) and the Land Reformers, pricked up their ears at the news that the workingmen of New England were to meet in convention, and prepared to converge on Boston to urge more "fundamental" reforms than the ten-hour day and higher wages.

Two hundred and seven delegates assembled in Faneuil Hall, Boston, on October 16, 1844, for the first New England Convention. Mechanics from the New England towns made up the vast majority, but there were delegates present from Brook Farm (George Ripley, Parke Godwin and L. W. Ryckman) and from the land reform movement (George Henry Evans, Thomas Devyr and Alvan E. Bovay). Both groups of reformers addressed the convention and stressed the need for adopting their particular program as a means of escaping the horrors of the onrushing factory system.

The convention bestowed its blessings on both programs. Over the opposition of some of the working class delegates, it adopted resolutions calling for the freedom of public lands and endorsing Fourierism. A unanimous vote, however, was given in favor of a resolution urging the establishment of producers' co-operatives as the method to put an end to "the present system of labor" in which capital secured the reward which should only belong to the laborer.

The convention adopted a resolution calling for a ten-hour law and organized a permanent association of New England workingmen to press for legislation that would prohibit any corporation from employing any person more than ten hours a day.

Unfortunately, the second convention, held in Lowell, on March 18, 1845, elected L. W. Ryckman president of the Association and George Ripley chairman of the executive committee.* This was a sure sign that nothing would be done in the legislative field. For, although both were sincere men, they were interested in a more "fundamental" reform than a shorter working day. In addition, Ryckman, a typical utopian, abhorred the use of any tactics that would antagonize the upper classes. "My object is not to array one class against another," he said sweetly, "but, by a glorious unity of interests, make all harmony and ensure universal intelligence, elevation and happiness." [37]

On May 28, 1845, the next convention of the newly organized Association met in Boston. The Associationists completely dominated the scene and most of the time was spent discussing the virtues of Fourierism. The ten-hour day was occasionally mentioned but solely in passing and nothing of a practical nature to advance the cause closest to the New England workingmen emerged from the convention.

By now, however, the workers were about fed up with the domination of their movement by utopian reformers. They had the greatest respect

---

* The convention adopted a constitution for the New England Association. The membership of the Association was to consist of delegates from all local associations who were to pay twenty-five cents into the general fund. Representation was as follows: one delegate for up to fifty members; one for every additional fifty up to five hundred; and thereafter, one for every one hundred members. Article 9 of the constitution read: "Female Labor Reform Associations shall be entitled to all the rights, privileges and obligations secured by this Constitution."

for their sincerity and devotion and agreed with their denunciations of the capitalist form of production, but they wanted immediate redress of grievances—not a paradise in the distant future. And they resented the fact that the reformers ignored their demand for shorter hours and were paralyzing the one organization which could achieve a ten-hour day. Sensing this attitude, the *Voice of Industry*, edited by Lowell labor leaders, called upon the utopians to re-evaluate their role in the New England Association.[38]

But the Associationists were determined to have their way. They still insisted that "nothing short of an entire revolution in society [could] remove the evils which the laboring people suffer." Minor questions like the ten-hour day were unimportant, said President Ryckman, and it was time the workers of New England realized that the Workingmen's Association "aimed at something more fundamental" than a shorter working day.[39] That the workers did not see it this way was of no importance.

However, the New England Workingmen's Association was, for a time, rescued from the reformers. By the time the Association met in Lowell on October 29, 1845, the Fourierist movement in America was on the decline, President Ryckman and the entire Brook Farm contingent not even attending the convention. The land reformers were also absent, having by this time lost interest in the New England labor scene. Working-class control of the New England Association was restored, and beginning with this convention the movement for a ten-hour day was revived. At subsequent conventions it was asserted in no uncertain words that the reduction of the hours of labor was "the great, prominent object of the workingmen of New England." * [40]

TEN-HOUR STRIKES

During this critical period in New England, an event of major importance was taking place in Western Pennsylvania. In the cotton mills of Pittsburgh and Allegheny City, factory girls were earning the magnificent sum of $2.50 for seventy-two hours a week. Unable to endure this any longer, on September 15, 1845, five thousand girls, described as the "prettiest girls and bone and sinew of Allegheny City and Pittsburgh,"

* Other issues, however, were not ignored. As we shall see below, the New England Workingmen's Association took a forthright stand in opposition to slavery. Moreover, at the Lynn Convention (January, 1846), the delegates expressed their opinion on a rumor of an impending war with England. "So far as regarding the laboring man on the other side of the water as our enemy and shooting him as such," they resolved, "we regard him as our friend and will do all in our power to better his condition." Norman J. Ware correctly refers to this declaration as "an early American advance toward internationalism." (*Young America*. December 13, 1845; *The Industrial Worker, 1840-1860*, p. 218.)

went on strike for the ten-hour day. They held out for almost a full month, but, desperate, some of the girls decided to go back to work. But they did not remain at work long. Strikers went from factory to factory, broke open the gates, seized the girls at the machines and dragged them outside. At the largest of the mills, Blackstock's factory, they were joined by what was known at that time as the "men's auxiliary." How it functioned and what happened at Blackstock's is described by an on-the-spot reporter of the Pittsburgh *Journal:*

"They were now in full force. A whole legion of men and boys accompanied them, as auxiliaries, to be used in case they were required. Thus prepared, flushed with conquest,...they marched to the scene of *the great struggle*—the Battle of Blackstock's Factory.

"On their arrival, they saluted the enemy with three shouts of defiance and an universal flourish of sticks and bonnets. After a minute or two spent in a reconnoitre, they moved forward in a solid column of attack, on the...pine gate of the yard.

"In a moment the gate was forced open. But the defenders were determined on a heroic defence, and the assailants were thrown back and the gate again closed. A second time the assault was made with a similar result.

"Both parties now took time for breath, and opened negotiations. The factory girls demanded the instant expulsion of the girls at work. The people inside obstinately refused the terms, and both parties again prepared to decide the matter by the uncertain chances of the field.

" 'They say they won't—let's try again!,' and encouraging each other with loud cries, the legions marched to the imminent breach. For a moment, the combat was a doubtful one. The garrison made a stubborn resistance—but what could you expect from pine boards? ... The gate gave way—'hurra! hurra!', and in a moment the yard was filled, the fortress was taken by storm, and the garrison were prisoners of war. ...

"We are informed that the manufacturers have expressed a great deal of dissatisfaction with reference to the conduct of the Police, on Monday, during the disturbances. It seems to us that this is unjust. It was utterly impossible for any ordinary police force to have maintained order. There were hundreds of the male friends of the operatives standing round— ready to interfere whenever it should become necessary.... 'Let 'em hit one of them gals if they dare, and we'll fetch them out of their boots!' said a grim double-fisted fellow on our right, while they were breaking open Blackstock's." [41]

The sight of hundreds of women daring to break open the factory gates and toss out the strikebreakers by main force antagonized the conservative middle class groups who believed that ladies should always behave like ladies. And so the factory girls found it impossible to gain public support, without which they were destined to fail—for they did not have the means to hold out for any length of time. The employers were adamant, contending that they would not decrease the working hours as long as New England mills continued to operate on a thirteen or fourteen-hour basis. They promised, however, that the moment the ten-hour day was instituted in the New England mills, they would introduce it in Pennsylvania.

The Pittsburgh girls turned to their sisters and brothers in the New England Workingmen's Association and urged them to intensify their fight for the ten-hour day, assuring them that in Western Pennsylvania arrangements had been made "for continuing the warfare." [42]

This appeal did not go unnoticed in New England. The members of the Workingmen's Association had anxiously followed the Pennsylvania strike for they were discussing at this very time the plan of action outlined by John C. Cluer. This plan, it will be remembered, provided for a conference between employers and workers to establish the ten-hour day by joint agreement, petitions to the legislatures if the conference failed, and finally—as a last resort—a general strike.

An effort had been made to get the manufacturers to meet with the workers in a convention and discuss the reduction of hours. The New England Workingmen's Association had even appointed a committee to arrange a conference for this purpose, but the employers ignored the request, and so point one in Cluer's program had failed. The question then arose as to what step should be taken next.

Some groups in the Association favored concentration on petitions and legislative action. But an important group advocated resort to strikes, culminating in a general strike, a second Independence Day, on July 4, 1846. Thus the Association adopted a resolution urging the local unions and associations "to commence raising a fund" to be used for the coming strikes for the ten-hour day. This plan was also favorably accepted at the Association's conventions. [43]

The Western Pennsylvania factory girls' strike in September, 1845, was regarded by the New England workers as the opening gun in the movement for a general strike, and they sent assurances of sympathy and support to the strikers. But the failure of the strike was fatal to the movement for a second Independence Day. The fact that 5,000 workers had been unable, despite their militant struggle, to gain a victory, discouraged the proponents of a general strike and lent weight to the arguments of those leaders who urged reliance on petitions and mass pressure. The girls in Lowell and Manchester were adamant in their resolve to continue with their plans and even set July 4, 1846, as the day for the general strike. However, the movement received little support.

TEN-HOUR LAWS

From this time on, the movement for the ten-hour day depended almost entirely on legislative action. Petitions, printed by the *Voice of Industry*, were forwarded to various towns in New England, where they were distributed by local workingmen's associations or female labor reform associations. After thousands of signatures were secured, the petitions were forwarded to the state legislatures with the added request that action be taken promptly to prevent the workers from hastening "on through pain, disease and privation down to a premature grave." [44]

In Massachusetts, this petition crusade resulted in the appointment by the state legislature of special committees to investigate conditions in the factories and to report on the need for legislation for shorter hours. But the legislature had taken care to appoint only corporation men to these committees and their reports were in keeping with the character of the bodies. One committee reported that its investigation had convinced it that "everything in and about the mills and the boarding houses appeared to have for its end health and comfort," and that it was "fully satisfied that the order, decorum and general appearance of things in and about the mills could not be improved by any suggestion of theirs, or by an act of the Legislature." * [45] Another committee admitted that there were abuses in the factory system and that working hours were too long, but felt that no legislation was necessary. "Labor," it declared, "is intelligent enough to make its own bargains and look out for its own interests without any interference from us." The evils in the factory system would be eradicated in due time through a "progressive improvement in art and science, in a higher appreciation of man's destiny, in a less love for money, and a more ardent love for social happiness and intellectual superiority." [46]

The committee was simply asserting in a legislative document what all the spokesmen for the wealthy were trying to impress upon the working classes and their allies among progressive reformers—that nothing could be done by the government or by the workers themselves to improve their conditions. "Legislation can do nothing," said R. C. Waterston in an address in 1844 on the causes and prevention of poverty, "combinations among the working classes could probably effect no permanent remedy. It must be left to the justice and mercy of the employer." [47]

Several states did yield to the workers' insistent demands for legislation to reduce the working hours. The first ten-hour law was passed by

---

* Nevertheless, evidence of the appalling plight of the workers and the terrible health conditions of the factories was revealed in the testimony of witnesses, and, when published, did much to destroy the myth concerning the so-called "Beauty of Factory Life."

the legislature of New Hampshire in 1847, and a year later Pennsylvania and Maine also passed ten-hour laws.

In urging the enactment of a ten-hour law, the legislative committee in New Hampshire argued that a shortening of the working day was advantageous to the employers for they "would realise a greater profit, even in less time, from laborers more vigorous and better able to work, from having had suitable time to rest." [48] Evidently the employers in New Hampshire and Pennsylvania were not entirely convinced by the logic of this argument for, at their insistence, clauses were inserted into the statutes which permitted employers to draw up special contracts with workers for more than ten hours. Even before the laws were passed, employers submitted these contracts to their workers and informed them that they had the alternative of either signing and continuing to work or refusing to sign and going jobless. They also threatened that the names of the workers refusing to sign would be sent to all the corporations in the district so that it would be impossible for them to gain employment in other factories.

In spite of the terror of the blacklist, the workers fought valiantly to preserve the ten-hour laws by agreeing among themselves not to sign the special contracts. Pledges were signed in many factories in New Hampshire and Pennsylvania, which stated:

"That on and after the 15th day of September next, we will work no more than the legal number of hours each day.

"That we will sign no contracts to work more than 10 hours per day.

"That to the support of these resolutions we pledge our lives and sacred honor." [49]

DECLINE IN NEW ENGLAND

The workers in New Hampshire were not able to maintain these pledges. The power of the corporations was too great. Workers who refused to sign were discharged, and when they went elsewhere to seek employment, they found all doors closed to them. Since the New England Workingmen's Association had ceased to be an effective labor organization, it could not support the workers in their determination not to sign special contracts. By 1847 the New England Workingmen's Association—now called the New England Labor Reform League—passed again into the hands of utopian reformers. The workers lost interest in the movement and in March, 1848, the organization came to an end.

The Female Labor Reform Associations came to the same end. In January, 1847, the name of the Lowell union was changed to the "Lowell Female Industrial Reform and Mutual Aid Society." The aim of the organization was to appeal to the "self-love" of the factory girls and to "their higher natures." Through enlightenment and education, the factory girls, "doomed to eternal slavery" under the capitalist system, would be brought together to end a "state of society which debases the masses to a level with the serfs of the old countries."

The language reveals an understanding on the part of working women of those days that their plight had its roots in the economic system.* But, like the utopians who influenced their thinking, the girls worked along lines which necessarily prevented them from putting their ideas into effect. They believed, for example, that through enlightenment and education alone, people could be rallied to support the immediate measures in the interest of the working class as well as a new social order.[50] But more than enlightenment was needed to cope with the power of the corporations.

UPSURGE IN PENNSYLVANIA

In Pennsylvania, however, the story was quite different. Here the influence of the utopians was negligible, and here, too, the workers had not allowed their militant spirit to wane. In 1848, corporations in Western Pennsylvania tried to force factory workers to sign special contracts permitting employers to extend the working hours beyond ten hours a day. The workers refusing to comply with this request, employers closed their factories and announced that they would not open them until the workers signed contracts permitting a twelve-hour day. They also threatened to move their machinery out of the state.

This was early in July, 1848. Three weeks passed and still the workers held out. Finally, toward the end of the month, about one hundred despairing workers agreed to sign the contracts and returned to work. "The factory opened," said a Pittsburgh paper, "steam was got up, and machinery started." The employers rejoiced too soon. They had quite forgotten what had happened in 1845. But the workers had not. Once again they marched to drive out the "scabs." The women strikers, armed with axes, began to hack away at the factory gate "with true Amazonian vehemence and vigor." Unable to cut their way into the yard because of iron supports on the gate, they decided to take the factory by storm. They rushed to the gate, tore off the boards, fell upon a detachment of Allegheny police, and captured the factory. The strike-breakers were forced to leave their benches and march out with the strikers.[51]

---

* The same understanding was revealed in a resolution adopted by the women loom weavers in Philadelphia in May, 1848. The resolution called for a revision of "the iniquitous system by which those who toil most receive least and those who toil least receive most," and resolved to "see labor organized on that basis preached by St. Paul so that if anyone would not work, neither should he eat."

Many of the girls were arrested and brought to trial, charged with destroying property. During the trial the girls made it quite clear that it had not been their intention to seize the factory; all they wanted to do was to get at the "scabs." "We went there to get our rights," said Mary Fulton; and Elizabeth Haggerty added: "We went to get the girls out; we went to get them out the best way we could." The girls were found guilty and sentenced to jail. The employers, of course, looked upon this as a victory and felt that the verdict would put an end to a strike which had already caused "serious injury to the whole community by deterring new investments and inducing withdrawal of some already made." [52]

The employers were mistaken. The strike lasted until August 28— when the ten-hour day became a fact, but the workers were forced to accept a 16 per cent reduction in wages. At first many of the girls refused to go back under these conditions. But after all the workers involved in the strike had discussed the issue fully, it was decided that the achievement of the ten-hour day was in itself a major victory and that the battle could now be continued to raise wages to the twelve-hour rate. Soon after, this too was accomplished.

ACTIVITY IN THE 'FIFTIES

Agitation for the ten-hour day continued during the 'fifties, but the movement was different from that of the preceding decade. In the 'forties, the agitation for ten-hour laws in Massachusetts had been carried on mainly by the workers themselves and the leadership had come from factory operatives and mechanics. In the 'fifties, however, the leadership was entirely in the hands of middle-class reformers and political figures.

Although the ten-hour movement of the 'fifties relied mainly on legislative enactments, collective agreements between employers and workers became more frequent. In 1853, for example, all factory workers in Media, Pennsylvania, won the ten-hour day "by joint contract between the employer and employed." At a mass meeting to celebrate this achievement, the workers appointed two of their leaders to make a tour of the New England states to lecture on the need to build strong unions and adopt collective bargaining procedure in the struggle for the ten-hour day. These delegates, said a reporter on the Lowell *American,* "made a good impression and helped the cause." [53]

The ten-hour movement of the 'fifties secured the enactment of a number of laws but, like those of the 'forties, they were meaningless because they either were not enforced or had the "special contract" feature. New Jersey in 1851 declared ten hours of work in certain industries to be a "legal day's labor," but made no provision for penalties to be enacted for working an "illegal" time. That same year Rhode Island passed a ten-hour law but was careful to specify that the ten-hour day was "legal" only when it was not "otherwise agreed by the parties." Two years later Connecticut followed suit and provided that "ten hours should be a legal day's labor in mechanical or manufacturing establishments unless otherwise agreed." [54]

After ten years of struggle, the workers in Massachusetts were not able to secure a ten-hour law. They could have attained the type of law adopted in New Hampshire—with the "special contract" feature attached. Indeed, Linus Child, a leading factory agent and a power in the legislature, declared that he and his colleagues "had no objection to a law similar to the New Hampshire statute." It might cause some inconvenience, but it certainly could not be dangerous. "I had no doubt," he declared, "I could easily make such bargains with our help as to the hours of labor as would be entirely satisfactory to the proprietors of the mills." [55]

But the workers in Massachusetts would have nothing to do with "special contract" laws. What they wanted was a law stating flatly that ten hours was the working day. So, to obtain such a law, the movement in Massachusetts turned from reliance on petitions to organized political action. In 1851, the New England Industrial League, a revival of the labor reform associations of the 'forties, came into existence and called upon the workingmen of Massachusetts to organize and send delegates to a state convention to prepare for the fall elections. Nothing in the nature of statewide political action stemmed from this convention, but in Lowell, Benjamin F. Butler carried a town election on a ten-hour platform, winning in the face of the corporations' warnings that: "Whoever employed by this corporation votes the Ben Butler [ten-hour] ticket on Monday next will be discharged."

Encouraged by the results in Lowell, the leaders of the New England Industrial League—William S. Robinson, editor of the Lowell *American,* and William S. Young, former editor of the *Voice of Industry*—called a Ten-Hour State Convention for Massachusetts. At the convention, held on September 30, 1852, a State Central Committee was formed and authorized to prepare an address to the public; to get candidates running for office to pledge their support of the ten-hour movement; to collect funds for an educational campaign; and to organize local societies. No move was made to form an independent labor party, the convention deciding to confine its "organized political action" to the securing of written pledges from candidates of all parties to support a truly effective law to shorten the working day. All candidates were to be required to reply to the following question:

"Are you in favor of the Legislature prohibiting all corporations in the State from employing any person in laboring more than ten hours in one day; and will you use your best efforts to secure the passage of such a law." [56]

The election of 1852 in Massachusetts, in so far as the mill towns were concerned, revolved almost solely about the ten-hour issue. The candidates for governor and lieutenant governor signed the ten-hour pledge, as did the entire coalition (combined Whigs and Democrats) ticket for the Senate. The Whig Party itself bowed before the sweep of the ten-hour movement and announced that it was "desirous of the passage of a law . . . establishing ten hours of labor to be a day's work, not for one class or division of society, but for all the people of the commonwealth." After the elections, the ten-hour champions declared that they now controlled one-tenth of the lower house of the legislature. This was a significant advance but not enough to break the control of the corporations. Nor did the huge petition campaign which followed the election of 1852 succeed in curbing the corporations' influence in the legislature. In 1855 a legislative committee did actually report in favor of a compulsory ten-hour law, but as Charles Cowley points out in his *History of Lowell:* "The corporation managers in Boston . . . killed the bill by secretly buying up some of the most influential of its advocates." [57]

If the factory workers in Massachusetts had had greater political influence, the results of the legislative campaigns would probably have been different. Although men were entering the factories in greater numbers during the 'fifties, the majority of the factory workers were still women who could not vote. In 1853, for example, the Merrimac Manufacturing Company in Lowell hired 1,650 females as compared to 650 males. This was the typical ratio in the textile mills of this period, and throws a good deal of light upon the limitations imposed upon the political movement for the ten-hour day. Also, not all the men could vote, for many were immigrants who had recently come to America. In addition, the power of the corporations over the ballot box was intensified after 1853, when the Whigs in the state legislature repealed a secret-ballot law on the ground that it "insulted the manliness and independence of the laboring man." [58]

Although the ten-hour movement did not succeed in enacting a law, it did force many employers to grant important concessions. In an effort to reduce the ten-hour vote in the coming fall elections, employers in September, 1852, lowered the working day to eleven hours in the machine shops of five important industrial towns.* The following year

* The hours of women workers remained unchanged, however. Women, after all, could not vote.

the ten-hour system became "all but universal" in Worcester. Even the textile factories were forced to yield to this agitation, and in September, 1853, the corporations of Lowell, Lawrence, Salem, and other cities reduced the working day to eleven hours. Thereafter, as a general rule, the working day in the textile factories of Massachusetts lasted from 7 A.M. to 7 P.M., with 45 minutes for dinner, and on Saturdays the mills closed earlier.

POLITICAL ACTION IN NEW JERSEY

An extremely interesting and significant political movement in connection with the struggle for the ten-hour day got under way in New Jersey in 1847. Although by this time skilled workers in the trades had already gained the ten-hour day, they joined enthusiastically with factory workers and unskilled laborers to secure a law that would cover all industries in the state. Though the ten-hour issue was the spearhead of the movement, many other progressive reforms were advanced at the very same time. For example in September, 1847, a mass meeting was held in Trenton at which, in addition to recognizing ten hours as a full day's toil for every worker in the state, resolutions were also adopted calling upon the state legislature to pass laws restraining persons from employing children in factories for more than eight hours a day, providing opportunities for every child to obtain a good common school education. One resolution demanded the repeal of a state law which required property qualification for a juror, and another urged that "the state revenues derived from the Camden and Amboy Railroad, and Delaware and Raritan Canal companies should be appropriated for the support of public schools." After expressing these demands, the meeting asserted: "That we believe the above resolutions to embrace important Democratic principles, and that we will not support men for public offices who will not support them.[59]

Early in 1848, the Workingmen's Association of Trenton was formed by the "Friends of the Ten-Hour System." Throughout 1848 and 1849, the organization continued to call mass meetings to advance the ten-hour cause and such issues as the demand for the elimination of property qualifications for jurors and elective officers. At these meetings it was made quite clear that workingmen would not support candidates for the legislature who were not in favor of their measures.[60]

When the legislature, which convened in 1850, refused to adopt any of the workingmen's measures, the Trenton workers denounced that body and appointed a committee to address their fellow workingmen throughout the state on the advisability of calling a state convention. In addition, the workingmen of New Jersey were urged to form clubs and to vote for no man for any office who was not in favor of the reform measures.[61]

Both parties went out of their way to win the labor vote. The Democratic Party platform included several of the workingmen's demands and especially pledged to support a ten-hour law. In addition, the party nominated Charles Skelton, a shoemaker and leader of the workingmen's movement in Trenton, to represent that city in Congress. The Whig Party came out for a "free school system as will educate all," abolition of the freehold qualification for public office and for jurors, "equal taxation of every species of property protected by the laws," a law protecting the wife and offspring "of the honest debtor from the rigorous exactions of the oppressing creditor," and one "regulating the hours of labor in manufactories and protecting children working therein." [62]

Had not the existing parties taken such a stand it is likely that the workingmen of Trenton would have launched an independent labor party, as there was considerable agitation for such action. Instead the workingmen decided to interrogate candidates on both tickets as to their opinions on the measures advocated by labor. The replies proved that the politicians were beginning to respect labor's political strength in the community—for all candidates indicated that they would cast their votes in the legislature for the measures advocated by the Workingmen's Association. [63]

The election resulted in a victory for the Democratic Party—which meant that Skelton was elected to Congress. At the 1851 session of the state legislature, many of the reforms demanded by the Workingmen's Association of Trenton were enacted into law.* Leading the list was a law establishing the ten-hour day throughout the state.

RESULTS OF THE TEN-HOUR MOVEMENT

The achievement of ten-hour legislation in New Jersey was the result of day-to-day activities conducted by the working class—activities which continued in the face of heart-breaking disappointments. And this in essence is the whole story of the ten-hour movement during the years 1840-1860. A great deal of energy and organization went into the struggle to secure a shorter working day. To some historians the results of the ten-hour movement seem rather meager in view of the time and energy expended. But the movement was of great significance. It united the

---

* The Workingmen's Association of Trenton did not go out of existence after the legislation it sponsored was enacted. It met regularly every Saturday night to discuss leading political issues of the day. At one of these meetings, it is interesting to note, the discussion centered about the question: "Should the State take the works at the expiration of the present Charter of the Railroad and Canal companies?" (Trenton Daily *State Gazette,* May 12, 1852.)

working class—skilled and unskilled, mechanics and factory operatives —and created a strong tradition of organization. Although many workers had not yet benefited by the ten-hour day by the time of the Civil War, the movement for the ten-hour day in the years 1840-1860 was responsible for a distinct reduction in the number of hours normally worked each week.* By 1860, ten hours had become the standard working day for most skilled mechanics and unskilled laborers other than factory workers, although their working hours had also been reduced. In most Massachusetts factories, hours were reduced from thirteen to eleven,† and in New Hampshire, as a result of several militant strikes in which as many as 5,000 workers were involved, employers were forced to institute a ten and five-sixths hour working day.[64] It is true that machines were speeded up, yet the change from a thirteen or fourteen-hour day to a ten or eleven-hour day was a great step forward for the working class.

In 1830 the average working day in America had been twelve and a half hours. Thirty years later, the average working day was eleven hours. This reduction was not the result of a benevolent disposition of employers. It came because the workers had organized and fought militant campaigns. And with shorter hours, the workers could now devote more time and energy to strengthening their organizations for future campaigns to achieve a still shorter working day.

* The following table taken from the *10th Census*, vol. XX, p. XXVIII, is one of many items that could be cited to indicate this trend towards the reduction of hours worked each day.

Working Hours Each Day, 1840-1860

Year	Establishments Total number reporting	8 to less than 11		11 to less than 13		13 to less than 14	
		number	per cent	number	per cent	number	per cent
1840	69	36	52.2	25	36.2	8	11.6
1845	103	60	58.2	33	32.0	10	9.7
1850	173	104	60.1	63	36.4	6	3.5
1855	250	161	64.4	84	33.6	5	2.0
1860	350	235	67.1	107	30.6	8	2.3

† In some parts of the state, however, the thirteen-hour working day prevailed. in the factories until 1865.

CHAPTER 12

Trade Unions and Labor Struggles in the Fifties

The decade of the 'fifties witnessed a number of important developments in the labor movement other than those just described. During these years skilled workers in the manufacturing branches of industry and the building trades in many cities and towns laid the foundation of the labor movement which was to burst forth in its full strength during and after the Civil War. Although they were not indifferent to other issues, these workers were mainly concerned with the working conditions in their shops or factories, the wages paid by their employers, the hours of work, the kind of men their foremen were, the control of apprentices, the right to organize without being charged with conspiracy, mechanics' lien laws and anti-store order laws. The unions they organized formed only part of the larger labor movement of the period, but they were to give a sense of permanency to the struggles of the working class and to lend strength to the economic and political activities of labor. Represented primarily by local unions, workers during this decade also began to conduct their struggles through loosely formed nationals which in due time were to lead the way in the formation of a national labor federation.

LABOR CONDITIONS

While money wages rose during the 'fifties as a result of trade union struggles, real wages declined because of the great increase in the cost of living following the discovery of gold in California, and the dumping of $50,000,000 in specie on the nation's money market in a single year. From 1840 to 1860 prices increased 14 per cent. In only two industries—metal trades and woodworking—did wages keep on a level with the increased prices.[1] The *New York Tribune* of March 27, 1851, published a cost of living budget which estimated $10.57 as the minimum weekly budget for a family of five. Beside food, clothing, rent, and fuel, the only other expenditure provided for was "furniture and utensils, wear and tear," twenty-five cents, and newspaper, twelve cents. Horace Greeley remarked:

"I ask, have I made the workingman's comfort too high? Where is the money to pay for amusements, for ice cream, puddings, trips on Sunday up or down the river, in order to get some fresh air; to pay the doctor or apothecary, to pay for pew rent in the church, to purchase books, musical instruments?"

The following day wage scales show that Horace Greeley was not too extravagant in his estimates:[2]

Building		Iron, Steel and Metals	
Bricklayers	$1.88	Catchers, bar mills	$ .61
Carpenters	1.74	Roughers, bar mills	1.63
Joiners	1.74	Laborers	.89
Engineers	1.38	Blacksmiths	1.56
Hod carriers	1.00	Boilermakers	1.28
Masons	1.60	Machinists	1.37
Painters	1.73	Millwrights	1.63
Plasterers	1.75	Moulders	1.41
Plumbers	1.90	Pattern makers	1.41
Stone cutters	2.00		

Many women workers were fortunate if they earned more than two dollars a week in the 'fifties. "The worst feature about seamstresses' 'wages,'" said a report in the New York Tribune, "is the all too prevalent fashion of those who employ them never giving them their pay."[3]

The living quarters of the workers reflected their earnings. Henry David Thoreau was shocked to discover unskilled laborers in New England "living in sties, and all winter with an open door for the sake of light, without any visible, often imaginable, wood-pile, and the forms of both old and young are permanently contracted by the long habit of shrinking from cold and misery, and the development of all their limbs and faculties is checked."[4] Conditions were no better in New York City. Thousands lived in tenement houses which were no more than a collection of moldy walls, while at least twenty thousand people made up New York's cellar population.

LOCAL TRADE UNIONS

Workers were soon picking up the dropped threads of organization. At a workingmen's convention in New York City in June, 1850, delegates from forty-three trade unions were present. It was reported on the floor that the journeymen tailors were the only mechanics in New York still unorganized. Reports from Boston, Philadelphia, Newark, and Trenton told of organizing drives in those cities. Seamen from California spoke of the growth of trade unions in San Francisco. By August 1853, San Francisco had unions among the carpenters, painters, tanners, shipwrights and caulkers, longshoremen, tailors, teamsters, printers, bricklayers, steamship and steam boat firemen and coal passers, blacksmiths, riggers, and stevedores.[5] For the first time in American history, trade unionism stretched from coast to coast.

The newly organized unions called strikes, many of which were successful in raising the wage level. By 1854 strikes of workingmen became a regular feature of life in the nation's industrial centers. "Each spring," declared the *New York Tribune* of April 20, 1854, "witnesses a new struggle for enhanced wages in some if not most of the trades of this and other cities." Conservative organs charged that "the mania . . . spreading far and wide" was part of an international conspiracy which had "commenced in England," and had as its objects the overthow of sound government and private property.[6] These journals were promptly reminded by the more liberal press that the strike wave arose from basic contrasts in American society. Said the *Rochester Daily Union* of April 25, 1853, in an editorial entitled, "Restlessness of the Working Population":

"Gold has been flowing in, the Paper Money system has been expanding, and as an inevitable consequence, the price of almost everything produced or consumed by the working classes has gone up; but the price of Labor itself . . . has remained pretty nearly where it was years ago. . . . It is not less clear that those who buy Labor at the old prices and sell at the present enhanced prices, gain precisely as much as labor loses, taking the prices which ruled before the expansion as the proper standard of comparison. This is the main reason why vast fortunes are made by manufacturers and more particularly by sagacious operators in produce and real estate, when prices are advancing. . . . And it is this class of operators generally, whom you will first hear declaiming against strikes, and demanding that the law against combinations to obstruct trade and commerce, shall be rigorously enforced against those who resort to the only expedient they know of, to get an equitable advance of wages."

By 1854 skilled mechanics had raised their wages through militant trade union struggle to 25 per cent above the level of 1850. This militancy was well expressed by the bricklayers and plasterers of New York City in 1850 when they announced on May 23, 1850 that "after years of comparative slavery to the will of the capitalists and employers, [they] deem it a duty they owe ... to themselves and families, to unite together as an organized body for their mutual protection, for the purpose of obtaining a fair remuneration for their labor—such remuneration to be made permanent and uniform and not subject to the caprice of employers to take advantage at any time of our necessities or the scarcity of employment." "We," they argued, "like the rest of the working classes of the community, have rights. Our labor is the only commodity we bring into the market—it is our capital, our all, and we maintain, so long as we submit to the purchaser placing his own price upon our labor, we submit to the basest species of servitude." [7]

As in the 'thirties, American workers realized that sporadic struggles during crises could not secure adequate wages for their labor; hence they tried to build more permanent organizations by putting them on sounder financial bases. Hardly had they begun before the depression of 1854 broke the unions to which more than 200,000 members belonged. When the local unions began to revive in the spring of 1855, they were careful to create permanent relief funds. Before these funds could grow appreciably, the crisis of 1857 smashed most of the unions, though more unions than ever before survived as a result of their relief funds. By 1860 local unions were flourishing again only to be sharply checked by the secession of the southern states.

The history of the local unions of the 'fifties is one of shortlived organization and oft-repeated reorganization. But the factor which distinguished the labor movement of the 'fifties from that which preceded it was that at no time was the thread completely lost, nor was it thereafter ever to be completely lost.

The trade unions of the 'fifties were exclusive craft unions composed of skilled mechanics. Unskilled workers found it almost impossible to join these unions, and several of them such as printers, hotel waiters, shoemakers, and tailors excluded women from the unions and the trades. Some unions, however, allowed wives or daughters of members to work in shops controlled by the societies.*

Like their predecessors of the 'thirties the new unions concerned themselves with apprenticeship rules, initiation fees, wage standards, collective

---

* Some unions discovered during strikes the folly of excluding women from membership, and accordingly revised their hostile attitude towards working women. The Journeymen Tailors' Union of Cleveland called upon the very women they had excluded to assist them during a strike. "Some of the employers in the Tailoring business," they appealed, "have refused the demands of the men, on the ground of being able to hire the sewing women at their own prices. Therefore, Ladies, *Strike for Your Rights!*" The ladies struck, but reminded the men that one good turn deserved another. Thereafter the Tailors' Union of Cleveland allowed women to join. (See *Cleveland Herald,* August 19, 29, 1850.)

bargaining, and strike funds. Co-operative and mutual benefit problems were still an important part of union business in the early years of the decade. Gradually the skilled workers extricated their unions from the influence of the utopians, and concentrated on immediate trade union demands. In many ways the unionism of the 'fifties was more advanced than that of the 'thirties. Dues were collected systematically, and strike funds were accumulated. Single men were allowed five dollars a week tramping money, and married men received three dollars a week in addition to a dollar and a half for a wife and a half a dollar for each child under ten years. A number of unions rented halls where meetings were regularly held to conduct the business of the organization.

Sometimes the union hall served as a hiring hall or "house of call" where unemployed workers could register for jobs and employers could come for men. One of the leaders in the Operative Bakers' Union of New York was a Scotsman who had been active in the trade union movement in Scotland where "houses of call" had been set up by many unions. No doubt that it was through his influence that the Bakers' Union in July, 1850, inserted the following notice in New York newspapers:

"To Boss Bakers. The Operative Bakers' Union House of Call ... is now open at 127 Grand Street daily, from 6 A.M. to 9 P.M. and on Sundays from 3 till 9, and a keeper is always in attendance to give every facility to Bosses from city or country, either visiting or writing the House for men." [8]

The most important advance made by the trade unions of the 'fifties was that of collective bargaining. Though the unions of the 'twenties and 'thirties had disappeared, their achievements in collective bargaining were not forgotten. In 1847 a collective agreement was signed between the master carpenters and the Journeymen Carpenters' Society of Trenton, New Jersey. Commenting upon this agreement, the *Trenton Daily State Gazette* of April 24, 1847, praised the employers for their enlightened attitude in recognizing the right of workers to bargain for better living standards. "Men should always have a fair compensation for their labor," it continued, "and we believe it is seldom that they demand more."

As soon as they were organized, the unions of the 'fifties began to apply the principles of collective bargaining to the whole trade in order to establish a uniform wage scale for all workers. To win such an agreement unions would draw up a wage schedule which they regarded as fair and then insert notices in the press inviting "all generous employers" to meet with their committees to discuss the proposed wage schedule and negotiate an agreement binding on both parties.[9] The following is a typical notice:

"To the Merchant Tailors of New York—Gentlemen, You are respectfully requested to attend a meeting of delegates from the Journeymen Tailors' Society to be held at the Shakespeare Hotel on Monday, September 16 [1850], at ten o'clock for the purpose of discussing matters of mutual interest to both parties." [10]

Early in 1850 the Printers Union of New York appointed a committee to investigate labor conditions in the trade. Weekly earnings, wages of boys, number of hours of work, number of men employed, prices paid for different kinds of work, time and method of payment, and working conditions were investigated. This inquiry covered eighty offices, employing 850 journeymen and 300 boys, or about 50 per cent of the workers employed in the printing industry in New York. Using these facts the Printers Union drew up a careful report upon working conditions and advanced recommendations for improving them. Great stress was placed on the securing of a uniform wage scale throughout the city.[11]

In May 1850, the Printers Union delegated another committee to sound out employers on the question of an agreement that would establish a fair wage scale for all workers in the trade. The union took this step after a special committee appointed to study the question had "found a disposition to adopt any measures calculated to benefit the trade, quite as general among the employers as among the men." On October 26, 1850, employing printers and a union committee representing the stereotypers met at Styman's Hotel in New York City, and at the end of the meeting the employers handed a brief statement to the press announcing that they had accepted the wage scale demanded by the union.[12]

An analysis of many of the strikes in 1853 reveals that the employers took advantage of every chance to break the collective agreements. When the unions went under during the crisis of 1854, the agreements lapsed. Although the unions had to repeat their struggles for collective agreements, they were helped by their previous experience and the precedents of written agreements.

IMMIGRANT LABOR

One of the most serious problems facing organized workers in the 'fifties was the use of immigrant labor to destroy established wage scales. During the 'forties and 'fifties one of the greatest mass migrations of labor in modern times came to our shores. From 1840 to 1850, 1,713,251 immigrants arrived, while the number from 1850 to 1860 came to 2,598,214. Of the population of New York City in 1860, 47.62 per cent were foreign

born; of Chicago, 49.9 per cent; of Philadelphia, 28.93 per cent; of Pittsburgh, 49.99 per cent; of St. Louis, 59.66 per cent.

Many native American workers viewed this wave of immigration with
fear and hostility. The immigrant worker, protested American mechanics, comes to this country willing to "work for fourteen and sixteen hours
per day for what capital sees fit to give him." [13] "There are persons," said
the *Harbinger* of January 10, 1846, "who are constantly watching for
German emigrants who can work at cabinet making, even going on
board the ships before the emigrants have landed, and engage them for a
year at $20 or $30 and their board, or the best terms they can make."

These fears were carefully exploited by nativist politicians and newspapers as well as by employers who worked to split the unity of their
workers. Nativist propagandists during the 'forties and 'fifties blamed the
declining living standards on the immigrants. American workers, they
said, could not compete with foreigners who "feed upon the coarsest,
cheapest and roughest fare—stalk about in rags and filth—and are neither
fit associates for American laborers and mechanics nor reputable members
of any society." [14]

Some workers believed such propaganda, and not a few joined the
bigoted crusades against the foreign-born. Associations were formed to
advocate changes in the naturalization laws to make it more difficult for
the foreign-born to become citizens, and to check the immigration of
labor. Most influential among these workingmen's organizations was
the Order of United Americans, set up in New York in 1844 "as a
benevolent and patriotic society which promised to protect its members
both against a poverty-stricken old age and immigrant competition."
Only American-born workers could become members. Its women's auxiliary, the United Daughters of America, was formed in March, 1845.
The Order of United Americans had chapters in sixteen states and by
1855 claimed a membership of fifty thousand. It published a weekly newspaper, the *Order of United Americans,* and the *Republic, a Monthly
Magazine of American Literature, Politics and Art.* Both publications
attacked immigrant labor. [15]

Some native American workers never abandoned their prejudices, and
played a part in the anti-Catholic, anti-foreigner Know-Nothing Party
which arose in the middle 'fifties, but gradually most American workers
began to realize that it was as futile to restrict immigration to the United
States, "as it would be for a man to prevent the world from making its
accustomed revolutions." [16] On December 15, 1849, *America's Own,* a
leading labor paper, made this appeal:

"American mechanics, you who feel a real interest to benefit your
fellowmen, recollect that *you must unite as mechanics and as mechanics*

only.... The feeling of animosity which exists against foreign mechanics was originally started by employers to distract your attention from measures of importance and which would ultimately prove of real practical benefit to you."

Many unions worked out a program for the immigrant problem. The Operative Bakers' Union of New York City stated in its constitution that one of its reasons for existence was "to advise and protect all newly-arrived immigrant bakers." The smiths and wheelwrights of New York City declared in their constitution that "counsel, aid and procuring work for newly-arrived mechanics," was an issue which no American worker could ignore. Some unions went further. To prevent the abuse of immigrant workers by employers, they inserted advertisements in the principal papers of Europe, and passed out handbills before immigrant boarding houses to inform the newly arrived workers where to "get work at adequate wages, and to prevent their getting into the clutches of work-usurers." Usually the immigrants were urged to come to the union before seeking employment in order to secure good wages and at the same time assist in preserving conditions already gained by workers in the trade.[17]

In some of the trades the different nationalities formed separate unions, co-operating with each other when taking important action. Quite often several nationalities united within the same labor organization, as in the Upholsterers Union in New York which had among its membership in 1850 German-American, Irish-American, French-Canadian, English, and native American workers. The Tailors' Union of New York was made up of native American and German-American workers. At first they were not on the best of terms, but police brutality, impartial as to a worker's national origin, during a strike made for greater understanding. German tailors paraded outside the police station in protest against the imprisonment of their brother Americans. "We did not expect to find in this free country," said one of their placards, "a Russian Police, nor do we believe the people will sustain these officials in their evident abuse of power."[18]

Since many Irish immigrants were unskilled, they found it difficult to become members of the exclusive craft unions of the 'fifties. Though most of them had little previous experience in trade unionism, their generations of struggle in their native land had prepared the Irish workers for militant action in America. It is true that these activities often were vigorous outbursts against oppression which left no permanent organization. Few workingmen were as militant as the Irish canal and railroad workers in their strike struggles. Employers tried to justify their vicious help-wanted advertisements which announced "No Irish need apply," by saying, "When they receive employment, are not they the first to insist on higher wages [and] in the Cant language, to strike?"[19]

ENGLISH INFLUENCES

A considerable number of immigrants who came from England and Germany contributed their trade union experience to the labor movement in America. The Fall River mulespinners, all of whom had belonged to trade unions in England, spread the principles of trade unionism throughout the textile centers of New England. In the winter of 1850 the mulespinners of Fall River, Massachusetts, conducted a militant strike against a wage reduction. They organized a union, collected $20,000 for their strike fund by sending delegates to other New England textile towns, and with the help of the weavers started the publication of the *Trade Union and Fall River Weavers' Journal.* After six months of struggle, the strike was lost and the spinners were forced to seek employment elsewhere. And wherever they went, they carried with them the principles of unionism.

However, the mulespinners of Fall River were soon to reorganize their union, and in 1857, they went out on strike for a wage increase. They won a partial victory at once, and gained all of their demands by 1860. The Amalgamated Mulespinners Association formed in 1860 was a direct result of the work of the British spinners who had disseminated the ideas of organization throughout the New England textile towns.[20]

The influence of British trade unionists was especially strong in the mining regions where low wages and the system of paying wages by orders drawn upon company stores caused considerable discontent. The first miners' unions in America were organized by Englishmen who had been active in British unions. John Bates, an English miner who had been active in the Chartist movement, led the miners in Schuylkill County, Pennsylvania, when they formed the first miners' union in America. It was named the Bates Union, after its founder and president. In the spring of 1849 the Bates Union, 5,000 strong, started the first organized strike in the anthracite region to secure higher wages and the abolition of the store order system. The employers were forced to agree to the selection of a joint committee representing the union and the mine owners to which the issues were submitted. An agreement satisfactory to the union was suggested by the committee.

Following the strike, Bates was employed by the union as its field agent to organize the miners. His allowance was $12 a week and a horse and buggy. Before long he capitulated to the employers when in 1849 he introduced a resolution to the effect "That we believe our interests and the interests of our employers are so connected and identified that it would be impossible to separate them ..."[21] By the middle of 1850 the union was dead.

The tradition of unionism, however, was not dead, and in 1861 the

American Miners Association, an industrial union, was organized. Daniel Weaver, the founder of the union and a former Chartist, declared in an address in 1861 that the "necessity of an association of miners, *and of those branches immediately connected with mining operations,* having for its objects the physical, mental and social elevation of the miner, has long been felt by the thinking portion of the miners generally." Weaver stressed the need for unity of all national groups within the union: "One of America's immortals has said, 'To me there is no East, no West, no North, no South'; and I would say, Let there be no English, no Irish, Germans, Scotch or Welsh." [22]

THE GERMAN-AMERICAN LABOR MOVEMENT

In some communities German workers were the leading groups in the trade union movement. The St. Louis labor movement of the 'fifties was led by a group known as the 48'ers, referring to the Germans who fled their native land during the reaction which followed the defeated revolution of 1848. Too often German workers in other cities adopted a rigid and sectarian approach to the American workers, regarding them as politically immature, and not worth the time and energy involved in surmounting language barriers to reach them. Accordingly, the German workers set up their own trade union and co-operative movement. With the arrival of more astute leaders, the German labor organizations were fairly well integrated with other working class movements.

Leadership of the German-American labor movement was first in the hands of Herman Kriege who came to America in 1845. Kriege had been associated with Karl Marx and Frederick Engels in Europe, but he lost their confidence when he unreservedly joined the land reform movement and took an active part in the National Reform Association founded by George Henry Evans. Kriege's influence in America soon disappeared.

In 1850 this leadership passed to Wilhelm Weitling who had arrived in this country late in 1846. Weitling had taken an active part in the revolutionary movement in Europe, and in 1846 had joined the German Workingmen's Society to which Marx and Engels belonged. He had come to America at the invitation of a group of German land reformers but before long he returned to his native land to fight in the Revolution of 1848. The revolution was short-lived and in 1849 Weitling returned to the United States. Here he started the publication of a labor paper, *Die Republik der Arbeiter* (the *Republic of the Working Men*), and helped to centralize the various German labor organizations. Under his guidance the Central Committee of the United Trades in New York was formed in April, 1850. The amalgamation meeting was made up of delegates representing the following organizations: the bakers, shoemakers, cabinet makers, tailors, upholsterers, turners, carvers, mechanics, bonnet makers, and furriers. Representatives also came from a branch of the American Protective Union, the Social Reform Union, and from labor unions in Williamsburgh and Newark. The total membership represented in the Central Committee of United Trades was about 2,400.

Similar bodies were organized in other cities, and a movement arose calling for a general workingmen's convention of German workers. A call for such a convention went out in September, 1850, and in the following month the first national convention of German-American workers was held in Philadelphia. Representatives from labor unions came from St. Louis, Baltimore, Pittsburgh, Philadelphia, New York, and Buffalo, and from general unions in Louisville, Williamsburg, Newark, Cincinnati, Marysville, Detroit, Rochester, Dubuque, and Trenton. Weitling, the guiding spirit of the convention, estimated that the total membership of the affiliated unions was 4,400. Among the topics discussed were education, political organization and Weitling's pet scheme, labor exchange banks.* The new organization was called the General Workingmen's League.[23]

Attempts to apply the program adopted by the convention met with failure because of the split developing among the German workers. For one thing, the German-American labor movement was divided in 1851 by the efforts of August Willich and Gehrach Kinkel to divert the attention of the workingmen from economic struggles in America to the task of raising funds to aid the revolutionary movement in Germany. Meanwhile, Weitling was attempting to convince the workers that the adoption of his labor exchange idea would solve all of their problems. To Weitling the labor movement was an instrument through which to spread this scheme. Like other utopians, Weitling regarded the struggle for hours and wages as unimportant compared to the movement for a co-operative system of industry. Trade unions, he said, were useful only because they brought workers together and made it easier to convert them to the larger program. Political action was also of little use, for the politicians would always betray the working class.

Most German workers disagreed with Weitling as soon as they began to understand his limited outlook on immediate questions confronting them, and they were antagonized by his domineering attitude. In an article in the June 19, 1852, issue of his *Republik der Arbeiter,* Weitling admitted that in May, 1852, the General Workingmen's League had only three hundred reliable members. Some time later, when trade union issues

---

* The labor exchange bank was an institution in which each producer could deposit his product in the central depot, and receive in exchange a paper certificate of equivalent value, which would enable him to purchase, up to its face value, any articles at cost in the bank store.

were becoming uppermost in the League, Weitling withdrew in disgust, and from then on to his death in 1871 he lost all interest in the labor movement.

New life was brought to the German-American labor movement through the leadership of Joseph Weydemeyer, a Communist, who had been in close contact with Marx and Engels in Europe.[24] Weydemeyer came to the United States in 1851 when he was thirty-three years old, and devoted his life to directing the emerging socialist movement in this country. Equipped with the understanding of a Marxist, and in close contact with Marx through correspondence, Weydemeyer saw the weaknesses of the narrow tendencies among the German-American workingmen, the incorrectness of the revolutionary loan movement led by Willich and Kinkle and the inadequacies of Weitling's program for the working class.

In January, 1852, Weydemeyer started the publication of a journal to which he gave the title, *Die Revolution.** It was succeeded a year later by *Die Reform,* which Weydemeyer edited in collaboration with Dr. Gustave Kellner. In both journals Weydemeyer exposed the fallacies of prevailing theories among German-American workers. The revolutionary loan movement, he pointed out, was utopian, for it was impossible to create a revolution through stimulus supplied outside the country in which the social upheaval was to take place. Furthermore, the scheme was only succeeding in dividing the German-American labor movement. At the same time, Weydemeyer took issue with Weitling, explained the need for struggling for immediate demands, and the importance of combining economic and political issues in the labor movement. "There should be no division between economics and politics," wrote Weydemeyer in *Die Reform* of May, 1853, and to Weitling's cry that the politicians would always betray the workers, he replied that labor had to be active in politics, but in a different type of politics than that of the ordinary politicians. Labor had to lead other sections of the population in the struggle for economic and political reforms. "The laboring class," Weydemeyer

---

* On January 1, 1852, the following notice appeared in the New York *Turn-Zeitung,* organ of the Socialist Athletic Society (*Turnerbund*): "*Die Revolution,* a weekly edited by J. Weydemeyer, former editor of the *Neue Deutsche Zeitung* which was suppressed by the police in Frankfurt-on-the-Main, will appear every Sunday with the collaboration of the editors of the former *Neue Rheinische Zeitung,* Karl Marx, Friedrich Engels, Ferdinand Freiligrath, etc. The business office of the paper is at 7 Chambers Street."

Only two issues of this paper appeared. The first number was entirely devoted to a contribution forwarded by Karl Marx, his celebrated classic, *The Eighteenth Brumaire of Louis Bonaparte.* This outstanding Marxist historical work was not printed in Europe until 1869.

constantly emphasized, "is the foundation stone upon which must rest the main reliance of all movements for general and special reforms." [25]

But to achieve its goals labor had to be organized and united. Weyde-meyer saw quickly that the narrow sectarianism of the German-American workers isolated them from the main streams of the American labor movement. His aim, therefore, was to organize a united labor movement which would combine economic and political struggles. Late in 1852, Weydemeyer organized the Proletarian League in New York. In this organization were held the preliminary discussions on the need for estab-lishing a new labor movement. On March 18, 1853, the Proletarian League issued a call for a mass meeting of workers to be held in Mechanics' Hall in New York City. The call stressed the need for uniting the American working class for the struggle to improve labor's status. "If the working class is not united," the call asserted, "it will never gain its rights." It concluded:

"Only if all crafts stand together and act together according to *one* definite plan will it be possible to do away with the many evils that lower the workers to the level of beasts of burden.

"Forward to a great association of workers, not only to fight for higher wages and for political reforms, but for the creation of a platform which can unite all workers for the welfare of the working class. All workers should come to the meeting. Arise all like one man. All for one, one for all." [26]

The conference met on March 21, 1853, and organized the American Labor Union. The new organization announced that it sought to form a "Union of all laborers of the United States without regard to nationality, for the purpose of reforming the conditions of labor," and announced that "All laborers without distinction, whatever trade they may follow, can belong to this Union; all unions without regard to their aims, whether political, trade, beneficent or only social, can belong to this Union, if they only recognize the object of the Union." [27]

Among other things the platform dedicated the organization

"To fight with every means at our disposal and to put a stop by law to the competition among capitalists for labor-power as well as the com-petition of the workers among themselves.

"To take measures affording the workers protection, vis-a-vis their employers, from arbitrary actions such as wage-cuts, lengthening of the legally prescribed working week, and the like; and the same time enabling them to obtain by common efforts wage-increases, if necessary.

"Furthermore, to take measures making it impossible to exploit the workers by fraud and profiteering of all kinds....

"To emphasize the independence of the Workers' League of existing political parties." *

The new organization quickly based itself on ward organizations (first set up in March and April, 1853, in New York and later in other cities), and on trade unions. All types of workers could belong to the ward organizations, called the *Arbeiter All-Gewerke* (Workers of All Trades), which met weekly for discussions of political issues. Only workers of specific trades could belong to the unions, which were established on a craft basis. Both the ward organizations and the unions were represented on the Central Committee of the American Labor Union, but at first the former group had considerably more weight in the committee. Weydemeyer, as leader of the Central Committee, soon sought to change this situation, and pointed out that the American Labor Union had to base itself on the trade unions. Even as a political movement the Union would fail to grow unless it had strong trade union backing. Hence Weydemeyer suggested that the representation of the trade unions on the Central Committee be increased, and that special committees be established to organize trade unions among unorganized workers. Both suggestions were adopted and committees to organize tailors and shoeworkers were immediately established.[28]

The success of the New York conference inspired unity conferences in other cities and, in spite of the opposition of Weitling and his followers, the movement spread throughout the country. In September, 1853, a congress of English-speaking trade union representatives met in New York and formed the Amalgamated Society which adopted the platform of the American Labor Union. At Washington a few months later English speaking workers organized a national federation under the leadership of Sam Briggs. Its official name was the Workingmen's National Association and its official organ, the *Workingmen's National Advocate,* expounded the principles of the American Labor Union: the independent political organization of labor, organization of the unorganized workers into trade unions, and the unity of all workers in the country.

"We are aiming," wrote Sam Briggs, "not only to obtain the necessary wages for our work; we must think rather of raising the working class by placing it in the position in society to which it is entitled—by electing people from its ranks to all the law-making bodies of the nation... Let

* The stand of the conference on political action followed the position set down by Weydemeyer several months before the meeting convened. In an article in the New York *Turnzeitung* (No. 15, November, 1852), Weydemeyer had emphasized that none of the existing parties were really concerned with the needs of the working class: "There is one thing missing in the platform of the Democrats and the Whigs, as well as in that of the other splinter parties: the formulation of a *labor platform.* Yet that is an urgent necessity which must no longer be deferred."

our opponents scorn this proposal if they so choose; we, however, consider it our right and we have men who are completely capable of understanding that task." [29]

Unfortunately, the new national federation of American workers died the same year it was founded. Nor did the American Labor Union have a long life. The Central Committee discovered that the craft unions were still too indifferent to the problems of other workers and displayed interest only when their own welfare was vitally at stake. In December, 1857, the American Labor Union was revived in New York under the name of the *Allgemeine Arbeiterbund,* but it did not last beyond 1860. Weydemeyer, who was in Milwaukee and in constant contact with the Communist Club in New York,* gave whatever guidance he could to the revived movement. In 1860 the leadership of the movement went to the Chicago *Arbeiter-Verein,* perhaps the best German workingmen's association in the country, and here in the Middle West, Weydemeyer and his followers sought to continue their efforts to unite all workers in America into an organization combining trade union and political demands.[30] These efforts ended in temporary failure, but the educational work and experience of sound leadership had turned the German workers toward the American workers. Weydemeyer had planted the seeds of scientific socialism in America, and eventually his dream of an American labor federation which united native American and foreign born

* The Communist Club of New York was formed in October, 1857. Its constitution required all members to "recognize the complete equality of all men— no matter of what color or sex," and to "strive to abolish the bourgeois property system...and substitute for it a sensible system under which participation in the material and spiritual pleasures of the earth would be accessible to everyone and corresponding, as much as possible, to his needs." "The Club seeks," the Constitution continued, "by any means it might consider appropriate, by private conversation, public meetings, correspondence with American and European communists, the circulation of appropriate newspapers and books, to spread propaganda for its objectives." As soon as thirty members joined the Club, steps could be taken to establish new branches in different parts of the city. (*Statuten des Kommunisten-Klubs in New York,* Manuscript copy in Wisconsin State Historical Society, Labor Collection, Political Parties, Box 25.)

The Communist Club was a prime mover in the efforts made in the United States in 1858 to establish an international labor association in co-operation with similar movements in Europe. On April 22, 1858, an international meeting held in New York declared: "We recognize no distinction as to nationality or race, caste or status, color or sex; our goal is nothing less than the reconciliation of all human interests, freedom and happiness for mankind, and the realization and unification of a world republic." The Communist Club was active in organizing German-Americans in the International Association. It called for "the uniting of all partisans of the Revolution who advocate the overturn of existing state and social relationships as well as freedom and equality for all inhabitants of the earth. We preach the revolution in the interest of unlimited progress." (Karl Obermann, *Joseph Weydemeyer,* New York, 1946.)

workers, skilled and unskilled workers, an organization which combined working class political and trade union demands, would be realized.

The analysis of Weydemeyer's activities in *History of Labor in the United States* by John R. Commons and Associates (vol. I, pp. 617-19) is a notable example of anti-Marxist prejudice of the writers. Weydemeyer is pictured as an "agitator" who "sought to take advantage of the trade union agitation of the time and to use the unions as the basis of a general class-conscious organisation" and influence them to combine "both trade union and legislative demands." This effort to "introduce Marxian Socialism into the trade union movement," it is concluded, failed as soon as the trade unions understood its true character.

This analysis, of course, ignores the fact that Weydemeyer helped create the "trade union agitation of the time" by his consistent campaign against Weitling and others who regarded the trade union activities as unimportant. As a Marxist, Weydemeyer knew the importance of strengthening the trade union movement, but he also saw the weakness of ignoring legislative demands while the trade unions were battling on the economic front. He also believed that the trade union movement was not the exclusive property of the skilled craftsmen, and raised the issue of organizing the unskilled as well as the skilled. That his approach to the problems of the working class did not meet with a welcome reception from many craft unions of the 'fifties is true, but it is also true that the American workers had yet to learn through experience the correctness of the program Weydemeyer set down. And it was precisely as a Marxist that Weydemeyer was able properly to evaluate the weaknesses of the trade unions of his time. The fact that he raised these issues as early as the 'fifties is a tribute to his clear understanding of the cardinal problems confronting the American working class. Today, when labor has proved through its activities of the past decade the correctness of Weydemeyer's emphasis on the need to combine legislative and trade union demands and to organize unskilled as well as skilled workers, it is only fitting that due credit be bestowed upon one who understood these issues almost a century ago.

NATIONAL LABOR ORGANIZATION

Other attempts to federate the labor movement nationally were made during the 'forties and 'fifties, the most important of which was the Industrial Congress which met annually from 1845 to 1856. After 1848 the followers of George Henry Evans seized control of the organization and turned it into a propaganda agency for their program of land reform. Within a few years nearly all the trade unions affiliated with the Congress had dropped out; at the 1853 Congress there were only 25 delegates present and three years later the number had declined to 11 delegates. Soon afterwards the movement joined the long list of organizations which began with the purpose of uniting the working class nationally and ended as the exclusive property of a small band of utopian reformers.

City Industrial Congresses were set up by 1850 in every industrial center. At first these organizations attracted considerable trade union support (forty-six different labor organizations were represented at the first City Industrial Congress held in New York City on June 6, 1850). But here too the influence of the utopians became immediately evident, and soon most of the City Congresses came under the domination of the land reformers. Consequently many trade unions either refused to send delegates or withdrew their delegates. Eventually, the New York City Industrial Congress, the most influential of the organizations, was swal-lowed up by Tammany Hall.[31]

Although no significant national labor federation embracing different unions was organized during the 'fifties, national and international bodies of local unions within the same trade were formed. The rapid extension of markets, the ever-increasing urbanization of the population, and the growth of communication and transportation made their organization necessary, for these forces taught the workers that wage scales could not be maintained in one section of the country unless they were upheld in other sections.[32]

The printers were the first to start a national organization. In December 1850, a national convention of journeymen printers was held in New York City, attracting delegates from New York, New Jersey, Pennsylvania, Maryland, and Kentucky. A national executive committee was set up to carry on the activities of the union between conventions, and a series of resolutions was adopted to be sent to the local unions of the trade for their guidance. Printers' unions throughout the country were called upon to make the "regulation and adjustment of different scales of prices so as not to conflict with each other"; to issue traveling certificates to all members; to send a list of "rats" to every union to prevent disgraced members from joining other unions; to raise strike benefit funds; to loan money to sister unions in distress; and to limit the number of apprentices and provide a five year period of training for apprentices.

An address was drawn up for the Journeymen Printers of the United States outlining the aims of the National Union. It begins by referring to the "utter impotency of unorganized labor in a warfare against capital." Trade unionism, the address continued, was necessary ". . . to remedy the many disastrous grievances arising from this disparity of power," and as long as the present wage system continued, trade unionism would be necessary. Events had demonstrated that "an extensive organization, embracing the whole country, would secure to our own, or to any trade, a power which could be derived from no other source." Such a national organization would make it possible to regulate the scales of wages in different localities, and at the same time prepare the workers for their ultimate redemption through self-employment.[33]

This address stimulated the organization of printers' unions in several localities. "A Printers Union was formed in this city, on Saturday last," the Trenton *Daily State Gazette* of January 9, 1851, reported, "according to the recommendation of the National Convention of Printers, held in the City of New York, on the 2nd of December last." When the first annual convention of the newly organized National Typographical Union met in May, 1852, delegates from twelve cities were present, representing local unions from New York City, Albany, Philadelphia, Harrisburg, Boston, Richmond, Baltimore, Cincinnati, and Trenton. Four years later at the 1856 convention, delegates also came from Louisville, Memphis, New Orleans, Nashville, Buffalo, and Chicago.[34]

The printers always felt that in organizing nationally they were setting an example "to the laborers of all trades and vocations, who are anxiously awaiting the development of some sure plan of amelioration which they can all adopt." [35] Some eight or ten important national trade unions were organized in the period from 1853 to 1860.* Although this number is imposing, most of them did little more than meet and pass resolutions. The National Typographical Union, and the national unions of the machinists and blacksmiths, and the iron molders were notable exceptions. The machinists and blacksmiths had fifty-seven locals belonging to the national body in 1860, and in the same year, the iron molders added forty-seven locals to the parent organization.

In 1861 the *Cincinnati Daily Enquirer* referred to the National Molders Union as the "largest mechanical association in the world." [36] Before the crisis of 1857 the iron molders had been organized on a local scale, but after 1857, with the introduction of machinery and increased centralization and specialization in the industry, the leaders of the unions were convinced that to gain higher wages was possible only through a national organization. When William H. Sylvis, the recording secretary of the

---

* These organizations were the Upholsterers' National Union (1853); Hat Finishers' National Association (1854); Plumbers' National Union (1854); National Union of Building Trades (1854); National Protective Association of the United States (railroad engineers) (1855); Journeymen Stone Cutters Association of the United States and Canada (1855); Lithographers National Union (1856); Cigar Makers' National Union (1856); National Convention of Silver Platers (1857); National Cotton Mule Spinners' Association of America (1858); Machinists and Blacksmiths National Union (1859); Painters' National Union (1859); Cordwainers' National Union (1859). Nearly all of these unions were craft unions. The National Union of Building Trades, however, included house painters, stone cutters, plasterers, carpenters, bricklayers, plumbers, and masons.

important Philadelphia molders' union, suggested that a committee of the Philadelphia local address a letter to all locals on the advisability of having a national union, the suggestion was accepted and the letter sent. So favorable was the response that a call was issued for a national convention to be held on July 5, 1859.

Thirty-five delegates from twelve local unions came to Philadelphia for the first national convention of molders. No action was taken, and the convention adjourned to meet again in six months. A loose national federation had emerged, and even though it had only advisory powers, it was a step forward. A year later the National Union of Iron Molders came into existence, with Sylvis as its national treasurer. Largely through Sylvis' work this union became a model for other labor organizations. He saw to it that shop committees and shop chairmen were established in all local unions, and many unions copied with but slight changes the stirring address written by Sylvis in 1859 and embodied in the union's constitution as its preamble:

"In union there is strength and in the formation of a national organization, embracing every molder in the country, a union founded upon a basis broad as the land in which we live, lies our only hope. Single-handed we can accomplish nothing, but united there is no power of wrong that we cannot openly defy." [87]

The concept of national organization advanced by Sylvis could not as yet be fully applied because the panic of 1857 and the following depression had destroyed most of the local and national unions which had been organized during the preceding years. Only three national unions—the typographical, the hat finishers and the stone-cutters—had survived. The revival of trade unionism after the panic was seriously checked by secession and the outbreak of the Civil War.

UNEMPLOYMENT DEMONSTRATIONS

Although the panic of 1857 destroyed trade unions it did not destroy working class solidarity. All divisions between skilled and unskilled, native American and foreign-born, male and female workers disappeared in the face of common unemployment. At least two hundred thousand were unemployed in October, 1857, and thousands of foreign-born workers crowded the shipping ports, begging for a chance to work their passage back to Europe. "Every ship for Liverpool," said the *New York Times* of October 16, 1857, "now has all the passengers she can carry, and multitudes are applying to work their passage if they have no money to pay for it." *The North American* of Philadelphia said: "Those of the Irish who have returned to their native land, have done wisely." [38]

Instead of sitting around and waiting for the depression to end, unemployed workers in several cities organized to compel the municipal governments to relieve their distress. The movement of the unemployed in Philadelphia began with meetings in the local wards. At one of these ward meetings the workers said that they did not intend to stand by and hear their children crying for bread, "at a time when God has blessed our land with an abundance of all the necessaries of life." [39] Meeting separately, the German workers of Philadelphia stated that they were not going to "die shamefully without ever raising a hand to save ourselves and children." The German workmen proceeded to form an association to fight for unemployment relief. This association would be prepared "to act in concert with whatever associations might be formed among American workmen." [40] Although the ward meetings were held separately, they were leading to what the *North American* called "the first genuine demonstration in the way of a convention of the unemployed." [41] Before long a committee of twenty-four members, one for each ward, emerged which eventually assumed the name, the Central Workingmen's Committee. Both skilled and unskilled American born and foreign-born workers were represented on the committee.[42]

The committee visited the Mayor who informed them that "time would remedy the evil." Mass meetings, he assured the delegation, were of no value. Confidence was the thing. Confidence was "like the genial warmth of the sun which shed its rays upon the plants causing them to flourish." [43] To give a material base to the Mayor's confidence, the committee demanded that the Select and Common Council issue $4,000,000 in city warrants in small denominations to be used as currency. The Council was further urged to float a loan of $50,000,000 for public works. "In the midst of apparent affluence we are in want," went the memorial to the City Council, "and though surrounded by every external indication of wealth we need the common necessities of life." [44]

Meanwhile the unemployed were also organizing in Newark, New Jersey. On November 6, 1857, a notice appeared in the press calling upon the unemployed workers to meet on the Military Common. The meeting, held on November 8, was attended by several thousand workers. Speaker after speaker asserted that when there was "starvation in the midst of plenty," they would "blame any man who died of starvation." When one person said that such ideas were foreign and un-American, voices from the audience shouted, "If we have American spirit we would *fight* for bread." [45]

Before the meeting adjourned, the workers resolved that they did not want alms but the chance to work. A committee was elected to call upon the authorities of the city and ask them to furnish work for the unemployed. A similar committee was elected by the German workers at the meeting to act jointly with the other committee. The joint committee promptly petitioned the Mayor and the City Council for relief:

"Your petitioners, while they do not claim that our city authorities are the proper source to look for employment under *any ordinary circumstances* would nevertheless venture the suggestion that the unemployed industrious poor must receive assistance from some source, either through labor or charity." [46]

The unemployed movements in Philadelphia and Newark were dwarfed by what took place in New York. On November 2, 1857, an advertisement appeared in the New York press: "All workmen without employment are hereby notified to attend a meeting at Tompkins Square. Purpose of meeting—necessity for prompt, vigorous and decisive action to prevent our families from starving." [47]

This meeting was attended by 12,000 unemployed workers. It was composed, said a report in the press, "of Germans, Irish and Americans." The leading address was delivered by John H. Paul, an unemployed carpenter who roused the audience to cheers with the following statement:

"Who is it that does the mischief? Who that robs us of our bread? It is the men who oppress the laborer; it is the capitalists. This crew of thieves and robbers it is who are driving us to starvation. This is the political and social enemy in our midst, that is starving our families to death. How shall we obtain relief unless we organize against this band of thieves and robbers? Who shall say we shall not have it? Let us have union; let there be an organization formed in every ward at once; let us set aside all political and religious considerations." [48]

On November 5 a mass meeting of 15,000 met at Tompkins Square. A parade formed when an unemployed shoe worker urged the audience to go to the Merchants' Exchange "and tell them that we shall and must have work." Arriving at Wall Street, the thousands of unemployed paraded about the Stock Exchange, shouting: "We want work." [49]

In spite of the organized efforts of the movement for work or relief, no work or relief was granted, and a large group of desperate workers broke into the shops of flour merchants and took what they could find to feed their starving families. United States troops were called out to protect stores and to guard the Custom House and the Sub-Treasury. Some businessmen charged that the unemployed movement was led by "ultra-communistic radicals ... and other foreigners, who, though they have changed their soil and allegiance, still keep their nature intact and insist upon having food put in their mouths and labor into their hands." [50]

The demonstrations of the unemployed in Philadelphia, Newark, New

York, and other cities were instrumental in obtaining some form of public works to provide work and reduce the suffering of the workers.[51] In addition, these mass movements taught the workers the need for greater unity among skilled and unskilled workers, the need for political action to elect men to office who were sympathetic to labor, and the need for national unions to uphold wage schedules throughout the country.

REVIVAL OF UNIONISM

Some unions did not wait for the depression to end before organizing their struggles for higher wages, but formed new locals proving that trade union activity was possible during a business depression. In Philadelphia Robert Bruce of the printers' union went from meeting to meeting calling upon the workers to organize into trade unions. Partly as a result of his work, the machinists and blacksmiths organized a new union during the panic of 1857, and by the summer of 1858 they had expanded to include six locals, three in Philadelphia, one in Reading, one in Baltimore, and one in Wilmington.

At the most intense stage of the crisis in December 1857, the shoe workers of Philadelphia formed an organization, adopted a constitution and decided "ways and means for getting back the reductions in wages effected by the manufacturers because of the Panic." By April 1858, the Grand Association of Pennsylvania, organized in twelve separate associations, had made plans "to establish a National Representative body, as soon as a sufficient number of subordinate Associations are formed in the various states." [52]

In February 1859, the Grand Association of Pennsylvania called a general strike in the industry to restore wages reduced during the panic. The strike ended May First in a victory for the union. Attempts to divide the workers through national prejudice failed. A reporter for the *Philadelphia Ledger* wrote: "The bosses ... tried to divide the strikers by embittering the minds of the Germans against the Irish, and the Americans against the Irish. But in this, they had signally failed." [53]

Throughout 1859 and the opening months of 1860 the resurgent labor movement organized new local unions, formed the Machinists' and Blacksmiths' and the Iron Molders' National Unions, and in a great strike wave fought to raise wages to their pre-crisis level. The outstanding strike of this period was conducted by the New England shoemakers. A general strike had been waged in Philadelphia in the 'thirties, but the shoemakers' strike of 1860 covered almost all of New England, and its force was felt from Maine to Florida. No strike before the Civil War had been so extensive.

NEW ENGLAND SHOEMAKERS' STRIKE

The shoemaker of the 'fifties was no longer the skilled artisan living in a semi-rural community with his own garden, pig, and cow to provide food during slack seasons and repeated depressions. Machinery had been introduced into the industry, making it possible for boys and girls to do the work of craftsmen. While the cost of living rose, wages for shoe workers fell. Wage cut followed wage cut, and after a reduction in the fall of 1859 men were earning $3 a week.[54] Wages for women were lower, many women earning as little as $1 a week. *The Boston Traveller* told of a woman worker who put in sixteen hours a day and earned $1 a week. "She had six children to support," the reporter added, "but was afraid she would have to send them to Ireland or England." [55]

When the strike began, the shoe workers in most New England towns were unorganized, but in Lynn, the center of the struggle, the shoe workers had organized a Mechanics' Association in 1859, and the leaders of the association helped workers in other towns to organize during the strike. Alonzo G. Draper, James Dillon, and Napoleon Wood were the leading figures in the strike. Draper, who was twenty-four years old when the strike started, worked in the shoe industry and studied law in his spare time. When the Lynn Mechanics' Association was formed, Draper was elected chairman and editor of its paper, the *New England Mechanic*. James Dillon, who was thirty-five years old at the time of the strike, was born in Cheshire, England, coming to America in 1845. He started to work in the shoe industry in Lynn during the fall of 1846, and when the Mechanics' Association was formed, he was elected vice-president. Napoleon Wood, twenty-five years old, was Canadian born and had worked in Lynn since 1851. He left Lynn with a party of fifty in 1856 to go to Kansas "to aid in maintaining the rights of the free State men," but ill health forced him to return to Massachusetts. Wood was a leader in the Methodist Church, and throughout the strike he let it be known that the struggle for decent living standards was not in conflict with religious beliefs.[56]

Early in February 1860, the leaders of the Lynn Mechanics' Association called mass meetings in Lynn and Natick, Massachusetts, to determine what steps should be taken to raise wages above subsistence levels. The shoe workers decided to send a circular to all manufacturers informing them of a new wage scale and appointed committees to meet with the employers. The circular issued by the Natick shoemakers, dated February 13, 1860, stated that in requesting higher wages the workingmen had "the best interests of the manufacturers as well as our own and the world at large, at heart; inasmuch as the wealth of the masses improves the value of real estate, increases the demand for manufactured goods, and promotes the moral and intellectual growth of society." [57] When the manufacturers refused to meet with the workers' committees, Washington's birthday, 1860, was chosen as the beginning of the strike, because: "This day being sacred to the memory of one of the greatest men the world has ever produced, it is a fitting occasion for a blow in favor of the cause you are engaged in, and to refer to his history of patience and endurance, may inspire every one that has pledged his honor to persevere in the cause so vital to themselves and their families." [58]

Early in the morning of February 22, three thousand shoemakers met in the Lynn Lyceum Hall to prepare for the strike. The hall was crowded; reporters agreed that it was "the largest and most enthusiastic meeting of its kind ever held in New England." A committee of 100 was appointed to prevent expressmen from taking shoes to be finished elsewhere; another committee of 100 was to visit the shops of the city and post the name of anyone still working as a scab, and a vigilance committee was set up "to aid in preserving order, to see that no violence was done, to suppress intemperance, arrest disturbers, and co-operate with the municipal police."* All strikers were required by pledge to obey the orders of the vigilance committee members. [59]

Several hundred Natick workers met, resolved to strike, and marched through the streets singing this song to the tune of *Yankee Doodle:*

> *Starvation looks us in the face.*
> *We cannot work so low.*
> *Such prices are a sore disgrace,*
> *Our children ragged go.*

CHORUS

> *Up and let us have a strike*
> *Fair prices we'll demand.*
> *Firmly let us all unite,*
> *Unite throughout the land.*

> *The carpenters get up a strike*
> *The masons do the same.*
> *And we'll take hold with all our might.*
> *And elevate our name.* [60]

* Everywhere the strikers were careful to prevent intemperance in their ranks. In Haverhill, Massachusetts, for example, the strikers voted to notify all who sold beer or other intoxicating liquors to stop their sale, and the chairman was authorized to appoint a committee to see that there was no violation. It was also voted not to aid anyone from the strike fund who was found drunk. (*Haverhill Gazette,* March 16, 1860.) In speaking of the strikers the *Newburyport Daily Herald* of March 13, 1860 declared: "There is no rowdyism and no drunkenness in their ranks."

Within a few days shoe workers throughout New England had joined in the refrain, "Up and let us have a strike." Leaders of the Lynn and Natick strikers traveled to Newburyport, Haverhill, Marblehead and other towns in Massachusetts; to Salmon Falls, Farmington, Rochester, Dover, and Barrington in New Hampshire; to Berwick, Maine, to urge shoe workers to organize and strike. By the end of the month the strike was general in all the shoe towns. Mechanics' Associations had been organized in at least twenty-five towns, and close to 20,000 shoeworkers were on strike.[61]

Newspapers carried glaring headlines: The Revolution at the North. The Rebellion among the Workmen of New England. The Shoemakers' Strike—Progress of the Social Revolution. Beginning of the Conflict between Capital and Labor.[62]

The same newspapers played up the part women were performing in the strike. Editorial after editorial thundered that the shoemakers' strike was living proof of the demoralizing influence of the woman's rights movement. Were not these female strikers asserting that they were struggling for equal pay for equal work?[63] Socialism would be next!

The lady binders and stitchers of Lynn joined the strike a day or two after it started. At their mass meeting which voted to join the strike, a committee was set up to enlist all female workers. Several days later the committee called a mass meeting which was so well attended that many could not get in. Here Mrs. Greenleaf, a shoebinder, was the leading speaker. "She considered their cause," wrote a reporter, "a sacred one and precisely similar to that of the Jewish patriarchs who left Egypt because they were obliged to work for nothing and furnish their own materials." [64]

Elsewhere the women joined enthusiastically in the struggle saying that like the women of the Revolution, they would see the battle through. Many a reporter who observed the spirit of the women strikers was convinced that the strike could only end in victory. Thus a correspondent for the *New York Herald* wrote from Marblehead, Massachusetts: "The women are about taking part in the strike—and what the Marblehead women undertake they are bound to succeed in accomplishing." On another occasion he wrote of the women strikers in Lynn: "They assail the bosses in a style which reminds one of the amiable females who participated in the first French Revolution" [65]

If anyone doubted their spirit, these doubts disappeared after the great Ladies' Procession of March 8. The parade was scheduled to start at ten o'clock in the morning. At eight o'clock a driving snowstorm set in, and by ten the streets appeared impassable, but the women ploughed through the drifting snow, holding aloft their banners. Some of the slogans on the banners were blurred, but those who had the courage to watch the demonstration could clearly see: American Ladies will not be Slaves! Our Union is complete: Our success certain! Weak in Physical Strength but Strong in Moral Courage, We Dare Battle for the Right, Shoulder to Shoulder with our Fathers, Husbands, and Brothers! [66]

Ten days later the women paraded again in Lynn, this time in the sunshine. Delegations from Salem, Marblehead, Newburyport and other towns joined them, while two companies of infantry from Lynn and Marblehead and the fire companies of several shoe towns marched along. Ten thousand strikers paraded that day in a procession almost two miles long, and many thousand, including school children who had been dismissed for the day, lined the way. Everyone agreed that it was the "greatest labor demonstration ever made in New England." [67]

The employers tried to break the strike by threatening the German and Irish workers that the state legislatures would deprive them of their vote. As soon as they heard of this threat, the German workers of Natick met and unanimously resolved: "That neither the fear of losing our political influence nor the threats of our would-be masters will deter us from adhering to the rules of the Natick strikers until the battle is fought and victory won." [68]

In response to the Lynn employers, State Attorney General Phillips came to the shoe town on February 23 and convinced the Mayor who was at first friendly to the strikers to call out the light infantry and to request a contingent of police from Boston. When the workers heard that the Boston police were coming, they massed at the railroad station and greeted them with jeers, hisses, and shouts. Eight thousand people roared, "Go back home," "Put them out," "You are not wanted here," "No outside police." This indignation at the invasion of the Boston police was shared by the civic-minded citizens of Lynn. Businessmen contributed heavily to the strike fund, and large meetings were held at which "the firmest determination was expressed to sustain the movement." [69]

None were more determined in their support than the clergymen. Reverend Charles C. Shackford, pastor of the Second Congregational (Unitarian) Church told the manufacturers who attended his sermons that he believed them to be in the wrong and that they should accept the strikers' demands. Father Strain advised "every Catholic shoemaker not to lift a hammer while the Yankees were standing out for higher wages; and if any of the Yankees did not remain firm, to influence them, if possible, to be true to the objects of the strike." And Reverend Driver, the leading Negro preacher, spoke out again and again for the strikers. "If I understand them," he declared proudly, "I am with them." To his congregation he said: "You, my colored brethren, know how to sympathize with labor unrequited. The poor journeyman is the bird picked. His is now the cider juice in the press under the screw." [70]

Many employers were ready to pay the increased wages before the second week of the strike was over, but they refused to recognize the unions organized during the strike or to sign written agreements with the union representatives. The shoe workers replied that until the employers signed the agreement the strike would continue. Some employers did sign written agreements, as in Lynn where close to a thousand workers went back to work on April 10 when thirty manufacturers signed a written agreement advancing wages more than 10 per cent. The willingness of employers to grant wage increases without recognizing the unions split the movement, and many workers returned without waiting for a written agreement. Some held out for a week or two longer but finally returned to work without written agreements. Before calling off the strike, however, they published a statement which said that their main object, a fair remuneration for their labor, having been achieved, they were going back to work. They concluded that having formed "a permanent association for the protection of our interests" during the strike, they would continue to struggle until their organization was recognized.[71]

Thus, most of the strikers went back to work at increased wages, and a few of the unions had signed agreements. While most employers would not sign agreements or recognize the unions, unions now existed in many towns which had formerly been unorganized. As the *Haverhill Gazette* said on March 23, 1860, the most important feature of the struggle was the fact that "an Association of mechanics will grow out of the movement which will doubtless do much for the protection of the laborers in their rights."

LABOR AND POLITICS

During the panic of 1857 and the shoemakers' strike of 1860, there were frequent references to the failure of the labor movement to pay closer attention to politics. Scarcely a meeting of unemployed workers took place at which some speaker did not criticize the trade unions for their indifference to politics, saying that the refusal of the authorities to provide adequate relief was the result of the workers themselves "voting for parties which did them no good." Because the workers did not exert their proper influence at the ballot box, "no political party has ranged itself on the side of labor, but all have legislated for capital." [72]

Similar views were expressed during the shoemakers' strike by Gideon Howard, a shoemaker from Randolph, Massachusetts, who reminded the workers that "the journeymen shoemakers in Massachusetts numbered about 50,000 men and if they concentrated their political power they could do almost anything they wanted. They could make laws for the protection of the laborer." It was time that the trade unions began to think along political as well as economic lines, said other speakers, for experience had demonstrated that economic gains could be rendered valueless by legislation directed against the interests of the working class.[73]

This criticism was justified. The labor movement of the 'fifties had made many advances on the economic front: wage increases, collective bargaining agreements, recognition of the closed shop, and regulation of apprentices. On the political front the trade unions had less to show. Nothing in the 'fifties approached the workingmen's parties formed during the 'twenties and 'thirties.

Yet there were important exceptions. In July 1850 the teamsters of San Francisco met to set up an association one of whose objects was to "nominate a candidate for one of the vacancies in the Council, so that we may have at least one representative who will be in favor of protecting the laboring citizens." The meeting was held, the Teamsters' Association was formed, and James Grant was nominated as labor's candidate for the City Council. Grant, who was also the regular Democratic nominee, won the election by a large majority.[74]

Six years later in New York City a committee of trade unionists issued an appeal to all workingmen in the state urging them to defeat Erastus Brooks, candidate for governor on the American (anti-foreign born) party ticket. Brooks, said the appeal, had "rendered himself obnoxious to workingmen by his uniform hostility to the interests of labor and labor organizations," and it was necessary to teach politicians of his caliber that "the laboring man in this free country holds in his hands the political fortunes of the most wealthy and ambitious of his fellow-citizens." [75] After Brooks was soundly defeated, the trade unionists forgot about teaching other unscrupulous politicians the same lesson.

The trade unionists of Trenton, New Jersey, decided that last minute appeals during election campaigns were not enough, and in September 1858, they met and adopted a platform of principles which they would support "until the workingmen have their rights in political as well as civil matters." [76] A month later the Workingmen's Union of Trenton was organized. Sponsored by the leading trade unions in the community, its purpose was to express labor's voice on political questions. The working classes produced "all the wealth and blessings of civilized society," yet they "never enjoyed equal social and political privileges with those that work not, and yet consume the labor of others."

The objects of the organization were divided into two categories:

national and state. Their leading national demand was that government lands should be withheld from the hands of speculators and sold only to actual settlers in limited quantities and at cost. By seizing the public domain, the railroad companies and monopolies were "destroying the common heritage and closing up the only safe asylum for the laboring millions from the hand of oppression." Within the state the Workingmen's Union demanded that all revenues derived from chartered companies, "as they are the price of special privilege and belong to the people," should be appropriated to the support of the common schools of the state, and "as education is a primary want of a free people, these schools should be extended until knowledge shall be as free as the air we breathe." Legislation was demanded to make it easier for workingmen to secure their wages "without being subject to repeated delays and appeals," by giving mechanics and laborers permanent lien on property of employers to the full extent of their earnings. A radical change in the state judiciary was demanded to make justice for the working people less expensive, and, finally, a larger number of the public officers should be elected by the people.[77]

Having drawn up their platform, the workingmen of Trenton organized for political action. They appointed a committee to question all candidates for public office "to ascertain whether we shall be compelled to make a separate nomination or whether one or both of the present parties will endorse our platform."[78] All candidates questioned replied that they were ready to support the platform of the Workingmen's Union, and one candidate, James W. Wall, asserted that he recognized in the platform a reiteration of the principles involved in the struggle "which is continually going on between the advocates of special privileges, grinding monopolies, and those who from the foundation of the government have always opposed them." The *Trenton True American* hailed this stand and added that the movement started by the Workingmen's Union could be compared to the workingmen's parties formed during the Jacksonian era, which finally attained the public school system, abolition of imprisonment for debt, and the elimination of property qualifications for office and other democratic reforms.[79]

The readiness of all candidates to endorse the platform of the Workingmen's Union halted the movement for independent political organization. At a meeting on October 26, a motion for a labor ticket was lost, 33 to 18. At this same meeting the union resolved to add to its platform the demand that the state legislature alter the law on conspiracy "to allow workingmen to unite, peaceably in defense of their rights and interests, without being subject to legal prosecutions." Other demands were later added calling for the abolition of the store order system of paying wages, for the direct election by the people of all state officers except judicial officers, and for the direct election of United States Senators. This last demand is one of the earliest moves to achieve this reform.[80]

The Workingmen's Union failed to get these reforms enacted into law. But then all measures for the advance of democracy were being held up by the bolder and bolder aggressions of the slave power. Utopian experiments, producer and consumer co-operatives organized by trade unions, the struggle for the ten-hour day, the movement to extend the franchise, to elect all public officials, land reform, woman's rights, and all other reform movements of the period were engulfed by the rising tide of anti-slavery. "The American working people," wrote an active trade unionist of the 'fifties in later years, "were preparing for the dreadfully disastrous contest with the cotton lords who had usurped the government at Washington." [81]

CHAPTER 13

Labor in the Ante-Bellum South

During the pre-Civil War period the trade union movement practically stopped at the Mason-Dixon line, although a few trade unions were organized and successful strikes conducted in the ante-bellum South. Four labor organizations existed in New Orleans before the Civil War; the Mechanics' Society, the Typographical Society, the Screwmen's Beneficial Association,* and the United Laborers' Beneficial Society. Two of these organizations were mutual aid societies, but the Screwmen's Association and the Typographical Society were militant trade unions. In 1854, when it had 324 members, the Screwmen's Union won a strike which raised wages from $2.50 to $3.00 a day. In the same year the New Orleans Typographical Society waged a successful campaign against the Associated Press which took advantage of the depression by reducing wages 25 per cent. When the Associated Press resorted to importing strike-breakers from New York, the New Orleans *Daily Picayune* canceled the A. P.'s service. "We hold that the laborer is worthy of his hire," it declared, "and we can assure the public that we shall never be leagued with an association that has among its objects the deprivation of the laborer of a fair compensation for his services." [1] The split in A. P. ranks and the solidarity of the printers forced the employers to capitulate. On May 7, 1855, the *New Orleans Commercial Bulletin* announced:

"Of course everybody knows that the Associated Press has been compelled to succumb to the Typo Union. We have struck our colors, not ignominiously, but from sheer necessity. We have been overwhelmed by numbers and there is no disgrace for the weaker party to yield to the stronger.... All past questions between our compositors and ourselves are reconciled and the *entente cordiale* is fully established." [2]

---

* Screwmen were workers who packed cotton bales into the hold of a ship.

249

These trade union successes do not obscure the fact that southern workers did not contribute much to the early development of the American trade union movement. The three and a half million slaves in 1860 could not organize into trade unions or bargain collectively for higher wages, shorter hours, and better working conditions. And whenever the free, white workers tried to organize they found the bitter resistance of the slave power.

SLAVERY

The organization of slave labor in the ante-bellum South was based on the task system and the gang system.* The former was used on rice and tobacco plantations, and meant that the daily quantity of work to be done was divided into "quarter hands," "half hands" or "three-quarter hands" according to the strength of the workers. In theory the work required of each slave was not too hard, but in practice the slaves were usually required to perform other tasks when their labor in the fields was finished. Lieutenant Anburey who visited a tobacco plantation where the task system was in force described its operation in his diary:

"They [the slaves] are called up at day break, and ... are drawn out into the field immediately, where they continue at hard labour, without intermission till noon, when they go to their dinners, and are seldom allowed an hour for that purpose.... After they have dined, they return to labour in the field, until dusk in the evening; here one naturally imagines the daily labour of these poor creatures was over; not so, they repair to the tobacco houses, where each has a task of stripping allotted which takes them up some hours, or else they have a quantity of Indian corn to husk, and if they neglect it, are tied up in the morning, and receive a number of lashes...." [3]

Cotton was produced by the gang system. The slaves worked under the constant supervision of overseers who used drivers to set the pace. From sunup to sundown the slavers worked in the cotton fields, six days a week.

"The hands," wrote a resident of Mississippi, "are regularly roused, by a large bell or horn, about the first dawn of day, or earlier so that they are ready to enter the field as soon as there is sufficient light to

* The labor of ditching, trenching, cleaning the waste lands, and hewing down the forests on the plantation was usually done by Irish laborers, for the Negro's life was too valuable to be risked at this work. The Irish were also the chief element among the roustabouts on the steamers carrying the cotton bales. "The niggers are worth too much to be risked here," replied a captain to an inquisitive passenger. "If the Paddies are knocked overboard or get their backs broken, nobody loses anything." (Ulrich B. Phillips, *American Negro Slavery,* New York, 1918, p. 302.)

distinguish the bolls.... The hands remain in the field until it is too dark to distinguish the cotton, having brought their meals with them." [4]

Wherever there were as many as twenty slaves, it was common to employ an overseer. If he produced plenty of cotton, the owners never asked how many slaves he killed. His wages were ordinarily from $200 to $600, but a real driving overseer often got $1,000. He might ruin the land, overwork young and old alike—if he could get so many bales to the hand, all was overlooked. To get the requisite number of cotton bags, he used the whip regularly. "It must be very disagreeable to have to punish them as much as you do," the traveler Frederick Law Olmsted remarked to an overseer. "Yes, it would be to those who are not used to it, but it's my business and I think nothing of it. Why, sir, I wouldn't mind killing a nigger more than I would a dog." [5] *

The account books of the slave owners give a good index to the general standard of living of the slaves. In 1795, a South Carolina planter estimated "... the expense for a negro including duty, board, clothing, and medicines ... [at] from twelve to thirteen dollars per year." Thirty years later, General Thomas Pickney wrote: "The average annual expense of plantation slaves in the lower county of South Carolina, extracted from the account of several executors and attornies, for four successive years, amounts to $35 per head." But this figure included, in addition to food and clothing, taxes, overseers' wages, medicinal costs, "ploughs, tools, nails, locks, hinges, fish-hooks, pipes, salt, etc." James L. Watkins, a statistician for the United States Department of Agriculture, has estimated that the annual cost of medical care, feeding, and clothing adult slaves working in cotton fields in 1822 came to $23.10.

In 1845, forty-eight sugar planters in Louisiana informed the Secretary of the Treasury that the cost of furnishing their prime field hands with food, medical treatment, and clothing was thirty-three dollars, and for other slaves, eighteen dollars a year. Nine years later a table was published in J. D. B. De Bow's *Resources of the South* which placed the cost of feeding a slave "... as deduced from fifteen years' experience" at seven dollars and fifty cents annually, or about two cents a day. [6] No wonder Frederick Law Olmsted wrote after a tour of the South in 1856: "In fact, under favorable circumstances, on the large plantations the slaves' allowance does not equal in quality or quantity that which we furnish the rogues in our penitentiaries." [7]

* In January, 1854, the British consul at Charleston, in a private letter, wrote: "The frightful atrocities of slave holding must be seen to be described.... My next-door neighbor, a lawyer of the first distinction, and a member of the *Southern Aristocracy*, told me himself that he flogged all his own negroes, men and women, when they misbehaved.... It is literally no more to kill a slave than to shoot a dog." (Laura A. White, "The South in the 1850's as seen by British Consuls," *Journal of Southern History*, Vol. I, Feb. 1935, p. 33.)

RESISTANCE

Unquestionably there were Negroes who accepted their oppression; there were some household slaves who did not share with their brothers and sisters an unalterable hatred of slavery. But for two centuries the slaves struggled by every conceivable means to gain their freedom. While this struggle could at no time take the form of trade union struggle, there are few pages in the history of the working class which are more important than the battles waged by the Negro slaves against their bondage, and no history of the American labor movement can omit this story.

These struggles took two forms: individual acts of resistance and collective action. A striking example of the first method is seen in a letter from a Louisiana overseer to the absent owner:

"As to the difficulty with Summer," he writes, "it arose from my having hit his wife a few light licks when backward to proceed to work after which I proceeded to the field where Summer left his work to the distance of 20 or 30 yards with his Cane Knife in his hand & very much enraged, and said that he was not going to put up with it and that I was an unjust man, and that I might go get my gun, kill him and bury him but that he was not going to put up with any other punishment to himself or family...." [8]

Rather than put up with brutal punishment some slaves killed their masters or overseers and then committed suicide. Slave suicide as a form of resistance was so common in some parts of the South that documents containing advice to planters on the handling of slaves always devoted considerable space to the subject. One such document explained that slaves often "stifle themselves by drawing in the tongue so as to close the breathing passage, others take poison, or flee and perish of misery and hunger." [9] Other documents warned planters to guard against the tendency of slaves to murder their own children to prevent them from growing up in bondage. In one instance a father and mother mutually agreed to "send the souls of their children to Heaven rather than have them descend to the hell of slavery." After killing their children both parents committed suicide. Another slave mother destroyed with her own hands every one of her thirteen children "rather than have them suffer slavery." [10]

Other slaves adopted the more effective method of collective action by stopping work in protest against whippings and other forms of brutality. One such stoppage is discussed in a letter from a Georgia overseer to the absentee owner of the plantation:

"Sir, I write you a few lines in order to let you know that six of your hands have left the plantation—every man but Jock. They displeased me with their work and I gave some of them a few lashes, Tom with the rest. On Wednesday morning they were missing. I think they are lying out until they can see you or your uncle Jack." [11]

Generally the slaves who stopped work fled to nearby swamps and forests and sent back word that they would not willingly return until they were assured a redress of grievances. John Holmes, an ex-slave, told how he ran off and hid in the swamp after an overseer threatened to whip him, and remained there until he was given a guarantee that he would not be beaten. "At last," he writes, "they told all the neighbors if I came home they wouldn't whip me. I was a great hand to work and made a great deal of money for our folks." [12] A planter in North Carolina held out the following promise to slaves who had run away to the swamps and refused to return until promised freedom from punishment: "If any or all of these will return to my plantation and to a sense of their duty in a reasonable time, I pledge myself to forgive them." [13]

Tens of thousands of slaves fled and never returned, most of them escaping to the North.* Escape called for tremendous courage and endurance because the fugitive slave had to travel at night through hundreds of miles of hostile territory, hide in swamps and forests, and gradually make his way to freedom. Theodore Weld, a leading Abolitionist, wrote of one slave who escaped to New York in 1838: "He had come 1,200 miles from the lower part of Alabama, traveling only at nights, feeding on roots and wild berries. He swam *every river* from Tuscaloosa [Ala.] to Pennsylvania." [14]

A typical advertisement in a Southern newspaper reveals the dangers facing a fugitive slave: "Fifty Dollars Reward. Ran away from the subscriber, living in Franklin County, North Carolina, on the 12th of January, 1817, a Negro man named Randol about 26 or 27 years of age.... It is expected he has some marks of shot about his hips, thighs, neck and face, as he has been shot at several times." [15]

No story of the runaway slaves is complete without the inclusion of the heroic unity between Negro and white that maintained the Underground Railroad. The Underground Railroad was a network of an unknown number of routes stretching northward from the upland country of North Carolina, Tennessee, Virginia, and Kentucky into Canada. W. W. Siebert estimates that there were twelve routes across Ohio alone, and that by 1840 every northern state from Wisconsin and Illinois east-

* According to Professor W. B. Hesseltine, "Between 1830 and 1860 as many as 2,000 slaves a year passed into the land of the free along the routes of the Underground Railroad." (*A History of the South*, New York, 1936, p. 258.)

ward was crossed by slaves on their way to Canada or into regions in the United States where they could be relatively safe from the kidnappers and agents of the planters.[16] Most slaves did not feel safe until they were in Canada as is testified to in the following song:

> I'm on my way to Canada,
>   That cold and dreary land;
> The sad effects of slavery,
>   I can no longer stand.[17]

A number of former slaves worked with the Underground Railroad either as agents or conductors, the most famous of whom was Harriet Tubman. After her escape from slavery, she determined to return to the South and rescue her aged parents, her brothers, sisters, friends, and any slave who would follow her to freedom. "But I was free and they should be free," Harriet Tubman said soon after she reached the North. "I would make a home in the north and bring them there."

She engaged a northern assistant to write to a free Negro in Maryland who could read and write, and who was willing to help slaves escape. The letter contained a code passage with a biblical reference. "Read my letter to the old folks," it went, "and tell my brothers to be always watching unto prayer, and when the good old ship of Zion comes along, to be ready to step aboard."

Learning that her father was in trouble because he had helped a slave to escape, Harriet collected funds and returned to the South. She found that her father was to be tried the next week, so, as she put it, she "removed his trial to a higher court," by bringing her parents to Canada.

Harriet Tubman made nineteen journeys to the South, rescuing about three hundred slaves herself and inspiring other thousands to escape. By 1856 there was a price of $25,000 on her head. Thomas Wentworth Higginson, a New England leader of the Abolitionist movement called her the "greatest heroine of her age," while the Negro slaves hailed her as the "Moses of her people." [18]

Many of the slaves who escaped from the plantations did not go North, but found refuge in the swamps, mountains, and forests of the South. Here they lived in communities which became the centers for expeditions against nearby plantations. The Norfolk Herald of May 12, 1823, stated that the citizens of the southern part of Norfolk County, Virginia, "... have for some time been kept in a state of mind peculiarly harassing and painful, from the too apparent fact that their lives are at the mercy of a band of living assassins against whose fell designs neither the power of the law, or vigilance, or personal strength and intrepidity can avail. These desperadoes are runaway negroes commonly called outlyers...." [19] Frequently these outlyers were the leaders of the slave uprisings.

Slave insurrections were not accidental or unplanned events in the life of the South. With historical records far from complete, at least 250 insurrections which involved ten or more slaves have been reported during the history of American Negro slavery. Southern society was organized around the need to suppress the Negroes by force of arms. Each plantation had its private arsenal, and groups of plantations had a private army of patrollers who rode the country roads at night. As Governor Robert Y. Hayne of South Carolina put it: "A state of military preparation must always be with us a state of perfect domestic security. A period of profound peace and consequent apathy may expose us to the danger of domestic insurrection." [20]

One southern newspaper admitted that the slave-owners never felt safe. "We of the South," it said, "are emphatically surrounded ... by a dangerous class of beings ... who would repeat Santo Domingo* if they were made to believe that death would not follow their insurrection." [21] But many slaves rose up in revolt even though they knew that death might probably "follow their insurrection." Nat Turner, the great Negro leader, told of one slave who joined his insurrection: "I saluted them on coming up, and asked Will how came he there, he answered, his life was worth no more than others, and his liberty as dear to him. I asked him if he meant to obtain it. He said he would, or lose his life."

A slave captured during Gabriel's revolt in Virginia in 1800 showed the same spirit in his testimony before the trial court:

"I have nothing more to offer than what George Washington would have had to offer had he been taken by the British officers and put to trial by them. I have ventured my life in endeavouring to obtain the freedom of my countrymen, and am a willing sacrifice to their cause and I beg, as a favour, that I may be immediately led to my execution. I know that you have pre-determined to shed my blood. Why then all this mockery of a trial?" [22]

Since many of the leaders of the slave insurrections were Negro mechanics or artisans, it was not surprising that the following program was urged by a committee of slave-owners as a means of controlling the slaves more effectively. "The great fundamental principle should be that the slave should be kept as much as possible to agricultural labors. Those so employed are found to be the most orderly and obedient of slaves.... There should be no black mechanics or artisans, at least in the cities." [23]

* The reference is to the slave revolts in Santo Domingo during the 1790's and early 1800's under the leadership of Toussaint L'Ouverture. It resulted in the establishment of the Negro republic in Haiti.

Few strikes before the Civil War were better organized than were some of the slave insurrections.* Denmark Vesey's revolt in South Carolina in 1822 was so carefully organized that even the slave-owners admitted that for care and discipline and extent, there had been nothing to compare with it. A free Negro, Vesey was determined to help his people. He refused the advice of slave-owners that free Negroes should return to Africa. He wanted to stay "and see what he could do for his fellow-creatures."

Vesey organized the slaves for revolt, reading aloud to them "from the Bible how the children of Israel were delivered out of Egypt from bondage." A contemporary record tells us: "Even whilst walking through the streets in company with another, he was not idle; for if his companion bowed to a white person, he would rebuke him and observe that all men were born equal, and that he was surprised that any one would degrade himself by such conduct, that he would never cringe to the whites nor ought any one who had the feelings of a man."

Six months before the blow was to be struck in Charleston in July of 1822, Vesey and his colleagues had recruited close to 9,000 slaves and free Negroes within a radius of fifty miles of the city. Each slave had a task. One was the armorer who made about two hundred and fifty pike heads. Another slave fitted the pike heads to handles. Still others spotted all stores which contained arms. All slaves who tended or were near horses were given instructions as to where to bring the animals. In spite of all their secrecy, informers entered the organization. Peter Poyas, a slave carpenter, warned the rebels: "Take care and don't mention it to those waiting men who receive presents of old coats, etc., from their masters, or they'll betray us." While the insurrectionists were laying their final plans to spread through Charleston, occupy the arsenal, and restore freedom to every slave, a house servant discovered the plot and reported it. Other betrayals came from slaves who had agreed to act as spies. One hundred and thirty-one Negroes were arrested, and thirty-five were executed. Others were banished or transported to different states.

The slave-owners never knew how many slaves were involved in the insurrection. Peter Poyas and another slave were chained to the floor of a prison cell and brutally tortured to force them to tell the names of other rebels. Wearied through pain, and wanting to save his life, Poyas'

* There is evidence of the existence in December, 1860, of a widespread secret organization of slaves in South Carolina, dedicated to secure freedom. J. R. Gilmore, a visitor in the region, observed: "... there exists among the blacks a secret and wide-spread organization of a Masonic character, having its grip, password, and oath. It has various grades of leaders, who are competent and *earnest* men and its ultimate object is *Freedom*." (Edmund Kirke [J. R. Gilmore], *Among the Pines,* New York, 1862, pp. 20, 25, 59, 89, 90-91, 301.)

companion finally began to yield: "Peter raised himself, leaned upon his elbow, looked at the poor fellow, saying quietly: 'Die like a man,' and instantly lay down again. It was enough; not another word was extorted." Later, when the slaves were awaiting execution, Peter Poyas told them, "Do not open your lips; die silent as you shall see me do." All obeyed.[24]

The greatest slave uprising before the Civil War was the Nat Turner insurrection in Southampton County, Virginia, in 1831. Born a slave in 1800 in that state, Nat Turner was a deeply religious person and believed that he received God's word to free his people. Early in 1831 he planned the strategy for a general uprising to begin in Southampton County, and then to spread throughout the South. On the night of August 21, 1831, the uprising began seventy miles from Richmond. Armed with broadaxes and scythe blades, the slaves marched to battle, gaining recruits from plantations on the way. For a time they were successful, but the combination of state and Federal troops was too powerful. Turner evaded arrest for more than six weeks but was finally captured and tried, and on November 11, 1831, he was executed. Of the other Negroes who were brought to trial, 17 were executed and 12 transported. During the uprising, 57 whites and 73 Negroes were killed.

After Turner's revolt, the slave-owners were haunted by insurrections. "They live in constant fear upon this subject," observed a contemporary. "The least unusual noise at night alarms them greatly. They cry out, 'What is that?', 'Are the boys all in?'" Negroes suspected of plotting insurrections were murdered, and the death sentence was imposed upon any person convicted of arousing among Negro slaves "a spirit of insurrection, conspiracy or rebellion." The legislatures tightened the laws against persons aiding runaway slaves, greatly restricted emancipation, limited even more the activities of free Negroes and prohibited the teaching to slaves of reading and writing. A Georgia law asserted that if any person should teach a slave to read and write, the slave should be punished by fine and whipping; the offending teacher was to be punished by fine not exceeding five hundred dollars and imprisonment. It also provided that "if one free negro teach another, he is to be fined and whipped at the discretion of the court! Should a free negro presume to preach to, or exhort his companions, he may be seized without warrant and whipped thirty-nine lashes, and the same number of lashes may be applied to each one of his congregation." [25]

Some measures were taken to reduce the danger of insurrection by decreasing the exploitation of the slaves. South Carolina re-enacted a law originally passed in 1740, limiting slave labor to 15 hours in the spring and summer and 14 hours in the fall and winter. Most of the states declared that no work was to be done on Sunday except that which was absolutely necessary. Georgia provided penalties for the master who overworked his slaves, and Louisiana decreed that slaves should be permitted two hours for dinner from May until November, and one and one-half hours during the remainder of the year. These were ineffectual safeguards, but their presence on the statute books shows that although the slave insurrections never succeeded, they were not complete defeats, any more than were the unsuccessful strikes of the northern workers.

WHITE WORKERS AND SLAVERY

The spirit and courage of the insurrectionists inspired many Abolitionists in their struggle to end slavery, and the ferocity with which the rebellions were crushed convinced new masses of people that slavery must be abolished. Consequently, the slave-owners sought allies among their non-slaveholding neighbors. On June 30, 1855, the *North Carolina Standard* argued that "persons who own no slaves are inseparably associated either by blood, affinity, interest and business relations with those who do; and whatever contributes to weakening the power of the South in this respect, or to impair the safety and value of the institution must fall in the end with equal force—with equal ruin upon all." [25]

Only a small percentage of the white population of the South derived their profits from the sweat and toil of Negro slaves. Not more than half a million southern whites in 1860 maintained slaves who with their families numbered less than three million. The total white population of the slave states was nine million; thus, less than one-third of the white people of the South derived any benefit from the institution of slavery. Economic power was concentrated in a few thousand families who lived on the best lands and received three-quarters of the returns from the yearly exports. The Federal Census of 1850 revealed that a thousand families received over fifty million a year while all the remaining 660,000 families received only about sixty million. [26]

Slavery was a blight to the whole South. Thousands of poor whites were living under conditions which were "only to be compared with that of the Roman plebeians in the period of Rome's extreme decline." They lived in abandoned outhouses cultivating the old fields of large plantations, land which the owners had left because it was too unprofitable for slave labor.* William Gregg, a public-spirited citizen of South Caro-

---

* Slavocracy's leading publicist, J. D. B. De Bow, frankly admitted: "The non-slaveholders possess generally but very small means, and the land which they possess is almost universally poor and so sterile that a scanty subsistence is all that can be derived from its cultivation, and the more fertile soil being in the hands of the slaveholders, must ever remain out of power of those who have none." (James D. B. De Bow, *The Industrial Resources, etc. of the Southern and Western States.* New Orleans, vol. II, p. 106.)

lina, estimated that at least one-third of the white population of his state lived under these conditions if not worse. *De Bow's Review* in 1860 estimated several million poor whites for the entire South. These poor whites on the soil were not the only poor whites in the South. William H. Seward argued in his famous speech, the "Irrepressible Conflict," that slavery was an evil not only because it loaded the Negroes down with chains, but because it was "scarcely less severe upon the freeman to whom only because he is a laborer from necessity, it denies facilities for employment and whom it expels from the community because it cannot enslave and convert him into merchandise." [27]

An Alabama planter boasted: "On my own place, I have now slave carpenters, slave blacksmiths, and slave wheelwrights, and thus I am independent of free mechanics." [28] Despite the high prices paid for slaves, and the relative inefficiency of slave labor in industry, employers found slave labor much cheaper than free labor. The De Kalb mill in Georgia reported that a Negro worker cost $75 a year in contrast to $111 required for a white operative, while the Saluda mill near Columbia, South Carolina, in which 128 adult slaves and children operated 1500 spindles and 120 looms, reported a saving of 30 per cent. During the 'fifties slaves employed in a cotton factory at Jackson, Mississippi, were allowed twenty cents a day for board, while white workers received thirty cents. As far north as Baltimore, slave mechanics offered such serious competition to skilled German artisans that many of them were forced to leave the city.[29]

The largest ironworks in the South, the Tredagar Iron Works in Richmond, Virginia, employed slave labor. When Robert Anderson took over the failing business in 1847, he replaced most of the free workers with slaves. "From the difficulty of controlling in a slave state the white labor *employed at high wages* in the manufacture of iron," he wrote, "I have come to the conclusion to introduce slaves to a great extent, having satisfied myself by experiment of the practicability of the scheme." By 1848 the company was making a $98,272 profit, and Anderson was preaching "that all iron establishments in a slave state must come to the employment of slaves." [30] *

---

* By the middle 'fifties, however, the use of slaves in industry on an extensive scale proved unsuccessful. One student who has examined this question offers the following reasons for this failure:

"Slaves transplanted from the plantations to the factories failed to make productive mill hands, for, since they were hired out for the period between planting and picking, the constant alteration between the land and loom prevented even a gradual accumulation of industrial skill.

"This could be obviated by the outright purchase of slaves, but that in turn entailed even greater difficulties. First, buying slaves meant a larger immediate outlay of capital. It was estimated that the initial investment would have to be

Slaves were not only preferred because of their cheapness but as one owner of a cotton factory in Fayetteville, North Carolina, reported: "With the blacks there is no turning out for wages, and no time lost in visiting masters, and other public exhibitions." [31] The ever-increasing competition of slave labor led to unemployment among free white workers and forced wages to the subsistence level of a slave. In August, 1855, the Raleigh, North Carolina *Arator* estimated that there were many hundreds and thousands of working class families who were "existing upon half starvation from year to year. . . . There are many in this city whose wives and children are suffering for the want of food and raiment, who, if they remain here, are doomed to drag out a miserable existence. . . ." William Gregg constantly spoke of the "mass of unemployed white labor" in the South.[32]

By 1860 the wage scales in the South were the lowest in the nation. The daily wage in 1860 for day laborers in the North was about $1.11, whereas in most southern states it was between 77 and 90 cents. The daily wage for carpenters in the North for the same year was about $2, while in many southern states it did not exceed $1.56. While operatives in Georgia cotton factories were earning $7.39 a month, workers in textile mills in Massachusetts doing the same work were getting $14.57.[33]

Hand in hand with unemployment and low wages was the stigma upon manual labor which developed in the slaveholding states. Free labor could have no social standing in a society where labor was considered degrading and unworthy of a white man. "The great curse of slavery with us," wrote Ebenezer Pettigrew, a prominent North Carolinian, "is not the fanatical notion of its sinfulness, but the rendering manual labour and pursuits degrading in the eyes of prominent gentlemen, who had rather cheat than work." [34] Few immigrants came South because they were looked down upon in a society where "to labor is to slave, to work like a Negro." [35] For the same reason a group of New England factory girls who had been induced to come south by bonuses and higher wages, "found their position so unpleasant, owing to the

increased by as much as 50 per cent, and that in the face of constant insufficiency of funds. Secondly, bought labor was precisely the factor industry could not endure. The ownership of slave labor would freeze southern industry at the start, denying it the capacity to expand and contract with relative ease. While an increase in production would demand a much larger outlay for the purchase of additional slaves, any slight depression, on the other hand, would bring relatively great losses. Slaves, unlike free labor, could not be 'fired' and thrown onto the open market; on the contrary their maintenance persisted, independent of profit or loss. Moreover, the forced sale of Negroes in a depressed market, like that of any other superfluous commodity, would entail great losses. Conversely, during prosperous periods, the competitive demands of manufacturers and planters would serve to inflate the price of slaves." (Fabien Linden, "Repercussions of Manufacturing in the Ante-Bellum South," *North Carolina Historical Review*, vol. XVII, Oct. 1940, pp. 326-27.)

general degradation of the laboring class," that they returned to the North.[36] Other workers who came south left because there were no opportunities for their children in the trades. Charles Lyell, an English traveler in America, noted the following conversation which took place in Columbus, Georgia, in the late 'forties: "Several New Englanders who have come from the north to South Carolina and Georgia, complain to me that they cannot push on their children here as carpenters, cabinet makers, blacksmiths, and in other of such crafts, because the planters bring up the most intelligent of their slaves to these occupations." [37]

When the white workers in the Tredagar Iron Works went on strike in 1847, they were promptly prosecuted and summoned to court. The same thing happened in New Orleans a few years later when longshoremen turned out for higher wages.[38] Only the printers were successful in maintaining labor organization because the printing trade was one of the few in which there was no serious competition from slave labor. In general, however, strikes could not be successfully conducted in a slave-holding community. "The South," Roger W. Shugg points out, "was hardly of a mind to bargain with workers of one race when it owned so many of another." [39]

Much of the labor activity of free workers in the South before the Civil War was directed towards keeping Negro slaves out of mechanical pursuits. This does not mean that white and Negro mechanics constantly clashed. In many places in the South, white and Negro mechanics worked side by side with little friction. The *Georgia Federal Union* of March 18, 1836, reported that "ten or fifteen white mechanics and some twenty or more Negroes [are] working well" in a boat-building establishment. Six years later, the English traveler, J. S. Buckingham, was impressed by the fact that in the cotton mills of Athens, Georgia, where white and Negro workers were working together, there was "no difficulty among them on account of colour, the white girls working in the same room and at the same loom with black girls and boys of each colour, as well as men and women, working together without repugnance or objection...." [40] White and Negro mechanics worked for years in the same workshops in St. Louis, before the Civil War, and rarely was there any antagonism between them.[41]

Yet the pre-war period in the South was one of unremitting effort on the part of white mechanics to curtail or prevent the employment of Negro artisans. At first they relied on petitions. Thus, in 1830, a group of unemployed stonecutters of Norfolk, Virginia, petitioned the Navy Department in Washington to stop the employment of Negro slaves in the construction of a drydock for the Navy. They were men of families, they declared, and found it impossible to keep their children from starving, when forced to compete with slaves. They could not but help "view this engagement of Negroes as a most grievous imposition, detrimental to the laboring interest of the community and subversive to every principle of equality."

When the Navy Department asked the engineer why he employed slaves, he promptly replied that he was saving money for the government. Negro slaves cost 72 cents a day at a time when white stonecutters were asking from one and a half to two dollars a day. Of almost equal importance, he argued, was the fact that he was teaching the slaveholders that they could successfully use their slaves on industrial projects. "It is important to this state," he concluded, "where slaves constitute so great a portion of the laborers, that Virginians should learn how the blacks may be made so much more valuable than has hitherto been thought." Convinced by these arguments, the Navy Department approved of the employment of slaves on the project. The stonecutters of Norfolk appealed to Congress but they received no support.[42]

Occasionally white mechanics protested against the introduction of Negro slaves as this practice would soon reduce their wages. When the workers in the Tredagar Iron Works turned out to prevent the use of slaves in the industry, they were told that their demands "struck at the root of all the rights and privileges of the masters," and were "pregnant" with the evils of abolition. Slave labor remained.[43]

Finally, the white mechanics turned to political action. At first they exerted little influence, but as their pressure increased some legislation was enacted. In 1845, the legislature of Georgia made the employment of a Negro mechanic or mason, whether slave or free, illegal. Similar legislation was being considered in other states, and so strong became the popular feeling against the use of Negro slaves in industry, that C. G. Memminger, a leader in southern politics, predicted that "ere long we will have a formidable party on this subject." [44]

The slaveholders were alarmed. Any restriction of the use of slaves not only limited their power and authority but removed an important source of profit, for the planters often turned to industry in times of crisis, to hire out their idle slaves. A victory for white labor would establish a precedent. If left unchallenged, it would lead only to more and more restrictions on the authority of the slave owners. L. W. Spratt, editor of the *Charleston Standard,* wrote:

"They will question the right of masters to employ their slaves in any works that they may wish for.... They may acquire the right to determine municipal elections. ... Thus the town of Charleston, at the heart of slavery, may become a democratic power against it." [45]

Their reasoning was logical. The protest movement against the use of Negro slaves in industry organized white mechanics in the South, and once they were organized they called for democratic reforms. As a result of the pressure exerted by the working class, a number of democratic reforms were achieved. It was the industrial workers who were chiefly responsible for the abolition of imprisonment for debt in Virginia and Maryland, and for the incorporation into the constitutions of these states in 1850-51 of provisions dealing with the property rights of married women.[46] In Georgia, the Mechanics' Associations forced the state legislature to pass a law in 1853 providing that the legal day for all white persons under 21 years of age in all cotton, woolen, and other manufacturing establishments or machine shops should be "from sunrise to sunset, the usual and customary time for meals being allowed."[47] This was the only piece of labor legislation enacted in the South during the pre-Civil War era.

The struggle for *ad valorem* taxation as a more equitable tax system reached considerable intensity in North Carolina. Although slaves from the age of 12 to 50 were taxed five and three quarters cents per hundred dollars of their value, land was taxed twenty cents and workers' tools and implements were taxed one dollar per hundred dollars. A worker from Raleigh, North Carolina asked in 1860: "Is it no grievance to tax the wages of the laboring man, and not tax the income of their employer?"[48]

The leader for equalized taxation was Moses A. Bledsoe, a state senator from Wake County. When he supported the recently formed Raleigh Workingmen's Association in 1858, the slaveholders read him out of the Democratic Party, but in 1860 he ran as an independent and was elected. The *ad valorem* campaign was a direct challenge to the political and economic privileges of slavery.[49]

The change from attacking the slave to attacking slavery came about very slowly, and many white workers never made the transition. Yet, in 1860, Alfred E. Matthews noted in a report of his journey through the South: "I have seen free white mechanics obliged to stand aside while their families were suffering for the necessaries of life, when slave mechanics, owned by rich and influential men, could get plenty of work; and I have heard these same white mechanics breathe the most bitter curses against the institution of slavery and the slave aristocracy."[50] Virginia workers were calling for a constitutional convention which would "bring the downfall of wire-drawing politicians and the rising up of respected laborers. Then will the old aristocracy be known as the dust that it is, and productive industry meet the reward that it merits."[51]

The mechanics and working men of Lexington, Kentucky, a slaveholding state, adopted the following resolution at a public meeting in the spring of 1849; and at the same time ordered the publication of 20,000 copies of an address on emancipation:

"Resolved, That the institution of slavery is prejudicial to every interest of the State, and is alike injurious to the slaveholder and non-slaveholder;

that it degrades labor, enervates industry, interferes with the occupations of free laboring citizens, separates too widely the poor and the rich, shuts out the laboring classes from the blessings of education, and tends to drive from the State all who depend upon personal labor for support. That while we recognize the right of property in slaves under existing laws, we hold that the laboring man has as full a right to his occupation and the profits of his labor, as the master to his slaves; and as slavery tends to the monopoly of as well as the degradation of labor, public and private right require its ultimate extinction." [52]

Not until the 'fifties did the alliance between the poor whites and slaves begin to extend throughout the South. Southern papers began to attack the "malicious whites" in the cities who were helping the slaves to organize rebellions. The Galveston, Texas, *News* of December 27, 1856, warned the planters to watch out for "white men who are constantly inciting our slaves to deeds of violence and bloodshed." [53] Four years later, a large group of planters in Alabama met to discuss the danger created by "low down poor whites" who were joining with slaves in plots to overthrow slavery after which land, mules, and money would be redistributed. The *Mobile Mercury* commented that "slaves are constantly associating with low white people who are not slave owners. Such people are dangerous to the community." [54]

Equally dangerous to slavery were the German-American Communists who organized opposition to slavery in a number of southern states. Adolph Douai, who later became a leading Marxist, published a weekly Abolitionist paper, the *San Antonio Zeitung*, from July 5, 1853, to March, 1856. Before the *Zeitung* started publication there were several small anti-slavery bulletins published by an association of German workingmen in San Antonio, all of whom were Communists and most of them followers of Wilhelm Weitling. [55] Though the Texan slave owners drove Douai out of the community, they could not, as they learned during the Civil War, destroy his anti-slavery ideas.* During the war, a leaflet was distributed in San Antonio, Texas, by a group of German-American Communists, calling upon the people to rise up against the Confederacy. Although the revolt did not materialize, General McCullock, writing to Jefferson Davis from San Antonio, admitted that the "tract speaks the sentiments of a large portion of the population here, many of whom are doing all they can to injure our cause secretly and would do so openly if they dared." [56]

---

* In 1868 Douai received a newspaper from Texas which carried the following announcement in bold type at the head of the first column: "This paper, edited and set by negroes, is being printed on the same press from which Dr. Douai for the first time advocated the emancipation of the negroes in Texas. Let this serve him as a token of gratitude of the colored race that they preserve the memory of his efforts for their freedom." (Morris Hillquit, *History of Socialism in the United States,* New York, 1903, p. 191; *New Yorker Volkszeitung,* No. 4, 1888.)

SLAVERY'S DILEMMA

As the 'fifties drew to a close the small oligarchy of slave owners faced an ever-increasing class war. "It is this great upheaving of our masses," wrote J. H. Taylor, a South Carolinian in 1850, "we have to fear, as far as our institutions are concerned." "The people," observed a citizen of Montgomery, Alabama, ten years later, "are divided into two classes—the rich and the poor who are as distinct and separate as the North Pole is from the South Pole." [57]

The slave owners faced still another dilemma in the 'fifties. To keep slaves out of industry meant to open the way for the rise of a free working class which was by nature hostile to the planter aristocracy. To permit the slaves to work in the factories would weaken the entire slave system, for experience had demonstrated that slaves engaged in industry speedily became leaders of struggles for freedom. Furthermore, the use of slaves in industry, which had seemed extremely feasible in the early 1840's, proved unsuccessful in actual practice.

The slave owners met these problems by throwing their full weight against the rise of industry in the South. Those who advocated the growth of southern industry complained bitterly of the opposition of the slaveholders who, "relentlessly hostile to the rising 'menace,' fought determinedly to block the establishment of factories." [58] The nature of the "menace" was stated simply by the *Morehouse Advocate,* a Louisiana paper: "The great mass of foreigners who come to our shores are laborers, and consequently come into competition with slave labor. It is to their interest to abolish slavery, and we know full well the disposition of man to promote all things which advance his own interests." [59] The *Charleston Standard,* a leading slaveholders' organ, agreed. "A large proportion of the mechanical force that migrate to the South," it declared in the 'fifties, "are a curse instead of a blessing; they are generally a worthless unprincipled class—enemies to our peculiar institutions—pests to society, dangerous among the slave population, and ever ready to form combinations against the interests of the slaveholder, against the laws of the country, and against the peace of the commonwealth." [60]

Horace Greeley in 1853 said that the slaveholders were quite logical in opposing the entrance of workers from the North into the cotton kingdom. "Every free laborer taken to the South," he observed, "is a fresh nail in the coffin of slavery." [61] By stifling the rise of industry, the slave owners were able for the time being to retard the growth of the free working class in the South, but they could not prevent workers in the North from driving nails in the coffin of slavery. Though slow to become active in the struggle, northern labor was to do more than its share to hasten the burial of human bondage in America.

CHAPTER 14

Northern Labor and Slavery

The struggles of American labor before the Civil War for higher wages, shorter hours, and better working conditions were interlocked with the struggle against Negro slavery. Eventually the wage workers had to throw all their strength into that struggle for they now understood that not until slavery was smashed could the working class advance.

This understanding did not come about overnight. From the very outset of the struggle against chattel slavery there were groups of workers ready to join in the demand for the end of human bondage in America. The platforms of many of the labor parties formed in New York state during the early 'thirties contained planks calling for the abolition of Negro slavery, "the darkest, foulest blot upon the nation's character." [1] Included in the "Workingmen's Prayer" submitted in 1830 by the trade unions of Massachusetts to the State Legislature was the appeal: "May the foul stain of slavery be blotted out of our fair escutcheon; and our fellow men, not only declared to be free and equal, but actually enjoy that freedom and equality to which they are entitled by nature." [2]

Thomas Wentworth Higginson writes in his memoirs that the antislavery cause was "far stronger for a time in the factories and shoe shops [of New England] than in the pulpits or colleges." Higginson was not referring to the capitalists who owned these factories and shops. These businessmen had a lucrative market in the cotton kingdom. What a New York businessman told an Abolitionist in 1835 was repeated by his colleagues in Boston and Lowell, where, as in the Empire City, there was a "triple entente between the 'Lords of the Lash,' the 'Lords of the Loom,' and the 'Lords of the Long Wharf.'" [3]

"We cannot afford, sir, to let you and your associates endeavor to overthrow slavery. It is not a matter of principle with us. It is a matter of business necessity. We mean, sir, to put you abolitionists down, by fair means if we can, by foul means if we must." [4]

266

That conservative businessmen would use foul means to put down the Abolitionists did not surprise workingmen. Foul means were always used to break strikes. During the campaign in Congress by the slave owners and their northern allies to deprive the Abolitionists of the right of petition, the Philadelphia Trades' Union observed that the petitions of the Abolitionists and those of the trade unions in behalf of the ten-hour day received the same treatment.[5] William Leggett, acting editor of the *New York Evening Post* and a spokesman for the labor movement during the Jacksonian era, attacked the government's interference with the mail privileges of the anti-slavery journals, and warned the workers that their journals would be next.[6] When the Mayor of Philadelphia prevented Frances Wright from lecturing in that city on the subject of slavery, the *National Laborer* stated:

"The people need not be surprised at this, when they remember that it is the same Mayor who demanded the enormous bail of $2,500 for the appearance of the Schuylkill laborers to answer the charge of riot, who were afterwards discharged because there was no crime found against them." [7]

UNCERTAINTIES

There was a growing conviction among the workingmen that to preserve their own civil and political liberties they had to support the struggle for the democratic rights of the Abolitionists to fight slavery. The Lowell girls said as much when they organized a Female Anti-Slavery Society in 1832, and when a few years later they campaigned for signatures to petitions urging the abolition of slavery.[8] This anti-slavery agitation was their atonement for working on raw materials produced by slave labor. Southern businessmen threatened the employers that if their workers did not stop their anti-slave agitation, they would buy clothing and shoes elsewhere. The employers fumed, but the Lowell and Fall River factory girls still held their annual fairs at which they raised money for the Abolitionist movement, and many a Mechanics' Association bade the Abolitionists Godspeed in their undertaking.[9]

There were workingmen who believed that the isolated activities of mechanics' associations and factory girls should be developed into a nation-wide campaign by free labor to bring an end to chattel slavery in America. In 1836, the Working Man's Association of England, parent body of the Chartist movement, addressed an appeal to American workers urging them to begin such a campaign. Their proposal was seconded by Lewis G. Gunn, a Philadelphia labor leader, who issued the following appeal to the workers of America:

"As long as the pulse beats in my frame the poor Negro in chains shall have my sympathy and much of my attention. . . . Let me entreat you also never to forget the slave. . . . Our Voice should *thunder* from Maine to Georgia, and from the Atlantic to the Mississippi—the voice of a nation of *Republicans* and *Christians* demanding with all the authority of moral power, *demanding* the immediate liberation of the bondsmen." [10]

The English workingmen and Gunn were disappointed by the slim results of their appeals. Most workers were not yet ready to join a campaign to abolish slavery, and some were more willing to attack the Abolitionists than the slave owners. Many obstacles had yet to be overcome before the wage workers of America could assume their proper role in the struggle to end slavery.

Some workers in the 'thirties feared that the slavery question would cause a split in the Democratic Party, thus strengthening the foes of Jacksonian democracy. The slave owners were an important section in the Democratic Party, and fear of alienating them was expressed by leading trade unionists like Ely Moore, president of the New York General Trades' Union, who declared that support of the Abolitionist movement by the working class would be disastrous for the Jacksonian movement. If the Democratic Party were split, he said, "the pro-Bank, anti-Jackson aristocracy will have realized its fondest and most cherished hope." [11]

Even when the Democratic Party was passing more and more under the domination of the slave owners, many northern workers still hesitated to support the anti-slavery movement for fear of splitting the party. This was especially true of Irish-American, German-American and other foreign-born workers who were constantly menaced by movements clamoring for legislation restricting immigration and extending the naturalization period required for citizenship. The Democratic Party opposed such laws, whereas the Whig Party, notoriously hostile to the foreign-born, openly sponsored these measures. A split in the Democratic Party, they believed, would mean the triumph of the anti-foreigner, anti-Catholic elements who hid their un-American principles behind the slogan of Americanism.

To the fear of splitting the Democratic Party was added the fear that emancipation would bring thousands of Negroes to the northern states, increasing the competition for jobs and sending wages and living standards down. The northern allies of the slave owners played on these fears. In New York City where business connections with the cotton kingdom were most highly developed, merchants, bankers, politicians and the pro-southern "satanic press" initiated a well organized campaign to convince the working class that the freedom of the slaves would "lower the conditions of the white laborer," that the Abolitionists were, therefore, the enemies of the Northern white workers.[12] The slave owners by keeping the Negroes enslaved were their true friends. To many workers who had a hard time supporting their families these arguments were given weight by the hiring of non-union free Negroes to replace members of trade unions.[13] *

Probably none were more influenced by this pro-slavery propaganda than were the Irish-American workers who were mainly unskilled and could easily be replaced by Negro labor. The Catholic press often took the lead in disseminating the type of propaganda which played upon the natural fears of workers. Thus the *Freeman's Journal,* which was for a time the official organ of the Archbishop of New York and had a wide circulation among Irish-American workers, regularly attacked abolitionism "as an import from England," and charged that the emancipation of the slaves would ruin the white workers in the North. The point of view was typical of the stand taken in an important section of the Catholic press towards the slavery question, and undoubtedly exerted great influence on Catholics throughout the nation. Since the Catholic Church did nothing to counteract this influence it acquired the reputation as being a "protagonist of slavery." [14]

Some steps towards counteracting this reputation were taken by Catholic workers in Ireland. In 1841 an appeal was addressed to Irish-Americans signed by 70,000 Irishmen, with Daniel O'Connell, the great Irish liberator, and Father Matthew, the prominent temperance leader, sponsoring the appeal. It denounced slavery and urged the Irish in America to identify themselves with the Abolitionists. "Irishmen and Irishwomen, treat the colored people as your equals, as brethren. By all your memories of Ireland, continue to love Liberty—hate Slavery—*Cling by the Abolitionists*—and in America you will do honor to the name of Ireland." [15]

After the appeal, a series of meetings was organized by Irish workingmen in Boston and New York to which Abolitionist leaders were invited. At one such meeting in Faneuil Hall, Boston, Wendell Phillips, the Abolitionist orator, read the O'Connell appeal to thousands of Irish workers who enthusiastically applauded every paragraph and shouted negatives to his questions: "Will you ever return to his master the slave who once sets foot on the soil of Massachusetts? (*No, No, No*) Will you ever raise to office or power the man who will not pledge his effort against slavery? (*No! No! No!*)" [16]

---

*In a number of instances, however, Negro and white workers worked and went on strike together. Thus white carpenters and caulkers and Negro caulkers employed in the Navy Yard in Washington joined in a strike in July, 1835. (Michael Shiner Diary, July 28, 1835, Library of Congress, manuscripts division.) Shiner, a free Negro, worked in the Navy yard with white workers from 1812-1865.

Had the O'Connell address received the support of the Catholic Church and the Catholic press it would have had more influence in Irish-American circles. But Archbishop Hughes of New York denounced O'Connell, expressed doubt as to the genuineness of the Irish appeal, and said that genuine or not it was the duty of every Irishman in America to resist and repudiate it with indignation as a foreign interference "on questions of domestic and national policy." Most Catholic papers continued their campaign to convince white workers that the Abolitionist program meant that after emancipation the Negro workers would crowd out the white worker.[17]

LABOR AND THE ABOLITIONISTS

The Abolitionists did little to overcome the fears of the working class regarding the so-called dangers of Negro emancipation. In fact they did a good deal to convince many workers that they were concerned only with the welfare of the Negro slaves and considered the problems of free labor as insignificant. In the first issue of the *Liberator* William Lloyd Garrison denounced the trade union movement as an organized conspiracy to "inflame the minds of our working classes against the more opulent." "Trade unions," he declared, were "in the highest degree criminal," for they led workers to believe that their employers were their enemies. "Perhaps," he added, "it would be nearer the truth to affirm that mechanics are more inimical to each other, than the rich toward them." [18]

Garrison was not alone. The *National Anti-Slavery Standard,* official organ of the American Anti-Slavery Society, declared in 1847 that no true Abolitionist could have any sympathy for those who denounced wage slavery as an evil. Even Wendell Phillips, who was later to fight for the freedom of the wage slaves, shared this view. Workers in the North, he wrote in 1847, had no real need for trade unions, for they were "neither wronged nor oppressed." And even if they were, they had "only to stay at home ... and soon diminished supply will bring the remedy." [19]

Fortunately, Phillips quickly changed his mind. A year later he opposed a resolution calling for the boycotting of products of slave labor on the ground that it was "wrong to purchase or use the product of *unpaid* labor." Phillips argued that if this was the justification for purchasing only the products of free labor then one logically would have to abstain from buying many other commodities besides cotton "since there was much labor in the world which though, perhaps, a little better paid than that of the slaves, was still unpaid, uncompensated, in any just sense." He pointed to the women shirtmakers, the factory operatives, the miners of England, and the laborers of Ireland as examples of workers who were "miserably underpaid" and whose "portion of the net profit of their several manufactories was far too small, unjustly so." "I call payment," he added, "that which secures the necessaries of life—some time and means of mental improvement and something against age and sickness. This every industrious human being deserves for a day's work." [20]

After some time more and more Abolitionist leaders adopted Phillips' viewpoint. Frederick Douglass, the great Negro Abolitionist leader, spoke out frequently in behalf of the efforts of wage workers to organize for improvement of their conditions.* He was hailed by trade unionists and invited by the journeymen printers' union of Rochester to attend an anniversary celebration of Benjamin Franklin's birthday. Horace Greeley was another opponent of slavery who did much to affect a rapprochement between Abolitionists and sections of the labor movement. Greeley denounced Abolitionists who refused to treat their workers decently and even turned down an invitation to an anti-slavery convention because of the indifference of many of the delegates to the problems of northern wage workers.[21]

But until the viewpoint of some of the leaders of Abolitionism towards the problems of free labor underwent a change, really cordial relations between them and most wage workers were almost out of the question. These workers definitely resented what they regarded as the tendency of Abolitionists "to stretch their ears to hear the sound of the lash on the back of the oppressed black," at the same time that they were deaf to the cries of the oppressed wage workers in the North. Devoted as she was to the anti-slavery cause, Sarah Bagley was forced, nevertheless, to denounce the Abolitionist leaders for their failure to concern themselves also with the plight of wage workers in the North. "What of the ten thousand girls," she asked Garrison, "who without any warning were turned out on the streets of Lowell, to go where they pleased and as they willed?" Other workers took up the cry and called upon the anti-slavery men to see to it at their conventions "that the rights of the white slaves of the North are not forgotten." Still others condemned those Abolitionists who expressed "pity for the southern slave, but would crush with an iron hand the white laborer of the north." [22] Such an attitude was expressed in the concluding verse of a poem published in many labor papers describing the death of a factory girl from starvation:

---

* Douglass spoke out just as frequently in criticism of the refusal of the trade unions to organize free Negro mechanics or even allow them to work in the same shops with white workers. "How sad it is," he declared in 1851, "that our white fellow-countrymen cannot find a class of original and heaven-sanctioned principles, which while they should be all sufficient to sustain the rights of white men should serve the opposite purpose for black men." (*Frederick Douglass' Paper*, June 26, 1851.)

That night a Chariot passed her,
While on the ground she lay;
The daughters of her master,
An evening visit pay,
Their tender hearts are sighing,
As Negroes' woes are told;
While the white slave was dying,
Who gained their father's gold.[23]

WAGE SLAVERY AND CHATTEL SLAVERY

Most workers agreed readily that chattel slavery was an abominable crime but they felt that their conditions in northern shops and factories were no less abominable. Slavery, as they saw it, did not consist of names but of facts. It mattered little to them whether the lash was of leather or of want and poverty. Said the Manchester, New Hampshire, *Operative* in 1844:

"A great cry is raised in the northern states against southern slavery. The sin of slavery may be abominable there, but is it not equally so here? If they have *black* slaves, have we not *white* ones? Or how much better is the condition of some of our laborers here at the north, than the slaves of the south? It may be said that he enjoys his *liberty;* but how many of our workingmen, how many of the operatives in our mills, enjoy anything worthy of the name of liberty?

"...Our laborers may work as the capitalist dictates, or not, but if they do not, they must starve! And if they work, the capitalists derive *nine elevenths* of the products of their labor. How much better, then, we ask, is the condition of some of our *white,* northern laborers, than some of the black southern slaves?" [24]

Robert Dale Owen, Albert Brisbane, and Horace Greeley opposed not only Negro slavery but all forms of slavery. Their ideas are incorporated in the following statement adopted at a meeting of 25,000 New York workingmen held in January, 1845:

"To slavery in the abstract, slavery in the concrete, to slavery absolute, slavery feudal, and the slavery of wages; to slavery where it is, and where it is not; from the first Israelite who leaned his ear against the door, and was pierced with his master's awl to the last son of Adam who shall wear the badge of servitude; to Slavery we are utterly opposed under every phase and modification, and so with firm and solemn purpose will remain until our lives end." [25]

There were some in the ranks of labor who argued that the workers should concern themselves primarily with the struggle against wage slavery. The *National Laborer* stated on September 17, 1836, that while it opposed "slavery in every form, either over the *body,* mind, color or degree," it felt that it was "the duty of organized labor to begin to secure to the workingmen the right of disposing his own labor at his own price, and to make that price just and equivalent to his toil." But it was the return of George Henry Evans from retirement to lead the land reform movement that marked the influence within the working class of the idea of precedence of the fight against wage slavery. Unlike the Owenites and the Associationists who fought against all forms of slavery simultaneously,* Evans and other land reformers took the position that the abolition of wage slavery was the only important problem facing the working class. Since the controversy over Negro slavery detracted the workers from the main problem confronting them, they had better forget about chattel slavery. Then could they triumphantly devote all their time and energy to the one program which would abolish wage slavery—land reform!

Evans also urged the Abolitionists to join his crusade instead of frittering away their time with petitions to Congress. Land reform, he assured them, would lead more quickly to the abolition of chattel slavery than would any number of petitions and mass meetings. Thus Evans predicted that if Congress passed a land reform law in 1850, the following wonderful situation would exist in the South twenty years later:

"In the Southern States chattel slavery is gradually dying out under the operation of the Free Public Land Law.... The emancipated Negroes have formed a settlement on the Public Lands almost large enough for a State and are debating whether they shall follow their brethren to Liberia or ask to be recognized as an independent State." [26]

To justify his theory that wage slavery should be abolished first, Evans followed the arguments of the slave owners and their northern allies whose favorite defense of slavery was the contrast between the "poor, miserable, manacled, starving, naked," free worker of the North and the happy slaves of the South, "surrounded with every comfort for animal indulgence," cared for in sickness and in old age by a benevolent master. "Free laborers," wrote George Fitzhugh, a prominent Southern apologist,

* On June 21, 1845, *The Harbinger,* organ of the Associationists, offered the following advice to the Abolitionists: "We are convinced, that if the leaders in the Abolition movement would embrace in their attacks, the two kinds of slavery the most prevalent in this country—chattel slavery at the south, and the slavery of capital, or the wages system at the north—black slavery and white slavery—this extension would give them immense additional power."

"have not the thousandth part of the rights and liberties of Negro slaves." [27]

Though Evans never openly justified slavery he supplied the slave press with useful arguments. He argued that to free the Negro people for wage slavery would be a great disadvantage to the slaves as they would exchange their "surety of support in sickness and old age," for poverty and unemployment.[28] Abolition of slavery, he maintained, would harm the northern worker by throwing millions of black workers on the labor market, driving down the wages of the whole working class. Thomas Devyr, one of Evans' disciples said: "Emancipate the white man first—free him from the thraldom of his unsupplied wants and the day this is done, we'll commence the manumission of the much wronged black man within our borders." [29]

This contention that freeing the slaves under the wage system would threaten northern workers met with approval among some Irish-American laborers, and Evans' radical sounding words impressed groups of German-Americans. It is extremely doubtful that many northern workers accepted Evans' statement that wage workers were worse off than Negro slaves. Why was it, they asked, that so many slaves risked their lives to escape their "security"? And why was it that no free Negroes in the North were known to have run the other way?

Organized workers understood the fundamental distinction between chattel and wage slavery; wage workers could organize and struggle legally to improve their conditions. An operative mechanic wrote in the *Democrat* of March 24, 1836:

"The observation has been made on the floor of Congress, that 'the mechanical and laboring population of the north are a parable class to the slaves of the south.' So long, however, as that class retains their power which they yet possess to right their wrongs peaceably through the ballot boxes, such assertions tend but to exhibit the ignorance or rashness of those that gave utterance to them."

Almost twenty-five years later, in February, 1860, a worker expressed the same idea at a meeting of striking shoe workers in Lynn, Massachusetts:

"You know we are not a quarter as bad off as the slaves of the South, though we are by our foolishness ten times as bad off as we ought to be. They can't vote, nor complain and we can. Then just think of it, the slaves can't hold mass meetings, nor 'strike' and we haven't lost that privilege yet, thank the Lord." [30]

In New England where the land reformers had little influence, the organized workers rejected Evans, and the New England Workingmen's Association urged the slaves to revolt for freedom, justified their right to do so, and called upon northern workers to refuse to join in any military movements to crush these revolts.

"We recommend to our brethren to speak out in thunder tones, both as associations and as individuals, to let it no longer be said that the Northern laborers, while they are contending for their rights, are a standing army to keep three million of their brethern and sisters in bondage at the point of the bayonet." [31]

On May 9, 1848, a mass meeting of trade unionists was held in Faneuil Hall in Boston, in honor of the European Revolutions of 1848. Among the resolutions adopted was one which stated: "While we rejoice in the organization of free institutions in the old world, we are not indifferent to their support at home, and we regret the despotic attitude of the Slave Power at the South, and the domineering ascendancy of the Money Oligarchy are equally hostile to the interests of labor and incompatible with the preservation of popular rights." [32]

"Down with both chattel slavery and wage slavery!" was the slogan of the day among the New England workers. How strongly they opposed slavery was expressed in 1852 by George W. Putnam, an Abolitionist field organizer in New England. "The factory operatives," he wrote to Garrison, "felt that the northern capitalist was closely akin to the Southern slaveholder, and that the design of the Slave Power and the Money Power is to crush both black and white." [33]

A follower of Evans addressed the delegates to the New England Workingmen's Association in 1846. Like Evans, he urged them to forget slavery in the South and to abolish wage slavery in the North through land reform. The delegates disagreed, and resolved that: "American slavery must be uprooted before the elevation sought by the laboring classes can be effected." [34] The organized workers in New England said in 1846 what Karl Marx was to say years later: "In the United States of North America every independent movement of the workers was paralysed so long as slavery disfigured a part of the Republic. Labour cannot emancipate itself in the white skin where in the black it is branded." [35]

Before Marx, Elihu Burritt, the "learned blacksmith," explained in his addresses to workers that slavery degraded free workers by forcing them to compete with chattel slaves, that in the minds of northern capitalists the condition of slaves was accepted "as the base line, the point of departure of their operations; that, somehow it must determine the compensation and honor for free labor." [36] Burritt was not the only New

England thinker to recognize these truths. "Many of the wisest of the labor men," wrote George E. McNeill, a contemporary trade unionist, were "of the opinion that no great progress could be made until after the destruction of the chattel slave system." [37] The New England labor press frequently stressed the same theme. The *Voice of Industry* editorialized in 1847:

"The question of slavery is in truth a question of labor. Whenever the rights of labor are discussed or upon whatever department of labor reform we insist the influence of slavery is arrayed against us. ...."

One year later, the *New Era,* a Boston workingman's paper, expanded on this theme:

"You cannot touch a single question of general policy in which slavery does not get some moral thrust. It cannot be avoided. Slavery must be extinguished....Whatever may be the question...this enormous dragon has something at stake....We go for direct and internecine war with the monster...." [38]

It was too much to expect, however, that most workers would accept so advanced a position in 1848; indeed, the majority of workers did not at any time before the Civil War advocate that "slavery must be extinguished." But gradually, more and more workers learned through experience that from the standpoint of their own class interests they too had to "go for direct and internecine war with the monster."

IMPACT OF SLAVERY EXTENSION

What brought the workers to an understanding of this position was that slavery did not remain in the South awaiting the day that the emancipated wage slaves would turn their attention to abolishing it. It expanded into territories outside of the slave states, and threatened to continue expanding indefinitely unless checked. It soon became apparent to most workers that if they followed Evans' advice and ignored the issue of chattel slavery, they would awake one fine morning and discover that all the land that was to emancipate them was in the hands of the slave owners. And if they continued to remain indifferent to this question, they would awake another morning to find themselves reduced to slavery.

In 1844 the Jacksonville, Alabama, *Republican* stated, "The balance of power is already against us. Under the circumstances the addition of Texas with its slaves is the only means of saving the South." [39] A year later, the slave owners secured the annexation of Texas. In 1846, they provoked a war with Mexico for more territory for slavery and for more political power in the government. Four years later by threatening to secede from the Union, they terrorized enough conservatives in the North, particularly the businessmen engaged in southern trade, to block the Wilmot Proviso which would prohibit the existence of slavery in any part of the territory acquired from Mexico. By beating the drums of secession a bit louder, the slave owners extended slavery into Utah and New Mexico, and gained a more effective fugitive slave law. These victories did not satisfy the slave power. In 1854 the slave owners secured the repeal of the Missouri Compromise of 1820, and opened to slave settlement a region that Congress had declared free. In 1857 the Dred Scott decision ruled that slavery could not be prohibited in any territory of the United States, and that slavery had to be protected by the government in these territories.

At first many workingmen were not alarmed by the conquest of the slavocracy. Some agreed with George Henry Evans that the annexation of Texas was only another phase of the "contest between rich and avaricious planters, and rich and avaricious manufacturers, for exclusive privileges." [40] The *New Era of Industry,* however, was alarmed at the aggressions of the slave power. "Every succeeding day only renders the question of slavery more vexing.... Its ugly face peers up from every cranny and dog-hole into which it has attempted to hide it." [41]

At workingmen's meetings in New York City in 1844 and 1845 opposition was voiced to the annexation of Texas "without provision for the extinction of slavery within her borders.... To admit Texas as a slave territory into this Union would, in the opinion of this meeting, have a tendency to strengthen the institution of slavery." [42] In New England workingmen led by Elihu Burritt organized meetings to protest the annexation of Texas. The *Manchester Operative* in August 1844, stated:

"We have heretofore held our peace in regard to the annexation of Texas, for the purpose of seeing whether our Nation would attempt so base an action. We call it base, because it would be giving men that live upon the blood of others, an opportunity of dipping their hands still deeper in the sin of slavery.... Have we not slaves enough now? Are not two-thirds of our population now in abject slavery? In the South we hear the clanking chains and heart rending pleadings of the sons of Africa that they may have freedom—while in the north the voice of our laboring classes ascends up to heaven in earnest prayer, that they too may be free from the galling yoke of aristocratic power. What a picture our country presents—then why add more of this corrupting evil to the already heart-sickening fact of slavery and bondage?" [43]

Irish workers in large numbers demonstrated in New York, Boston, and Lowell against the annexation of Texas, showing that although they were unwilling to join the Abolitionists, they were opposed to the extension of slavery. Irish workers were also present at a meeting called by New York workingmen in May 1846 to oppose the Mexican War. This meeting branded the war as a scheme of the slave owners and their allies who lived "in such luxurious idleness on the products of the workingmen." They demanded of President Polk that further hostilities be avoided by withdrawing American troops "to some undisputed land belonging to the United States." [44]

Speaking through their delegates at the 1846 convention of the New England Workingmen's Association, the organized workers of New England denounced "the foul disgrace" of extending the area of slavery, and pledged that they would "not take up arms to sustain the Southern slaveholder in robbing one-fifth of our countrymen of their labor." [45]

The division in the ranks of the workingmen on the slavery question continued through the controversy over the Wilmot Proviso. The German-American workers, meeting in a national convention when the debate over the proviso was reaching a climax in Congress, did not adopt a single resolution on chattel slavery. The opportunism of Wilhelm Weitling, and of Herman Kriege, a land reformer who outdid Evans in his insistence that wage workers ignore the slavery question, was mainly responsible for this silence. [46]

Other workers who advocated land reform at first adopted the attitude of their leaders. According to the leaders, the Wilmot Proviso was humbug to cover up the extension not of Negro slavery, but of white slavery. All slavery would end through land reform. "But as the politicians have not the most distant idea of elevating the masses, and as this would do it, they wish to raise new and unimportant issues to draw people's attention from the Land Proviso, so as to perpetuate the greatest Slavery of all Slavery, poverty under the accursed system of Land Monopoly." [47]

A similar stand was taken by the New York City Industrial Congress in the summer of 1850 when it declared that the contest in Congress was "one in which we as workers take no special interest, except in so far as the American Union may be endangered thereby, sincerely believing that it is only a contest between the capitalists of the South and the North as to which shall have the most chattel slaves or the most wage slaves. Resolved, That we consider the freedom of the Public Lands of the first importance." [48]

There is considerable evidence that even that section of the working class in the land reform movement was becoming concerned over the aggressions of the slave power. In June, 1850, the National Industrial Congress condemned slavery as a "moral, social, and political evil." They resolved, "That we are opposed to the further extension of Slavery, and view with abhorrence the idea that to satisfy the South, and to secure the perpetuation of the Federal Union the people of the United States must agree ... that the Slave as well as the Free Area shall be extended. Slavery can never be a bond of union and of freedom." [49]

After the Compromise of 1850, the Sons and Daughters of Toil of Philadelphia, a land reform organization, attacked Congress for having "degraded labor by enacting Fugitive Slave Bills [and] Compromise Acts." This organization affirmed "That Labor on the Soil, in the workshop or factory is, and of right ought to be free without reference to sex, color, or condition." [50]

When the infamous Kansas-Nebraska bill to repeal the Missouri Compromise was introduced into Congress, few workers were silent and none were indifferent.* New leaders had emerged from the German-American workers who immediately joined the small group of anti-slavery men and women who were fighting the battle of freedom and civilization. Chief among these leaders were the Communists, followers of Karl Marx who had come to this country after the defeat of the Revolution of 1848 in Germany. With Joseph Weydemeyer as their leader, they soon became the most effective opponents of slavery in the labor movement. The Communist Club of Cleveland, Ohio, resolved late in 1851, to "use all means which are adapted to abolish slavery, an institution which is so wholly repugnant to the principles of true Democracy." [51] Communist clubs "contributed liberally toward spreading the light on this question and they were so downright in their opposition to the slaveholders as to call any of their members promptly to account who fell under the slightest suspicion of sympathizing with the South." [52]

The Marxists set out to convince the working class that free labor could not emancipate itself as long as chattel slavery existed, that the expansion of slavery "would immensely undermine the power of free labor," and that unless the slave power was smashed, slave labor would become the dominant labor system in the factories and shops of the North as it was fast becoming in the fields of New Mexico. [53]

---

* A worker who was very active in the struggle against slavery during the 'fifties remarked years later that the reduction of working hours had much to do with the vigorous role labor played in the anti-slavery movement after 1854. "In 1854," he wrote, "the country was in the throes of the great contest which ended in Civil War. The audiences all over the land were largely composed of the same class of people who rushed tumultuously into the village church, but they were not working fourteen hours, only ten. I suggest the inquiry to those who resist the reduction of the hours of labor, could a population of fourteen hour men have conducted the debate on the conflict, as we did. I say emphatically No. The history of our country for the last half century would have been reversed. Some disgraceful compromise between Liberty and Slavery would have intervened to the postponement of the noble ideas now before us." (Edward H. Rogers, *Autobiography,* Manuscript copy written in 1902, in Wisconsin State Historical Society, Chapter V.)

THE SLAVEHOLDERS' PROGRAM

The penetrating analysis of the Marxists was proved by tne insane logic of the slave owners. Enslave them all, Negro and white workers alike, they cried. Why be troubled with a free working class? Keep labor on a level with beasts of burden, for as soon as "the mere laborer has the pride, the knowledge, and the aspirations of a free man, he is unfitted for his situation." Slavery was "right, natural and necessary" for all workers, regardless of their complexion. "Slavery is the natural and normal condition of the laboring man," ranted the *Charleston Mercury*. "Master and slave," it stated, "is a relation in society as necessary as that of parent and child, and the Northern States will yet have to introduce it. The theory of free society is a delusion." [54]

Free society, the slave owners argued, was not only a delusion but a danger. In a free society "greasy mechanics" and "filthy operatives," who were "hardly fit for association with a Southern gentleman's body-servant," organized trade unions, engaged in strikes and other subversive activities. Abolitionism was only one of the many isms in the North. From the anti-slavery movement flowed "inexorably common schools, socialism and all other isms." None of these movements could develop in the South. Slavery, boasted one planter, protected the South "from the demands for Land Limitation ... anti-rent troubles, strikes of workmen ... diseased philanthropy, radical democracy and the progress of socialistic ideas in general."

Northern capitalists should institute the system of slave labor in the North. It would relieve them of all anxieties caused by workingmen's parties, trade unions, and German Marxian Socialists who "insolently form associations and devise plans to improve our homely American institutions into the likeness of the bloody and drunken dreams of French and German liberty." Only an alliance between the northern capitalists and the slavocracy could arrest the forces of abolition whose hidden object was the overthrow of all forms of property and the establishment of communism. Eventually, they argued, the northern capitalists would learn that slavery was necessary for them. [55]

It is true that these proposals to replace free labor with slavery in the factories and shops of the North were in direct conflict with the trend of capitalistic development in the United States. Wage labor was a necessity for this development, and slavery had no place in an economy of factories, railroads, and advancing technology. This did not, however, make the danger any less real for the northern workers. They knew that slave labor was rapidly replacing free labor in southern industry, and they were constantly reminded of this fact by their employers and the commercial press whenever they organized to raise wages and reduce working hours.

As early as 1844 workers in Fall River textile mills were told by the mill owners: "You must work as long and as cheap as the Slaves of the South, in order to compete with the Southern manufacturer." [56] Four years later the *Philadelphia Daily Republic* warned striking workingmen in Pennsylvania that if they did not put an end to their demands for increased wages and shorter hours, northern manufacturers would move to the South and use slave labor in production:

"Manufactures are practicable, safe and successful in the South," it declared. "Slave labor can [be] and is employed in them, and—that labor is cheaper than the labor of the free white man, cheaper than the pauper labor of Great Britain.... It is true that slaves are inferior laborers, where, without motive, interest, or any feeling of duty, they must be left to their discretion and cannot be overseen, as in small farming and other solitary occupations, but wherever they can be worked in gangs, and superintended as in the cotton field, forge, furnace, and large cotton and woolen factories, compulsion can easily be made to supply the place of zeal and interest...." [57]

In short, the degrading and paralyzing effects of chattel slavery were definitely threatening the status of every free worker in the United States. Color was no longer the barrier between the Negro slave in the South and the free white worker in the North. As one pro-labor paper put it: "They [Negro slaves] are valuable because they *can* be carpenters, and blacksmiths, and masons, etc., and hence every white laboring man in the country is compelled to have a direct interest in the question of the chattelization of labor." [58]

Organized labor took up the challenge. More than ten thousand workers in Newark, New Jersey, in 1856, at an anti-slave rally passed the following resolution:

"Resolved, That we view with jealousy and suspicion the bold attempts which the Slave Power of the country is now making to degrade the laboring and producing classes of the people by establishing its system of chattel labor in the Free territories of the West; and that...we would repel and resent the efforts to introduce the black slaves into our workshops....Resolved, That the people in this city have abundant reason for sustaining Free and Independent labor...and our influence shall never be given to substitute for it slave labor." [59]

At Manchester, New Hampshire, a protest meeting against the "Nebraska Infamy" was crowded with workers. In Pittsburgh, the workers held a mass meeting to oppose the admission of slavery into Nebraska. Late in February, 1854, five thousand mechanics and workers met at the Broadway Tabernacle in New York City and resolved that the Nebraska Bill was "a base breach of compact and an attempt to degrade free labor."

They further resolved: "That we the mechanics and workingmen of New York heartily concur in the stern protests against the threatened repeal of the Missouri compromise." [60]

A few days later the German-American workingmen of New York City took a similar stand, and at a mass meeting of the *Arbeiterbund* on March 1, 1854, a resolution introduced by Joseph Weydemeyer received the unanimous approval of several thousand German-American workers. It asserted that since the Nebraska bill favored "capitalist land speculation" at the expense of the people, authorized the "future extension of slavery," and withdrew vast tracts of land making it unavailable for any future homestead bill, the German-American workers of New York, who "have, do now, and shall continue to protest most emphatically against both black and white slavery" had no choice but to "solemnly protest against this bill and brand as a traitor against the people and their welfare everyone who shall lend it his support." [61]

Similar meetings were held by workers in New Jersey, Illinois, Pennsylvania, Ohio, Massachusetts, Michigan, Vermont, Connecticut, Indiana, and Wisconsin. Each meeting adopted resolutions castigating the slave power and opposing the Nebraska Bill. The workers of Philadelphia resolved that "We are opposed to the introduction of the curse and infamy of Human Slavery into the Virgin Territory of the North." Shortly after the repeal of the Missouri Compromise, the National Industrial Congress met in convention and reversed their former stand that chattel slavery was of minor importance to the working class. They now correctly said that chattel slavery was first on labor's agenda, and they called upon the workers of the North to demand "the immediate repeal of the Nebraska Bill, the Fugitive Slave Law, and the restoration of the Missouri Compromise." They voted that "in the future we will have no representative in our State or National Councils who has not plighted his sacred honor to resent the aggressions of the southern slave power, and to stand by the liberties of the citizens who elected him to power." [62]

EMERGENCE OF THE REPUBLICAN PARTY

At the time that the National Industrial Congress pledged to support for political office only those candidates who would oppose the aggressions of the slave power, a new political party, dedicated to this purpose, was emerging. Out in Ripon, Wisconsin, Alvin E. Bovay, formerly the secretary-treasurer of the National Industrial Congress and a leader of the workingmen's movement in New York, was uniting liberals and reformers, disgusted with the Whig and Democratic parties, into a new political organization dedicated to fight the further extension of slavery and pledged to support a free land program. Upon this new political organization, Bovay bestowed a name which his former leader, George Henry Evans, had used as far back as 1846. At that time Evans had predicted that within a decade there would be but two political parties in America, "the great Republican Party of Progress and the little Tory Party of Holdbacks." [63]

Evans had used land reform as the dividing line between the two parties, but by the time Bovay gave the name "Republican Party" to the organization which emerged in Ripon, the campaign for land reform and opposition to the extension of slavery had become inseparable. Slaveholders knew that a Homestead bill would prevent the expansion of slavery and give political strength to the anti-slavery forces. The *North Carolina Standard* said that it opposed the Homestead bill because it would bring in new states in the Senate "to vote us down upon every question affecting our vital interest, and finally to control the government absolutely." * Representative Branch of North Carolina said that it was dangerous to slaveholders because it was supported by the labor movement and was therefore "the first step...towards introducing communism and socialism." [64]

The Republican movement spread rapidly throughout the Northwest and soon became an influence in the industrial centers of the East. A general realignment was taking place in American political life. Democrats who refused to stay in their party when it was dominated by slave owners, and Whigs who were fed up with their party straddling the slavery question, were looking for a new political organization. Conservative Whigs who surrendered at every threat of the Slave Power moved into the Know-Nothing movement, finally ending up in the Democratic Party. The newly formed Republican Party represented a coalition of different classes united by their opposition to the future encroachment of the Slave Power.

Important sections of the northern capitalists joined the Republican Party after it got under way and contributed considerable sums to its campaign chest. These industrial and mercantile capitalists were determined to wrest the control of the government from the slaveholders and their northern allies. To these capitalists, owners of cotton and woolen mills and iron furnaces, a victory for the Republican Party meant protective tariffs, government subsidies for the construction of railroads, opportunity to exploit the rich resources of the public domain, a national banking system, and a uniform currency. These measures were long overdue,

---

* For several years, northern manufacturers had also opposed a Homestead bill on the ground that it would induce workers to leave for the West, thereby creating a labor scarcity in the East. Increased immigration and the desire to extend internal markets gradually caused the manufacturers to support a Homestead bill.

but as long as the slavocracy dominated the government they could not be achieved. It was time, thought these capitalists, that the planter aristocrats were removed from political influence, and the interests of northern capitalism advanced. Said a newspaper spokesman for the northern bourgeoisie: "If no measures of protection and improvement of anything North or West are to be suffered by our Southern masters, if we are to be downtrodden and all our cherished interests crushed by them, a signal revolution will eventually arise." [65]

Not all northern capitalists recognized the fact that slavery hindered the industrial development of the South, but men like John Murray Forbes, the anti-slavery Boston capitalist; Congressman Thaddeus Stevens, the progressive Pennsylvania iron-master; Nathaniel Banks and John Sherman, the political representatives of Northern industry, realized that slavery was "the foe of all industrial progress and of the highest material prosperity." [66] Fear of losing southern trade and the fear of secession caused most mercantile and many industrial capitalists to support the anti-Republican movement. William M. Evarts, a leading Republican, said in 1860 that "the great share of the bankers, the great share of the moneyed interests of the Northern states ... are combined with the slaveholders in support of slavery." These moneyed interests also feared that if the slave holders were deprived of their property rights of taking slaves into the territories, a broader attack on all property rights would follow. They agreed with the *New York Herald* when it declared on October 26, 1860, that once the Republicans were victorious the workers "would soon turn their attention to the goods and chattels of their wealthier neighbors, having been long taught by the leading republican journals the doctrine of the communists that 'all property is robbery.' "

The *Boston Courier* spoke for those who believed that the Republican Party jeopardized property rights.

"The truth is," it stated on April 1, 1860, "that Republicanism is neither more nor less than Radicalism. We do not mean that all Republicans are radicals. Far from it—but the operation of its doctrines are to this end. It is a struggle to escape from all restraints of order and law, and as a consequence you will find the whole body of speculatists upon morals, religion, government and social revolution in its ranks. The Negro and his condition are mere incidents of the main question."

The doctrines of the Republican Party, the conservatives believed, were already arousing the working class. How else explain the militant unemployment demonstrations during the panic of 1857 and the great shoe strike of 1860? These were, reasoned the conservatives of the North, the logical result of Republican doctrines. It was useless for the Republicans to protest that they did not advocate the abolition of slavery, to oppose the use of force and violence, to condemn men like John Brown for trying to organize slave revolts. Narrow class fears closed the minds of many businessmen whose broad class interests should have swept them into the Republican Party.

Nor did the working class as a whole support the Republican Party. Many still remained within the Democratic Party because of its friendly attitude towards the foreign-born, and continued to battle inside that party for a policy in favor of free soil and against the further expansion of slavery. Quite a few native American workers joined the Know-Nothing movement. Some workers refused to join the Republican Party because it meant that they would have to join hands with capitalists who were exploiting workers and who called out the militia to break strikes. These men, said one worker, had no sympathy either for the white man or the Negro. Their only aim in joining the Republican movement was "that capital shall obtain political power to direct the legislation of the Federal Government as it does now that of New England, and thus enable the few to govern the many." [67]

Many workers understood that their hostility to their employers should not prevent them from supporting the Republican Party against the slavocracy, and they knew that most capitalists actually regarded the Republican Party as too radical, fighting its candidates tooth and nail. They understood that as long as the slavocracy dominated the government there was no hope of a Homestead Act, and enough workers fought for land reform to make this issue of importance to labor. Nor did they feel that protective tariff legislation would benefit the industrialists alone, for they sincerely believed that it would protect American labor from the "ruinous competition with the cheap labor of the old world," and enable capitalism in America to provide more jobs. The German-American Marxian Socialists also contended that measures such as protective tariffs which accelerated the growth of capitalism in America merited labor's support because the development of capitalism was the precondition for the growth and maturing of the labor movement. The *New York Tribune* was correct when it said on October 9, 1858: "The working men, with very few exceptions, desire a Protective Tariff, and they begin to see that the Slave Power is not inclined to accord one, hence they incline to the belief that a few years of Northern ascendancy would be wholesome."

While some workers regarded the Republican Party's stand on slavery as too conservative, and only the annihilation of slavery would satisfy them, to most workers, as to most small farmers, the basic issue was not the extermination of slavery but the prohibition of its spread to new areas. *Die Soziale Republik,* organ of the *Arbeiterbund,* expressed the prevailing working class opinion when it stated on April 24, 1858 that "The present question of the present moment is not the abolition of slavery, but the prevention of its further extension."

ELECTION OF 1856

In the campaign of 1856 labor played a leading role. Workingmen marched in Republican torchlight processions carrying banners which featured the leading slogans of the campaign: "Free Soil, Free Labor, Fremont," and "We Won't Work for 10 Cents a Day." Many prominent '48'ers and labor leaders addressed workingmen's meetings using as their chief theme the second of these slogans. Slave labor in the South, they maintained, drove down the wages of southern free workers. If slavery were permitted to expand into the North ten cents a day would soon be the prevailing wage.

In its appeal to the labor vote the Republican Party reminded the common people that they alone could be relied on to save the country because the majority of the capitalists opposed the new political movement. The capitalists could not be relied upon, for the moment the slaveowners threatened secession, men of wealth forgot their convictions and assured the planter-aristocrats that they would "do anything, submit to anything, to preserve the Union." It was necessary for the workers "to rise up against this combined power of money and barbarous brutality." "Farmers, Workingmen," the Republicans appealed, "it is for you to save the country from the combination which threatens to exclude white laborers from the Territories and hand them over to the sole occupancy of slaves and slave-breeders." [68]

This Republican appeal for the labor vote was not campaign oratory, for it was in keeping with the origins of the new party and its platform— an end to the spread of slavery, federal aid for internal improvements, a Homestead Act, and the preservation of civil and political liberties. In the campaign of 1856 a Republican Party pamphlet could honestly say: "The present political contest differs from all previous ones in its direct bearing upon the interests of the laboring class. Other important issues have borne more directly upon capitalists and corporations." The pamphlet then inquired if workingmen thought it possible to serve their interests by voting "for that party candidate whose avowed policy it is to bring slave labor into direct competition with that of free men?" [69]

That masses of American workers understood the issues in the campaign of 1856 is proved by an address issued by 25,000 workingmen of Pittsburgh including native Americans, German-Americans, and Irish-Americans; iron molders, textile workers, coal miners as well as carpenters, printers, masons, and other skilled mechanics. It bore the title,

"Address of the Workingmen of Pittsburgh to the Fellow-Workingmen of Pennsylvania," and went, in part:

"The undersigned, workingmen of the city of Pittsburgh, convinced that our interests as a class are seriously involved in the present political struggle, send greetings to you, our fellow-workingmen of Pennsylvania, asking you to aid in the protection of our common rights, now in great peril....

"Let us look at the facts:

"In another section of our country, exists a practical aristocracy owning Labor, and made thereby independent of us. With them Labor is servitude and Freedom is only compatible with mastership. They despise us 'Greasy Mechanics,' 'Filthy Operatives,' and 'small Farmers doing their own drudgery' and 'unfit to associate with a Southern gentleman's body servant'—and being gentlemen no doubt believe what they say. The political power of that section is in their hands, from the ignorant and depressed conditions of our fellow-workingmen there—the 'poor whites' as they call them. These aristocrats desire to extend this system over all the Territories of the nation. To extend it over the Territories is to give them supreme power over the government, and then they will extend it over us.

"Free workingmen of Pennsylvania, shall they do it? The present Presidential contest is to decide."

Could the workingmen cast their votes for the Democratic Party? No, said the workers of Pittsburgh. The Democratic Party was no longer the champion of the rights of man. The present Democratic Party was "fighting the cause of the slaveholder." If this party were successful the slaveholders would take over the Territories. Once the slaveholders enter the Territories, there would be no inducement for the workingmen to go there, for how would their children be educated? "Slavery," said the address, "abhors the 'abomination of free schools.' Knowledge for the rich; ignorance for the poor...." *

No hope then, argued the Address, could be found in the program of the Democratic Party. The only hope of the workers was the Republican

* The Address was not overstating its case because the following remarks appeared in the *Richmond Enquirer,* February 22, 1856: "We have got to hating everything with the prefix 'free'—from the free negroes down and up through the whole catalogue of abominations, demagogueries, lusts, philosophies, fanaticism, and follies, free farms, free labor, free niggers, free society, free will, free thinking, free love, free wives, free children, free schools.

"But the worst of these abominations, because when once installed, it becomes the hotbed propagator of all—is the modern system of free schools. A little learning is a dangerous thing to all conservatism of thought, and all stability in general affairs."

Party which opposed the extension of slavery into the territories, and denied the authority of Congress, or any Territorial Legislature, or any individual, or any association of individuals to give legal existence to slavery in any Territory of the United States.

"Here, fellow workingmen, we find *our* platform, and under this banner we have enlisted to fight the battle of the rights of man. If we have spoken the truth then join us. . . . We have all laid aside minor differences in the face of a great danger which has overshadowed minor questions, and have pledged ourselves to an alliance for the preservation of the Territories against Slavery. We have been met with the cry of sectionalism, fanaticism, abolitionism; but we are not alarmed. On our side, proclaiming the same principles in language too plain to be misunderstood, are Washington, Jefferson, Franklin, Adams, Monroe, Jackson, Clay and Webster. With these guides we feel that we have not gone astray. . . .

"Think freely on this great question. Cast away your old prejudices, beware of designing leaders. Study the truth for yourselves, satisfy your minds on the basis of facts, and common-sense alone, and then strike for yourselves, your fellow-workingmen, your country and the Right." [70]

This Address is probably the most representative statement of the position of most northern workers on the slavery question before the Civil War. It does not call for the abolition of slavery, but neither does it attack the Abolitionists. It emphasizes the point uppermost in the minds of most workers: if slavery were permitted to expand, labor in the North would be reduced to the level of the Negro workers in the South. *"To extend it over the Territories,"* says the Address, *"is to give them supreme power over the government, and then they will extend it over us."*

A few months after the election of James Buchanan, the Democratic candidate, the Supreme Court rendered the Dred Scott decision which ruled that slavery could go into any territory of the United States. The Mechanics and Workingmen's Central Union of New York City condemned the decision, saying that it was definite "evidence of the settled determination of Slavery to make itself legal in all of the States," and through the power of the Supreme Court to deprive free labor of the ability to protect itself "against the competition of slave labor." [71]

FIGHTING REPUBLICAN CONSERVATISM

Although the Republican Party was defeated in the Presidential election of 1856, it made an impressive showing, and in the next three years it gained added strength in many parts of the North and West. Nowhere was this more apparent than in Pennsylvania whose electoral vote was to be vital in the campaign of 1860. In 1858 the People's Party, the name assumed by the Republican organization in Pennsylvania, carried the city election in Philadelphia and the state election. Both victories, said the *Philadelphia North American* on September 27, 1858, were won because the People's Party was "devoted to the interests of our own working classes." Its slogan, "Popular Sovereignty and Protection to American Industry," won the support of workers and industrialists of Pennsylvania, for the panic of 1857 had convinced them that it was necessary to link protection of free labor from the competition of slave labor with protection of American labor from the competition of the cheap labor in Europe.

There were some misgivings about the protection plank because it was attracting conservative groups into the party who were already trying to tone down the party's stand on slavery.[72] Their frantic attacks against John Brown confirmed these misgivings. Northern workers held mass meetings to express sympathy for John Brown. In Ohio, the Social Working Men's Association of Cincinnati, made up of many German Marxists, drew up a set of resolutions which declared: "The act of John Brown has powerfully contributed to bring out the hidden consciousness of the majority of the people." [73]

The German-American workingmen were also the first to remind the Republican Party leaders of their responsibilities to the common people. They were particularly suspicious of certain conservative elements in the Republican Party who had formerly been connected with the anti-foreign born Know-Nothing movement. In 1858 these groups induced the Republican majority of the Massachusetts state legislature to pass the notorious Massachusetts Amendment withholding suffrage from the naturalized for two years. Unless these conservatives were checked, they would dictate the Republican platform and nominate the Republican candidates in 1860.

On March 13, 1860, two months before the Republican Party's convention met in Chicago to nominate its Presidential candidate, the German-American workingmen of New York City called a special meeting to discuss the issues of the campaign. Here they adopted an important set of resolutions in which they announced their "determined opposition to all efforts for the extension and perpetuation of slavery," condemned any infringement on the rights of immigrants by extending the naturalization period, and called for the immediate passage of a Homestead Act. Only when it nominated candidates on "the above principles," they declared, could they "go hand in hand with the Republican Party." Before adjourning, the German-American workingmen issued a call for a national conference to discuss the issues before the American people and to take steps to prevent conservative forces from taking over the Republican Party.

Two days before the Republican convention opened, a momentous and much-neglected national conference of German-Americans met in the *Deutsches Haus* in Chicago. It was a broad conference representing all classes within the German-American population, with representatives of the workingmen playing a leading part. Joseph Weydemeyer, representing the German-American workingmen's movement of Chicago, was one of the most forceful and persuasive speakers at the conference. Dr. Adolph Douai, who had just escaped from a pro-slavery mob in San Antonio, Texas, where he had edited an anti-slavery paper, worked closely with Weydemeyer. Their influence is seen in the resolutions adopted by the delegates.

These resolutions, based upon those passed previously by the German-American Republican workingmen of New York City, requested the German-American delegates to the national Republican convention to submit five principles to that body as the sentiment of the majority of the German Republican voters of the Union, and "to use all honorable means to secure their recognition in proper form by the national convention." These principles included opposition to the Massachusetts Amendment, a call for the passage of a Homestead law and the demand that Kansas be admitted into the Union as a sovereign state without slavery. In reference to the Republican Party stand on the slavery question, the resolution declared: "That while we firmly adhere to the principles of the Republican Party as they were laid down in the Philadelphia platform of 1856, we desire that they be applied in a sense most hostile to slavery."

And again: "We pledge ourselves to support any aspirant for the Presidency and Vice-Presidency who stands on this platform, and has never opposed the Republican platform of 1856, nor has ever been identified with the spirit of the Massachusetts Amendment." [74]

These resolutions were printed immediately after they had been accepted by the delegates to the Republican convention, thus serving notice that the German-Americans, a large number of whom were trade unionists, would give their votes to the Republican Party only if its platform and candidates opposed Know-Nothingism and the further expansion of slavery. These votes could not be shrugged off lightly. It was generally acknowledged that the German-Americans could determine the outcome of the election in a number of crucial states.

Just how much influence this document exerted on the Republican convention cannot be accurately determined. William L. Baringer, who has made a careful study of the Republican convention of 1860, thinks that the influence was substantial. "According to the silence of dozens of convention witnesses concerning the German convention," he writes, "it would seem they had no influence on the convention's deliberations. But their pressure can be seen in the platform and the rapid decline of Bates as Seward's leading opponent." [75]

LINCOLN AND LABOR

He should have added that the influence of the *Deutsches Haus* conference can be seen in the rapid rise of Abraham Lincoln as Seward's leading opponent and in Lincoln's subsequent nomination as the Republican standard-bearer. This nomination, it has often been said, was merely the result of pure accident plus vote-swapping, logrolling and wire-pulling. This ignores the fact that Lincoln already possessed a mass following among the small farmers and workingmen who made up the bulk of the Republican Party. Swedish workers in the Middle West spoke affectionately of *"arbetaresonen* Lincoln" (Lincoln, the son of the workingman), and German workers in Illinois showed their devotion to Lincoln by organizing early in 1860 Lincoln-for-President clubs. In April 1860, the *Baltimore Turnzeitung,* central organ of the German Turner Bund of the United States, in which workingmen predominated, came out for Lincoln for President. "Under a standard-bearer like him," it stated, "the Republican Party will be certain of victory." [76]

The stand taken by the *Turnzeitung* may come as a surprise to those who have been led to believe that Lincoln was a political nonentity in 1860. Lincoln had already endeared himself to the foreign-born workers by the strong stand he took in opposition to the Know-Nothing movement. In 1855 Lincoln denounced Know-Nothingism and refused to endorse fusion between the Republican and Know-Nothing parties.

"Of their principles," he wrote, "I think little better than I do of those of slavery extensionists. Indeed I do not perceive how any professing to be sensitive to the wrong of the Negro, can join in a league to degrade a class of white men. I have no objection to fuse with anybody provided I can fuse on grounds which I think right."

Thereafter Lincoln lost no opportunity to blast away at the Know-Nothing movement. He spoke frequently of the contributions Germans, Irish, French, and Scandinavians had made to American civilization, and said that to him the true mark of American democracy was the fact that "men that have come from Europe themselves or whose ancestors have come hither and settled here" could find themselves "equal in all things" in this country. To permit the Know-Nothings to triumph would endanger the finest features of American institutions.

Lincoln had also opposed the Massachusetts Amendment. In a letter dated May 17, 1859, to Dr. Theodore Canisius, a prominent German-American editor, Lincoln said that he was against the adoption of the Massachusetts provision "in Illinois, or in any other place where I have a right to oppose it." He added, "I have some little notoriety for commiserating the oppressed condition of the Negroes and I should be strangely inconsistent if I would favor any project for curtailing the existing rights of white men, even though born in different lands and speaking a different language from my own." The letter received wide publicity and aroused great enthusiasm for Lincoln among German-American and other foreign-born workingmen.

The same enthusiasm was aroused among workers by Lincoln's clearcut opposition to the further extension of slavery and by his sympathetic understanding of the problems of the laboring people. No other national political figure of the stature of Lincoln defended labor as strongly as Lincoln did in his New Haven speech of March 6, 1860, in reference to the great shoe strike then in progress: "I am glad to see that a system of labor prevails in New England under which laborers can strike when they want to, where they are not obliged to labor whether you pay them or not. I like the system which lets a man quit when he wants to, and wish it might prevail everywhere. One of the reasons why I am opposed to slavery is just here. . . ."

Lincoln's stand on slavery was one that was understood and appreciated by the workingmen. He was not an Abolitionist, but he opposed slavery and its further extension. In March, 1860, he said: "If you give up your convictions and call slavery right . . . you let slavery in upon you. Instead of white laborers who can strike, you'll soon have black laborers who can't."

Probably no speech Lincoln delivered before the Civil War aroused as much enthusiasm for him among the workers as the one he made in September, 1859, at a State Fair sponsored by the Wisconsin Agricultural Society. Lincoln attacked the mud-sill theory of labor which meant that a "blind horse upon a treadmill is a perfect illustration of what a laborer should be," and that "the education of laborers is not only useless, but pernicious and dangerous." Such a theory was itself useless, pernicious, and dangerous. Free labor, said Lincoln, was the chief bulwark of America's freedom, and it was labor, not capital, which was "the source from which human wants are mainly supplied." The mud-sill advocates put capital first and labor last. Lincoln said he stood for the opposite point of view:

"... that labor is prior to, and independent of capital; that, in fact, capital is the fruit of labor, and could never have existed if labor had not first existed; that labor can exist without capital, but that capital could never have existed without labor. Hence ... labor is the superior ... greatly the superior to capital." [77]

ELECTION OF 1860

It is not an exaggeration to say that the Republican Party fought its way to victory in the campaign of 1860 as the party of free labor. In speech after speech Carl Schurz asserted that "the Republican Party stands emphatically as the party of free labor," and explained its philosophy in a single sentence: "To man—his birthright; to Labor—Freedom; to him that wants to Labor—work and independence; to him that works—his dues." Henry Wilson, an anti-slavery leader and now a Republican Congressman from Massachusetts, defined the issue of the campaign: "On the one side is arrayed the Republican Party, vindicating the dignity of free labor and asserting the rights of the toiling millions; while its antagonist is a false Democracy, reviling the laboring man as a slave, and prostituting itself to the interests and purposes of a purse-proud oligarch." [78]

Never before in American history had a political party made such a conscious effort to win the votes of the workingmen as did the Republican Party in 1860. Republican newspapers referred to the party ticket as the workingman's ticket. The name, said the *Boston Journal* of June 15, 1860, was justified because both Lincoln and Hannibal Hamlin, the Republican vice-presidential candidate, "sympathize with the workman in his wants and aspirations. Remembering their own hard toil they could not fail to foster the interests of free labor whenever opportunity offered." Ben Wade, a Republican leader, justified the term "Workingman's ticket" with the statement, "Abe Lincoln is the very incarnation of American labor." [79]

Three main issues were stressed by the Republican Party in its effort to gain the labor vote. It opposed the further extension of slavery which would open up the territories to free labor and defend labor from the competition of slave labor; it favored the passage of a Homestead Act which would cut down the competition for jobs in the industrial cities; it stood for protective tariff legislation which promised labor a favored position. A typical Republican appeal went:

"Working Men! You who need remunerative labor and Homesteads, Vote for the friends of both as is demonstrated by past acts not words. The Republicans hold that the natural conditions of all the Territories is freedom, and that they should be kept free; that the landless should have free homes in the Territories and that American industry should be protected." [80]

The party's opponents charged that the Republicans ignored the welfare of free labor because "all their sympathies are involved in their tenderness for the Ethiopian race.... They shut their eyes to the squalor around them, and shed crocodile tears over the imaginary ills of slaves in the South." [81] But the Democrats soon realized that this argument was wasted on workers who saw issues of immense importance in the Republican platform. They then proceeded to whip up a "Reign of Terror." Lincoln's election, they said, would bring secession and ruin, throwing thousands of workers out of employment. The *Columbus Daily Ohio Statesman* of November 2, 1860, warned the workingmen of Ohio:

"The election of Lincoln, if such a disastrous event should take place, will inflict a blow upon every workingman in the North who needs, for the support of himself and family, constant employment and the highest wages he can now obtain. If, therefore, the laborers in Ohio desire themselves and their fellow workmen to remain independent and prosperous, they will vote unhesitatingly for that Presidential candidate who is the true friend of free labor, and who can, if they do their duty, defeat Lincoln in Ohio."

The second argument the Democrats used was that victory for Republican "abolitionism" would soon bring thousands of free Negroes to the North to compete with white workers. Even free Negroes in Boston were warned to vote against Lincoln because the emancipation of the slaves following a Republican victory would endanger their jobs. On November 1, 1860 the *New York Herald* issued a special appeal to Irish and German laborers which was reprinted in many newspapers:

"If Lincoln is elected you will have to compete with the labor of four million emancipated negroes. His election is but the forerunner of an ultimate dissolution of the Union. The North will be flooded with free negroes and the labor of the white man will be depreciated and degraded."

Many employers supplemented these appeals with warnings of their own. The *Newark Daily Advertiser* reported on November 7, 1860, that employers of that city were making "no secret of inducing their numerous workmen to vote for the anti-Republican candidates on pain of immediate dismissal in case of their defeat." New York business firms engaged in southern trade handed out circulars to their workers warning them to vote against Lincoln. "By doing so," these circulars promised, "you will take care of yourself and your family. But if the Republican candidate for President is elected the South will withdraw its custom from us and you will get little work and bad prices." [82]

The Republicans urged the workers to hold fast and refuse to be intimidated. "Wide Awake! Workingmen Attention!" the *New York Tribune* of October 28, 1860, appealed. "German fellow-citizens, be on your guard. Stand firm for Lincoln and Liberty. Be not frightened into voting the Fusion ticket * by the parasites of slavery." The German workers proved that they would stand firm for Lincoln. The German clothing workers in Brooklyn were called together by their employers and advised to vote against Lincoln if they wished to continue at work. Instead of listening to their employers, Socialist workers took over the meeting which resolved that bosses who refused to pay higher wages and imported scabs to break strikes should not be listened to in political matters. Joseph Weydemeyer addressed the workers during the meeting, urging them to vote for Lincoln and to support tariff legislation.[83]

The anti-Lincoln "Reign of Terror" failed. Of course, there were workers who cast their votes for the Democratic candidates. William H. Sylvis of the Molders' Union voted for Stephen A. Douglas as did many Irish voters.† A vote for Douglas was not, however, a vote for slavery because Douglas led that section of the Democratic Party which came closest to the Republican Party in its opposition to the extension of slavery and its demand for Free-Soil in the territories. But not all Irish-American workers supported Douglas. In New York, Boston, and Philadelphia there were Irish Republican rallies for Lincoln. An Irish-American workingman of Philadelphia said that he and hundreds of others like him had determined to leave the Democratic Party. They were convinced, he declared, that the party of the slave power could not defend free labor. "I attached myself to the Democratic Party for the reason that the party professed to be the friend of the laboring man and particularly those of foreign birth. I have been long enough in the party to know that their professions are false, and made only to delude the ignorant in order to secure their votes and when secured, their rights and interests are ignored...." [84]

The activity of German-American workingmen to elect Lincoln was tremendous. From New York to St. Louis mass rallies were held in all the cities by these workers for the election of the Republican candidate. Swedish workers were no less active. The *Chicago Press and Tribune* paid tribute to the German and Scandinavian workers "for the zeal and

---

* The Fusion ticket refers to the consolidation of the anti-Republican parties (the Douglas-Bell-Breckenridge forces) into one ticket of presidential electors. The combined ticket, it was believed, could defeat Lincoln in New York. (See Philip S. Foner, *Business and Slavery: The New York Merchants and the Irrepressible Conflict*, Chapel Hill, N. C., 1941, pp. 172-207.)

† Part of the Irish workers' reluctance to support Lincoln was caused by the wide circulation of the *Impending Crisis* by the Republican Party. Hinton Rowan Helper's *Impending Crisis* attacked the Irish-American population as supporters of slavery. "We can well afford to dispense with the ignorant Catholic element of the Emerald Isle..." he wrote, "there is so little difference between Slavery, Popery, and Negro-driving Democracy, that we are not at all surprised to see them going hand in hand in their diabolical works in humanity and desolation." (*The Impending Crisis of the South: How to Meet It*, New York, 1860, p. 173.)

energy with which they worked yesterday to put the finishing touches to the noble service they have rendered in the whole canvass." The Chicago *Arbeiter-Bund* won special praise for working ceaselessly in rallying labor's support for the Republican ticket.[85]

It is impossible to determine how many workers voted for Lincoln. This much is certain. There was strong labor support for Lincoln in Pennsylvania, Missouri, Illinois, Ohio, and New England. The labor vote in Boston, Philadelphia, Cincinnati, Lowell, Chicago, and Trenton went for the Republican candidate, and even in New York City, the northern extension of the cotton kingdom, a considerable vote for Lincoln was registered in working-class districts.[86]

Republican spokesmen admitted the importance of the labor vote in Lincoln's victory. "We owe a debt of gratitude to the laboring men who gave us this victory," said one New York Republican. And Rufus Andrews, a leading Republican, said that Lincoln's election has "been affected by the laboring men, the party will try to repay them by a Homestead Act and a protective tariff." [87]

Lincoln's election marked the end of an important stage in the struggle against slavery. Thus far the struggle had been mainly concerned with preventing its spread to the territories. A small but influential group of men and women had also pushed forward the movement for the abolition of slavery, but most people were as yet not prepared to accept their position.

In the great coalition formed to prevent the expansion of slavery, labor was an important and in some respects a decisive factor. At first it was slow to act, because of the hostility of many Abolitionist leaders toward working class demands, because of affiliation with the Democratic Party, because of fears that emancipation of the slaves would increase competition in the labor market, and because of the confusion created by the pseudo-revolutionary ideas of George Henry Evans and other land reformers. But once these obstacles were overcome the working class assumed its proper place in the coalition against the slave power.

The workers had tipped the scales to end the political domination of our national life by the slave power. Soon the workers were to join in a great people's war, out of which would come the annihilation of slavery, an unfettered capitalism, and a stronger labor movement.

CHAPTER 15

Labor and the Civil War

Three days after Lincoln's election, on November 10, 1860, the German paper that was closest to the labor movement, the *New Yorker Demokrat,* outlined in an editorial the tasks facing the progressive forces:

"We have taken part in the campaign not as party-adherents, not for self-seeking reasons, but because the Republican Party is closest to our point of view and because we consider its victory a guarantee that still greater victories for the cause of humanity can be achieved in the future. It is therefore our special task to see to it that what has been achieved with our help is not again undone but is built up still more; and if reactionary elements in the party of Reaction intend to do that, we must form a counterweight to them and press forward to further gains."

This warning was timely.

Late in February, 1861, shortly before Lincoln's inauguration as President of the United States, a convention of slave owners set up a provisional government at Montgomery, Alabama, with Jefferson Davis as the president of the Confederate States of America. Knowing that their movement to destroy the Union was unpopular among the majority of the southern white population, the secessionists refused to put the question even before a restricted southern electorate. "We live under an oligarchy," said the Mississippi *Natchez Courier* of February, 1861, "that has not yet dared to trust the people as to a say to its consent." [1] While the slave oligarchy was engineering secession and preparing for war, President Buchanan did nothing but pray that all would be well in the end, and northern businessmen, worried over tumbling markets and repudiated debts, were urging Congress to grant the slaveholders any concession that would bring them back into the Union. Naturally these appeasers wanted to get the support of the workers. As early as November 14, 1860, the pro-slavery *New York Herald* had appealed:

"The events transpiring about us create in the most stoical minds apprehensions of financial trouble of a serious nature, and it is the duty of all classes, great and small, to do all that lies within their power to calm the troubled waters. Above all, there should be an expression of sentiment by the working men—the bone and sinew of the North—in such a way that the South will see that the rabid republicans, who, with their mad cry of elevation of the negro, would destroy the prosperity of the nation, cannot rely upon them to back them up in this wild crusade, that will land us—Heaven only knows where. Let, therefore, the working men in this metropolis and in every city and town in the Northern States assemble in mass meeting as early as possible and there give utterance to their true sentiments upon the issues of the day...."

LABOR AND THE SECESSION CRISIS

Within a few weeks mass meetings of workingmen were held in many parts of the country, but the sentiments expressed were seldom to the liking of the *Herald,* which defended the right of the southern states to secede and endorsed any and every concession to slavery.

Workingmen of Louisville, Kentucky, at a mass meeting sponsored by the Iron Molders' Union, December 27, 1860, elected a Committee of Thirty-Four to arouse the workers of the nation to preserve the Union. The resolutions adopted at the meeting stated that the workers' "material prosperity ... hopes of happiness and future security depend upon the continuation of the Union as it is." They called upon their brethren to "unite in one solid column for a single purpose—the preservation of the Federal Union," to let the "disorganizing traitors who are now at the Federal capital plotting treason against the greatest and best government instituted by man know that under the circumstances of our position, furnishing as we do, the nerve, the strength, the skill, in the multiplied industrial interest of the country, and at necessity's call freely breasting the tide and brunt of war, we will not desert the gallant old ship of Union, freighted as she is, with the liberty, happiness and prosperity of more than twenty-five millions of human beings so long as one timber remains above the surging sea, or one shred of the glorious emblem of our national unity is to be seen at her masthead." In the future the workingmen of Louisville "will not support for office any man who is or may be known to entertain disunion sentiments." [2]

These resolutions were not seen as fit to print by the *Herald,* but the Cincinnati *Commercial* on January 4, 1861, said of them: "The heaviest blow which the secessionists of Louisville have received was from the workingmen of that city." At the same meeting a committee was appointed to draw up a National Address to Workingmen. This committee was made up of representatives of Louisville's leading labor organizations: the Molders, Machinists and Blacksmiths, Typographers, Bricklayers, Carpenters, Stonecutters, Cabinet-makers, Plasterers, Piano Makers, Boiler-makers, Cigar-makers, and Coachmakers. Even business was represented in the person of John Gillis, a merchant engaged in the Southern trade. His presence might explain in part the fact that the Address, unlike the resolutions, conjured up the horrors of Civil War, and urged the adoption of the Crittenden Compromise.* In spite of this weakness, the Address stated that all workingmen believed that the preservation of the Union was essential to the welfare of the country and the future happiness of the working class, and that the election of Lincoln did not justify any attempt to destroy the nacion. It called upon the workers to organize meetings in every Congressional district and demand the resignation of all members of Congress who were "now by their action imperilling the safety of the Union." Some time later the workingmen were urged to send delegates to a national labor convention to be held in Philadelphia on February 22, 1861.[3]

The Address had a wide influence; meetings of workers were held in Evansville and New Albany, Indiana, Chicago and Alton, Illinois; Pittsburgh and Philadelphia, Pennsylvania; Nashville, Tennesee; Winchester and Wheeling, Virginia, as well as in other industrial towns. Of great importance were the meetings in Maryland, Virginia, and Tennessee, for at these meetings the convictions of southern free labor were expressed. The tone of their resolutions revealed a uniform hostility to the secessionist oligarchy.[4] At a workingmen's meeting in Baltimore, the secession movement was condemned, the Union and the Constitution upheld, and James Touchstone, a leading anti-slavery figure in Maryland's labor movement, was elected as a delegate to the Philadelphia convention. Elsewhere in Maryland, miners, mechanics, and laborers calling themselves "upholders of the Union and the Constitution" met to oppose secession.[5] A meeting of mechanics and workingmen of Frederick County, Virginia, attacked the "fanatics" of the North, and "the gasconading folly and sinister selfishness of the demagogues of the South." It characterized the secession of South Carolina "as ill-advised, unjust, and disrespectful to her sister States of the South," and stated that "the dismemberment of the Union would entail upon us a longer and blacker train of woes than has ever yet, in the Providence of God, afflicted any people." [6] In Nashville, Tennessee, a free labor convention declared their "undying love for the Union," and called secession "treason ... by designing and mad politicians, calculated to flood the Valley of the Mississippi with the blood of freedom." [7] The workingmen of Portsmouth, Virginia declared:

* The Crittenden Compromise provided that the area from the Missouri River to California be divided along the line of 36° 30′—slavery forever prohibited north of it and protected by Congressional legislation south of it; that whenever any area was ready to enter statehood, it should be admitted free or slave as its people decided, and that Congress be deprived of its power to abolish slavery where it existed or to interfere with the interstate slave trade.

"We look upon any attempt to break up this Government or dissolve this Union as an attack upon the rights of the people of the whole country, and tending to destroy the position of equality assumed by us all [and] we hold that the constitution of the United States is not a league or compact between the States in the Sovereign capacity, but a Government proper, founded on the adoption of the citizens and itself; and that no power short of convention of the whole Union assembled according to the provisions of the Constitution has power to absolve the citizen from his allegiance to the United States."

They concluded their meeting with an appeal to their brethren throughout the country "to stand by the Constitution and the Union as the sheet anchor of their hopes." [8]

North of the Mason-Dixon line workers were also holding meetings and passing resolutions against secession. "We frown diligently upon the traitrous action of South Carolina and other States," the workingmen of Wilmington, Delaware, declared, "in attempting to alienate a portion of this Union from the common brotherhood." [9] A pro-Union meeting of the workers of Newark ended with three cheers for the flag, the Constitution, and for Major Anderson who was holding Fort Sumter. [10] Over in Philadelphia meetings of workingmen were being held in various shops and factories, culminating on January 26 in a parade and mass meeting. Some of their banners read: "The workingmen of the Pennsylvania Steam Engine and Boiler Works are moving forward for the Union." "The Union is the keystone of the country." "The Union and the Crittenden resolutions." "We want Working Men not talking men in Congress." "Our political machinery is out of order; mechanics must repair it." [11]

The theme of the mass meeting was "Union and Compromise." When the Crittenden proposals were read by the chairman, many in the audience shouted opposition "to the phrases proposing the extension of the Missouri Compromise line to the Pacific." [12] There was protest also over the dictatorial manner in which the chairman who was a superintendent of the Pennsylvania Railroad brushed aside the demand for a nay vote on the Crittenden proposals. Jonathan Fincher, the well-known leader of the Machinists' and Blacksmiths' Union, severed all official connection with the meeting because of the way in which the milk and water resolutions had been gagged through. [13] The last resolution was a fair statement of the position of labor: "That if after all fair and honorable means have been exhausted without effecting the desired object so earnestly cherished by all Union-loving citizens, we, as workingmen, will sustain the Federal Government in all just and legal measures to enforce the laws of our land and nation." The *Philadelphia*

Inquirer commented on January 20, 1861, "They are first for peaceable compromise, and if that fails, then and not till then, they are for employing force to maintain the Government."

If resistance to the slave power was the common conviction of the organized workers, it certainly was not the maximum demand as is seen in the convention in Pittsburgh in January, 1861, called by the Typographical Union, whose slogan was "No Compromise with Traitors." The convention told the government not to yield an inch to those who threatened and bullied, but "to execute its laws against all traitors." [14] A mass meeting of mechanics and laboring men of Easton and Newcastle, Pennsylvania, denounced "Secession and all Compromise," and called upon the administration to take necessary steps "in favor of the Constitution and the enforcement of laws." [15] A workingmen's meeting in Cincinnati early in February, 1861, declared: "The Union must be preserved in its integrity by the enforcement of the laws in every part of the Union by whatever measures may be necessary." [16]

Lincoln was met at his hotel in Cincinnati while en route to his inauguration by a delegation from the German Workingmen's Society which numbered two thousand members. Among the delegates were those implacable foes of slavery and the slave power, the Marxian Socialists. One of them, Fred Oberkleine, delivered the address to Lincoln in which he said that the free workingmen of Cincinnati were opposed to all "compromises between the interests of free labor and slave labor."

"We, the German free workingmen of Cincinnati, avail ourselves of this opportunity to assure you, our chosen Chief Magistrate, of our sincere and heartfelt regard. You earned our votes as the champion of free labor and free homesteads. Our vanquished opponents have in recent times made frequent use of the term workingmen and workingmen's meetings in order to create the impression that the mass of workingmen were in favor of compromises between the interests of free labor and slave labor.... We firmly adhere to the principle which directed our votes in your favor.

"If to this end you should be in need of men, the German free workingmen with others will rise as one man at your call ready to risk their lives in the effort to maintain the victory already won by freedom over slavery."

Lincoln assured the delegation that he agreed with these sentiments and observed that "the workingmen are the basis of all governments for the plain reason that they are the most numerous...." [17]

Opposition to secession always raised the question of labor's independent political action as the best way of dealing with the appeasers in the halls of Congress. A labor convention was called in Cincinnati to which came delegates from every trade union in the city. They met on February 16, formed a labor party, nominated a workingmen's ticket for city officers and announced:

"Resolved, That experience has plainly told no reliance can be placed on party politicians. We, therefore, urge upon the laboring masses the propriety—yea, the imperative necessity of severing party connections, and uniting in organizations from which men can be chosen to administer the laws in an impartial spirit and whose highest aim will be the promotion of our individual interest and the advancement of our country's good.

"Resolved, That as upon the laboring classes depends the future of our country, in the present crisis we will not desert it, but will lend our aid to sustain the Government in saving the Union from the awful calamities which have overtaken it through the schemes of designing men, and which, if not averted will eventuate in our common ruin." [18]

Late in February, 1861, the National Convention opened in Philadelphia. Beginning on February 22 with a "Grand Workingmen's Parade," more than fifty trade unions of Philadelphia led by the molders, machinists and blacksmiths, car builders, carvers, turners, coach-makers, wagon-makers, and wood-workers, participated in this great demonstration. The National Convention was national in name only because only delegates from eight states were present. This comparatively small representation was countered by the fact that these eight states, Pennsylvania, Maryland, Kentucky, Virginia, Tennessee, Indiana, Ohio, and Delaware were states closely united to the South by historical and economic ties.

Isaac Van Houten of the Pennsylvania railroad car shops was elected president, and the convention opened its sessions. Many of the speakers called for labor's activity in political affairs. A Mr. Wolf from Kentucky called for the immediate formation of a united party of workingmen and farmers to save the union. "What we want to have as our representatives are the workmen, mechanics fresh from the shop and farmers fresh from the field." His proposal was endorsed by other delegates. J. N. Burns, representing Philadelphia labor, called for workers from their benches to represent the common people in Congress and carry on the battle against secession.

On the following day the resolutions committee presented its report which contained eight resolutions. They (1) endorsed the Crittenden Compromise, (2) announced devotion to the Union and opposition to all traitors, North or South, (3) attacked secession as dangerous and repugnant to all workingmen, (4) warned politicians that the workers were determined to replace them with men from the shops and factories, (5) condemned a policy of coercion which would lead to civil war, (6) called for the repeal of the "personal liberty" laws in several northern states which were aimed at preventing the return of fugitive slaves to the South, and (7) urged the organization of state associations of workingmen in each of the thirty-four states. An eighth resolution provided for the establishment of a committee of 34 to organize the workers of the country for political action.[19]

These resolutions were adopted, permanent officers elected, and July 4, 1861, was set as the date for the next national labor convention to be held in Louisville. Just as the convention was about to adjourn, James Touchstone, the delegate representing the workingmen of Baltimore, demanded to be heard in order to submit resolutions which he considered "proper to emanate from a representative from a Slave State." He prefaced his resolutions with a stirring address against the traitors who had brought the crisis upon the people.

The *Philadelphia Inquirer* carried the following report of the address:

"It was a crying shame that treason was allowed to show its head all over the land. The Senate and the House of Representatives had been polluted by the presence of avowed traitors, and persons in high and low places had perjured themselves. Treason, as black as any imp of darkness, now stalks through the land, as if in habiliments as pure as those of angels. The workingmen are interested in denouncing the treason. It was inaugurated by aristocrats whose only aim was to place their feet on the necks of the mechanics.

"It is urged by these Disunionists that they are actuated by a desire to repel Northern aggression, but two wrongs, nor a multitude of wrongs, never made a right, and in this it will never do. It is a plain out-and-out usurpation of the rights of the people by nabobs and aristocrats, and it would be more honorable in the new Confederacy so as to acknowledge it, than to endeavor to deceive the people by a contemptible subterfuge. Those who have started the movement have not done so for the purpose of redressing wrongs, but for the purpose of overturning constitutional liberty and upon its ruins to rear a despotism. This could be seen by following them in their actions thus far. They have increased the taxation. How will workingmen like that? They propose to interfere with the elective franchise, by requiring a property qualification. How will mechanics like that? They have elected a President for 10 years, and propose to allow him a pension on his retirement. How will the mechanics like that? The workingmen should raise their voices against these invasions of their rights."

Touchstone moved the adoption of his resolutions which called for the support of the Constitution and for all measures the national government might deem necessary to "sustain the lawful authority in putting down traitors, who would destroy the rights of the people by overturning the Government." One resolution said "that Cotton is not king, but that the people of the United States are sovereigns," and another resolution stated: "That this convention sympathize with their brother workingmen of the seceded States, and they pledge them their efforts to regain their constitutional rights, which have been wrested from them by violence." [20]

As the resolutions were read they were greeted by tremendous applause, and many voices called for their adoption, but it was finally decided that it was inopportune to adopt them at a time when important negotiations to settle the crisis peacefully were under way in Washington. Reporters at the convention admitted that although a compromise policy was endorsed the support given to Touchstone proved that the majority of the delegates favored preserving the Union by force if necessary.[21]

The National Convention adjourned on February 23, 1861, never to meet again.*

A large section if not the majority of the workingmen sought to preserve the Union through compromise with the slave owners. This mistaken belief did not come from the working class but was forced on it by other influences. Businessmen, politicians, and newspapers friendly to the slaveowners played upon the fears of unemployment. Unless the South were persuaded by concessions to remain in the Union, said these northern allies of slavery, business would go to pieces and mass unemployment would be the future of the working class. The drop in business following the secession of South Carolina and the widespread unemployment resulting from the crisis made these arguments plausible, particularly to the unorganized workers who were suffering the most.[22]

Where the economic ties with slavery were strongest, in cities like New

---

* The Committee of 34 did continue its activities for a time. According to William H. Sylvis, its corresponding secretary, the committee expected to organize the workingmen for independent political action. In March, 1861, Sylvis wrote: "The business of this committee is to perfect and perpetuate an organization among the industrial classes of the city and State for the purpose of placing in positions of public trust, men of known honesty and ability; men who know the real wants of the people, and who will represent us according to our wishes; men who have not made politics a trade; men who, for a consideration, will not become the mere tools of rotten corporations and aristocratic monopolies; men who will devote their time and energies to the making of good laws, and direct their administration in such a way as will best serve the interests of the whole people." (James C. Sylvis, *The Life, Speeches, Labors and Essays of William H. Sylvis*, Philadelphia, 1872, p. 45.) It is obvious that neither Sylvis nor the other trade union representatives on the Committee of 34 realized that the destruction of the slave system was a precondition for effective independent labor political action. Soon enough, however, events themselves were to bring this sharply to their attention.

York, Philadelphia, and Boston, the working class was strongly influenced by businessmen who were ready to surrender every democratic principle to keep their profitable trade relations with the South. Several of the workingmen's anti-war, pro-compromise meetings in these cities were controlled by these businessmen or their politicians. In Philadelphia the workingmen's movement for compromise was organized by businessmen and trade union leaders. As the movement developed, the businessmen gained considerable control over it.[23] The same thing happened in New York and Boston where merchants in southern trade and anti-Republican politicians organized so-called workingmen's meetings which put the blame for the secession crisis on the Abolitionists and called for any concession to the slaveowners.[24] Only one worker was allowed to address a meeting at Faneuil Hall, Boston, and when his remarks were thought to be too pro-Union and too strongly opposed to secession, they were stricken from the record. All the other speakers, just as at the so-called workingmen's meeting held in Brooke's Hall in New York City, were Democratic politicians.[25]

An analysis of the pacifist stand of many workingmen on the eve of the Civil War must consider the anti-war campaign conducted for more than a decade by Elihu Burritt. Burritt in July, 1846, formed the League of Universal Brotherhood devoted to "the elevation of man, as being, as a brother, irrespective of his country, color, character, or condition." Its members, mainly workingmen, pledged never to enlist in any army or navy, or to render any voluntary support or approval "to the preparation for or prosecution of any war, by whomsoever, for whatsoever purpose, declared or waged."

A year later Burritt published *A Way-Word to the Working Men of Christendom* signed "By a Working Man of America":

"Working Men of the United States! Voters of a young Republic! What example will you set at the polls to the hard-working myriads of your brethren in the old world who lack your right of suffrage to enthrone the sanguinary monster, War! Shall your great officers of the nation be peace and your exactors, righteousness? Or shall garments rolled in blood and fiendish feats of human butchery, qualify your candidate for the highest honor within the nation's gift?" [26]

Burritt's pacifist ideas led him to compromise with the slaveowners up to the point of allowing them to secede.

To prove that they meant what they said when they had petitioned Congress to crush the traitors by force, many workers joined military associations and offered themselves to the Federal government. Most of these associations were formed by German workingmen, but some, like the Columbian Association set up in New York City, were organized by

Irish workers.[27] On February 5, 1861, Colonel Edward F. Jones informed the Governor of Massachusetts that the Sixth Massachusetts Regiment "made up mostly of men of families, who earn their bread by the sweat of their brows," was prepared to defend the country's flag whenever the call to arms was issued.[28]

It is important to understand that the division in working class circles during the secession crisis revolved only about the question of *how* the Union was to be preserved. There was no division on the important issue, "The Union must and shall be preserved." If peaceful methods failed, the workingmen in nearly all cases were prepared to resort to arms to put down the rebellion. A contemporary workingmen's paper summed it up: "The great industrial masses of the nation are of the Union and for the Union, although some of them [in the South] have been betrayed by wicked leaders into a rebellion in which they have no heart, and by which they endure only hardship and suffering." [29]

TO ARMS!

When President Lincoln called for volunteers after the attack on Fort Sumter, April 12, 1861, workingmen were the first to place their names on the rolls of volunteers. Carpenters, painters, shoemakers, tailors, clerks, mill operatives, printers, and other workers left their jobs unfinished. The Mechanics' Phalanx of Lowell, led by Captain James N. Horse, a carpenter, won a $100 prize for being the first organization ready for camp.[30] Lumbermen in Wisconsin were among the first to enlist and soon became the famed "piney boys" of the 23rd and 29th Regiments.[31] The 34th Regiment of New York which departed for service in July, 1861, was made up, according to the *New York Tribune,* "principally of farmers and mechanics." [32] The De Kalb regiment, consisting entirely of German clerks, left for service on July 8, at which time the Garibaldi Guard, made up of Italian workingmen of New York, was also ready to depart. "The Polish Legion" organized by Polish workingmen of New York late in April, 1861, and a company of Irish workers moved to the front a few weeks later.[33] As the reports of enlistments by Irish workers of Boston and New York increased, the *New York Tribune* expressed joy at the disappointment of the "friends of ... Jeff Davis [who] reckoned upon any assistance from the Irish population of the North." [34] Thousands of Irish workers later joined the army after the following appeal by the Phoenix Regiment of the Empire Brigade:

"The Phoenix, the mother of brave Irishmen, calls upon the children of 1428 to rally around her Green Banner, and marching side by side with the Stars and Stripes, carry the music of the Union to the utmost boundaries of the land." [35]

Investigations conducted during and immediately after the war reveal that before the conflict was over, workers constituted almost half of the northern armies, a ratio greatly out of proportion to their number. At the close of the war a Senate report calculated that between 500,000 and 750,000 men had left the industries of the northern states for the armed forces.[36] Since the total number of men employed in northern industries was 941,766, more than 50 per cent of the workers had left for military service. B. A. Gould's *Investigation in the Military and Anthropological Statistics of American Soldiers,* published in 1869, tells a similar story. Gould states that of every 1,000 soldiers in the Union Army, 421 (252 mechanics, 6 printers, 165 laborers) belonged to the working class. The number per 1,000 for those engaged in agriculture was 487; in the professions, 16; and in commerce, 35. In industrial states like Massachusetts and Connecticut, the percentage of workers was much higher. For Massachusetts, Gould's table lists 502 mechanics, 9 printers, and 186 laborers per 1,000, making a total of 697 as against 140 for agriculture. For Connecticut the figures are 411 mechanics, 7 printers, and 203 laborers per 1,000 making a total of 621.

Gould's statistics for volunteers are also significant despite the fact that he lists no figures for New York or Rhode Island. Of 409,676 volunteers listed for whom occupations were given, 103,708 were mechanics, 49,464 were laborers and 2,664 were printers making a total of 155,836 workers. According to Gould's careful study, 38 per cent of all those who volunteered or about 383 per 1,000 were laboring men. The figures for recruits are more revealing even though the figures from Rhode Island, Minnesota, and Oregon are omitted. Of 229,641 recruits, 64,221 were mechanics, 59,161 laborers, 1,499 printers, making a total of 124,881 laboring men. In other words, 54 per cent of the recruits were workers.[37]

Other studies substantiate Gould's conclusions. Thus a report of Major Poore of the Massachusetts Eighth Regiment giving the occupational composition of the regiment reveals that of the 803 men listed, at least 476 were workers as compared to 22 farmers, 48 clerks, 17 merchants, 31 small tradesmen, five gentlemen, and 10 professional men. Again, of the Fifteenth Battery of Lowell, the occupations of the volunteers show 60 workers, 22 farmers, three merchants, two students, one agent and one gentleman.[38]

The above figures prove that labor responded in more than full measure to the call to arms.* As Major John W. Mahan said in 1865:

* Employers frequently complained that because of the number of workers who left for the armed forces industry was being drained of its manpower. The *Boston Commercial Bulletin* reported on July 18, 1863, that the draft was taking so

"Who was it rallied around the flag in 1861 when Fort Sumter was surrendered? Who was it left without bounty, and without price, that left their homes to sustain the honor of the republic? I tell you that it was the bone and muscle of the Country; and from that time to this, on every bloody battle field, they have proved their devotion to it." [39]

Among these workers were thousands of trade unionists. Entire local unions had enlisted at Lincoln's call for volunteers. In Brooklyn the Painters' Union resolved to fight as a unit "for the maintenance of the flag of our country." [40] A Philadelphia local union entered the following in its minutes: "It having been resolved to enlist with Uncle Sam for the war, this Union stands adjourned until the Union is safe or we are whipped." [41] From the Boston Printers' Union 100 members went to the army and navy to do their duty "in support of the flag of the free," and members of the Printers' Unions in the 11th Massachusetts Regiment so distinguished themselves that they received special citations.[42] The National Typographical Union had to disband Local 23 of Wisconsin because of the large number of members in the army. The Spinners' Union of Fall River, Massachusetts, practically disappeared during the war, and one local of the Iron Molders Union which had 384 members in February, 1861, had lost 97 members within a few months due to enlistments.[43] So many men who belonged to the International Machinists and Blacksmiths Union had left to fight that the number of locals was sharply reduced. By action of the national convention all members of the union in the armed forces were exempted from payment of dues for the duration of the war.[44] Many companies in the regiments of the Illinois Volunteers were composed of members of the Miners' Union, and the American Miners' Association, organized two months before the attack on Fort Sumter, sent large numbers of its members into the ranks.[45]

The Socialist movement in America contributed heavily to the armed forces. The Turner organizations, made up largely of German-Socialist workingmen, the *Arbeiterbund,* and the Communist Clubs sent more than half their members to the Union Army. In New York the Turners

---

many workers from the boot and shoe industry that it was badly hampered and that some establishments were forced to close down. In December, 1863, thirty-five Boston capitalists addressed a memorial to Secretary of War Stanton in which they complained: "In the free states the great numbers already drawn from the workshops and fields have seriously embarrassed many branches of the industry upon which the production of the country depends...." (Quoted by James F. Rhodes, *History of the United States from the Compromise of 1850,* Vol. V, New York, 1905, p. 205.)

Unquestionably unemployment stimulated enlistments but many historians have exaggerated its influence.

organized a regiment in a few days after Lincoln's first call for volunteers, and in many communities they sent one or more companies. There were three companies of Turners in the First Missouri Regiment, and the Seventeenth consisted almost entirely of Turners. In the assault of Camp Jackson, the German Socialists of Missouri fought under their red regimental banner on which they had inscribed the symbol of a hammer smashing a handcuff.[46]

The statistical records of the men who fell defending the nation do not tell who were trade unionists, but the unions informed the public when one of their members died in the service of his country. The following notice inserted in the press by the Stone and Hollow-Ware Molders Union No. 1, of Philadelphia, is typical:

"Whereas, it has pleased Almighty God in his province to remove from our midst our late fellow member, Quarter Master's Sergeant, David Johnson, we would bear witness to his high character as a man, as a moulder, and a soldier; always ready to protect his fellow-men or his country, he was among the first who united themselves to protect our interest, and when his country needed his service, among the first to enlist under his stars and stripes, and met his death from a wound received at Briston Station; therefore be it Resolved, that it is with unfeigned regret that we hear of his death, and hope that his zeal may animate all our members." [47]

One of the first regiments to move to the defense of Washington was recruited by William H. Sylvis. Because of his wife's objections (he had four small children), he did not join the company, although he was offered a commission as a first lieutenant. Several months later, he organized a militia company of molders, and when Pennsylvania was threatened with invasion, the molders' company was the first to offer its services. Sylvis served as orderly sergeant with the company for several months.[48]

Martin Boyle, a leader of the Miners' Association, raised a company of volunteers of which he was elected captain. So valuable were his services that the colonel of the regiment asked him to recruit another company.[49] John M. Farquahr, president of the National Typographical Union, enlisted in the Union army as a private in the 89th Illinois and rose to the rank of major. Robert Williamson Keen, leader of the Tailors' Union in Philadelphia and later a charter member of the Knights of Labor, enlisted at the outbreak of the war for three months' service in the Twenty-Second Pennsylvania; re-enlisted in the Ninety-ninth Pennsylvania for three years, was wounded severely at the battle of Fredericksburg, December 13, 1862, and took the field again when he recovered. Samuel Langdale Leffingwell, president of the Cincinnati Typographical Union, was commissioned a major in the Thirty-first Ohio in August,

1861, and fought in the Union army throughout the entire war, receiving his honorable discharge on June 11, 1865. Isaac J. Neall, ex-President of the National Molders' Union, was wounded, re-enlisted and became a captain, while Francis Rosche, national ex-treasurer, was killed in action.[50]

Many Socialist leaders joined the Union army and some attained positions of high rank. Joseph Weydemeyer, one of the outstanding leaders of the German-American workingmen, enlisted when the Civil War began and received a captaincy commission. Later, because of his work in recruiting an entire regiment of German-American workers, as well as for other distinguished service, he was commissioned a colonel and assigned by Lincoln as Commander of the military district of St. Louis. August Willich, a close friend of Karl Marx, rose to the rank of colonel and in 1862 became a brigadier-general. Robert Rosa, who had been an officer in the Prussian army before he became a member of the Communist Club of New York, was major of the Forty-Fifth Regiment of New York. Fritz Jacobi enlisted as a private, and attained a lieutenancy commission before he died on the field of Fredericksburg.

A great number of the rank-and-file trade unionists and labor and Socialist leaders in the Union army were foreign born, and quite a few of them had not yet become citizens, but they did not hesitate to offer their lives to their adopted country. Most of them, like the Italian workingmen who had fought under Garibaldi, brought with them military experience obtained through service in the armies of Europe.

FIGHTING FOR WHAT?

The following section of a resolution adopted on May 2, 1861, by the Troy local of the International Molders' Union is a representative statement of the reasons which motivated most workers who joined the Union Army after the firing upon Fort Sumter:

"Whereas a goodly number of the members of the Troy Iron Molders' Union have enlisted in the army of the United States for the austensible [sic] purpose of maintaining the supremacy of Law and Order and defending the Constitution so wisely drafted by the Sons of '76 and also the Federal Capital and last but not least to protect that good old flag, the Stars and Stripes. . . ." [51]

Men like Weydemeyer and Willich knew from the outset of the war that it could not be won unless the Negro people were emancipated. Other workers shared their views. One worker wrote home to his union brethren early in the war: "I tell the boys right to their face that I am in the war for the freedom of the slaves." And William H. Sylvis, who had supported Douglas in the election of 1860, said that "from the day the first gun was fired, it was my earnest hope that the war might not end until slavery ended with it." [52]

The logic of waging a people's war successfully made the workers understand that the abolition of slavery was necessary for military victory. Thousands of Negro slaves were being used in southern factories, iron foundries, machine shops, munition plants, and textile mills to produce the means of war for the Confederacy. Many thousands more were used in the cotton and corn fields, releasing white southerners for the battle-front. The slaveowners boasted that the institution of slavery would win the war for them. The *Savannah Republican* stated:

"They [the Northern people] forget the peculiar character of our institutions, the permanency of our industrial system, the fact that the labor of the South is not, as elsewhere, the fighting element of the State. When wars occur in Europe or at the North, you take the laboring man from the plough, the workshop and the factory to fight for them. Production, to the extent of the force required, must accordingly cease. In the Southern, and especially the cotton growing States, the case is entirely different. A wholly different system of labor prevails. Our cotton-fields are tilled by slaves, and Georgia alone might send twenty-thousand troops to the field, without diminishing the production of her staple to the amount of a hundred bales." [53]

When in August, 1861, General John C. Fremont issued his order freeing the slaves of rebels in Missouri, many workers in Pittsburgh, Lowell, and other industrial communities hailed his action, and the chorus of disapproval which came from these workers when Lincoln revoked the order was tremendous. Anti-slavery men reported that in many cities where a few months before only a handful of Abolitionists could be found among the workingmen, there were now hundreds of workers who understood the need "for prosecuting the war till slavery is wiped out." [54]

As the cry for emancipation developed among the workers, the northern allies of the slavocracy tried to frighten them by threats and stories of disaster. Unless the workers opposed the plot of the Abolitionists to have slaves overrun the North, all would be lost. Already, said the traitors of the Civil War, employers had discharged white workers to make jobs for escaped slaves. On June 5, 1862, the Pennsylvania *Indiana Democrat* published a false report that workers at the Cambria Iron Works "threw down their tools and quit work" after "worthless runaway negroes of the South" were employed for twenty-five cents a day. "Our friends can see in this the beautiful workings of the Emancipation policy of President Lincoln." [55]

Though the paper was forced, by the very men who were supposed to have struck, to retract the article as a lie, the Copperhead press throughout the North printed the story and wrote impassioned editorials protecting white workers from the southern menace. Here and there workers were taken in by their propaganda, and a mass meeting in Quincy, Illinois, adopted resolutions stating that they would not tolerate the competition of free Negro workers.[56]

The letters, telegrams, and petitions to President Lincoln in behalf of emancipation defeated the Copperhead campaign. The *Iron Platform,* a New York workingman's paper, gave in November, 1862, the reason that had compelled it to call for the freedom of the slaves:

"There is one truth which should be clearly understood by every workingman in the Union. *The slavery of the black man leads to the slavery of the white man.* . . . If the doctrine of treason is true, that 'Capital should own labor,' then their logical conclusion is correct, and all laborers, white or black, are and ought to be slaves." [57]

Educated by the people and prodded by military necessity, Lincoln was beginning to see that emancipation was "absolutely essential for the salvation of the Union, that we must free the slaves or be ourselves subdued." Instead of deferring, as in the past, to pro-Southerners like General George B. McClellan who warned that "any expression of radical views upon slavery would rapidly disintegrate our armies," Lincoln now listened to the cry coming from factories and fields, *"Emancipate, Emancipate."* [58]

ENGLISH WORKERS AND THE CIVIL WAR

This cry was not confined to the workers and farmers of the United States, but it came from the people of Europe as well. "It was not the wisdom of the ruling classes," said Karl Marx, "but the heroic resistance to their criminal folly by the working classes of England, that saved the West of Europe from plunging headlong into an infamous crusade for the perpetuation and propagation of slavery on the other side of the Atlantic." [59]

Of all nations, England was the most influential in the Civil War. Not only did she possess the biggest navy in the world, but France was quite willing to co-operate with her in whatever policy she adopted toward America. As Lord John Russell informed George M. Dallas, the American minister to England, the two countries had formally agreed "to take the same course as to recognition, whatever the course might be." [60] When the news of the Battle of Bull Run reached Europe proving that the South had an army which could win battles, England recognized the belligerency of the Confederacy, and on the day that the American Ambassador, Charles Francis Adams, reached London, Queen Victoria issued her "Proclamation of Neutrality." This was the first step that the Confederacy believed would lead to military intervention in its behalf.

That the intervention never came was in part the result of Russia's refusal to join England against the North. Also, the businessmen of England were of a divided mind because their country was dependent upon the North for wheat, and English businessmen were making huge profits from both contestants.[61] By far the most important force in preventing recognition of the Confederacy and intervention in its behalf were the heroic efforts of the English workers. "In England," wrote Thurlow Weed who spent a great deal of time in the British Isles during the Civil War, "the commercial cities, the capitalists, and as a rule, the aristocracy were against us. But they did not have their way. The working classes were with us." [62] Karl Marx wrote to the *New York Tribune:* "It ought never to be forgotten in the United States that at least the working class of England from the commencement to the termination of the difficulty have not forsaken them." [63]

A slaveholder had warned William Russell of the *London Times* that when cotton no longer came to England, the workers would starve and would soon clamor for intervention to break the northern blockade. By 1862 but a small fraction of American cotton got through the blockade. The great textile centers closed down, and unemployment spread to other industries. On February 11, 1862, the *London Times* reported 900,000 people out of work of a population of 20 million in England and Wales. A few months later it was estimated that 31.8 per cent of the population of many industrial cities were unemployed.[64] A letter printed in the *London Times* in April, 1862, tells of the suffering of the workers:

"I am living in the centre of a vast district where there are many cotton mills, which in ordinary times afford employment to many thousands of 'hands,' and food to many more thousands of mouths. With very rare exceptions quietness reigns. . . . Hard times have come, and we have had them sufficiently long to know what they mean. We have fathers sitting in the house at mid-day, silent and glum, while children look wistfully about, and sometimes whimper for bread which they cannot have. We have the same fathers who, before hard times, were proud men, who would have thought 'beggar' the most opprobrious epithet you could have hit them with, but who now are made humble by the sight of wife and children almost starving, and who go before 'relief committees' and submit to be questioned about their wants with a patience and humility which it is painful, almost shocking to witness. ... But harder than this, our factory women and girls have had to turn out, and plodding a weary way from door to door, beg a bit of bread. ...

"To see the homes of those whom we know and respect, though they are but workingmen, stripped of every bit of furniture—to see long cherished books and pictures sent one by one to the pawn shop, that food may be had—and to see that food almost loathsome in kind, and insufficient in quantity, are hard things to bear. But these are not the worst things. In many of our cottage homes, there is nothing left by the pawning of which a few pence may be raised, and the mothers of us 'Lancashire lads' have turned out to beg, and ofttimes knock at the doors of houses in which there is as much destitution as there is in their own; while the fathers and lads themselves think they are fortunate if they can earn a shilling or two by street sweeping or stone breaking." [65]

These workers and their dependents did not, as the slaveholders expected, clamor for intervention on the side of the Confederacy. By supporting the North the English workers knew that they were strengthening their own struggles for freedom, for as one English worker at a trade union meeting in London said, "The cause of labour and liberty is one all over the world." [66]

On November, 1861, Captain John Wilkes, commander of the American warship *San Jacinto,* stopped the British mail steamer, *Trent,* and removed two Confederate commissioners, Mason and Slidell, and their secretaries. The Tory press in England seized upon the incident and demanded that war be declared against the North. The British government immediately threatened to do this unless the men were released at once. The corrupt press of France urged Louis Napoleon to side with England.

Although most English workers could not vote, they made their influence felt through meetings and demonstrations. At public meetings throughout the country, the workers insisted on settling the *Trent* affair through arbitration. At one such meeting in Brighton, Mr. White, an influential member of Parliament, said, "It is due to the working class to mention that they are the originators of this meeting and that all the expenses of organizing it are borne by their Committee...." [67] At a meeting in Marylebone, the most populous district of London, the following resolution was unanimously adopted: "This meeting resolves that the agents of the rebels, Mason and Slidell, now on the way from America to England, are absolutely unworthy of the moral sympathies of the working class of this country, since they are slaveholders as well as the confessed agents of the tyrranical faction that is at once in rebellion against the American republic and the sworn enemy of the social and political rights of the working class in all countries." [68]

Mr. Gilpin, M.P. for Northampton declared in January, 1862, that "there was not a man of sufficient eloquence or ability who could obtain the adoption in any fairly gathered meeting of the workingmen of this country, in any part of the kingdom, a resolution in favor of slavery." [69] Nor was there any use in arguing that breaking the blockade through intervention would restore prosperity. The answer of the workers was clear: "No matter what the suffering we may endure, no matter what the sacrifices we may have to undergo, we will not allow our Government to depart from the strict principle of neutrality on behalf of the slaveholding Confederacy." [70]

But one argument did have influence and did succeed in confusing many workers. Why suffer, said English papers friendly to the South, why endure misery and hardships for a cause the North itself does not champion? The North was not fighting to free the slaves. Did not McClellan assure the slaveholders when he took command that they should have no fear that the Union army would interfere with slavery? Did not McClellan promise them that he would crush with an iron hand any slave insurrection? Had not Lincoln revoked the orders of Generals Fremont and Halleck to free the slaves in their districts? The view that the war between the North and South was over slavery was as impudent as it was untrue. Why starve and sacrifice for a war that was being fought between Republicans and Democrats over protective tariffs and banking systems? Why not restore British prosperity by breaking the northern blockade? [71]

Pushed by the common people of America, and anxious to inspire the working class and middle class in Europe to oppose all efforts of their governments to aid the Confederacy, Lincoln began to move. On March 13, 1862, he approved an act of Congress forbidding army and navy officers to use their forces to return fugitive slaves, any officer violating the order to be dismissed from the service. A month later slavery was abolished in the District of Columbia, with compensation for the owners. On June 9, 1862, the Senate passed a bill providing suffrage for free Negroes in Washington, and a day later a resolution passed through Congress securing fugitives the right of trial by jury and placing the burden of proof upon the claimant to establish his ownership of the slave and his loyalty to the Union. Then on September 22, 1862, Lincoln issued a preliminary Emancipation Proclamation which announced that all slaves belonging to persons who were still in rebellion on January 1, 1863, would be free.[72]

Although these steps aroused joy among the common people of America and England, they still feared that reactionary forces might stop emancipation at the last moment. Then began an avalanche of petitions, letters, and telegrams from working class and farming districts in America urging Lincoln to stand fast and carry through emancipation. In England too the workers were determined to encourage Lincoln to continue until slavery was abolished.

When, on January 1, 1863, President Lincoln signed the Emancipation Proclamation, Confederate hopes for English intervention received a crushing blow. From London, Henry Adams, son of the American Ambassador to England, sent a joyful dispatch to his brother: "It is creating an almost convulsive reaction in our favor all over this country. The *London Times* [is] furious and scolds like a drunken drab. Certain it is, however, that public opinion is very deeply stirred here and finds expression in meetings, addresses to President Lincoln, deputations to us, standing committees to agitate the subject and to effect opinion, and all other symptoms of a great popular movement peculiarly unpleasant to the upper classes here because it rests on the spontaneous action of the laboring classes." [73]

Four weeks after the Proclamation, Henry Adams wrote again to his brother: "I went last night to a meeting of which I shall send you a report; a democratic and socialistic meeting, most threatening and dangerous to the established state of things; and assuming a tone and proportions that are quite novel and alarming in this capital. And they met to notify the Government that they will not tolerate 'interference against us!' " * [74]

The organizers of this meeting were Karl Marx and Frederick Engels. From the outbreak of the war Marx and his followers supported the North because they knew that the destruction of slavery in America would unfetter American capitalism, expand bourgeois democracy in America and Europe, thus making possible the further advance of the working class movements the world over. Marx was convinced that

* On March 26, 1863, Adams attended a large meeting of trade unionists at St. James's Hall in London. The report which he submitted to the State Department remained unpublished until 1942. In the report Adams emphasized that the meeting was attended by about 3,000 persons, "all, with the exception of a few invited guests, the members of the working classes, or, technically, skilled laborers." The speakers, he went on, "were all laboring men, trained no doubt in their own Unions to declamation, but evidently themselves sprung from the heart of the people...." The speakers emphasized "that their interests and those of the American Union were one; that the success of free institutions in America was a political question of deep consequence in England, and that they would not tolerate any interference unfavorable to the North. There could be no mistaking the manner in which the audience echoed these sentiments of the speakers, nor could any one doubt what was intended." (Charles I. Glicksberg, ed., "Henry Adams Reports on a Trades-Union Meeting," *New England Quarterly*, Vol. XV, December, 1942, pp. 724-28.)

the North could win only if it conducted the war in a revolutionary manner for the annihilation of slavery.[75]

On September 28, 1864, the first international organization of labor was formed, the International Workingmen's Association. Two months later the General Council of the Association organized a series of workingmen's meetings in London to protest against the anti-Union attitude of the English government. How important this work was to American interests was admitted by Senator George Hoar of Massachusetts speaking in Congress in 1879:

"The International Association of European and American workingmen has this title to respect among other, that it has established among the nations of the world a relation, that it has recognized a kindred between man and man, growing out of the common bond of labor, greater, more powerful, more binding than any mere national attachment, or than any tie which connects the subject to the sovereign. America is the last nation that ought to be ungrateful for that sublime accomplishment. In the darkest days of our own war, when the governing classes of England would have been glad to have joined the emperor of France in recognition of the Southern Confederacy, what prevented it was the angry growl of the workingmen of Lancashire, saying to the English Government, 'We love the workingmen of North America a great deal better, we are more nearly allied in interest and in feeling to the workingmen of America, than we are to the aristocracy of England; and although we have borne many things from you, one thing we will not bear, that you shall array the power and might of England against the cause in which those American workingmen are engaged!' "[76]

CONTRIBUTIONS OF NEGRO WORKERS

By their deeds at the front and in production, the northern workers proved worthy of their English brothers, and by their service to the Union cause during the war the Negroes proved that they earned their freedom. Even before the Emancipation Proclamation, Negro slaves had helped the Union army at every opportunity. Slaves assisted the Federal armies as they marched south, bringing Union commanders valuable information and sabotaging the Confederacy's war effort. The capture of the Confederate steamer, *Planter,* by Robert Smalls is one example of the heroism and resourcefulness of the Negroes during the Civil War. The captain and the white crew absent, Smalls took command of the ship and disguised as the Confederate captain gave the proper signal to Fort Sumter, getting beyond the range of its guns before the ruse was discovered. The *Planter* was delivered to the Federal fleet outside Charleston harbor.

So valuable was the information which Negro slaves gave to Union generals that Confederate commanders often sent out large detachments to clear the country of "Yankee Negroes." In Missouri, slaves were particularly active in aiding the Union officials to root out guerilla bands. Once the entire command of General Banks was saved from a surprise attack by the action of a mounted slave who raced ahead of Confederate troops to give warning of their approach.[77]

Several months before the Emancipation Proclamation, Negroes were serving the Union cause by constructing fortifications and entrenchments, working even when they had no shoes to drive their shovels into the ground. Others were employed in building railroads, cutting wood to supply fuel for steamboats, and loading and unloading government boats. They were also in the blockading service of the Union army, working as carpenters, stevedores, pilots, gunners, and ordinary seamen.[78]

Escaped slaves frequently supplied valuable information concerning Confederate activities. In December, 1861, two Negroes visited the *USS Monticello,* anchored off Wilmington, North Carolina, and gave a detailed description of the Confederate fortifications at New Inlet and Zeek's Island. After the capture of these fortifications, the navy paid tribute to the assistance rendered by the slaves. Equally useful were the Negro slaves in securing supplies for the northern armies in enemy country. They helped cavalry commanders replace worn-out horses, and brought cattle, food, and forage to troops who could not advance for lack of supplies.[79] As early as May 1, 1862, the *New York Tribune* urged Union commanders to use slaves as scouts and spies and warned officers who refused their help that they were depriving the Union army of important allies. "They know the country; they are accustomed to midnight journeys through forest, swamp and thicket avoiding the highways; they are accustomed to keep out of sight and hearing and to find food where a white man must go without."

When the arming of Negroes became law, thousands joined the colors. By 1864 about 186,017 Negroes were serving as Federal troops, of whom 134,111 were from slave states. Of this number 68,178 gave their lives. Commenting on this fact the *New York Tribune* said on December 26, 1865: "The Negro gave one in three of his number to the cause of freedom. Did we, with all our valor, do half as well?"[80]

Negro soldiers endured shameful discrimination. They received less pay than white soldiers until July, 1864; few Negroes were commissioned as officers, and many were forced to perform arduous tasks in addition to fighting. Nevertheless, following the leadership of Frederick Douglass, who urged his people not to permit discrimination to blind them to the full significance of the war, Negroes continued to join the army and fought with distinction. Negro soldiers fought in 198 battles and skirmishes. In May, 1863, General Banks assured Lincoln that the "Victory at Port Hudson could not have been accomplished at the time it was, but for their [Negro troops'] assistance." [81] This regiment of Negro troops had been assigned to storm the key position of the Rebel works, and so intrepid was their charge that it won nationwide admiration.

"Until I joined the Negroes," wrote John Worthington Ames, who assumed command of a Negro regiment in August 1863, "I never saw the enemy's works carried by assault, I never saw guns captured and never knew of captured guns to be used against the enemy; our Negroes have never failed in all these things." [82] Similar testimony came from Colonel Thomas Wentworth Higginson, who commanded a detachment of Negroes in Florida. "It would have been madness," he wrote in February, 1863, "to attempt with the bravest white troops what [I] successfully accomplished with black ones." [83]

It was in guerilla fighting that the Negro soldiers excelled. Squads of Negro troops went into "Rebeldom," destroyed supply stores, salt works, munition dumps, and brought out lumber and other supplies needed in the North. They always brought back new recruits for the Union army. A North Carolina paper in 1864 reported that it was "difficult to find words of description ... of the wild and terrible consequences of Negro raids in this obscure theatre of war." [84]

No one gave more brilliant service than that remarkable woman, Harriet Tubman. No one knew the country better than she; her years of working in the "Underground Railroad" had given her matchless knowledge. In 1863 the army agreed that she give up her work as a nurse in military hospitals and organize a guerilla brigade to operate in South Carolina. Selecting a group of former slaves who were familiar with the country, she and Colonel Montgomery began operations. How they worked is told in the following dispatch which appeared in the *Boston Commonwealth* of July 10, 1863:

"Harriet Tubman

"Col. Montgomery and his gallant band of 300 black soldiers, *under the guidance of a black woman,* dashed into the enemy's country, struck a bold and effective blow, destroying millions of dollars worth of commissary stores, cotton and lordly dwellings, and striking terror to the heart of rebeldom, brought off near 800 slaves and thousands of dollars worth of property, without losing a man or receiving a scratch. It was a glorious consummation."

After the expedition, the new recruits were addressed by Colonel Montgomery who was "followed by a speech from the black woman, *who*

*led the raid and under whose inspiration it was originated and con-
ducted."*

When Lincoln was pressed by defeatists, in 1864, to abandon the use
of Negro troops and discharge those already in service, he replied:

"There are now in the service of the United States near two hundred
thousand able-bodied colored men, most of them under arms, defending
and acquiring Union territory. . . . Abandon all the Posts now garrisoned
by Black men; take two hundred thousand men from our side and put
them into the Battlefield or cornfield against us, and we would be compelled to abandon the war in three weeks." [85]

From the ranks of the workingmen, white and Negro alike, had
come a large portion of the men who did the actual fighting in the Civil
War. It was on a note of pride that the *Boston Daily Evening Voice,*
organ of the trade unions of New England, concluded an elaboration of
labor's contribution to northern victories. On December 27, 1864, it
declared: "Thousands of laboring men have marshalled themselves
under the flag of the free to maintain the integrity of the Government
and vindicate the supremacy of the law. To prevent the dismemberment
of our glorious republic they have abandoned their occupations and
their homes, and are making a sacrifice of blood on the altars of their
country. The strong right arm of the workingman is our country's sure
defence in her hour of trial. Every battlefield attests their devotion tc
country and their love of freedom."

CHAPTER 16

Labor and the Copperheads

Labor's contribution during the Civil War at the battlefront and in the rapidly expanding factories of the North is one of the most inspiring chapters in American history. But historians have either neglected labor's role or have regarded it only in its connection with the Draft Riots. These riots, they contend, were proof that labor did not champion the war, "gave it only sullen support throughout and rejected its idealistic purposes." [1]

LABOR AND THE DRAFT

The truth is that labor did not oppose conscription but rather its class character, the drafting of the poor and not of the rich, of men and not of wealth. This attitude of labor was articulated both by *Fincher's Trades' Review,* the outstanding labor journal of the time, and by William Sylvis, the foremost labor spokesman of his period. The labor paper declared: "For the sake of the country let the conscription come. But let it come upon the rich as well as the poor." [2] And Sylvis argued that had the workers said they would not enter the army, Congress would have ordered the armed soldiers to enter the workshops "and forced us into the army and *that would have been perfectly right....* Now, if it wanted money, could it not have done the same thing? If it has the right to take every man, has it not the right to take every dollar also?" [3]

But the Conscription Act, adopted in 1863, was discriminatory. It contained a clause which made it legally possible to evade service by providing a substitute or by paying a $300 commutation fee. The result was, as the *National Anti-Slavery Standard* pointed out, that the Act granted "a virtual release from the draft for the comfortable class." [4] So unusual was it to find a wealthy capitalist or his son in the armed forces that those who served were regarded almost as social outcasts.

Judge Mellon of Pennsylvania, founder of the Mellon fortune, told one of his sons who wished to serve that it was "only greenhorns who enlist." [5]

That workingmen should have been agitated by the injustice of the Conscription Act was hardly surprising. Nevertheless, the trade unions and the labor press urged workers to abide by the law while campaigning to amend it. In the main, this advice was followed, especially by the organized workers. But a small section of the working class, chiefly the unorganized, succumbed to Copperhead propaganda.

The Copperheads took full advantage of the class nature of the Conscription Act. Posing as friends of labor, they denounced through their press the provision which permitted all who "possess $300 in 'greenbacks' filched from the *people*" to escape military service.[6] Handbills carrying the words of the "Song of the Conscripts" were circulated by the thousands in the summer of 1863, in the labor sections of New York and other cities. A typical excerpt went:

> *We're coming, Father Abraham, three hundred thousand more,*
> *We leave our homes and firesides with bleeding hearts and sore;*
> *Since poverty has been our crime, we bow to thy decree;*
> *We are the poor who have no wealth to purchase liberty.*[7]

What would the workers fight for? the Copperheads asked. And they replied: "to enable 'abolition capitalists' to transport Negroes into northern cities in order to replace Irish workers who were striking for higher wages." [8] The *New York Copperhead* urged workingmen to obey only "Laws which give the poor equal privileges with the rich," while the *Daily News* wrote: "The people are notified that one out of about two and a half of our citizens are to be brought off into Messrs. Lincoln and Company's charnel house. God forbid! We hope that instant measures will be taken to prevent this outrage." [9]

The treasonable campaign of the Copperheads helped to incite bloody and destructive draft riots. On July 13, 1863, a few days after the opening of recruiting, a mob in New York City wrecked the main recruiting station. For three whole days the mob roamed through the city, destroyed shipyards, railroad and street car lines, closed factories and machine shops, attacked the homes and offices of leading Republicans, and killed and wounded an undetermined number of Negroes. Before the riot was quelled, upward of four hundred were killed and wounded, and property estimated at $5,000,000 in value was destroyed.[10]

The rioting spread to other cities. In Troy, New York, three hundred men from the Rensselaer Iron Works and the Albany Nail Works marched through the streets declaiming against the draft, sacked the *Times* office, threatened to burn the African Church, broke open the jail and released the prisoners. In Hartford, Indiana, and in Port Washington, Wisconsin, and in some of the mining districts of Pennsylvania, recruiting boxes were smashed and commissioners driven out of town. Here, in the mining areas, workers' indignation was heightened when it was suspected that mine operators had influenced officials to set a higher quota for the mining districts in order to break the miners' union.* [11]

The Copperheads had partly attained their objective. "Without premeditated organization," they boasted, "the working classes protested in force against the Federal draft which would ... tear from dependent families their sole support." [12] But the Democratic-Republican Workingmen's Association of New York, composed of representatives from the Typographical, Hatters, Carpenters, and Cabinetmakers unions, exposed the Copperhead contention.

"The workingmen of New York did not originate the riots of 1863," declared the Association after a careful investigation. "They were the result of long and careful labors on the part of a class of leaders who succeeded in arousing the prejudices of a small number but sufficient to produce great and direful results.... The workingmen of New York are not rioters. A few reckless and dissolute men, who vibrate between the penitentiary and the dark dens of crime, are not the representatives of the workingmen of the metropolis." [13]

At workingmen's mass meetings, it was pointed out that only a small fraction of the working class had joined the rioters, that most workers in the mob had been dragged out of their shops by the threat that resistance would mean death. The very communities which resisted conscription had previously furnished plenty of volunteers, most of them workers. And it was further revealed that the Irish had already furnished more troops to the federal armies in proportion to their number than had native born Americans. Speakers referred to the magnificent battle record of New York's famous "Fighting Sixty-Ninth" and of other brave Irish regiments.[14] At a meeting in New York City, Patrick Keady, the president of the New York Practical House Painters Association, read the text of a letter he had sent to the members of the union, most of them Irish workingmen:

"I do not for a moment suppose that any of you took part in the late riots. You are too well aware of your own interest to do that; but you can in many ways exercise your influence to prevent recurrence of such

* The fact that a leading Provost Marshal in charge of conscription in Pennsylvania was a notorious anti-union mine operator added weight to the suspicion. (William A. Itter, *Conscription in Pennsylvania During the Civil War*, unpublished doctoral dissertation, University of Southern California, 1941, p. 144.)

disgraceful scenes as were then enacted—scenes which proved that it was not the honest workingmen that engaged in this, but thieving rascals of this and adjacent cities, who have never done a day's work in their lives, and who came here for the purpose of plunder and not to resist the draft....

"I ask you then as a friend, to do all in your power to prevent a repetition of this loss of life and wholesale destruction of property which must ever result from the enactment of such scenes.

"I have read the lists of those who have been arrested, and I do not notice the name of a single painter among them. This is certainly very creditable when it is known that many painters live in this city. Will you keep this record unstained? Will you do all in your power to induce others who are not present to do the same?" [15]

Trade unionists pointed out that during the height of the disorders a group of Socialists braved the fury of the mob and distributed a leaflet exhorting the workers to "Stand by the Union, the Constitution and the Laws! ... Keep honestly at your work!" [16]

Stand by the Union! This slogan rose again and again throughout the war from the trade unions and the labor press. When President Lincoln issued a call in October, 1863, for 300,000 more men, *Fincher's Trades' Review* promptly appealed to workingmen to respond for "Unless we rally round the flag, boys, we shall have no country." [17] More than three months later, the same labor paper greeted another draft with "pride at knowing it [labor] is competent to honor the call." This time the labor paper took occasion to warn the imperialist European governments, particularly those of England and France, to "take heed how they trifle with the wishes of a nation of freemen, who are willing to stake their existence upon their attachment to a principle." [18]

COPPERHEAD PROPAGANDA

Were it not for the activity of organized labor and its press, the Copperheads might have succeeded in their treacherous drive to paralyze totally the war effort of the government of the United States. The Copperheads, moreover, did not limit their machinations to provoking riots. They also launched a campaign for a negotiated peace with the slave aristocracy. "Stop the War!" shrieked Cyrus H. McCormick, the reaper and harvester magnate and a leading Copperhead. "Declare an armistice! Call a convention and consider terms of peace...." [19]

For the Copperheads feared the Civil War as a revolutionary war which aimed at a "Reign of Terror similar to that which disgraced the French Revolution." The Abolitionists, they said, were "fanatics and revolutionists," whose ultimate objective was a socialist society. [20]

At the same time they posed as champions of labor's interests, contending that labor had nothing to gain and everything to lose by supporting and continuing the war. The substitute clause in the Conscription Act, cried the Copperheads, was merely "one more evidence of the administration's disposition to grant favors to the wealthy at the expense of the poor." Moreover, they argued, the government's policies permitted the owners of industry to intensify their exploitation of the poor. The war was creating in America "a system like that of England, which pauperizes the masses and robs them of the rewards of their toil to feed a pampered aristocracy." Already it had enriched the few at the expense of the many, made "the rich richer and the poor poorer," and forced the worker "to take [as] pay for his labor a depreciated currency which enhances his living one, two and in some cases three hundred per cent." To make matters worse, the Copperheads continued, the Emancipation Proclamation had loosed thousands of Negroes upon the North who crowded white workers out of jobs, cheapened the cost of labor and formed an army of strike-breakers "to put down the white laboring classes." [21]

WARTIME CONTRASTS

It is a tribute to labor's understanding of the deeper issues of the Civil War that so few permitted themselves to fall prey to Copperhead propaganda, for there was truth in the assertion that the rich were getting richer and the poor poorer. The start of the war found business in the midst of a crisis caused by the loss of southern markets and the repudiation of close to $300,000,000 of southern debts. But the picture changed when the government placed orders for war supplies.

A new class of millionaires arose, whose fortunes were largely the product of the worst corruption in all of American history. Guns sold to the government by fraudulent contractors exploded in the hands of the soldiers. For sugar the government often received sand; for coffee, rye; for clothing and blankets, a shoddy material made of refuse stuff and sweepings of the shop; and for shoes a composition of inferior leather with paper soles. [22] Sailors were sent to sea in ships built of green timber, "fitted with engines good only for the junkshop," but George Morgan's commission from selling such ships totaled $95,008 for a period of four and one-half months. Soldiers wore uniforms which disintegrated in the rain, but contractors amassed fortunes by supplying these outfits to the government. Others made millions through illicit trading with the enemy.

At the same time the worker's living standard was drastically lowered. Food, clothing, and rent soared under the impact of speculation and inflation, while wages either remained the same or rose very slowly. Wholesale prices of manufactured products rose in 1863 to 59 per cent above those of 1860; in 1864 to 125 per cent; and in 1865 to 107 per cent.[23] Translated into basic necessities, the increases were even more startling. Milk was sold for 1½ cents a quart in New York City in 1861; it was 10 cents a quart in 1864. Butter selling for four cents a pound in April, 1861, was 25 cents a pound in November, 1864. A barrel of mess beef which was $6 in the winter of 1861 rose to $13 in the winter of 1864. Coal cost $5.50 a ton in the winter of 1861; three years later it was $11.[24] In 1864 the *New York Tribune* admitted that while the cost of living had doubled, "wages are only from 12 to 20 per cent higher than they were before the war, and there is absolute want in many families, while thousands of young children who should be at school are shut up at work that they may earn something to eke out the scant supplies at home." [25] *

Congressional legislation and fiscal policies contributed to heighten labor's distress. In 1862 Congress passed a Homestead Act which granted 160 acres of the public domain to anyone who would cultivate it for five consecutive years. Here at last was the measure labor had been demanding in common with western farmers since the days of George Henry Evans' land reform crusade. But the act also provided that an individual cultivating the land could purchase it at $1.25 an acre within six months. Before many settlers could avail themselves of the opportunities offered by the Homestead Act, dummy "settlers" operating for land speculators staked out and recorded claims, and six months later exercised their option to buy. Before long most of the best homesteads passed into the hands of land speculators.

But this land grab was only an aspect of a general campaign of plunder. To the Union Pacific, Central Pacific, and Northern Pacific railroads, chartered between 1862 and 1864, Congress turned over more than 70,-000,000 acres of the public domain, while another 140,000,000 acres were given to the states. These lands, too, were soon appropriated by speculators.

Fraud, corruption, land grabbing—such were the origins of many American fortunes. And these fortunes were further swelled by the government's fiscal policy. Greenbacks issued during the war depreciated in value until they sold for as little as forty cents on the dollar. Since this paper money was accepted as legal tender for the purchase of government bonds, those with funds on hand rushed to invest. Profits were estimated at three to four hundred per cent. Thus, while soldiers and

* Toward the end of the Civil War, labor's condition began to show improvement, partly as a result of increases in "take-home pay" due to increased employment, and partly as a result of trade union struggles.

workers were paid in greenbacks worth no more than fifty or sixty cents, Congress assured the bondholders that they would be paid in dollars worth one hundred cents.[26]

Profits were further augmented by the Contract Labor Law of 1864. This legalized contracts made abroad to bring workers to America, assured businessmen that these workers would not be drafted for the armed forces, and gave legal sanction to the American Emigrant Company which acted as an agent for employers in America. Before leaving Europe the workers signed a contract with the Emigrant Company, which almost reduced the immigrants to the status of indentured servants.* [27] Before its repeal in 1868 the act supplied industry with thousands of workers who were frequently used as strikebreakers.

Incensed by the "Act to Encourage Immigration," labor made it clear that while it did not desire to prevent the entrance of foreign workers, it did object to their being used to cut wages and break strikes.

"By united effort and harmonious combination," said *Fincher's Trades' Review* of June 6, 1863, "we have so far elevated the standard of wages as to secure a moderate share of the comforts which can alone alleviate a life of toil; and that man who knocks at a shop door for the purpose of taking the place of another, at a less price, we not only pronounce a human ingrate, but an enemy of the human race."

WARTIME STRIKES

Labor regretted the strikes which impeded the prosecution of the war. Hence it pleaded with employers to settle grievances peacefully and to grant increases in wages, and appealed to the government to control prices and to reduce living costs to pre-war levels. "We, on the part of the laboring millions," promised *Fincher's Trades' Review,* "will accept the wages of peace, if they be accompanied by peace prices, for all the necessaries of life; but if we must pay *war prices,* we must have *war wages.*" [28]

But the government did nothing to control prices. Indeed, its financial policies, as we have seen, only helped to aggravate conditions. And most employers were too conscious of their favored position to listen to appeals of reason and patriotism.

Labor had no alternative but to strike. Labor leaders, among them

---

* The law provided "That all contracts that shall be made ... whereby emigrants shall pledge the wages of their labor for a term not exceeding twelve months, to repay the expenses of their emigration, shall be held valid in law, and may be enforced in the court of the United States ... and such advances shall operate as a lien upon any land thereafter acquired by the emigrant." (*United Statutes at Large,* Vol. XIII, p. 386.)

William Sylvis, recognized that strikes were "unfortunate." But "what, then, are the workingmen to do?" asked *Fincher's Trades' Review.* And Sylvis expressed the sentiments of many workers when he said: "But if the issue is forced upon us we must accept it. If capitalists will persist in their efforts to drive us to the wall, and reduce us to beggary and want, and deprive us of the rights due to every citizen, and their persistence leads to open war, upon them must rest the responsibility." [29]

It was significant that during most of the strikes the workingmen placed the onus on capital. They inserted paid advertisements in the press, listing the increases in the cost of living, and pointing to the recalcitrance of "their employers, who were gaining enormous profits on government contracts." It was "as loyal citizens, sound uncompromising Union friends of the Government [and] as respectable mechanics," that they appealed for public support in the struggle that had been forced upon them.[30]

Many employers, of course, hastened to put pressure on the government to forbid turn-outs and to place strikers under arrest. The same men who were severely injuring the conduct of the war by their corrupt practices now pleaded that unless the authorities came to their assistance, production for the armed forces would be seriously hampered. The coal operators of Missouri, for example, who had raised the price of coal, proposed during a strike in 1863 that since the government was "materially interested in having a full and constant supply of coal," the Union army should be sent in to disperse the strikers.[31]

Union generals quickly responded to such appeals from employers. In April, 1864 Major-General William Rosecrans issued General Order No. 65 from his headquarters in St. Louis, which prohibited the organization of men engaged in war production, forbade picketing, guaranteed military protection for scabs, and blacklisted those who dared to engage in organizing unions. A similar order was issued by General Burbridge in Louisville, Kentucky. He was said to be "in the confidence of the employers, [and] aware of all their plans." *

* There were a few generals who were friendly to the laboring classes. The outstanding example was General Benjamin F. Butler. When Butler arrived at New Orleans with Federal troops, he found thousands of unemployed workers facing famine and starvation. The price of food had risen to levels that were entirely beyond their means, what with bread selling at 20 cents a loaf and flour at $14 a barrel. Butler proceeded to fix prices, and levied a tax on confederate bondholders and traders to aid the unemployed. When the wealthy protested, Butler told them bluntly: "The poor must be employed and fed, and you must disgorge. It will never do to have it said, that while you lie back on cushioned divans, tasting turtle, and sipping the wine cup, dressed in fine linen, and rolling in lordly carriages, that gaunt hunger stalked in the once busy streets, and poverty flouted its rags for the want of the privilege to work." They disgorged

These orders were enforced. At Cold Springs, New York, Federal troops were used to break a strike in the R. P. Parrott Gun Works where the workers were demanding an increase in wages. Four of the workers were arrested, held seven weeks without trial, not permitted to return to their homes, and they and their families driven from the town. In St. Louis striking machinists and tailors were forced back to work at the point of a bayonet. In Tennessee General Thomas had two hundred striking mechanics arrested and "deported." [33] Troops were used to break' the strikes of the engineers on the Reading Railroad, and of the Miners Association in Tioga County, Pennsylvania.

That speculators and contractors who fattened on the sorrow of the nation should have won the ear of the government sent waves of anger through the working class. Did not the workingmen in the Union army have enough to do in fighting "the enemies of their country, without being made to war against their brethren at home?" [34] asked *Fincher's Trades' Review.* "Has it come to this, that the Government we all love, and to protect and uphold which at least a quarter of a million of our fellow-laborers have sacrificed their lives and a million more today brave the foe that would destroy it, must array its armed citizens against their fellow-citizens because of a difference among civilians?" [35]

Prominent trade unionists of the period ceaselessly reminded the government that every action taken against labor in favor of capital was a means of feeding Copperhead propaganda in working-class circles.[36]

FAILURE OF THE COPPERHEAD CAMPAIGN

Realizing that the Confederacy had no chance of winning tne war the Copperheads intensified their drive for an immediate termination of the war through a negotiated peace. Unless the workers acted quickly to end the war on terms agreeable to the South, they warned, the coalition of the capitalists and the government would impose on them a worse bondage than that supposedly suffered by the Negro slaves.[37] "Peace will stay the slaughter," said the New York *Daily News* on June 1, 1864, "will put a stop to further demoralization—will put an end to starvation prices for labor...."

But the Copperheads failed to incite labor to acts of disloyalty. While some workingmen were infected with the propaganda of the Copper-

to the amount of $350,000. The money was spent to aid the poor. $70,000 worth of food was distributed monthly to 9,707 families, $2,000 a month was used to support five asylums for orphans and widows, and $5,000 a month went to Charity Hospital. Meanwhile, Butler provided work relief for the unemployed. More than a thousand men were hired by the city authorities to clean the streets and repair the wharves. (See Howard P. Johnson, *New Orleans Under General Butler,* unpublished doctoral dissertation, Yale University, 1937.)

heads,* labor in the main rejected their overtures. It too wanted the war to end quickly, but the war, it said, had to be fought to a victorious conclusion. A "Union Man" in the ranks of the Federal Army wrote to *Fincher's Trades' Review,* urging it to rally labor on the home front against a negotiated peace. The letter was endorsed by trade unions throughout the North. It said:

"We are out here voluntarily, sacrificing all the comforts of home, the society of our friends, and all we hold dear in this world to maintain the constitution and the Union against a cursed Rebellion which, gaining strength through many years of secret treachery, threatened at one time to overwhelm our land.

We, the soldiers of the Union, looking back to the many battle-fields crimsoned with the blood and whitened with the bones of thousands of our murdered comrades, with the very ground beneath our feet crying for vengeance, cannot ask for peace on any other terms than the entire subjection of the Rebels in arms against the best Government God ever gave to man." [38]

Behind the battle front labor assured the government of its determination to help in the crushing of the rebellion. Late in August 1864, the Machinists' and Blacksmiths' Union met in convention at Philadelphia. Few workers had suffered so severely at the hands of capitalists and of government officials. Nevertheless, the Machinists and Blacksmiths voted that the way to end the suffering of the working class was to crush the Confederacy on the battlefield. Its resolution read:

"Resolved, That our rights and interests as working men, besides our duty to our families, our duty to our fellow workmen (who are in the army by thousands) and our duty to our country as citizens requires that we should use every means in our power to aid our government in its efforts to suppress this most wicked and unnatural Rebellion.

"Resolved, That however much we may differ on questions of minor importance, when it comes to the question of the life or death of the great Republic, we workingmen will stand as a unit in defense of the

* Virginia-born Elisha W. McConas, a trade unionist connected with the Copperhead movement, was able to influence the Chicago Trades' assembly to endorse a proposal that the war be terminated on the ground that it was unimportant to workers. "The present war," went a resolution written by McConas for a workingmen's meeting in Chicago, "was not caused by the laboring men of the North, nor fought under their direction, nor continued for their interests—their only part being to bear its burdens and shed their blood in the ranks." (*Chicago Tribune,* April 27, August 22, 24, 1864.) The Machinists and Blacksmiths Union of Chicago refused to associate itself with the anti-war movement led by McConas, and openly accused it of being under Copperhead control. (See *Chicago Tribune,* August 22, 24, 1864, and *Fincher's Trades' Review,* Oct. 8, 1864.)

sentiment of the immortal Jackson: 'The Union must and shall be preserved.' " [39]

Scores of similar resolutions can be cited.[40] They all record the failure of the Copperhead campaign to transform the workers' hatred of profiteers and capitalists into a hatred of the war itself. This failure, be it noted, was due in no small measure to trade union leaders and to the labor press. These always sought to impress the workingmen with the need to distinguish carefully between the government and the capitalists.

No one more bitterly denounced the use of troops to break strikes than William Sylvis; yet he always refrained from casting the blame on the administration and on Lincoln, arguing that "they have never seen but one side of the question. It is our duty to show them our side, and then if they allow such things we can blame them." As an illustration, Sylvis cited the case of the Schuylkill Miners Union. Because the workers themselves did nothing to bring their grievances before the administration, the employers succeeded in convincing the authorities at Washington that the miners had associated together "for disloyal purposes." It was labor's duty, therefore, Sylvis argued, to educate the administration.[41]

Fincher's Trades' Review agreed with Sylvis. It was not Lincoln, it declared, but "upstart officials who have taken undue advantage of the place they have disgraced" upon whom should be placed the blame for the outrageous wrongs labor suffered. The labor paper was convinced that once the President was informed of the real issues in the dispute he would take his stand with labor.[42]

LABOR TURNS TO LINCOLN

To Lincoln, then, the workingmen turned to redress their grievances. A committee of working women who had visited him reported that he was "deeply impressed with the tale of their sufferings and wrongs." With much feeling, said the report, he told the quartermaster: "I shall consider myself personally obliged if you can hereafter manage the supplies of contract work for the Government made up by women so as to give them remunerative wages for their labor." [43] Again, when workers in the shipyards struck for higher wages, Lincoln suggested that heads of the army and navy settle the strike by bargaining with labor. In December, 1863, Commodore Montgomery, a navy officer who had refused to listen to delegations of workingmen in the Brooklyn Navy Yard and had discharged men for union activity, was replaced by Admiral S. H. Stringham. "This appointment," wrote a union official, "gives general satisfaction and it guarantees that the Administration means to do right by their employees." The new commander reinstated the discharged men.[44] A year later union printers in St. Louis appealed to Lincoln when General Rosecrans sent troops to break their strike. In their appeal the strikers reminded the chief executive of the words he had uttered in 1860: "Thank God, we have a system where there can be a strike." Lincoln ordered that "servants of the Federal Government should not interfere with legitimate demands of labor," and that the soldiers be withdrawn.[45]

But the deepest enthusiasm for Lincoln among the workingmen was evoked by the report of an interview in the White House between the President and a delegation of the New York Machinists and Blacksmiths Union. In the fall of 1863, some 7,000 members of that union went out on strike for higher wages to meet the mounting rise in the cost of living. The employers appealed to Washington for an extension on their contract to enable them to break the strike. Instantly the union sent a committee to Washington to see the President. The account of the interview, given by a correspondent who accompanied the delegation, read as follows:

"We were received in a manner that shows conclusively the worthy old gentleman had not left all his sympathies for laboring men with his maul and wedges in the prairie State. After hearing our statement, he told us that he could do nothing as President, but as Abraham Lincoln, his sympathies were with us, and further, having been raised in a rural district, he had never participated in a strike. The only one he had ever beheld was a strike among the shoemakers of Haverhill, Massachusetts, ... in which the shoemakers succeeded in beating the bosses. As to the present strike, he considered the employers the first strikers as they refused to accept the terms offered by the men, and compelled the latter to cease work ... and now that both were on strike, let the best blood win. He then recommended the committee to call upon the Secretary of the Navy and, to insure prompt attention, gave them a note to the Secretary, asking an immediate interview, which upon presentation was granted.... The Secretary assured our committee that no extension of time would be granted by anyone in his Department, as Congress alone possessed the power to grant it."

The committee's report to the membership of the union "was received amid vociferous cheers, and the meeting adjourned with three times three for the President, the Navy Department and fair play." [46]

Some time later the Machinists Union, hearing a rumor that the contracts of the employers had been extended, sent another delegation to Washington. Malcolm MacLeod, a member of the delegation, wrote an account of their visit for *Fincher's Trades' Review.* Lincoln told the committee that he knew nothing of the contracts, and again advised them to see the Secretary of the Navy. In addition, he gave the trade unionists a note reading "Secretary Welles—Please see and hear these gentlemen. (Signed) A. Lincoln."

"Mr. Lincoln," MacLeod continued, "also made inquiries about our wages—what we received now and what we demanded. After answering him, he said 'It must be hard for workingmen. I do not live in a large way, although I am here. But it costs me 100 per cent more than it did two years ago.'"

When asked by the delegates where his sympathy lay in the strike, Lincoln replied that as President he could not officially take sides. But he added: "I know the trials and woes of working men, and I have always felt for them. I know that in almost every case of strikes, the men have just cause for complaint."

The committee saw the Secretary of the Navy who, according to Mac-Leod, "was much cooler to us than his boss." Nevertheless, the trade unionists were assured that their employers had received no extension on their contracts. MacLeod concluded his account with a statement that was to be repeated for many months in working-class circles:

"It is but faint praise to say that the President deserves the hearty thanks of all the working men throughout the country for the kind and courteous manner in which he treated their humble representatives. If any man should again say that combinations of working men are not good, let him point to the Chief Magistrate—kindly and frankly treating a working men's committee. I will never dress to see old Abe, working clothes will do." [47]

Lincoln was often slow in dealing forcefully with the Copperheads (he even revoked General Burnside's order which suppressed the vicious *Chicago Times*). But the Copperheads might have had greater success in turning labor against the war had not the workingmen known that they could appeal for redress to the White House.

ROLE OF THE LABOR PRESS

Basically, the Copperhead campaign among the workingmen failed because the vast majority of them understood that their fate was being decided on the battlefields. For promoting this understanding much credit belongs to the labor press, to papers like *Fincher's Trades' Review* and the *Iron Platform*. The first reiterated that the very right of workers to organize was involved in the struggle. Therefore, it contended, while labor had to organize to lift the burdens of the war off its back, it also had to make every sacrifice necessary to insure victory. That sacrifice would be easier to bear if labor realized that the rebellion was nothing more than an "attempt ... to establish a government on the destruction of the rights of labor," and if it clearly understood that it was fighting not only for its own future, but for workingmen throughout the world. "Our example," said *Fincher's,* "has created new-born hopes in the oppressed of every land and extorted concessions to the people of all countries." Labor could not afford to let this be destroyed.[48]

The second, the *Iron Platform,* edited and published by members of the New York Typographical Union, developed the same theme. The war, this workingmen's journal repeated in issue after issue, was not merely a question of what class or political party should control the government. It was not only an issue of internal improvements and of homestead acts, however important these were:

"Our contest has a greater issue than these involved, and it is of the utmost importance that every working man understand it clearly. If he would be a freeman, and enjoy the blessings of liberty for himself and his children—if he would be true to himself and to the working men of the South—if he would be true to the interests of Labor throughout the world he must work and vote to overthrow rebellion and treason and maintain the government at every cost."[49]

The *Iron Platform* also mobilized working-class support for win-the-war candidates. In October, 1861, it campaigned for the election of the People's Union Candidates, nominated at conventions of Pro-Union Democrats and Republicans in New York State. "Vote for no Party, and no Party ticket," it appealed to the workingmen of New York City. "But let the workingmen of this great city vote in one solid body for the People's Union Candidates.... Let our votes prove that we hold the Union dearer than Party politics."[50] And the People's Union candidates swept the election.

A year later the *Iron Platform* urged the formation of a Democratic-Republican Party in New York, which would unite win-the-war Republicans and Democrats. Unfortunately, the Democratic Party refused to co-operate, and the votes were split.[51]

The refusal of the Democratic Party in New York to unite on a win-the-war program led to the formation of the Democratic League in May, 1863. It consisted of Democrats loyal to the government who supported candidates on the basis of their pro-war attitude. William Oland Bourne, editor of the *Iron Platform,* was the labor representative on the Executive Board of the League.[52]

WORKINGMEN'S DEMOCRATIC-REPUBLICAN ASSOCIATION

Early in 1864, the editors of the *Iron Platform* broadened their pro-war activity when they joined with other trade unionists to organize the Workingmen's Democratic-Republican Association of New York. Similar Associations were later established in Chicago, Boston and Philadelphia and all were linked by correspondence committees.[53] Their objectives were to unite Republican and Democratic Workingmen in support of Union candidates, to educate the workers on the fundamental issues of the war, and to rally the working class behind the administration. In March, 1864, the officers of the Association visited President Lincoln, and brought him the assurance of labor backing. In reply Lincoln declared that the interests of no class were so deeply involved in the war as were those of the workers. He urged them to "beware of prejudice, working division and hostility among themselves," and referred regretfully to the fact that during the draft riots in New York some working people had been killed by other working people. Then Lincoln said: "It never should be so. The strongest bond of human sympathy, outside of the family relation, should be one uniting all working people of all nations and tongues and kindreds." [54]

In the crucial Presidential campaign of 1864, the Workingmen's Democratic-Republican Association campaigned energetically to secure the re-election of Lincoln. In a letter addressed to General George B. McClellan, the Democratic candidate, the Association reminded him that the interests of labor "as a class" were at stake in the war. The nation, the letter continued, was engaged "in a death struggle of democracy against aristocracy and despotism." The outcome of the Presidential election, therefore, was of crucial importance to the workingmen. Finally, it posed the following questions to McClellan:

"1. If you are elected President will you consider yourself to be the President of the American Union in its territorial extent as it existed before the first ordinance of secession?

"2. Will you, as President, adopt the most vigorous measures against foreign and domestic enemies?

"3. Do you consider the American Union in its territorial extent as it existed before the first ordinance of secession?

"4. Will you, as President, recognize the Southern Confederacy as an independent nation in order to take the first steps toward the negotiation of peace?" [55]

But the hero of the Copperheads refused to answer. Publicizing this fact, the Workingmen's Democratic-Republican Association intensified its drive to re-elect Lincoln. It was significant that a number of trade unions broke with the tradition of non-participation in politics and joined the Association in the campaign.

Thus the Mechanics Union in New York City called a special membership meeting at the request of the Association and took an unprecedented step. As the president of the union put it in a public letter:

"The time has come when every man, no matter how humble, ought to vote intelligently. We are not allowed to discuss politics in our meeting rooms. However, we organized as a political body for the coming contest, and ... it was moved to indorse the Union ticket.... After some discussion, the motion to indorse was carried almost unanimously." [56]

Some pro-Union observers feared that "the high prices of provisions" would drive the workingmen into the Copperhead camp,[57] but a careful examination of the files of the *New York Daily News* during the entire campaign, reveals no reported instance of any trade union or association adopting resolutions favoring peace, or approving McClellan's candidacy.*

Lincoln swept all but three states. The American people had determined to win the war and to save the Union.

VICTORY

In the name of the workingmen of Europe the General Council of the International Workingmen's Association sent an address, penned by Karl Marx, to President Lincoln congratulating the American people on his re-election and expressing satisfaction that it should have fallen to him to lead his country in a war which marked the beginning of a new era for the working class. "From the commencement of the titanic American strife," wrote Marx, "the workingmen of Europe felt instinctively that the Star Spangled Banner caried the destiny of their class." Hence they had borne "patiently the hardships imposed upon them by the cotton crisis, opposed enthusiastically the pro-slavery intervention—importunities of their betters—and from most parts of Europe contributed their quota of blood to the good of the cause." [58]

In the United States, too, the workers had borne patiently the many hardships of the war. Copperheads abetted the southern slavocracy and made every effort to exploit for their own purposes the indignation of the

*The "Workingmen's United Political Association of the City and County of New York," was formed early in the summer of 1864 to campaign for McClellan. But it was little more than a front for the Democratic Party, and it attracted none of the numerous trade unions in New York. The president of this paper organization, McDonough Bucklin, was an organizer of the Democratic Party. (See *New York Daily News,* Aug. 5, 1864; Joseph Adam Sagat, *Northern Labor in the National Conflict, 1861-1865,* unpublished M.A. thesis, 1939, University of Wisconsin, p. 114.)

working class against profiteering. But their campaign failed. The workers continued to contribute to Union victory by toiling ten or twelve hours a day in coal pits and at steel furnaces, building ships, laying tracks, operating the looms and the shoe factories. It can truly be said that without the support of labor the Civil War might have ended in the victory of the slavocracy which believed that all workers should be slaves. William H. Sylvis epitomized labor's role in the Civil War when he said before the delegates to a convention of the International Molders Union held in Chicago in January, 1865:

"I presume it is hardly necessary for me to enter into any arguments to prove that the workingmen, the great body of the people, the bone and muscle of the nation, the very pillars of our temple of liberty are loyal; that, I take it, would be sheer mockery, would be adding insult to injury; for the evidence of our loyalty one need only point to the history of the war; to the fact that while armed treason and rebellion threatened our institutions with destruction, while the proud and opulent of the land were plotting the downfall of our government, the toiling millions stood like a wall of adamant between the country and all its foes." [59]

The war over, the workers of America served notice on the ruling classes that in the future they intended to claim their just share in the democratic institutions they had fought to preserve. Among the resolutions adopted at a mass meeting of Boston workers held at Fanueil Hall on November 2, 1865 was the following:

"... We rejoice that the rebel aristocracy of the South has been crushed, that ... beneath the glorious shadow of our victorious flag men of every clime, lineage and color are recognized as free. But while we will bear with patient endurance the burden of the public debt, we yet want it to be known that the workingmen of America will demand in the future a more equal share of the wealth their industry creates ... and a more equal participation in the privileges and blessings of those free institutions, defended by their manhood on many a bloody field of battle." [60]

CHAPTER 17

The Labor Movement, 1861-1866

During the early Civil War years trade unionism was all but defunct. Many of the unions which had managed to survive the panic of 1857 and the secession crisis were well-nigh deprived of members after the first call for volunteers. Those that continued to show signs of life were seriously affected by the early war depression.

National unions fared as badly as local labor organizations, and those with southern locals were especially weakened. By the end of 1861 many of the Iron Molders' locals were about extinct; the national convention called for January, 1862, did not even meet. So discouraged was I. S. Cassin, national president of the Machinists and Blacksmiths, that he did not even attend the national convention called for November, 1861. At this convention, in Pittsburgh, the union's national secretary, Jonathan Fincher, found only a few optimistic delegates. Their optimism was considerably strained when they learned from Fincher that only thirty locals were still in good standing, as compared with eighty-seven in November, 1860, and that membership had declined from 2,717 to 1,898 since April, 1861.[1]

Yet even in these difficult months, when the situation for organized labor appeared hopeless, a number of organizations showed signs of life. In New York, Boston, and Philadelphia, many unions held fairly regular meetings and maintained a more or less continuous organization. Some unions even took steps to raise wages. But in the main, trade unionism was on the decline.

CAUSES OF TRADE UNION REVIVAL

But a new day for American labor was approaching. By the middle of 1862 the early war depression was all but over, and business and industry were beginning to flourish as never before. Workingmen failed to reap any benefits from the good times that began in late 1862. Soaring prices rendered the vast majority of them worse off than they had been in 1860. To wage earners, alone of all classes in American society, the war had brought ever-increasing hardships.

The great changes taking place in the every-day life of the working-man made organization a matter of utter necessity. "The time has now arrived," said the shoemakers of Philadelphia in November, 1863, "when it is absolutely necessary that an organization should be formed in our trade, for the regulation of our wages and the protection of our rights in general. The high prices of provisions, fuel, clothing, etc., render it imperative that we should have an advance on our present wages ... and this cannot be done without organization." [2]

High prices were not the only reason for organization. Capital was becoming so powerful during the war that unless labor organized it would find, at the end of the conflict, that "capital and capitalists will have the industrial classes *completely* within their grasp." [3] Now was the time to begin, for the scarcity of labor owing to enlistments and continued drafts assured the workers that it would be difficult if not impossible for employers to replace union men with non-unionists. Jonathan Fincher observed in December, 1863, that "at no time in the history of labor, perhaps, have passing events placed before workmen so many advantages. There are few idle—work is plenty." "Organize! Organize!" he appealed, "organize in every village and hamlet, and become tributary and auxiliary to district, county, state and national trade organization." [4]

Long before this call was issued the revival of trade unionism had started in earnest. Unions that had continued to hold meetings during the early period of the war rapidly gained new members after the summer of 1862. Many trades re-established effective unions, drew up new constitutions, set forth demands for higher wages and more satisfactory working conditions, and, when employers refused concessions, went out on strike to secure these demands. By the beginning of 1863 the revival was in full swing, and scarcely a week passed without the formation of a new union in some part of the country. Frequently the fact of its organization and its wage demands were announced simultaneously. A fairly large percentage of the unions formed in 1863-64 were organized during or immediately after a strike. The *Springfield Republican* of March 26, 1863, remarked that "the workmen of almost every branch of trade have had their strikes within the last few months.... In almost every instance the demands of the employed have been acceded to. The strikes which have all been conducted very quickly ... have led to the formation of numerous leagues or unions." The San Francisco *Evening Bulletin* reported that "striking for higher wages is now the rage among the working people of San Francisco," and added that the strikes were invariably successful and led to the organization of trade unions.[5]

During this turbulent period not all strikes had as their purpose the securing of higher wages to meet the rising cost of living. The introduction of machinery in specific trades was the cause of many strikes. As skills disappeared with technological advances, replacement became a problem in several trades. No longer was it a question of limiting the number of apprentices in relation to the skilled mechanics; now it was a question of the loss of jobs and of constantly declining wage standards. American workers fought to prevent the introduction of machinery and the spread of the factory in the mistaken belief that only in this way could they maintain their status.

The struggle was useless. The floating grain elevators introduced in New York harbor in the winter of 1861-62 accomplished in one hour the work formerly done in ten hours. In July of 1862, two thousand laborers stopped work and demanded an end to the elevators. The Grainmen's Protective Union of New York appealed to the grain merchants to settle the strike by abandoning the use of machinery and restoring the former method of carrying out the work. "We do not ask or claim any increase of wages. The usual rate of wages we have been earning for 20 years is all we ask. We ask only that we still be allowed to work as we have heretofore, industriously, peacefully, usefully to ourselves, our families, and the whole mercantile community." [6] The strike failed. Nor were the street cleaners or blacksmiths successful in their strikes for similar demands.[7]

American workers learned quickly that the solution to this problem was not in fighting the new machines but in collective action to improve their conditions. This understanding was reflected in the columns of *Fincher's Trades' Review* in the summer of 1863. For weeks its major theme was the headline, *"The Upheaving Masses in Motion."* In their November, 1863, appeal to the shoemakers of Philadelphia, the organizers informed their brethren in the factories that "nearly every trade in the city has organized and obtained an advance, varying from 10 to 15 per cent." Unless the Sons of Crispin did likewise, the "finger of scorn" would be deservedly pointed at them. Common laborers, factory workers, and even preachers joined the ranks of organized labor during this upsurge of unionism. The *Philadelphia Public Ledger* of February 19, 1862, carried the following notice: "The Regular Stated Meeting of the Local Preachers' Union will be held this evening...at 7½ o'clock."

WOMEN WORKERS

No wage-earners had greater need for organization than the working women. Women in government and private employment were paid 50 per cent of the wages of men workers for the same work, and in some industries they were often not even paid for their work.* When Richard F. Trevellick conveyed to a mass meeting of workingmen in Detroit the plight of the working women, the audience, although profoundly moved, could not decide on a program. This is not surprising as there was sharp division among all workingmen on the question of women workers. "We will resist," said the Secretary of the Journeymen's Tailors' Association of St. Louis, "any attempt to introduce female apprentices by encouraging them to leave service and other employments more congenial to girls than mixing with men in a workshop from morning to night." [8] *Fincher's Trades' Review* at first supported this backward attitude, contending that since women were paid half as much as men their presence in the trade would soon result in forcing down the wage levels of workingmen. The workers in the armed forces, it argued, "will esteem it a poor reward for all their sacrifice, to find [when the war is over] every avenue choked up by their wives and daughters at half paying prices." [9] Yet Fincher, the paper's editor, like other alert trade unionists, soon realized that this negative attitude could not solve the problem. The war required the services of working women, and events proved the futility of fighting to force them back in the homes. To prevent wages in the trades from sinking to the level of women's wages it was necessary for the men to help organize the women into trade unions and raise their wage standards. Hence Fincher began a campaign in September, 1863, to convince workingmen that a "more just compensation of female labor" was the surest road to the maintenance of wage levels. He urged the women to organize into trade unions, assuring them that workingmen would help them, "for no person claiming to be a *man* would shrink from any duty assigned him in such a cause." [10]

Two months after this appeal, a mass meting of working women, held

* Surveys of wages of working women in New York City during the Civil War revealed shocking conditions. Girls engaged in sewing umbrellas earned three dollars a week by working from 6 a.m. to midnight, and from these wages employers deducted the cost of needles and thread. Tassel-makers who made six dollars a week in 1853 made about four in 1863 by working from 6.30 a.m. to 10 p.m. Sewing girls who made underwear earned about seventeen cents for a twelve-hour day in March, 1864. Girls who made cotton shirts received twenty-four cents for a similar day's work. And the women had to furnish their own thread even though the price of spools had risen from four to ten cents. (See *New York Tribune*, Oct. 9, 14, 1863; *New York Herald*, Nov. 14, 1863; *New York Tribune*, Mar. 22, 1864.)

in New York City, received the co-operation of many workingmen's unions in the city, and several delegates shared the platform with the women. Most of these unions later voiced their approval of the resolution adopted by the meeting and voted to give financial assistance to the organizing drive. The resolution recommended that "an organization be commenced for the purpose of uniting the working women of the City of New York in a movement for increasing the prices now paid them for labor." [11]

While these efforts were being made to organize women into the trade union movement, another type of woman's organization was coming into existence. Late in 1863 the Working Women's Protective Union was formed in New York City. It owed its existence to a visit by a New York workingman to Moses S. Beach, the editor of the *New York Sun*. He had urged the editor to join him in a movement to aid the working women of the city, many of whom were starving. Moved by his story, Beach called upon the working women of New York to attend a meeting which was to be held at the Military Hall. The night of the meeting found an overflowing hall, in which sat hoop-skirt makers, shirt sewers, vest makers, sewing machine operators, press feeders, silver-burnishers, photographers, and umbrella sewers. Their average wage, a survey at the meeting revealed, was between $2 to $3 a week. A committee of working women was appointed to consult with a committee of men to devise means of securing higher wages and other measures of relief. Out of this committee's report grew the Working Women's Protective Union.[12]

The Protective Union conducted a placement bureau which received 6,422 applications during the first ten months of its existence. To prevent overcrowding in some trades, the union also trained women in many new occupations, and taught seamstresses who worked by hand to run a sewing machine for which work the pay was higher. In 1864, the Union placed 3,500 women; the next year the number was 3,608.[13] Although it made an earnest effort to secure better wages and shorter hours for the women it placed, it did not always succeed as it relied solely on "that sympathy and for the support which are due to the otherwise defenceless condition of the working women." [14]

But the Union was successful in supplying working women with legal protection. A chief grievance was non-payment for work and the vicious practice of deducting a considerable portion of the wages for so-called imperfect work. Largely through the activity of the Protective Union, a law was passed providing for imprisonment of employers guilty of not paying working women.* Deductions from wages for supposedly im-

* This law did not entirely end the abuse because employers could get around the law by transferring their businesses to their wives or other women.

perfect work was met with prosecution of the guilty employers, and by 1870 the union's threat to prosecute was enough to force the employer to pay wages in full. In 1880 the treasurer of the union reported that the organization had settled 27,292 disputes since 1864, and that twenty thousand of them were settled out of court. A total of $24,647.49 had been recovered, the sum of $3.38 being the average recovery. No woman was ever charged for these legal services.[15]

The New York Union was not the only working women's relief association formed during these years. Others were organized in Chicago, St. Louis, Indianapolis, Boston, and Philadelphia. The latter, organized in 1864, called upon the women "to make known the prices received, the number of hours worked, and other particulars," promising that none of the names would be exposed. Gathering sufficient information to prove its case, the association brought pressure upon government officials to secure wage increases for women working in arsenals and on government contracts.

None of these protective associations were trade unions, but they encouraged women workers to protest and to organize. The Philadelphia Association announced its desire "to organize women into protective associations" and published the *Women's Journal* to further the cause of trade unionism among working women.[16]

One of the earliest women's trade unions was formed by a thousand umbrella sewers of New York City and Brooklyn, a most exploited group of women workers. Paid from six to eight cents for each umbrella, they made twelve umbrellas by working from 6 o'clock in the morning until past midnight. In addition, they had to pay for their own needles and thread. In October, 1863, these women struck for an extra two cents for sewing umbrella covers. Many employers acquiesced, but others held out and the organization was too weak to bring the strike to a successful conclusion.

A "Ladies Cigar Makers Union" was organized in Providence, Rhode Island, early in 1864, and in September of that year it voted to boycott an employer who hired strike-breakers.[17] In April, 1864, the sewing machine operators in New York City organized a Working Women's Union, which combined benevolent features with trade union principles. "We have organized," said the secretary of the union, "to improve our social condition as far as possbile, and in no case to allow employers to reduce our wages, and lastly, as soon as we have the numbers and the fund, to have an advance of wages and shorter hours." Early in 1865, this union held a large mass meeting under the chairmanship of its president, Miss M. Trimble. A number of prominent men trade unionists addressed the meeting, pledging their organizations' support. William Harding, president of the New York Trades' Assembly, assured the ladies that the city central labor body was ready to aid them, and only asked in return that they induce their gentlemen friends who did not belong to a trade union to do so immediately. "If they do not join," he said, "then have nothing to do with them, and tell them you do not wish to associate with any gentleman who refuses to aid in a movement calculated to benefit his fellow-man." At the meeting eighteen new members were admitted to the union. As they were sworn in, the members formed a ring about them, singing:

> Welcome sisters, to our number,
> Welcome to our heart and hand;
> At our post we will not slumber,
> Strong in union we shall stand.[18]

MORE AND BIGGER UNIONS

The wave of organization which started in the summer of 1862 grew in intensity from month to month, and by the spring of 1864 it had reached unprecedented heights. Fincher wrote jubilantly on October 29, 1864: "At the time we commenced our publication of the *Review,* our old subscribers can bear witness that scarcely one-tenth of the different trades possessed the advantage of complete organization.... And now contrast our advertising columns with those of the first six months of the *Review,* and you will find an array of organized Trade Societies that evinces a great moral power, which is both feared and respected." In June, 1863, the trade union directory occupied only half a column; six months later it filled two columns: four and a half columns in October, 1864, and by May, 1865, it had grown to a seven-column page.

The notices reveal that 20 trades embracing 79 unions were organized in December, 1863; 40 trades and 203 unions by June, 1864; 53 trades and 207 unions by December, 1864, and 61 trades with about 300 unions in November, 1865. It is estimated that in 1864 about 200,000 workers belonged to trade unions. Although the majority of them were in the leading industrial states, New York, Pennsylvania, and Massachusetts, San Francisco boasted of more than twenty-five unions in 1864, and unions were also developing in the South. The first trade union organized in Houston, Texas, the Houston Typographical Union, No. 87, was formed during the Civil War, and in Wheeling, West Virginia, trade unions first appeared in 1863. On March 10, 1863, the Wheeling *Intelligencer* informed its readers that the "workingmen of the fourth, fifth, and sixth wards are getting up a union."[19]

The Civil War years also saw the rise of national trade unions. The opening of trunk railway lines was developing a national market, and the terrific competition for this new market caused employers to reduce labor costs. Skilled journeymen were often dismissed and their places filled with boys and women who were paid extremely low wages. On December 12, 1863, *Fincher's Trades' Review* observed that the profound economic changes taking place made the combination of local unions into national and even international bodies imperative.*

"Our vast occupations," it declared, "are influenced by the most distant sections of the country, and in some cases by our neighboring nations. Thus of what avail would be a union in New York City even if comprising within its limits all of the craft there employed, if the mechanics of surrounding cities, such as Philadelphia, Boston, Baltimore, Providence, Albany, Newark, Jersey City, etc., were not pledged to the same obligations as their friends in New York. Let a surplus of that peculiar kind of labor arise in either of the other cities, and forthwith New York becomes flooded with an opposing current over which the organization has no control."

More than twelve national unions were organized from 1860 to 1886; † by 1870 no fewer than thirty-two national unions were in existence. Not all were fully national in representation and not all were similar in organization or philosophy. They ranged from the militant molders' national union to the conservative Brotherhood of Locomotive Engineers which was opposed to strikes in general. Many of the national unions soon collapsed, only to be replaced by others. Still, nationwide trade unionism in America, growing out of the establishment of economy on a national scale, had come to stay.

The national unions of the 'sixties produced many of the outstanding leaders of the labor movement. One of the greatest labor leaders in American history, William H. Sylvis, came from the Molders; the Machinists and Blacksmiths claimed Ira Steward who became the leader of the eight-hour day movement, and Jonathan Fincher, editor of *Fincher's Trades' Review;* Richard Trevellick, a tireless labor lecturer and organizer, belonged to the Ship Carpenters and Caulkers; Robert Schilling, an

* The introduction of machinery also influenced the rise of some national unions. The Knights of St. Crispin, founded March 7, 1867, at Milwaukee, Wisconsin, and soon to become the largest labor organization in the country, was organized primarily to protect journeymen from the competition of unskilled workers ("green hands") resulting from the introduction of machinery during the 'sixties. It sought to save for its members the jobs left after technological innovations had occurred. (See Don D. Lescohier, *The Knights of St. Crispin, 1867-1874*, Madison, Wisc., 1910.)

† American Miners' Association (1861), Locomotive Engineers (1863), Sons of Vulcan (iron puddlers) (1862), Telegraphers (1863), Plasterers (1864), Cigar Makers (1864), Hat Makers (1864), Carpenters and Joiners (1865), Bricklayers and Masons (1864), Journeymen Tailors (1865), Painters (1865), Curriers (1864), Ship Carpenters and Caulkers (1865). Some of these unions were called "international," since they also included organized workers in Canada.

active figure in the labor movement for more than thirty years, first worked with the coopers. Particularly well represented are the printers from whose ranks came J. C. Whaley, Alexander Troup, John Collins, and A. C. Cameron, all of whom were active in the National Labor Union, the last named also editor of the *Workingman's Advocate* of Chicago.

It is manifestly impossible within space limits to trace in detail the story of the growth of all the national unions of this period. But no account of the labor movement would be complete without an examination of the rise of the Iron Molders' International Union during the era of the Civil War, for it was justly regarded as the "most powerful in number, resources and completeness," and the most ably led of all the trade unions in America.

THE MOLDERS

Early in 1862 William H. Sylvis started to rebuild the National Molders' Union by writing to leaders of local molders' unions still functioning. The national convention, which had not met since the war, was reconvened at his insistence in Pittsburgh in January, 1863. Twenty delegates from fourteen locals attended, whose first act was to elect Sylvis national president. The convention revised the constitution completely, and adopted as its name the Iron Molders' International Union. Great emphasis was placed upon centralized organization, for in the past the national union had been a loosely united federation of autonomous locals. Often their constitutions were in conflict with each other and with that of the national body. Under Sylvis' leadership the convention of 1863 ended this diffuseness. Local union constitutions were to conform to that of the national union, and the by-laws of the local bodies were to be subject to the authority of the national union.

These amendments to the constitution marked an advance in trade union organization. So too did the system of finances which included annual membership dues and funds from sale of union cards and charters. This system, administered by Sylvis, placed the union on a sound financial basis. He set up a card index system at the molders' national office to enable the national leadership to know who was in the union, who was paid up, and who was in arrears. He also insisted that when a member changed from one local to another, he should be cleared up financially in the previous local before he could receive a new union card. Much of this had been on paper before, but Sylvis really enforced it.

The handling of strike funds had also been inefficient before Sylvis became president. An excellent administrator, Sylvis knew that the national union could never function properly unless it had a national treasury. He insisted, therefore, on a special strike fund to be raised through a compulsory per capita tax.[20]

Sylvis fought against the calling of outlaw strikes, even though he knew that many local union leaders opposed him. All strikes, he demanded, must be authorized, and only then could they be fully supported by the national organization. Don't strike, he told the union members, until you are well organized, and then strike hard. Outlaw strikes, he argued, were an evil, because they wasted the workers' strength in impetuous and futile struggle. A strike to be successful had to be prepared for in advance, and fought through in an organized manner to the end. Only such tactics made for victory.[21]

Many of the trade union principles practiced by Sylvis had been thought of before but they had not been effectively applied. No earlier union had so concerned itself with setting up a tightly knit, carefully planned national body with a sound system of finances, an adequate dues system, effective strike relief, a simplified and uniform card system, the circulation of lists of strikebreakers and the distribution of regular reports on prices, rents, wages, and piecework rates.

Sylvis left Philadelphia on February 3, 1863, to reorganize the old locals and to organize new ones. He traveled throughout the country and in parts of Canada, covering about ten thousand miles.* His original capital of $100 was soon gone, and he had to depend on the small sums given him by the molders. James C. Sylvis, his brother, wrote: "He wore clothes until they became quite threadbare and he could wear them no longer ... the shawl he wore to the day of his death ... was filled with

---

* Sylvis made three trips in 1863, covering more than one hundred molding centers. During his first trip, which took four months, he visited Central and Western Pennsylvania, the Ohio Valley towns, Missouri, Illinois, Michigan, Canada, Erie, and Buffalo and Rochester, New York. His second trip was completed in six weeks. He visited Albany, Troy, Rochester, Erie, Cleveland, and Pittsburgh. His third trip carried him from Newark through Ohio to Detroit and finally into Canada. His total expenses for these three trips were $900.03, of which $620.90 was for travel and $279.13 for his own and his family's needs.

In 1864 Sylvis also made several organizing trips during which he covered every New England community where a union could be organized, visited Baltimore and went west to Chicago. (For detailed accounts of his trips, see Jonathan Grossman, *William Sylvis, Pioneer of American Labor*, New York, 1945, pp. 57-72, 70-74; and Sylvis' letters in *Fincher's Trades' Review*, August-October, 1863, February-May, 1864.)

Sylvis' tours were the topic of conversation in progressive circles all over the country. In July, 1868, Elizabeth Cady Stanton, leader of the Woman's Rights movement, wrote admiringly: "Since his first election as President of the I.M.I. Union in 1863, he has visited nearly all the cities, towns, and villages in the United States, attended hundreds of meetings, public and private, and made the acquaintance of many hundred thousand workingmen." (*The Revolution*, July 2, 1868.)

little holes burned there by the splashing of molten iron from the ladles of molders in strange cities, whom he was beseeching to organize." [22] Yet Sylvis was never happier. "I shall ever look back upon the scenes and incidents of 1863," he wrote after the tours, "as the happiest of my life." [23] For had he not organized 19 new unions, reorganized 16 locals which had disappeared after 1861, and placed 12 others on a firm foundation? When he was re-elected president by the national convention of 1864 he summed up the year's work: "From a mere pigmy, our union has in one short year grown to be a giant; like a mighty oak it has grown up in magnificent proportions with its giant branches stretching out in every direction, reaching into every corner of the continent where our trade is known." [24]

In 1863 the national union had a membership of 2,000, in fifteen locals, representing eight states; two years later its membership had increased to 6,000 in 54 locals from eighteen states, the District of Columbia, and Canada. Its total income had been $1,600 in 1863; in 1865 it had risen to $25,000.[25] "Out of all the charters issued since the commencement of my administration two years ago," Sylvis reported in 1865, "but one has been returned; showing a degree of prosperity and stability unequalled in the history of any similar organization on the continent." The union, he added, had brought its members something more than increased wages and the closed shop.*

"The benefits secured by *our* union aside from an increase in wages are beyond calculation. A strong desire for mental cultivation has infused itself throughout the entire body. Schools, libraries, reading and lecture rooms and other institutions for the diffusion of useful knowledge are springing up among us ... a feeling of brotherhood everywhere exists; an interest in each other's welfare had broken down to a vast extent that selfishness that used to exist among us; a feeling of manly independence has taken the place of that cringing and crawling spirit that used to make us the scorn of honest men." [26]

The work of Sylvis influenced many national unions, though not all of them followed the highly centralized form of organization adopted by the molders. His highly successful organizing tours stimulated other national unions to send traveling organizers into the field, contributing much to the growth of these unions. It is not without reason that William H. Sylvis is called America's first national labor organizer and pioneer labor leader.†

* Between 1865 and 1867, the Molders' Union established the closed shop in most of the foundries of the country. A molder without a "union card" found it practically impossible to secure work. (Grossman, *op. cit.,* pp. 84-87.)

† Sylvis was not only a remarkable labor organizer and an excellent trade union administrator and strategist. He was also a profound student of labor issues and

THE LABOR PRESS

The wartime revival of trade unionism was helped by, and in turn aided, the development of a labor press. During the decade 1863-1873 about 130 daily, weekly, and monthly journals representing labor and advocating labor reform were started. The principal papers were *Fincher's Trades' Review*, founded June 6, 1863, in Philadelphia; the *Workingman's Advocate*, the first issue of which appeared in Chicago, on July 1, 1864, during the printers' strike; the *Daily Evening Voice*, the official organ of the Workingmen's Assembly of Boston and vicinity, published in December, 1864 by locked-out printers; the *Daily Press* published in St. Louis on a co-operative basis by striking printers. The *Weekly Miner*, established in Belleville, Illinois, by John Hinchcliffe on May 23, 1863, was the official organ of the American Miners' Association. It was to be "devoted to the advancement of the interests of the working classes generally, and of the hitherto neglected coal miners especially." [27]

-----

problems. Experience in the class struggle as well as analysis of economic theories guided him in the development of a labor philosophy. He was keenly aware of the existence of the class struggle, and dismissed as "mere humbug" the conception of identity of interest between employers and workers. He rejected the theories of the classical economists—Adam Smith, Malthus, John Stuart Mill and others whom he dubbed economists of the "higher order." His wage-theory was simple: wages had to provide workers with a decent living standard and had to be sufficient to enable them to overcome disasters in the shape of unemployment, "lost time, sickness, medicine, doctor's bills." "And what," he asked of those who glibly assured workers that if they were frugal all would be well, "if the husband and father should be sick—the body prostrated by racking pain, and the mind frenzied with apprehensions of a starving family? Who shall describe his agony—who can comprehend his misery?" (James C. Sylvis, *op. cit.*, pp. 395-97.)

Charity and philanthropy, Sylvis argued, were not the answers to labor's needs. "Wealth, alarmed by the cries of anguish," he remarked, "gathers the poor into almshouses, and eases her conscience by feeding them upon offals and selling their dead bodies to the dissecting room to defray a portion of the expense." (James C. Sylvis, *op. cit.*, p. 363.) Higher wages, not charity, was Sylvis's demand. Yet this was only part of his program for labor. This also included shorter hours; better working conditions; a higher social status; co-operative enterprises to abolish the wage system; improvement of the lot of the female laborer; decent housing to replace tenements; international labor solidarity; independent political action; land reform; abolition of convict labor; establishment of mechanics' institutes and of a bureau of labor statistics and currency reform. Not all of his ideas were thought out clearly, but every cause he championed was motivated by one desire—to advance labor's cause. His entire life was devoted to this cause and his greatest reward was a favorable response to his appeals from the working class. "It is a matter of honest pride to me," he once wrote, "to know that my humble efforts in the cause of humanity and social reform, are appreciated by fellow workingmen everywhere." (*Fincher's Trades' Review*, August 8, 1863.) Sylvis died poverty-stricken. He did not have even one hundred dollars at the time of his death and his family had no way of paying his funeral expenses.

During and shortly after the Civil War, labor papers appeared in Denver, Indianapolis, Nashville, and Minnesota; Columbus, Kansas, and in Concord, New Hampshire; several papers appeared in the metropolitan centers like San Francisco, St. Louis, Chicago, Boston, and New York. Jonathan Fincher proposed in 1865 a national daily labor paper to the *Workingman's Advocate,* the Buffalo *Miner,* the Buffalo *Sentinel,* and the New York *Trades' Advocate,* but only John Hinchcliffe, editor of the *Miner,* endorsed the proposal. Cameron refused, saying that the *Advocate* was well established, and that it could serve the labor movement of the Middle West better than a national labor paper.[28]

Fincher's Trades' Review, the official newspaper of the Philadelphia Trades' Assembly and of the Machinists and Blacksmiths, was the most influential labor paper of the Civil War era. Jonathan Fincher, its editor and publisher, outlined its policy in the first issue, on June 6, 1863: "To espouse labor, in all conflicts to be on the side of labor. To sustain the government and all properly enacted laws." To the women it promised a "sufficient space to embrace a fair choice of literature made up of every variety, calculated to secure our paper a hearty welcome to the family circle."

Every Saturday the paper appeared with its four large pages, seven columns to the page. One column was devoted to the progress of the war, and the entire front page was usually devoted to stories written by workingmen. Editorials, trade news, trade union notices and articles by the foremost labor leaders of the day made up the rest. The *Review* was a national labor organ. Representatives of the Molders, Printers, Ship Carpenters, Stone Cutters, Cabinet Makers, Carpenters, Hatters, and Shoemakers unions were on the editorial board.[29]

Fincher accepted no paid advertisements, hoping to keep the paper going by subscriptions and donations from unions, and at no time during its three years was the *Review* free from financial worries. Its subscription rate of two dollars a year was not enough to meet expenses even in December, 1865, when it claimed a paid circulation of eleven thousand with readers in thirty-one of the thirty-six states, the District of Columbia, three Canadian provinces and eight English cities.[30] A number of unions raised funds for the paper at picnics, balls and parties, while other unions contributed from their treasuries. To meet the increasing debt Fincher in June, 1864, began to charge for trade union notices, but the efforts to finance the paper failed, and on August 18, 1866, the last issue came off the press.

Fincher's Trades' Review was one of the best labor papers published in the United States, but its great weakness was its stand against political activity. Fincher justified this opposition by saying that political activity created a fraternal feeling between two antagonistic classes and restrained the worker from "asserting and maintaining those rights so essential to the comfort of himself, his family, and his fellow-workingmen." [31] When labor followed this advice by limiting itself to simple trade unionism, it discovered that the employers were making good use of the business of politics to deprive the worker of his essential rights.*

The *Workingman's Advocate,* published weekly from 1863 to 1877 by A. C. Cameron in Chicago and Cincinnati, did much to overcome Fincher's insistence that labor stay out of politics. In the issue of April 21, 1866, Cameron dedicated his paper to the cause of independent political action by labor. "So far as we are concerned, from this day henceforth, the policy of the *Advocate* will be to aid in the formation of a Workingman's Party, independent altogether of either political faction; to have our representatives in every branch of the State and National Legislatures taken from our own ranks; men ... whose interests and sympathies in behalf of the producing classes are stronger than their devotion to capital or party."

In subsequent issues Cameron constantly kept a labor party before his readers. One day he would have an editorial on proportional representation, and on the next day he might run a column explaining why workingmen should always be preferred as candidates since they knew without being told the needs of the workingmen. Although the *Advocate* later overemphasized political action and lost itself in the maze of currency reform, it merited the tribute accorded to it by Samuel Gaul, president of the Bricklayers' National Union, when he called it an "able and earnest journal in the cause of labor." [32]

All labor papers of this period were agreed on the need for mass education of the working class and called for labor schools, libraries, reading and lecture rooms. "To ameliorate the condition of the working classes," the *Belleville Miner* declared, "it is only necessary to educate them, that they may better understand the relation they bear to other classes of society." [33] *Fincher's Trades' Review* argued that the great revival of trade unionism during the war period would amount to little unless it was accompanied by mass education of the newly organized workers: "There should be a series of instructive lectures, the tenor of

---

* In reply to criticism of his stand on political action, Fincher wrote: "We have always advocated the use of a negative rather than a positive power politically or a non-voting power than a supporting power—a plan by which the political action of workingmen would not be pinned to the robes of any demagogue, and, at the same time, be free to vote to a political death any representative who would betray them." (*Fincher's Trades' Review,* July 1, 1865.) He failed to show why representatives should concern themselves with the interests of workingmen who refused to exert any influence in the election of candidates.

which should be the vindication of the correctness of our position as combinations; also the necessity of the movement." [34] *

With inadequate financial backing the labor papers could not compete with the commercial press in general news coverage, yet their influence was considerable. "The *Review*," said Jonathan Fincher in November, 1865, "in a financial point of view, is a failure, yet, as a progressive movement in the cause of right and justice, it has been an unquestioned success, as a glance at the Labor movement of today, as compared with it three years ago, will amply demonstrate." [35] Sylvis fully agreed. "Not until their advent," he declared in discussing the value of labor papers, "did we make the slightest advance towards equalizing wages with the cost of living nor would our best efforts to establish the eight-hour law or to accomplish any other reform have availed us anything without their aid." Without an independent labor press, he added, workingmen would have been powerless to cope with the employers' offensive against labor's right to organize. [36]

THE EMPLOYERS' COUNTERATTACK

By the summer of 1863 the employers had begun their counter-offensive against organized labor. Employers' associations had existed before in America, but never had there been such united action on their part. Local employers' associations were formed in most industrial communities, and though they dealt with other matters, their chief purpose was the destruction of the trade union movement. They locked out and blacklisted trade unionists, and refused to re-employ any worker who would not sign his name as a guarantee that he had left the union. In December, 1863, the Association of Engineers of New York, which represented nineteen firms, issued a secret circular which read:

"We are opposed to every combination which has for its object the regulation of wages. For the next ninety days the proprietors of each establishment represented in this Association refuse to employ any machinists other than those now employed in their respective establishments excepting any one who shall bring recommendation from his present employer that he has been honorably discharged." [37]

The typical employers' association of the Civil War era was local,

* One of Fincher's chief aims in his paper was to demolish the myth that American workers did not need to trouble with building labor organizations since they would soon be able to rise out of their class and become employers. The vast majority of wage-earners, he argued, would always remain members of the working class. Hence, if they wished to have a decent standard of living, they had to organize and conduct an unrelenting struggle to wrest better conditions from their employers. (See especially *Fincher's Trades' Review*, June 6, 13, 1863.)

although larger federations did exist in a few industries. The Albany Foundry Association organized in 1859 to resist the Molders' Union, and proposed to employers in other cities the formation of a National Founders League, but it was not until March, 1866, that a national organization, the American National Stove Manufacturers' and Iron Founders' Association, was founded.* In 1863 the "Iron Founders' and Machine Builders' Association of the Falls of Ohio" appeared and declared its intention to communicate "with all the parties engaged in similar business to that of the members of the Association and suffering the same grievances." [38] The efforts of the molders to secure wage increases to meet the rising cost of living constituted these grievances.

Employers' associations were also formed by Buffalo shipowners, St. Louis merchant tailors, Brooklyn master mechanics, Massachusetts nail manufacturers, Boston master plumbers, western railroads, and others. In Detroit, employers of various kinds co-operated in anti-union activities through the "Employers' General Association of Michigan."

A large section of the press aided the employers' associations in their anti-labor crusade. Few were the editors who did not praise these associations as patriotic organizations seeking to protect the hard-working laborers of America from the unscrupulous foreign agitators who, they said, made up the bulk of the trade unions. James Redstone, the editor of the *Indianapolis Evening Gazette,* was one of the few. When asked by the Iron Founders' and Machine Builders' Association of the Falls of the Ohio to join them in fighting the International Machinists and Blacksmiths Union, he replied: "My answer, then, is that I will have nothing to do with any scheme that has a tendency to oppress honest labor, and I think any combination against workingmen would bring the same result as controls the workingmen of Europe. God grant this may never happen here." [39]

Employers during the Civil War did not confine themselves to blacklists, lockouts, and "yellow dog" contracts; they secured the co-operation of the federal and state governments. The federal government encouraged

* In announcing its formation the Association proclaimed:

"Resolved, That it is expedient and necessary to the protection of the interests of the iron founders of this country, to organize themselves into a National Association for the protection of their general interests, the promotion of a friendly feeling and mutual confidence among the members, and especially for the purpose of resisting any and all actions of the Molders' Union, which shall in any manner interfere with our right to control our own workshops, and to manage our own business.

"Resolved, that we will proceed at once to introduce into our shops all the apprentices or helpers we deem advisable, and that we will not allow any Union Committee in our shops, and that we will in every way possible free our shops of all dictation or interference on the part of our employees." (*Boston Daily Evening Voice,* March 13, 16, 17, 20, 23, 1866.)

the importation of foreign contract labor to break strikes, while Union generals used military force to disperse or to imprison strikers. Among government officials, Lincoln alone was openly friendly to organized workers, and his sympathetic understanding of labor's problems on several occasions stopped the savage attack upon trade unions by government officials and military commanders.

Labor suffered greatly at the hands of the state governments, several of them permitting employers to use convict labor. In 1864 I. G. Johnson, owner of the Spuyten Duyvil iron foundry in New York City, took over the foundry at Sing Sing, and paid the State of New York 40 cents a day for the labor of each convict. Three dollars was the union rate. That Johnson did not succeed in killing the powerful Spuyten Duyvil Molders' Union was due to the successful struggle organized by Sylvis.[40] But other unions did not fare so well when faced with this competition.

Continuing their offensive, these employer groups introduced bills in several state legislatures to curb combinations of workingmen and to outlaw the right to strike. Minnesota, early in 1863, was the first state to pass a law which made a striker interfering with workmen liable to a $100 fine or six months' imprisonment.* Bills were introduced in the legislatures of New York and Massachusetts in the spring of 1864 to prevent "intimidation" or interference with workmen, but they were defeated by organized labor.† The Illinois legislature was so friendly to the coal operators that when the latter needed assistance in breaking the 1863 strike of the Miners Association, it hurriedly enacted measures, later known as the La Salle Black Laws, which prohibited any person, by threat, intimidation, or otherwise, from preventing an-

---

* Minnesota and Pennsylvania also passed laws allowing the ejection of the families of strikers from company-owned houses. And the latter state passed an act in February, 1865, empowering railroad companies to employ a private police force, which was later extended to coal and iron companies. The legislation set up communities which were actually outside the state law and reduced workers in these communities to a feudal status. The coal and iron police had all the powers of metropolitan police officers, and provided employers with a private army to combat organized labor. (See Jeremiah P. Shaloo, *Private Police with Special Reference to Pennsylvania*, Philadelphia, 1933, pp. 58-61.) Many state governments revived conspiracy laws and invoked them against unions, compelling labor organizations to waste their funds in high legal expenses. Conspiracy cases were most frequent in New York, New Jersey, and Pennsylvania.

† A few bills were introduced in state legislatures to ameliorate the worker's lot. Wisconsin passed a law, after much pressure from organized workers, to prevent employers from holding up workers' wages. Laws were also passed in New York, New Jersey, and Pennsylvania to abolish the store-order or scrip-payment system. Unfortunately, as Fincher pointed out, these laws "were evaded in just those counties where the store-order system was wide-spread." (*Boston Daily Evening Voice*, Mar. 17, 1865, and *Fincher's Trades' Review*, June 27, 1863; Jan. 27, 1864.)

other person from working, on penalty of a fine up to $100 Any two or more persons who combined for the purpose of preventing others from working during a strike were liable to a penalty of a fine up to $500 or imprisonment in the county jail up to six months.[41] A union miner wrote: "In the name of God, what is this country coming to? On the one hand, they are trying to set the black men free, and on the other hand these worthy gentlemen would like the Miner to sign away his freedom!"[42]

LABOR TIGHTENS ITS RANKS

It was clear to trade unionists that few local unions had the funds or the numbers to resist the attacks of employers' associations. Only co-ordinated activity and labor solidarity could meet the offensive. What was needed was a strong federation of trade unions. Such a federation, said *Fincher's Trades' Review* on December 19, 1863, is "needed *now* at this time because capitalists are entering into a combination to force *labor* to submit to their dictum still more than ever."

Out of this crisis emerged the next step forward in the development of American trade unionism—the formation of city central labor bodies known usually as trades' assemblies. The first was formed at Rochester, New York, February, 1863; the second and third in Boston and New York three months later. Later in the year trades' assemblies were organized in Albany. Buffalo, Louisville, Philadelphia, Pittsburgh, St. Louis, and San Francisco. Before the end of the war there were more than thirty assemblies extending throughout the manufacturing centers of the country from the New England States to California.

Many of these assemblies grew out of strike movements, for it was then that the workers saw the power of the employers' combinations, and realized that their only answer was greater labor solidarity. The appeal for a trades' assembly in San Francisco came after the failure of the tailors' strike for higher wages in June, 1863. "We hold that labor, the chief source of wealth, can receive its merits only by the united and earnest efforts of its devotees," the call declared. The same idea was expressed in New York City where a meeting had been called to organize a trade union. "To find protection," said a trade union speaker, "each trade must organize by itself and then come into a central organization."[43]

Throughout the Civil War it was the local trades' assembly rather than the national trade union to which the workers turned for a solution to their problems. With the exception of the molders, printers, machinists, and blacksmiths, the national unions were not beyond the stages of initial organization. Even the members of many national organizations still regarded the local federations as their main source of support. A typical assembly was the New York City Assembly. Its aims were to unite the strength of the many trades and industrial organizations to defend the rights and promote the workers' interests; to create a co-operative feeling among workers so they could act in a united manner promptly and perseveringly; to discuss laws that might be considered infringements of labor's rights and to devise means to abolish or amend them; to adjust difficulties between employers and workers, but to aid any organization which was forced to go on strike; to see that only those employers who paid union wages and conformed to union rules received the patronage of union men.[44]

With the exception of the Trades' Assembly of Rochester, the city federations had no strike funds, but all helped the striking unions to collect money. Their influence and prestige were also of some value. In Philadelphia, for example, the trades' assembly intervened during an important strike of printers by asking politicians friendly to labor to bring pressure upon the employers. Their appeal was heeded, and the employers finally granted the demands of the union. The trades' assembly of San Francisco helped the Iron Molders' Union to checkmate the plan of the Employers' Association to bring in strike breakers during its strike in April, 1864. When the strike breakers reached the Isthmus of Panama they were met by representatives of the San Francisco Trades' Assembly, and by molders and boilermakers. So persuasive were the representatives in explaining the reason for the strike and the meaning of the employers' offensive to all workingmen that the strike breakers, on their arrival at San Francisco, refused to scab and applied for membership in the union. The employers acknowledged defeat, and granted the wage increases.[45]

Another weapon that the trades' assemblies utilized was the boycott, known at this time as "non-intercourse." Richard Trevellick, president of the Detroit Trades' Assembly and president of the Caulkers' International Union, described a typical boycott:

"All the trades unite for this purpose, and when a case of oppression is made known a committee from the Trades' Assembly calls upon the offender and demands redress. If the demand is not complied with every trade is notified, and the members all cease trading at the obnoxious establishment. Sentinels are placed around notifying people of the facts, and in every case the offender is brought to terms." [46]

When not engaged in exerting pressure upon employers, the trades' assemblies were busy with the tasks of organization and education. To the trades' assemblies goes the honor of being the organizing center of the surging trade union movement during the Civil War. Several trades' assemblies not only appointed agents to organize unorganized workers,* but designated special officials to start co-operative stores to help keep down the cost of living. The assemblies of Albany, Boston, Chicago, and Troy sponsored co-operative grocery stores, but the Troy Assembly also maintained a "Workingmen's Emporium," a small department store which was well patronized by trade unionists.[47] In addition, the Troy Assembly established a free library and reading room at which lectures were delivered by leading trade unionists. William Sylvis attended the great picnic run by the Troy Assembly to raise money for the library and reading room. He described the event in a letter to *Fincher's Trades' Review* of September 10, 1864:

"It was without doubt, the greatest thing of the kind ever held in the country. From $1200 to $1500 over the expenses will be realized. If some of the old fogies of the Philadelphia Trades' Assembly had been present, I think their optics would have been expanded by the size of the pewter plates.... The workingmen and women of this city are alive to their interests...."

POLITICAL ACTION

An outstanding example of united political action during the Civil War was the campaign of the trades' assemblies of New York State to defeat the Hastings-Folger anti-strike bill introduced in the early spring of 1864. Entitled, "An Act to Punish Unlawful Interference with Employers and Employees," the measure made any person or combination of persons "who, by force or threats of force, of any kind ... prevent workers from accepting employment, or one, from employing such workmen, ...that he may desire to employ ... to be guilty of misdemeanor and suffer jail up to one year or a fine up to $250 or both." [48] The Chamber of Commerce of New York City and the employers in upstate districts who were bent upon destroying the molders' and machinists' unions

---

* Soon after its origin, the Rochester Trades' Assembly, formed by the Carpenters' and Joiners' Union, the Typographical Union, the Iron Molders Union, the Cutters' Union, and the Painters Union, set up a committee on organization "for the purpose of assisting members of any trade who may desire to organize a union and connect themselves with the Assembly." By December, 1863, the committee had added five new unions to the membership of the Assembly: the Machinists and Blacksmiths, the Coopers, the Tailors, the Tinsmiths and the Shoemakers. One trade unionist wrote from Rochester late in 1863: "Trades' unions here about are in a flourishing condition—more so than we have known for years. This is mainly due to the beneficial influences and workings of our Workingmen's Assembly." (*See Fincher's Trades' Review*, Dec. 19, 1863, and John C. Gleason, *The Labor Movement in Rochester 1820-1860*, unpublished M.A. thesis, University of Rochester, 1940, pp. 96-98.)

lobbied for the passage of the bill whose provisions were so severe, according to William Sylvis, "that every trade organization in New York State would have been crushed out of existence." [49]

The defeat of the Hastings-Folger Bill is an inspiring episode of the Civil War. It begins with a letter to the press from Martin A. Kelly, president of the Carpenters' Union No. 5 of New York City:

"In connection with many workingmen of this city I have seen with alarm the attempt about to be made to encroach on our already greatly abridged rights and privileges as shown forth in the bill on 'Strikes' lately introduced into the Senate by Mr. Hastings. There are some among us who think that the matter will die out of its own want of life; but I am not one of that class. Looking back on the experience of that past as shewn in legislative enactments, and feeling that but little if any dependence can be placed on the honesty or virtue of many of those who fill the chairs in the legislative halls, I feel that prompt and efficient action is required on the part of the workingmen throughout the State to defeat such an obnoxious measure. As the time is approaching when the Grinding Committee will be organized, it is necessary that we should act promptly to defeat this bill...." [50]

Kelly's proposal was discussed at a special meeting of the New York Trades' Assembly which voted to send a delegation to Albany and to hold a mass meeting against the proposed anti-strike law. This meeting was held April 7, 1864, in Tompkins Square Park. Forty trade unions were represented, ranging from the powerful Iron Molders Union No. 11 of Spuyten Duyvil to the newly organized Furriers' Union of New York City. At noon the marchers assembled at their trade union headquarters and then marched in a body to the park. Three stands were erected, two for the English and one for the German speakers, all draped with American flags and with union banners. When the meeting opened there were at least 15,000 trade unionists in the audience, each with a white satin badge designating his union. [51]

Prominent trade union leaders of New York addressed the meeting, reviewing labor's part in winning the war, and asked if it were proper for the legislature to reward workingmen for their devotion by aiding employers to smash the trade unions. John Van Wart, president of the Coopers' Union of New York City, exclaimed: "Why is it that they seek to crush the workingmen? It is from the working classes they got men to fight the battles of the country and to sustain the American flag. Shall these men suffer for the bread necessary to sustain them?"

The meeting warned any legislator voting for the hated measure that he would be signing his political death warrant. "The laborers of New York," said T. J. Roberts of the Coopers' Union, "have risen in their might, and they are determined that any man who favors the bill should not be supported for any political offices. They will tell their legislators that they are the bone and sinew of the country, and that the men who seek to cower them down to be slaves at their feet will be hurled from power." Shouts of, "We will send them to hell next election," greeted this statement. Thomas Cooper, a leading trade union official in New York, called for greater alertness on the part of workingmen during all political campaigns. The resolutions adopted called upon all honorable members of both houses to vote down the premeditated outrage, and added that "should this bill be allowed to proceed further, the working classes throughout the States are earnestly requested in addition to other means to register the names of all members found voting for the same, for future action." [52]

Meanwhile the trades' assemblies of Troy, Rochester, Albany, and Buffalo were organizing similar protest meetings. The Buffalo meeting denounced the bill as "uncalled for ... especially in times like the present, when the workingmen, with their lives in their hands, are rallying to the defense of the Union and Constitution, while capital (with a few honorable exceptions) is staying at home in ease and comfort, having with its ill-gotten wealth extorted from labor, purchased a substitute, while the mechanic has left his home and those dear to him too often without either means or protection." The meeting closed with the warning, "We will hold to a strict account each of our representatives in the Senate and Assembly, and will repay them for their labors at the ballot-box." [53]

As a result of these mass protests throughout the state the bill was recommitted to the Senate Judiciary Committee on April 12, and the Legislature adjourned soon after with no further action taken on the bill. Celebrations were held in the streets of New York City, Albany, Buffalo, and Troy.

A NATIONAL PERSPECTIVE

The defeat of the anti-labor bills in New York and Massachusetts revealed the power of the trades' assemblies, yet the employers' offensive grew more intense. By the close of 1864 employers' organizations resisted and fought the efforts of many workers to gain wage increases and improved working conditions. The *Boston Daily Evening Voice* of December 24, 1864, reported that a 25 per cent decrease in wages had been forced upon workers in nail manufacturing establishments in Massachusetts by employers' associations. The following spring the Rensselaer Iron Works of Troy, at the request of the state employers' association of iron founders, cut wages a dollar a day, and in Brooklyn the employers' association of boss plasterers forced a reduction of fifty cents a day from a wage of $3.50.[54] All this was the beginning of a national campaign against trade unionism. Sylvis quoted a capitalist who late in 1864 had warned him that: "the day is not far distant when the condition of the workingmen will be worse than ever before. The day will come when men who are now active in the labor movement will be forced upon their bended knees to ask for work.... A spirit of retaliation has been aroused in the bosom of every employer, the fruits of which are now being manifested in the widespread and universal organization of capitalists for the avowed purpose of destroying your unions." [55]

By the middle of 1864 it was becoming clear to a number of trade union leaders that local trades' assemblies could not individually meet the employers' offensive successfully. "This is not a war between any particular *trade* and *capital*," said one labor leader. "It is a war between the sons of toil, who represent labor, and their employers who represent *capital*." The form of organization, he continued, had thus to correspond to the new character of the struggle, which meant that the workers in all the states had to act in a united manner through a national labor federation.[56]

Not until the war was over did a consciousness for national labor solidarity really begin to make headway; nevertheless, several attempts to achieve such a federation were made during the war years.* In 1861 the Machinists and Blacksmiths International Union selected a committee "to request the appointment of a similar committee from other national or grand bodies and meet them, fully empowered to form a National Trades' Assembly," but the outbreak of the war shelved this proposal for a national labor federation. Sylvis persuaded the national convention of the molders in 1864 to endorse the old proposal of the machinists and blacksmiths for a national trades' assembly. Members of the machinists and blacksmiths union of Albany urged their parent body to join the molders in a campaign for a national labor federation. They were more than willing to "expend [their] last dollars, time and talent, also, to protect the rights of mechanics from being untrammeled throughout the length and breadth of the land." [57]

The initiative for the creation of a national labor federation came not from the national trade unions but from the trades' assemblies. In Louisville, Kentucky, delegates to the city trades' assembly had held frequent discussions during the winter of 1863-1864 on the need for such a federation. The delegates, said one trade unionist, "beheld capital organizing for the overthrow of the labor movement of the age, and

---

* The New York State Workingmen's Assembly, organized in 1865, was an intermediate step between city and national organization.

they felt that it was their imperative duty to do all in their power to fortify, strengthen and build up the cause of labor, and bring the contest that is now going on to an end, in favor of labor." They concluded that if workingmen "derived benefit by being formed into Trades' Assemblies that they would derive more benefit if they could form an International League." [58] The corresponding secretary of the assembly was accordingly instructed to send a letter to the trades' assemblies of the United States and Canada, asking their opinion in regard to the calling of a national convention.

In August, 1864, this letter was followed up by a call issued by Robert Gilchrist, president of the Louisville Trades' Assembly and League of Friendship inviting all officers and members of trades' assemblies to attend a convention to be held on September 21 in Louisville, Kentucky:

"Are not capitalists and employers of almost every city organizing themselves into unions, and is it not patent to every one that their object is the overthrow of our organizations? Are we to shrink with fear when we behold this spectacle? We answer no ... it should stimulate us to powerful exertions. ... Should the employers by combination attempt to overthrow any one branch of the trades, the other branches or organizations of mechanics would make the cause of the trade or branch struck at, their cause, and would lend their aid and sympathy to that trade."

By combining their strength the organized workers would become so powerful "that the capitalists or employers will cease to refuse our just demands." [59]

Only twelve delegates from eight trades' assemblies were present when the convention met in Louisville; however, the interest was widespread. The Troy Trades' Assembly sent a letter to the convention explaining that only the time element had prevented the sending of a delegate; it congratulated the Louisville assembly and wished the delegates God-speed in the glorious work which they had commenced. [60]

The chief work of the convention was the drawing up of a constitution and a set of resolutions. The purpose of the new organization, the International Industrial Assembly of North America, was to adjust the disagreements between employers and workmen in a manner that "may be mutually beneficial." Strikes were to be avoided "except when they became absolutely necessary." When such strikes did occur the convention provided for a treasury for the "practical benefit of any organization of workingmen which may be struck by the capitalists unjustly." For this purpose the International Industrial Assembly was empowered to levy a per capita tax of five cents for every organized workingman "through the various trades' assemblies of America and to be kept in their treasuries subject to the order of the International body."

Many of the problems of the American worker were truly reflected in the resolutions of the Louisville Convention. One resolution called upon the trades' assemblies to work for legislation outlawing the store-order system and abolishing the competition of prison labor. An attempt, however, to endorse the formation of a labor party was defeated, although the recommendation was contained in the report of the committee on the constitution. Another resolution urged the assemblies to help the sewing women. A third praised the movement for consumers' co-opera-tives and recommended to the trades' assemblies that they set up co-operative grocery stores. Still another advised the assemblies to hire salaried traveling organizers subject to orders from the International Industrial Assembly. A resolution was also adopted favoring the creation of a national Department of Labor in Washington "officered by men who are of and with labor."

Perhaps the most important statement to come out of the convention was the special resolution affirming the right of workingmen to be their own judge of the value of their labor, and the compensation they were entitled to receive. "We claim this as an inherent right vested in man—a birthright—we pledge our sacred honor as men to maintain at all hazards and under all circumstances." [61]

Before the International Industrial Assembly adjourned it planned to hold its next convention in Detroit in May, 1865, but the meeting never took place because not enough workers as yet understood the need for national organization. Influential leaders like Sylvis and Fincher were convinced that a national federation based upon trades' assemblies would never be strong enough to meet the employers' offensives. Fincher argued that the Industrial Assembly had no power to organize labor in districts where no trades' assemblies existed, "from the simple fact that the Assemblies are the creatures of the local Trades' Unions." Only a national federation based upon national trade unions could perform this task, for they would "carry with them acknowledged authority and power to bind the organizations." [62]

A. C. Cameron, editor of the Chicago *Workingman's Advocate*, took issue with Fincher. Commenting on the Louisville convention he answered that the International Assembly was superior to the national trade unions because "there are thousands of mechanics and workingmen on this continent who never have been, and never will be represented in an International Union of their particular branch of labor." [63] At the time this was written the national unions were too few in number to speak for a considerable portion of the working class, and the strong national unions were too busy meeting the attacks of employers' associations

In view of these circumstances, it is clear why the International Industrial Assembly was short-lived.

TOWARDS AN EIGHT-HOUR DAY

Even while the Louisville convention was in session, an issue was emerging which would supply the spark for the formation of a strong national labor federation after the war. Although this issue was not stressed at Louisville, the delegates had not ignored it, for one of the resolutions passed at the convention declared it "a propitious time" to begin a nationwide agitation to make eight hours the legal working day. The struggle for the eight-hour day did not begin in earnest until the war was over, but like every major issue advanced by the labor movement in the post-war years, its origins can be traced to the period before the war. While the war continued, preparations were being made for the tremendous campaign that would get under way as soon as the rebellion was smashed.

Although American labor during the first half of the nineteenth century confined its demands on hours to the ten or nine-hour day, there were occasional statements on the eight-hour day: thus the *National Laborer* declared on November 19, 1836, that it would not halt its agitation for a shorter working day now that the mechanics of Philadelphia had secured a ten hour day. "We have no desire to perpetuate the ten hour system," it said, "for we believe that eight hours daily labor is more than enough for any man to perform."

During the 1850's the demand for the eight-hour day increased; at a mass meeting of New York trade unions in the opening year of the decade it was unanimously resolved that "eight hours is a just and sufficient number of hours for any man to work." And in Philadelphia an organization called the Assembly of Associated Mechanics and Workingmen was founded in 1851 to win the eight-hour day.[64] The organized caulkers of Boston adopted the eight-hour system on May 24, 1854, and in the next few years several other labor organizations did likewise. By 1859 the Machinists and Blacksmiths National Union recommended to its locals that they consider the eight-hour day; this proposal was repeated at its 1860 convention. The following year the National Molders' Union appointed a committee to outline a plan by which "agitation for the eight hour system may be brought about." It reported that many molders favored the universal adoption of the eight hour system, convinced that it would "tend to the amelioration, enlightenment and education of the laboring classes."

But the first significant organizational steps taken by American labor to secure the eight-hour day occurred in 1863. At its convention that year the Machinists and Blacksmiths Union endorsed the eight-hour day, terming it "the most important change to us as workingmen to which all else is subordinate." At the same time the Boston Trades Assembly took a similar stand, and both organizations appointed committees with a combined budget of eight hundred dollars whose duties were to start an educational and lobbying campaign for the reform.[65] On October 10, 1863, *Fincher's Trades' Review* joined the campaign, and said that "today we have nailed this banner to our masthead, *viz:* 'Eight Hours for a Day's Labor.' "

Following their accustomed pattern, the commercial press charged that the leaders of the eight-hour day were foreign-born.[66] Naturally, foreign-born workers played an important part in the movement, but the causes were not in the national origin of its supporters, rather were they rooted in American industrial conditions. As for the leadership, it was supplied by a native American wage earner and a loyal member of the Machinists and Blacksmiths Union. This man was the Boston machinist Ira Steward, whom the socialist *Labor Standard* called the "originator and author of the Eight Hour Movement." [67] It was Steward who convinced the Machinists' and Blacksmiths' Union and the Boston Trades Assembly in 1863 to start the great campaign. It was Steward who transformed this campaign for a shorter working day from one conducted by isolated organizations into an integrated demand for state and national legislation. It was Steward who developed the main ideas justifying the demand for shorter hours.

Ira Steward decided to devote his life to the cause of a shorter work day when in 1850 as a youth of nineteen he worked twelve hours a day as a machinist's apprentice. He was discharged by the company when he began to agitate for shorter hours. This experience increased his will to advance the struggle for a shorter working day; in pamphlets, letters to newspapers, lectures, and appearances before legislative committees he advanced his arguments. Employers and the commercial press were not convinced, but intellectuals and workers and many political figures were. After a five-hour talk with Ira Steward, Senator Charles Sumner changed his vote in favor of an eight-hour law. Reverend Jesse H. Jones admitted that his opposition to the proposal for an eight-hour day disappeared when he had heard Steward lecture. "There are no college professors," he declared, "nor writers on political economy, whose works I have met, but could learn wisdom at his lips on the political economy of the labor question." [68]

Steward's main theory was that the "habit, customs, and opinions of the masses" represented the strongest power in the world. Labor's demands were small, he contended, because long hours gave the workers little chance to realize that they needed more. A worker who labored fourteen hours a day had neither the imagination nor the energy to demand higher wages. He was so debased by excessive toil that he could think only of food and sleep. "How can they be so stimulated to demand higher wages," asked Steward, "when they have little or no time or strength to use the advantages which higher wages can buy or procure?" If hours were reduced, the leisure time would create new motives and desires. In order to satisfy these new habits, wages would have to move upwards. "Change and improve the daily habits of the laborers," he said, "and they will raise their own pay in spite of any power in the universe; and this can only be done by furnishing them with more leisure or time!" [69]

Again and again Steward stressed his main thesis in order to convince workingmen that wages would not be lowered if hours were reduced. He even popularized a little couplet, written by his wife Mary B. Steward, which assured workers:

Whether you work by the piece or work by the day,
Decreasing the hours, increases the pay.[70]

To Steward the eight-hour day was more than a means of securing higher wages and more leisure; it was essential for the preservation of American democratic institutions from the "corruptions of capital, through its control of the literature, politics, and daily press of the country." A shorter working day would make it impossible for capital or corporations to deprive the laborer, against his will, of the time and opportunity necessary to study the institutions of his country.

Further, argued Steward, the eight-hour day was indispensable for the removal of *all* hardships imposed upon the working classes and the precondition for a new and better social order. In the first place it would make the masses discontented with their lot when their leisure opened their eyes to dress, manners, and surroundings of the wealthy. Secondly, leisure would give the workers time to study various proposals to change the existing social order. "If the hours of labor are not reduced," said Steward, "laborers will never be able to consider the many measures necessary to wholly emancipate them from slavery and ignorance and the vices and poverty." Thirdly, an eight-hour day would unite skilled mechanics and unskilled laborers "for their own emancipation," for "give the masses time to come together and they cannot be kept apart." Finally, only through a "higher standard of popular intelligence" could the capitalist system be superseded by a more just social order. "The eight-hour system," promised Steward, "will put the man who made the shoes, and the man who bought them, together; and they will compare the prices paid for the labor, and the sale of the shoes; and observing the difference will begin to think."

Out of this thinking would emerge the demand for producers and consumers' co-operatives by means of which the capitalist system would be put out of business. As Steward saw it, the eight-hour day, by bringing higher wages, would help labor take the first step "on that long road which ends at last in a more equal distribution of the fruits of toil," for wages would continue to increase "until the capitalist and laborer are one." Hence, "the way out of the wage system is through higher wages resultant from shorter hours." [71]

To argue, as did Steward, that the eight-hour day would "secure such distribution of wealth that poverty shall finally become impossible," [72] and that it would bring about the end of the wages system, and put a stop to "Idleness, Speculation, Class Legislation, Financial Convulsions, Intemperance, Prostitution, and War," was to echo the Utopians of the 'forties.* It was naïve, moreover, to believe that the habits, customs, and opinions of the masses were the force that could compel employers to grant labor's demands. The power to compel such concessions lies in the power of trade unionism and the independent political organization of the working masses.

Steward, although an active member of the Machinists and Blacksmiths Union, did not believe that the shorter working day could be gained through trade union action. While he did not oppose agreements with employers for a shorter working day, he believed that they did not accomplish much. Such agreements, he argued, might secure the eight-hour day for small groups of workers, but the great mass of unorganized workers would not be affected. Moreover, these unorganized workers through their longer hours would soon weaken the position of the organized workers. If a law were passed compelling all to work eight hours, all capitalists would be required to introduce the shorter working day. Since the new wants created by leisure would make certain that workers would ask for and receive higher wages, it would soon bring the low-standard laborer up to the level of those who enjoyed a higher wage-standard.

In keeping with his emphasis on legislative action, Steward urged the

* In an unpublished manuscript entitled *Meaning of the Eight Hour Movement*, Steward argued that it was a distortion of his views to say that "merely establishing the Eight Hour System for Labor, will create all these blessings." "Our ideas," he continued, "is that until the working classes have *more time* outside their daily tasks, little else need be tried in the way of Social or Political Reform in the Northern States... Every scheme for progress waits upon that of more leisure for the Producing Classes." (Manuscript copy in Ira Steward Papers, Wisconsin State Historical Society.)

An occasional statement of this type, however, did not do much to dispel the belief that Steward's thesis was that the eight-hour day would bring about the millennium.

workers to change the slogan, "Vote Yourself a Farm," to "Vote Yourself an Eight-Hour Day." Before an election, all candidates should be asked, "Will you, if elected, use all your influence to secure the eight-hour system for every laborer and mechanic ... and at the rate of pay usually allowed in the ten-hour system?" [73]

Steward did not consider the trade unions capable of leading this political struggle. Not only did a number of them forbid political discussions, but few of them represented sufficient workers in the trade to unite all labor. Very few unions would agree to abandon all other issues and concentrate *only* on the demand for the eight-hour day; therefore Steward organized in Boston in 1864 the first eight-hour organization, the Workingmen's Convention, later called the Labor Reform Association. Its aim was the eight-hour day as the first step in the emancipation of the American working class. That same year in Europe, the constituent convention of the International Workingmen's Association, led by Karl Marx, declared that the "limitation of the work-day is the first step in the direction of the emancipation of the working class." [74] *

The eight-hour movement spread rapidly. From 1865 to 1867 hundreds of eight-hour leagues were formed; in California alone more than fifty leagues functioned early in 1868. By this time statewide organizations, known usually as Grand Eight-Hour Leagues, were in existence in Illinois, Indiana, Michigan, and Iowa. Though their main strength came from the workers, many farmers and other non-wage earners joined the leagues. Nearly all unions in New York City were represented in 1866 in the Central Eight-Hour League formed in that city, and Thomas

* There is nothing to indicate that Marx and Steward were in contact with each other during this period, but it is clear that the father of the eight-hour movement in America had great respect for the work of the founder of scientific socialism. In an undated letter to F. A. Sorge, leader of the American Marxist movement in the post-Civil War era, Steward describes the pleasure with which he was reading Marx's *Capital*, and particularly the chapter dealing with the hours of labor. "I want this translation of Karl Marx *to be read*," he continues. "With this idea, which is always before me, I have been much troubled at the passages that are to English speaking people, obscure. The average reader will not struggle long to understand. And the ability of Dr. Marx leads me to believe that in his own language, he was clear and easily comprehended. Had I been able to spend the time from my own writing I would have made after my own ideas, an abridgement or an abstract of the chapters that precede the 'Working Day.' Especially as the most obscure passages are in the first part of the manuscript. I shall quote from the Dr. several passages to help introduce and make his name more common to our readers. I never knew how much he had said on the Hours of Labor." (Letter in Ira Steward Papers, Wisconsin State Historical Society. Emphasis in original.) An abridged English edition of *Capital*, Vol. I, was published in the United States in 1877, translated by Otto Weydemeyer, son of Joseph Weydemeyer. The authoritative English translation of Vol. I was made by Samuel Moore, under the editorship of Frederick Engels, and was published in 1895.

Clark, President of the Carpenters' and Joiners' National Union, was its Vice-President.[75]

During the war, labor's agitation for the eight-hour day had been a contribution to post-war planning. Few of the advocates of the shorter day had demanded that it begin while the war was still being fought, for the workers understood that it would impair the war effort and delay victory. Their main argument was that the eight-hour day would help solve unemployment which was bound to come as soon as the war was over. Another strong argument was that if the national and state governments provided for the future inauguration of the shorter work day, morale in the armed forces would be heightened.[76] Political rhetoric vaguely promising everything to the returned veterans was not enough. "While no one disputes the claims of our noble soldiery to proper care when the war is over," asked *Fincher's Trades' Review,* "what preparation is being made to aid them in the least?" It was only proper that labor should demand that eight-hour laws go into effect when the war was over. "Let the mechanics and laborers in the ranks of our armies repeat the cry until it echoes from Texas to Maryland." [77]

Unmoved by these logical and patriotic appeals, Congress and the state legislatures were too busy obeying unscrupulous business interests which were robbing the public domain. Millions of acres of public lands were already in the hands of speculators; thus soldiers and sailors were being robbed of a large part of the land on which many of them had intended to build a new life. The predictions of the eight-hour advocates were soon a reality. A correspondent writing in *Fincher's Trades' Review* of June 17, 1865, stated, "As was to be expected, the returned soldiers are flooding the streets already, unable to find employment." They were joined in their search by workers who had formerly been employed on war orders. A description of conditions in the shoe industry told of "terrific competition between laborers for work" and the consequent reduction of wages.[78]

"Had Congress, in its wisdom, passed an enabling act," editorialized *Fincher's Trades' Review* on July 22, 1865, "declaring that a reduction of hours should take place on the return of Peace, then there would have been an opening for our brave associates; but now they are dependent upon the liberality of men never known to let slip an opportunity to line well their own pockets at the expense of the comfort and happiness of others."

The prevailing conditions, far-sighted labor leaders argued, called for a united struggle by workingmen and returning soldiers for the establishment of the eight-hour day. "With judicious management," one observer reminded the trade unions and the eight-hour leagues, "the thousands of returned soldiers, mainly workingmen before the war, can be induced to swell their ranks and add to their effectiveness." [79] In several communities this advice was taken seriously and joint organizations of trade unionists and veterans of the Union army came into being. At a meeting in July, 1865, delegates from several trade unions and from veteran soldiers' associations of Massachusetts met in convention and voted to organize local eight-hour leagues throughout the state. Several local organizations were soon formed to advocate "the claims of the soldier and laborer." [80]

The solution to unemployment, many workers believed, lay in the shorter working day which would distribute the available jobs. Other workers were convinced that in producers' co-operatives and monetary reform they would find the solution. Steward's program united even if only temporarily all workers who advocated a shorter working day.* To be sure, a few organized workers did not join the eight-hour crusade, fearing that a reduction in working hours would lower their pay. But they were definitely in the minority. Resolutions, mass meetings, and numerous strikes made the eight-hour question "the grand issue of the day" for the American working class in the years immediately following the Civil War. As Karl Marx observed, the movement "ran with express speed from the Atlantic to the Pacific, from New England to California." [81] The Carpenters and Joiners were speaking for the American worker when they declared at their National Convention in 1867: "We consider the most important issue at present before the laboring classes to be a reduction in the physical hours of labor...." [82]

By unifying workers all over the country around a single issue the struggle for the eight-hour day provided the stimulus for the formation of a national labor federation.

One of the most effective arguments for eight hours as a legal day's work was that even if this was not secured, the battle would compel all employers to institute the ten-hour day.

CHAPTER 18

The Labor Movement, 1866-1872

The manifold aspects of the labor movement immediately following the Civil War can best be understood by a study of the rise and decline of the National Labor Union and an examination of the issues with which this labor federation concerned itself. By examining at the same time the stand taken by national and local trade unions on these issues, it will be possible to determine to what extent the position adopted by the National Labor Union was representative of the trade unions themselves.

FOUNDING THE NATIONAL LABOR UNION

The National Labor Union grew out of the consciousness that the local efforts of workers could never remedy the evils they suffered. It was evident that "only by nationalizing their struggle, and by establishing a unity among the working classes throughout all states," could the workers hope to win a better life.[1] The effects of the Civil War upon American economic life made this evident. As the *Rochester Daily Union and Advertiser* pointed out on September 5, 1866, in urging the establishment of a national labor federation:

"The longer action is delayed, the more difficult it will be for the workingmen to secure the end they seek. Capital is centralizing, organizing and becoming more powerful every day. The late war and what has grown out of the war, made Capital stronger. It has made millions all at the expense of the labor of this country, and the capital thus concentrated is to be used in a greater or less degree to defeat the objects sought by the workingmen."

Though the National Labor Union did not fully succeed in establishing the much needed "unity of action among the working classes throughout all states," the story of its rise and decline calls for extended analysis because almost every basic problem facing the modern American labor movement was deliberated upon at its conventions, and because it is impossible to understand the philosophy of the post-Civil War labor movement unless one delves into the history of this organization.

Several attempts were made to set up a national labor federation after the failure of the International Industrial Assembly in 1864. In February, 1866, William Harding, president of the Coach Makers' International Union; William Sylvis, president of the International Molders' Union, and Jonathan Fincher, secretary of the Machinists and Blacksmiths Union, met in Philadelphia to discuss the need for a national federation of labor. At their invitation delegates from all local and national trade unions were invited to a preliminary conference in New York City. Eleven delegates, most of whom came from New Jersey and New York, answered the call and met in New York on March 26, 1866, to plan a National Labor Convention, to be held on August 20, in Baltimore. A committee headed by William Harding was appointed to work with the Baltimore Trades Assembly in planning for the convention.

Calls were sent to the officers and members of the various Trades Assemblies, Workingmen's Unions, Eight-Hour Leagues, and labor organizations throughout the country, inviting them to send delegates. The movement for an eight-hour day, the call said, had assumed an importance which demanded "concerted and harmonious action on all matters pertaining to the prosecution of labor reforms." It was therefore necessary that a National Congress be held "to form a basis upon which we may harmoniously and concertedly move in its prosecution." And the most effective manner of winning a reduction in the hours of labor to eight per day, would be the special business to come before the Congress.[2]

THE FIRST CONGRESS

On the opening day of the convention, August 20, 1866, a great banner stretching the length of the Rayston building greeted the delegates: "Welcome to the Sons of Toil, from the North, South, East and West." Sixty delegates were present of whom thirty-eight were sponsored by forty-three local trade unions, twelve from eleven trades assemblies, six from four eight-hour leagues, two from an international, and one from a national union. According to the estimate of the *New York Times,* more than 60,000 people were represented by the fifty-nine organizations which had sent delegates. Although the majority came from the eastern states, Chicago, Detroit, and St. Louis were represented by three delegates each. Of the local unions, the building trades had the largest representation, followed by the ship-carpenters, molders, and machinists. Only the Curriers and Coachmakers National Union sent official delegates, but four officers of three other national unions had been sponsored by such organizations as the Boston Workingmen's Assembly, and the Workingmen's Union of St. Louis. In addition, Jonathan Fincher and W. C. Otley, secretary and president respectively of the Machinists' and Blacksmiths' Union, President White of the Bricklayers, and President Shaw of the Carpenters and Joiners were present throughout the proceedings and were given the privilege of the floor. All told, there were at least eleven officials from six national unions in attendance.[8]

Much of the work of the congress was done in committees such as the Committees on Permanent National Organization, Trade Unions and Strikes, Co-operative Associations and Convict Labor, Eight-Hours and Political Action, and Resolutions. A special committee was appointed to prepare an "Address to the Workingmen of the United States."

The Committee on Trade Unions and Strikes, headed by Andrew C. Cameron, editor of the *Workingman's Advocate,* urged the organization of the unorganized, skilled and unskilled, into trade unions, and further recommended the formation of unions in all localities and trades where none existed. An international organization in every branch of industry was also recommended. Realizing that many unskilled laborers could not enter existing trade unions, the committee called for their organization into a general Workingmen's Association which would be affiliated to the National Labor Congress with the right of representation in the Congress. The committee's long report on strikes characterized them as "productive of great injury to the laboring classes," and advised labor to oppose strikes except as a last resort "... when all amicable and honorable means have been exhausted." It proposed that arbitration take the place of strikes, and that each trades' assembly appoint an arbitration committee to which all disputes between employers and workers be referred.

The report of the committee was adopted unanimously, and found its final expression in two major resolutions; the first declared it to be the imperative duty of every worker to join a labor organization, and where none existed to organize one. It called upon every union to be represented in a trades' or workingmen's assembly, and to assist in forming national and international organizations in the trade. The second resolution deprecated strikes, and urged that all honorable means be exhausted before such action was taken.[4]

Political action was brought before the convention by the report of the Committee on Eight Hours and Political Action which proposed that each locality should determine for itself whether to nominate an independent ticket of workingmen or to work with existing political parties. A few delegates argued for the rejection of the report, contending that political action was outside the sphere of trade union activity, and that to adopt the committee's report would make the congress a political organization. Edward Schlegel, representing the German Workingmen's Association of Chicago, was greeted with a burst of applause when he said that the report did not go far enough, and he called for the repudiation of the two old parties and the immediate formation of a new party of labor. "A new labor party *must* be formed," he said, "composed of the elements of American labor. We are shy of fighting the old political parties but should not be. If we are right let us go ahead. The Free Soil Party originated with a few thousand voters; but if it had not been formed, Lincoln would never have been elected President of the United States."

His arguments carried the convention which instructed the committee to amend its report for a stronger stand on independent political action. The amended report asserted that history had proved that the working class could have no confidence in the existing political parties. The time had come for the workers "to cut themselves aloof from party ties and predilections, and organize themselves into a National Labor Party," whose first objective would be the enactment of an eight-hour law by Congress and the state legislatures. Wherever a workingman was found eligible for any office, the committee recommended that he be preferred. Opponents of political action were instrumental in getting the report sent back to the committee, where the stand for a National Labor Party was watered down to the vague instruction that steps to form such a party "shall be put in operation as soon as possible." In this form, the report was accepted by a vote of 35 to 24.[5]

Although the reports of the committees on Trade Unions and Strikes and on Eight Hours and Political Action received the major attention of the Congress, many important questions facing the labor movement were taken up. The Congress called for a boycott of goods made by convict labor unless wages paid were equal to those demanded by the trades unions. Resolutions urged the abolition of slums and the improvement of housing conditions; asserted that the public domain be available to public settlers only; recommended the formation of mechanics' institutes, lyceums, and reading rooms; asked the workers to give full support to the labor press,* and advised unions to set up co-operative workshops, assuring them that co-operation was a "sure and lasting remedy for the abuses of the present industrial system." One resolution

---

* Several papers were specifically mentioned as meriting the support of the Workingmen: the *Workingman's Advocate* of Chicago, the *Daily and Weekly Voice* of Boston, the *Daily Union* of Detroit, the *Molders' International Journal* of Philadelphia, the *Herald* of Troy, the *Industrial Advocate* of St. Louis, and *Die Reform* (German) of Chicago.

concerning working women pledged individual and undivided support to the sewing women and daughters of toil in the land, and appealed for their hearty co-operation.[6]

Many issues of importance not only to labor but to the nation as a whole, such as land reform, housing, and education, were discussed.

"Altogether," commented Horace Greeley in the *New York Tribune* of August 27, 1866, "the convention has thoroughly represented the intelligence, education and enterprise of the workingmen of the Union, and its influence should be general and permanent.... The meeting, deliberations and conclusions of a Labor Congress representing laborers in different sections of our country, mark an era in our history."

A penetrating comment was also made by Karl Marx in a letter to a friend in America on October 9, 1866: "I was afforded great joy by the American Workers' Congress at Baltimore which took place at the same time as the Geneva Congress of the International Workingmen's Association. The slogan there was organization against Capital, and remarkably, most of the demands I drew up for Geneva were also put forward by the correct instinct of the workers."[7]

A striking illustration of this remarkable coincidence is revealed in the stand taken by both conventions on the eight-hour issue. The Baltimore Congress declared on August 16, 1866, that "the first and great necessity of the present to free the labor of this country from capitalistic slavery is the passing of a law by which eight hours shall be the normal working day in all states of the American Union." Two weeks later, the Geneva Congress of the International Workingmen's Association re-solved that "a limitation of the working day is a preliminary condition without which all further attempts at improvement or emancipation must prove abortive.... The Congress proposes eight-hours as the legal limit of the working day." The resolution then went on to say: "As this limitation represents the general demand of the workers of the North American United States, the Congress transforms this demand into the general platform of the Workers of the World."[8]

There were several shortcomings in the Baltimore Congress which before long were to hurry the organization into its decline. One mistake was the attitude it took toward strikes as "productive of great injury to the laboring classes." While it is true that several strikes in 1865-66 had resulted in setbacks, these strikes had heightened working class solidarity of which the Baltimore Congress itself was an expression. Although there was agreement among trade unions that strikes should be used only as a last resort, many trade unionists had little confidence in a national labor federation committed to arbitration as a substitute for strikes. Then, there was no provision for the financial assistance of unions engaged in strike struggles.*

Another major defect was the convention's failure to take any position on organizing Negro workers. It could be said that the call for the organization of all workers, skilled and unskilled, covered the question, but had not the congress realized the special exploitation of the woman in industry? Its failure to concern itself in the same manner with the Negro workers was but part of its general lack of understanding of the special problems facing the Negro people. Thus the congress ignored the battle over Reconstruction, confining itself to saying that the "speedy restoration of the agricultural interests of the South is of vital importance to the laboring men of the North." [9]

By condemning all existing parties the congress seemingly washed its hands of the most significant political issue facing the Negro toilers —the relation of the Republican Party to their struggle for land and political rights.

Another weakness was that no provision was made for the effective functioning of an organization. To William H. Sylvis, who had been unable to attend the convention because of illness, the failure to work out a comprehensive plan of national organization was a serious sin of omission. He summed up the congress by saying: "The fact is the Convention met, held a five days' session, built a splendid track, placed upon it a locomotive complete in all its parts; provided an engineer and numerous assistants, placed them upon the footboard, told them to go ahead and then suddenly adjourned without providing wood and water to get up steam; and there the whole machine will stand until the third Monday in August, 1867, when it is hoped that there will be such a coming together of workingmen as will astonish the oldest inhabitant and that the work so nobly begun at Baltimore will be completed." [10]

STRENGTHENING THE NATIONAL LABOR UNION

Some of these defects were remedied at subsequent conventions. At the Chicago convention of 1867, seventy-one delegates representing sixty-four organizations were present. Ten delegates came from as many eight-hour

* Actually, the National Labor Union had no funds to speak of, and was so poor that it did not even publish its own proceedings. Treasurer John Hinchcliffe received only $205.21 during 1866 from the local tax for running expenses and expended $187.25. Had it not been for its devoted secretary, C. W. Gibson, an eight-hour champion, the organization would not have been able to function. Gibson gave unstintingly of his labor and his own money to keep the organization alive. Without clerical aid he wrote 1,387 letters, distributed 2,157 printed letters and 5,816 addresses and circulars. He received only $75.38 from Treasurer Hinchcliffe and spent $791.62, supplying the difference from his own pocket. J. C. C. Whaley, the organization's president, was little more than a figurehead.

leagues, and twelve from thirteen trades' assemblies. The number of local unions had decreased—twenty-seven delegates coming from thirty-three unions as compared with the Baltimore figures of twenty-eight and forty-two respectively. But the number of national unions officially represented increased from two to six, the printers, bricklayers, coachmakers, iron molders, tailors and cigar makers sending delegates.[11]

Since the past year had demonstrated weaknesses in organization, the convention adopted a constitution. The president was empowered to appoint organizers to establish associations of workingmen, the members of which were to sign a pledge subscribing to the constitution and platform of the central body. Funds needed for the activities of the national organization were to be collected from member trade unions in accordance with the size of their membership.[12]

This new constitution strengthened the organization, but it was not until 1868 when Sylvis was elected president that a real effort was made to build the National Labor Union. In December of that year the Executive Committee met in Washington, and decided to authorize Sylvis "to take the field to canvass the principal cities and towns of the country, for the purpose of discussing and disseminating the principles of the National Labor Union, and forming branch Unions to cooperate therewith." [13] Soon after, Sylvis, accompanied by Richard Trevellick, started his organizing tour of the South. During their three-month tour they organized twenty-six branches of the National Labor Union. Sylvis sent encouraging messages to the official organ of the union, the *Workingman's Advocate* of Chicago. "We talked of the benefit of trades' unions, cooperation, the National Labor Union, etc.," he wrote from Mobile, "and the people seemed much interested." [14]

The state chairmen of the National Labor Union were inspired by this success and started organizing drives of their own. Robert Hodkin, state chairman for Michigan, issued an appeal to workingmen to form a labor union in each ward, township, or school district: "Seven workingmen or other good citizens," he wrote, "who favor our views and who mean earnest work in the cause of labor reform can form a Union." The group had but to send its application to William H. Sylvis with the charter fee of $5 and the names of the president, secretary, and five or more of its members.[15] The report from the various states during 1868 and early 1869 were enthusiastic. The chairman for Ohio reported that he had organized twenty labor unions. "I assure you," he added, "that I shall not drop it here. I intend to keep the ball rolling until there is a Union in every town." [16] Similar letters came to the *Workingman's Advocate* from organizers in other states. Early in 1869 the *Chicago Tribune* quoted the membership of the National Labor Union at 800,000, although Sylvis himself put the figure at 600,000.[17] Both estimates were greatly exaggerated, but membership was soaring to high levels.

In its discussion of the 1868 convention of the National Labor Union, the *New York Herald* had commented: "Their philosophic and statesmanlike views of the great industrial questions might be adopted by our Solons at Washington and politicians generally with infinite benefit to trade and business prosperity of the whole community." Sylvis agreed wholeheartedly with this observation. He was determined that labor's new-found strength should be heard from in Washington, so during the Congressional session of 1868-69 he appointed a committee of five to represent the National Labor Union in Washington. Its function was "to watch over the interests of our Union, lay our plans and objects before Congressmen and Senators, and to take advantage of every opportunity to help along the work." [18] For the first time in its history the American worker had a lobby in the nation's capital.

Just what had been done and what was still to be done by the National Labor Union can best be answered by discussing the following issues before labor: (1) the eight-hour day; (2) organization of working women and woman's rights; (3) organization of Negro workers; (4) international labor unity; (5) co-operatives and currency reform; and (6) political action.

THE EIGHT-HOUR DAY

Before the adjournment of the Baltimore Convention in 1866, a committee consisting of one representative from each state, headed by John Hinchcliffe, the president of the convention, had arranged to meet with President Andrew Johnson. Hinchcliffe presented Johnson with a list of the objectives of the Baltimore meeting and appealed for his co-operation to secure the eight-hour day, to limit the grants of public lands, and to end the system of convict labor. The President remained silent on the eight-hour question, but asserted that he was "in favor of the shortest number [of hours] possible that will allow the discharge of duty and the requirements of the country." [19]

On June 25, 1868, the campaign of the National Labor Union, the eight-hour leagues, and trade unions came to fruition. Congress passed an eight-hour day for laborers, mechanics, and all other workmen in federal employ. For the first time since the order of President Martin Van Buren in 1840 establishing the ten-hour day for government employees, labor's demands had been officially recognized by the federal government.

However, the high hopes raised by this victory were not realized. Some department heads reduced wages in proportion to the change in hours. An Act passed in July, 1862, had provided that government wages should conform to those of private establishments in the immediate vicinity of the shipyards. Using this law, Secretary Bone of the Navy reduced the wages of all Navy Yard mechanics 20 per cent. He was upheld by Attorney-General Evarts and his successor, Attorney-General E. R. Hoar. The latter also ruled that the eight-hour law did not affect contractors on government jobs.[20]

Labor denounced these decisions. "There seems to be no desire on your part nor among your superiors at Washington to do anything for the people," Sylvis wrote to the Attorney-General. "Congressmen and Senators," continued Sylvis, "may raise their wages with impunity. . . . Swindling railroad corporations, land rings, gold rings, whiskey rings, bondholders' rings, and the representatives of other kinds of swindles can receive kind words and privileges, but workingmen must be insulted and take back seats." But it would not always be so, he warned; fortunately, workingmen still held the ballot in their hands, and by a "judicious use of it" would finally gain what was justly due them but "now withheld by those placed in official positions by our votes."[21] Mass meetings of trade unions and eight-hour leagues unanimously pledged themselves "never to give up the struggle until eight-hours become the established principle in this country."[22]

President Grant, who had ignored Sylvis' request that he speak out for an honest construction of the eight-hour law in his inaugural address, was compelled in 1869 to pay more attention to the demands of labor. He issued an executive order that "no reduction should be made in the wages by the day to such laborers . . . on account of such reduction in the hours of labor." On May 29, the *Workingman's Advocate* flashed the joyful news to labor: *Victory at Last. Eight Hours a Legal Day's Work*.

But so flagrant were the violations that by 1872 Grant had to repeat the order. Congress on May 18, 1872, conscious of the approaching elections, appropriated funds to pay the wages lost because of "improper interpretation" of the law by officials, but there were still no provisions for the enforcement of the law, and officials continued to ignore it.[23]

What labor thought of this continuous defiance of the law was well expressed in 1874 by the Workingmen's Council of the United States: "The government of the United States in taking pains to enforce its financial and other laws made in favor of the rich, while deliberately and impudently violating the Eight-Hour Law in favor of labor, shows itself to be a tyrannous fraud, fit only to be despised by honest men."[24] Two years later the Supreme Court ruled that the eight-hour law did not prevent the government from making agreements with labor "for more or less than eight hours."[25]

More and more workingmen were becoming discouraged and pessimistic, and felt that the struggle to secure a national eight-hour law had been just so much wasted effort. This mistaken attitude was challenged by the German Socialist trade unionists who in their journal, the *Arbeiter Union,* explained that the importance of the law reducing the workday to eight hours lay in the fact that the highest legislative body "has recognized the necessity of reducing the work-day, and sanctioned in principle and by law the demand for a shorter work-day for the entire nation." [26] Officials could violate the law, but the principle that the national government could step in and by legislation provide for the welfare of the working people would remain.

The eight-hour law passed by Congress had stimulated the passage of similar legislation in the states. In California a petition twenty-two feet long containing 11,000 names was presented to the legislature early in 1866, asking that an eight-hour law be passed. When the measure passed the Assembly but was defeated in the Senate, the trade unions changed their tactics. A union would designate a day after which its members would work but eight hours, and then notify employers that they were expected to agree to the new schedule. A typical advertisement appeared in the *Weekly Los Angeles Republican* on July 18, 1868, which notified the employers that for Carpenters, Bricklayers, Stone Masons, Plasterers and Painters of the Mechanics' League of Los Angeles, eight hours would "constitute a legal day's work without reduction from present rates ... from and after the 10th Day of August, A.D. 1868." [27] Alexander M. Kennady, leader of the eight-hour movement on the Pacific Coast, reported in 1868 that every trade union in California which deemed it expedient to adopt the eight-hour system "obtains it by the simple passage of a resolution. There is no strike. Employers accept the notice." [28]

The California legislature finally yielded to the pressure for an eight-hour law, and on February 22, 1868, a huge torchlight parade celebrated its passage. Each trade union's place in the line of march was determined by the date on which it had obtained the shorter workday. First came the ship caulkers who had secured the eight-hour day in December, 1865. The plumbers and gas fitters carried a banner with the date, July, 1867, followed by the machinists, ironworkers, brass finishers, and their apprentices, all of whom were still working more than eight hours. [29]

By 1868 six states and several cities had already passed eight-hour laws. Workingmen throughout the nation hailed these laws and joined in the popular refrain:

> *Let all now cheer, who never cheered before,*
> *And those who always cheer, now cheer the more.*

But the cheers soon were hushed because the state laws were but empty promises. An eight-hour law had been enacted in New York in

1867, but Governor Fenton refused to help enforce it. When the New York Workingmen's Assembly asked the governor to issue a proclamation calling upon employers to observe the law, he replied, "It would be an act of unwarranted assumption to issue a proclamation requiring its observance." [30]

Although employers could not stop the passage of eight-hour laws, they succeeded in emasculating these laws by inserting nullifying clauses. *Fincher's Trades' Review* had warned against such legislation early in the campaign for the eight-hour day. Labor should be on its guard, it had declared on June 27, 1863, against attempts to set aside the law: "We demand a positive law, that neither the employer nor journeyman can evade."

Most of the laws were full of loopholes. One passed in California provided for an eight-hour day in "all cases within this state, unless otherwise expressly stipulated between the parties concerned." The Illinois law was to be effective only where there was "no special contract to the contrary." [31] After the passage of these laws employers informed their workers that only those who signed contracts agreeing to work longer hours could hold their jobs. Private industry was quick to follow the example set by the national government, and wage-cuts invariably followed reduction in hours. Ira Steward appealed to the Massachusetts legislature in 1871 to enact an eight-hour law which would prohibit reductions in pay in order to prove to the workers that an eight-hour system would really increase wages.* The workers "must first be satisfied by actual experiment that wages cannot possibly be reduced by the reduction proposed." So much for Steward's idea that the eight-hour day would automatically bring higher wages! "For all practical purposes," reported a committee of the National Labor Union, "the eight-hour laws might as well have never been placed on the statute books, and can only be described as frauds on the laboring class." [32]

Labor was learning that legislation was not enough. In some states, organizations were formed to retain the eight-hour day, and strikes were called to enforce the law. In April, 1868, shortly after an eight-hour law had been passed, the coal companies in Schuylkill County, Pennsylvania, posted notices requiring workers to sign contracts to work longer than eight hours. The miners struck. Delegations of miners, laborers, and mechanics met and drew up a statement opposing all contracts which nullified the state law. More than 25,000 people took part in the strike,

---

* In 1869 Steward wrote: "What we Eight Hour men want, first of all, is National, State, and Municipal Experiments which shall prove to the entire satisfaction of the majority, that *the Eight Hour System cannot and will not reduce wages.*" (*Meaning of the Eight Hour Movement,* Manuscript copy in Ira Steward Papers, Wisconsin State Historical Society.)

and although it failed, the spirit aroused by the strike resulted in the forming of the Workingmen's Benevolent Association of Schuylkill County.[33] The bricklayers of New York City struck in 1868 because the state authorities had not carried out the provisions of the eight-hour law. Though the fourteen-week strike failed, 1800 men did succeed in obtaining the eight-hour day.

Three years later, the trade unions of New York City started a campaign for the enforcement of the eight-hour law. More than twenty thousand workers joined in the parade. The painters' union float expressed the mood of the march. The float, preceded by a cannon, carried the slogan: "Peacefully if we can, forcibly if we Must. When peaceful efforts fail, then the Revolution." [34]

The following spring, a three-months' strike of a hundred thousand workers resulted in ten unions, most of them in the building trades, securing the eight-hour day. This victory was celebrated on June 10, 1872, with a parade of more than 150,000 workers. So effective was this parade that the *New York Times* could only observe: "It would be a matter of interest to inquire what proportion of the thousands pouring that long column of strikers... were thoroughly American." [35]

The success of New York labor stimulated the workers throughout the nation. On May 22, 1872, the *New York Tribune* reported that strikes for the eight-hour day were being won in scores of cities, among them Jersey City, Philadelphia, Buffalo, Chicago, and Albany. Thus by 1873 the organized struggles in various states had secured the adoption of the eight-hour day either by compelling the enforcement of legislation or by agreements with employers. But with the panic of 1873 most of these gains were swept away.

However, the eight-hour movement had not been fruitless. By unifying labor throughout the nation it made other gains possible. The struggles of the 'sixties and early 'seventies had taught the workers that legislative gains could be kept only when backed up by alert and militant unions. Of great importance was the understanding gained in the struggle that labor must enter politics as an independent force. In 1868 Alexander M. Kennady said of the movement for a shorter working day in California:

"...By far the most important result of this eight hour agitation—to those who look forward to the day when labor, organized and effectively drilled, shall assume its legitimate sphere in the body politic—is visible in the marked improvement in the character of the men engaged in the movement. A few years ago the working population of California were in a chaotic state—disorganized, and at the mercy of capitalists—with very rare exceptions. Today, nearly every branch of skilled industry has its union, fixing its own rate of wages, and regulating its domestic differences. A spirit of independence, and a feeling of mutual confidence inspire its members, in place of the craven fear and mutual distrust which formerly animated them." [36]

WOMEN WORKERS AND WOMAN'S RIGHTS

Despite the growth of trade unionism among women workers toward the latter part of the Civil War, the conditions of most working women had not greatly improved. "Badly as our workmen and mechanics may be treated," said the *National Workman* of February 23, 1867, "it is no secret that the condition of females who are obliged to work for a living is far worse." Unfortunately, the attitude of many male trade unionists to these females was still one of open hostility. They believed that working women were only aggravating the difficulties created by post-war unemployment, and were convinced that the easiest solution would be to drive women out of the trades and bar them from joining the unions.

The war, however, had rendered such a simple solution impossible. Economic necessity had brought thousands of women into industry, many of whose husbands had been killed or seriously wounded in the conflict. Employers read with interest the report of General Travis Elias Spinner who had introduced 1,500 women into government offices during the war. Not only was the experiment a success, but he reported that women were "doing more and better work for $900 per annum than many male clerks who were paid double that amount." [37] If women can do the same or better work for half the cost of male labor in government employment, why wouldn't this also apply to other occupations?—asked the wary employers.

It did! In 1868 the *Workingman's Advocate* reported that a careful survey of the problem had proved that in nearly all trades women were being introduced in order "to undermine prices, that character of labor being usually employed ... at a lower rate than is paid for male labor in the same kind of work." The result was a general depression of the wage scale to the level of the low wages paid to women.[38]

Workingmen could blame the wage-cuts upon women, but this hostility did not halt the increasing use of workingwomen. If the wage standards of male mechanics were to be defended, women workers had to be organized into unions. A resolution adopted in June, 1865, by the New York Journeymen Tailors' Union urged its members to "make every effort necessary to induce the female operatives of the trade to join this association, inasmuch as thereby the best protection is secured for ourselves as well as for the female operatives." [39]

Since many unions were not prepared to accept women, they were often forced to form their own organizations. During the post-war era unions were formed by women cigar-makers, collar workers, tailoresses and seamstresses, umbrella sewers, cap makers, textile workers, printers, furnishers, laundresses and shoe-workers. A number of organized work-ingmen helped the women establish these unions, and prominent trade union leaders spoke frequently at meetings called to assist the women trade unionists. When the boss shoemakers of Utica, New York, an-nounced that they would not employ women who joined the Daughters of St. Crispin, an outstanding women's trade union of the time, several hundred Knights of St. Crispin threw down their tools and went on strike. When the Collar Workingwomen's Association of Troy, New York, another outstanding woman's trade union, called a strike to defend the organization against the efforts of the employers to smash it, it received financial assistance from the men's trade unions in the city. The molders' union, which itself had been aided by the Collar Working Women's Union, donated five hundred dollars and pledged to "continue the same for weeks to come rather than see such a brave set of wenches crushed under the iron heel of these laundry nabobs." [40] A member of the mold-ers' union wrote in the *Rochester Union and Advertiser* for May 16, 1866:

"We all know that many of these working girls and women have lost their husbands, brothers, fathers, and lovers in the late struggle for the life and existence of our common country; and is it not too bad now to see monied corporations—money which they have made, many of them by furnishing the enemies of the government with means to take the lives of our soldiers—is it not too bad, I say, to see these corporations trying to deprive these widows and orphans, that they have helped to make, of the means to earn an honest living? But corporations, they say, have no souls, and have nothing to answer for."

Although most unions still did not permit women to join their ranks directly, preferring to have them organize separate locals, a few organ-izations discovered that only full equality for women would solve their problems. The Cigar Makers' International Union altered its constitution in 1867 to admit women to membership and took special action a few years later to organize women into the same union as men. A similar development occurred in the National Typographical Union. At its 1854 and 1855 conventions, it condemned the employment of women com-positors. When the delegates assembled for their 1869 convention, they were presented with an appeal from the Women's Typographical Union No. 1 of New York, organized in 1868 by the New York Typographical Union.

This document is a remarkable statement of the problems of working women. It explained that there were a large number of women working at the trade whose interests were totally neglected, and reminded the male trade unionists that the status of these women was "a detriment to the trade, and disastrous to the best interests of all printers." Their labor had been used during strikes to defeat the organized male workers, but when that had been accomplished, they had been set adrift by the employers, and their necessity constantly compelled them "to work at a price at which they cannot earn a living and which tends to undermine your wages." Believing that "the interests of labor, whether that labor be done by male or female, are identical, and should receive the same protection and the same pay," the women compositors had formed their own union. They had been inspired "by the assistance, exertions and praiseworthy example" of the New York Typographical Union. They now appealed to the International Union to recognize their organization and seat their delegates at the convention.[41]

The appeal was accompanied by a set of resolutions adopted by the New York Typographical Union, recommending the recognition of the women's union. In addition, it was endorsed by Robert McKenchie, president of the International Union. In his report to the convention he stated that the recognition of woman labor was one of the most important problems before the delegates, and showed, by referring to the assistance the printers of New York had received from women compositors in their strikes, that the existence of local unions often depended on the attitude they adopted toward the women in the trade.

The delegates were impressed. They voted unanimously to accept the credentials of the delegates from the Women's Typographical Union No. 1 of New York as well as to assist women in the formation of separate local unions. A year later they reaffirmed this stand, and, in addition, elected Miss Gussie Lewis of New York to the position of Corresponding Secretary of the National Typographical Union.[42] At its 1872 convention a committee appointed to consider the question of women printers reported that "the experiment of establishing separate unions for females has resulted unsatisfactorily ... chiefly because a difference has resulted from the two scales (men and women) of prices in force." It was therefore decided that the union should favor the principle that "there should be no difference in compensation paid to competent workers, based upon a difference of sex." To give this ruling force, it was also decided not to grant any more charters to "female unions," and a recommendation was made to all locals "to admit female printers to membership upon the same footing, in all respects, as males."[43] From that time on women joined the union directly and were accorded equal rights with male members.

This friendly attitude to women workers was, to a considerable extent, influenced by the National Labor Union. At its founding convention in 1866 the organization had pledged its "individual and undivided support to ... the daughters of toil in this land." Two years later, at its 1868 convention, it commended Kate Mullaney, director of the Troy Collar Workingwomen's Association, for her "indefatigable exertions" on behalf of female laborers, and elected her as assistant secretary of the organization. In addition, the convention advised women "to learn trades, engage in business, join our labor unions or form protective unions of their own, and use every other honorable means to persuade or force employers [to] *do justice to women by paying them equal wages for equal work.*" [44] For the first time in American history a national labor federation had voted for equal pay for equal work.

To Karl Marx this progressive stand made the National Labor Union one of the most significant organizations in the world labor movement. Thus he wrote to a friend in America: "Great progress was evident in the last Congress of the American Labor Union in that among other things it treated working women with complete equality. While in this respect the English, and the still more gallant French, are burdened with a spirit of narrow-mindedness. Anybody knows, if he knows anything about history, that great social changes are impossible without the feminine ferment. Social progress can be measured exactly by the social position of the fair sex." [45]

The woman suffrage movement, anxious to secure the assistance of the labor movement, turned naturally to the National Labor Union. Four delegates from women's labor associations came to the 1868 convention: Susan B. Anthony and Mary Kellogg Putnam of the Workingwomen's Protective Unions, Nos. 1 and 2; Mary MacDonald of the Women's Protective Union of Mt. Vernon, New York; and Elizabeth Cady Stanton, secretary of the Woman's Suffrage Association. All the delegates were seated except Mrs. Stanton, whose credentials were referred to the convention. Those opposed to Mrs. Stanton argued that a suffrage association was not a labor organization as stipulated by the by-laws. Susan B. Anthony, the foremost woman's rights leader, came to the defense of her colleague and warned the delegates: "We cannot elevate the men until the women are brought up also. To do this, the ballot must be given them." She was strongly supported by William Sylvis who, in recommending the seating of Mrs. Stanton, declared: "She is one of the boldest writers of her age and has done more than anybody I know to elevate her class and my class too, and God knows they need elevation." [46]

After many speeches a decision was reached to accept Mrs. Stanton's credentials, the vote being 44 to 19. When eighteen delegates threatened to leave the convention and resign from the National Labor Union, a qualifying resolution was adopted; it asserted that the admission of Mrs.

Stanton as a delegate did not mean that the National Labor Union had endorsed "her peculiar ideas," nor committed itself on the question of female suffrage. Another defeat was suffered by the suffragists when the delegates rejected a recommendation of the Committee on Female Labor that their resolution should include the phrase, "secure the ballot."

While the woman suffrage leaders were disappointed by the convention's rejection of their proposals, they were deeply impressed by the positive steps to assist working women, regarding these as the beginning of a "new era in Workingmen's conventions." Mrs. Stanton said that the "interests of the country would be safe in hands like these," and that the discussions at the Congress "were superior to those of any body of statesmen ever assembled on this continent." [47]

However, the relations between the woman's rights leaders and the National Labor Union did not remain cordial for long. At the 1869 congress, Susan B. Anthony of the Workingwomen's Protective Association and Martha Walbridge of the Excelsior League No. 3 of Massachusetts submitted credentials. M. R. Walsh of the New York Typographical Union No. 6, objecting to the seating of Miss Anthony, presented a resolution from his local which said that it would be "an insult to our entire organization to admit her as delegate." The resolution accused her of having used the Workingwomen's Protective Association as a strike-breaking agency, supplying women compositors to replace men who were on strike.[48]

Miss Anthony admitted the charge, and justified her action by the statement that this was the only way women could get experience in the trade. That many delegates understood this dilemma is seen in the first vote which showed a 55-52 majority for her admission. This decision was later reversed, and her credentials were returned by a vote of 62-28. On August 26, 1869, *The Revolution,* a journal owned by Miss Anthony, declared: "The worst enemies of Women's Suffrage will ever be the laboring class of men. Their late action towards Miss Anthony is but the expression of the hostility they feel to the idea she represents."

This attack was not a just one, for the speeches at the convention prove that the opposition was not to Miss Anthony but to her defense of scabbing which was "sacrificing the very cardinal principles for which the unions were formed." [49] Men like Sylvis, Trevellick, and other leaders of the National Labor Union were the foremost advocates of woman suffrage. "Why," asked Sylvis, "should women not enjoy every social and political privilege enjoyed by men? The time, I hope, is not far when universal suffrage and universal liberty will be the rule all over the world." [50] * R. W. Hume, another leader of the National

* Unquestionably Sylvis' sudden death on July 27, 1869, on the very eve of the 1869 convention of the National Labor Union, set back the movement for co-

Labor Union, was as forthright. "Nothing but the success of the labor cause can right their wrongs," he wrote, "and its success depends largely on their acquisition of their political and legal rights. We can trust our wives, sisters and daughters to help us at the ballot boxes to overthrow mammon." [51]

But all members of the National Labor Union were not so advanced. Some still believed women to be inferior to men and unfit mentally and temperamentally to vote. Others believed that suffrage was only incidental, and that in advocating equal pay for equal work, the National Labor Union had "acknowledged all the correlative rights of women, including property and suffrage." Still others maintained that it would take too long to secure female suffrage. "Our business is with those who are already voters." [52] Such narrow views did much to antagonize the woman's rights advocates, but Miss Anthony and some of her colleagues also adopted a narrow viewpoint by condemning backward workers instead of educating them.

The split between Miss Anthony and the National Labor Union did not affect the latter's interest in the problems of the working women. It continued to encourage the organization of women workers, and always sought their co-operation. Organizers for the National Labor Union invited working women to all meetings conducted by the local and state labor unions, and urged them to become members. At its 1870 congress one of the four women delegates, Mrs. Willard of the Sewing Girls Union of Chicago, was elected second vice-president of the National Labor Union. A year later Mrs. Willard, now representing the Working Women's Union of the same city, was re-elected. [53]

While not yet ready to endorse woman suffrage, the National Labor Union had become a champion of woman's rights. It had pledged its

operation between labor and the women's rights leaders. The *American Workman* declared on September 4, 1869: "We are inclined to think if Mr. Sylvis had been living, the opposition to Miss A[nthony] would not have taken the organized and active and persistent shape it did. Certainly, the views of the late president and Miss Anthony accorded in all essential points; and the influence of *The Revolution* has been constantly in line with the support of the body to whom she had credentials as a delegate. Mr. Sylvis . . . warmly endorsed her paper."

It is true that the women's rights delegates were not interested primarily in labor problems, but the *American Workman* was quite correct in pointing to the progressive attitude generally adopted by *The Revolution* to these problems. This weekly journal, owned by Susan B. Anthony and edited by Elizabeth Cady Stanton and Mr. Parker Pillsbury, commented on April 16, 1868: "The contest between labor and capital has commenced. Capital is absorbing more than its share of the profits of trade. Labor is defrauded of its just dues. The rich are becoming richer and the poor poorer every day." It constantly reminded the trade unionist "that all their efforts for self-extrication and elevation are vain until the claims of the more oppressed working women are recognized." (*The Revolution*, July 23, 1869.)

aid to organize women workers; it demanded that the eight-hour law apply to women workers; that Congress and the state legislatures pass laws providing equal pay for equal work for women in government employ; it adhered to the principle of equal pay for equal work in all industries; it accepted women delegates on an equal basis with men, appointing them to important committees, and electing them to positions of leadership in the organization.

But with all this, the status of working women in 1873 was not much better than that of a decade before. Only two of the thirty or more national unions admitted women—the printers and the cigar makers. Women found it impossible to organize separate unions that could maintain their organization, and by 1872 most of the women labor organizations had disappeared. The organizing of the American working woman still remained to be done, and it was to take many years of struggle before the majority of organized workers would understand the words of R. W. Hume, a leader of the National Labor Union and a leading Socialist. A long and careful study had convinced him, he said in 1870, that the condition of the working woman of America could never be advanced until organized workingmen understood that labor's success depended basically "on strengthening the weakest part of the labor forces, for the main strength of the capitalist class consisted in the divisions existing in labor's ranks." [54]

CHAPTER 19

The Labor Movement, 1866-1872

(Continued)

Two years after the close of the Civil War the National Labor Union addressed American trade unionists: "Negroes are four million strong and a greater proportion of them labor with their hands than can be counted from among the same number of any other people on earth. Can we afford to reject their proffered co-operation and make them enemies? By committing such an act of folly we would inflict greater injury upon the cause of labor reform than the combined efforts of capital could accomplish.... So capitalists North and South would foment discord between the whites and blacks and hurl one against the other as interest and occasion might require to maintain their ascendancy and continue the reign of oppression." [1] The address advocated unity of Negro and white.

The confusion existing among American workers on this question impeded the progress of the trade union movement for generations. Preoccupied with their own struggles to gain higher wages and to halt the employers' offensives, organized workers of the North did not understand that their future was being influenced by the outcome of the struggle for democracy in the South.

LABOR AND RECONSTRUCTION

Immediately after the Civil War the Negro toilers in the South found their new freedom little different from their former bondage. The plantation owners were still the masters, and old restrictions limiting the liberty of free Negroes were still enforced. Following a tour through the South shortly after the war, Carl Schurz, liberal German-American leader, reported that the former slave owners still regarded and treated the freedmen as their natural property, and that the prevailing attitude among the former masters was that the "Negro exists for the special object of raising cotton, rice and sugar *for the whites,* and that it is illegitimate for him to indulge like other peoples in the pursuit of his own happiness in his own way." [2]

Although the Negroes had joyfully hailed the Emancipation Proclamation, they demanded in addition to political and civil rights a material base for their freedom. Concretely they asked for land—forty acres and a mule. This democratic demand, monstrous and ridiculous though it appeared to the ex-slave owners and their allies in the North, was as natural as the slogan, "Vote Yourself a Farm," of the northern white workers during the 'forties. To the Negro workers ownership of land meant freedom from masters and overseers and the system of control that characterized slavery. "We will still be slaves," was their common refrain, "until every man can raise his own bale of cotton, and say: 'This is mine.' " [3]

With rare exceptions, however, the Negro masses did not get land. Instead, under President Johnson they received the "Black Codes" * which the Freedman's Bureau reported to Congress "actually served to secure to the former slaveholding class the unpaid labor which they had been accustomed to enjoy before the war." [4] In most states the Freedman's Bureau was successful in getting the Black Codes wiped off the statute books. But by its inability to redistribute the land among the Negro masses, the Bureau was unable to give an economic base to southern democracy. The Negroes were finally forced to return to their former owners when the Freedman's Bureau threatened with a vagrancy charge all laborers without contract or employment. "This device," General Tillson of the Bureau said, "worked like a charm." [5]

Negro conventions met in the South during the summer and fall of 1865 to protest against the Johnson governments and the Black Codes. Most of the delegates at these conventions were plantation workers, but city artisans often played an important part. For the first time in

---

* Under the Black Codes a Negro who was not at work was arrested and imprisoned. In order to pay off the prison charges and fines he was hired out. If a Negro quit work before his contract expired, he was arrested and imprisoned for breach of contract and the reward to the person performing the arrest was deducted from his wages. Some of the codes also provided that if a Negro laborer left his employer he would "forfeit all wages to the time of abandonment." Negro children whose parents were considered too poor to support them were bound out as apprentices, girls until 18 years of age and boys until 21. In Mississippi the code provided that if a Negro could not pay taxes to care for the poor, he would be regarded as a vagrant and hired out, and clearly asserted that the laws under chattel slavery were to be in full force again "except so far as the mode and manner of trial and punishment have been changed and altered by law." (Vernon L. Wharton, *The Negro in Mississippi, 1865-1890,* Unpublished Ph.D. Thesis, University of North Carolina, 1939, pp. 145-50; Paul Lewinson, *Race, Class and Party,* New York, 1932, pp. 32*ff.*)

American history the Negro people in the South were entering the political life of the nation and they asked only that the government recognize the rights of Negroes as citizens of a republic whose life they had helped preserve. They demanded a "fair and remunerative reward for labor," free education for their children, protection of their families, and the repeal of the Black Codes.[6] "These," said a resolution adopted at the Colored People's Convention of South Carolina meeting in Charleston in November, 1865, "are the rights of free men, and are inherent and essential in every republican form of government." [7]

While the Negro masses in the South were fighting Johnson's policies, Abolitionists were organizing a national campaign to stop him from returning the slaveholding oligarchy to power. Allied with them in this great campaign were many northern industrialists who understood that their control of the national government depended upon crushing the landed aristocracy and establishing democracy in the South. Johnson's plan threatened to nullify the political and economic results of the war. A union of northern and southern Democrats and groups of discontented farmers of the West threatened the power of the Republican Party, the political representative of the industrial bourgeoisie. Protective tariffs might soon be replaced by free trade; the national banking system might be abolished, and the currency system would certainly give way to cheap money. Little wonder that the men who had gained control of the government during the war and hoped now to use their political power to protect their gains and to develop an industrial America, began to realize that only by championing the cause of democracy in the South would the victories of the Civil War be safeguarded.[8]

These were some reasons why the Radical Republicans opposed Johnson's plan, and why they later climaxed their program with the Reconstruction Acts. The first of these measures was passed in February, .867, and provided that the Negroes be enfranchised, that leading Confederates be disenfranchised, and that new constitutional conventions be called to frame state constitutions embodying universal manhood suffrage, these constitutions to be approved by a majority of the citizens and by Congress. Then the southern states would be readmitted into the Union.

In this struggle against the southern oligarchy, what was the position of the labor movement? Some trade unionists, especially the German workingmen, joined the coalition of Abolitionists and industrialists in opposing Johnson's Reconstruction plan. No man, they believed, should be deprived of suffrage "merely on account of his race, color, creed, or length of purse." The former slaveholders, one trade unionist declared, were "the worst set of capitalists known to the civilized world; men who did not stop to advocate that capital should *own* its own labor and that the normal condition of the poor man was that of a slave, whether he be white or black." The men who were seeking to crush the black workingmen would, if they were victorious, soon destroy the white laboring man. Uriah S. Stephens, soon to head the Knights of Labor, emphasized early in the Reconstruction period the necessity of "securing the right of suffrage and a right to the *soil* for the liberated freemen of the South." [9]

The stanchest opponent of Johnson's policies in labor's ranks was the *Boston Daily Evening Voice*, official organ of the Workingmen's Assembly of Boston and Vicinity. It charged that the former slaveowners were ·determined to keep the Negro people "under a despotism worse if possible than slavery itself." "No workingman," it warned, "should be found with that party."

"Leaving the question of Negro suffrage to the whites of the former rebel states is an abandonment of the cause of the defenceless freemen by the Government he has served.... There should be no reconstruction without the full recognition of the Negro's manhood, and there should be an energetic superintendence of affairs in the late rebel states till they may be trusted with government." [10]

Week after week the *Voice* continued to attack those ready to surrender, to give clear arguments to the confused, to lead its readers in the struggle against Johnson's disastrous policies:

"We ask workingmen to consider that this [Johnson's] plan will degrade black labor and cheapen it, and will consequently cheapen white labor....Put the black laborer in a position to act like a *man,* and he will get a fair price for his work, in which case we will risk but that his white competitor will get a fair price too; but make a dog of him, and he'll get a dog's pay, and we white men, compete as best we may, will not get much better." [11]

Industry was moving to the South, the *Voice* argued, and it was vital to the northern workers that southern workers were paid a decent wage. If they worked for "serf's wages," the standards of the North would decline. Hence the rights of labor, North and South, had to be maintained. [12]

"The Negroes, by emancipation," it argued, "enter into the field of free labor, and become competitors with white workingmen. They must, therefore, on the principles of the workingmen's movement, be elevated to the intelligence and rights which white workingmen enjoy, so that they can co-operate with them, or they will operate against them by underworking. To secure that elevation the right of suffrage is indispensable.... If the workingmen have learned anything, it is that there can be no hope of their success but in union—the union of all who labor, and that intelligence is the first requisite to success. How mad and suicidal, then, to hold up one hand for the degradation of the Negro, while the other is raised for the elevation of the white laborer! Capital knows no difference between white and black laborers; and labor cannot make any, without undermining its own platform and tearing down the walls of its defence.

"The whole united power of labor is necessary to the successful resistance of the united power of capital. Otherwise, those left out of the union are forced, in self-defense, to take a position antagonistic to their brethren or class, and become co-operators with the enemy. If the Trades' Unions of white men exclude black men, black men are obliged to underwork, and thus injure the cause of the white men. On the same principle, it is a damage to the cause of white labor that black labor should be ignorant and degraded...." [13]

Some labor journals attacked the *Voice,* notably the *Detroit Daily Union,* which charged that if "Negro suffrage is agitated" the prejudices in the minds of workers would cause division and conflict. The *Voice* answered the charge: "We could certainly be tender of the people's prejudices, but as we have shown, we are engaged in a great work, in which the question of the Negro or manhood suffrage—of universal freedom, of consistent democracy—is fundamental and vital. We *must* teach truth—We *must* walk in the light or we are sure to stumble and come short of our aim." [14]

The majority of the workers did not agree with the *Voice.* Whether the economic life of the South was to be based on free labor or semi-serf labor did not concern them. Most workers still thought of Andrew Johnson as the poor tailor of Tennessee who had introduced a Homestead Bill in Congress in the 'fifties and fought for its passage in 1862. They hailed the presence in the White House of one who had been a worker, believing with the Philadelphia Trades' Assembly "that he will exercise the prerogatives of his office for the maintenance and advancement of the General Government, and *also for the benefit of the working classes.*" [15] Because Johnson was sympathetic to some of labor's demands, many workers were willing to overlook the fact that he was restoring the former slaveholders to political power. When Johnson ordered the adoption of the eight-hour day in the government printing office, the labor press hailed him as the champion of the working class who was helping "to free the white slaves of the North." His countermanding of an order of the War Department which had reduced the wages of its employees received praise from mass meetings of trade unions for having "again manifested his sympathy for the workingmen." The *National*

Workman gave him the following tribute, "All honor to the President for his practical sympathy with labor." [16]

At the same time workers were suspicious of the groupings in the alliance which were fighting Johnson's policies of Reconstruction. Most northern Abolitionists, unlike Wendell Phillips, were indifferent to the demands of organized labor, and particularly hostile to the eight-hour day. That the leading group in the democratic coalition was the industrial bourgeoisie was enough to alienate a large section of organized labor, for to many workers the immediate enemy was not the old slavocracy but the new one. "No sooner had the heroic devotion of the sons of toil been proven on a hundred battlefields," said the *Working-man's Advocate,* "no sooner had they vindicated the right of the Republic, by virtue of its bloody baptism, to take its rank among the nations of the earth, or the shackles been stricken from the limbs of the *colored* slaves of the South, than a hell-born plot to enslave the white mechanics of the North was concocted."

The strategy of the industrialists and financiers, it continued, was to divert the attention of the masses from the "struggle between capital and labor," and thus "distract the public mind from matters of vital importance to the toiling masses." Meanwhile the financiers and industrialists would continue their seizure of the public lands, and saddle an unjust monetary system on the nation. By the time the workingmen woke up and turned their attention from events in the South to developments in the North, the conspiracy would have succeeded, and instead of a Republic, America would be a land ruled by financial and industrial monarchists.[17] Labor leaders did not understand that unity with industrialists for a progressive national program did not require labor to abandon its independent economic struggles against them.

Labor's unclarity was reflected in Sylvis' opposition to the program of the Radical Republicans. While Sylvis was on an organizing tour through the South in 1869, the new Reconstruction governments were introducing public education, developing social legislation of great significance to the poor people, white as well as Negro, and in many other ways bringing a more democratic way of life to a region formerly controlled by a handful of wealthy aristocrats who had always been oblivious to the welfare of the masses. But in his dispatches to the *Workingman's Advocate,* Sylvis showed little understanding of the revolutionary changes occurring in the South, and expressed no sympathy for the Reconstruction policies of the Republican Party.[18]

Yet Sylvis understood that the Negroes had not been fully emancipated by the Civil War. "No man in America rejoiced more than I at the downfall of Negro slavery," he said in 1868, "but when the shackles fell from the hands of those four millions of blacks, it did not make them *free;* it simply transferred them from one condition of slavery to another; it placed them upon the platform of the white workingmen and made all slaves together. We are now all *one family of slaves together* and the [labor] reform movement is a second emancipation proclamation." The labor reform movement, according to Sylvis, was the new anti-slavery movement, and its objective was to abolish slavery "in every corner of our country." [19]

Sylvis believed that in an independent labor party lay the immediate future of the Negro people. But the former slaves refused to support a labor party that ignored their basic demands: the protection of political and civil rights, land distribution, and equal economic opportunities. Nor would they vote for a labor party when their votes were necessary for the victory of the Republican Party. For the Republican Party, despite its serious limitations, did at that time represent the future of the Negro people. A victory for the Democratic Party would have meant the loss of all the democratic gains they had already won.

Failing to see any difference between the two major parties, labor refused to support the revolutionary elements among the Radical Republicans. This policy weakened the Radical Republicans, made their alliance with the Negro people more unstable, and strengthened the enemies of labor. Had the labor movement and its allies among the western farmers continued to exert their influence upon the industrialists and financiers in the Republican Party, as they had done in the years before the Civil War, the overthrow of progressive governments in the South might never have occurred.

ORGANIZATION OF NEGRO WORKERS

Another obstacle to the necessary alliance between white and Negro labor was the hostility of organized white workers to Negroes already in industry in the North and to those who were now entering industry in large numbers. Negro mechanics had always been an important part of southern industry. It is estimated that in 1865 there were 100,000 Negro mechanics in the South as compared with 20,000 white mechanics. In the tobacco, brick-making and ship-caulking industries as well as in railroad construction and on the docks Negro workers were employed in large numbers. [20]

Conditions were different in the North; there the Negro workers formed but a small part of the working class. Once the war was over Negro workers came North in ever increasing numbers. Like their brothers who had preceded them during the war, they met with discrimination which barred their advance in the skilled trades. Many unions turned down their applications for membership, and not a few ordered their members to refuse to work in shops employing Negro mechanics. These discriminatory policies were carefully kept alive by propagandists who insisted that this migration would increase unemployment and that the Negro workers would reduce wage scales which were already declining.[21]

The Washington, D. C., local of the bricklayers union called a strike at the Navy Yard in 1869 because several Negro workers had been hired. Six members of the local were expelled because they had worked with Negro workers. One member of the union openly disagreed with this policy. "For my part," he declared, "I believe in elevating the Negro, not for his sake, but for our own, and if he goes forth and cannot get into a local union, he will go to work for any one at any price." [22] But this worker was the exception. "It will take time," said the *Workingman's Advocate* on December 11, 1869, "to eradicate the prejudices of the past; to overcome the feelings which, it may be, the teachings of a lifetime have inculcated."

The question of Negro labor was first raised by the National Labor Union in the "Address to Workingmen" issued just before the Chicago Convention in 1867. In this document Cameron brushed aside the objections of those who feared the prejudices of some of the members. He insisted that "delicate as the question may be ... it would be a sad dereliction to pass it by unnoticed." What is wanted, he continued, "is for every union to help inculcate the grand ennobling idea that the interests of labor are one; that there should be no distinction of race or nationality; no classification of Jew or Gentile, Christian or infidel; that there is one dividing line, that which separates mankind into two great classes, the class that labors and the class that lives by others' labor." [23]

A vigorous debate took place at the 1867 convention on the issue of organizing Negro workers. The discussion was on the report of the Committee on Colored Labor, headed by A. W. Phelps, whose own union, the New Haven Carpenters and Joiners, excluded Negroes. The report declared that it recognized the importance of the subject and the danger of Negro competition, but since the problem was "involved in so much mystery" it proposed that the question be referred to the next convention.

Trevellick and Sylvis disagreed, calling for the admission of Negroes into the labor movement because without such unity trade unions would be "killed off." Trevellick insisted that the Negro worker would be an asset to the trade union movement because he had "stood his ground nobly when a member of a trades' union." Van Dorn, representing the Boot and Shoemakers Union of Chicago, supported Trevellick and urged the admission of the "black worker as a duty to a common brotherhood."

Though the convention recommitted the report, the committee continued to evade the issue. Its final statement was that since the constitution did not specify that Negro workers could *not* belong to the National Labor Union, there really was no need to discuss the question.[24]

On August 7, 1867, the *Boston Daily Evening Voice* in its discussion of the whole convention paid particular attention to the debates on the admission of Negroes to the labor movement.

"The debate on the question of Negro labor was also very discreditable to a body of American labor reformers," it declared. "The question should not have come up at all, any more than the question of red-headed labor, or blue-eyed labor. Of course, the Negro has the same right to work and pursue his happiness that the white man has; and of course, if the white man refuses to work with him, or to give him an equal chance, he will be obliged, in self-defence, to underbid the white, and it is a disgrace to the Labor Congress that several members of that body were so much under the influence of the silliest and wickedest of all prejudices as to hesitate to recognize the Negro. When we need to get rid of prejudices and learn to take catholic views, they have nailed their prejudices on to this platform. We shall never succeed till wiser counsels prevail and these prejudices are ripped up and thrown to the wind."

At the 1868 convention the problem was again evaded, but a new factor was emerging which made further evasion impossible. Negro workers were forming their own associations and were engaged in militant strikes.* In 1867 a wave of strikes swept the South. A strike on the levee in Mobile early in 1867 spread to other industries, resulting in some of the most stirring mass demonstrations of southern history. About the same time the Negro longshoremen in Charleston formed the Longshoremen's Protective Union Association and won their strike for higher wages. After the strike the Charleston *Daily News* referred

---

* In several cases white and Negro workers struck together. One observer wrote from New Orleans in 1865: "I thought it an indication of progress when the white laborers and Negroes on the levee the other day made a strike for higher wages. They were receiving $2.50 and $3.00 a day, and they struck for $5.00 and $7.00. They marched up the levee in a long procession, white and black together." (J. T. Trowbridge, *The South: A Tour of its Battlefields and Ruined Cities, etc.* Hartford, Conn., 1866, p. 405.) The strike was won after the workers were out for little more than two hours. It is significant to note that the strike was conducted by the Screwmen's Union of New Orleans, which before the war had refused to allow its members to work with Negroes.

to the association as the "most powerful organization of the colored laboring class in South Carolina." In February the dock workers of Savannah, Georgia, nearly all Negroes, won their strike to have the city council repeal a poll tax of $10 on all persons employed on the wharves.[25]

The *National Workman* of February 9, 1867, commented on the victory in Savannah: "This is not the first time since their Emancipation that they have resolutely asserted and vindicated their rights. The fact is the black man likes to be paid for his work just as well as the white man, and are rapidly learning how to secure their demands."

By 1869 the growth of Negro labor organization had been so rapid that there was a need for central bodies to unite the scattered locals. Hence, on July 19, 1869, the first state labor convention gathered in Baltimore. Delegates from the work benches and the trade unions throughout the state answered the call which had been posted in churches and printed in Negro newspapers.

Isaac Myers, a Baltimore caulker, explained in his welcoming address that the chief aim of the movement was to organize the Negro mechanics of Maryland. A state organization was necessary not only because many trade unions barred Negroes, but also because self-organization was the Negro mechanics' only hope for higher living standards. Myers concluded that only labor organization could preserve the power of their ballot. Out of this convention came a permanent organization, with Isaac Myers as its president, and representatives from each trade present constituting an executive board. This new central labor body was the dynamic center of organization for Negro workers throughout the nation.[26]

At the Baltimore convention the delegates had to make a far-reaching decision. Should they continue their struggle for admission, on equal terms, to the existing trade unions, or should they organize into separate trade unions? They decided to do both. Delegates were appointed to attend the convention of the National Labor Union in Philadelphia in August, and at the same time the organization issued a call for a national Negro labor convention to be held in Washington the following December.

Thus between the 1868 and 1869 conventions of the National Labor Union the Negro workers had organized on a wide scale, and by their successful struggles had proved that they were a necessary part of American trade unionism. In his letters to the *Workingman's Advocate* from various parts of the South, Sylvis wrote enthusiastically about the organization of Negro workers. He was convinced that "careful management, and a vigorous campaign, will unite the whole laboring population of the South, white and black, upon our platform." He regarded the winning of Negro support for the program of the National Labor Union as one of the major questions before the 1869 convention.

"If we can succeed in convincing these people," he wrote from Wilmington, North Carolina, "that it is in their interest to make common cause with us in these great national questions, we will have a power in this part of the country that will shake Wall Street out of its boots." [27]

Sylvis died before the 1869 convention of the National Labor Union, but the convention reflected the new trends he had discussed. Among the 142 delegates, nine were Negroes.* For the first time the National Labor Union adopted a plan for the organization of Negro workers. The resolution, introduced by Horace Day of New York, declared: "The National Labor Union knows no North, no South, no East, no West, neither color nor sex on the question of the rights of labor, and urges our colored fellow members to form organizations in all legitimate ways, and send their delegates from every state in the Union to the next congress." Not only was this resolution passed, but a special committee was appointed to "organize the colored men of Pennsylvania into labor unions." [28]

The convention listened intently to several speeches delivered by the Negro delegates. They heard Robert H. Butler of the Colored Engineers Association of Maryland say that Negro workers were not looking for "parlor sociabilities, but for the rights of mankind." They heard Isaac Myers, delegate from the Colored Caulkers Trade Union Society of Baltimore, deliver one of the most magnificent addresses ever made by an American trade unionist. He opened his address by paying tribute to the delegates for their awareness of the need for unity between Negro and white workers. "Silent, but powerful and far-reaching is the revolution inaugurated by your act in taking the colored laborer by the hand and telling him that his interest is common with yours." He then gave a brilliant analysis of the need for unity. "Slavery, or slave labor, the main cause of the degradation of white labor, is no more. And it is the proud boast of my life that the slave himself had a share in striking off the one end of the fetters that bound him by the ankle, and the other that bound you by the neck."

Negro workers, he continued, desired above all an equal opportunity to labor under conditions similar to those enjoyed by white workers.

* Five of the Negro delegates represented the United Laborers and Hod Carriers Association of Philadelphia. The others were: Isaac Myers of the Colored Caulkers' Trade Union Society of Baltimore, Ignatius Gross of the Colored Molders Union Society, Robert M. Butler of the Colored Engineers Association of Maryland, and James W. Hare of the Colored Painters' Society of Baltimore.

They wished to receive wages which would "secure them a comfortable living for their families, educate their children, and leave a dollar for a rainy day and for old age." And they were more than ready to offer full co-operation in the common struggle. It was true, he admitted, that such co-operation had not always been evident in the past, but this was because the workshops had been shut to the Negro, and trade unions had barred him from membership. Hence the Negro worker had been compelled to put his labor on the market for whatever he could secure. But all that was past. "We mean in all sincerity a hearty co-operation. . . . Where we have had the chance, we have always demonstrated it. We carry no prejudice. We are willing to let the dead past bury its dead." "Mr. President," he said in conclusion, "American citizenship for the black man is a complete failure if he is proscribed from the workshops of the country." [29]

The unity achieved at the convention stirred the Philadelphia correspondent of the *New York Times:*

"When a native Mississippian and an ex-confederate officer, in addressing a convention, refers to a colored delegate who has preceded him as 'the gentleman from Georgia,' when a native Alabamian, who has for the first time crossed the Mason and Dixon line, and who was from boyhood taught to regard the Negro simply as a chattel, sits in deliberate consultation with another delegate whose ebony face glistens with African sheen [sic], and signs the report of his colored co-delegate, when an ardent and Democratic partisan (from New York at that) declares with a 'rich Irish brogue' that he asks for himself no privilege as a mechanic or as a citizen that he is not willing to concede to every other man, white or black—when, I say, these things can be seen or heard at a national convention, called for any purpose, then one may indeed be warranted in asserting that time works curious changes.

"And all this was seen and heard in the City of Philadelphia during these August days in this year of grace 1869. Who shall say now, that prejudices, no matter how strongly they may have been implanted in the human breast, may not be rooted out?" [30]

The *Workingman's Advocate* called upon the labor movement to follow the example of the National Labor Union and put an end to the exclusion of Negroes from trade unions. Several organizations instantly responded. At a convention of the New York Workingmen's Assembly early in 1870, President Jessup lauded the actions of the Philadelphia Congress, and called upon the affiliated unions to organize colored workmen. The Negro workers, he said, would "no longer submit to occupy positions of inequality with the whites in the trades and professions." Several months later at the 1870 convention of the Carpenters and

Joiners National Union, President Phelps stressed the same theme, and called upon the delegates to repeal a resolution adopted the year before which pronounced it "inexpedient" to admit Negroes as members or to organize them under the National Union because of "the prejudice of many of our members against the colored people." "I think," said Phelps, "the time has arrived when we can no longer afford to shut out of our unions colored mechanics. We must all strike hands in a common cause." After some discussion, the convention resolved to invite all carpenters and joiners "no matter what may be the color of their skin," to form new local unions, and urged each existing local union "to admit such colored members as in their judgment they deem best." [31]

Few trade unions were willing to follow the carpenters and joiners. When the committee appointed by the Philadelphia Congress of the National Labor Union reported on its work it stated that many trade unions would not accept Negro mechanics, and proposed that Negroes be organized into "Jim Crow" locals. The International Typographical Union at its convention in 1869 had before it the case of Lewis Douglass, son of the Negro leader, Frederick Douglass. Lewis Douglass had been denied membership in the Washington branch of the Columbia Typographical Union. Several delegates denounced this action as contrary to the principles of the union. And though a counter-resolution objecting to the admission of any Negro into the organization was defeated by a vote of 57 to 38, the convention sustained the action of the Columbia Union.[32] Again at the 1870 convention the Douglass case came before the convention, where a committee was appointed to bring in recommendations on the admission of colored printers. All that the committee would report was that it regretted that the Negro question had ever been introduced into the union. They did, however, recommend that the question of admitting or rejecting colored printers be left entirely in the hands of the locals.[33]

Referring to the Douglass case, the *Printers' Circular,* organ of the Typographical Union, declared, "That there are deep-seated prejudices against the colored race no one will deny; and these prejudices are so strong in many local unions that any attempt to disregard or override them will almost inevitably lead to anarchy and disintegration ... and surely no one who has the welfare of the craft at heart will seriously contend that the union of thousands of white printers should be destroyed for the purpose of granting a barren honor of membership to a few Negroes." [34]

This capitulation set a pattern for other unions in which the Negro workers were not so few in number, and the *National Anti-Slavery Standard* reported that some local unions in New York were inserting the word, *white,* in all places where the character of the members was described. [35]

NEGRO LABOR CONVENTIONS OF 1869

The Negro workers were not content to praise the unions which were admitting colored workers, nor to condemn those which still clung to ancient prejudices. A national congress had been called for December by the Maryland State Convention of Negro Workers. The object of the convention was to "consolidate the colored workingmen of the several states to act in co-operation with our white fellow workingmen in every state and territory of the Union, who are opposed to distinction in the apprenticeship laws on account of color, and to so act co-operatively until the necessity for separate organization shall be deemed unnecessary." [36]

Of all the conventions held in various states to elect delegates and prepare a program, the most advanced was the one held in Columbia, South Carolina, on November 25, 1869. Among the delegates were wage laborers from plantations, sharecroppers, and urban mechanics and laborers. A number of delegates from colored labor unions were also present. Although Negro political leaders attended the convention, it did not concentrate on party politics. Instead the convention devoted itself to determining "how the laboring men, the producers of wealth of the State, those on whom the whole people must depend for their prosperity, may be secured in their rights and advanced in their social and material interests." A printed circular was distributed to the delegates listing the questions they would be called upon to discuss: What were the wages in the various counties, and what wages should be paid? What share of the crop was received by the sharecroppers, and what share should they receive? How did the planters treat the laborers, and what should be done to prevent planters from defrauding their workers?

Discussion revealed shocking conditions and showed why the organization of Negro toilers was imperative. Many employers, said the delegates, refused to pay their laborers wages, and others cheated their workmen in every way. One delegate reported: "Our people cannot buy decent clothing, nor buy medicine, nor send children to school. The planter says, when the crop is gathered, 'Now, I get two-thirds—you get one-third. You owe me so much, and so much, and this comes out of your third.' And then the man has left but two or three dollars. The magistrates do not do justice. The white men swindle and swindle, and the magistrates say the white man is right every time. We cannot get justice."

The delegate from the powerful Colored Longshoremen's Protective Union answered the question, "What can and ought to be done to prevent these wrongs?" by advising Negro laborers everywhere "to form unions and insist on an advance of wages." Through organization, he said, the Negro longshoremen of Charleston had secured a large advance of wages, and their experience had proved that to "secure increased wages there must be organization and united action." Once unions were formed, it was necessary to press for chartered rights and laws to protect labor organizations. This proposal was applauded, and a committee was appointed to set up unions in the various counties. During this discussion a communication was received from white laborers in Edgefield county, expressing sympathy with the objectives of the convention and the plan to organize unions in the counties. They hoped that the measures adopted by the convention "would benefit all classes of laborers."

Before the convention adjourned a Committee on Permanent Organization and delegates to the National Colored Labor Convention were appointed. In response to the criticism that there were no trade unionists among the officers of the Permanent Organization, those men already nominated withdrew and names of men "now actually engaged in farming or in some mechanical occupation" were substituted. I. F. Clark, president of the Colored Longshoremen's Protective Association of Charleston, was elected vice-president of the new organization. "The longshoremen," said the delegate who made the nomination, "are the pioneers in this great labor movement, and well deserve the honor." [37]

Because the working class delegates could not afford the trip to Washington, the representatives to the National Colored Labor Convention were almost all political leaders and lawyers. Only nine of the fifty-four delegates from the South who attended the first National Colored Labor Convention in Washington on December 5, 1869, were workers; the rest were lawyers, preachers, teachers, and merchants. But some of the northern delegates were truly representative of Negro labor. The delegates from New York City had been elected at a meeting held early in November at Zion Church, at which were represented 400 waiters, 7 basket-makers, 32 tobacco twisters, 50 barbers, 22 cabinet-makers and carpenters, 14 masons and bricklayers, 2 rollers, 6 molders, 24 printers, 50 engineers and 500 longshoremen. [38]

THE NATIONAL COLORED LABOR UNION

Although non-working class delegates were in the majority at the Washington Convention, it fulfilled the *New York Tribune's* prediction of November 26, 1869, that it would be the "largest in point of numbers, influence and intelligence of any similar body of colored men, ever assembled in this country." Samuel P. Cummings, leader of the Knights of St. Crispin and one of the white delegates to the convention, described for the *American Workman* the ability and the understanding displayed by men "who ten years ago were slaves on the plantations of the South." The convention proved, he stated, that the day was not far distant when the Negro workers would join their white brothers "in all honest efforts to make the interests of labor the paramount interest in our legislation, state and national." [39]

Isaac Myers' efforts to gear the congress to trade union issues was not entirely successful. A debate developed over the question of admitting delegates who held credentials from the Massachusetts Labor Reform Party. J. M. Langston, a prominent Negro lawyer and Republican Party leader, opposed their admission, charging that they were plotting to break up the Republican Party. Should they be allowed to advocate the cause of a labor party at the convention, he argued, the body might desert the Republican Party and thus turn it against the Negro people.

Langston's views were not shared by all the delegates, some of whom rebuked him "for denouncing white delegates because of color." The credentials of the delegates were received. George T. Downing, the acting chairman, reminded Langston that while the Republican Party deserved respect and support for its part in overthrowing slavery, it was by no means above reproach. "We think it should have been more consistent," he continued, "more positive in its dealings with our and the country's enemies. ... We should be secured in the soil, which we have enriched in our toil and blood, and to which we have a double entitlement." [40]

Despite the advice of the *Workingman's Advocate* to break their ties with bogus politicians and co-operate with the National Labor Reform Party, the platform of the convention was silent on the question of independent labor action and concentrated on the problem of discrimination and exclusion from the trades and workshops. Discrimination was branded by the convention as an "insult to God, an injury to us, and a disgrace to humanity." [41] Co-operative Negro workshops were proposed as a remedy against the "exclusion of our people from other workshops on account of color." The platform also endorsed a liberal immigration policy, but denounced the importation of Chinese labor as "slavery in a new form." Negro workers were urged to seek education, to avoid the "evil of intemperance," and to form workingmen's associations in every state. [42]

Isaac Myers was elected president of the National Colored Labor Union whose structure closely resembled the National Labor Union to which it had voted affiliation. An executive committee, the National Bureau of Labor, with its headquarters in Washington, was to lead the national body between annual elections. It was to meet once a month, had power to grant charters to various organizations in different states, and with the president was empowered to "advise and superintend the organization of labor unions, land, loan, building and co-operative associations generally in the different states." The Bureau of Labor was also responsible to "give especial attention to protecting the rights of the workingmen of the various organizations chartered by the National Labor Union by bringing about such legislation in the several states as may be necessary for the interest and advancement of the condition of the laboring classes." [43]

In February, 1870, the Bureau issued a prospectus containing the chief demands of the Negro people; it called for a legislative lobby to fight for legislation which would gain equality before the law for Negroes; it proposed an educational campaign to overcome the opposition of white mechanics to Negroes in the trades; it recommended co-operatives and homesteads to the Negro people.

A vigorous campaign was organized by the National Colored Labor Union to win these demands. Its official newspaper, the *New National Era,* popularized the program, and constantly stressed the need for the organization of Negro labor, often sponsoring labor meetings. Isaac Myers went on a tour of the South to organize local associations of Negro workers, while Sella Martin was elected the delegate of the National Colored Labor Union to the Congress of the First International to be held in Paris.

Speaking in Washington on April 11, 1870, Myers told an audience of Negro workers that unless they organized they would be soon ousted from the skilled trades and left as "servants, the sweepers of shavings, the scrapers of pitch, and carriers of mortars." A week later in Norfolk, Virginia, he urged the organization of white and Negro workingmen in the same unions. The day had passed, he said, "for the establishment of organizations based upon color. We are organized for the interest of the workingmen, white and colored, and to do this, let the officers be composed of both white and colored men." * Wherever he went on his organizing tour, Myers appealed to the Negro workers to join trade unions and to establish co-operative associations. On more than one occasion white as well as Negro workers came to listen to the militant leader of the National Colored Labor Union.[44]

These activities were hailed by the *Workingman's Advocate* as the "grand inaugural movement ... to consolidate the colored element of the Southern states" which would "ultimately have but one result—a

---

* D. Collins, a white labor leader, also addressed the meeting, declaring that "if the laboring society was established ... wages would be much better for both white and colored." (*Norfolk Journal,* reprinted in *New National Era,* April 28, 1870.)

clear alliance with, and an endorsement of the principles of the National Labor Union." [45] However, the difficulties that stood in the way of this clear alliance were not overcome. The controversy started by Langston at the first convention of the National Colored Labor Union to bar the seating of white delegates boomeranged at the 1870 congress of the National Labor Union when four Negro delegates presented their credentials: Isaac Myers; Josiah Weare, of the United Hod-Carriers and Laborers' Association of Philadelphia; Peter Clark of the Colored Teachers Co-operative Association of Cincinnati, Ohio, and John M. Langston.

No sooner were their names announced than objections were raised to seating Langston. Alexander H. Troup, treasurer of the National Typographical Union and the Boston Workingmen's Assembly, and Samuel P. Cummings of the Knights of St. Crispin, led the movement. Their opposition to Langston was purely a political one, and both made it clear that they were opposed to Langston's admission because they believed that his sole purpose was to influence the session in behalf of the Republican Party, and that he had done his best at the Negro Labor Congress to create division between black and white workers. After considerable discussion, which proved that the objection was political and not racial, Langston was denied a seat by a vote of 49 to 23.

When the resolution for a third national political party came up, Isaac Myers opposed it, with the defense that the Republican Party was the friend of white and colored workers while the Democratic Party was the foe of the entire working class. "While the Republican Party is not the beau ideal of our notion of a party," he said, "the interests of workingmen demand that they shall not hazard its success either by the organization of a new party or by an affiliation with the Democratic Party." Since legislation for the benefit of the working class could only be obtained through the Republican Party, he declared, the National Labor Union would serve the working people best by affiliating with the Republican Party. [46]

The resolution for a Labor Party was carried, and the platform stated that "inasmuch as both the present political parties are dominated by the non-producing classes, the highest interest of our colored fellow-citizens is with the workingmen, who, like themselves, are slaves of capital and politicians." But as the same platform ignored their basic demands, the Negro people continued their support of the Republican Party. The action of the National Labor Union convention in endorsing a Labor Party marked the end of unity between the two national organizations of labor. At its next convention the Negro Labor Congress separated from the National Labor Union and proclaimed its allegiance to the Republican Party.

The call to this convention, published in the *New National Era* of November 17, 1870, was directed "To the Colored Workingmen of the United States, Trades, Labor and Industrial Unions."[47] In his opening address, Myers stated that Negroes did not desire a separate union based on color, and reaffirmed his belief that the "condition of the white laborers will be mutually advanced by co-operation with the colored laborers." Little was done at the convention to further labor unity other than instructing delegates from the southern states to organize labor unions. The major emphasis was on political questions, and the election of Frederick Douglass as president of the congress was another proof that the National Colored Labor Union was rapidly becoming an appendage to the Republican Party.[48]

Nevertheless, the activities of the organization after the convention proved that the domination of the non-labor elements did not mean that the movement had lost its interest in economic problems. Several unions were formed in the South and there were struggles for wage increases. In March, 1871, state officers of the Labor Union called a convention to form a Laborers Union Association of the state of Texas.* Workers of both races met in convention at Houston on June 8. Similar conventions were held in Tennessee, Alabama, Georgia, and Missouri, but none of these led to the forming of permanent labor organization.

In several communities the Labor Union stimulated Negro and white workers to form a number of local unions which won several strikes. It helped to organize the Longshoremen's Association, No. 1, of Baltimore on June 26, 1871. A committee of the Labor Union had led the struggle of these Negro longshoremen to secure a wage increase and improvements in working conditions. It sent a petition to the Master Stevedores asking them to advance wages from twenty to twenty-five cents an hour, "the present rates being insufficient to support ourselves and families." Their demands were granted by the Master Stevedores, and an agreement was signed.[49]

Had the National Colored Labor Union combined its political activities with these daily struggles of the Negro masses, it would have become a great force in the nation, but Isaac Myers gradually receded into the background and Frederick Douglass soon became the spokesman of the movement. He stressed only the need to support the Republican Party, calling it the "true workingmen's party of the country." † [50]

---

* The call went in part: "All are alike interested in this great work—the white man as well as the black. Ours is a common interest, and the sickly sentimentality which induces distinctions by reason of color, in this great work is entirely ignored. There is labor sufficient for all, and all are invited to attend." (*New National Era,* May 11, 1871.)

† Douglass spoke and wrote frequently in support of labor's demands for shorter hours and higher wages, but his bitterness over the refusal of many trade unions

The efforts to build a solid alliance between white and Negro workers in the years immediately following the Civil War ended in defeat. The leaders of the National Labor Union and Negro labor leaders like Isaac Myers understood the significance of the issues at stake. But the constituent local unions and trades' assemblies often refused to apply the progressive steps taken at the conventions of the National Labor Union. Moreover, the leaders themselves were not mature enough to understand the special problems brought to them by the Negro people. But they understood that until they could help solve these problems the American labor movement could not rise to its full stature. The *Workingman's Advocate* put it succinctly on May 7, 1870: "We firmly and honestly believe that the success of the labor movement for years to come depends on the co-operation and success of the colored race.... Their interests are our interests; our interests are theirs."

---

to permit Negro workers to join their ranks, and his belief that an independent labor party would injure the Negro people by helping to defeat the Republican Party, turned him against the unions. But he understood that the future of Negro workers was closely connected with that of the entire working class. "Their cause," he declared in 1883, "is one with the labor classes all over the world. The labor unions of the country should not throw away this colored element of strength.... It is a great mistake for any class of laborers to isolate itself and thus weaken the bond of brotherhood between those on whom the burden and hardships of labor fall. The fortunate ones of the earth, who are abundant in land and money and know nothing of the anxious care and pinching poverty of the laboring classes, may be indifferent to the appeal for justice at this point, but the laboring classes cannot afford to be indifferent. ... Experience demonstrates that there may be a slavery of wages only a little less galling and crushing in its effects than chattel slavery, and that this slavery of wages must go down with the other." (*Address to the People of the United States, Delivered at a Convention of Colored Men, Louisville, Kentucky, September 24, 1883*, pp. 12-13.)

CHAPTER 20

The Labor Movement, 1866-1872

(*Concluded*)

The same period which saw the first attempt in our country of an alliance of workers irrespective of their sex or color also witnessed an advance in international labor solidarity. The European workers' heroic support of the American Union during the Civil War initiated this trend. After the war the magnificent struggles of European workers, ably led and inspired by the International Working Men's Association, were reported in the American labor press. *Fincher's Trades' Review* featured reports of "the working of Labor Reform in the older countries of the world,"[1] and announced on April 8, 1865, that it would begin publishing extracts from foreign labor publications in the hope that its "exertions" would "eventually secure a *grand union of the working trades of the world.*"

INTERNATIONAL LABOR UNITY

The *Workingman's Advocate* carried a column in each issue with the heading "From the Old World: Progress of the Labor Movement." At the start of the Franco-Prussian War, this paper printed the full text of the September 8, 1870, address of the International Working Men's Association drafted by Karl Marx.[2] When Marx wrote *The Civil War in France,* originally an address to the General Council dealing with the Paris Commune, the *Advocate* reprinted it serially from July 15 to September 2, 1871. For an entire year beginning with the November 26, 1870, issue, this paper published a long series of articles by Wilhelm Liebknecht, German Socialist deputy and member of the First International. The activities of the American section of the International were also followed, and letters written by F. A. Sorge, its secretary, appeared frequently in its pages. Although A. C. Cameron did not support affiliation of the National Labor Union to the First International, his paper helped to create sentiment for such a step in American trade union circles.

The *National Workman,* organ of the New York Working Men's Assembly, devoted much space to news of European labor affairs, and the decisions of the General Council were always fully reported.[3] Nor was the *Arbeiter Union,* organ of the General German Working Men's Association, formed by German Socialist trade unionists in New York, without influence. Many of its articles and editorials relating to international labor were translated and reprinted in other labor papers. This paper, ably edited by Adolph Douai, a leading American Marxist, constantly stressed the need for international labor unity: "The solidarity of the working classes of both hemispheres has long been evident. The sufferings of one are the sufferings of the other, and there are common causes for the suffering of both." [4]

It was mainly through the influence of the leaders of the German socialist trade unions, all of whom were outstanding figures in the American labor movement, that men like Sylvis, Trevellick, and Jessup became aware of the International Working Men's Association and understood the need for international labor unity. Sylvis declared again and again "that the interests of labor are identical throughout the world ... a victory to them will be a victory to us." John W. Browning, another leader of the National Labor Union, assured the Cuban people "that the American labor movement sympathized with them in their struggle for freedom." [5]

Both Sylvis and Jessup helped cement international labor solidarity within their own trades. Sylvis corresponded with leaders of the molders' unions in England, Ireland, Scotland, and Wales with a view to halting the importation of strike-breakers, and checking the emigration of molders sponsored by the American Emigrant Company. Unable to obtain such co-operation, Sylvis appealed directly to the members of these unions. In a circular issued for distribution in England and Scotland he warned them that the stories circulated by the Emigrant Company concerning their opportunities in America were false. Although nothing definite emerged from these efforts, the experience convinced Sylvis "that international labor unity must be effective and that united action on all matters concerning labor must be achieved." Such unity, he was certain, would destroy the power of the capitalists "to supplant working men struggling for their rights in one portion of the world by the importation of help from another." International solidarity of labor, he predicted, "could build up a power that would defy the world." [6] In a reply to a communication from William J. Jessup, secretary of the New York Ship Joiners' Association, R. Applegarth, secretary of the London Society of Carpenters and Joiners, suggested an amalgamation with the

London Society. "Our objects and yours are identical. Our sympathies would naturally be the same." He reminded Jessup that the Amalgamated Society of Engineers in England had branches in several American communities.

The *National Workman,* on printing Applegarth's letter, approved of his proposal for an international union, and urged the New York Ship Joiners to accept the invitation. Such international affiliations, it stated, would end the competition of foreign workers fostered by employers. Capitalists, it went on, had agents working for them in other countries. Why then should not working men unite in the same way? [7]

Affiliation of American labor with European labor was again brought up at the founding congress of the National Labor Union in 1866. The request to send a delegate to the Geneva Congress of the First International was turned down because there was not time enough to send a delegate. However, the congress wished them "Godspeed in their glorious work." A year later, at the 1867 congress, affiliation with the International was an important issue. President William J. Jessup moved to affiliate and was supported by Sylvis. Although the congress voted against affiliation, it decided to send Richard F. Trevellick to the next congress of the International,* and adopted a resolution promising its co-operation to the organized workingmen of Europe in their struggle against political and social wrongs. [8]

Two events in the years immediately following strengthened the possibilities of an alliance between the National Labor Union and the International Working Men's Association. In April, 1869, the General Council of the International received a communication from the New York Compositors Union requesting its help in checking the importation of European strikebreakers. The Council voted to aid the union. This action aroused great respect in American trade union circles for the International. Another display of international solidarity arose that same year when the dispute over the "Alabama Claims" † threatened war between the United States and Great Britain. The Address of the General Council, written by Marx and addressed to Sylvis as president of the National Labor Union, said in part:

"Yours is the glorious task of seeing to it that at last the working class shall enter upon the scene of history, no longer as a servile following but as an independent power, as a power imbued with a sense of

* Trevellick was unable to collect enough money to make the trip.

† The "Alabama Claims" involved American grievances against Great Britain during and just after the Civil War, especially the losses caused by the Confederate vessel, the *Alabama,* fitted out in Liverpool. The controversy was settled by the Treaty of Washington signed May 8, 1871.

its responsibility and capable of commanding peace where their would-be masters cry war."

In his response, Sylvis said that labor's struggle was a common one the world over. In behalf of the working people of the United States, he extended the right hand of fellowship to the International and "to all the downtrodden and oppressed sons and daughters of toiling Europe." [9]

The death of Sylvis in 1869 was a great blow to international labor unity.* After his death, the National Labor Union at its 1869 convention, voted to send a delegate to attend the Basle Congress of the International. In the fall of that year, A. C. Cameron, the delegate selected, made the trip to Europe with funds advanced by Horace Day, the currency reformer, who was assuming a leading role in the National Labor Union. Cameron brought back several proposals made by the International for united action with the National Labor Union. One proposal called for the establishment of an Emigrant Bureau by both organizations which would correspond with trade unions and emigrant associations in Europe, obtain and forward information on the conditions of labor and the existence of strikes, "and otherwise aid the one high purpose of all who work for our reform . . . that of the complete unity and enfranchisement of labor everywhere." Another proposal provided that the General Council of the International should "endeavor to prevent workmen being engaged in Europe to be used by American capitalists against the workmen of America." [10]

These proposals were well received by the 1870 congress but it voted against affiliation. Cameron's report influenced many delegates to vote against affiliation because he placed great importance on the differences between American and European labor. The program of the International was more advanced than anything advocated by an American trade

* Among the letters of mourning which poured into the National Labor Union upon the news of Sylvis' death was the following from the General Council of the International Workingmen's Association, dated August 18, 1869, signed by Karl Marx and other leaders of the International.

"The sad tidings that death has so unexpectedly and prematurely removed your honored and able President, William H. Sylvis, a loyal, persevering and inde-fatigable worker in the good cause among you, have filled us with indefatigable grief and sorrow. The great brotherhood and sisterhood of toil can but ill afford to lose such tried champions in the bloom of life as him whose loss we mourn in common. But though able counsellors and tried leaders are not over abundant, we find consolation in the knowledge that there are others in your ranks willing and able to serve you in his stead and with the same zeal and devotion. We are reassured that your present session will select the right men for the right place and make arrangements that will enable you to continue the great struggle with-out any interruption and insure its success." (*Workingman's Advocate,* Sept. 18, 1869.)

union. This, said Cameron, was understandable i*ı* light of the "institutions and state of society in Europe [which] are a legitimate offspring— the inevitable offshoot of despotism." In America the situation was altogether different; here the evils were due not to the nature of the government, but to bad administration. In Europe a revolutionary change was necessary, while in America all that was required was "a just administration of the fundamental principles upon which the government is founded." Hence the methods employed by the International, though necessary in Europe, "could not and did not apply to the state of affairs existing in our country."[11]

Sylvis had also recognized that conditions in Europe were quite different from those in America. But he knew that essentially "the war of poverty against wealth" was the same the world over; that the proposals of the International Working Men's Association for co-operation with the National Labor Union were based upon issues which concerned American workers as much as those in Europe. He believed, therefore, that affiliation with the International would strengthen the National Labor Union.*

The closest the National Labor Union came to joining the International was a resolution passed at the 1870 convention which asserted: "The National Labor Union declares its adherence to the principles of the International Working Men's Association, and expects to join the said association in a short time."[12] The expectation was never realized.

THE FIRST INTERNATIONAL IN AMERICA

American sections of the International Working Men's Association were organized by Socialist groups in this country. In October, 1867, the Communist Club of New York founded by F. A. Sorge, Conrad Carl, and Siegfried Meyer in 1857, became a section of the International in America. By 1872, there were about thirty sections and five thousand members of the First International in the United States. Sections were formed in Chicago, San Francisco, Washington, D. C., New Orleans, Newark, Springfield, and New York City. Among the New York sections, one was French, one Bohemian, four German, and two native American. The majority of the membership in America, observed F. A. Sorge, were "plain wage workers and handicraftsmen of every possible trade." †[13]

---

* For an interesting analysis of similarities between the International and the National Labor Union, see George Wilkes, *The Internationale: Its Principles and Purposes,* New York, 1871, p. 5.

† The records of the Philadelphia section give an interesting picture of its membership composition. This section was formed on October 9, 1871, by "a few of

In 1869, the powerful German General Working Men's Union became Section 1 of New York. Founded in this city in October, 1865, by fourteen Lassalleans, its first constitution stated that its founders regarded Ferdinand Lassalle "as the most eminent champion of the working class, for the purpose of reaching a true point of view on all social questions." †￼ In keeping with his philosophy, the constitution declared that "the effective and intelligent use of the ballot ... will eventually lead to the emancipation of the working people from the yoke of capital." Evidently the Union took its Lassalleanism lightly, for it was criticized by the General Workingmen's Union in Germany, a Lassallean organization, for being too Marxist. In 1868 the union and the Communist Club merged, and the Social Party of New York and Vicinity was formed. Sorge became its president.

Early in 1869, the Social Party was admitted to the National Labor Union as Labor Union No. 5 of New York. Its delegates were present at

---

those who toil by day for food, raiment and shelter for themselves and families." Among the founders were a shoemaker, a weaver, a clerk, a teacher, a photolithographer, two tailors, a machinist, a manufacturer, a doctor, a civil engineer, a seamstress, and a milliner. The members of the section from its organization to January, 1873, consisted of seven machinists, five shoemakers, six physicians, a civil engineer, a coachmaker, a medical instrument maker, a harness maker, an architect, a manufacturer, a tailor, a dentist, a brass worker, two law students, a sculptor, two carpenters, a house painter (eighty years old), a purifier of oil, a stonecutter, a bookkeeper, an artist, a hatter, a pyrotechnist, two dealers, a watchmaker, a teacher, a housekeeper, a cabinet maker, a builder, a photographer, two printers, a seamstress, an attorney-at-law, two bricklayers, and a shoe tool manufacturer. (*Minute Book of Section 26 of Philadelphia of the International Workingmen's Association*, October 9, 1871-January, 1873, Mss Wisconsin State Historical Society.)

† Ferdinand Lassalle, German Socialist labor leader, played a prominent part in the founding of the *Allgemeine Deutsche Arbeiterverein* (General Association of Gorman Workers), organized on May 23, 1863. In his *Open Letter to the Workers' Committee of the Leipzig Workers' Association,* which he had written in February, 1863, Lassalle laid down the two main demands of the Association: universal suffrage and state credits for producers' co-operatives. His absorption in political action and his theory of the "iron law of wages," namely, that the worker receives, on the average, only the *minimum* wage, because there are always too many workers, led him to ignore economic struggles and the trade union organization of wage earners. Political action, he believed, would solve the problems of the working class, for through it the workers could compel the government to help them by granting them capital or credit with which they might organize producers' co-operatives. Lassalle's historical service, wrote Marx, was that he "reawakened the workers' movement in Germany after its fifteen years of slumber," and Lenin observed that Lassalle's main contribution was that he "converted the working class from an appendage of the liberal bourgeisie into an independent political party." But Marx, Engels, and Lenin showed that Lassalle was forced into serious concessions to Prussian reaction, and weakened the trade union organization of the working class. (See Karl Marx and Frederick Engels: *Selected Correspondence, 1846-1895,* New York, 1942, pp. 82-83, 146-52, 193-97, 250-51, 332-39.)

the 1869 and 1870 conventions, but after the latter congress the organization withdrew in order to concentrate on the American sections.[14]

In December, 1870, three New York sections formed a provisional central committee for the United States, with F. A. Sorge as its secretary. A few months later, in May, 1871, ten sections were represented in the central committee, eight from New York and two from Chicago. The committee, officially called the North American Central Committee of the International Working Men's Association, issued several addresses to trade unions and labor societies in the United States inviting them to affiliate. To become affiliated, the trade union or labor society had to acknowledge and defend the principles of the International Workingmen's Association, and remit annual dues of two cents per member for the General Council and five cents per member for the Central Committee. The program stressed the fact that the economic emancipation of the working classes was "the great end to which every political movement ought to be subordinate as a means." The failure hitherto to achieve this end was due to "the want of solidarity between the manifold divisions of labor in each country and from the absence of a fraternal bond of union between the working classes of different countries." [15]

Not many trade unions responded to these invitations to affiliate. Replies came, however, from middle class reformers, a fact which fostered internal dissensions within the American section of the International, and forced the Central Committee to devote much time to their solution. Sorge had his hands full trying to expel Victoria Woodhull and Tennessee Claflin, two ardent women suffragists and preachers of free love, who with members of the defunct New Democracy or Political Commonwealth, an organization of American intellectuals who advocated voluntary socialism to be achieved by a referendum, organized in the summer of 1871 Section No. 12 in New York City.

Sorge and other Marxists championed the cause of woman suffrage, but were opposed to intellectual reformers who insisted on "intruding themselves into the ranks of labor either for intellectual purposes or for advancing some hobbies of their own by the aid of the working people." *

---

* Sorge and other Marxists were especially enraged by the publication of a denunciation of Marx and a distortion of Marxism in *Woodhull & Claflin's Weekly*, organ of Section 12. "Your paper," wrote Sorge to the editors, "professedly sustains the I.W.A., and is read by a not inconsiderable number of members and friends of the International." Hence it should not "give publicity . . . to anything regarding the International Workingmen's Association except authentic information." (*Woodhull & Claflin's Weekly*, September 23, 1871.)

Although this paper did contain some news of importance to labor and the Internationals, the bulk of the space was devoted to lengthy discussions of Free Love, Sexual Freedom, Spiritualism, Universological Science, and similar questions. (See issues of February 11, 1871, and April 18, 1874.)

Sorge wrote the General Council: "The intention of politicians and others is now pretty clear—to identify the I.W.A. in this country with the woman's suffrage, free love, and other movements, and we will have to struggle hard for clearing ourselves from these imputations." [16]

Due to Sorge's skillful leadership, Section 12 and other American sections dominated by middle-class reformers were expelled by the General Council in London. In July, 1872, after a special committee appointed by the Council to investigate affairs in America had voted to order the expulsion of Section 12, a meeting of the American section in Philadelphia declared themselves in complete harmony with the General Council. The expulsion of the intellectual reformers put new life into the American sections. "The ground is prepared," said the Federal Council of the American sections in 1873, "for cultivation and it is now the duty of the pioneers of the labor movement, not to waste time and work, as often has been done, in experiments or odious quarrels, but to organize the workingmen as a class, and to create that class feeling, which never will allow the laborer to leave the organization out which leads to the great aim of the International Workingmen's Association—the Emancipation of Labor." [17]

The influence of the early Marxian groups organized into the American sections of the International far outweighed their number. The Provisional Central Committee established close relations with the New York State Workingmen's Assembly and with the Miners' Benevolent and Protective Association of Pennsylvania. Section 1 of New York appointed a special committee in October, 1869, to organize trade unions among Negro workers, and several weeks later gained the admittance of these Negro labor unions to the Workingmen's Union, the central labor body of New York City.[18]

The American sections organized mass meetings to welcome the Fenian leader, O. Donovan Rossa, when he came here in 1871 to organize support for Irish freedom. They sponsored demonstrations in support of the Communards in Paris, and after the Commune was defeated extended their welcome to the fugitive Communards. When the International marched in the eight-hour parade held in New York on September 13, 1871,* they were greeted everywhere along the line with cries of *"vive la Commune."* On December 18, 1871, a number of leading trade unions in

---

* In April, 1873, the Federal Council of the American Federation of the International Workingmen's Association sponsored a meeting of trade unions in New York to devise steps for the enforcement of the eight-hour law. The meeting, attended by fifteen unions, set up the Eight-Hour Enforcement League. (See Call for the meeting in *Papers of the Philadelphia Section of the American Federation of the International Workingmen's Association,* Mss., Wisconsin State Historical Society, and *New York Sun,* Apr. 23, 1873.)

New York joined in a demonstration with the American sections to protest the execution of three prominent Communards. On these occasions, Negro workingmen marched in a contingent of the International.[19]

During the unemployed struggles after the panic of 1873, as we shall see below, the International was the organizing center. Thus, in spite of the failure of the National Labor Union to affiliate with the International Workingmen's Association, this movement made its influence felt in the ranks of the American working class.

THE CO-OPERATIVE MOVEMENT

At the early conventions of the National Labor Union, the eight-hour day, organization of Negro workers, woman's rights, and international labor unity were the important issues. But as the employers' offensives during and after the Civil War increased, a number of leading trade unionists, including William H. Sylvis, concluded that the newly arisen trade unions could not by themselves solve the problems of the working class. Trade unions, they argued, could not halt the increasing use of machinery which was displacing skilled workers. Nor could trade unions maintain wage standards, for employers were constantly reducing wages, and the unions were forced just as constantly to strike. But strikes, went the argument, did not solve the problem. Even when they were successful, strikes only provided a temporary relief since employers soon robbed them of their gains. Certainly the misery accompanying even a successful strike was not compensated for by the meager returns of victory. Neither trade unions nor strikes would enable workers to halt their degradation under the wage system or to attain permanent security.[20] *

A new weapon had to be found that would enable workers to meet the counter-offensive and put an end to labor's degradation by opening the way for its elevation to its rightful place in society. That weapon was co-operation. As the *Printers' Circular* emphasized: Co-operatives were "the only true protection which the working man has against the overshadowing influence of capital." [21] As in the 'forties and 'fifties, two types

* The disastrous set-backs suffered by the Molders in 1867-68, when many strikes were lost, stimulated the movement for co-operatives. If this outstanding American trade union could barely survive the ferocious assaults of organized employers' associations, what could less powerful unions do? So, at least, many workers reasoned. Disillusionment with strikes as a major union tactic caused men like Sylvis to become disillusioned with trade unions altogether and to reach the conclusion that "no permanent reform can ever be established through the agency of trade unions. . . ." (*Workingman's Advocate*, December 12, 1868, February 13, July 3, 1869.) One should not overlook the influence of the Lassallean Socialists, who were not at all concerned with the building of strong trade unions, in causing several American labor leaders to change their objectives.

of co-operative enterprises were advocated: consumers' co-operatives and producers' co-operatives. Of what value were wage increases when the rise in the cost of living robbed the workingmen of their wages and forced them to borrow money to feed, clothe, and house their families? Only co-operative stores could solve this question. With the profits made through the co-operatives, associations of workingmen could buy co-operative workshops and factories.

Great importance was placed on these producers' co-operatives. Successful producers' co-operatives run by the trade unions would give them the necessary funds with which to meet the offensives of employers. They would be yardsticks for industry, and the employers would be forced to adopt the decent working standards instituted by the co-operatives. Moreover, they would prevent employers from discriminating against workers who were active trade unionists, for they would find it futile to persecute men who could find in co-operatives, "cities of refuge." Thus would the co-operative become the workers' "mailed fist," and employers could be told, in the language of one worker, "that if they did not change their policy they would be supplanted as manufacturers by the very men ... they had proposed to starve into submission." [22]

Co-operation, ran the theory, was more than a supplement to trade unionism; it was the lever through which the workers could be rendered "independent of the capitalist employer," and the present iniquitous system of wages that conceded the laborer "only so much of his own production as shall make comfortable living a bare possibility," and which made life a "ceaseless degradation, a daily martyrdom, a funeral march to the grave," would be abolished. It would bring in a new civilization in which "reason directed by moral principle" would prevail and a universal brotherhood of man would flourish. In the future society each worker would "have a comfortable home—a happy fireside—a competency for his family, the just fruits of his toil...." [23]

Discussion of co-operatives filled many columns of the labor press during the Civil War. Sylvis' discussions at molders' conventions of the importance of co-operation and his illustrations of what had been accomplished by the Rochdale Pioneers of England, were published in *Fincher's Trades' Review*. So too were the speeches and letters of Thomas Phillips, a Philadelphia shoemaker who was interested in the Rochdale experiment and in trade unionism. Although some co-operative stores based on the Rochdale plan were founded during the war years,* it was generally

---

* The Rochdale Society was organized by twenty-eight workers, active supporters of Owenism and Chartism, in 1844. In the beginning, its store was open two evenings a week and sold small stocks of groceries. Gradually other stores were founded, a federation organized, corn mills established and a wholesale society created. Although Rochdale was essentially an association of consumers, it also

agreed that the principles of co-operation would have to wait for victory.

Beginning with 1866 these principles were put into practice. During the next few years co-operative associations were established by unions of the bakers, coachmakers, collar-makers, molders, shipwrights, machinists and blacksmiths, ship-carpenters, caulkers, boiler makers, shoemakers, hatters, plumbers, tailors, printers, and seamstresses. Negro unionists entered the field of co-operation, seeing in it a solution to their exclusion from work-shops.[24] The most spectacular co-operative ventures organized during this period were set up by the Molders' Union. At its national convention in 1866 it endorsed the principle of co-operation and urged the local unions to form co-operative foundries. When in March, 1866, the iron foundry owners of Albany and Troy posted notices in their foundries announcing that they would not allow a union committee in the shops, and would introduce all the helpers and apprentices they desired, the Troy union retaliated by organizing a co-operative foundry. With the assistance of William Sylvis, the local issued subscriptions for stock, raised twenty-six thousand dollars, purchased real estate, and opened shop.

For a time the venture was a success. During the first six months of co-operation, about thirty-five molders were constantly employed. In addition to their regular pay, they received two dollars a day as their share in the co-operative's profits. For an eight-hour day the workers earned about thirty dollars a week during the summer season, and twenty-five dollars during the slack winter season. Nowhere in the trade were wages and conditions comparable. And the co-operative made profits—six thousand dollars during the first six months, and seventeen thousand dollars during the following year when the number of workers employed was more than doubled.

The success at Troy inspired Sylvis to call for similar co-operatives in all parts of the nation so that "peace and prosperity will reign among the molders throughout the land." He looked forward to the day when the "blaze and smoke of a thousand foundries" organized by the union would afford havens for the "storm-tossed toiler." Two years after the establishment of the Troy foundry, eleven co-operative foundries existed in the United States and more than twenty others were in the process of organization. Sylvis was determined that most of the energy of the Molders' International Union be used in creating a chain of foundries all over the country. Thus, the International Co-operative Association of Pittsburgh was organized. At its 1868 convention, the union changed its name to the Iron Molders' International Protective and Co-operative Union of North America.[25]

---

owned factories, workshops, mills, steamship lines, and other industries. The Society operated on the basis of a plan devised by Charles Howarth, whereby profits were divided among purchasing members according to amount of purchases.

The molders soon discovered that in order to exist in a competitive world, co-operative foundries had to abandon co-operative principles. Stockholders demanded more and more profits, and to meet these demands the co-operatives were forced to reduce wages, lengthen working hours, and abolish union standards. Instead of becoming yardsticks for private capitalists to follow, many co-operatives served as models for employer offensives against labor.[26]

Co-operatives organized by the carpenters, printers and other unions were short-lived.* They were denounced in the press as examples of French communism. Industrialists sold at a loss to prevent them from developing a market. Often poor management added to their difficulties. But the chief difficulty was the securing of capital. Co-operatives had to persuade men with money to invest in enterprises whose object was to abolish the wage system. Naturally, the bankers asked for a high rate of interest, and soon the entire co-operative movement degenerated into joint stock companies more interested in making profits than in emancipating labor.

MONETARY REFORM

The less thoughtful did not see in the failure of the co-operatives proof of the bankruptcy of their theories. It was not the theory but the inability to get capital that caused the failure of the co-operative ventures.† While the control of credit and money remained in private hands, laborers could not "by any system of combination or co-operation secure their natural rights." It was necessary to restore the nation's monetary system to the people; once this was achieved, capital at a reasonable rate of interest

---

* However, not all co-operatives were failures. A co-operative shoe factory set up by the Knights of St. Crispin in Philadelphia was said to be in a very flourishing condition in 1871. A co-operative established by the Coopers' Union of Minnesota in 1870 soon owned seven shops which produced most of the barrels for the flour mills of the city. (See *Philadelphia Public Ledger*, Jan. 1, 1871; American Economic Association, *Publications*, Vol. I, pp. 129ff.)

† Sylvis reached the conclusion that state aid was essential for successful co-operatives; at the 1867 convention of the National Labor Union he proposed the following plan which the delegates enthusiastically adopted: "Whereas, the Congress of the United States have from time to time made appropriations of large sums of money and grants of public land for the social benefit of Railroads and other monopolies ... be it Resolved that we respectfully petition Congress at its next session to appropriate $25,000,000 to aid in establishing the eight hour system, co-operation." (*Boston Daily Evening Voice*, August 27, 1867.) Sylvis was unconsciously echoing Lassalle's statement to the German workers: "The State must come to your rescue. ... The State ought to regard it as its holiest duty to assist in making certain the possibility of your self organization and association." (Ferdinand Lassalle, *Open Letter to the National Labor Association of Germany*, translated by Hohn Eihnamm and Fred Bader, Cincinnati, 1879, p. 22.)

would be available for co-operative enterprises, and the workingmen would be able to secure the "bulk of what they produce." Thus did the failure of co-operatives help the labor movement lose itself in the wilderness of monetary reform.

The initial ideas of the post-Civil War advocates of currency reform in the ranks of the labor movement were largely derived from Edward Kellogg, a prosperous drygoods merchant in New York City. Losing his fortune in the panic of 1837, Kellogg began to study the evils of the monetary system. His first treatise, *Currency, the Evil and the Remedy,* was published in 1843 in the *New York Tribune.* Six years later he published his major work, *Labor and Other Capital.* The monetary laws of the United States, wrote Kellogg, were responsible for labor's degraded status. These laws allowed bankers to create and loan money, and by simply withholding capital, bankers could bring about a scarcity of money which, in turn, would give them the high interest rates they were concerned with. The results of these laws were disastrous to the people of America.

Kellogg believed that workers were powerless to improve their living standards as long as they ignored the "fundamental reform," the lowering of the interest rate. To achieve this "fundamental reform," he proposed that the government should establish a "National Safety Fund" with one or more branches in every state. This fund would be used to issue paper money based on real estate and bear a fixed rate of interest of one per cent. By lending money this governmental lending institution would force private agencies to lower their interest rates. It would mean that "all agriculturists, manufacturers, mechanics, planters, in short all who wish to secure a support by honest industry," could get all the capital they needed at a low interest rate. And since the Safety Fund would make it possible for trade unions to get cheap capital, the "fundamental reform" would lead painlessly to the abolition of the wage system.[27]

Kellogg's fundamental reform did not impress the labor movement of the 'fifties, recovering, as it was, from the utopian schemes of the 'forties. Too many sad experiences with paper money issued by wildcat banks had made labor skeptical of paper money theories. But during the 'sixties and 'seventies many workers, farmers, and some industrialists believed that the time had come for a reform in the monetary system. The greenbacks of 1862 had depreciated, but the bankers had used these greenbacks to buy government bonds which were redeemable in gold and paid interest in gold. "The manner in which the public debt is funded," said the *Coopers' Monthly Journal* in March, 1871, "presents, by the high rate of interest, stronger inducements to moneyed people to invest in U.S. Bonds, than to putting in their capital into industrial, commercial, and manufacturing enterprises." Co-operatives set up by workingmen faced the same difficulty of securing capital at low interest rates; hence both in private industry and in their own "self-employment" undertakings, workers were confronted by the same problems of finance and interest rates.[28]

Such was the setting after the Civil War when Alexander Campbell, a delegate to many conventions of the National Labor Union, published several pamphlets outlining Kellogg's monetary theories. Overnight Kellogg's work became the bible of the labor reformers. Cameron reprinted whole chapters of his *Labor and Other Capital* in the *Workingman's Advocate,* and Sylvis became so convinced of Kellogg's proposals that he stated on November 16, 1868, that "when a just monetary system has been established, there will no longer exist a necessity for trade unions." [29]

Though the monetary reform program of the National Labor Union was based on Kellogg's theories, it was not identical with them. The organization called for the abolition of the national banking system, demanded that the rate of interest should be fixed by the government instead of by the banks, and called upon the government to reduce the rate of interest on its bonds to three per cent and at the same time make them convertible into greenbacks which would be legal tender at the option of the holder. The government was to lend paper money directly to its citizens, on security of a business or property, at about one per cent rate of interest. Thus co-operatives would be able to obtain capital at a fixed and reasonable rate of interest, and small businessmen would secure funds to stay in business, thereby providing employment for unemployed workers.

Some of the enthusiastic advocates of currency reform in the National Labor Union had more in mind than providing capital for co-operatives. Their plan was to do away with Wall Street and the "cursed" banking system which they believed were responsible for the misery of the working class. The principal enemy of the laboring masses thus became the "financial oligarchy" and not the rising industrial bourgeoisie which was organizing the powerful offensives against the trade unions. The struggles of workers for higher wages and better conditions became, in the minds of the monetary reformers, insignificant when compared to the struggle to break the power of the "money aristocracy."

Ira Steward understood the danger of the currency panacea to the labor movement. He warned that consciously or not the monetary reformers in the labor movement were "doing the work of the capitalist classes better than they could do it for themselves." Employers had no objection to workers devoting their time and energy to currency reform as long as it kept their minds off the basic questions of wages and hours. It was to the interest of the capitalist class, Steward argued, "to fix public attention upon the economic humbugs, the settlement of which in the best way, leaves the laborer a laborer, the capitalist a capitalist, between whom there is an irrepressible conflict." [30]

But Steward's arguments did not convince Sylvis, Trevellick, Cameron, and other advocates of currency reform, and by 1867 these leaders felt that in the National Labor Union's financial program lay the future of the American working class. "Our objective point," declared Sylvis, "is a new monetary system, a system that will take from a few men the power to control the money, and give to the people a cheap, secure, and abundant currency. This done, and the people will be free. Then will come such a social revolution as the world has never witnessed...." [31] Even though it represented a sincere desire of socially conscious working class leaders to achieve a better social order, currency reform could not and did not bring freedom to the workers. Instead it helped hasten the death of the national labor federation which had been the main hope of a better life.

POLITICAL ACTION

It was legislation, said the *Arbeiter Union*, that had "created the unjust monetary system which turns the product of labor over to capital." How but through political action could a "just monetary system that will fairly distribute the products of labor, be established?" [32] Confirmed currency reformers, many leaders of the National Labor Union now concentrated more and more of their energies on political action, ignoring at the same time all issues which could not be affected by such action. Their mistake was not that they took up political issues but that they picked the wrong issue and ignored the economic struggles of the workers.

The attitude of the trade unions toward political action during and immediately after the Civil War was not consistent. Some unions forbade their membership "under any pretence whatever [to] introduce or discuss political questions," and justified this ban with the argument that dissension over the support of candidates at elections would split the unions. [33] But this did not mean that trade unionists should remain aloof from politics. Political activity by the workers was necessary, but it had to be conducted outside the union. [34]

Many trade unions recognized the limitations of such an approach and political as well as economic issues were raised at all meetings. The Carpenters and Joiners, the Coopers, the Plasterers, the Cigar Makers and the Miners unions were but a few of the labor organizations whose conventions featured discussions of the need for political action. At the convention of the State Union of Carpenters and Joiners of Massachusetts in January, 1866, such discussion was followed by the adoption of a series of resolutions calling for greater political activity by the organized workers of the Bay State. "Resolved," went the concluding resolution, "that we declare that we will demand, maintain and defend our rights, not only in the work-shop and the dusty field of toil, but also in the halls of the State Legislature, in the Courts of Law, and in the Congress of the United States." [35]

Because the nature of their industry demanded legislative intervention, and because of their experience in England with the movement to secure such legislation, the miners of Pennsylvania were among the most polit-- ically minded and alert workingmen in the country. Founded by John Siney in 1868, the Miners and Laborers Benevolent Association, formerly the Workingmen's Benevolent Association of Schuylkill County, soon became an effective collective bargaining force, securing a trade agreement with the coal operators in 1869 and 1870. Through its political activities, the union secured the passage of a law by the state legislature in 1869 legalizing trade unions. The law stated that it was lawful for any and all classes of mechanics, journeymen, tradesmen, and laborers "to form societies, and associations for their mutual aid, benefit, and protection, and peaceably to meet, discuss, and establish all necessary rules and regulations to carry out the same—all acts or parts of acts inconsistent herewith are hereby repealed." [36] Since the law did not free workers or their unions from liability to prosecution for conspiracy, the Workingmen's Benevolent Association fought for a new law to exempt workingmen and their unions from the conspiracy laws. This was achieved in 1872 when a law was passed by the state legislature "to relieve workmen, laborers, and journeymen from certain prosecutions and indictments for conspiracy under the civil laws of the Commonwealth."

The first mine inspection bill was passed by the legislature in April, 1869, after a vigorous campaign in which the union brought the issues to the people of the state. This act provided for the "better regulation and ventilation of mines, and for the protection of the lives of the miners in the county of Schuylkill," and authorized the governor to appoint an inspector of mines. The miners fought for a law covering the entire anthracite region, but the Legislature listened to the mine owners who claimed that the mines in the other counties did not require ventilation or inspection. A few months later the Avondale (Luzerne County) disaster in which 109 miners lost their lives, aroused public opinion to demand a more effective mine inspection law which would apply to all the anthracite mines in the state. When the legislature convened, delegates from the Miners' Union went to Harrisburg and stayed there until a new law was passed. [37]

Not all trade unions were as active politically as the Miners' Union, but the eight-hour question, the importation of Chinese labor, and the use of the conspiracy doctrine to attack labor organization were compelling reasons for trade unions to consider political action. When neither of the major parties showed any interest in measures demanded by the workingmen, the trade unions in many states took the lead in forming independent political parties. In California the trade unions formed the base of a third-party movement organized to meet the threat of Chinese labor, and in Massachusetts the Knights of St. Crispin, anxious to secure legal recognition by incorporation, helped to start and gave full support to the state Labor Reform Party.[38]

In 1869 the Massachusetts Labor Reform Party won an amazing victory. With an organization formed three weeks before election day and without funds or newspaper support, the party elected one of its candidates to the state senate and twenty-two to the lower house, polling 13,000 votes in the state. Overnight, the party became an important factor in American politics. The Republican Party, in self-defense, reproached the workingmen, saying that it had "accomplished more for the elevation of the laborers of America than had been accomplished before since the government was framed"; hence it viewed "with surprise and indignation the claim of any other organization to arrogate to itself the title of 'labor party.'"[39]

Undaunted by the pique of the Republican Party, the workingmen of Massachusetts prepared to enter the gubernatorial campaign of 1870. It selected as its candidate for Governor, that great American, Wendell Phillips. Unlike many of the Abolitionists, Phillips had always regarded the abolition of slavery as but one aspect of the emancipation of mankind, and when slavery was abolished, he devoted much of his time to labor reform. As early as November 2, 1865, Phillips delivered an address at Faneuil Hall in Boston in favor of the eight-hour day, in which he said:

"It is twenty-nine years [this] month since I first stood on the platform of Faneuil Hall to address the citizens of Boston. I felt then that I was speaking for the cause of the laboring man, and if tonight I should make the last speech of my life, I would be glad that it should be in the same strain,—for laboring men and their rights."[40]

Phillips conducted an active campaign but the combined votes of the Labor Reform and the Prohibition Party were 21,946, as against 79,549 for the Republicans, and 49,536 for the Democrats. One reason for the defeat was the lack of organization which even Phillips' eloquence could not overcome. Like most labor parties of this period, there was little political activity between elections, and at election time there was no local organization to get out the vote.

The state convention of the Massachusetts Labor Reform Party was held at Worcester on September 4, 1871. Four hundred and twenty-five delegates were present, including about ten women. Phillips welcomed the delegates and made the keynote speech. "Under all flags," he said, "there is one great movement. It is for the people *peaceably* to take possession of their own.... We come by the right of numbers to take possession of the government of the earth."

The platform, drawn up by Phillips, opened with the words: "We affirm as a fundamental principle that labor, the creator of wealth, is entitled to all it creates." In the resolutions, war was declared on the wages system which "enslaves the workingman," on the present system of finance "which robs labor, and gorges capital," on the lavish grants of land to speculating companies, and on the system of enriching capitalists "by the creation and increase of the public interest-bearing debt." Demands were raised for the eight-hour day, and for the discontinuance of the forced importation of Chinese labor. Another demand read: "Whenever women are employed at public expense to do the same kind and amount of work as men perform, they shall receive the same wages." [41]

E. M. Chamberlin, who had headed the state ticket in 1869, was the candidate of the Labor Reform Party for governor. Though Phillips refused to run for public office, he stumped the state once again for the Labor Party.

"When we get into power," said he, "there is one thing we mean to do. If a man owns a single house, we will tax him one hundred dollars. If he owns ten houses of like value, we won't tax him one thousand dollars; but sixty thousand dollars; and the richer a man grows, the bigger his tax, so that when he is worth forty million dollars, he shall not have more than twenty thousand dollars a year to live on. ..." [42]

The Labor Party received 6,848 votes. Phillips attributed the small vote to intimidation by employers. When speaking at meetings attended by factory workers, he said, none of them dared sit on the platform or introduce him for fear of being reported by spies. There was a good deal of truth to this, but the main reason for the defeat is to be found in the decline of the Knights of St. Crispin and other unions in New England during this period. [43]

In 1872 the Massachusetts Labor Reform Party split into two small hostile groups: the Labor Union headed by Phillips, and the Eight-Hour League lead by Ira Steward and George McNeill. The split occurred over the eight-hour question. Steward regarded it as the only question of significance to labor, and he particularly opposed the currency issue. Wendell Phillips, influenced by the writings of Edward Kellogg, was moving more and more toward currency reform. When he insisted that the platform of the Labor Party lead off with a demand for a new monetary system, the eight-hour advocates walked out and set up their own organization.[44] This conflict between the currency reformers and the eight-hour advocates seriously weakened various state efforts at independent political action. Each group believed that its program alone would emancipate the working class. But the workers were losing interest in labor parties headed by men concerned primarily with advancing their pet theories.[45]

The rapid decline of the state labor parties does not mean that they had accomplished nothing. The very fact that labor was acting independently forced the existing parties to be more attentive to the demands of the workingmen, and some significant gains for labor were won. The formation of the Massachusetts Bureau of Labor Statistics in 1869 is an example. The *Workingman's Advocate* of August 5, 1871, stated that this victory alone justified the formation of a labor party in Massachusetts, for the Bureau had done more to advance the principles of labor reform than could have been accomplished in years by the usual methods of agitation. The facts were before the people. They knew the "depths not only of their own but their neighbor's degradation under the iron heel of monopolized capital. . . ."

At the 1867 convention of the National Labor Union a resolution was adopted which read: "The time has arrived when the industrous classes should cut themselves aloof from party ties and predilections and organize into a National Labor Party."[46] A year later, at the 1868 convention, a committee was appointed to formulate a platform for the proposed National Labor Party. Bowing to the insistence of those delegates who opposed independent political action, the convention agreed that the new party would not participate in the forthcoming Presidential campaign; however, the Declaration of Principles, modeled after the Declaration of Independence, was made public. Nearly two-thirds of the document dealt with currency reform. In addition to advocating that the national banking system be abolished and that the rate of interest be fixed by the government, it demanded land grants to actual settlers only; a Department of Labor; an honest and intelligent expression of Congress on the eight-hour question; a liberal system of railroads, express, water transportation, and telegraph communications "under the management of the general government for the benefit of the people. "We earnestly ask," the platform concluded, "the co-operation of the whole people, white and black, male and female, to unite and assist, in bringing into operation the principles above set forth."[47]

The first organizational step was taken at the 1870 congress, when, despite the opposition of several delegates, an executive committee for the National Labor Reform Party was selected and authorized to decide upon a date for the calling of a nominating convention. The committee, consisting of delegates from fourteen states and headed by Cummings of the Knights of St. Crispin, met in Washington early in 1871, and recommended that the convention be held the following October. Later it was decided to postpone the meeting until February 22, 1872. One result of the delay was a split within the executive committee, one group calling a conference in December, 1871, and announcing a national convention to be held on July 4, 1872, to nominate candidates for the National Reform Party. This group was not recognized by the National Labor Union, and President Trevellick announced that it had no authority to act separately.[48]

About one hundred delegates, representing fourteen states, attended the nominating convention held February 22, 1872, in Columbus, Ohio. Most of the delegates had never attended a convention of the National Labor Union, and only about twenty-five of them were connected with organized labor. One of these twenty-five was John Siney, leader of the organized miners in the anthracite districts of Pennsylvania.

The currency reformers dominated the convention, making the greenback program the major demand of the new party. Other resolutions called for the eight-hour day, the granting of public lands to settlers only, an end to the immigration of forced Chinese labor, and the reduction of the tariff, "so as to admit free such articles of common use as we can neither produce nor grow, and lay duties for revenue mainly upon articles of luxury."[49]

The main business before the convention was the nominating of candidates. The Republican Party had split, one wing calling itself the Liberal Republicans. Politicians anxious to be nominated at the Liberal Republican Party convention to be held in April were interested in the proceedings at Columbus, for they knew that if they could come to the Liberal Republican convention with the support of a section of labor, their chances for victory would be greater. There was considerable behind-the-scenes manipulation at Columbus by representatives of political figures, few of whom had previously displayed much interest in the welfare of labor.

When David Davis of Illinois, one such political figure, was nominated as the Presidential candidate of the National Labor Reform Party, a controversy developed. Several local workingmen's committees adopted resolutions ignoring the nominations at Columbus, and called for a new convention. Horace Day and Ezra Wood, both active in the National Labor Union, denounced the choice of Davis, and announced their intention of supporting the forthcoming Women's Rights Convention and its candidates for the Presidential campaign.[50]

Davis had welcomed the "unexpected honor" of being labor's candidate, but when the Liberal Republican convention nominated Horace

Greeley, he lost interest and informed the National Labor Reform Party that he could no longer serve as its standard bearer. Thereupon a call was issued to all delegates who had attended the Columbus convention urging them to appear at a conference to be held in New York on July 30. Thirty-five individuals answered the call and joined in the adoption of a resolution asserting that the "working classes of the country have nothing to choose between President Grant and Horace Greeley." At a meeting in Philadelphia on August 22 to elect a new candidate it was voted to send delegates to attend a convention of Democrats who had refused to go along with their party in supporting Horace Greeley. Unprincipled politics led to the choice of Charles O'Connor of New York, a leading defender of slavery and foe of the Negro people, as the candidate of the National Labor Reform Party. O'Connor was also nominated at the rump Democratic convention to which the Labor Reform Party had sent delegates. Small wonder that the party received 29,489 votes in the election.[51]

Meanwhile, another group which had refused to join the dissident Democrats held its own conference in Columbus. Twelve delegates, led by A. C. Cameron, decided that it was "inexpedient at this late day" to nominate candidates to fill the vacancy caused by the unexpected withdrawal of David Davis and Joel Parker.[52]

DECLINE OF THE NATIONAL LABOR UNION

This fiasco of 1872 ended the brief existence of the National Labor Union. In a letter to Karl Marx in 1870, F. A. Sorge had stated the fundamental reason for the early decline of the Union: "The National Labor Union which had such brilliant prospects in the beginning of its career, was poisoned by Greenbackism and is slowly but surely dying." A year later he observed: "The leaders of the National Labor Union have learned nothing and, it is to be feared, will never learn to under-stand the labor question." [53]

Influenced by the Lassallean Socialists in America, many of the leaders of the National Labor Union had reached the conclusion that the ballot box alone would "correct all the evils of which we complain." They overlooked the all-important truth that without trade unions behind it, political action often accomplished nothing for the working class. The experience with the eight-hour laws proved this if it proved anything at all. It was most regrettable, therefore, that Cameron, Trevellick, and other leaders of the National Labor Union did not pay close attention to the following letter from Albany, New York, which appeared in the *Workingman's Advocate* of February 5, 1870:

"Since trade unions have flourished, a wonderful change having come over the spirit of reality in our State Legislature, we now demand our rights, and, so far they dance attendance on us. We get members of that body to present bills we wish passed, and tell them all that if we fail to get justice at their hands we will place our direct representatives there to grant it at the next session. And we've asked and got the Assembly Chamber to hold a workingman's mass meeting. The honorable Assembly of the Empire State adjourned to let those horrid conspirators, those trade union men, hold a meeting."

This dispatch showed the direct relationship existing between trade unions and labor's political influence. But the currency reformers learned nothing from this experience.

The rapid decline of the National Labor Union can be observed in the composition of its conventions. At the 1868 Congress, five national unions—the Typographical, Molders, Machinists, Carpenters, and Bricklayers—sent eight delegates. Fifteen came from thirteen trade assemblies, and forty-three local trade unions sent as many delegates. At the convention in 1869, three national unions, the molders, printers, carpenters and joiners, sent delegates, and six trades' assemblies, five state labor bodies, and fifty-three local unions were represented.[54]

After the 1869 convention the Workingmen's Assembly of New York State announced that it disagreed with the sentiment of the leaders of the National Labor Union that "no permanent reform can ever be established through the agency of the Trade Unions." That same year the Carpenters and Joiners' National Union joined in criticizing the leaders of the National Labor Union for their negative attitude toward trade union action, and voted to send no more delegates to the Labor Congress.[55]

During 1870-71, all trade unions severed relations with the National Labor Union. Three national unions—the molders, shoemakers, and printers—sent delegates to the 1870 congress, and thirty-four local trade unions and eight trades' assemblies were also represented. Few of these organizations were represented again. The delegates from the National Typographical Union reported that they "failed to discover anything in the proceedings that entitle the Congress to representatives from a purely trade organization." [56] William Jessup reported to the Workingmen's Assembly of New York that the National Labor Union had lost sight of its original objectives. He compared the 1870 convention with that of 1866, stating that at the first Congress:

"...Every delegate represented some branch of mechanical pursuit; at the last convention we find a strange mixture of mechanics, workingmen, ministers, lawyers, editors, lobbyists, and others of no particular occupation, some intent upon organizing a political labor party, others using their efforts to defeat that measure and benefit existing parties. With so much difference in the aims of the representatives, the convention could be none other than it was—unharmonious." [57]

In 1871 the Bricklayers and the Cigar Makers national unions severed relations with the National Labor Union. The Cigar Makers said that it was "inexpedient hereafter to have any more connection with the Labor Congress, for the reason of it being an entirely political institution, and no benefits deriving therefrom." [58] At the 1871 convention there were only two delegates who could be said to represent a labor organization, the iron molders local union of Ottawa, Illinois, and the Mechanics State Council of California. The majority of the twenty-two delegates were agrarian reformers.

The seven delegates who attended the 1872 Congress decided to form a new association "whose primary object shall be to discuss questions of a non-political character." A committee of three, composed of Trevellick, Cameron, and M. A. Foran of the Coopers' International Union, was designated "to open a correspondence with the presidents of the various State, National, and International Trade and Labor Unions requesting them ... to take into consideration the expediency of calling a National Industrial Congress. ..." [59] The National Labor Union was a thing of the past.

Despite its short life, the National Labor Union was an important stage in the development of the American labor movement. It had crystallized the most significant issues for workers in this period, and through its educational activities had helped to rally labor throughout the nation around these issues. It was among the first organizations in the world to raise the question of equal pay for equal work for women and to place them in positions of leadership. It was the first American national labor federation to welcome Negro delegates. The first American labor body to have a strong lobby in Washington, it urged the creation of a Department of Labor; it directed attention to the need for the shorter workday and co-operated to establish the eight-hour system in the federal and state governments. It directed activity to rectify unjust legislation; it fought the unjust grants of land to the railroads, and called for the restoration of the public domain to the people. It was recognized as the representative of American labor by the International Working Men's Association, and sent an official delegate abroad to attend a convention of that body. It assisted in the launching of a number of state labor parties and of the first National Labor Party in the history of the American labor movement.

The program of that party, monetary reform, was disastrous, but the existence of such a party, dominated though it was by a petty-bourgeois ideology, proved that an important section of the working class was ready to act independently in national politics. While it over-emphasized political action and monetary reform and ignored trade unionism in its last years, the National Labor Union brought to the attention of the American people the fact that the government of the United States was becoming more and more dominated by industrial and financial monopolist interests, and that to preserve American democratic institutions a great people's movement was necessary which would unite workers, farmers, and small producers.*

* Since this book was published in 1947 the most important new work on the period of the Civil War and Reconstruction in relation to organized labor is David Montgomery, *Beyond Equality: Labor and the Radical Republicans, 1862–1872* (New York, 1967). Dr. Montgomery discusses in detail the labor reform movement, and concludes that while the Radical Republicans were concerned with the problems of Negro equality, they were less so with the demands of wage earners in the North; that this in turn helped bring on the eclipse of Radicalism, and that even though it did not entirely succeed in obtaining its ends, the labor reform movement had by the end of the Civil War decade established itself as a source to be reckoned with in American political and economic life. In general, Dr. Montgomery's discussion is in keeping with that presented in the present volume, but he differs with me on a number of issues. This can be easily traced in the index of Dr. Montgomery's volume under Foner, Philip S.

CHAPTER 21

The Birth of the Knights of Labor

Though the Knights of Labor did not become an important force in the labor movement until after the period under discussion, its beginnings belong to the era of the National Labor Union. A small group of garment cutters in Philadelphia in 1869 organized a new body called the "Noble and Holy Order of the Knights of Labor." The impetus for its organization came out of the failure of the Garment Cutters Association of Philadelphia which had been organized in 1862.[1] Uriah Stephens, one of its active members, was convinced that the decline of the union was due to a lack of secrecy. "I am determined," said Stephens, "to make an effort to institute something different. When the dissolution takes place I shall make an effort to get some good men together and originate something that will be different from what we have ever had."[2] That something different was the first local assembly of the Knights of Labor, whose establishment was an event of immense import in the American labor movement.

On December 9, 1869, a resolution was adopted to dissolve the Garment Cutters Association, and, immediately after the dissolution, Stephens and eight other former members became the charter members of the new organization. All took a pledge of secrecy, and a committee was appointed to draw up a secret plan for the government of the new organization. On December 28, the new association adopted the name, the Knights of Labor. On January 6, 1870, officers were elected, Stephens being chosen Master Workman, the title of the presiding officer, while James L. Wright became the Venerable Sage, or the retiring presiding officer. Other officers were Worthy Foreman, the Unknown Knight, Recording Secretary, Financial Secretary, and Treasurer. The initiation fee was set at $1.00.[3]

RITUALS OF THE KNIGHTS OF LABOR

Many of the trade unions of this period had elaborate titles for their officers and high-sounding ceremonies, but none of them carried this practice as far as did the Knights of Labor. When a candidate—and until 1878 only wage-earners could become members—was invited to join the Knights, he attended a secret meeting where he was first asked three questions: "Do you believe in God, the Creator and Father of all? Do you obey the Universal Ordinance of God, in gaining your bread by the sweat of your brow? Are you willing to take a solemn vow binding you to secrecy, obedience, and mutual assistance?" If the applicant said yes, he was asked to take a pledge to obey all laws, regulations of the order, and promise to "defend the life, interest, reputation and family of all true members of this Order, help and assist all employed and unemployed, unfortunate or distressed Brothers to procure employment, secure just remuneration, relieve their distress and counsel others to aid them, so that they and theirs may receive and enjoy the just fruits of their labor and exercise of their art."

After the pledge, the new member was taken to the "base of the sanctuary," the meeting room, to receive instructions of the Worthy Foreman. Here he was told that the organization of labor was made necessary by the fact that in every trade, capital had its "combinations, and whether intended or not, they crush the manly hopes of labor, and trample poor humanity in the dust." The Knights meant "no conflict with legitimate enterprise, no antagonism to capital," but they were aware that men "blinded by self-interests" overlooked the rights of others, "and sometimes even violate the rights of those they deem helpless." To prevent such violation, the Knights intended "to create a healthy public opinion on the subject of labor (the only creator of values), and the justice of its receiving a full, just share of the values or capital it has created." They would support all laws which sought "to harmonize the interests of labor and capital ... and also those laws which tend to lighten the exhaustiveness of toil." They did not approve of general strikes, but if it should become "justly necessary to enjoin an oppressor, we will protect and aid any of our members who thereby may suffer loss and as opportunity offers, extend a helping hand to all branches of honorable toil." [4]

When the candidate had been told the objectives of the Knights of Labor, he was turned over to the Venerable Sage who explained the secret organization of the order, such as the grips, the passwords, and how to know when an assembly would meet. The last bit of information was very important, for until 1878 or 1879 the name of the order was never referred to as such. It was known as the "Five Stars" or as the "Five Asterisks," since it was represented in printed documents by five asterisks thus —* * * * *. Calls for meetings were often chalked upon sidewalks and fences in mysterious symbols which were clear only to the initiated. The symbol 8 $\frac{148}{8000}$ meant Local Assembly No. 8000 would meet on August 1, at 8 o'clock.[5]

ROLE OF URIAH S. STEPHENS

To understand the meaning of the initiation ceremonies, it is necessary to know something about Uriah S. Stephens. The *Journal of United Labor,* the official organ of the Order, in its obituary of Stephens on February 15, 1882, declared: "All through our rituals and laws will be found the impress of his brain, and inspiration of his keen insight into the great problems of the present hour."

Stephens was born in 1821 at Cape May, New Jersey, and was trained for the Baptist Ministry. During the Panic of 1837, he was forced to abandon his studies, and became apprenticed to a tailor. Later, he taught school in New Jersey and, in 1845, moved to Philadelphia where be became a tailor. A vigorous opponent of slavery and the slavocracy, he joined the Republican Party immediately after its formation and campaigned for Fremont and Lincoln.[6]

Stephens' activities during the early 'sixties are not too well known. One story has it that he went to Europe where he came in contact with prominent Marxists, and it has been recorded that he brought back from Europe when he returned to America a copy of *The Communist Manifesto* by Marx and Engels. Stephens is said to have told a contemporary that he found that the pamphlet "contained pretty much everything I had thought out myself, and I used it largely in the preparation of the Declaration of Principles of the Order." [7] This story is questioned by Professor Norman J. Ware, historian of the Knights of Labor, who doubts that Stephens ever traveled to Europe or received copies of Marx's writings. Certainly there is little in Stephens' philosophy of labor that has anything in common with Marxism, and he himself was opposed to the policies of Sorge and other American Marxists and was against "having anything to do with them either individually or as a body." [8]

Stephens put great emphasis on the word, "solidarity." Labor, he argued, had to be powerful and unified to cope with the strength of organized capital. The only organization of labor which would meet the power of capital was one which united workers of all trades, and was universal in its scope. Trade unions, he believed, were too narrow, both in composition and in their fields of operation. Instead of uniting all workers, they barred the unskilled, the Negroes, and other groups of workers. Since all workers, Stephens maintained, had common interests, they should logically belong to a common society and be united by their bonds of "universal brotherhood." [9]

This unity could be won through three principles: secrecy, co-operation, and education. Secrecy had a triple purpose: it would protect the worker from anti-labor employers; it would prevent employers from discovering the plans of the workers, and, finally, secret rituals would bring home to the new member the importance of the organization he had just joined. In the secret sanctuary of the meeting room all craft, religious, national, racial, and political differences disappeared. Here the wage-earner could think and act as a wage-earner, and not as a white or Negro; American, European, or Asiatic; Democrat or Republican; Catholic, Protestant or Jew. "Creed, party and nationality," Stephens once said, "are but the outward garments and present no obstacle to the fusion of the hearts of worshippers of God, the Universal Father, and the workers for man, the universal brother." [10]

Stephens did not confine his attention to improvements within the wage system. He believed that a major objective of the Knights was to achieve "the complete emancipation of the wealth producers from the thraldom and loss of wage slavery." [11]

Through co-operation the Knights would achieve better conditions, and the gradual substitution of the co-operative system for capitalism. Improvement of working conditions would come through trade assemblies based on craft union organization, and the replacement of the capitalist system by the co-operative system was the task of the mixed assemblies that united workers regardless of craft. [12]

Education, Stephens believed, would play a large part in achieving the immediate and ultimate objects of the Knights of Labor by breaking down the prejudices and antagonisms which still divided the working class. Within the secret sanctuary of the Knights of Labor, members were taught that workers, regardless of their different occupations, had common aims and interests. Education would also prepare the members to act politically because only when the membership understood the principles of political economy and politics could they be effective in the life of the nation.*

---

* Stephens' emphasis on education is reflected in an interesting procedure adopted by the early Knights. When a member entered the vestibule or anteroom of the meeting room he came upon a small, triangular table on which a basket full of cards was placed. To obtain admission to the sanctuary or meeting room, the member had to write his name on a card. The aim was to compel each member to learn to read and write, and Terence V. Powderly, later the outstanding leader of the Knights, observed that he knew of over one hundred men in Scranton who were influenced by this card system "to take a course in writing so that they could

"Political economy," said Stephens, "may and should be freely and exhaustively discussed in the Local Assembly. In this way, and in this alone, can members become thoroughly informed as to their rights as citizens, both in the abstract or higher laws of God, and legally, or in the present laws of the land. In this way the justice or injustice of their surroundings are made more apparent, and they are enabled more intelligently to discharge the duties of citizenship, exercise the elective franchise, and realize exactly where they stand, and where they consistently belong." [13]

Stephens' aim was to unite all workers in a general mass organization regardless of sex, race, creed, or color. "I do not claim any power of prophecy," he is reported to have said, "but I can see ahead of me an organization that will cover the globe. It will include men and women of every craft, creed and color; it will cover every race worth saving." [14] In stressing the need for unity and solidarity in the ranks of labor, Stephens was obviously far in advance of many labor leaders of the period who spoke and fought only for the interests of their particular craft. Again, in emphasizing the importance of education and discussions of current political and economic issues, he was far ahead of those trade union leaders who urged that only questions of wages, hours, and working conditions concern the membership of labor organizations.

Yet Stephens was more a humanitarian than a trade unionist. The organization he wished to build was not a trade union, but a mass fraternal lodge, a working class Masonic order. And his belief that secrecy, education, and co-operation alone would create labor solidarity and solve the workers' problems stamped him as a visionary dominated by utopian ideas.

EARLY STRUCTURE OF THE KNIGHTS OF LABOR

Although Stephens criticized the trade unions of the period because they were "too narrow in their ideas and too circumscribed in their field of operations," [15] the early local assemblies of the Knights of Labor were local craft bodies. No one but a garment cutter who could prove that he had served a specified time as an apprentice was admitted to Local Assembly No. 1. Women were not eligible for membership, and it was not until 1882 that women were initiated into the Order. "Compared with the trade unions of that day," writes Terence V. Powderly, "the first assembly of the Knights of Labor was far behind them in toleration

---

not only write but read their names and other things beside." (*The Path I Trod*, New York, 1940, p. 54.)

and fellowship." [16] The main emphasis in the early assemblies was on a rigid craft organization.* Not until the Order expanded into the coal and iron regions of western Pennsylvania did these exclusive craft ideas begin to break down, and only then did the Knights of Labor make substantial progress. To understand this change in the organization of the Knights of Labor, we must turn our attention to the long depression of the 'seventies.

---

* The idea of solidarity was expressed in the practice of allowing members of other crafts to join the garment cutters local. These men—known as "sojourners" —did not participate in discussions of trade matters and did not pay dues, but would become organizers among their own kind of workers to form new assemblies. The first sojourner was admitted in 1870, and the second assembly, organized on July 18, 1872, was set up by ship carpenters and caulkers of Philadelphia who had been sojourners in Local Assembly No. 1. The fact that the second assembly was not formed until 1872 is proof that the Order grew very slowly at first.

CHAPTER 22

The Long Depression, 1873-1878

Despite the post-Civil War depression, real wages increased during 1865-73 due to the great activity of labor through trade unions and political organizations. The Bureau of Labor Statistics of Pennsylvania stated that the wage increases of organized workers during this period were 40 per cent higher than those of unorganized labor.[1] When, in September, 1873, the banking house of Jay Cooke and Company closed its doors, the situation changed completely. Overnight the entire credit structure of the country crumbled, and before the end of the year over five thousand commercial failures had been reported.

DECLINE IN UNION MEMBERSHIP

Throughout the following six terrible years unemployment was on the upgrade. The New York Association for the Improvement of the Condition of the Poor estimated that by the end of 1873 one-fourth of the working force, or about 43,750 persons in New York City were out of work. Similar agencies in other industrial centers reported the same conditions.[2] In 1877-78 three million workers were unemployed, and at least one-fifth of the working class was permanently unemployed. Two-fifths worked no more than six to seven months in the year, and less than one-fifth was regularly employed.[3] One New York worker asked in the fall of 1877: "What are our carpenters doing? Nothing! What are our bricklayers doing? Nothing. What have they to live on the coming winter? Nothing." [4]

Few were the unions that weathered the storm of this long depression. Of the thirty national unions in existence when the crisis broke in 1873 there were only eight or nine by 1877. The machinists and blacksmiths union lost two-thirds of its members; the coopers national union decreased from 7,000 members in 1872 to 1,500 in 1878; the cigar makers' national union from 5,800 in 1869 to 1,016 in 1877, and the typographical national union from 9,797 in 1873 to 4,260 in 1878. The Knights of St. Crispin with a membership of about 50,000, early in 1872, had practically no members in 1878.

In New York City, trade union membership decreased from about 45,000 in 1873 to 5,000 in 1878. The total trade union membership of Cincinnati in 1878 was about 1,000, and Cleveland, an important trade union center before the depression, was a non-union city in 1878.[5] While there are no reliable statistics as to the total trade union membership in the United States on the eve of the depression, it has been estimated that about 300,000 workers belonged to trade unions early in 1873. In his testimony before the United State Industrial Commission in 1900, Samuel Gompers estimated the total trade union membership in 1878 at 50,000.[6]

Lockouts, blacklists, legal prosecutions, and "yellow dog" contracts were used by employers to smash the trade unions. When a delegation of French trade unionists visited America in 1876 to join the national celebration of the centennial of the Declaration of Independence, they were shocked to discover that "in this great American Republic" many workers were afraid to serve on delegations to welcome them, fearing that it would label them as trade union members. A union member, they were told, was "hunted like a mad dog." In their report to the trade unions of France, the delegates remarked that this experience had convinced them that capital was as much the master in America as in Europe.[7]

PERSISTENCE OF UNIONISM

Trade unionism, however, was not crushed. The National Trade Association of Hat Finishers of the United States of America not only kept alive but retained a closed shop during the depression. And the Sons of Vulcan organized twenty new forges in 1874. A year later the union won a bitterly fought strike. In 1876 the United Sons of Vulcan (puddlers); the Associated Brotherhood of Iron and Steel Heaters (roughers, rollers and catchers); the Iron and Steel Roll Hands Union, and the United Nailers, united to form the Amalgamated Iron and Steel Workers.[8]

In the bituminous or soft coal mining industry the depression years saw the formation of the Miners' National Association of America modeled after the British union of the same name. All workers employed in and around the mines could become members. Founded in October, 1873, the union grew steadily in spite of the depression. By May, 1874, it had gained about 25,000 members. "Our hope," wrote John Siney, head of the organization, in May, 1875, "is that we will continue to grow till all who toil in the mines of the country will be good and efficient members of the Miners' National Association." [9]

These successes were the exceptions. In vain did the trade union journals remind the workingmen "that in those places where the union flourishes wages are higher than where there are no unions." [10] The refusal of employers "to give men work who would not leave the union" forced workers out of the labor organizations. [11]

Several attempts during the depression years to form national labor federations ended in failure. The Industrial Congress, founded by a convention of trade union delegates * on July 15, 1872, went to pieces two years later. Its founders had pledged that the new federation would not engage in independent political action, or "deteriorate into a political party . . . or a refuge for played out politicians." [12] The Congress tried to help the unions engage in strikes, and even sent out organizers into the field, one of whom was Terence V. Powderly, soon to head the Knights of Labor. In 1874 the Industrial Brotherhood, a secret labor federation, fused with the Industrial Congress, contributing to the congress its ritual, constitution, and name. The preamble to this new organization, called the Industrial Brotherhood, placed great importance on political action, and on the struggle for a national greenback currency issued directly to the people and interchangeable for government bonds bearing not over 3.65 per cent interest. Other demands included equal pay for equal work, the eight-hour day, the abolition of the contract system on public work, laws for the promotion of safety and health measures, monthly wage payments, and wage-lien laws. [13] The last meeting of the Industrial Congress was held in 1875, the only national trade union represented being the Typographical Union. Its most important action at this convention was the designating of July 4, 1876, as the day the eight-hour system was to go into effect by a "united movement on the part of the working masses of the United States." [14]

Following the dissolution of the Industrial Brotherhood several futile attempts were made to establish a national labor federation. Thus, from 1873 until 1878 when the Knights of Labor became a national factor in the American labor movement, there was no national labor body to lead the unions in meeting the offensives of the employers.

* Seventy delegates attended the convention. Forty-four came from five national unions (Coopers, Machinists, Molders, Sons of Vulcan, and Knights of St. Crispin). Other delegates included representatives of miners, cigar makers typographical, and tobacco workers.

DEPRESSION LIVING

"It is but necessary for one to make a tour of the city during the hours of seven to eight A.M., and five to six P.M.," wrote a New York trade unionist in the *Toiler* of July, 1874, "and observe the various jobs that are in progress and the number of men working in violation of the eight-hour rule.... Men cannot afford to walk about long in idleness, and consequently are obliged to accept any term offered." In the building trades where the eight-hour day and daily wages of $2.50-$3.00 had become common before the depression, a ten-hour day and daily wages of $1.50-$2.50 were the prevailing standards in October, 1875. By this time, the former powerful bricklayers, stone-cutters, carpenters, plasterers, and painters unions of New York had almost ceased to exist.[15]

Between 1873 and 1880 wages in the textile industry were reduced 45 per cent. In 1871 the wage of male weavers in Pennsylvania was $2 per ten-hour day, and of females $1.16. By 1878 the rates had been reduced to $1.23 and 99 cents a day respectively. Railroad workers suffered wage-cuts of between 30 and 40 per cent during the period 1873-77. The earnings of furniture workers dropped 40 to 60 per cent between 1873 and 1876.[16] As early as the summer of 1874 the Coopers' Union of New York reported: "The situation is deplorable. There is no standard of wages, each man working for what he can get, and all at low wages."

A letter addressed by the Central Committee of the Tradesmen's Union of Philadelphia to "Fellow Workmen" in the summer of 1874 declared:

"The sufferings of the working classes are daily increasing. They will soon be thrown into the deepest misery and affliction ... Soon one-third only of the actual number of workingmen will be able to get employment, while the other two-thirds, homeless and hungry, will look out in vain for the better times prophesied by a lying press.... In the middle of the summer we are en masse thrown out of work. Those who still are employed have to submit to constant reductions of wages, until the price of their labor falls to nothing." [17]

It is true that the prices of consumer goods also declined and that real wages, therefore, did not drop as low as money wages. But this was more than counterbalanced by the widespread unemployment. During the first three months of 1874 about 90,000 homeless workers, two-fifths of whom were women, were lodgers in New York City's police station houses. They were called "revolvers" because they were not permitted to spend more than one or two days a month in any one station-house. They slept huddled together in their damp clothes on hard benches, and were turned out hungry at daybreak. This method of providing for workers evicted from their homes was properly called "utterly barbarous and heartless" by a reporter who visited the station houses.[18] But the well-housed and well-fed condemned "the over-generous charity of the city" in providing even the hard benches be-cause it "might sap the foundation of that independence of character, and that reliance on one's own resources." The entire business, said the *Nation,* was "thoroughly communistic." [19]

As the crisis deepened, the plight of thousands upon thousands of homeless workers, the tramps of the 'seventies, grew worse. They lived in shacks and gleaned the garbage heaps for food. A reporter for the San Francisco *Mail* visited one of the communities of homeless workers on the Pacific Coast. He asked an aged worker who was extracting from a pile of ashes food "that a humane man would hesitate about throwing to his dog": "Can't you find any work?" The old man looked up and answered:

"Work, sir? Do you think if we could find work we would live here and have to fight for our meals with the dogs of the city? All the men here go every day from wharf to wharf and hunt the whole city over for a job at any price. Two bits would be gladly taken for a day's work, but we can't get anything.

"Several of the other dumpies drew near, and a tall, fine looking fellow who had been washing himself in a can of water, said: 'I have lived on this lot for three months, eat and sleep here, and I have never let a day go by that I have not walked mile after mile to get a job. Some weeks I have made a dollar, and weeks I have not made anything. I have offered to work for one-half the price that Chinamen [*sic*] get in any branch of hard labor. But no use. No one would take me. I don't get drunk. I don't steal, but I have got either to starve or live on such stuff as this.' " [20]

Go West? The *Workingman's Advocate* explained why the workers could not go West. "In the first place, many of them have not the means to take them there, and in the second place they have nothing with which to till the land when they get there.... If they could cultivate the soil, without oxen, or horses, or implements of agriculture or could live on grass, and shrubs, and wild fruits while their first year's crop were growing, going West might be a valid question worth considering." [21] Where, after all, could the worker secure $14 to $16 to pay for initial fees and commissions, money to cover transportation for 500 or 1,000 miles, the price of draft animals and implements, and sus-tenance for the first few years until enough food could be grown to feed his family and pay his expenses? "Transportation alone for a family of five," Professor Fred A. Shannon estimates, "would be the equivalent of half a year's wages." [22]

Some workers did go West during the depression years; a local of carpet weavers in Philadelphia moved *en masse* to Leavenworth, Kansas, when they were told that there were jobs in the community. Others who were planning to go West were dissuaded by appeals from trade union leaders in Chicago, Detroit, and St. Louis, to the labor press. Don't come West, they counseled. The western cities were "over-run with mechanics and others in want of employment." [23] A worker who had returned from a trip to the West where he had been in search of work wrote to the *National Labor Tribune* of September 7, 1875:

"Twelve months ago, left penniless by misfortune, I started from New York in search of employment. I am a mechanic, and am regarded as competent in my business. During this year I have traversed seventeen States and obtained in that time six weeks' work. I have faced starvation; been months at a time without a bed, when the thermometer was 30 degrees below zero. Last winter I slept in the woods, and while honestly seeking employment I have been two and three days without food. When, in God's name, I asked for something to keep body and soul together, I have been repulsed as a 'tramp and vagabond.' "

Instead of going West many workers were coming East, and many more left for Europe and South America. In August, 1876, an advertisement appeared in the *New York Sun* calling for one hundred stone-cutters and masons who would be ready to go to Scotland for two years work with passage paid. So many workers answered the call that the police had to be called to keep order. A year and a half later, in February, 1878, the newspapers carried the story that the *S.S. Metropolis* had sunk on its way to South America with a boatload of laborers from the United States. "One hour after the news that the ship had gone down arrived in Philadelphia," the *New York Tribune* reported, "the office of Messrs. Collins was besieged by hundreds of hunger-bitten, decent men, begging for the places of the drowned laborers." [24]

It should not be concluded that workers were not interested in becoming farmers in the West. Of all the suggestions made by workingmen to the Congressional Committee of 1878 appointed to investigate the "Depression in Labor and Business," the one most frequently advanced urged that a loan or subsidy be granted by Congress to enable the unemployed to take up a claim under the Homestead Act, and begin farming.[25] No proposal gained greater support from labor than the bill introduced in the House of Representatives in 1878 by Benjamin F. Butler which would allow a family, expressing the desire to undertake farming in the West, "to have expended for their benefit the first year of settlement a sum not exceeding twelve hundred and fifty dollars," in addition to transportation to the public lands.[26] The bill was labeled a communistic proposal and promptly forgotten. Even the *New York Tribune* was forced to admit that it was up to Congress to provide for the homeless and the starving. "It is useless to ignore this miserable, gaunt fact which stares us in the face at every corner," it said on February 7, 1878. "It is not to be dispelled any longer by soup-houses on the one hand, organized precautions against tramps on the other.... How the unemployed mechanics and laborers have got through this winter, God only knows.... Are they all to sink down permanently into tramps and paupers?"

The *New York World* outlined its program for the unemployed: "The American laborer must make up his mind henceforth not to be so much better off than the European laborer. Men must be content to work for less wages.... In this way the workingman will be nearer to that station in life to which it has pleased God to call him." [27]

American labor, however, was not convinced that God had decreed that all who work shall starve, and their great unemployed demonstrations were proof of their conviction.

UNEMPLOYED DEMONSTRATIONS

The rallying force in the struggles of the unemployed were the American sections of the International.* Toward the end of October, 1873, the Federal Council of the North American Federation of the International Working Men's Association, which combined all sections of the First International in the United States, issued a manifesto in leaflet form. After explaining the extent of unemployment and suffering of the working class, it proposed the following program:

"We submit and recommend to you the following plan of organization, put into effect already successfully by our German fellow-workers:

---

* Even before the crash in September, 1873, the International was active in rallying the unemployed to demand relief. In March, 1872, a mass meeting of the unemployed, called together by the New York Sections of the International, was held in Tompkins Square. The slogans on the banners of the demonstrators read: "The Unemployed Demand Work of the Government," "Eight Hours Our First Right," and "Eight Hours, Peaceably if We Can, Forcibly if We Must." One of the resolutions adopted by the meeting read: "We hereby demand of the government that a National Labor Bureau be established for the purpose of instituting all the various branches of useful industry, guaranteeing employment to all persons who cannot find it elsewhere, upon equitable principles of time (not exceeding eight hours per day), and compensation, and that the products be sold to the people at cost." (*Woodhull & Claflin's Weekly*, March 23, 1872.) The resolution embodies the basic principle advanced by the advocates of the full-employment bill.

"The workingmen of one, two or more blocks form a district club, the district clubs combine to form ward committees, the ward committees will form a central body by deputizing three (3) delegates from every such ward committee.

"The united workingmen thus organized will make the following demands to the respective authorities: (1) Work to be provided for all those willing and able to work, at the usual wages and on the eight-hours plan; (2) An advance of either money or produce, sufficient for one week's sustenance, to be made to laborers and their families in actual distress; (3) No ejectment from lodging to be made for non-payment of rent, from December 1st, to May 1st, 1874." [28]

In the tenth ward of New York City, the German workers had set up an unemployed council early in November, 1873, and proceeded to gather information on the extent of unemployment and the needs of families who were in distress. A little later a mass meeting of German workingmen was held, and a central committee elected to co-ordinate the activity of all the unemployed of the city. At the same time the trade unions of New York went into action. A meeting of trade union representatives took place on November 15, 1873, to demand the employment of mechanics and laborers on public works. A resolution was adopted calling upon the City of New York to request a loan of $10,000,000 "from the National Government to help out labor," and a petition was forwarded to Congress which asserted that "all penniless, homeless and involuntary idle people are the wards of the nation and should not be suffered to roam through the streets neglected and uncared for." It further recommended that the government "operate all industry in which it has jurisdiction, ... and that it employ all members of the working class." All profits of these businesses were to be applied to the reduction of taxes.[29]

A meeting at Cooper Institute on December 11, 1873, called by the trade unions and sections of the International in New York, was crowded to the doors and an overflow audience waited outside to hear its decisions. Inside the hall, banners proclaimed: "The Unemployed Demand Work, Not Charity." "When Working Men Begin to Think Monopoly Begins to Tremble." "Equal Laws and Homes for the Industrious." The *New York Times* condemned these slogans as "decidedly communistic." [30]

The meeting approved the following suggestions from the organizing committee: (1) Public approval of all bills before they become law; (2) No individual be allowed to have more than $30,000; (3) Eight hours constitute a working day. In addition, a resolution was unanimously adopted which declared:

"Whereas, we are industrious, law-abiding citizens, who have paid all taxes and given support and allegiance to the government,

"Resolved, that we will in this time of need supply ourselves and our families with proper food and shelter and we will send our bills to the City Treasury, to be liquidated, until we shall obtain work and pay for our work."

Before adjourning, the meeting elected a Committee of Safety in which the International and trade unionists were represented. The central committee appointed at the German mass meeting and the Committee of Safety agreed to co-operate.[31]

Mass meetings of unemployed workers took place in other cities as well, the American sections of the International playing a leading part in most of them. In Chicago, 5,000 workers, at a meeting on December 21, 1873, sponsored by the International and the trade unions, drew up a petition which demanded employment for all those willing and able to work, at the rate of eight hours a day and a living wage. It called for the extension of food and money to the unemployed through a committee appointed by the workers.

On the following day twenty thousand unemployed workers marched through the streets of Chicago to the City Hall. Calling upon the authorities, their representatives demanded "bread for the needy, clothing for the naked, and houses for the homeless." Several years before, over a million dollars had been contributed to the Relief and Aid Society for the victims of the great Chicago fire. About $700,000 remained of the fund, and the delegation requested that it be turned over to assist families who were in need; and that they be represented on the committee which would select the families to receive assistance, because they knew who was hungry.

A conference of the Mayor of Chicago, a committee of the Common Council, representatives of the workingmen, and the Relief and Aid Society met on December 26, 1873, but the Society refused to turn over its funds to the City Treasury. Thereupon the committee representing the workingmen called another mass demonstration and a mass committee marched on the Relief and Aid Society to appeal for relief. At first the Society refused to grant this committee an audience, but when a thousand workers sought admittance to the building they changed their mind. Believing that the workers were ignorant and superstitious, the Society ruled that only those who submitted to vaccination would obtain relief. So many workers appeared before the Society's doctor, that the police had to be called. Finally the Society gave up its struggle and announced that during the first week of 1874 it would provide relief for families of unemployed workers. About 9,719 families were provided with some form of subsistence. But the City Council never kept its promise to aid the unemployed.[32]

Meanwhile in New York City the joint committee formed by the Central Committee and the Committee of Safety representing trade unions and sections of the International, was organizing the unemployed, calling mass meetings and demonstrations. This activity was to culminate in a demonstration of the unemployed on January 13, 1874. Originally it was planned to terminate the parade in front of City Hall, but when this was forbidden, Tompkins Square was chosen. By the time the first marchers entered the Square, New Yorkers were witnessing the largest labor demonstration ever held in the city. The Mayor, who was expected to address the demonstration, changed his mind and, at the last minute, the police prohibited the meeting. No warning, however, had been given to the workers, and the men, women, and children marched to Tompkins Square expecting to hear Mayor Havemeyer present a program for the relief of the unemployed. When the demonstrators had filled the Square, they were attacked by the police. "Police clubs," went one account, "rose and fell. Women and children ran screaming in all directions. Many of them were trampled underfoot in the stampede for the gates. In the street bystanders were ridden down and mercilessly clubbed by mounted officers." Hundreds of workers were seriously injured, and several were arrested and sentenced to prison for attacking the police.[33]

The Committee of Safety called mass demonstrations to protest police brutality, and to release Christian Moyer who had been imprisoned on the charge of attacking the police at Tompkins Square.

But the unemployed movement could not withstand this severe trial, and it began to lose its momentum. In a number of wards representatives of Tammany Hall took over leadership of the movement in order to stifle any atttempt at mass action, and soon its influence made itself felt in the Committee of Safety. By the fall of 1874 the endless squabbles within the Committee of Safety resulted in the unemployed losing interest.[34]

LASSALLEANS AND MARXISTS

Had the American sections of the International been united, they might have prevented the disintegration of the unemployed movement, but the American Socialist movement was anything but a unified body. During the depression years the conflict between the Lassalleans and the Marxists in America broke out again, intensified by the migration to the United States of several thousand German workers who had fled the reaction in Germany following the Franco-Prussian war. The moment they arrived in America the ideological conflict that had divided the working class in Germany was transplanted to this country.

The conflict manifested itself in the strategy to be followed in organizing the working class for its emancipation. To the Lassalleans the disintegration of the trade unions was proof that only political action would serve the working class during the depression. Unemployment demonstrations, they also argued, were of no value unless they led to the formation of a labor party, and once this was accomplished there was little need for any further concentration on mass meetings and demonstrations of the unemployed.[35]

The Marxists did not reject political action; they believed that every class struggle was a political struggle, but they held that the time was not yet ripe for the formation of a workers' party strong enough to influence the elections. The trade unions, they contended, were the cradle of the labor movement, and it was the duty of the American sections of the International both to revive existing trade unions and to help in the organization of new ones. The demonstrations of the unemployed should be continued regardless of whether or not they led to a labor party, for such demonstrations secured relief for homeless and hungry families, stimulated the workers to think along socialist lines, and presented opportunities to bring home to workers the importance of building trade unions.[36]

After 1873 the Lassallean influence found its expression in the organization of the Labor Party of Illinois in the West, and the Social-Democratic Party of North America in the East. The Labor Party, established after the unsuccessful mass demonstrations of the unemployed in Chicago in December, 1873, had met with empty promises. By February, 1874, it was publishing a weekly organ, *Vorbote,* edited by the Lassallean, Karl Klinge. *Verbote* placed great stress on the fundamental Lassallean demand—state aid to co-operative societies. In keeping with Lassallean principles it announced that the Labor Party would have nothing to do with trade unionism, since "it never led to any lasting betterment for the workingmen in the several trades." [37]

The Social-Democratic Party of North America, founded in 1874 by the Lassalleans, emphasized in its original platform that workingmen must concentrate their efforts upon political action. But within the movement were a number of Marxists who constantly stressed the importance of combining trade union and political activities. As a result of their influence, the party gradually approached the ideas of the International.[38]

While the Lassalleans, both in the West and in the East, were devoting their energies to the formation of labor parties, the sections of the

International which adhered to Marxist principles were seeking to become part of the American labor movement. They had a measure of success in 1875 when the United Workers of America, an organization of Irish workingmen led by J. P. McDonnell, affiliated to the International. That this affiliation of Irish workingmen to the International did not develop into a major trend in the labor movement was due in no small measure to the shortcomings of many Marxists in America. Too often, as Sorge often said, they simply transferred to America what they had learned in Germany without attempting to understand the differences between the two labor movements. Many of them made no effort to learn English, and confined their activities to German-speaking workers. Some even had a contempt for native American workers, regarding them as theoretically backward.[39]

"The Germans," wrote Engels a decade later, "have not understood how to use their theory as a lever which could set the American masses in motion; they do not understand the theory themselves for the most part and treat it in a doctrinaire and dogmatic way, as something which has got to be learnt off by heart but which will then supply all needs without more ado. To them it is a *credo* [creed] and not a guide to action. Added to which they learn no English on principle. Hence the American masses had to seek out their own way...."[40]

For a time it seemed that the split between the Lassalleans and the Marxists would be healed. The Labor Party of Illinois and the Social-Democratic Party of North America met with complete failure at the ballot-box, thereby vindicating the Marxist contention that premature political action before the workers were organized into trade unions was futile. Applying the lessons of this experience, the advocates of trade union action in the Social-Democratic Party increased their influence. At a party convention in 1875 a resolution was adopted which asserted that "under the present conditions the organization of working people into trade unions is indispensable, and that each party member is obliged to become a member of the Union of his trade, or to aid in establishing a trade union where none exists." The *Socialist,* English organ of the Social-Democratic Party, hailed the resolution, and called for "the defense of the trade unions and their principles upon every occasion, in order that the reorganization of society may be speedily accomplished."[41]

THE SOCIALIST MOVEMENT UNITES

Appeals for unity in the socialist movement poured into the labor press during 1875-76. The following, which appeared in the *National Labor Tribune* of September 25, 1875, was typical:

"Throughout the United States there exist numerous organized bodies of workingmen who declare the present political and social systems are false, and require to be changed from their very foundation; that the present degrading dependence on the capitalist for the means of livelihood is the cause of the greater part of the intellectual, moral and economic degradation that afflicts society; that every political movement must be subordinate to the first great social end, *viz.,* the economic emancipation of the working classes. Roughly stated, this is the creed of an immense number of workingmen, and they are the principles held in common by the organized bodies above referred to, but there are minor points on which we differ. To clear up these points of difference, and unite all the various bodies in one grand, invincible organization, has for some time past been the earnest desire of us all, and now it seems that this desire is about to be realized. From all quarters comes a cry for unity. Suggestions have been made to hold a congress in some convenient place, for the purpose of deciding upon a common plan of action, but the time and place of meeting is not yet fixed. Many persons hostile to the cause of labor—and notably the editors of the stock-jobbing press—have sought to bring this radical labor movement into disrepute by persistently asserting that the movement is French, German or Russian, but nothing can be further from the truth. Just as well might these venal writers assert that the 'law of gravitation,' because it was discovered by Newton, is therefore an English movement. For all men who know anything about social science know that the emancipation of labor is neither a local nor a national, but a social problem embracing all countries in which modern society exists. We are workingmen born or naturalized in the United States, therefore such attempts to make aliens of us, only show to what depth of villainy our opponents will proceed. 'Divide and conquer!' has ever been the cry of the oppressor, and it has been successful through all the ages; but now the working classes are rallying to the voice of common sense. . . ."

Unity within the socialist movement was formally established in July, 1876, when delegates from nineteen American sections of the International met in Philadelphia and dissolved the International Working Men's Association.* A few days later, a meeting of socialist organizations was

* Before dissolving, the delegates adopted the following declaration:
"Fellow Working Men:
"The International Convention at Philadelphia has abolished the General Council of the International Workingmen's Association, and the external bond of the organization exists no more.
" 'The International is dead!' the bourgeoisie of all countries will exclaim, and with ridicule and joy it will point to the proceedings of this convention as documentary defeat of the labor movement of the world. Let us not be influenced by the cry of our enemies! We have abandoned the organization of the International

held at Philadelphia to form a united party. The platform of the new party, called the Working Men's Party of the United States, adopted the trade union policies of the International, but conceded to the Lassalleans' request that a national instead of an international organization be established. "We work for the organization of trade unions," the platform stated, "upon a national and international basis to ameliorate the condition of the working people." Since political liberty without economic independence was an empty phrase the party was to direct its energies first to economic issues. Participation in politics was to be delayed until the party was "strong enough to exercise a perceptible influence," and even then only in towns or cities where demands of a purely local character were presented which were not in conflict with the party's platform and principles.[42]

The program of the unity congress was a victory for the Internationalists led by Sorge, but there were several shortcomings which were to weaken the party's influence. The national executive committee, to be located in Chicago, was dominated by the Lassalleans. Furthermore, P. J. McGuire, who led the Social-Democratic Party delegates, succeeded in putting through a proposal empowering the executive committee to permit local election campaigns wherever possible. Frequently the committee refused to follow the mandate of the platform with respect to organizing workers into trade unions, but instead led the workers fruitlessly to the polls.

No sooner had the Working Men's Party begun to function than the old conflict between Lassalleans and Marxists broke out anew.* McGuire,

for reasons arising from the present political situation in Europe, but as a compensation for it we see the principles of the organization recognized and defended by the progressive workingmen of the entire civilized world. Let us give our fellow workers in Europe a little time to strengthen their national affairs, and they will surely be in a position to remove the barriers between themselves and the workingmen of other parts of the world.

"Comrades, you have embraced the principle of the International with heart and love; you will find means to extend the circle of its adherents even without an organization. You will find new champions who will work for the realization of the aims of our association. The comrades in America promise you that they will faithfully guard and cherish the acquisitions of the International in this country until more favorable conditions will again bring together the workingmen of all countries to common struggles, and the cry will resound again louder than ever: "'Proletarians of all countries, unite!'" (International Arbeiter-Association, Verhandlungen der Delegirten-Konfernz zu Philadelphia, 15 Juli, 1876, pamphlet, New York, 1876, pp. 8ff.)

* The Marxists, however, made every effort to maintain unity within the Working Men's Party of the United States, reminding the Lassalleans that factional struggles only weakened the socialist movement. "What a spectacle," appealed Adolph Douai, "for our common bitter enemies to see the two socialist workingmen's factions fight each other instead of the common enemy." (Labor Standard, March 31, 1877.)

speaking for the Lassalleans, maintained that political action was the most important method of organizing the American workers for their emancipation. "We cannot successfully preach trade unionism in these hard times," he argued. "Workingmen—members of our Party—find it difficult to pay even their ten cents a month to keep up the Party. How then can they support a Trades' Union, costing three times as much as the expense of membership in our Party? One form of labor organization in these hard times can exist only at the expense of the other." And if trade unions could really help workers solve their problems, he concluded, what use was there for a Working Men's Party? [43]

The Marxists took issue with McGuire. They admitted that the trade unions were not broad enough to include all workers, but insisted that it was the duty of the Socialists to broaden them. To the question: why have a workingmen's party if trade unions are successful, they replied:

"There is every use for our party. It can do the work which the Unions cannot *at present* accomplish. It can agitate and create intelligence on economical questions. It can make war on the errors of the past. It can arouse the people to the necessity for union and action. It can show itself the party of intelligence and wisdom by helping along every labor union, by working and agitating for the thorough advancement of labor which can only be affected in *labor* organization. It can hurry the masses into their unions, and the latter it can hurry on to centralized action. If we are to hurry the birth of a better future we must strive for a healthy present. Let us not be foolishly selfish because our party is not the entire labor movement. It is only an advanced guard." [44]

The English journal of the Working Men's Party of the United States, the *Labor Standard,* understood the role it should play in American life, and in issue after issue, it appealed to trade unionists to remain in their unions, called upon non-unionists to join labor organizations, and urged members of the Working Men's Party to organize their fellow workers. Even after J. P. McDonnell, editor of the paper, had been censored by the Lassallean-dominated national executive committee for his emphasis on trade unionism and the space he was giving to trade union activities, he continued to call for the revival of the trade unions. Articles from the pens of Frederick Engels and George Eccarius, a member of the International in England, brought home to the readers of the *Labor Standard* the news of trade union activities and labor struggles in Europe. And no paper mirrored the great strike struggles that took place in America as effectively as did this journal of the Working Men's Party of the United States. [45]

CHAPTER 23

Challenging the Great Depression

The American workers did not take unemployment and wage cuts passively, but organized militant struggles to protect their interests. In the textile, coal mining, and transportation industries, workers waged great strikes against the offensives of the employers during this chaotic period.

TEXTILE STRIKES

Fall River, which by 1874 had become an important center of New England's textile industry, was the scene of the most militant strikes in that industry. In the fall of that year wages were reduced 10 per cent, followed a few months later by another cut. After the first cut, the mulespinners revived their union, hired a secretary, and called mass meetings of all spinners, weavers, and card-room hands. The latter group, most of whom were women, formed their own union, at the same time that the weavers set up the Weavers' Protective Association.

Encouraged by promises of support from spinners' locals in New Bedford and Lawrence, Massachusetts, the Fall River workers decided to go on strike if the wage-cuts were not rescinded. A delegation from the spinners', weavers', and card-room workers' unions visited the manufacturers and presented the demand for the rescinding of the wage cut. The employers rejected the demand and refused to discuss arbitration of the question on the grounds that arbitration was un-American.[1]

When the card-room women heard of this refusal, they met separately and voted to strike whether the men did so or not. Soon the men joined the strike and by February, 1875, more than three thousand workers had stopped work. All workers not affected by the walk-out were taxed to support those on strike. After a month of struggle the employers agreed to rescind the cut on April 1, and the strike was called off.[2]

But by the time summer rolled along the manufacturers were again trying to restore the 10 per cent wage cut. Again the workers called a strike and by August nearly every mill in the city was closed down, and the walk-out had assumed the character of a general strike in the industry. This strike, called the "Great Vacation," lasted for eight weeks and ended in the workers' defeat. When the strike had stretched into its third week the discouraged workers decided to call it off. But when they discovered that the employers were now demanding more than the 10 per cent cut, they continued to hold out. On September 27, 1875, the strikers marched to the City Hall to demand bread for their starving children. They were greeted by three companies of militia and a cordon of police who prevented them from presenting their demands. For many years after, September 27 was marked in Fall River by mass meetings to commemorate these textile strikers.

Late in October the workers returned to the mills, accepting the wage cut, and signing the "yellow-dog" contracts or "iron-clad oaths," as they were called at the time. All workers who had addressed public meetings or in any way had helped lead the strike, were blacklisted.

The defeat wiped out the unions of the weavers and card-room operatives.* The spinners, however, kept their organization alive. They signed the "yellow-dog" contracts, but privately declared that they recognized no agreement forced upon them by the hunger of their children.[3]

THE LONG STRIKE OF 1875

The defeat of the textile workers came shortly after an equally crushing defeat suffered by the miners in the "long strike of 1875." In 1868 the Workingmen's Benevolent Association was formed, with John Siney as its president. By 1869 the union had thirty thousand members, about 85 per cent of the workers in anthracite mines. That very year, after a prolonged strike against a wage cut, the mine owners in the anthracite district signed an agreement which recognized the union as the bargaining agency for the miners and provided for a sliding scale of wages based on the prevailing price of coal.† A minimum wage regardless of

* Before dissolving their organization, the weavers assigned their slender funds to their leaders so that they could move to other communities.

† In the Lehigh region the miners were to be paid according to the price of coal at Elizabethport, New Jersey, and in the New York market. When coal sold at $5 a ton in this market, the miners would receive their minimum pay, and for every dollar coal advanced above that price they were to be given an increase of 15 per cent. In the Schuylkill region, where coal was shipped to Philadelphia rather than to New York, wages were to be determined by the price of coal at Port Carbon. When coal sold for $3 a ton at Port Carbon, the Schuylkill miners would receive their minimum wage, and for every advance of 25 cents above that price,

the price of coal was also agreed upon. From that time on, up to 1875, the coal operators tried each year to force a wage cut. The agreement signed on July 29, 1870, by the Anthracite Board of Trade and the Workingmen's Benevolent Association, the first written contract ever drawn up between miners and operators in America, worked out disastrously for the miners. The union accepted a proposal that wages should advance or decline 8¼ per cent for each 25 cent change in the price of coal, with the minimum basis of $2 a ton. The contract also provided for a cut in the base pay of contract miners whose wages were high, ranging from 10 per cent for those with net earnings of $100 to 40 per cent for those earning over $200 a month. A victory, however, was scored by the union in the agreement when the operators agreed not to "discharge any man or officer for actions or duties imposed on him by the Workingmen's Benevolent Association." [4]

Unquestionably the union was dazzled by the prospect of wage increases under the new agreement if the price of coal rose. Unfortunately, the price fell rapidly and, in the very first month following the acceptance of the new contract, the miners saw their wages cut 8¼ per cent. By December, 1870, their wages had been reduced 24¾ per cent. In subsequent agreements adopted in 1871, 1872, and 1873, the principle that wages should slide downwards as well as upwards in relation to the price of coal was retained, but the union was successful in raising the minimum wage. Thus although the price of coal dropped during these years, the miners were at least able to maintain a certain minimum wage. The operators, therefore, were determined to smash the union and the principle of a minimum wage.

Franklin B. Gowen, renowned labor-hater, was the leader of the coal operators. He was president of the Philadelphia and Reading Railroad, which, through its subsidiary, the Philadelphia and Reading Coal and Iron Company, had gained control of the largest collieries in the anthracite district. Since the Schuylkill and Mahoning coal fields depended on the Philadelphia and Reading Railroad for an outlet to a market, Gowen was able to dictate a labor policy to the other coal operators.[5] This coal baron was ready to commit any crime to smash the militant Workingmen's Benevolent Association, or, as it was now called, the Miners' and Laborers' Benevolent Association. He imported contract labor and hired company police and labor spies. At the same time, he posed as the friend of the laboring man, condemning the union as a despotic organization "before which the poor laboring man has to crouch like a whipped

they would secure a 5 per cent increase in wages. (See Andrew Roy, *A History of the Coal Miners of the United States,* Columbus, Ohio, 1907, pp. 76-78, and Marvin W. Schlegel, "The Workingmen's Benevolent Association: First Union of Anthracite Miners," *Pennsylvania History,* vol. X, October, 1943, pp. 246-47.)

spaniel before a lash, and dare not say that his soul is his own." The leaders of the union, he said, were foreign agitators, "advocates of the Commune and emissaries of the International." [6]

For three years Gowen prepared his offensive. Not all coal operators were ready to join his drive against the union, as they knew the stabilizing effect of union policies on the industry. But it was not long before Gowen eliminated this small group from the industry, and in December, 1874, the operators started their attack by announcing a 20 per cent wage cut for contract miners, a 10 per cent cut for laborers, demanded that the minimum basis be eliminated and insisted that wages be further decreased 8 per cent for every 25 cents coal dropped below $2.50. It was clear, however, that this announcement was made to provoke the union into a strike during which the operators hoped to destroy the organization. One of the leaders of the Miners' and Laborers' Benevolent Association told a *Philadelphia Times* reporter that the war was not against wages as much as it was "directly against our organization." A Mahoney City correspondent wrote to the *Miners' Journal*: "It is well known that the coal market can afford to pay last year's prices, but it seems that the wages question is not the trouble, but the disbanding of the M. & L.B.A." [7]

John F. Walsh, an English miner who had fought three years in the Union Army, led the strike which soon followed. The ruthless Gowen, who was also president of the powerful Anthracite Board of Trade, later admitted in a report to his stockholders that he had spent four million dollars to break the strike, and defended his action by saying that the money had been well spent because he had rescued the company "from the arbitrary control of an irresponsible trades union." [8] Gowen was assisted by the Governor of Pennsylvania, who quickly sent in troops to break the strike.

The miners had little money, but they had the sympathy of workers throughout the country. The Industrial Congress passed a resolution tendering "heart-felt sympathies to the miners now locked out, and earnestly requested all organized bodies of workingmen throughout the country to forward to the Treasurer of the Congress as generous financial assistance as their circumstances will permit." Later the president of the congress issued another appeal to the workers of America saying that the miners were "engaged in a contest with the most powerful Anti-Trade Union combination that has ever been formed in this country," and that, "these miners are fighting the battles of labor in this country." Similar appeals were issued by various sections of the International Working Men's Association. [9] *

---

* The Marxists enthusiastically supported the miners' strike, but at the same time reminded the strikers that they would not succeed basically in changing

Only a small amount of money was collected, and so the miners had to rely on their own small resources and their magnificent spirit. That spirit is expressed in a song that was written during the struggle:

> *In eighteen hundred and seventy-five, our masters did conspire*
> *To keep men, women, and children, without either food or fire.*
> *They thought to starve us to submit with hunger and with cold,*
> *But the miners did not fear them, but stood out brave and bold.*
>
> *Now two long months are nearly o'er—that no one can deny.*
> *And for to stand another month we are willing for to try.*
> *Our wages shall not be reduced, tho' poverty do reign*
> *We'll have seventy-five basis, boys, before we'll work again.*[10]

Before many weeks had passed, the miners in the northern anthracite fields accepted the wage cuts and returned to work,* but the miners in the southern and middle fields carried on. "Since I saw you last," wrote a miner during the strike, "I have buried our youngest child, and on the day before its death there was not a bit of victuals in the house with six children." [11]

"The miners," wrote Andrew Roy, later mine inspector of Ohio, "made heroic sacrifices such as they had never made before to win the strike. In the closing weeks of the contest there were exhibited scenes of woe and want and uncomplaining suffering seldom surpassed. Hundreds of families rose in the morning to breakfast on a crust of bread and glass of water, who did not know where a bite of dinner was to come from. Day after day, men, women, and children went to the adjoining woods to dig roots and pick up herbs to keep body and soul together...." [12]

With part of the miners supplying coal, the operators were able to hold out until starvation forced the remaining miners to yield. The union

---

their conditions as long as they fought only "for wages, or for limitation of working hours." "Let the soil be ours!" they appealed. "Let the factories with all their machines be ours! When in possession of these means, then also what is produced by and of them is ours! Then there will be no more need of strikes to increase the income from our labor, which our labor-masters now reluctantly hand over to us, but every person will have the full income of his or her labor, and their full share of natural products. Therefore let us inscribe on our banners: 'Down with work for wages! Arise and battle for possession of the materials.' " (*National Labor Tribune*, Sept. 25, 1875.)

* The existence of two miners' unions was a factor in the defeat of the strikers. The W. B. A. was on friendly terms with the national organization and even exchanged membership cards with the Miners' National Association. But its members, especially in the Schuylkill and Lehigh regions, refused to abandon the older union and enter the new national organization. As a result locals of each union existed side by side in the same regions and, though they worked together, the unity of the anthracite miners was considerably weakened.

agreed to the wage cut but demanded that its authority for fixing the rates be recognized. The operators refused and the strike continued until June when hunger finally had its way. "We are beaten," admitted John Walsh, "forced by the unrelenting necessities of our wives and little ones to accept terms which, as we have already told the Coal Exchange and the public, we could never under any other circumstances have been forced to accept." [13] Wages were cut 20 per cent; signed agreements did away with provisions for weighing the coal; the union was broken, and Walsh and other union leaders were forced to leave the region. Seven months after the end of the "long strike" the president of the Miners and Laborers Benevolent Association sadly admitted that "the organization is decimated as it never was before; it is weak and tottery in most places, and in many has gone altogether out of existence." The miners dolefully sang:

> *Well, we've been beaten, beaten all to smash,*
> *And now, sir, we've begun to feel the lash,*
> *As wielded by a gigantic corporation,*
> *Which runs the commonwealth and ruins the nation.*[14]

The "long strike" also brought an end to the once-promising future of the Miners' National Association. John Siney and other leaders of the Association had been opposed to the strike, and while the strike was in progress Siney had told the executive board that strikes provided the "source of most of our troubles," and were the "cause of degrading our own class." Conciliation and arbitration were the best means of solving conflicts between capital and labor.[15] Siney overlooked the fact that he was dealing with employers who were dead set against unions, and no matter how willing unions were to compromise, the workers were confronted by a coalition of industry which received government support.[16]

Siney's own experience in the strike should have convinced him of this fundamental error. After the strike in Clearfield County, Pennsylvania, had lasted three weeks, the operators imported strike-breakers. A mass meeting was held to protest the action, at which Siney was present although he did not participate in the discussion. On May 12, 1875, he was arrested on charges of conspiracy. Twenty-six other union leaders, including Xeno Parkes, field organizer for the Miners' National Association, were arrested on the following day.

Their trial once again was proof that the common law was still being used by the courts against the people. In his charge to the jury Judge John Holden Owes held that "any agreement, combination or confederation to increase or depress the price of any vendible commodity, whether labor, merchandise or anything else, is indictable as a conspiracy under the laws of Pennsylvania." The law was "part of the common law which our forefathers brought with them from the mother country, and the same law under which the people of this State have lived since the days of William Penn."

After the men in the Joyce-Maloney case had been convicted of riot and conspiracy, Judge Owes said in pronouncing the sentence: "I find you, Joyce, to be the president of the Union and you, Maloney, to be secretary, and therefore I sentence you to one year's imprisonment." * [17]

In a desperate effort to keep the Miners' National Association alive, Siney turned to the panacea of producers' co-operatives. But the membership did not have the capital, nor did they agree with their leadership that such co-operatives would harmonize labor and capital. The Association disintegrated in 1876 without having opened a single mine of their own, and the members of the organization began to look to the Knights of Labor for leadership. [18]

Gowen and his associates were not satisfied with the destruction of the Workingmen's Benevolent Association only. They were bent on smashing all organized activity of the miners. For did not these workers still sing their song?:

When the men go back to work, they must all be determined, To prepare for a struggle in some future day.

THE MOLLY MAGUIRES

As wage cut followed wage cut, the miners fought back, led by an Irish fraternal and patriotic organization, the Ancient Order of Hibernians. They had belonged to the Order when their union was strong, but now it became their secret organizational center. In most studies of American labor history the secret activities of the miners after the strike of 1875 have been associated with acts of violence in eastern Pennsylvania that began in 1862 and continued for twenty years. These crimes are said to have been committed by a secret society, the Molly Maguires.

Recent research has revealed a different story. It is now established that there was no society in America calling itself the Molly Maguires, that this name was tagged to the Ancient Order of Hibernians by the commercial press whose purpose it was to help the coal operators crush all organization in the mining industry; that the Philadelphia and Reading Company hired the Pinkerton spy agency not to save society from a band of terrorists but to spread terror; that during the 'sixties

---

* As a result of labor's indignation and political pressure, a law exempting labor combinations from the charge of conspiracy was enacted at the next session of the Pennsylvania legislature.

and early 'seventies the operators had subsidized secret armed vigilante societies in Pennsylvania to murder and terrorize miners. As many miners were killed by these gangsters as were mine foremen and bosses by miners.

No account of the offensive against labor during the long depression would be complete without a discussion of the trials of the so-called "Mollies"—men accused of murder and terror in the coal region. Gowen was state prosecutor in a number of cases. If the Molly Maguires are eradicated, said Gowen, "we can stand up before the whole country and say: 'Now all are safe in this country; come here, with your money; come here with your families and make this country your residence; help us to build up this people and you will be safe.' " [19]

The evidence against the accused men was supplied by James Mc-Parlan, the Pinkerton spy who testified that he discovered the murder plots of the Molly Maguires. His testimony was corroborated by disreputable characters who secured immunity for their own crimes. Several witnesses who testified for the accused miners were indicted for perjury and sentenced at once to serve two and one-half years in the county prison. As a result even close friends of the defendants were reluctant to testify in their behalf.

It was generally admitted in the press that the corroborating witnesses for McParlan contradicted themselves so often and told such incredible tales that no one could be convicted on their testimony in an honest trial. John Kerrigan, a witness who testified that he had joined several of the men on trial in killing a man named Yost, was accused by his own wife of killing the man himself and then accusing "innocent men to suffer for his crime." Another witness for the prosecution declared that he had had a view of the faces of the men who had killed Thomas Sanger, a mine foreman, and he was certain that the man who had committed the crime was Thomas Munley because Munley sat in the court room in the same "peculiar and constrained manner" as had the five men seen on a fence about 500 feet distant on the morning of the murder. Gowen admitted in his summation that the witness had not been asked if he recognized Munley by his face.[20]

When another witness testified that she had only seen the side view of the murderer and that the "side view looks like the man" on trial, Gowen said to the jurors, "There are mechanical appliances that render identification instantaneous. The art of the photographer has discovered a method whereby, in an instant of time or less than an instant, in a pulsation of the heart, in the winking of an eye, you can take the picture of a man while he is moving at full speed before you. Why should not the eye of this woman be able to do the same thing?" [21]

Another witness recalled that the murderer had a slight mustache, but could not remember the color of his hair or eyes. His testimony was as reliable as that of his cronies:

"*Q.* Had you ever seen the man before?
A. I never saw him before that morning.
Q. Did you know him at all?
A. No, I did not know him at all.
Q. Have you ever seen him since?
A. Yes, sir.
Q. Munley, stand up. Is that the man?
A. That is not the man I can recognize at all." [22]

But Munley was convicted.

Practically all of the evidence was based upon McParlan's statements, and, as the defense pointed out, it was not "until the emissary of death, James McParlan, had made his advent into this country" that the crimes began. McParlan's subsequent career was not so successful. In 1906 as chief of the Denver division of the Pinkerton agency, he was hired by the state of Idaho to find the murderers of ex-Governor Frank Steurenberg. As a result of his evidence, William Haywood, Charles Moyer, and George Pettibone, leaders of the Western Federation of Miners, were arrested in Denver, Colorado, kidnapped and taken to Boise, Idaho, where they were charged with the murder. During the trial of Big Bill Haywood, Harry Orchard testified that he had killed the ex-governor at the instigation of the union leaders, and had been influenced by McParlan to turn state's evidence. Under Clarence Darrow's brilliant cross examination, Orchard revealed that he had been carefully coached by McParlan. Darrow proved that McParlan had used Orchard the way he had used Kerrigan in the Molly Maguire cases to railroad labor leaders to their death.[23]

The mass movement in defense of Moyer, Haywood, and Pettibone was instrumental in securing their freedom; absence of such a mass movement in the Molly Maguire trials made possible the carrying out of lynch sentences. The *Labor Standard* and the *Irish World* exposed the plot of the coal operators but these papers were not influential enough to organize a movement great enough to save the condemned men.*

* Protest meetings were held in many industrial centers. A mass meeting in Philadelphia spoke out "against the hasty and inhuman manner in which the so-called 'Molly Maguires' have been sentenced to death." On January 13, 1877, a mass meeting of New York workingmen, called by the Working Men's Party, adopted a set of resolutions which asserted that the charges against the condemned men were "chiefly based upon the testimony of an infamous person named McParlan, who has been actively engaged in the service of the mine owners"; accused the mining corporations with having "endeavored to cover with odium the working men of Pennsylvania for the purpose of diverting attention from their own cruel and outrageous robbery of the workmen." (*Labor Standard,* Jan. 20, Feb. 24, 1877.)

The *Miners' National Record* refused to aid the men on trial, and the *National Labor Tribune* argued that if the labor movement joined in condemning the accused men, the commercial press would be convinced that organized labor did not approve of violence.[24]

On June 21, 1877, the first group of condemned men were brought out in pairs for execution. Roarity, Carroll, Duffy, and Munley were executed in succession. "I have nothing to say, gentlemen," Carroll declared when asked to make a statement, "only that I am innocent of the crime I am charged with." Other executions followed within a year, and the legal murders were over on January 14, 1879, when Sharp and McDonnell were hanged. These two men were executed just as a messenger arrived with a telegraphic reprieve from Governor Hartranft. The messenger was not admitted to the scene of the execution, and the men were dead by the time the reprieve was placed in the hands of the proper authorities. Reporters stated that the reprieve seemed to have been timed to arrive just too late in order that the Governor might win labor support while he performed the work cut out for him by the coal companies.[25]

The men whose lives had been "sworn away" by labor spies and perjurers, the *Irish World* observed in June, 1877, "were mainly leading intelligent men whose direction gave strength to the resistance of the miners to the inhuman reduction of their wages." [26] A week later, the *Miners' Journal,* the operators' organ, corroborated this statement, and gave away the conspiracy. Referring to the men who had been executed the day before, it declared: "What did they do? Whenever prices of labor did not suit them they organized and proclaimed a strike." * [27]

* The most recent study of the Molly Maguires is by J. Walter Coleman, *The Molly Maguire Riots: Industrial Conflict in the Pennsylvania Coal Region,* published in 1936. This is in some ways a curious book. The author states that he had made a careful examination of the records of the cases and of the files of local newspapers, but hesitates to draw logical conclusions from the evidence he presents based on this research. He admits that the fact that the Pinkerton Archives are not accessible to students renders it difficult to dismiss the charge that a conspiracy was entered into between the Philadelphia and Reading Company and the Pinkerton officials to manufacture evidence to convict a group of militant labor leaders, and he agrees that the subsequent activities of McParlan, particularly in the Haywood-Moyer-Pettibone frame-up, show that the Pinkerton detective was quite ready to enter into such conspiracies. He also acknowledges that the men prosecuted "were closely associated with the labor movement in the anthracite region, and as leaders in this movement they were obnoxious to the interests of the employers of labor," and that "for this reason" they "were exterminated by means of funds furnished by leading mining and railroad companies of eastern Pennsylvania." (pp. 171-72.) Furthermore, he agrees that the trials were travesties of justice. Yet he reaches the conclusion that the "responsibility for many of the violent deeds committed as a phase of labor disturbances is not to be fixed by earthly judges." (p. 175.)

To this writer it is clear that Anthony Bimba's *The Molly Maguires* published in

THE GREAT STRIKES OF 1877

All over the country employers shared the glee of the mining and railroad companies of Pennsylvania. During the years when textile workers and miners were suffering serious setbacks, the progressive governments in the South were being overthrown and replaced by governments dominated by planters and industrialists. With good reason the *Commercial and Financial Chronicle* could report to northern capitalists anxious to invest in the South that conditions were ideal, for "this year [1877] also labor is under control for the first time since the war." [28]

Every industrial and trade report echoed the words, "labor is under control," and employers were now consumed with the hope that workers would no longer dare to resist wage cuts and ask for better working conditions. But in the summer of 1877, a short month after the first condemned men in Pennsylvania had been executed, our country experienced one of the most widespread and militant strikes in its history.

The railroad workers had felt the impact of the depression as keenly as any group of workingmen in the country. Their wages had been cut steadily until average weekly earnings amounted to five to ten dollars a week. Irregular employment reduced their wage still more. Men with families were permitted to work only three or four days a week, most of which time had to be spent away from home at their own expense. After paying a dollar a day to the company's hotel, they frequently returned home with as little as thirty-five or forty cents. To make matters even worse, the men often had to wait two, three, and even four months for wages which were supposed to be paid monthly.* [29]

Not even the docile and fraternal organizations of railroad workmen, the Brotherhood of Railway Conductors and the Brotherhood of Locomotive Firemen and Enginemen, were tolerated by the companies. Union men were blacklisted, grievance committees were refused hearings, and the Pinkerton spies were so active that workers were afraid to talk to one another.

The spark which set off the explosion was the notice of another 10

1932, which Coleman admits is "substantiated by authentic documents," has come closer to the truth in concluding that the evidence makes it possible for "earthly judges" to see that the entire case was a conspiracy of reactionary employers against a militant labor movement.

* Even the conservative organ of the Brotherhood of Locomotive Engineers acknowledged that the railway workers had good cause to complain of their conditions. Several months before the panic it inquired: "Are not railway employees in this year of grace, 1873, enduring a tyranny compared with which British taxation in colonial days was as nothing, and of which the crack of the slave whip is only a fair type?" (*Journal of the Brotherhood of Locomotive Engineers*, April, 1873, p. 162.)

per cent wage cut, to take effect on the Pennsylvania Railroad on June 1, and on many other lines a month later. This cut was brazenly announced as the railroad officials knew that the workmen had no militant organizations to lead them, and that thousands of unemployed were begging for work. But these officials had overlooked the fighting tradition and the temper of American workers.

A reporter for the *Baltimore Sun* described the spirit of the strikers and their families in his account of the strike on the Baltimore and Ohio:

"The singular part of the disturbances is the very active part taken by the women, who are the wives and mothers of the firemen. They look famished and wild, and declare for starvation rather than have their people work for the reduced wages. Better to starve outright, they say, than to die by slow starvation." [30]

Another thing the rail operators overlooked was the fact that a great many people in America bitterly hated the railroads. Rate discriminations against individuals, firms, and whole communities; stock manipulation, bribery, corruption, and the wholesale robbery of the public domain had so infuriated the people that they welcomed the chance to aid the strikers. Even the commercial press which attacked the strikers with unprecedented fury was forced to admit that the vigor of the strike was due in no small measure to the fact that the railroad men were joined by farmers, miners, and small businessmen who shared a common hatred of the companies.

The *New York Tribune* declared: "It is folly to blink at the fact that the manifestations of Public Opinion are almost everywhere in sympathy with the insurrection." [31] The "insurrection" had started on the Baltimore and Ohio Railroad early in the morning of July 16, when forty Baltimore and Ohio firemen and brakemen on freight trains stopped work. A freight train was halted at Camden Junction, outside of Baltimore. The police moved in and dispersed the strikers.

Suddenly the strike spread all along the line. At Martinsburg, West Virginia, 1,200 brakemen and firemen seized the depot and stopped all freight trains, allowing only passenger and mail trains to move. When the Mayor of Martinsburg had the leaders of the strike arrested, a large crowd leaped into action and soon they were released. Delegations of miners from the surrounding towns poured into the city to help stop any further arrests.

The strike spread to other points in West Virginia. In the town of Keyser, white and Negro railroad workers met together and voted to join the strike. They had "soberly considered the step," and had finally decided that "at the present state of wages which the company had imposed upon us, we cannot live and provide our wives and children with the necessities of life." [32]

Vice-President King of the Baltimore and Ohio appealed to Governor Matthews of West Virginia to break the strike, and the Governor dispatched the National Guard. The militia, composed of laborers and farmers, not only refused to shoot workers who were derailing freight trains, but fraternized with the railroad men, offering them their weapons.[33] Unable to rely on the militia, Governor Matthews wired President Hayes for federal troops. On July 19, a day after he received the request, Hayes dispatched troops to West Virginia, under the command of General French.[34] This marked the first time in our history that federal troops were used to suppress a strike in peace time.

The reporter for the *New York World* wrote to his paper from Martinsburg: "It has been well observed that if the rights of the strikers had been infringed or violated instead of that of the Railroad corporations, it is probable that Governor Matthews would have hesitated a long while before he would have thought it his duty to call on the president for aid." [35]

General French arrested the leaders of the strike and reported to Washington that everything was quiet. But the strike was far from crushed. It spread to other parts of West Virginia and extended into Ohio and Kentucky. Canal boatmen, miners, and other workers turned out to redress their own grievances as well as to assist the railroad men. In Louisville, Kentucky, a gang of Negro sewermen stopped work, and with picks, shovels, and hoes on their shoulders marched through the streets, urging all other laborers to join them. "Before night," wrote a correspondent from Louisville, "there were several hundred, including some whites." [36]

Meanwhile troops were being mustered in at Baltimore to be sent against railroad workmen and miners at Cumberland, Maryland, who had stopped trains coming from Martinsburg. As the troops marched to the station they were followed by several thousand Baltimore workmen who protested the sending of militia to Cumberland. When these workmen tried to prevent the departure of the troops, the militia fired into the crowd, killing twelve and wounding eighteen. "The determined temper of the soldiers," wrote a correspondent for the *New York Times*. "is evinced by the circumstance that all the men killed were shot through the head or heart." [37]

The Maryland governor's plea to President Hayes for federal troops was also answered immediately, and with the aid of the troops the company started to operate the trains. Any worker who pleaded with a strikebreaker was instantly arrested; every group of strikers who sought to stop trains from moving was immediately fired upon. Such tactics,

reported the *New York Times,* "disheartened and subdued the mob." [38]
By July 22 the wholesale killings and arrests, the regular troops, militia
and police, the vigilante groups and the terror whipped up by the commercial press broke the strike on the Baltimore and Ohio.

The strike that had begun on the Baltimore and Ohio in Maryland
and West Virginia spread to lines in Pennsylvania, New York, New
Jersey, Ohio, Illinois, Missouri, and California. The strike reached great
intensity in Pittsburgh, for it was supported by all classes in the city. The
only railroad between Pittsburgh and New York charged such exorbitant
rates that the small businessmen as well as the rest of the population
were filled with rancor against the railroad companies.

Wage cuts were only one of many grievances of the men on the Pennsylvania railroad; a few days after it had announced the new wage
schedule, the company ordered that the number of cars taken out by
one crew be increased from eighteen to thirty-six. Not only did this
double-header edict mean twice as much work for less pay, but it meant
that half of the workers would be fired.

Shortly after the men were notified of the new wage-cut, a committee
of engineers visited Tom Scott, president of the Pennsylvania Railroad,
and agreed to accept the reduction in wages if it would be rescinded
when business improved. This agreement was not accepted by the workmen who began to organize secretly under the leadership of R. H.
Ammon, a young brakeman. They organized a secret industrial union,
known as the Trainmen's Union, composed of engineers, conductors,
brakemen, and firemen. A strike was set for July 27, 1877, but as the
day approached, the engineers backed out and it looked as if the entire
movement would fold up. Then came the news of the strike on the Baltimore and Ohio and the double-header edict of the Pennsylvania, and so
the Trainmen's Union went ahead with its plans to strike.[39]

At Pittsburgh the strikers used the same tactics developed by the
Baltimore and Ohio strikers. Large groups, including striking miners
from Wilkensburg and unemployed workers from Pittsburgh assembled
on the tracks and prevented the movement of freight trains, allowing
only passenger and mail trains to pass. On July 21, Sheriff Fife, backed
by the Pittsburgh militia, read the riot act to strikers on the Pennsylvania
tracks. The sheriff was helpless when the workers refused to budge,
as the militiamen refused to disperse the strikers.[40]

A mass meeting called by the Trainmen's Union resolved not to go
back to work until the wage reductions were rescinded, the double-
header edict withdrawn, and all strikers re-employed. Delegations from
Pittsburgh businessmen and from near-by mining towns assured the
strikers of their support. The situation in Pittsburgh was tense, yet even
the reporter from the *New York Times* admitted that the strikers had

"behaved well" and that only freight trains had been stopped. Instead of meeting with the union, the company called for more troops. The Governor ordered the Philadelphia militia be sent to Pittsburgh. Colonel Tom Scott praised the Governor and publicly boasted that he would settle "this business with Philadelphia troops." [41]

Scott was confident that his militiamen, fresh from banking centers and mercantile influences, would not fraternize with the "mob." En route to Pittsburgh, the militiamen boasted that they were going to clean up the city. Even the *Army Journal* admitted that the Philadelphians were "spoiling for a fight." [42] They soon had their chance. When they tried to arrest the leaders, the people resisted. They greeted the soldiers from the rival metropolis with groans, hoots, and hisses. A few boys hurled two or three stones at the militia. The troops replied by firing directly into the crowd, killing twenty people—men, women, and children. Twenty-nine people were wounded. A Grand Jury investigation termed the action, "an unauthorized, willful, and wanton killing... which the inquest can call by no other name but murder." [43]

The community was enraged. Thousands of workers from the rolling mills, coal mines, and factories hurried to the scene of the killings. Crowds surrounded the soldiers, driving them into the railroad roundhouse. All night the troops were besieged by an aroused citizenry determined to avenge the murder of the workers. The roundhouse burst into flames, and the troops were forced to withdraw. The Union Depot at Pittsburgh and the terminals of the Pennsylvania Railroad were also afire! [44] Just who set the fires is still in doubt, but the *National Labor Tribune* charged on September 15, 1877, that both the strikers and troops had played into the hand of conspirators "who aimed and seemed to have hit the bull's eye to replace the worn-out rolling stock, etc., and save a big corporation from bankruptcy at the public expense."

Scare headlines in the commercial press increased national apprehension. On July 22 the *New York World* reported on Pittsburgh: *"Pittsburgh Sacked. The City Completely in the Power of a Howling Mob!"* Its news column told its readers that Pittsburgh was "in the hands of men dominated by the devilish spirit of communism." President Hayes ordered soldiers to guard Washington. A proposal was made at a cabinet meeting to declare the State of Pennsylvania in insurrection, and to call for 75,000 volunteers.

Newspapers, clergymen, and public officials vehemently declared that the strike was another Paris Commune, "an insurrection, a revolution, an attempt of communists and vagabonds to coerce society, an endeavor to undermine American institutions." [45] Reacting to their own headlines, the newspapers called for more bloodshed. The strikers, said the *New York Tribune,* knew but the logic of force; it was futile to show mercy to the "ignorant rabble with hungry mouths." To the *New York Herald* the mob "is a wild beast and needs to be shot down." The *New York Sun* recommended a diet of lead for the hungry strikers, while the *Nation* called for federal sharpshooters.

The strike on the Erie Railroad in New York began on July 20, when firemen and brakemen turned out to protest the firing of workers who had met with management on the rescinding of the wage cut. Before the cut, the average wage on the Erie was about twenty-three dollars a month. When the strike was called, the company denounced Donahue, the leader of the strike, as a "dangerous character who holds and disseminates communist views." [46] The strike spread to Hornellsville, to Jervis, Corning, Troy, Buffalo and to Erie, Pennsylvania, finally involving the New York Central and Lake Shore Railroads.

Whenever the militia was called out, it fraternized with the strikers. At Buffalo a company of the militia went over to the strikers, and at Elmira the local troops were reported to be "in open sympathy with the strikers." [47] An officer of the 69th New York regiment informed the *Labor Standard* that many members of the regiment "composed of Irish workingmen [were] in perfect sympathy with their oppressed fellow workmen." The officer continued: "Many of us have reason to know what long hours and low pay mean and any movement that aims at one or the other will have our sympathy and support. We may be militiamen, but we are workmen first." [48]

William Vanderbilt, president of the New York Central, ordered the wage cut on his road rescinded and promised the Buffalo strikers a 25 per cent wage increase if they went back to work. At the same time he distributed $100,000 to the strikers and unemployed workers of the New York Central. However, the men never got the wage increase.[49]

Like a circle in a great pool, the strike widened every hour moving farther and farther westward until it reached the Pacific Coast. To ward off the strike the Central Pacific Railroad in San Francisco rescinded a 10 per cent wage cut which had gone into effect on June 1. Several shipping companies granted concessions for the same reason. Unfortunately demagogues were able to side-track the strike movement into anti-Chinese riots.[50]

As the strike wave spread from the Atlantic to the Pacific, from the Canadian border to the Mason-Dixon line, the cry of communism became louder and louder. The railroad strike was said to be the work of agents operating for the Working Men's Party who had learned their lessons "from the Socialist leaders in the Old World." They were using the strike as a signal for a revolutionary uprising to overthrow the government and establish an American Commune.[51] Actually, because of the disruptive work of the Lassalleans in preventing effective trade union work, the newly organized Working Men's Party had had little contact with railroad workers prior to the strike.[52] Party leaders and Socialist leaders like those on the *Labor Standard* had predicted a major upheaval on the railroads, and consequently were not caught unawares by the great strike actions in the summer of 1877. As soon as the strikes were called, the National Executive Committee of the Working Men's Party ordered all sections to call mass meetings, to offer "resolutions for an eight-hour law throughout the Union, for the abolition of all conspiracy laws, and for the purchase by the Federal government of the railway and telegraph lines." In Philadelphia, Newark, Paterson, Brooklyn, New York, and other eastern cities, the Working Men's Party sponsored mass meetings which expressed their support of the strikers and condemned the government for helping the railroad operators break the strikes. A mass meeting called by the Working Men's Party in San Francisco was attended by 10,000 people who expressed their sympathy "for the families and friends of those who have been shot down while fighting the battle of oppressed labor." [53] Before the meeting was over, a gang of hoodlums broke it up by trying to turn it into an anti-Chinese demonstration.

In Cincinnati the Working Men's Party appointed a committee to contact the railroad men, and worked closely with the strikers, while in Chicago and St. Louis it was in the leadership of the strike. In Chicago, as in other western cities, it took on the aspect of a general strike. On July 24, workmen at the Michigan Central freight yards downed tools. Soon workers in other yards stopped work, and during the day most factories and shops in the city were shut down. On the following day police charged the strikers at the Michigan yards with guns and clubs, arresting the leaders. But terror could not stop the spreading strike wave. Eight hundred coal miners in St. Clair and Madison counties turned out demanding an increase in wages, an eight-hour day, and payment twice a month. They expressed sympathy with the railroad strikers in Chicago and pledged to render whatever assistance they were called upon to give. In Cairo, Illinois, a number of Negro stevedores struck for an increase in wages from twenty to thirty cents an hour. Their demands were granted, but before returning to work the Negro workmen pledged full co-operation to the strikers in other parts of the state.[54]

On July 25, the *New York Times* announced: *The City in Possession of Communists.*

The Working Men's Party had helped arouse the workers of Chicago. Two days before the strike started on the Michigan Central the party had held an emergency conference after which it issued a call for a mass meeting to be held the following day. About 20,000 workers answered the call, many of them marching to the demonstration with banners on which were written: *"We Want Work Not Charity." "Why Does Over-production Cause Starvation?" "Life by Work or Death by Fight."* [55]

George Schilling and Albert R. Parsons were among the leaders of the Working Men's Party to address the meeting. Parsons urged support for the railroad workers who were on strike in the eastern states but said nothing about a strike in Chicago, nor is there any evidence that the party had anything to do with the walkout of the switchmen of the Michigan Central. Once the strike had begun, however, the party appointed an executive committee to help in the general strike. This committee immediately issued circulars calling upon all workers to unite with the railroad men by shutting down every shop, factory, mill, and lumber company in the city. The members of the party among the cigar and furniture workers took the lead in spreading the strike. Throughout these turbulent days the Socialist leaders, especially Albert Parsons, moved among the strikers telling them to remain peaceable but firm, and signing up hundreds of workers who wished to join the Working Men's Party. [56]

Chicago's mayor and police force stopped warning workers, and on July 26, a pitched battle took place between police and strikers at the Halsey Street Viaduct, which ended when a contingent of cavalry charged the crowd with drawn swords, killing twelve and wounding several score. Chicago had become a second Pittsburgh. The Board of Trade organized "citizen patrols," and federal troops armed with re-peating rifles came to the city from the Sioux country. Parades of strikers were broken up, leaders of the Working Men's Party were arrested, and workers' headquarters demolished. In the street fighting, between thirty and fifty men were killed and almost one hundred wounded. Gradually, the strike in Chicago was crushed, and on July 28 freight trains moved under military guard. [57]

Meanwhile events were moving so fast in St. Louis that the *Republican,* the city's leading newspaper, exclaimed: "It is wrong to call this a strike; it is a labor revolution." [58] Here, the Working Men's Party issued an announcement calling a mass meeting for July 22. "We are asking the public to condemn the government for its action in sending troops to protect capitalists and their property against the just demands of railway men." Several thousand workers attended the meeting which condemned the government for allying itself with capital and against workers "who are attempting to secure just and equitable reward for their labor." The meeting agreed that "we will stand by them in this most righteous struggle of labor against robbery and oppression, through good and evil report, to the end of the struggle." [59]

A mass delegation was formed to visit a meeting to be held by railroad workers in East St. Louis. When the delegation came to the river which divides the city, they decided to cross by ferry since the bridge was run by a monopoly. Inspired by the delegation from the Working Men's Party, the railroad men voted to quit work the following day. An executive committee representing one man from each road was appointed and empowered to set up sub-committees for each separate branch of the industry—brakemen, firemen, switchmen, trackmen, sectionmen, wipers, and blacksmiths. Before adjourning, the meeting adopted a resolution calling on the men not to drink liquor during the strike, and suggesting that if anyone should become intoxicated his friends should take him home.[60]

The company offered to restore wages at the scale that existed on May 15, but the strikers demanded the wages paid prior to January 1, 1877. On July 23 freight trains were ordered stopped. Passenger trains were permitted to move, and special care was taken to let all mail trains through. When the executive committee learned that the men on the Missouri Pacific had decided to go back to work after gaining their demands, it visited these workers and urged them to stay out until a general settlement had been made. They refused. Whereupon, the executive committee left, only to return the next day with an engine and two flat cars carrying several hundred strikers. The men formed into line and marched with fife and drums to the Missouri Pacific shops. This was most effective; the workers stopped and joined the strikers. Demonstrations were organized on a city-wide scale, railroad strikers going from shop to shop urging the workers to join them. A prominent part in these demonstrations was played by the Negro workers who worked on the levee. One reporter, on July 26, wrote from St. Louis:

"This afternoon great crowds of strikers and some 300 Negro laborers on the levee visited a large number of manufacturing establishments in the southern part of the city, compelling all employees to stop work, putting out all fires in the engine rooms and closing the buildings.... The colored part of the crowd marched up the levee and forced all steamboat companies and officers of independent steamers to sign pledges to increase the wages of all classes of steamboat and levee laborers sixty to one hundred per cent." [61]

As the strike spread throughout the city, it was directed by the Working Men's Party, which first sponsored a parade embracing 1,500 workers. When the procession ended, a mass meeting was held and resolutions were adopted expressing support of the strike, calling upon the strikers to prevent disorder and violence and not to give up the strike until the eight-hour day and living wages for the laboring men of St. Louis had been secured. Later, a committee was set up to organize a general strike. This committee, officially known as the Executive Committee, United

Working Men of St. Louis, was under the leadership of members of the Working Men's Party.[62]

The first act of the Executive Committee was to call for a general strike for wage increases, for the eight-hour day, and for a law prohibiting the labor of children under fourteen. Many firms instantly granted their workers wage increases. But this was not enough; the strike mounted. By July 29, all places of business in the city were closed. At first the city authorities practically left the Executive Committee in charge of the city. When the receivers of the St. Louis and South Eastern railroad asked Mayor Overstolz to arrest the strikers, he refused, because of his "inability to do so."[63] But very soon, the city authorities joined with committees organized by prominent merchants to suppress the strike. The St. Louis Gun Club contributed shot-guns, and five thousand muskets came from other sources. Some $20,000 was raised by a committee of merchants to arm a force of one thousand men.

When Governor Phelps threatened to declare martial law, the Executive Committee urged him to convene the Legislature and speak out for the passage of an eight-hour law and for a measure prohibiting the employment of children under fourteen years of age. "Nothing short of a compliance to the above just demand," the Committee declared, "will arrest the tidal wave of revolution."[64] Militiamen, police cavalry, armed vigilantes, and federal troops took control of the city. The headquarters of the strikers was raided, seventy-three men were arrested and forty-nine imprisoned with no charges placed against them. The members of the Executive Committee were arrested on charges of conspiracy, and the high bail of $3,000 for each man forced them to remain in prison. The mass movement broken, the strike was soon crushed. Four members of the Executive Committee were sentenced to a five-year prison term and fined $2,000 each.[65] By August 2, the strike was over. Here and there, the companies adjusted some of the grievances but those who went back to work found the wage reductions still in effect. Many returned to their jobs feeling that they had gained nothing from the two weeks of struggle, but there were others who remembered with great satisfaction the sight of "white and colored men standing together, men of all nationalities in one supreme contest for the rights of workingmen."[66]

The American capitalists drew a lesson from the national strike wave. They saw the importance of a militia controlled by wealthy men, a larger standing army, and more and better armories. During the next few years the militia in several states was centralized, more armories strategically built, and conspiracy laws enacted against the trade unions.

Labor learned two fundamental lessons from the great strike: first, that future success would depend upon effective national organization along trade union and political lines. The role of the local, state, and national governments in crushing the strike convinced workers that no reliance could be placed on either of the major parties. Second, labor realized that executive committees set up during a struggle and scattered mass meetings were not enough. Strikers with hungry families to feed required swift relief payments. Hastily established committees could not meet this need. The railroad strike proved the necessity of strong unions with an adequate dues system to meet strike expenses.*

* Since this book was published in 1947 a number of new works have appeared on the miners' labor unions in eastern Pennsylvania and the Molly Maguires. Most important of these are: Marvin W. Schlegel, *Ruler of the Reading: The Life of Franklin B. Gowen* (Philadelphia, 1947); Clifton K. Yearley, *Enterprise and Anthracite* (New York, 1961); Wayne G. Broehl, *Molly Maguires* (New York, 1964), and Harold W. Aurand, *From the Molly Maguires to the United Mine Workers: The Social Ecology of an Industrial Union, 1869–1897* (Philadelphia, 1971). A number of these works accept the accounts of those who have maintained that there was a terrorist element among the Ancient Order of Hibernians known as the Molly Maguires and that this element did in fact conspire to commit a number of murders before and after 1872. In general, however, they reject the view that the Mollies were intimately connected with coal unionism. My own view still is that there were actually no organized terrorist groups in the coal regions, that even individual terrorists had no connection with unionism among the coal miners, and that fundamentally the entire Molly Maguire issue was a frameup engineered by Franklin B. Gowen. In any case, one of Dr. Aurand's points is well worth quoting. He notes: "The Molly Maguire investigation and trials were one of the most astounding surrenders of sovereignty in American history. A private corporation initiated the investigation through a private detective agency; a private police force arrested the alleged offenders; the coal company attorneys prosecuted them. The state provided only the courtroom and the hangman."

CHAPTER 24

Independent Political Action, 1873-1878

The rapid disintegration of the political parties formed under the leadership of the National Labor Union caused many workers to lose interest in independent political action. On the other hand, during the hard times following the panic of 1873, a feeling was mounting in the labor movement that trade unions were powerless to remedy labor's grievances and that independent political action alone could aid the wage-earners. In June, 1875, the *Iron Molders' Journal* admitted that "hundreds of the ablest men in the [labor] movement have lost hope as to the power and willingness of workingmen to fight capital to the bitter end, through the organization known as trades unions. . . . Hence we find them no longer urging the organization of labor into Trade and Labor Unions, but urging organization for political purposes. . . ." [1]

THE RISE OF GREENBACKISM

Leadership for independent political action during the depression came from farmers rather than from wage-earners. Several independent parties emerged in the western states between 1873 and 1875. That their appeals for united action with the workers were welcome can be seen in an article in the *National Labor Tribune,* published in Pittsburgh and edited by John P. Davis, a leader of the Knights of Labor in Western Pennsylvania. In 1875 Davis wrote: "Farmers of the West, we welcome the hour when we can take your hand. The mechanic of the East, the vast army of laborers, stand waiting for the tocsin to sound, when they can, with you, rise up and possess this land and this government." * [2]

* Unity between farmers and workers in the 'seventies was strengthened by the activities of the Order of the Sovereigns of Industry, which grew out of the Patrons of Husbandry (the Grangers), an educational, social, and mutual aid society for farmers. The Order was mainly concerned with establishing consumers' co-operatives

As the depression grew worse and trade unions disintegrated, trade union leaders and labor journals called upon the workers to join with the farmers in an independent political movement to destroy the money power. If only the government could be forced to issue greenbacks and aid workers' co-operatives by advancing credit at 3 per cent instead of the 12 per cent charged by the bankers, all would be well! The issuance of greenbacks would speedily end the depression. "Let the government print its own money, and ... pay it out to our starving people, the actual workingmen, for their labor in enterprises to be run and owned by the people at large through their hired agents," declared the *National Labor Tribune.* "It is not necessary that the railroads should be built, owned and controlled by private corporations. Let the government build railroads.... Let us issue greenbacks for that purpose, and employ idle labor." [3]

To some sections of the working class, the greenback movement was not viewed as a mere inflationary movement. Essentially it was regarded as the opening wedge toward greater industrial democracy and a better social order. In the Greenback Party, however, none of these principles were emphasized, for labor had little influence in the movement. The party was mainly interested in more money to secure higher prices and was not concerned about changing the social order.

The Greenback Party emerged from a series of conventions in 1875. Most of the representatives at these conventions were farmers and lawyers,

---

for the distribution of necessaries of life among wage-earners, and was "designed for the laboring classes, especially working men and women." (Circular entitled "Private Instructions to Deputies and Masters" in Thomas Phillips Papers, Wisconsin State Historical Society.) The Order co-operated in several cases with the Patrons of Husbandry, and even united with the Patrons to maintain a co-operative store. "The Farmers and Sovereigns," went one circular issued by the Order, "act as a unit in all purchasing as far as practicable. In a word they join hands and concentrate the power of both organizations. This simple fact gives the Sovereigns a great advantage over all other organizations in matters of making contracts. This brings directly to the homes of working people a saving that cannot be secured in any other way." (Circular entitled "Union of Grangers and Sovereigns" in Thomas Phillips Papers, Wisconsin State Historical Society.) Another circular declared: "It [the Order] is and will continue to be, in thorough sympathy and hearty co-operation with the Patrons of Husbandry, both being parts of one great whole, whose destiny is to work out a better future for the industrial classes of this country." (Circular, dated January, 1874, in Sovereigns of Industry Papers, Wisconsin State Historical Society.)

The total membership of the Order in 1875-76 was said to be 40,000, of whom 75 per cent were in New England and 43 per cent in Massachusetts. Its decline started in 1875 and by 1878 it was passing out of existence. (See Commons, *op cit.,* Vol. II, pp. 171-75; E. M. Chamberlin, *Sovereigns of Industry,* pp. 150-54; J. Butterfield to John Samuel, Worcester, Mass., January 31, 1877, *Ms.,* John Samuel Papers, Wisconsin State Historical Society.)

but a few leaders of unions that had gone to pieces during the depression were usually present. At a convention in Cleveland in March, 1875, John Siney; Richard F. Trevellick; Robert Schilling of the National Coopers' Union; A. C. Cameron; and C. W. Thompson, the Negro trade union leader from the Tobacco Laborers' Union of Richmond, Virginia, were present.

The convention adopted a platform built on financial reform and set up a new party. The money question, it asserted, "more deeply affects the material interest of the people than any other question in issue before the people." Payment of the national debt in greenbacks, and the issue of interconvertible legal tender currency bonds bearing not more than 3.65 per cent per annum, were demanded. The new independent party became known immediately as the Greenback Party.

In September, 1875, a conference took place in Cincinnati, representing a movement led by Horace H. Day, a wealthy philanthropist who had been active in the National Labor Union. Day had refused to attend the Cleveland convention as it was not representative of labor. In spite of Day's objections, the Cincinnati Conference voted to fuse with the Independent Party. The contribution of the Cincinnati conference was a demand that was to appear in every Greenback platform until 1879—the repeal of the resumption of the specie payment act which had been passed in June, 1875.

Labor was represented at the first national convention of the Greenback Party which met in Indianapolis, May, 1876, in the person of Trevellick, A. C. Troup, and John Hinchcliffe, but the convention was dominated by farmers, lawyers, businessmen, and politicians. Little recognition was accorded labor, either in representation on committees or in the platform; for, would not a repeal of the resumption act and the issuance of greenbacks end unemployment automatically? [4]

The Greenback Party devoted its major campaign to winning support in the rural districts. A few labor papers, such as the *National Labor Tribune* and the *Workingman's Advocate,* conducted a campaign for its national and state tickets. In the mining districts of Pennsylvania, Trevellick, Davis, Drury, and other leaders of the Knights of Labor organized Greenback clubs and sponsored meetings for the party candidates.[5] Most of the work of organizing working class support was done by John P. James, secretary of the Miners' National Association. James tried very hard to win over the Socialists, and debated vigorously with members of the Working Men's Party on the importance of the Greenback movement to the laboring man. In July, 1876, the Working Men's Party adopted a resolution urging their sections to refrain from political action in the forthcoming campaign, and to support none of the parties in the field because they were dominated either by capitalists or by quacks.* James asked the Socialists to revise their stand, contending that lumping the Greenback Party with other parties was unjustified. "It is purely a struggle of right against might," he wrote to the Labor Standard, "labor against capital, and every laborer in this country who is a voter ought to have his place in the lists of the Independents." [6]

A few Socialists endorsed James' proposal, arguing that, with all its limitations, the Greenback Party was "inculcating a hatred of monopolies and monied despotism, laying bare their rascalities and robberies, sloughing off the old party politicians, giving new men and new ideas and preparing the way for the final victory of labor." Most Socialists disagreed with this stand, contending that the platform of the Greenback Party benefited not the working class so much as it did the demands of the real estate speculators and politicians. The financial demands of the party, when enacted into legislation, would not solve labor's problems, for the Greenbackers were only interested in the extinction of the national debts through the issuance of greenbacks. Peter Cooper, its presidential nominee, was, to be sure, a humanitarian, but he did not represent the working class. The Greenback Party, argued the Socialists, was ignoring the reign of terror in the South in which the Ku Klux Klan was forcibly denying the Negro the right to vote and forcing them into a state of semi-slavery. No party, said the Labor Standard, which overlooked the problems of one section of the working class deserved the support of any worker.[7]

The Socialists were correct in 1876 when they refused to endorse the Greenback movement. At this time the new party offered little to workers and embraced but few of them in its ranks. The vote in the 1876 elections was proof that labor was far removed from the Greenback political movement. Chicago gave Cooper 251 votes out of more than 62,258; Cincinnati, 21 votes out of 47,000. In Philadelphia, 10 votes were cast for Cooper; in Pittsburgh, 93; in New York City, 289; and in Brooklyn, 50. The highest labor vote for Cooper came from the counties in Pennsylvania, scene of the "long strike" of 1875. Schuylkill County gave Cooper 1,238 votes; Luzerne County, 600; Dauphin County, 397; and Mercer County, 400 votes.[8] Little wonder that the National Labor Tribune which had predicted a "political revolution in the labor vote"

* The Working Men's Party was following a policy adopted at a congress held at Philadelphia in April, 1874, of the American sections of the International Working Men's Association. The resolutions on political action rejected "all cooperation and connection with the political parties formed by the possessing classes, whether they call themselves Republicans, or Democrats, or Independents, or Liberals, or Patrons of Husbandry (Grangers), or Reformers, or whatever name they may adopt." (Circular issued by the International Working Men's Association, Wisconsin State Historical Society.)

POLITICAL ACTION, 1873–1878 479

was sorely disappointed. "The results of the election," it said, "are sickening." [9]

LABOR PARTIES AND GREENBACKISM

The terror which broke the great strikes of 1877 had taught the workers that living conditions could not be improved if the armed forces of the government were to be used to crush labor activity. Determined to nominate and elect men who would stand by the working class, the wage earners turned to independent political action. The workers' parties which sprang up all over the country, in almost every industrial center between New York and San Francisco, were at first independent of the Greenback movement. Soon a great many of them fused with the Greenbackers because of the close relationships that had been built up during the strike between the workers, farmers, and small businessmen. The farmers had shown their solidarity with the strikers in their battle against the hated railroad corporations. When the strikers in Scranton set up a relief store, they were supplied with food by the farmers. "The farmers in the surrounding country," reported the *Scranton Republican,* "have proved themselves very generous, and in many instances have donated batches of potatoes to the cause. They are dug up and hauled to the store by committees appointed for that purpose, and afterwards distributed wherever required." [10]

On July 23, 1877, the Breadwinners League of New York called upon trade unionists, labor reformers, grangers, and Greenback men to unite for the formation of an independent party. As the platform for the new party the League suggested four demands: First, that the government should "immediately take control, own and operate the railroads"; second, enactment of labor laws for the protection of workingmen; third, instant resumption of public works "with government funds" to provide employment for unemployed workers, and, fourth, repeal of all National Bank charters and issuance of greenbacks in their stead.

"Citizens," the call concluded, "Organize! Unite with us, and we will redeem the nation from bond, bank and railroad monopolies, by converting every city in this vast, rich, idle country into an actual workshop; every acre of its broad land into a farm, every mine into a source of life instead of a Potter's Field to its workers." [11]

This appeal stated the principles upon which political activity was to be conducted in many American communities during the next two years. This activity was a fusion of two programs: the demand for financial reform, and the demand for labor laws.

The first Greenback-Labor fusion took place in Pennsylvania in the very heart of the district where the railroad strike had been most extensive and violent. On August 13, 1877, a meeting in Pittsburgh, sponsored by the trade unions, formed the United Labor Party. Its platform included the typical demands of the Greenbackers, and called for protective tariff legislation, labor bureaus in the state and national governments, abolition of contract convict labor, workmen's compensation legislation, child labor laws, abolition of conspiracy laws applying to labor organizations, distribution of public lands to settlers only, and the establishment of courts of arbitration for the settlement of disputes between labor and capital.[12]

Late in August, the Greenback Party of Pennsylvania and the United Labor Party appointed a joint committee to organize a united movement and write a common platform. The platform which emerged from this conference kept the original financial demands of the Greenback Party, adding a number of the labor demands raised by the United Labor Party. The two parties now fused. Most of the candidates nominated for offices had been nominated a few weeks before by the Greenback Party, but a number of labor men were added to the ticket. All of the labor men who ran for office under the Greenback Labor emblem were influential leaders in the Knights of Labor.[13]

The fall election of 1877 saw an effective organization to gain public support for labor candidates and to bring out the vote. The work was conducted by Greenback clubs which sprang up in those districts where the railroad strike had been fought and in centers where the Knights of Labor were influential. "Twenty new Greenback clubs," the *New York Tribune* reported on August 13, 1877, "have been organized around Pittsburgh and in the vicinity of Pottsville in the past few days."

A similar fusion movement was taking place in Ohio. On September 13, a convention called by the executive committee of the Working Men's Party of Columbus, Ohio, met in that city. The convention voted to fuse with the Greenback Party and form a national party if the Greenbackers agreed to certain conditions. The Greenback candidates nominated the previous June were to be withdrawn, new candidates selected by a joint convention, and labor demands added to the Greenback platform. The Greenback Party accepted these conditions and a new convention was held. Stephen Johnson, whom the party had nominated for governor, was renominated, but the other candidates were selected from the ranks of the workingmen. A new platform was drawn up which advocated repeal of the Resumption Act and the National Banking Act and restriction of the issuance of money to the government, a graduated income tax, complete control by the government over all corporate bodies, and abolition of paying wages in store scrip.[14]

The Working Men's Party of Cincinnati remained aloof from the

Greenback movement. Meeting in convention on August 12, it refused to join with this party, and nominated a full ticket for state officers. For School Commissioner, it nominated a Negro, the superintendent of schools in the Negro section. During the railroad strike Superintendent Clark had supported the strikers, and on several occasions had addressed mass meetings organized by the railroad men.[15]

In New York a Labor Reform Convention was held at Troy on October 9, following an appeal of the Breadwinners League issued during the railroad strike. This convention nominated an independent ticket for state officers and drew up a platform of labor reforms. John J. Junio of Syracuse, a cigar maker and trade union leader, was nominated for the office of Secretary of State; George A. Blair, of New York City, a leader in the Knights of Labor, State Controller; and Ralph Beaumont, shoemaker, State Senator. The labor demands in the platform called for reduction in the hours of labor; abolition of the contract system of prison labor; prohibition of manufacture in tenement houses; establishment of a bureau of labor statistics, and state ownership and management of railways. The financial plank favored "a currency of gold, silver, and United States Treasury notes which should be a full legal tender for all debts, public and private, and the retirement of national-bank bills." [16]

Such a mild proposal for currency reform prevented the Greenbackers from proposing fusion, although at its state convention the party did place some of the Labor Reform candidates on its ticket. A few weeks before election, the Labor Reform Party set up a complete election organization in the up-state counties where large numbers of workers were employed in the shops and railroad yards.

"Here in Elmira," wrote a reporter for the *New York Times,* "every ward has its 'Labor Reform Headquarters' in which well-attended meetings are held each night. In the words of one of the best-known Republicans in this part of the State, there has never been so complete and thorough a political organization since the days of the Know Nothing party. Each county has been divided into districts, which are in turn subdivided into wards and precincts, and in each of the divisions so made there are regular constituted and recognized leaders, whose duty it is to make the closest possible canvass of the districts allotted to their charge.... Nearly all the men connected with the movement are workers in shops and factories." [17]

The party's own newspaper, the *Elmira Daily Bazoo,* printed a pledge daily, which each worker in the area was asked to sign, promising to vote for labor candidates. One of the questions asked of all candidates was the attitude he had taken during the railroad strike.

An analysis of the election returns in 1877 reveals the impetus the railroad strike had given to the movement for independent political action. The vote polled by Stephen Johnson, the Greenback-Labor candidate for governor of Ohio, was almost 17,000, more than five times the Greenback vote of the preceding year. More than half of the votes were polled in those counties which covered the industrial cities of Toledo, Cleveland, Youngstown, Canton, and Columbus; another quarter of the vote came from railway towns and industrial counties in the northeastern area of the state. In Toledo the city ticket and some of the candidates on the county ticket were swept into office. Toledo sent two Greenback-Labor men to the lower house of the legislature.

In Pennsylvania the Greenback-Labor Party polled 52,854 votes, seven times more than the Greenback vote of the preceding year, and nearly 10 per cent of the total vote cast. The vote came mainly from the anthracite and bituminous counties, the counties through which the Pennsylvania railroad ran, and those adjacent to New York, the territory of the Erie railroad. These counties contributed about 25 per cent of the total vote. The *New York Tribune* commented on the voting: "The coal-miners and other rough and communistic characters went to the polls under the lead of their secret society officers and carried their ticket by 3,000 majority." [18]

The Labor Reform Party of New York polled over 20,000 votes, ten times the vote of the Greenback Party in 1876. Steuben county, which contained the town of Hornesville, the center of the Erie strike, and Chemung county, which included Elmira, gave the party 4,666 votes or little less than one-fourth of the total vote. Rochester, another highly industrialized area, contributed 23 per cent of the total vote.[19]

THE NATIONAL GREENBACK-LABOR PARTY

The election returns in 1877 speeded up the organization of a national independent political movement. During the campaign unity had already developed between Greenback and Labor forces, particularly in the heavily industrialized states. In Pennsylvania and Ohio the two groups had united and local Greenback-Labor organizations had been formed. The Baltimore and Louisville, Kentucky, Working Men's parties favored unity with the Greenbackers. In New Jersey and Massachusetts both political groups had endorsed the same candidates, and in New York the Labor Reform Party had already worked together with the Greenback forces in the elections.

Not long after these elections, a call was issued for a "national convention of labor and currency reformers" to be held in Toledo in

February, 1878. The call had been sent out by D. B. Sturgeon, of Toledo, Ohio, chairman of the State Executive Committee of the National Party in Ohio, and was signed by prominent Greenbackers. Farmers, small businessmen, and workers discussed the coming convention and looked forward to a new political party that would speak and act for the plain people.

One hundred and fifty delegates, most of them from Pennsylvania, Ohio, Indiana, and Illinois, attended the convention. Although such leading figures from the labor movement as Robert Schilling, Uriah S. Stephens, Richard Trevellick, and Ralph Beaumont were delegates, the convention was run by such men as E. P. Allis and E. A. Boynton, prosperous manufacturers; and Walter P. Groom, secretary of the New York Board of Trade and editor of the *Mercantile Journal*. While Trevellick was honored with the temporary chairmanship, the permanent chairman was Francis W. Hughes, leader of the Greenback forces in Pennsylvania.

The platform of the new National Party opened with a vivid account of the state of the nation: "Business income and wages reduced, unparalleled distress inflicted upon the poorer and middle ranks of our people, the land filled with fraud, embezzlement, bankruptcy, crime, suffering, pauperism and starvation." These conditions, it stated, were caused by "legislation in the interests of, and dictated by, moneylenders, bankers, and bondholders." Nothing was said about the industrial capitalists who had slashed wages and forced their workers to sign "yellow dog" contracts. There were the usual Greenback demands except that the interconvertible 3.65 bonds were not mentioned. The labor demands called for legislation reducing the hours of labor, national and state bureaus of labor and industrial statistics; abolition of contract prison labor, and prohibition of the importation of labor.[20] This mild program was attacked by the *New York Tribune:* "Of course, all reasonable men can see that the Toledo resolutions mean communism. The coming party is bent upon complete social and financial revolution." [21]

During the winter and spring of 1878 unity among the different groups in the party was strengthened. Greenback clubs were organized in working class and farming districts; Greenback newspapers gained an enormous circulation, and Greenback pamphlets were carefully read and discussed by workers all over the country.

"It is not an uncommon scene," wrote a Pennsylvania correspondent of the *New York Tribune,* in the spring of 1878, "to find a company of unemployed miners at street-corners in Pottsville or Tamaqua, talking about the currency and general politics. One of the company who can read takes up a newspaper or a currency pamphlet, and discloses to his little crowd of listeners, what it contains, and when he finishes they all join in a free open-air discussion." [22]

In several states workingmen's associations became Greenback clubs, and trade unions joined in recruiting members for the new movement. Wherever a local assembly of the Knights of Labor existed there was certain to be a number of Greenback clubs. In New York City the leaders of the Working Men's Union actively spread the doctrines of the new party.

That the party's organizing work, helped by many volunteers, was effective is seen in the spring elections of 1878. In February of that year, Terence V. Powderly, soon to be Grand Master Workman of the Knights of Labor, was elected Mayor of Scranton. The Democrats and Republicans had formed a joint citizens' ticket to defeat Powderly's "Labor Reform or Molly Maguire ticket." "Down with this Communistic Oligarchy," cried the *Scranton Republican*. This paper dreaded the future of Scranton "with a succession of Powderlys in the Mayor's offices and a non-tax-paying irresponsible rabble in power." Powderly's defeat was "as certain as we look for the setting sun." Following Powderly's election the *Scranton Republican* explained that "hundreds of workingmen have been attracted into the meshes of communism." [23]

In the spring elections in New York State the new party, called the United Workingmen and Greenback Party, elected mayors in Elmira, Auburn, Utica, and Oswego, polled more votes than the Democrats in Rochester and Syracuse, and elected supervisors in seventeen counties. These victories were the fruit of careful organization work conducted by workingmen in up-state communities. From Elmira, Auburn, Rochester, Utica, and Oswego came "Greenback workingmen missionaries to the counties near at hand" to lecture to the farmers on the necessity of supporting the independent party candidates.

"The speakers," wrote a reporter for the *New York Tribune* from Elmira, "were almost exclusively mechanics who worked in the shoe factories or machine shops of this city. After laboring at the bench 8 or 10 hours in the day, they would drive a dozen miles into the country, make a speech at a school-house or in the open air, return at or after midnight, and report for duty in the shop at the customary hour the next morning. In this way meetings were held in every school district of this county and Greenback clubs were formed in many of the towns." [24]

Despite the headway it was making, the Greenback-Labor movement was nevertheless splitting apart. As early as May, 1878, the basic antagonisms within the party were developing into a crisis. At the Pennsylvania state convention, held that month, a split was narrowly averted. The labor delegates suffered a setback when Powderly was defeated by David Kirk in the election of chairman of the convention. Their major defeat came when the convention rejected Thomas Armstrong, publisher of the *National Labor Tribune,* as the candidate for governor and nominated Samuel Mason, a lawyer, who had no connection with the labor movement. It turned out later that he was the lawyer for the Pennsylvania Railroad.

To make matters worse, the platform had fewer labor demands than had been advanced by the party during the previous year. It asked for the reduction of the hours of labor and the abolition of the contract system in prisons. But John Siney saved the day. Had it not been for him, the convention would have split. "There are but two parties in the field," pleaded Siney, "the party of the skinners and the skinned, the party of the robbers and the robbed. Come then, let us work together as laborers, as greenbackers, as all opposed to the rule of politicians of either the Republican or the Democratic party." [25]

The conflict in Pennsylvania was mild compared to that of New York. Late in July 1878 a convention was held in Syracuse for the purpose of solidifying the statewide Greenback-Labor Party and nominating a state ticket. Four separate delegations claiming to represent the movement came from New York City. Three delegations came from Brooklyn, three from Troy, three from Albany, and two from Buffalo. A stormy debate over the seating of the New York City delegations ended with the exclusion of all the delegates of that city. *The Nation* reported that the conflict was one between the "city and the country, the city representing mainly the 'Labor Reform' and the country the 'greenback' faction of the new party." The composition of the state executive committee set up by the convention revealed that the Greenbackers dominated the party, for two-thirds of the members were currency reformers and only one-third were labor representatives. Nor was labor itself united; a labor leader like John J. Junio of Elmira openly stated that he considered that the "settlement of the Greenback question is the settlement of the labor question." Most of the candidates nominated by the convention were Greenback politicians with little influence in the labor movement, and here, as in Pennsylvania, the platform contained fewer labor demands than that of a year ago. [26]

The state platforms of the Greenback-Labor parties generally reflected the strength of the working class in the movement. In Maine, where there was little or no labor support, the platform was financial and agrarian, and in Indiana the only labor resolutions were those asking for ventilation of mines and establishment of wages as a first lien on the property of corporations. In Ohio, Missouri, Illinois, and Massachusetts, where there was more labor participation, a good deal of attention was given to labor demands even though the financial reforms dominated the platforms. In Ohio, Andrew Roy, a leading figure in the miners' organizations, was nominated for Secretary of State, the most important office to be filled. Ben Butler, who had considerable labor support in Massachusetts, was the party's candidate for governor. He was later nominated by the Democratic Party as well.[27]

Many platforms which contained demands for labor also contained denunciations of the "red flag of Communism imported from Europe which asks for equal division of property."[28] That the working men did not believe in this Redbaiting is seen in a catechism distributed in leaflet form by working class Greenback clubs. Entitled, "The Epistle of Nathan the Wise," the leaflet went in part:

"Then said the People to the Wise man, What is Communism?"

"And the Wise man answered them never a word but bent his head over a paper and wrote upon it.

"And the multitude questioned him the more, saying, What is this thing called Communism? Tell us we beseech thee.

"And the Wise man answered them and said, Not to gather and keep in my stores fine bread and fine meats, wine and fruits, treasures of gold and silver, and precious stones of which I have not need, nor cunning garments made by work ... when my brother fainteth for a crust. This is communism.

"And a woman murmurs, Is this not Christianity?

"And an aged Rabbi spoke, So taught Moses and the prophets from the beginning.

"And one from the land of Celestial muttered, So taught Confucius six thousand years ago.

"And the Wise man said, Peace! Trouble not your hearts for a word. It is humanity."[29]

The vote in the fall of 1878 represented the high point of the movement; some 1,060,000 votes were cast for the Greenback-Labor candidates for Congress, and fifteen representatives were sent to Congress, six from the East, six from the Midwest and three from the South. The Congressional vote in Pennsylvania was almost 100,000, or about 14 per cent of the total vote. Again the anthracite region contributed the largest share of the vote, although the vote fell 3,000 votes below that of 1877. In Luzerne county the vote for the National Party dropped from 14,538 to 9,674, and in Dauphin county from 3,923 to 1,468. Dissatisfaction over the choice of candidates was responsible for this decline.[30]

Fundamentally the alliance of Labor and the Greenbackers was unstable. To Greenback advocates, labor's demands were of little importance because the Greenback theory stated that financial reform would solve all problems. Many Greenbackers weakened the coalition by such non-sensical statements as: they would have nothing to do with "Communism or trades-unions, which are a kind of labor corporation." The maximum demands of the Greenbackers were well put by one delegate to a Green-back-Labor convention: "All we want is greenbacks, a national money, and an honest government." [31]

But the workers wanted much more. A writer for the *Atlantic Monthly* conducted a survey in the fall of 1878 to discover what workers expected to gain through the Greenback-Labor movement. Speaking to workers in Pennsylvania, New York, and New Jersey, he found that these workers were "all agreed in their belief in 'absolute money'...in desiring the government to become the employer of the people by con-structing public works to an enormous extent and in thinking that it should own and operate railroads, canals, and telegraphs for the benefit of the people; in favoring government ownership of land, legal pro-hibition of large accumulation of wealth by individuals, and the sub-stitution, to a great extent, of the will of the people, as expressed each year (or each day), for fixed constitutional provisions and limitations." Other common demands were: the shorter work day, all public officials to be elected by direct elections, a graduated income tax, public works, proportional representation.[32]

By 1879 the only group left of a once powerful combination of workers and middle class elements was the farmers. In 1880, the Green-back leaders called a conference to which came representatives from the Knights of Labor, the Greenback-Labor party, the California Working Men's Party, the Working Men's Party of Kansas, the Chicago Eight-Hour League, and the Workingmen's Union. The participation of the Socialists occurred after a long struggle led by Adolph Douai who maintained that in spite of the "currency humbug," the labor demands of the Greenback-Labor coalition were important. As masses of American workers were in the movement, it was necessary for Socialists to par-ticipate in the movement to salvage the good and make war on its short-comings. "How can they hear us," asked Douai, "if we shut ourselves up in our closet? How can they read our declarations, if they cannot get at them? And when they read them, do they not need explanation from us before they can fully understand them?" [33] Ironically enough, by the time the Socialists had made up their minds to work with the Greenback-Labor coalition, the workers had already left the movement.

At the conference the Socialists were isolated, and the mild plank they had introduced against monopoly was skilfully sidetracked by a parliamentary trick. The platform's labor planks demanded the enforcement of the national eight-hour law, regulation of prison labor, prohibition of child labor under fourteen years of age, and payment of wages in cash.[34]

In the election campaign for the presidency of the United States, conducted by the Greenback-Labor coalition, James B. Weaver, its candidate, made special appeals to the farmers by calling for the regulation of railroads and the reservation of public lands to actual settlers. Despite broad organizational support in rural districts, Weaver polled only 300,000 votes. No campaign had been organized among the workers, Weaver doing most of his campaigning in the South. By 1882 the coalition had fallen apart and Weaver was advising the party leaders to schedule his addresses in rural areas only, because the cities were hopeless.[35]

CHINESE EXCLUSION

While the Greenback-Labor movement engaged the energies of the workingmen of New York, Pennsylvania, Ohio, and other eastern and mid-western states, workers in California were joining an independent political party whose purpose was the elimination of the Chinese from American life. Most Americans had welcomed the Chinese when they first came to America in large numbers during the gold rush of '49. In 1852 the governor of California had called the Chinese the "most desirable of our adopted citizens," and recommended that land be given them "to induce further settlement." However, emigration was stimulated by steamship companies which found the importation of Chinese workers highly profitable, and by contract companies which were thus able to supply American employers with a cheap supply of workers to break strikes.

In 1870 seventy-five Chinese were employed to break a strike of the Knights of St. Crispin in North Adams, Massachusetts. The employer threatened that he would continue using "coolie" labor in order "to free himself from the cramping tyranny of that worst of American trades-unions—the Knights of St. Crispin." The Philadelphia *North American* urged employers to emulate their colleague in North Adams and use this cheap labor which cost less than six dollars a month. The *Boston Commonwealth* agreed: "These 'Celestials' belong to no striking organization—do not care to be out at nights—don't worry about their pay—do not presume to dictate to their employers." [36]

There were two attitudes toward the Chinese in the labor movement. One view was that since "a nation's wealth consists chiefly in its labor, which is its capital," American workers should welcome anyone, "China-

man, African, or native of any country *coming voluntarily* to this soil."
Opposition to the Chinese, by dividing the working class, only served the
interests of employers. Instead of denouncing the so-called "yellow menace," American workers should organize the Chinese and prevent employers from using them to reduce wage standards. Not for an instant
should they confuse the struggle against unfair immigrant labor competition with anti-foreign prejudices.[37]

Those who proposed this correct approach to the problem were few.
Even A. C. Cameron, who was far in advance of other labor leaders in
his belief that Negro and white workers should unite, took a wrong
stand on the question of Oriental immigration. "Yes," he wrote in the
Workingman's Advocate of June 12, 1869, "bring them along, Chinamen,
Japanese, Malays, and monkeys, make voters of them all; acknowledge
them as men and workers; mix them all up together, water down the
old Caucasian race." The *Arbeiter Union,* ably edited by Adolph Douai,
criticized these expressions of race hatred, but agreed that Chinese immigration should be stopped because their living standards were so low
that it would take a hundred years until they absorbed western civilization.[38]

With such an attitude coming from the advanced leaders of the
labor movement, it is not surprising that so many workers opposed the
Burlingame Treaty of 1868 under which the United States and China
recognized the right of their citizens to emigrate to the other country.
No sooner was the treaty ratified than the labor movement began a
campaign to have it abrogated. This demand was advanced at each
congress of the National Labor Union after 1868, and was made one
of the planks of the National Labor Reform Party. The presence in
America of Chinese labor, said the Labor Party, "is an evil, entailing
want and its attendant train of misery and crime, and should be
prohibited...."[39]

DEMAGOGY'S BRIEF SWAY IN CALIFORNIA

Most of the Chinese laborers who had been brought to America lived
in California, and here, once the great railroads were completed, they
entered the trades, moving gradually from unskilled to skilled occupations. The completion of the railroads, throwing thousands of men out
of work, brought on the problem of unemployment several years before
it had become a serious problem in other parts of the country. Demagogues were able to convince many workingmen in California that
unemployment was due to "coolie competition," and Chinese workers
working for incredibly low wages gave these arguments plausibility.
Many manufacturers and merchants who were beginning to feel the

effects of competition from Chinese business men in America joined in building up the bugaboo of the "yellow menace." [40]

On July 22, 1877, the workingmen of San Francisco met to express sympathy for the railroad strikers at a meeting sponsored by the Working Men's Party of the United States. Neither the speeches nor resolutions adopted by the gathering mentioned the Chinese question. But before the meeting was over, hoodlums disrupted the gathering by demanding that the speakers say something about the "Chinese menace." When the meeting refused to be intimidated, the gang departed, making Chinatown their target. For several days the hoodlums wandered about the city, attacking Chinese laborers and demolishing Chinese laundries. The riots were finally quelled by a Committee of Safety which had organized a "pick-handle brigade."

One of the members of the "pick-handle brigade" was an Irish drayman, Denis Kearney, well known for his sympathies with the employers, his attacks upon the working class, and his boasts that he had amassed a fortune from business ventures. Kearney had decided that his political future would be best advanced by joining a workingmen's movement. He tried to join the Working Men's Party of the United States but was rejected as an enemy of the working class. He then decided to form his own organization, and with a small following he set up the Workingmen's Trade and Labor Union of San Francisco in August, 1877. Three months later, in October, he founded the Working Men's Party in California, with himself as president.

His party proposed "to wrest the government from the hands of the rich and place it in the hands of the people, where it properly belongs," aimed to destroy land monopoly in the state, to provide "decently for the poor and unfortunate," and declared its intention "to destroy the great money power of the rich by a system of taxation that will make great wealth impossible in the future." These planks were a mask for the party's disruptive aim: "We propose to rid the country of cheap Chinese labor as soon as possible and by all means in our power, because it tends still more to degrade labor and aggrandize capital." [41]

The Kearney party made rapid headway; ward clubs were organized throughout San Francisco; meetings on the sand-lots were held every Sunday night, and thousands of unorganized workers joined the Working Men's Party of California. Its prestige among workingmen increased when some leaders of the Socialist Working Men's Party of the United States united with the Kearney party. Soon most of the members of the Socialist movement in San Francisco had joined Kearney's party, giving it considerable strength.

The *Labor Standard* urged all Socialists to fight against the slogan "The Chinese Must Go," and to expose Kearney as a demagogue who was preventing a proper solution of the Chinese problem. Importation of Chinese workers for anti-labor activity, the *Labor Standard* went on, must be opposed, but Chinese workers in America should join with other workers to raise their wages through trade union activity. "You can look in your shoe shops," wrote Caleb Tilley, an Eastern Socialist leader, to the party in California, "for some of the men that were made tramps not by Chinese, but by a more powerful enemy, an enemy that has no heart, no soul, that never hears your dying groans, capital." [42]

Early in January, 1878, Kearney and his associates were arrested and imprisoned for using language "having a tendency to cause a breach of peace." [43] Having become a "martyr" by his brief imprisonment, Kearney was now convinced that no one would dare to oppose his leadership. But his high-handed and dictatorial tactics evoked resentment even among his own followers. Members of the Working Men's Party of California were infuriated by his practice of visiting ward-club meetings, accompanied by a gang of husky and noisy henchmen who would promptly disrupt any gathering that met with his displeasure. With the aid of his trained hoodlums, Kearney deposed ward-club officers who criticized his tactics and appointed leaders who were subservient to him. "I am the voice of the people," he is reported to have said. "I am the dictator until the people put some one else in my place. I owe the people nothing, but they owe me a great deal." [44]

Rumor that the "voice of the people" was "owned and run" by anti-labor interests and that he had promised to put a stop to the movement if the business men of San Francisco handed over $5,000, was also creating an opposition to Kearney and his closest associates. Furthermore, the local trade unions gradually became hostile to Kearney because, opposed to organized labor, he gave the trade unions no representation in the party.

For a while Kearney was able to retain control of the party by expelling all members, including a number of Socialists, who opposed his policies. He gained control of the first convention of the Working Men's Party of California, held in San Francisco on January 21, 1878, but was not able to stop the adoption of a platform which departed from Kearney's disruptive politics. The platform stated that since the government of the United States was controlled by the capitalists, the rights of the people were ignored. "Coolie" labor was denounced as a curse to the land and a demand for its restriction and abolition was raised. Other demands urged that ownership of land be granted only to settlers; that the financial system should be consistent with the needs of the agricultural, manufacturing, and mercantile industries and not the needs of bankers, merchants, and brokers; that the eight-hour day be the legal working day; the farming out of convict labor be halted, and all labor on public works be paid prevailing wages. It also advocated that an end should be put to the growth of millionaires and monopolists, through taxation, and that the President of the United States, the Vice President and the United States Senators be elected directly by the people. Finally, it called for a system of compulsory education, secular in character, to be set up nationally. "There should be instituted in all our public schools lectures, at stated intervals, whose primary aim should be to uphold the dignity of labor and mechanical avocations as paramount to all other walks in life." [45]

During the early months of 1878 the party grew rapidly throughout the state, becoming a power in local elections. In a special election in Santa Clara county, on February 19, 1878, the Working Men's Party candidate for the assembly was elected, defeating the candidates supported by the Democrats and Republicans. A month later, the Working Men's Party elected the mayor and city attorney of Sacramento.

Like the Greenback-Labor movement, the decline of the Working Men's Party of California set in after its greatest victories. After March, 1878, the party split into Kearney and anti-Kearney factions, and wherever the two factions nominated separate candidates in municipal elections, defeats were suffered. Other factors hastened its disintegration. A number of candidates elected by the party were old-line politicians or manufacturers, and once in office they disregarded the organization's principles and voted for measures denounced by the workingmen.

By May, 1878, two executive committees had been set up. The anti-Kearney forces, many of whom were trade unionists, issued an address to the people of California, accusing Kearney of being a dictator, of "selling out to the enemy," and of "acting as an irrepressible disorganizer and an enemy of the party, persuading men to folly, riot and disorder, breaking up clubs, and otherwise damaging and disgracing the party." [46]

From this point on the story of the Working Men's Party of California is largely one of internal dissensions and petty squabbles. A few victories were won in this period of dissension—a new state constitution was adopted mainly through an alliance between the Working Men's Party and the Grangers, and in 1879 the party elected Isaac S. Kalloch, Mayor of San Francisco. But in 1880 the Working Men's Party failed to elect its candidates and soon after it fused with the declining Greenback-Labor Party.

The Working Men's Party of California, though it degenerated into a racket, and the Greenback-Labor movement, controlled though it often was by manufacturers and politicians, had far-reaching consequences. Both brought the question of monopoly to the fore, and were influential in arousing public support for a number of important labor demands. Both movements were instrumental in forcing old established parties to listen more attentively to the demands of the common people. This consequently resulted in the passage of laws in various states establishing bureaus of labor statistics, ending the farming out of convict labor, setting up systems of compulsory education, and abolishing payment of wages in anything but lawful money.

THE SOCIALIST MOVEMENT

The Unity Congress of the Socialist factions in 1876 did not end the conflict between the Lassalleans and the Marxists. The Lassalleans were determined to ignore the mandate of the congress that political campaigns should be organized only when the party was "strong enough to exercise a perceptible influence." The defeat of the great strikes of 1877 was seized upon by the Lassalleans as proof that the ballot box was the only effective weapon with which to fight the capitalist class. Strikes and unemployment demonstrations, they argued, could never succeed because the moment they began to be successful the government sent in the police, the militia, and the army to crush the movements. Since the government officials could not be removed by trade union action, only an independent political party representing the exploited masses could change the situation. Once the state was captured through the ballot a socialist society would be close at hand.[47]

Aided by the general trend toward political action following the railroad strike, the Lassalleans or "political action" Socialists were able to persuade many sections to ignore the decisions of the Union Congress and to rush into politics. At first the results were very favorable. In the autumn municipal and state elections of 1877 the Socialist vote increased considerably: in Chicago the vote was 7,000; Cincinnati, 9,000; Buffalo, 6,000; Milwaukee, 1,500; New York, 1,800; Brooklyn, 1,200, and New Haven 1,600.

At the Working Men's Party convention held in Newark on December 26, 1877, the "political action" Socialists gained complete control of the movement.* Its name was changed to Socialist Labor Party and the constitution and declaration of principles were completely revamped. All obstacles to immediate campaigning were removed, and the main purpose of the party, it was now asserted, was the mobilization of the working class for political action. In a subsidiary statement it was affirmed that the party "should maintain friendly relations with the trade unions and should promote their formation upon socialistic principles." But it was made quite clear that the chief function of the Socialist Labor Party was the organization of political campaigns. Its guiding

* J. P. McDonnell of the *Labor Standard* and his followers stayed away from the convention.

principle became: *"Science the Arsenal, Reason the Weapon, the Ballot the Missile."*

The new party met with considerable success at the polls during the spring and fall elections in 1878. The vote in Chicago in the spring election was about 8,000 and two Socialist aldermen were elected. The following fall the Socialists in Chicago elected four members to the legislature, one senator and three assemblymen. In St. Louis three Socialists were elected to the legislature, and in New York the Socialist vote was 4,000 or twice the vote polled in the previous election.[48]

Naturally, the "political action" Socialists regarded the election results as a vindication of their position. But in reality it was not the Lassalleans who were responsble for these victories as much as it was the Marxists or "trade union" Socialists, who had opposed the Lassallean concentration on political action only. Swallowing their disagreement with the Lassalleans, the Marxists in Chicago,* St. Louis, and New York mobilized their trade unions behind the Socialist candidates, distributed leaflets on election day, and in every possible way united trade union and political action groups. In Cincinnati, however, where the Lassalleans held sway, no connections with the trade unions were established. Consequently the Socialist vote actually declined after the fall of 1877.[49]

Subsequent elections proved that the Marxists had been correct when they warned that a rush to the ballot box without careful preparation in advance and without trade union support would never secure lasting results. The Socialist vote in the autumn elections in 1879 was disappointing, falling in Chicago from 12,000 to 4,800. The "political action" Socialists shrugged off the result with statements that the return of "good times" made an end to socialist success inevitable and that "the workingmen are still blind and thoughtless." The return of "good times" was "rapidly drawing the plundered toilers back into their old paths" and causing the Socialist vote to dwindle. But even Phillip Van Patten, Lassallean leader of the Socialist Labor Party, was forced for the time being to admit the correctness of the Marxist position:

* The key man in achieving a coalition of the trade unions and the Socialist Party in Chicago was Albert R. Parsons. He was both an active Socialist and a militant trade unionist, being elected president of the Amalgamated Trade and Labor Unions of Chicago and Vicinity. By no means a thorough student of Marxism, Parsons did at this time favor both economic and political action. By forming trade unions and voting independently at the polls, he declared, the workers would "ere long call a halt to the increasing power of aggregated wealth which is surely turning our fair America into a land of paupers, tramps and dependent menials." (Alan Calmer, *Labor Agitator: The Story of Albert R. Parsons*, N. Y., 1937, p. 38; and Albert Parsons' *Scrapbook, Mss.*, Wisconsin State Historical Society.)

"The only reliable foundation today is the trade union organization," he wrote, "and while political efforts of a spasmodic nature will often achieve temporary success, yet the only test of political strength is the extent to which trade union organization backs up the political movement." [50]

By 1880 the organized Socialist movement was splitting wide apart into irreconcilable factions. The trend was away from the "political action" Socialists, and was hastened by two events that occurred in 1880. During the spring elections in Chicago, the Socialist candidate for alderman in the Fourteenth Ward, Frank A. Stauber, emerged victorious only to be fraudulently deprived of his seat by the election judges. Although Stauber was finally allowed to obtain his seat, the incident convinced many Socialists that little faith could be placed in the ballot as a method of achieving a new social order because successful Socialist candidates would simply be prevented from taking office.

Soon after this occurrence the Socialist Labor Party split over the manner of participation in the Presidential election of 1880. The majority was in favor of fusion with the Greenbackers, and the party, it will be remembered, participated officially in the Greenback convention which nominated James B. Weaver. One wing, however, insisted upon nominating independent Socialist candidates, and in Chicago this group, headed by Albert R. Parsons, nominated its own local ticket. [51]

Disillusioned with political action and losing faith in voting as a weapon for achieving a socialist society, some of the leaders of the Socialist movement split away from the party. One group swung sharply to the right and began to advocate a type of unionism which would have nothing to do with politics. Another group advocated abandoning the ballot, educational "propaganda by word," the struggle for immediate demands through the trade unions, and substituting physical force, arming of the workers, and "propaganda by deed." * The ranks of the evolving anarchist movement were swelled by the arrival of Socialists

* As far back as 1875, a small group of German Socialists in Chicago had formed an armed club which came to be known as *Lehr und Wehr Verein*. The attack on the workers during the great strike of 1877 by the police, the militia and the United States Army resulted in the spreading of the movement started by the club. Although most of the members of these armed groups belonged to the Socialist Labor Party, the national executive committee of the party denounced such organizations on the ground that they gave a false picture of the objectives and policies of the Socialist movement. In 1878 all members of the Socialist Labor Party were ordered to leave these clubs, but this order was resented by Socialists in Chicago and intensified the schism in the party. (Morris Hilquit, *History of Socialism in the United States,* New York, 1912, p. 213; A. Sartorius Freehern von Waltershausen, *Der Moderne Sozialismus in den Vereinigten Staaten von Amerika,* Berlin, 1890, pp. 158-60; Commons, *op. cit.,* Vol. II, 280-81.)

who had been forced to flee from Germany after the passage of the Anti-Socialist Exceptional laws in October 1878.

Soon Social-Revolutionary clubs made their appearance in New York, Boston, Philadelphia, Milwaukee, and Chicago, composed of foreign-born workers who had belonged to the Socialist Labor Party or who had recently arrived from Germany. Eventually the new organizations were to federate and form the Revolutionary Socialistic Party. This party's platform, adopted at a convention in 1881, urged the organization of trade unions on "communistic" principles and asserted that aid should be given only to those unions which were "progressive" in character. The platform also denounced the ballot as "an invention of the bourgeoisie to fool the workers" and recommended independent political action only in order to prove to workers "the iniquity of our political institutions and the futility of seeking to reconstruct society through the ballot." The chief weapons to be used in combating the capitalist system were "the armed organizations of workingmen who stand ready with the gun to resist encroachment upon their rights...." [52]

Very few workers in America were full-fledged anarchists. In the main those who were influenced by the anarchist philosophy, were class-conscious, militant trade unionists, who had lost faith in the efficacy of the ballot as a result of the increasing use of troops and local police to crush strikes, the wide-spread corruption in politics, and the inability even to seat labor candidates when they were elected to office.

After the election of 1880 the Socialist movement split into several groups. One group tried to rebuild the badly shattered Socialist Labor Party. Another group developed pure anarchism in New York and other eastern cities under the leadership of Johann Most, who arrived in this country from England in 1882. Out in Chicago and other cities of the Middle West, Albert H. Parsons and August Spies led a group which combined trade unionism with anarchism, and in the Rocky Mountain and Pacific Coast labor movement, Burnette G. Haskell, a lawyer who hated his profession, and Joseph R. Buchanan, a leader of the Knights of Labor, proposed propaganda by deed and emphasis on education and trade unionism as the means to achieve "a universal revolution from the throes of which the New World will be born." Almost unnoticed, another group was beginning to develop the principles which would powerfully affect the destinies of the American working class, the pure and simple trade unionism, the "new unionism" of the American Federation of Labor.

CHAPTER 25

Beginnings of the Modern Labor Movement, 1878-1881

During the long depression of the 'seventies, the trade unions in many industries lost the majority of their members, but at no time did trade unionism disappear. The *Iron Molders' Journal* reminded employers that though the labor movement was exhausted "the spirit of resistance to wrong, which is the spirit of Trade Unionism, will never die while labor can be wronged, either by individuals or the law." [1]

REVIVAL OF TRADE UNIONISM

Business began to revive by the middle of 1878, and a year later industrial recovery was in full swing throughout most of the country. These next few years were to bring huge profits to the Carnegies, Rockefellers, Goulds, and Morgans as trusts and monopolies concentrated the economic life of the nation more and more in their hands. But to labor, the revival of industry did not automatically bring higher wages, shorter hours, and better working conditions. As a result of the struggles of organized workers, the length of the working day had been reduced from the fourteen and fifteen hours common earlier in the century. In a few rare instances, early in the 'eighties, workers had won even the eight-hour day, but most workers were still as far from the eight-hour day as they had been in the 'sixties. Most New England textile workers in 1883 had an average working day of a little over ten hours. Bakers in the same year worked from 80 to 120 hours a week; organized cigar makers from 55 to 60 hours a week; unorganized cigar makers from 66 to 90 hours a week and transportation workers in most urban centers from 90 to 100 hours a week. [2]

Samuel Gompers, President of the Federation of Trades' and Labor Unions of the United States and Canada, estimated that wages in 1883 were lower than those of 1870. The average annual wage for industrial workers in the five most important manufacturing states, New York, Massachusetts, Ohio, Pennsylvania and Illinois, Gompers asserted, came to less than four hundred dollars.[3] Wage statistics gathered in the period do not fully coincide with Gompers' estimates, but they substantiate his conclusion that a considerable number of American workers lived in poverty. The average annual living cost of a working class family in 1883 was put at $754.42, while the average income of a worker was $558.68.[4]

The unions which came through the depression of the 'seventies formed the foundation of the modern labor movement. There were eighteen national unions in 1880, half of which had been formed before the crisis. Beginning in 1879 four unions increased their membership as follows:[5]

	1880	1881	1882	1883
Bricklayers	303	1,558	6,848	9,193
Printers	6,520	7,931	10,439	12,273
Cigar Makers	4,409	12,000	11,430	13,214
Carpenters and Joiners		2,042	3,780	3,293

Fully as important as the growth in membership of the national unions was the rise after 1879 of city central bodies in every important industrial center. "In all the principal cities," went a report of September 1880, "the trade unions are allied for mutual assistance with Central Councils or Trades' Assemblies."[6] There were a few trades' assemblies which extended over an entire county, such as the trades' assemblies of Essex County and Passaic County, New Jersey, and Allegheny County, Pennsylvania. Local central councils of the building trades were organized in a few cities, the council in New York having twenty-five unions. Another type of city federation was the United German Trades, formed in New York, Chicago, Milwaukee, St. Louis, and other cities where there was a large German working class.[7]

The United German Trades were closely related to the Socialist Labor Party, supported its candidates for office and helped circulate socialist papers. The influence of Socialists in the trades assemblies was not confined to the German central labor bodies alone. Many of the trades assemblies were organized by Socialist trade unionists, and the *Bulletin of the Socialist Labor Party* was not exaggerating when in September, 1880, it stated that the establishment of city central labor bodies all over the country "has been accomplished mainly by the efforts of Socialists who influence and in some places control these assemblies, and are respected in all of them." Nor was Lucien Sanial, leader of the Socialist Labor Party in New York, painting a false picture when he wrote in September, 1879:

"We dare say that trade unionism in many of the largest cities of

America... would be small indeed if our own men, the Socialists, did not, as active members of their respective trade unions, infuse into them that life and spirit of which these organizations give from time to time some startling evidence." * [8]

It was due to the Socialists in the trade unions of New Orleans, Galveston, Houston, and Savannah, that the trades assemblies in these cities admitted unions of Negro workers on an equal basis with other unions. In the same cities federations were organized of unions of long-shoremen, draymen, yardmen, cotton classers and markers, scale hands, weighers and re-weighers, pressmen, and crewmen to which Negro and white workers were equally eligible. This democratic policy adopted by the Southern Central Trades Assemblies and water-front federations did much to break up the antagonism between white workers and Negro workers. In November, 1883, a parade of the unions composing the Central Trades and Labor Assembly was held in New Orleans. Ten thousand workers marched in the line, representing all countries, colors, and industries, and the demonstration was so successful that it was repeated in 1884 and 1885. [9]

The trades' councils took the lead in negotiating agreements between employers and striking unions and in the enforcement of boycotts. All of them were active on the political front, some through independent political action and others by promoting labor legislation. To cite but one case: in 1882 the Trades Assembly of San Francisco set up a legislative committee to propose labor measures, interrogate candidates for office, and lobby for legislation at the state capitol. The committee drew up a list of questions which were submitted to all candidates for public office, covering such issues as employers' liability, factory inspection, postal savings banks, government ownership of railroads, free textbooks, weekly payment of wages, and the abolition of child labor. Union members were

* The following letter sent by P. J. McGuire, formerly a Lassallean Socialist but now a confirmed trade union Socialist, to Phillip Van Patten, leader of the Socialist Labor Party, gives a vivid illustration of Sanial's point and indicates the origin of the Carpenters National Union. It was sent from St. Louis on April 15, 1881: "Our carpenters' strike is a glorious success. Liebkeit and I managed it. I have got Liebkeit active at work in the movement. We have raised our wages to $3 per day and after two weeks strike we now have only 82 men out on strike, where over 800 were out this day a week. Next Monday we go to work. We have given two weeks' gratis to hold them out and the carpenters will do anything for us. Last Sunday we had a mass meeting of over 1,000 carpenters. Bigger trades meeting never was held in St. Louis.... We have got lots of new members for our union. Last night organized carpenters union of 70 men in E. St. Louis. I received letters from all cities asking me for information and asking me to organize a National Carpenters Union. I will do so." (*Socialist Labor Party Correspondence, Mss.,* Wisconsin State Historical Society. See also Gerhard Segur, P. J. Fitzpatrick, S. Robert Wilson, to Phillip Van Patten, December 1, 1879, June 2, December 4, 1880, *Socialist Labor Party Correspondence.*)

urged to support only those candidates who replied favorably to the questionnaire.[10]

Through their political activities the trades' assemblies often prevented state legislatures from enacting anti-labor laws and forced the passage of legislation demanded by organized labor. Thus several trades' assemblies succeeded in stopping the passage of anti-labor conspiracy laws, and many were successful in their campaigns to secure the establishment of bureaus of labor statistics and the enactment of labor laws.

Perhaps the most important activity of the trades' assemblies was the promotion of organization campaigns among the workers of their communities. Through the efforts of the San Francisco Trades Assembly the following trades were organized in the early 'eighties: hodcarriers, patternmakers, boilermakers, foundry laborers, machinists, beer bottlers, custom cutters, metal roofers and cornice-makers, cartmen and coal haulers, blacksmiths, bag and satchel-makers, house-movers, coopers, brass molders and finishers, ship painters, plumbers and gas fitters, marble cutters, varnishers, marble polishers and rubbers, stair-builders, wharf-builders, watchmakers, painters, and expressmen. Similar results were achieved by trades' assemblies of other cities.[11]

By uniting the local unions at a time when many of them were not yet affiliated with their national organizations and when no effective national labor federation yet existed, the trades' assemblies established labor solidarity and guaranteed success to many campaigns to organize the working class, to secure better living standards and to achieve the passage of labor legislation.

THE INTERNATIONAL LABOR UNION

Important as the activities of the trades' assemblies were, they confined their work for the most part to the skilled workers. The organization of the unskilled as well as the skilled workers was undertaken during this period by two organizations: the International Labor Union and the Knights of Labor. Although its life was only five years and did not survive 1882, the International Labor Union is important for what it represented and what it attempted to do. It was the first great effort to organize all unskilled workers in one union and by uniting them with the trade unions of skilled workers to achieve nationwide labor solidarity irrespective of nationality, sex, race, creed, color, or religion.

The International Labor Union was organized early in 1878. It developed from a united front established about this time between several former International and eight-hour leaders. Disgusted with the domination of the Working Men's Party of the United States by the Lassallean "politicals," Sorge, McDonnell, Douai, and Otto Weydemeyer, son of Joseph Weydemeyer, joined with Ira Steward, George E. McNeill, and George Gunton to campaign for immediate demands around the slogan, "Shorter Hours and Higher Wages." Their strategy was to build a mass working class organization whose aim was the abolition of the wage system.

At a conference early in 1878, J. P. McDonnell and George E. McNeill organized a provisional central committee of the International Labor Union with members in eighteen states. Among them were Albert R. Parsons and George Schilling of Chicago; Otto Weydemeyer of Pittsburgh; F. A. Sorge of Hoboken, New Jersey; George Gunton and Ira Steward of Massachusetts. An executive board of seven, with George E. McNeill as president, functioned for the provisional central committee when that body was not in session. The central committee prepared a Declaration of Principles, this platform representing a compromise of the two groups that had combined to form the organization.[12] The part dealing with principles and ultimate aims was the product of the Steward wing of the coalition. It declared that:

"The wage system is a despotism under which the wage-worker is forced to sell his labor at such price and such conditions as the employer shall dictate.... That as wealth of the world is distributed through the wage system, its better distribution must come through higher wages and better opportunities until wages shall represent the earnings and not the necessities of labor; thus melting profit out of existence, and making co-operation, or self-employed labor, the natural and logical step from wages slavery to free labor.... That the first step towards the emancipation of labor is a reduction of the hours of labor, that the added leisure produced by a reduction of the hours of labor will operate upon the natural causes that affect the habits and customs of the people, enlarging wants, stimulating ambition, decreasing idleness, and increasing wages...."

The part of the platform dealing with demands was a joint product of the two groups on the Provisional Committee:

"We therefore, severally agree to form ourselves into a Committee known as the Provisional Central Committee of the International Labor Union, whose objects shall be to secure the following measures: the reduction of the hours of labor; higher wages; factory, mine and workshop inspection; abolition of the contract convict labor and truck systems; employers to be held responsible for accidents by neglected machinery; prohibition of child labor; the establishment of Labor Bureaus; labor propaganda by means of a labor press, labor lectures, the employment of a general organizer, and the final abolition of the wage system...."

Tactics were distinctly influenced by Sorge, McDonnell and the other former Internationals on the Provisional Committee:

"The methods by which we propose to secure these measures are:
"1st. The formation of an Amalgamated Union of laborers so that members of any calling can combine under a central head, and form a part of the Amalgamated Trades' Union.
"2nd. The establishment of a general fund for benefit and protective purposes.
"3rd. The organization of all workingmen in their Trades Unions, and the creation of such Unions where none exist.
"4th. The National and International amalgamation of all Labor Unions." [13]

It may seem surprising that Marxists were ready to accept that part of the platform dealing with principles and ultimate aims. Certainly Sorge and his colleagues had no illusion that the wage system would be abolished automatically through the eight-hour day. Unlike Steward they did not believe that the capitalists would voluntarily abandon their ownership of the means of production and turn their factories over to the workers as soon as their profits had been absorbed into the wages of the workers through the operation of the eight-hour day. But the Marxists and the eight-hour leaders did agree on two principal points in the program: the wage system was a despotism, and the "first step towards the emancipation of labor is a reduction of the hours of labor."
Sorge and his colleagues were ready to make concessions because they regarded the eight-hour movement led by Steward as "an oasis in the desert of the Currency Reform humbug." Further, the Marxists believed that the International Labor Union provided the means by which the majority of American workers, skilled and unskilled, could be organized into trade unions and through their struggles come to see more clearly the need for socialism.[14]
The object of the International Labor Union was to build a mass labor organization. "The International Labor Union," said President McNeill, "presents a plan by which the unorganized masses and local unions can become affiliated." Its aim, he said, was "to band together Jew, Greek, Irishman, American, English and German, and all nationalities in a grand labor brotherhood." Through it the trade unions would "be stimulated into a new and more vigorous life," and in it workers of any nationality, creed, or color would join hands together "until freedom shall be achieved for all." [15] Adolph Douai hailed McNeill's statements and stressed the special need of carrying the principles of the International Labor Union to Negro workers in the South:

"The Negro population of the South deserves our kindest and most careful attention. They are almost the only laboring people there. Few of them are anything but wage slaves. Without their gathering into our fold, one half of this country must remain adverse or indifferent to our movement. Beginning with their enlightenment in our purposes in such places as Baltimore, Washington, Louisville, St. Louis, and wherever our Labor Unions are spreading, we might achieve what otherwise cannot be done. We might loosen the hold of their white employers on them." [16]

Although the founders of the movement intended an organization that would unite all unskilled workers in America,* the International Labor Union was dominated by textile workers, a great many of whom were workingwomen. The repeated wage reductions in the textile industry during the depression years as well as the long working day, made these workers ready for organization. As soon as McNeill, McDonnell, Gunton, and other leaders of the International Labor Union carried the message of organization to textile labor, unions sprang up in every textile center from Vermont to New Jersey, and strikes immediately followed. Many of these strikes were spontaneous, and some were led by other organizations, but all were influenced by the International Labor Union.

The great strikes of the texile workers during 1878-80 in Paterson and Passaic, New Jersey, Clinton and Cohoes, New York, and in Fall River, and other cities, are indications of the great labor solidarity that was built in the short and brilliant career of the International Labor Union. The strike of 1880 in Cohoes, New York, ended in a complete victory, the strikers gaining a 10 per cent wage increase and fifty minutes for dinner. More than five thousand workers struck, most of whom were members of the International Labor Union.[17] Led by the International Labor Union, the 1878-79 strike in Fall River was one of the greatest in American history. It was carefully prepared for several months by the local branch, and by the time of the walk-out to secure higher wages and the nine hour day, over 5,000 workers had joined the organization. On May 8, 1878, during the course of the strike, twenty-five thousand workers marched in a parade held under the auspices of the International Labor Union, and raised as their slogans:

* "The object of the International Labor Union," wrote Carl Speyer, general secretary of the International Union, two years after it was organized, "is chiefly to organize the unskilled laborers, those are often dangerous competitors to mechanics and consequently the Trades Unions are benefited by the existence of the International Labor Union and fully sympathize with us and assist us where they can. To induce mechanics to join us would be interfering with the Trade Unions who regard the International Labor Union as an associate." (*Papers of the International Labor Union, Mss.*, Wisconsin State Historical Society.)

"We want less work and more pay. We want to work nine hours a day. We want a full hour for noon. We want these things and we want them soon. Peace! There is no Peace! There shall be no peace until our 15 per cent is restored. In Unity is Strength! Join the International Labor Union." [18]

But the many strike failures caused a rapid decline in the membership of the International Labor Union. By February, 1880, there were no more than 1,500 members in the organization, and a year later it went to pieces. In 1881 there remained but one branch in Hoboken, New Jersey, where F. A. Sorge lived.* In 1883 Sorge reorganized the branch as the International Labor Union of Hoboken "to unite the members of the International Labor Union, for the purpose of aiding the trade unions of New Jersey in attaining favourable labour laws." [19] Four years later when Sorge left Hoboken for Rochester, New York, the branch dissolved. At no time did the International Labor Union have more than 8,000 members, but many times that number belonged to it for short periods and were influenced by its principles. These workers were to carry their labor solidarity and class consciousness into the organization of the Knights of Labor.

THE KNIGHTS OF LABOR

Immediately following the Civil War, the Knights of Labor was not an important force in the labor movement. It began to make its influence felt during the depression years. Late in 1873 an attempt was made to co-ordinate the existing local assemblies. Local Assembly No. 1 issued the call to all assemblies asking them to elect delegates to a convention for the purpose of founding a district assembly. At this convention, District Assembly No. 1 was set up in Philadelphia, comprising 31 local assemblies, and the ritual was put into written form. Having established a permanent central body, the order, hitherto confined to Philadelphia, began to expand into New Jersey and western Pennsylvania. "The Order is moving westward," the *National Labor Tribune* informed its readers early in 1875. A little later it announced: "The Secret Order of Labor has taken a deep hold on the workingmen of the country.... The order is spreading silently, like the rising of a tide.... It is Labor's

---

* In February, 1880, Carl Speyer listed the following branches of the organization: Omaha, Nebraska (English branch), Council Bluff, Pennsylvania (English branch), St. Louis, Missouri (English branch), Carterville, Illinois (English branch), Pittsburgh, Pennsylvania (German branch), Hoboken, New Jersey (German branch), Paterson, New Jersey (English branch), Paterson, New Jersey (Silkweavers branch No. 14). (*Papers of the International Labor Unions, Mss.,* Wisconsin State Historical Society.)

coming salvation.... The door is open to all good men, and they are welcomed as brothers by a brotherhood of toilers, who are making the elevation of Labor their religion." [20]

In 1874, District Assembly No. 2 of Camden, New Jersey, was founded; and in August, 1875, District Assembly No. 3 was organized in Pittsburgh. From this center organizers moved into surrounding regions including West Virginia.

The growth of the Order during these years was uneven. Groups joined and left in quick order when they found that the organization did little to raise wages. Most recruits came from unattached local unions that had never belonged to a national trade union, or from national trade union locals that had been disrupted during the depression. Thus the large locals of the Miners' National Association, the Machinists and Blacksmiths National Union, and the Knights of St. Crispin moved in and out of the Order. The universal membership idea of the Order was well suited to the mining industry which had always been organized along industrial lines, and its early secrecy permitted the miners to continue in the labor movement after the defeat of the "long strike" of 1875.[21]

Since the Knights of Labor had no platform (before 1878), constitution, or Declaration of Principles, organizers for the Order—called preceptors—could promise workers that by joining the organization every problem facing them would be solved. Naturally, when the promised results were not forthcoming, workers became disillusioned and left. It was inevitable, therefore, that a demand should arise for the establishment of a national organization which would "bring order out of chaos, unite the widely separated parts of the society, and direct the movement along well defined harmonized lines." [22]

A very important impetus toward centralization within the Order was provided by the secrecy issue. The commercial press was quick to associate secret labor organizations with the Molly Maguires, and the cry was raised that the Knights of Labor, a branch of the "Mollies," was plotting to overthrow the government of the United States. Added to this was the fact that the Catholic Church made it quite clear that it was hostile to all secret societies and especially to those with rituals and vows which might conflict with the confessional. The Knights of Labor had been founded by Protestants, but when it moved into the mining districts of Pennsylvania the Order gained many Catholic members. The hostile attitude of the priests in these counties to the Order affected its growth and quickly brought the secrecy issue to the fore.[23]

When the Pittsburgh convention in 1876, referred to above, failed to unify the existing labor organizations and create a consolidated national organization, the Knights decided to set up an independent national organization of their own. A convention for this purpose, called by District Assembly No. 1, met in Philadelphia in July, 1876. The convention was attended by 35 delegates, 22 of whom came from Philadelphia and Reading. Pittsburgh, which felt that it rather than Philadelphia was the real center of the Order, was not even represented. The convention did not take up the question of changing the policies of the Order—including secrecy—but adopted a constitution for a national body which was to be known to outsiders as the National Labor League of America. The League was empowered to control the secret ritual, which it could modify by a two-thirds vote. All other powers remained with the district assemblies.

A second convention, called by District Assembly No. 3 and attended only by its followers, met at Pittsburgh in May, 1877. The most important action taken at this meeting was the declaration that the name and object of the Order should be made public and the provision that a new Catholic member could, "if he considers it his duty," confess to his father confessor.[24]

It was the great strike of 1877 which proved the need for the centralization of the Knights of Labor. The Knights had participated as individuals in the strike, but Terence Powderly insisted that the only influence the Order exerted officially was to counsel moderation, peaceful methods, and avoidance of contacts with radical elements. As more and more workers moved into the Knights of Labor, following the strike, the need for centralization increased. By the end of 1877, eleven new district assemblies had already been set up, bringing the total to fourteen. The Order now extended into New York, Massachusetts, West Virginia, Ohio, Illinois, and Indiana, as well as Pennsylvania and New Jersey.

With District Assembly No. 3's consent, District Assembly No. 1 sent out a call for a convention to meet at Reading, Pennsylvania, January 1, 1878, "for the purpose of forming a Central Assembly ... and also for the purpose of creating a Central Resistance Fund, Bureau of Statistics, Providing Revenue for the work of organization, establishment of an Official Register, giving number, place of meeting of each assembly, etc. Also the subject of making the name public. ..."[25]

The Reading convention set up a central national form of organization for the Knights of Labor and adopted a set of principles which, with some slight changes, served as the constitution of the Order throughout its existence. It called attention to the "alarming development and aggressiveness of great capitalists and corporations [which] unless checked, will lead to the pauperization and hopeless degradation of the toiling masses." If the workers were "to enjoy the full blessings of life," they would have to "check ... unjust accumulation and the power for evil of aggregated capital." This could only be done when the workers were organized. The goal of the Knights of Labor was "to bring within the fold of organization every department of productive industry," and "to secure to the toilers a proper share of the wealth that they create."

The platform advocated a bureau of labor statistics; co-operative institutions, both productive and distributive; reservation of public lands for actual settlers; weekly pay for employees; mechanics' liens; the abolition of the contract system on public works; arbitration of labor disputes; the adoption of laws providing for the health and safety of those engaged in mining, manufacturing, and building industries; the recognition by incorporation of trade unions; prohibition of the employment of children under fourteen years of age; equal pay for equal work for both sexes; prohibition of the importation of foreign contract labor; establishment by the government of a national currency, "issued directly to the people without the intervention of any system of banking corporations, which money shall be legal tender in payment of all debts, public or private"; organization by the government of postal savings banks; ownership by the government "of all telegraphs, telephones and railroads"; and finally "the reduction of the hours of labor to eight per day, so that the laborers may have more time for social enjoyment and intellectual improvement, and be enabled to reap the advantages conferred by the labor-saving machinery which their brains have created."

The preamble of the Knights of Labor followed closely the preamble and platform of the Industrial Brotherhood organized during the depression years. Strike action was deplored, and the preamble states that most of the objectives in the platform "can only be obtained through legislation." The Knights regarded monopoly as an evil and wanted it abolished. The way to do it, they believed, was through government ownership of the railroads, telegraphs, and telephones; elimination of the private banking system, and substitution for it by a postal savings bank.[26] Not until a co-operative society took the place of the wage system would the inevitable tendency toward monopoly be halted. The Order had to be the instrument "through which in time *financial* and industrial emancipation of the World's Workers from *Corporate Tyranny* and *Wages Slavery* is to be achieved." [26]

In spite of its confusion, the Order's platform advanced a program aiming at the organization of the entire working class and the abolition of "wage slavery." Its structure and methods, however, were not suited to the attainment of these objectives, and were frequently detrimental to the satisfaction of other specific demands.

The constitution adopted by the Reading convention set up a national body styled the "General Assembly of the Knights of Labor of North America," at whose annual meetings delegates from the various district organizations and unattached local assemblies would elect officers and decide questions of general policy. The General Assembly had "full and final jurisdiction" over the organization. It alone possessed the power and authority to make, amend, or repeal the laws and regulations of the Order; to decide all controversies arising in the Order; to issue all charters, traveling, transfer and final cards. It also had the power to tax the members for the maintenance of the Order.[27]

Constitutionally it appeared that the Knights had a highly centralized form of organization, but, actually, the local and district assemblies were virtually autonomous and did as they pleased. As a rule, the general officers acted only as they were forced to by the national trade unions, local and district assemblies. Centralization was more formal than real.[28]

The difference between theory and practice derived fundamentally from a conflict between the leadership and the membership. While the membership was finding that through strikes and boycotts they could secure important gains for labor, the leadership emphasized the futility of strikes and argued that only through self-employment could labor obtain lasting victories. Strikes could not solve labor's problem, said Terence V. Powderly in 1882, because "strikes cannot change the apprentice system, a strike cannot remove the unjust technicalities in the administration of justice, a strike cannot regulate the laws of supply and demand, for if it cuts off the supply it also cuts off the demand by throwing consumers out of work, thereby curtailing their purchasing power." [29] That same year, Robert D. Layton, general secretary of the Order, wrote jubilantly: "On the subject of strikes, I have discharged a duty. I promised myself and some of the Grand Officers some time ago, i.e., to give strikes a left handed blow somewhere near the stomach. I think if vigorous (although crude) language will unseat, or tend to dethrone his satanic majesty in our Order that I have as an individual did a little toward that end." [30] Both Powderly, who replaced Stephens as Grand Master Workman in 1879, and Layton frequently urged the Knights to remain at work and use the funds that would be consumed in strikes for the purpose of establishing co-operatives. Thus the failure of the strikes of the 'seventies led the leaders of the Knights of Labor to repudiate the strike except as a weapon of last resort.

At the first General Assembly in 1878 a sum of money was set aside as a Resistance Fund during strikes. Two years later, the General Assembly voted to have 10 per cent of the fund used for education, 60 per cent for co-operative purposes, and the remaining 30 per cent for strikes. This Assembly also outlined strike procedure. The first step called for the election of an Arbitration Committee by the Local Assembly involved in the strike. If this committee failed to adjust matters, the District Assembly with which the local was affiliated was to appoint a District Committee on Arbitration. If the dispute still remained unsettled, another committee was to be formed of one man from each of the nearest two district assemblies and a third from the district involved. If this committee failed to arbitrate the matter, the entire dispute could be referred to the Executive Board, the Grand Master Workman, and the Grand Secretary, whose decision would be final. "No strike," the General Assembly ruled, "undertaken without the sanction and orders of this joint body of General Assembly officers . . . shall be supported from the strike fund of this Order." [31] The leadership of the Knights hoped that this provision, by making it almost impossible to render financial aid to strikes, would turn the thoughts of the membership to co-operative projects and arbitration. But the members knew that without the use of the strike their efforts to improve their conditions would be fruitless.

When Uriah S. Stephens, the chief defender of secrecy, resigned his position of Grand Master Workman in September 1879,* it was not long before the Order became a public organization. The Grand Master Workman and the Grand Secretary were authorized by the convention of 1881 to issue a proclamation on January 1, 1882, to the workingmen of America informing them of the existence and objectives of the Order. The convention also deleted the oath from the initiation pledge substituting for it a simple promise, and voted to remove all spiritual passages and language from the ritual. [32]

Powderly did not bother to issue the proclamation because he said everyone knew of the existence and objectives of the Order. The real growth of the Order dates from the Detroit convention of 1881 where the secrecy of the organization was revoked with the secret ritual, however, continuing in practice. In 1878 the Order had 9,287 members; in 1879, 20,151; in 1880, 28,136; and in 1883, 51,914. Its period of greatest growth was during 1885-86 when more than 600,000 joined.†

* In 1878 Stephens had been nominated by the Greenback-Labor Party for Congress in the Fifth District of Pennsylvania. He resigned as Grand Master Workman of the Knights of Labor to devote his time to the campaign. After his defeat in the election, he was re-elected but resigned his position in 1879, explaining that "business and finance together render it impossible for me to be at Chicago. I do not feel that I can any longer bear the burden. It must rest upon other shoulders." (*Proceedings* of the General Assembly of the K. of L., 1879; Powderly, *Thirty Years of Labor*, p. 629.)

† In May, 1880 there were 38 District Assemblies (seven of which were not functioning) and 868 Local Assemblies in the Knights of Labor. The District Assemblies were distributed as follows: Pennsylvania, 8; New Jersey, 1; West Virginia, 4; Ohio, 3; Illinois, 4; Indiana, 1; New York, 1; Missouri, 1; Kentucky, 2; Maryland, 1; Iowa, 1; Alabama, 2; Massachusetts, 1; Colorado, 1.

The following were the Local Assemblies: Alabama, 19; California, 2; Connecticut, 2; Colorado, 17; Delaware, 5; Georgia, 1; Illinois, 58; Indian Territory, 1; Indiana, 23; Iowa, 13; Kansas, 15; Kentucky, 36; Minnesota, 2; Massachusetts, 11;

In February, 1883, Robert D. Layton, testifying before a Senate Committee investigating relations between labor and capital, stated that the membership of the Order was in West Virginia, Illinois, Ohio, Pennsylvania, New York, California, and Canada. Any person over eighteen years of age, he said, "working for wages, or who at any time worked for wages," could become a member. However, "no person who either sells, or makes his living by the sale of intoxicating drink, can be admitted, and no lawyer, doctor, or banker can be admitted." Did this mean, he was asked, that manufacturers could become members? "Yes," he replied, "manufacturers can belong to it," but local assemblies were to be "composed of not less than ten members, at least three quarters of whom must be wage-workers." [33] With the leaders of the Knights of Labor proclaiming the identity of interest between labor and capital, it is hardly surprising that employers were eligible for membership.

One reason the Knights of Labor succeeded in organizing assemblies where unions had failed was because there were not enough workers engaged in one trade to support a union, while any number of trades could be represented in the mixed assemblies of the Knights of Labor. In many communities, particularly in the rural districts, local assemblies arose in which there were almost as many occupations represented as there were members. The mixed assembly was well suited for the organization of the semi-skilled, the unskilled, and the day laborers.* It was to these workers that the Knights of Labor began to make its main appeal in the 'eighties because the trade unions had failed to organize them. The great slogan of the Order, "An injury to one is the concern of all," was to arouse thousands of workers all over the country.[34]

On August 15, 1880 the *Journal of United Labor* pointed with pride to the fact that many Assemblies had Negro members who "for fidelity to their obligations, strict attendance on all meetings, prompt payment of dues, good conduct, and all that goes to make good members and good citizens, ... are not excelled by any other class of men in the Order." † This development, it declared, was in keeping with the basic principles

---

Maryland, 18; Missouri, 35; Michigan, 2; New York, 23; New Jersey, 56; Ohio, 51; Ontario, 1; Oregon, 12; Pennsylvania, 396; Wyoming Territory, 1; West Virginia, 67; Wisconsin, 1. (*Journal of United Labor*, May 15, 1880.)

* "One great difficulty experienced by all single trade-unions has been the organization of isolated workers in localities where the number of those employed at such a trade was not sufficient to form a local body of their own. Under the Knights of Labor this difficulty is obviated, as they can join a mixed Local Assembly, which will enable any trade to thoroughly organize under one head." (*Journal of United Labor*, July, 1883, p. 520.)

† John W. Hayes, general secretary of the Order, estimated that in 1886 there were no less than 60,000 Negroes in the Knights of Labor. (Sterling D. Spero and Abram L. Harris, *The Black Worker: The Negro and the Labor Movement*, New York, 1931, p. 42.)

of the Knights of Labor as set forth in a decision of the Grand Master Workman in September, 1879 which announced: "The (outside) color of a candidate shall not debar him from admission; rather let the coloring of his mind and heart be the test."

"We should be false to every principle of our Order," the journal concluded, "should we exclude from membership any man who gains his living by honest toil on account of his color or creed. Our platform is broad enough to take in all."

Although the Knights believed that "industrial development had passed beyond the craftsman stage upon which the trade unions were founded," [35] the Order recognized that the skilled workers had special problems, and for some time tried to solve them. The first official expression of the Knights toward trade unions was made by Grand Master Workman Stephens before the second regular General Assembly in January, 1879. He urged the issuing of an address to the trade associations of the continent pointing out "the weakness and evils of isolated effort or association, and the useless and crushing competition resulting therefrom, unproductive of good to themselves and the public at large." He suggested the the trade unions be reminded of "the benefits of amalgamation and affiliation with our great brotherhood" and that a special effort be made toward "unifying *all* labor organizations into *one* grand consolidated body." [36]

A resolution was adopted providing "that trades organized as trades may select an executive officer of their own, who may have charge of their organization, and organize Local Assemblies of the trade in any part of the country, and attach them to the District Assembly controlling said trade." [37] These district assemblies were virtually national trade unions and would have their own officers and hold their own trade conventions. But at the next convention, in September, 1879, an opposite policy was expressed toward trade unions. The General Assembly heard the leader of the Order say, "No time should be lost or money spent in strikes or in the organization of separate trades or callings. Benefits resulting therefrom are but partial and evanescent. . . . Our first duty is the consolidation of all branches of productive labor into a compact whole." * There were two resolutions adopted on the

---

* Powderly used the experience of the depression years as an argument against the craft unions. The panic, he maintained, had proved that the distinction between skilled and unskilled workers was fictitious, for the skilled craftsman had seen that "he was no better than the man with the pick and shovel," insofar as securing employment at decent conditions was concerned. "All men who labor," he therefore concluded, "have been brought by the hard times to one level and should have the good sense to remain on that level. Most of the trades' unions have gone to the wall. What is the lesson taught? We want no trade unions." (*Journal of United Labor,* June 15, 1880.)

question of trade unions. One stated that the "establishment of Locals formed and conducted exclusively in the interest of any one trade is contrary to the spirit and genius of the Order as founded; and we recommend that Locals should admit workmen of all trades ... and also that all laws permitting such exclusive organizations be rescinded." The other resolution asserted that locals "conducted in the interest of any special trade must in all cases be subordinate to the District Assembly in whose territory they may be located, and all laws permitting trade District Assemblies to interfere with the control of the other District Assemblies over any Local Assembly in their district are rescinded." [38]

In 1882 the General Assembly returned to its original policy in regard to trade unions. Trade locals were now encouraged. The *Journal of United Labor* went out of its way to prove that the formation of "Trade Locals and Districts is and always has been from the first a part of the plan of the Knights of Labor." [39] The Window Glass Workers organized a powerful national assembly at a time when even trade locals were prohibited by the laws of the Order, and it was given the right to organize as a national trade union under the designation of Local Assembly No. 300. The Knights now encouraged this trend, assuring the trade unions that "they could protect the interests of their trade just the same ... and at the same time receive all the advantages of organization and association with all other branches of industry." [40]

Undoubtedly the discontent with the existing mixed district assemblies was instrumental in creating a more friendly attitude in the Knights of Labor toward the trade unions. One important factor in this change of mind was the emergence in 1881 of a rival organization, the Federation of Organized Trades and Labor Unions of the United States and Canada, the foundation stone of the American Federation of Labor.

THE "NEW UNIONISM" OF THE 1870'S

To understand the forces that created the Federation it is necessary to go back to the terrible years after the panic of 1873, and examine the activity of a small group of cigarmakers who were building the model for the "New Unionism" in the crafts. These men were Adolph Strasser, Samuel Gompers, Ferdinand Laurrell, Conrad Carl, and others. "From this little group," wrote Gompers in his autobiography, "came the purpose and initiative that finally resulted in the present labor movement. We did not create the American trade union, that is the product of force and conditions. But we did create the technique, and formulate the fundamentals that guided trade unionism to constructive policies and achievements." [41]

Samuel Gompers was born in the East End of London in 1850 of

Dutch-Jewish parents. His father was a cigarmaker whose home was his workshop. In the summer of 1863 the family migrated from the East End of London to the East Side of New York. Here Gompers helped his father make cigars in their home, attended lectures and classes at Cooper Union, and joined debating clubs, the Odd Fellows, and the union of his trade.

From 1873 to 1878 Gompers' intimate associates were Marxian So-cialists. The Cigarmakers Union of New York had many men who had been active in the revolutionary movements in Europe and were members of the International Workingmen's Association in America. In his auto-biography Gompers writes that the principles of the International ap-pealed to him "as solid and practical," and acknowledges that as a result of the influence of the Marxists there developed a clearer understanding of the principle "that the trade union was the intermediate and prac-tical agency which could bring wage-earners a better life." [42]

Whatever Socialist ideas Gompers picked up came from Socialists who were disillusioned with the Socialist movement. To Ferdinand Laurrell, a Swede who had been secretary of the International for the Scandi-navian countries, Gompers gave credit for his development as a trade union leader. Laurrell conducted discussion groups in the cigar shop where Gompers worked from 1873 to 1878, the only union cigar shop in New York, owned by David Hirsch, a German exile. Laurrell advised Gompers to attend Socialist meetings, "listen to what they have to say and understand them, but do not join the Party." [43] He warned him against "zealots and impractical visionaries," and reminded him again and again that the trade union was the cornerstone of the labor movement. " 'Study your union card, Sam,' " Laurrell is said to have told Gompers, " 'and if the idea doesn't square with that, it ain't true.' " [44]

Another disillusioned Socialist to whom Gompers was indebted was Adolph Strasser, president of the International Cigar Makers' Union in 1877. At one time Strasser had come under the influence of the Las-salleans and had been active in the Social-Democratic Party of North America. He was one of the men responsible for the unity which estab-lished the Workingmen's Party of the United States. Later he made a complete break with socialism and began to champion trade union demands only. [45]

The brutality of the American bourgeoisie had much to do with the swing to the right of those radicals of the 'seventies who were to be so prominent in the American Federation of Labor. Gompers, for example, witnessed the Tompkins Square outrage of 1874 and saved himself from police brutality by hiding in a cellarway. Instead of arousing his hatred, the incident convinced him that it was too dangerous to join the revolutionary movement. [46] The reactionary uproar which followed the great strike wave of 1877 intimidated a number of "Socialists." Hardly a day passed during the months following the railroad strike without some reference in the press to "the revolutionary demands of the trades' unions," to "the crazy communists of the trade unions" and to the efforts of "communist trade union movements to destroy American society." [47] Typical is the following from the *New York Herald* for May 11, 1878: "Further reports of movements, projects and programmes for the overthrow of everything by workingmen, more or less organized as labor leagues or Communist Societies are given in our columns today."

Not to be outdone, the *New York Tribune* ran a series of articles devoted to the theme, "The Growing Power of the Communists in the Country." In a leading article, one writer said that the Communists had captured and turned to their own purposes the powerful trade unions in the nation in preparation for a great general strike during which they would seize control of the country. The writer concluded that since trade unionism was now identified with communism, it was necessary to suppress all trade unions. The *Tribune* expressed the hope that the article would receive nationwide attention and would be reprinted in other papers. "Men who love order," it went on, "or have property to lose cannot afford to see with indifference the steady advances of communism in this country." [48]

Ex-Socialists like Adolph Strasser and P. J. McGuire set out to convince men who loved order that they had nothing to fear from the "New Unionism." In the oft-quoted testimony he gave to the Senate Committee on Education and Labor in 1883, Strasser showed how far he had traveled politically in one decade:

Question: "You are seeking to improve home matters first?"
Answer: "Yes, Sir, I look first to the trade I represent; look first to Cigars, the interest of men who employ me to represent their interests."
Chairman: "I was only asking you in regard to your ultimate ends."
Witness: "We have no ultimate ends. We are going on from day to day. We fight only for immediate objects—objects that can be realized in a few years." [49]

THE CIGAR MAKERS

Strasser and Gompers had worked together in the great strike of the Cigar Makers in 1877. During the depression the employers in the New York cigar-making industry began to transfer their work from the large shops to the tenement houses where wages were one-half of what they were in the shops. A sixteen hour working day was not unusual. By the middle of 1875 more than one-half of the cigars made in the city were produced in tenement houses. This change in production almost destroyed the union. In the winter of 1873 the union had close to 1,700 members; two years later it had dwindled to a handful of members. Strasser, Laurrell, Gompers, and their associates reorganized the union in the summer of 1875, and Gompers was elected the first president of the reorganized Local No. 144.[50]

Even before the depression, the New York union, unlike the international union which excluded unskilled workers, had been organized on an industrial basis and took in rollers and bunchers as well as the more skilled workers. This industrial form was continued after the union was reorganized. In 1876 the union had only 500 members, but among them were some of the best members of the Working Men's Party. A general strike of cigar makers was called in the fall of 1877 to abolish the tenement house system. From seven to ten thousand cigar makers, including most of the tenement house workers, rose against starvation wages and intolerable conditions in the tenement sweatshops.

Funds to aid the strikers came in from all over the country. A telegram from workers in San Francisco read: "Be of good cheer. Hold out. Money every week." The Cigar Makers' official journal welcomed the assistance coming from other workers and stated, "if poverty and actual starvation force us to yield the defeat will be not ours only but that of the working class generally." After 107 days of bitter struggle, the strike was called off. Work was resumed under old conditions, and the sweatshop in the tenement slums continued. "The evils of many years duration," said the *Cigar Makers' Journal,* "cannot be remedied in one day." [51]

The failure of the strike strengthened Gompers, Laurrell, and Strasser in their determination to remodel the Cigar Makers' International Union. They were convinced that the reason the American unions could not stand the shock of depression or lost strikes was because they were not conducted upon business principles.[52] Following the British trade unions, they resolved to rebuild the Cigar Makers International into a cohesive, financially stable organization. They proposed to give to the International officers complete authority over the local unions; to set high dues to build a financial reserve, to establish sick and death benefits, and a system of lending money to journeymen moving about in search of work.

These changes were introduced at a convention held in August, 1879, and incorporated in the constitution of the union. It also adopted the British principle of equalization of funds which authorized the International officers to order a local union with a good treasury to transfer some of its funds to another local union in financial distress.[53] Thus there arose a new Cigar Makers International Union which became the model for many American trade unions and laid down the principles upon which the American Federation of Labor itself was to be based.

In many ways the "New Unionism" was not new. William Sylvis had

LABOR MOVEMENT IN THE UNITED STATES

established centralized control in the Molders' International Union in the 'sixties, and many other national trade union leaders at the time sought to incorporate this feature in their organizations. Sylvis had stressed administrative efficiency, strike funds, and insurance features, although, unlike Strasser and Gompers, he never did so at the expense of labor solidarity. It is true, however, that most of the unions of the 'sixties and 'seventies still lacked centralized control, especially over strikes, and were not financially stable.

What was really new about the "New Unionism" of the Cigar Makers was that it was introduced at a time when the depression period had already convinced many trade unionists of the significance of centralization, financial stability, and efficiency in the labor movement. Throughout the hard times of the 'seventies there was constant discussion in the labor press of the lessons that could be learned from a study of the organization of British trade unions.* The failure of the great struggles that shook the country during the depression only served to strengthen the feeling that the unions that would emerge when the lean years were over would have to follow the pattern of the British unions.[54] The Cigar Makers were the first to transform this conviction into practice.

The new Cigar Makers International Union was not, as Gompers states, "the first constructive efficient American trade union organization";[55] to the Molders' International Union under Sylvis' leadership belongs that honor. But the Cigar Makers, unlike the Molders, broke completely with ultimate objectives like self-employment through cooperatives. The emphasis was solely on "practical methods" and "immediate demands." No nonsense like secret rituals, passwords, and mystical ceremonies. And above all no utopian schemes for financial reforms which would bring an end to the grievances of the working class overnight. The Cigar Makers held that "necessity has forced the labor movement to adopt the most practical methods. They are struggling for higher wages and shorter hours, which lead to a higher state of civiliation. No financial scheme or plan of taxation will shorten the hours of labor."[56]

Gompers, Strasser, and Laurrell, it has been claimed, based the fundamental concepts of their "New Unionism" on Marxist trade union principles.† It is true that Marx and Engels attached the greatest importance to the trade unions, and believed that they formed the cornerstone of

* Jackson H. Rolston made a tour of American cities in 1877 and 1878, lecturing to trade unions on "The English Trade Unions." (See *Labor Standard*, Nov. 2, 1878, for an account of his lecture.)

† John R. Commons, for example, asserts that the policies of the Cigar Makers' Union were based "on a Marxism revised to fit American conditions," and that "Gompers became even more class-conscious than Marx himself." (See his article "Karl Marx and Samuel Gompers," *Political Science Quarterly*, Vol. XLI, 1924, 283-85.)

the labor movement. But they believed that the trade unions were important because they served "as organizational centres for the broad working masses," and therefore called for "the drawing of all workers into their ranks." They also believed that the mission of the organized workers was to lead in the struggle for Socialism.[57] To the founders of the "New Unionism," however, the trade unions were meant to be "organizational centers" for the skilled aristocracy of labor in order to enable the craftsmen to protect their monopoly of the job at the expense of the unskilled and semi-skilled workers. To Gompers, moreover, high dues and huge treasuries, "grievance committees," "business agents," and apprenticeship rules became the essence of trade unionism. This unionism, soon to be carried over to the American Federation of Labor, was practical and efficient. Unquestionably, American trade unions were sorely in need of efficiency. But in introducing efficiency into their trade unions, Gompers and his associates robbed them at the same time of the principles of labor solidarity and a sense of direction.

In 1881, Gompers and Strasser began to show their contempt for trade union democracy. A group in Local No. 144 of the Cigar Makers' International Union, called the Progressives, began to campaign to oust Gompers and his associates, who were known as the Internationals, from the leadership of the local union. The Progressives—still Socialists —intended thus to block Strasser's and Gompers' high-handed conversion of the Cigar Makers Union into a pure-and-simple trade union for skilled craftsmen. But the immediate issue was the conduct of the political struggle against the tenement house system. They proposed a mass struggle, demonstrations, agitation, and, if necessary, independent labor candidates. The Internationals, they charged, wanted to endorse a "shyster" lawyer "who has belonged to parties of all shades and colors."

In April, 1881, the Progressives succeeded in electing their candidates to offices in Local No. 144. But Gompers and his fellow office-holders refused to recognize their defeat and simply rejected every demand to hand over the offices and the local's treasury. Strasser, the International president, who later described the Progressives as "anarchists" and "tenement house scum," sustained the Gompers clique.[58] Gompers himself justified his undemocratic action on the same ground that he was later to excuse a similar course of action as president of the American Federation of Labor. He charged that the opposition, being Socialists, were simply unfit to manage the affairs of the Union. "We trade unionists," he wrote in his autobiography, "felt rather apprehensive of the future as the unruly Socialist element increased in numbers." [59]

The Progressives left the International and with the assistance of District Assembly No. 49 of the Knights of Labor set up a dual union in New York, thus initiating a practice which the Socialists in the labor movement were unfortunately too often to follow. They quickly out-numbered the Internationals in New York, organizing the rollers, bunchers, packers, and the workers referred to by Strasser as the "tenement house scum."

The bitter struggle that ensued between the Progressives and the Internationals in the New York cigar-making industry, with Progressives scabbing on the Internationals and the Internationals scabbing on the Progressives, is a sorry episode in the history of the American labor movement that was to have far-reaching effects on the relations between the trade unions and the Knights of Labor. But it is a story that belongs to a later period. Meanwhile, it is worth noting that their quarrel with District Assembly No. 49 was responsible to some extent for the refusal of Gompers and Strasser to follow other national trade union leaders into the Knights of Labor.* Similarly, the struggle within the Cigar Makers' ranks was partly responsible for the formation of the American Federation of Labor.

THE FEDERATION OF ORGANIZED TRADES AND LABOR UNIONS

In April, 1881 the Paterson *Home-Journal,* a socialist paper, called upon the organized trade unions "to convene a Congress of labor in this country during the summer and to take active steps toward the organization of the unorganized." The main emphasis in this new federation, it urged, should be placed on the organization of the unorganized into trade unions for an effective struggle to improve the living conditions of the working class. "The failure of the past labor congresses," it concluded, "was that they gave their time and money to the propaganda of financial rather than industrial questions. At the last congress some six years ago, we uttered our protest against the danger, but with no avail. The question of finance has a place, an important place, but the question of economic organization of labor is paramount." [60]

The initial steps to found a federation of trade unions were taken neither by Gompers, nor by the Cigar Makers, but by a secret society in Indiana called the "Knights of Industry." Together with another secret body, the Amalgamated Labor Union, it issued a call for a conference at Terre Haute, Indiana, on August 2, 1881, "to effect a preliminary organization of an international Amalgamated Union." Ever

* Gompers had belonged to the Knights of Labor for a short period. "With other trade unionists I joined the Knights of Labor," he wrote in 1891, "for the purpose of confining that organization to theoretical educational work and to see that the Trade Unions were protected from being undermined or disrupted. This was as early as '75." (Samuel Gompers to N. E. Mathewson, Oct. 10, 1891, *Gompers Letter-Books, Mss.,* Vol. V, p. 158, Samuel Gompers Memorial Room, American Federation of Labor Building, Washington, D. C.)

on the watch for any move to establish a national labor federation, the Printers hailed the proposed conference and sent a delegate. The Cigar Makers resolved to support the conference but forgot to send delegates. There were more trades' assemblies than national trade unions, and more Greenbackers than trade unionists at the conference. One proposal on organization submitted to the convention called for a declaration against trade union organization. The trade unionists succeeded in securing an early adjournment in order to call another congress in the East where a greater number of national trade unions could be represented. This congress, it was finally decided, should be held in Pittsburgh, on November 15, 1881. The opening paragraph of the call developed the need for greater unity of the working class:

"Fellow-workingmen: The time has now arrived for a more perfect combination of Labor—one that will concentrate our forces so as to more successfully cope with concentrated capital.

"We have numberless trade unions, trades' assemblies or councils, Knights of Labor and various other local, national, and international unions. But great as has been the work done by these bodies, there is vastly more that can be done by a combination of all these organizations in a federation of trades."

In Great Britain and Ireland, the call continued, annual trades' union congresses were held, and the work done by these assemblies of workmen revealed that "only in such a body can proper action be taken to promote the general welfare of the industrial classes." A National Trades Union Congress in America could prepare labor measures for enactment into legislation by the United States Congress, "form a Congressional Labor Committee to urge and advance legislation upon measures wanted at Washington and report to the various trades," and organize "a systematic agitation to propagate trade union principles and to impress the necessity of protective trade and labor organizations and to encourage the formation of such unions and thus amalgmation into trade assemblies." By such activities "we could elevate trade unionism and obtain for the working classes that respect for their rights to which they are justly entitled." [61]

One hundred and seven delegates attended the Pittsburgh convention, and it was estimated in the contemporary press that the number of workers represented at the convention was close to half a million.[62] The Printers had the largest national trade union representation with 14 delegates; the Amalgamated Association of Iron and Steel Workers had 10; the Molders, 8; the Glass Workers, 6; the Cigar Makers, 5; and the Carpenters, 5. The remaining delegates came from 46 local assemblies of the Knights of Labor.

John Jarrett, president of the Amalgamated Association of Iron and Steel Workers, was elected chairman and Samuel Gompers became chairman of the Committee on Organization. This committee provoked the liveliest discussion at the convention when it reported in favor of a pure trade association to be known as "The Federation of Organized Trades Unions of the United States of America and Canada," to be composed of trades' unions only. Gompers' proposal was fought because it meant that the proposed labor federation would organize only skilled craftsmen and would not organize the entire working class, skilled as well as unskilled, Negro as well as white, and foreign-born as well as native born. Here is a sample of some of the discussion from the floor:

"Mr. Weber hoped that the name of the Federation would read so as to include all laboring people."

"Mr. Kinear: I want this organization to reach all men who labor, such as the longshoremen in our seaport towns. For that reason, I desire the article so amended as to read 'Trades and Labor Unions.' "

"Mr. Grandeson [the colored delegate] of Pittsburgh: We have in the city of Pittsburgh many men in our organization who have no particular trade, but should not be excluded from the Federation. Our object is, as I understand it, to federate the whole laboring element of America. I speak more particularly of my own people and declare to you that it would be dangerous to skilled mechanics to exclude from this organization the common laborers, who might, in an emergency, be employed in positions they could readily qualify themselves to fill."

"Mr. Pollinger: We recognize neither creed, color nor nationality, but want to take into the folds of this organization the whole labor element of this country, no matter of what calling; for that reason the name should read, 'Trades and Labor Unions.' "

"Mr. Dewey: I do make the amendment as suggested."

"Mr. Brant: That suits me exactly. I wish this Federation broad enough to encompass all working people in its folds." [63]

On a vote the amendment was unanimously adopted and the name changed to Federation of Organized Trades and Labor Unions of the United States and Canada. This was to remain its name until it was changed in 1886 to the American Federation of Labor.

After the name of the Federation had been decided, the delegates took up the report of the Committee on Platform. The first part of the report was a preamble outlining the reasons that made a Federation of Labor necessary. It is in sharp contrast to the theory of the identity of interest between labor and capital held by most leaders of the Knights of Labor.

"Whereas, A struggle is going on in the nations of the civilized world between the oppressors and the oppressed of all countries, a struggle between capital and labor, which must grow in intensity from year to year and work disastrous results to the toiling millions of all nations if not combined for mutual protection and benefit. This history of the wage-workers of all countries is but the history of constant struggle and misery engendered by ignorance and disunion; whereas the history of the non-producers of all ages proves that a minority, thoroughly organized, may work wonders for good or evil.... Conforming to the old adage, 'In union there is strength,' the formation of a Federation embracing every trade and labor organization in North America, a union founded upon a basis as broad as the land we live in, is our only hope." [64]

The class-conscious character of the preamble did not escape comment from the contemporary press. The *Pittsburgh Telegraph* observed that the preamble "breathes a spirit of conflict rather than pacification" and expressed the hope that it would be replaced by a new spirit, "the spirit of concord with capital." [65]

The resolutions proposed by the Committee on Platform called for incorporation of unions, compulsory education of children; prohibition of child labor under the age of fourteen years; uniform apprenticeship laws; enforcement of the National Eight-Hour Law; prohibition of convict contract labor; abolition of store order system of payment; mechanics' lien laws; repeal of conspiracy laws; establishment of a National Bureau of Labor Statistics; supervision of the railroad and telegraph companies of the country "with a view that their operations, as in the postal service, may be for the benefit of the people whose franchise they have secured"; reclamation by the government of railroad land grants forfeited for non-fulfillment of contracts, and reservation of the public domain henceforth exclusively for actual settlers; protection of American industry; prevention of the importation of foreign contract labor; and, finally, action by all trades and labor organizations to "secure proper representation in all law-making bodies by means of the ballot." [66]

There was some opposition to the abolition of child labor on the ground that its enforcement would be an interference with individual rights. Delegate after delegate arose to defend the resolution presenting vivid descriptions of the terrible effects of child labor upon society. "See what I have seen of the gigantic evils of this," said one delegate, "and if you had a hundred votes you would cast them for this resolution." Samuel Gompers reviewed the degradation of children in the tenement cigar shops and ended his speech by saying, "Shame upon such crimes; shame upon us if we do not raise our voices against it." The resolution was passed unanimously.[67]

Considerable opposition developed against the resolution favoring protective tariffs. "I am for free trade," said one delegate. "Protective tariffs are a party issue; it is of no importance to the country at large. Protective tariff means protection to the American manufacturer against the importation of foreign cheap goods, but it does not mean protection to the American laborer against the importation of foreign cheap laborers." The steel workers' delegates were for the tariff resolution which was finally adopted at their insistence.[68]

Two resolutions proposed by the Committee on Platform were ruled out of order by President Jarrett as foreign to the purpose of the congress.* These called for supervision over railroad and telegraph companies, and reservation of the public domain for actual settlers only. Several resolutions introduced from the floor were adopted. They demanded legislation for the inspection and ventilation of mines, factories, and workshops, sanitary supervision of all food and dwellings, laws making employers liable for all accidents resulting from their negligence or incompetence, and action by Congress "entirely prohibiting the immigration of Chinese into the United States." Only one delegate spoke against the Chinese immigration resolution, Mr. Cummin of Boston, and his defense was not free of chauvinism. Asserting that this country was and should remain "an asylum for the oppressed of the entire world," he said, "In behalf of the state I represent I cannot vote for any resolution against the Constitution of the United States. This is a free country and we should permit the Chinese to come over here. I do not believe that they would swallow us up." [69]

A good deal of discussion centered around a resolution introduced from the floor expressing sympathy with the people of Ireland in their struggle to free themselves from British oppression. The resolution said that the land in Ireland should be owned by the cultivators of the soil and that no person should be allowed to own more land than he could till. Gompers led the opposition to the resolution, saying that the land

* Jarrett's handling of the chair set a pattern which Gompers was to use effectively in later years to beat down the opponents of the A. F. of L. bureaucracy. The Pittsburgh *Commercial Gazette* commented upon it under the heading, "Applying the Gag Law," as follows: "As soon as a question had been stated he would ask 'Are you ready for the question?' Immediately the question would be called for by a number of delegates who thought that by so doing they would place the motion in proper shape for debate. But Mr. Jarrett was not of the same mind, and the last three sections of the 'plan' were railroaded through with a speed that was highly creditable to Mr. Jarrett's conception of the rule [adopted previously making it imperative for a vote to be taken whenever seven members were for the 'question'], but not entirely satisfactory to the delegates who thought that they should be permitted to air their opinions on every question that came before the house." (Quoted in Alfred P. James, "The First Convention of the American Federation of Labor: A Study in Contemporary Local Newspapers as a Source," *Western Pennsylvania Magazine of History and Biography,* Vol. VII, January, 1924. p. 41*n.*)

idea was incorrect and urging the convention not to commit itself to such a principle. Some delegates inferred that Gompers was disturbed by the press reports that he represented the Socialist element at the congress, and that he was making his general position clear by opposing the "socialistic" land resolution.[70]

The resolution was finally referred to a special committee, which reported a substitute proposal deploring "the unjust land laws that have been enforced against the Irish people in the past," and the "unjust imprisonment" that hundreds of Irishmen were suffering "in consequence of their heroic attempts to ameliorate the condition of her oppressed people." The statement concluded on the following note of internationalism:

"That we extend to these champions, battling in the cause of human liberty, our hearty sympathy, and that we also extend to the oppressed of all nations struggling for liberty and right, the same encouraging words of sympathy."[71]

The resolution was adopted.

The convention passed another resolution that is significant because it expressed the delegates' interest in the problems facing the farmers. This resolution denounced a public land bill submitted to Congress in February, 1880, which if enacted into law would have turned over the public domain to "western cattle kings and other capitalists" and forced farmers to rent their land "from the great landlords." The resolution further stated that "a vote in its favor by any member of Congress will be an act of treason to the interests of labor," and that all who voted for the measure "will be punished by the political opposition of the working class portion of their constituents."[72]

This platform invites comparison with that of the Knights of Labor. Both documents agreed that under capitalism the lot of the worker, unless organized, grew worse. Both emphasized the need for organizing the working class and using the ballotbox. The programs of the two organizations, moreover, had much in common. Both organizations favored the establishment of bureaus of labor statistics; health, safety, and employers' liability laws; mechanics' lien laws; legal incorporation of unions; prohibition of child labor; abolition of convict contract labor; and restriction of immigration.

There were also important differences. The Knights demanded government ownership of the systems of transportation and communication, but the new Federation did not. Nor did the Federation accept the monetary program of the Knights of Labor, indicating that it definitely regarded the industrial capitalist rather than the banker as the chief enemy of the wage-earners, and—unlike the Knights—had pretty nearly rid itself of the belief in financial panaceas. It is also significant that the Federation made no reference to producers or consumers co-operatives, and failed to recommend compulsory arbitration which the Knights supported. The Federation did concern itself with the question of apprenticeship laws and the "store system" of payment, neither of which appeared in the Knights' platform.

While many of the demands of the two organizations were identical, it is quite obvious that the Federation was more concerned with immediate gains under capitalism than in the solution of labor's problems through self-employment. "Grasp one idea," said Mark W. Moore, secretary of the General Committee of the Terre Haute convention, in a report to the delegates at the Pittsburgh Congress, "less hours and better pay, and carry it into all your work as the first principle." [73] The acceptance of this principle broke with the middle-class reformist conceptions of the 'sixties and 'seventies, brushed aside financial nostrums, and geared the labor movement for a realistic struggle to better the conditions of life.

After the report of the Committee on Plaform, the next important business to come before the congress dealt with the plan of representation at future conventions of the Federation. After considerable discussion a plan was adopted which gave the national trade unions the greatest representation. Local trades assemblies and councils could only send one delegate each, but national or international unions could send one delegate for one thousand or less members, two delegates for four thousand, three delegates for eight thousand.[74]

The Pittsburgh Convention elected a legislative committee of five consisting of Samuel Gompers, Richard Powers, C. F. Burgman, A. C. Rankin, and W. H. Foster which was instructed to organize a campaign to secure protective and other legislation favorable to the workers. The objectives of the newly-formed Federation were listed by the Convention as follows:

"1. The encouragement and formation of Trades and Labor Unions.

"2. The encouragement and formation of Trades and Labor Assemblies or Councils.

"3. The encouragement and formation of National and International Trades Unions.

"4. To secure legislation favorable to the interests of the industrial classes." [75]

Frank K. Foster, the Federation's first Secretary, summed up the meaning of these objectives in a letter to H. A. Cole of the Bricklayers' National Union. "The growing power of associated capital," he wrote, "must needs be met by associated labor. Federation is the motto of the future." [76]

REFERENCE NOTES

CHAPTER I

1. Edward Arber, ed., *Travels and Works of Captain John Smith*, Edinburgh, 1910, vol. I, p. 360, vol. II, p. 444.
2. Alexander Brown, *Genesis of the United States*, Boston, 1891, vol. II, p. 797.
3. Henry B. Dawson, ed., *Records of New Amsterdam*, Morrisania, 1867, vol. II, p. 278; Almon W. Lauber, *Indian Slavery in Colonial Times within the present limits of the United States*, New York, 1913, pp. 287-88.
4. Brown, *op. cit.*, vol. I, p. 353; Nathaniel B. Shurtleff, ed., *Records of the Governor and Company of the Massachusetts Bay in New England*, Boston, 1853, vol. I, p. 405.
5. *William and Mary Quarterly*, vol. XIV, pp. 152-53.
6. C. A. Herrick, *White Servitude in Pennsylvania*, Philadelphia, 1926, pp. 43, 47; Thomas J. Wertenbaker, *The Founding of American Civilization: The Middle Colonies*, New York, 1938, p. 198.
7. James E. T. Rogers, comp., *History of Agriculture and Prices in England, 1259-1793*, Oxford, 1866-1902, vol. V, p. 826.
8. Sir G. Nicholls, *A History of the English Poor Law*, London, 1910, vol. VI, p. 245. For a summary of English labor legislation of the period under discussion, see Richard B. Morris, *Government and Labor in Early America*, New York, 1946, pp. 3-9.
9. Philip A. Bruce, *Economic History of Virginia*, New York, 1907, vol. I, p. 579; A. E. Bland, P. A. Brown, and R. H. Tawney, eds., *English Economic History: Select Documents*, London, 1914, pp. 357-58.
10. Sidney and Beatrice Webb, *History of Trade Unionism*, London, 1930, pp. 249-50; Sir Frederic Morton Eden, *The State of the Poor*, edited by A. G. L. Rogers, London, 1928, pp. 24-28.
11. *The Laws and Acts of the Parliament of Scotland*, Edinburgh, 1682, vol. I, p. 810.

12. Arthur H. Thomas, ed., *Calendar of Plea and Memoranda Rolls, A. D., 1323-1364*, Cambridge, 1926, p. 225; Edward III, 9-11, *Statutes of the Realm*, vol. I, p. 367, vol. IV, pt. 1, p. 59.
13. Arnold T. Rogers, *Six Centuries of Work and Wages*, London, 1884, p. 398.
14. William Douglass, *Summary of the British Settlements in North America*, London, 1775, p. 206; Marcus W. Jernegan, *Laboring and Dependent Classes in Colonial America, 1607-1783*, Chicago, 1931, p. 47.
15. A. R. Newsome, ed., "Records of Emigrants from England and Scotland to North Carolina, 1774-1775," *North Carolina Historical Review*, vol. XI, April 1934, p. 132.
16. Philip S. Foner, ed., *Basic Writings of Thomas Jefferson*, New York, 1944, pp. 4, 17; A. E. Smith, "Indentured Servants: New Light on Some of America's 'First Families,' " *Journal of Economic History*, vol. II, May 1942, pp. 40-53.
17. Sister Margaret Patricia, "White Servitude in the American Colonies," *Records of the American Catholic Historical Society of Philadelphia*, vol. XLII, March 1931, p. 34; William Eddis, *Letters from America*, London, 1792, pp. 72-73.
18. Frank R. Diffenderffer, *The German Immigration into Pennsylvania*, Lancaster, Pa., 1900, pp. 206, 211-12, 262.
19. Quoted by Leila Sellers, *Charleston Business on the Eve of the Revolution*, Chapel Hill, 1934, p. 118.
20. Quoted by Charles M. Haar, "White Indentured Servants in Colonial New York," *Americana*, vol. XXIV, 1940, p. 374; *American Weekly Mercury*, Nov. 7, 1729; *New York Post Boy*, Nov. 6, 1752.
21. Stella H. Sutherland, *Population Distribution in Colonial America*, New York, 1936, pp. 119, 168-75; Morris, *op. cit.*, pp. 315-16; S. C. Johnson, *A History of Emigration from the United Kingdom, to North America, 1763-1912*, London, 1913, pp. 1-10.

CHAPTER II

1. John A. Mecklin, "The Evolution of the Slave Status in American Democracy," *Journal of Negro History,* vol. II, April 1917, pp. 106-07; William E. Dodd, "Emergence of our First Social Order," *American Historical Review,* vol. XL, Jan. 1935, pp. 227-28; W. W. Hening, ed., *The Statutes at Large,* Richmond, 1810-1823, vol. II, p. 481.

2. Herbert Aptheker, *Negro Slave Revolts in the United States, 1526-1860,* New York, 1939, p. 9; *New York Weekly Journal,* Jan. 5, 1735.

3. William Eddis, *Letters From America,* London, 1792, p. 70; Ebenezer Cook, *The Sot-Weed Factor,* London, 1708, pp. 6-7.

4. William H. Whitman, Record Commissioner, *The Colonial Laws of Massachusetts...* Boston, 1890, Body of Liberties, Sec. 87; *The Colonial Laws of New York,* Albany, 1894, vol. I, pp. 157-58; Morris, *op. cit.,* pp. 88-89 and Chapter IX, "The Legal Status of Servitude," pp. 390-512.

5. *New England Historical and Geneological Register,* vol. V, 1851, p. 161; George Francis Dow, ed., *Records and Files of the Essex County Quarterly Courts,* Salem, 1911, vol. I, pp. 27, 51, 57, 59.

6. Eddis, *op cit.,* p. 70; George Whitefield in *Pennsylvania Gazetteer,* April 17, 1740; I. N. P. Stokes, *Iconography of Manhattan Island,* New York, 1915-1928, vol. I, p. 865.

7. Nathaniel B. Shurtleff, ed., *Records of the Colony of New Plymouth in New England,* Boston, 1855, vol. I, p. 129; Eugene I. McCormac, *White Servitude in Maryland,* Baltimore, 1904, p. 52.

8. *Records and Files of the Essex County Quarterly Courts,* vol. I, pp. 6, 147.

9. Aptheker, *op. cit.,* pp. 17-18; Aptheker, "American Negro Slave Revolts," *Science and Society,* vol. I, Summer 1937, p. 517.

10. Samuel J. McKee, Jr., *Labor in Colonial New York, 1664-1776,* New York, 1935, pp. 161-63; E. B. O'Callaghan, ed., *Documents Relating to the Colonial History of the State of New York,* Albany, 1855, vol. V, pp. 39, 341.

11. Carl Bridenbaugh, *Cities in the Wilderness,* New York, 1938, pp. 37-38.

12. Benjamin Rush, *An Account of the Manners of the German Inhabitants of Pennsylvania,* Philadelphia, 1875, p. 10. See also *Boston News-Letter,* June 18-25, 1716, Oct. 31, 1763.

13. Adam Smith, *An Inquiry into the Nature and Causes of the Wealth of Nations,* London, 1845, vol. I, p. 34.

14. *New York Mercury,* Feb. 11, 1771.

15. McKee, *op. cit.,* p. 29; Bridenbaugh, *op. cit.,* p. 337; Richard B. Morris, "The Organization of Production during the Colonial Period," in Harold F. Williamson, *The Growth of the American Economy,* New York, 1944, pp. 60-62; Morris, *op. cit.,* pp. 38-41.

16. Richard B. Morris, *Government and Labor in Early America,* pp. 44-45.

17. U. S. Bureau of Labor Statistics, *Bulletin 499,* 1929, pp. 50-51; Talcott Williams, *Labor a Hundred Years Ago,* New York, 1887, p. 9; O'Callaghan, ed., *Documents Relating to the Colonial History of New York,* vol. IV, p. 707, vol. V, pp. 196, 343; Morris, *Government and Labor in Early America,* pp. 47-48.

18. McKee, *op. cit.,* pp. 11-12; Leonard Lundlin, *Cockpit of the Revolution,* Princeton, N. J., 1940, p. 27.

19. *Records of the Courts of Assistants, Massachusetts Bay Colony,* Boston, 1904, vol. II, p. 3; *Records and Files of the Essex County Quarterly Courts,* vol. I, p. 3; U. S. Bureau of Labor Statistics, *Bulletin 499,* p. 10.

20. *Pennsylvania Chronicle and Universal Advertiser,* March 27, 1769; John C. Miller, *Origins of the American Revolution,* Boston, 1943, p. 275.

21. Bridenbaugh, *op. cit.,* p. 201. For examples of protests of Southern wage-earners against the use of Negro slaves, see Yates Snowden, *Notes on Labor Organization in South Carolina, 1742-1861,* Columbia, S. C., 1914, p. 7; Allen D. Chandler, ed., *The Colonial Records of Georgia,* Atlanta, 1908, vol. V, pp. 378-79.

22. Charles Z. Lincoln, ed., *Messages from the Governors of New York,* Albany, 1909, vol. I, p. 260; *New York Journal,* Feb. 4, 1768. See also *Pennsylvania Archives,* 8th series, vol. II, p. 1477; Morris, *Government and Labor in Early America,* pp. 182-86.

23. *New York Post Boy,* March 19, 1753.

24. Robert F. Seyboldt, "Trade Agreements in Colonial Boston," *New England Quarterly,* vol. II, April 1929, p. 309;

Boston Weekly News-Letter, Feb. 12, 1741.

25. "Articles and Regulations of the Friendly Society of Tradesmen and House Carpenters, March 10, 1767," Broadside in the New York Public Library, Rare Book Room; *Minutes of the Common Council of New York,* New York, 1905, vol. II, p. 177; George W. Edwards, *New York as an Eighteenth Century Municipality, 1731-1776,* New York, 1917, pp. 90-91.

26. *Minutes of the Common Council of New York City,* vol. V, p. 15; O'Callaghan, ed., *Documents Relating to the Colonial History of New York,* vol. III, pp. 16, 309, 326, 328; Marianna G. Van Rensselaer, *History of New York in the Seventeenth Century,* New York, 1909, vol. I, p. 68; vol. II, p. 219.

27. *New York Mercury,* August 7, 1758.

28. *Georgia Colonial Records,* vol. I, p. 495.

29. Donald L. Kemmerer, "The Suffrage Franchise in Colonial New Jersey," *Proceedings of the New Jersey Historical Society,* vol. LII, 1934, p. 167; Carl Becker, *History of Political Parties in the Province of New York, 1760-1776,* Madison, Wisc., 1909, pp. 11-17; Carl and Jessica Bridenbaugh, *Rebels and Gentlemen,* New York, 1942, p. 14; *Proceedings of the Massachusetts Historical Society,* vol. XLIX, June 1916, p. 454.

30. Stokes, *op. cit.,* vol. IV, p. 536; Merle Curti, *Growth of American Thought,* New York, 1943, p. 45.

31. Henry W. Belknap, *Trades and Tradesmen of Essex County, Massachusetts,* Salem, 1929, p. 9.

32. Bridenbaugh, *Cities in the Wilderness,* p. 256.

33. Philip A. Bruce, *The Institutional History of Virginia in the Sixteenth Century,* New York, 1910, vol. I, pp. 644-75; Thomas J. Wertenbaker, *Torchbearer of the Revolution,* Princeton, N. J., 1940, pp. 8-14.

34. O'Callaghan, ed., *Documents Relating to the Colonial History of the State of New York,* vol. V, p. 322; Rev. A. G. Vermilye, *The Leisler Troubles of 1689,* New York, 1891, p. 25.

35. George W. Edwards, "New York Politics before the American Revolution," *Political Science Quarterly,* vol. XXXVI, Sept. 1921, pp. 586-602; *New York Gazette,* May 27, Oct. 14, 1734; *New York Weekly Journal,* Oct. 14,

1734; Handbill signed by Timothy Wheelwright and John Chissel, dated September 8, 1734, and "A Song—1734," both in the New York Public Library, Rare Book Room.

36. Edwards, *op. cit.,* pp. 587, 593; O'Callaghan, ed., *Documents Relating to the Colonial History of the State of New York,* vol. VI, pp. 7-8.

37. Albert B. Hart, ed., *American History Told by Contemporaries,* New York, 1898, vol. II, p. 198.

38. John C. Miller, *Sam Adams,* Boston, 1936, pp. 9-15.

CHAPTER III

1. Curtis P. Nettels, "The Menace of Colonial Manufacturing, 1690-1720," *New England Quarterly,* vol. IV, April 1931, pp. 240-66; Clarence V. Alvord, *The Mississippi Valley in British Politics,* Cleveland, 1917, vol. I, pp. 88-99.

2. John C. Miller, *Origins of the American Revolution,* p. 23.

3. Curtis P. Nettels, *Roots of American Civilization,* New York, 1938, pp. 17-22.

4. Moses C. Tyler, *Literary History of the American Revolution, 1763-1783,* New York, 1897, vol. I, pp. 100-01.

5. Charles M. Andrews, "Boston Merchants and the Non-Importation Movement," Colonial Society of Massachusetts, *Publications,* vol. XIX, 1916-1917, p. 259.

6. Jared Sparks, *Life of Gouverneur Morris,* Boston, 1832, vol. I, p. 25; H. C. Van Schaack, *Life of Peter Van Schaack,* New York, 1842, p. 47.

7. Philip Davidson, "Sons of Liberty and Stamp Men," *North Carolina Historical Review,* vol. IX, Jan. 1932, pp. 50-54.

8. *New York Gazette,* Nov. 7, 1765; Emerson Taylor, *Paul Revere,* New York, 1930, p. 70; Herbert M. Morais, "The Sons of Liberty in New York," in Richard B. Morris, ed., *The Era of the American Revolution,* New York, 1939, pp. 272-73; C. C. Jones, *History of Georgia,* Boston, 1883, pp. 61, 111; Fitch Papers, in *Connecticut Historical Society Collections,* vol. XVIII, 1920, pp. 384-85.

9. *Mss.,* Boston Committee of Correspondence, vol. VI, pp. 472-73, New York Public Library, Manuscript Division; William Cutter, *Life of Israel Put-*

nam, New York, 1861, p. 133; R. S. Longley, "Mob Activities in Revolutionary Massachusetts," *New England Quarterly*, vol. VI, March 1933, pp. 98-130; Elizabeth May Blake, *Opposition to the Stamp Act in New York City*, unpublished M. A. Thesis, Syracuse University, 1936, p. 38.

10. James K. Hosmer, *The Life of Thomas Hutchinson*, Boston, 1896, p. 238; Charles M. Metzer, "Propaganda and the American Revolution," *Mid-America*, vol. XXII, Oct. 1940, p. 252; John C. Miller, *Sam Adams*, p. 302; R. Frothingham, *Life and Times of Joseph Warren*, Boston, 1865, p. 137.

11. H. L. Calkin, "Pamphlets and Public Opinion during the American Revolution," *Pennsylvania Magazine of History and Biography*, vol. LXIV, Jan. 1940, p. 30; *South Carolina Gazette*, Sept. 22, 1768.

12. "A New Song—Address'd to the Sons of Liberty on the Continent of America, 1768," copy in the Library of the Historical Society of Pennsylvania; *New York Gazette*, Jan. 6, 1766.

13. Benson J. Lossing, *Pictorial Field-Book of the Revolution*, New York, 1860, vol. I, p. 482; R. J. Burker, "The Daughters of Liberty," *American Historical Register*, vol. I, 1894, pp. 29-36; *Boston Chronicle*, Sept. 28, 1769.

14. John C. Miller, *Origins of the American Revolution.* p. 344; *Ms.*, letter dated Boston, April 4, 1766, Rhode Island Historical Society.

15. W. W. Willard, ed., *Letters on the American Revolution*, Boston, 1925, p. 25.

16. Arthur M. Schlesinger, *Colonial Merchants and the American Revolution*, New York, 1918, pp. 382-87; John C. Miller, *Sam Adams*, p. 299.

17. Michael Kraus, "America and the Irish Revolutionary Movement in the Eighteenth Century," in Richard B. Morris, ed., *The Era of the American Revolution*, pp. 337-39; Willard, *op. cit* , pp. 121, 216; *Newport Mercury*, March 12, 1775.

18. Glenn C. Smith, "An Era of Non-Importation Associations," *William and Mary Quarterly*, Series 2, vol. XL, p. 94; *Gage Correspondence*, vol. I, p. 197.

19. Becker, *op. cit.*, p. 28.

20. Sellers, *op. cit.*, pp. 205-09.

21. Esther Forbes, *Paul Revere and the World He Lived In*, Boston, 1942, p.

187; Merrill Jensen, *The Articles of Confederation*, Madison, Wisc., 1940, p. 45; L. H. Gipson, Jared Ingersoll, New York, 1920, p. 270.

22. Philip Davidson, *Propaganda and the American Revolution, 1763-1783,* Chapel Hill, N. C., 1941, p. 77.

23. *Pennsylvania Magazine of History and Biography*, vol. IX, 1885, p. 196; vol. XXI, 1897, p. 478; vol. LXII, 1938, p. 306.

24. Quoted by Claude Van Tyne, *Loyalists in the American Revolution*, New York, 1902, p. 142.

25. Governor James Wright to Lord Dartmouth, Dec. 19, 1775, in *Georgia Historical Society Collections*, Savannah, 1873, vol. III, p. 228.

26. Quoted by Charles F. Millett, "Tory Imperialism on the Eve of the Declaration of Independence," *Canadian Historical Review*, vol. XII, Sept. 1931, p. 267.

27. Claude Van Tyne, *The Causes of the War for Independence*, New York, 1922, pp. 394-95.

28. *New York City during the American Revolution... Original Papers*, pp. 54-55 (Colonel Marinus Willet's narrative); John Adams, *Letters Addressed to His Wife*, Boston, 1841, vol. I, p. 42; Donald L. Kemmerer, *Pathway to Freedom: The Struggle for Self-Government in Colonial New Jersey*, Princeton, N. J., 1940, p. 327.

29. Worthington C. Ford, ed., *Journals of the Continental Congress*, Washington, 1904-1937, vol. I, pp. 86-89; Edward McCrady, *History of South Carolina in the Revolution, 1775-1780*, New York, 1901, p. 270.

30. Philip S. Foner, ed., *The Complete Writings of Thomas Paine*, New York, 1945, vol. I, pp. 30-31.

31. *New Jersey Archives*, vol. X, p. 179; John C. Fitzpatrick, "The Committees of Correspondence and Safety of the Revolutionary War," *Magazine of the Daughters of the American Revolution*, vol. LV, Nov. 1921, p. 617.

32. McCrady, *op. cit.*, pp. 39-40.

33. Herbert M. Morais, "Artisan Democracy and the American Revolution," *Science and Society*, vol. VI, Summer 1942, p. 236.

34. Carl Van Doren, *Mutiny in January*, New York, 1943, p. 43; Sterling *Mss.* lib. 4, f. 62, March 4, 1776, New York Historical Society.

35. *Pennsylvania Archives*, 1st. Series, Philadelphia, 1853, vol. VIII, p. 730.
36. W. B. Hartgrove, "The Negro Soldier in the American Revolution," *Journal of Negro History*, vol. I, April 1916, pp. 119-28.
37. Herbert Aptheker, *The Negro in the American Revolution*, New York, 1940, pp. 34-41.
38. Philip S. Foner, ed., *George Washington: Selections from his Writings*, New York, 1944, pp. 16-17.
39. *Ibid.*, pp. 59-60.
40. Charles Francis Adams, ed., *Familiar Letters of John Adams and His Wife Abigail Adams, During the American Revolution*, New York, 1876, p. 365.
41. C. J. Hoadley, ed., *Public Records of Connecticut*, Hartford, Conn., 1894, vol. I, p. 62.
42. Robert L. Brunhaus, *The Counter-Revolution .in .Pennsylvania*, Philadelphia, 1943, pp. 70-71.
43. G. H. Bryden, ed., *Letters to and from Caeser Rodney*, Philadelphia, 1933, p. 303; Elias P. Oberholtzer, *Robert Morris*, New York, 1903, pp. 51-56; Brunhaus, *op. cit.*, pp. 71ff.
44. Brunhaus, *op. cit.*, p. 58; Eugene P. Link, *Democratic-Republican Societies, 1790-1800*, New York, 1942, p. 26.
45. Carl Van Doren, *op. cit.*. pp. 213-14.
46. E. R. Turner, *The Negro In Pennsylvania*, Washington, 1911, p 92.
47. *Independent Journal*, Jan. 24, 1784; McCormac, *op. cit.*, p. 76; William Miller, "The Effects of the American Revolution on Indentured Servitude," *Pennsylvania History*, vol. VII, 1940, p. 136.
48. *National Laborer*, June 11, 1836.
49. *Fall River Mechanic*, July 6, 1844.

CHAPTER IV

1. *New York Advertiser*, Jan. 23, July 17, Sept. 8, Oct. 7, 1786.
2. *North American Review*, vol. XII, Jan. 1821, pp. 85-86; John Bristed, *America and Her Resources*, London, 1818. p. 54; Samuel Reznck, "The Rise and Early Development of Industrial Consciousness in the United States, 1760-1830," *Journal of Economic and Business History*, vol. IV, Dec. 1932, pp. 784 ff.
3. Philip S. Foner, ed., *Thomas Jeffer-*

son: Selections from his Writings, New York, 1943, p. 30.
4. Rezneck, *op. cit.*, p. 801.
5. Victor S. Clark, *History of Manufactures in the United States*, New York, 1929, vol. I, p. 380.
6. *Niles' Register*, vol. XII, June 28, 1817, pp. 286-87.
7. Frederick Engels, *The Condition of the Working Class in England in 1844*, London, 1936, p. 295.
8. Harry J. Carman, *Social and Economic History of the United States*, New York, 1934, vol. II, p. 18.
9. W. R. Bagnall, *Samuel Slater and the Early Development of the Cotton Manufacture in the United States*, Middletown, Conn., 1890, p. 44.
10. Caroline F. Ware, *The Early New England Cotton Manufacture*, Boston, 1931, p. 64; Jonathan Taylor Lincoln, "The Beginning of the Machine Age in New England: Documents relating to the Introduction of the Power Loom," *Bulletin Business History Society*, vol. VII, June, 1933, pp. 6-13.
11. Charles A. Wilson, *Waltham, Past and Present, and its Industries*, Cambridge, Mass., 1879, pp. 122-30; Melvin T. Copeland, *The Cotton Manufacturing Industry of the United States*, Boston, 1888, p. 38.
12. Vera Shlakman, *Economic .History of a Factory Town*, Northampton, Mass., 1935, pp. 31, 37, 48.
13. Blanche E. Hazard, *The Organization of the Boot and Shoe Industry in Massachusetts before 1875*, Cambridge, Mass., 1921, pp. 93-96, 112, 124 ff.
14. L. C. Hunter, "Influence of the Market upon Techniques in the Iron Industry in Western Pennsylvania to 1860," *Journal of Economic and Business History*, vol. I, Feb., 1929, pp. 241-81.
15. Quoted by Thomas C. Cochran and William Miller, *The Age of Enterprise*, New York, 1942, p. 6.
16. Michael G. Mulhall, *Industries and Wealth of Nations*, London, 1896, pp. 32, 292-98, 377-80.
17. *Senate Executive Document*, 39th Congress, 2nd Session, No. 2, p. 10; *Appleton's Annual Cyclopedia*, 1862, p. 699; *New York Evening Post*, July 10, 27, 1864.
18. Frederick Merk, *The Labor Movement in Wisconsin during the Civil War*, Madison, Wisc., 1915, pp. 170-71; *Fed-*

eral Census, 1870, Population, p. 793; Helen Campbell, *Women Wage Earners*, Boston, 1893, p. 101.

19. Peter Roberts, *The Anthracite Coal Industry*, New York, 1901, p. 19.
20. *Commercial and Financial Chronicle*, Jan. 13, 1866; Emerson D. Fite, *Social and Economic Conditions in the North during the Civil War*, New York, 1910, p. 165.
21. Stuart Daggett, *Chapters on the History of the Southern Pacific*, New York, 1922, pp. 199-221.
22. *Report of the Select Committee to Investigate the Alleged Credit Mobilier Bribery, February 18, 1873*, Washington, 1873, p. X.
23. *National Labor Tribune*, May 15, 1875.
24. Reprinted in Edward A. Wieck, *The American Miners' Association*, New York, 1940, pp. 256-57.
25. Philip S. Foner, ed., *Abraham Lincoln: Selections from his Writings*, New York, 1944, pp. 84-85.
26. James C. Sylvis, *The Life, Speeches, Labors and Essays of William H. Sylvis*, Philadelphia, 1872, pp. 98, 110, 112-13, 155-56, 448-450.

CHAPTER V

1. *American State Papers*, Finance, vol. IV, Washington, 1858, no. 662.
2. "Account of a Journey of Josiah Quincy in 1801," *Proceedings Massachusetts Historical Society*, Series II, vol. IV, 1888, p. 124.
3. Clark, *op. cit.*, p. 57; Stewart, *op. cit.*, pp. 20-23; Harriet H. Robinson, *Loom and Spindle*, New York and Boston, 1898, p. 6.
4. Sidney I. Pomerantz, *New York, An American City, 1783-1803*, New York, 1938, pp. 216-17.
5. John R. Commons, ed., *Documentary History of American Industrial Society*, Cleveland, 1909-1911, vol. III, p. 118.
6. Henry B. Fearon, *Sketches of America*, London, 1819, p. 404.
7. Frank Monaghan and Marvin Lowenthal, *This Was New York: The Nation's Capital in 1789*, Garden City, New York, 1943, pp. 80-81.
8. John R. Commons, "American Shoemakers, 1648-1895," *Quarterly Journal of Economics*, vol. XXIV, Nov. 1909, pp. 50 *ff*; Commons, *History of Labor in the United States*, vol. I, p. 104.

9. T. Earle and C. T. Congdon, eds., *Annals of the General Society of Mechanics and Tradesmen of the City of New York, 1785-1800*, New York, 1882, pp. 10-22; James G. Wilson, *Memorial History of the City of New York*, New York, 1892-93, vol. III, p. 16; Pomerantz, *op. cit.* p. 215.
10. Jonathan Boucher, *A View of the Causes and Consequences of the American Revolution*, London, 1797, p. 309.
11. Monaghan and Lowenthal, *op. cit.*, p. 77; Richard B. Morris, *op. cit.*, pp. 77, 81.
12. Richard B. Morris, *op. cit.*, pp. 77, 81-84.
13. Ethelbert Stewart, *A Documentary History of Early Organization of Printers*, Indianapolis, 1907, p. 6; Earle and Congdon, *op. cit.*, p. 381.
14. Commons, ed., *Documentary History of American Industrial Society*, vol. III, p. 364.
15. *National Advocate*, July 4, 1817; *Working Man's Advocate*, Oct. 18, 1845.
16. George A. Tracy, *History of the Typographical Union*, Indianapolis, 1913, pp. 19 *ff*.
17. Commons, ed., *Documentary History of American Industrial Society*, vol. III, p. 365; Stewart, *op. cit.*, pp. 47, 101.
18. Commons, ed., *Documentary History of American Industrial Society*, vol. III, p. 370.
19. *Ibid.*, p. 36; G. A. Stevens, *History of the New York Typographical Union, No. 6*, New York, 1913, p. 70.
20. Stewart, *op. cit.*, p. 101.
21. Commons, ed., *Documentary History of American Industrial Society*, vol. VI, p. 392; James Truslow Adams, *New England in the Republic, 1776-1850*, Boston, 1926, p. 346.
22. Stewart, *op. cit.*, pp. 24-25, 39, 52.
23. Commons, ed., *Documentary History of American Industrial Society*, vol. III, pp. 74-76, 369; Stewart, *op. cit.*, pp. 19-20; Stevens, *op. cit.*, pp. 45, 60.
24. Stevens, *op. cit.*, pp. 72-73.
25. *Ibid.*, p. 16.
26. Commons, ed., *Documentary History of American Industrial Society*, vol. III, pp. 364-66.
27. *Ibid.*, p. 294.
28. Stevens, *op. cit.*, pp. 72-73.
29. Commons, ed., *Documentary History of American Industrial Society*, vol.

III, pp. 83, 93, 97-98; Commons, *History of Labor in the United States,* vol. I, pp. 110-11.
30. Stevens, *op. cit.,* p. 47.
31. *Ibid,* p. 64; Stewart, *op. cit.,* p. 35.
32. *Sixteenth Annual Report of the Bureau of Statistics of Labor,* Massachusetts, 1885; Commons, ed., *Documentary History of American Industrial Society,* vol. III, p. 136.
33. Stephen Simpson, *The Working Man's Manual,* Philadelphia, 1831, p. 86.
34. Walter Nelles, "Commonwealth v. Hunt," *Columbia Law Review,* vol. XXXII, Nov. 1932, p. 1129.
35. Walter Nelles, "The First American Labor Case," *Yale Law Journal,* vol. XLI, Dec. 1931, p. 177.
36. Commons, ed., *Documentary History of American Industrial Society,* vol. III, pp. 167, 172, 177; Nelles, in *Yale Law Journal,* vol. XLI, p. 177.
37. Commons, ed., *Documentary History of American Industrial Society,* vol. IV, p. 16.
38. Stewart, *op. cit.,* p. 18.

CHAPTER VI

1. *Pennsylvania Packet,* April 29, 1786.
2. "Constitution of 1777, Article VII," in *United States Documents,* vol. XLI, pt. 1, pp. 2630-31.
3. "Arminus" in *Independent Gazetteer,* Oct. 9, 1784. See also "An Old Mechanic," in *ibid.*
4. C. W. Spaulding, *New York in the Critical Period, 1783-1789,* New York, 1939, pp. 107-08; Pomerantz, *op. cit.,* pp. 95-96; *New York Gazetteer,* April 15, 25, 1785; *New York Packet,* April 7, 21, 24, 27, 1785.
5. Spaulding, *op. cit.,* p. 177; John C. Miller, *Sam Adams,* pp. 378-79, Charles A. Beard, *An Economic Interpretation of the Constitution of the United States,* New York, 1913, pp. 241, 244, 247; *Pennsylvania Gazette,* July 9, 1788.
6. *Pennsylvania Gazette,* Oct. 3, Dec. 19, 1787.
7. Zachariah Chaffee, Jr., "The Bill of Rights Belongs to the People," *Bulletin of the American Association of University Professors,* Feb., 1942, pp. 92-93.
8. William A. Robinson, *Jeffersonian Democracy in New England,* New Haven, 1916, pp. 111-14.

9. *New York Journal,* March 5, 1794; *Dunlap's American Daily Advertiser,* Jan. 3, 1793; W. R. Fee, *Transition from Aristocracy to Democracy in New Jersey, 1799-1829,* Somerville, N. J., 1933, p. 44.
10. *New York Journal,* March 5, 1794, Oct. 11, 1796.
11. Link, *op. cit.,* pp. 91-92, 115.
12. *American Daily Advertiser,* August 2, 1794.
13. Link, *op. cit.,* pp. 166-71.
14. Quoted in *ibid.,* p. 158.
15. William Manning, *The Key of Libberty,* Bellevea, Mass., 1922, pp. 66-71.
16. Link, *op. cit.,* p. 151; Philip S. Foner, ed., *The Complete Writings of Thomas Paine,* New York, 1945, vol. I, p. 183.
17. Link, *op. cit.,* p. 151.
18. Vernon Stauffer, *New England Clergy and the Bavarian Illuminati,* New York, 1918, pp. 13-22; Timothy Dwight, *The Duty of Americans at the Present Crisis,* New Haven, 1798, pp. 20-21.
19. Quoted by John H. Wolfe, *Jeffersonian Democracy in South Carolina,* Chapel Hill, 1940, p. 144.
20. Quoted by Link, *op. cit.,* p. 96.
21. *Alexander Hamilton's Report on Manufactures Made to Congress, December 5, 1791,* Boston, 1892, p. 29.
22. Samuel Eliot Morison, *The Life and Letters of Harrison Grey Otis,* Boston, 1913, vol. I, p. 218.
23. Frank M. Anderson, "The Enforcement of the Alien and Sedition Laws," *Annual Report of the American Historical Association for 1912,* pp. 123-24.
24. Pomerantz, *op. cit.,* p. 129.
25. Glenn L. Bushey, "William Duane: Crusader for Judicial Reform," *Pennsylvania History,* vol. V, July 1938, p. 145.
26. *Columbia Law Review,* vol. XXXII, pp. 1163-64.
27. Dixon Ryan Fox, *The Decline of the Aristocracy in the Politics of New York,* New York, 1918, p. 88.
28. Henry Adams, *Documents Relating to New England Federalism,* New York, 1878, p. 392.
29. *Ibid.*
30. Quoted by Wolfe, *op. cit.,* p. 232.
31. *Independent Chronicle* (Boston), Jan. 4, 1808. See also Philadelphia *Aurora,* Jan. 29, Feb. 3, 5, 7, March 27, 1807, Nov. 21, 1808.
32. *Minutes of the Common Council of New York City,* vol. IV, pp. 699-701.

33. Claude G. Bowers, *Jefferson in Power*, Boston, 1936, p. 433.
34. *New York Evening Post*, April 30, 1808; Virginia D. Harrington, "New York and the Embargo of 1807," *Proceedings of the New York State Historical Association*, vol. XXV, 1927, pp. 144-45.
35. Bowers, *op. cit.*, p. 239; Henry Adams, *op. cit.*, p. 172.
36. T. S. Martell, "A Sidelight on Federalist Strategy," *American Historical Review*, vol. XLIII, April 1938, pp. 559-60.
37. *Richmond Enquirer*, July 28, 1807; *Niles' Register*, vol. III, Dec. 19, 1812, pp. 246-48; *New York Evening Post*, Feb. 20, 1812; *Newark Sentinel*, Sept. 21, 1813; Wolfe, *op. cit.*, p. 257 *n;* Stewart, *op. cit.*, p. 54.
38. *New York Spectator*, August 12, 28, 1814; Tracy, *op. cit.*, p. 44.
39. *New York Evening Post*, August 12, 28, 1814; *New York Spectator*, Aug. 12, 1814; *Niles' Register*, Vol. VI, August 27, 1814, p. 441; *Minutes of the Common Council of New York City*, August 15, 1814; W. E. Apgar, "New York's Contribution to the War Effort of 1812," *New York Historical Society Quarterly Bulletin*, vol. XXIX, Oct. 1945, pp. 203-12.
40. Benson J. Lossing, *Pictorial Field Book of the War of 1812*, New York, 1868, pp. 970-71.
41. William C. Nell, *Colored Americans in the Wars of 1776 and 1812*, Philadelphia, 1902, pp. 30-31.
42. John Spencer Bassett, ed., *Correspondence of Andrew Jackson*, Washington, 1927, Vol. II, pp. 118-19.
43. *Connecticut Courant*, Sept. 29, 1818.
44. Fox, *op. cit.*, p. 267 *n*. See Kirk H. Porter, *A History of Suffrage in the United States*, Chicago, 1918, pp. 47 *ff.* for a detailed account of the struggle to remove property qualifications for voting.
45. Philip S. Foner, ed., *Thomas Jefferson: Selections from His Writings*, New York, 1943, p. 20.

CHAPTER VII

1. *Niles' Register*, August 7, Sept. 4, Oct. 23, 1819; Samuel Rezneck, "The Depression of 1819-1822, A Social History," *American Historical Review*, vol. XXXIX, Oct. 1933, pp. 30-32.
2. H. A. Weed, ed., *The Autobiography of Thurlow Weed*, New York, 1884, vol. II, p. 19.
3. Mitchell Franklin, "Concerning the Historic Importance of Edward Livingston," *Tulane Law Review*, vol. XI, 1937, pp. 206-09.
4. Rezneck, *op. cit.*, pp. 39-42.
5. William Tudor, *Letters on the Eastern States*, Boston, 1821, p. 263; Commons, *op. cit.*, vol. I, p. 171.
6. *Pennsylvanian*, August 28, 1833; Commons, ed., *Documentary History of American Industrial Society*, vol. V, pp. 330-31.
7. *Working Man's Advocate*, July 15, 1830; Matthew Carey, *Appeal to the Wealthy of the Land*, 3rd edition, pp. 3-5.
8. Helen L. Sumner, "History of Women in Industry in the United States," in "Report on Condition of Woman and Child Wage Earners in the United States," *United States Bureau of Labor*, 1910, vol. IX, p. 125.
9. Matthew Carey, *Selected Excerpts*, vol. IV, p. 435 (copy in Library Company of Philadelphia); *Paterson Courier*, August 11, 1835; *State Papers*, Finance, vol. V, p. 817; Matthew Carey, *Letters on the Conditions of the Poor*, 2nd. edition, pp. 16-17; *Mechanics' Free Press*, June 19, July 31, 1830; *Boston Post*, Oct. 15, 1835.
10. Carrol D. Wright, *History of Wages and Prices in Massachusetts, 1752-1883*, Boston, 1885, p. 171.
11. *Manufacturers' and Farmers' Journal*, Jan. 25, 1822.
12. *The Man*, March 11, 1834; *Mechanics' Free Press*, Jan. 17, 1829; *Paterson Courier*, August 5, 12, 1835; *An Appeal to the Working Men of the United States on their own Condition and Amelioration, By an American Citizen*, Norwich, 1833, p. 8 (copy in American Philosophical Society's pamphlet collection); *Boston Post*, Oct. 22, 1835; *Newark Daily Advertiser*, August 10, 1835.
13. *Paterson Courier*, August 12, 1835.
14. *The Man*, March 11, 1834.
15. *The Louisianan*, April 1, 1823, quoted by Arthur Pearce, *The Rise and Decline of the Labor Movement in New Orleans*, unpublished M. A. Thesis, Tulane University, 1940, pp. 7-8.

16. *Columbian Centinel,* April 20, 1825; Commons, ed., *Documentary History of American Industrial Society,* vol. VI, pp. 77-79.
17. *Mechanics' Free Press,* June 21, 1828. This issue contains a reprint of the original pamphlet, no copies of which have been preserved. The fact that it was reprinted a year after its original appearance indicates the popularity of the pamphlet.
18. *Philadelphia Democratic Press,* June 14, 1827.
19. *Mechanics' Free Press,* Oct. 25, 1828; Commons, ed., *Documentary History of American Industrial Society,* vol. V, p. 87.
20. *The Co-operator,* April 3, 1832; *Boston Post,* Sept. 6, 10, 1832.
21. Seth Luther, *An Address to the Working Men of New England . . . ,* Boston, 1832, pp. 7-8; Commons, ed., *Documentary History of American Industrial Society,* vol. VI, pp. 81-83; United States Bureau of Labor, *16th Annual Report,* p. 725.
22. *Working Man's Advocate,* Oct. 4, 1834; *Paterson Courier,* August 5, 1833; *Mechanics' Free Press,* Jan. 17, 1829.
23. *Proceedings 1833 Convention, New England Association of Farmers', Mechanics' and other Workingmen,* pp. 7, 20, 321; John B. Andrews and Helen Bliss, "History of Women in Trade Unions," *United States Senate Document 645,* 61st Congress, 2d Session, vol. X, p. 12.
24. Seth Luther, *An Address to the Working Men of New England on the State of Education and on the Condition of the Producing Classes in Europe and America. With Particular Reference to the Effect of Manufacturing (as now Conducted) on the Health and Happiness of the Poor, and on the Safety of our Republic,* Philadelphia, 1836, 3rd edition.
25. Carroll D. Wright, "Report on the Factory System of the United States," U. S. House Misc. Doc. 42, part 2, 47th Congress, 2d Session, p. 44; *Working Man's Advocate,* Oct. 1, 1834.
26. *Working Man's Advocate,* Oct. 1, Dec. 17, 1830, Jan. 9, 1833.
27. *Ibid.,* Oct. 1, 1830.
28. Commons, *op. cit.,* vol. I, pp. 348-52, 396, 424, 478-84; *Commercial Bulletin and Missouri Register,* Dec. 9, 1835.
29. See list prepared by Edward B. Mittle-

man, in Commons, *op. cit.,* vol. I, pp. 472-84.
30. *National Laborer,* June 4, 1836; Andrews and Bliss, *op. cit.,* pp. 38, 42.
31. Shlakman, *op. cit.,* pp. 62-63.
32. *The Man,* March 8, 11, 1834.
33. *Boston Transcript,* reprinted in *The Man,* Feb. 20, 1834; *The Man,* Feb. 22, 23, 1834.
34. Rev. Wm. Scoresby, *American Factories and Their Female Operatives,* Boston, 1845, p. 61.
35. *National Laborer,* Oct. 29, 1836; *Boston Post,* Oct. 7, 1836.
36. Seth Luther, *An Address on the Origin and Progress of Avarice, and its Deleterious Effects on Human Happiness,* Boston, 1834, p. 3.
37. Andrews and Bliss, *op. cit.,* p. 43; *Lynn Record,* Jan. 1, June 18, 1834.
38. *Proceedings of the Government and Citizens of Philadelphia on the Reduction of the Hours of Labor, and Increase of Wages,* Boston, 1835, p. 9.
39. *National Laborer,* April 2, 30, May 7, 1836.
40. *Paterson Intelligencer,* July 29, 1935; *Newark Daily Advertiser,* July 28-30, August 10, 1835; Seth Luther, *op cit.,* pp. 42-46.
41. *New York Morning Courier and Enquirer,* June 3, 1833.
42. *National Laborer,* April 2, 20, 23, May 21, Nov. 5, 1836.
43. *Ibid.,* April 9, May 14, June 25, 1836.
44. Commons, *op. cit.,* vol. I, pp. 360, 364.
45. Reprinted in *National Laborer,* April 9, 30, 1836.
46. Commons, *op. cit.,* vol. I, p. 369.
47. *Journal of Commerce,* April 3, 1835; *Working Man's Advocate,* June 14, 1835.
48. *Newark Daily Advertiser,* Feb. 13, 1836.
49. *National Laborer,* Jan. 21, Dec. 24, 1836.
50. *Working Man's Advocate,* May 17, 1834.
51. *Ibid.,* Dec. 6, 1834.
52. *National Trades' Union* (New York), May 30, 1835; *National Laborer,* Nov. 12, 1836.
53. Commons, ed., *Documentary History of American Industrial Society,* vol. VI, pp. 232-33; *National Laborer,* Nov. 12, 1836.
54. *Boston Post,* April 17, May 6, 7, 1835; *Pennsylvanian,* August 8, 1835; Commons, ed., *Documentary History of*

American Industrial Society, vol. VI, pp. 94, 279, 280; Hartz, *op. cit.*, p. 405.

55. Commons, ed., *Documentary History of American Industrial Society*, vol. VI, p. 94.

56. Commons, *op. cit.*. vol. I, p. 417; *Pennsylvanian*, August 8, 1835.

57. *Working Man's Advocate*, July 25, 1835.

58. *Proceedings of the Government and and Citizens of Philadelphia on the Reduction of the Hours of Labor, and Increase of Wages*, Boston, 1835, p. 9.

59. Commons, ed., *Documentary History of American Industrial Society*, vol. VI, p. 39.

60. *Proceedings of the Government and Citizens of Philadelphia on the Reduction of the Hours of Labor, and Increase of Wages*, pp. 4-5.

61. Commons, ed., *Documentary History of American Industrial Society*, vol. VI, p. 39.

62. *Proceedings of the Government and Citizens of Philadelphia on the Reduction of the Hours of Labor, and Increase of Wages*, pp. 4, 8, 9-10.

63. *16th Annual Report of the Bureau of Statistics of Labor*, Massachusetts, August 1885.

64. *Newark Daily Advertiser*, August 10, 1835; *National Laborer*, April 9, May 26, 1836; *New York Evening Post*, March 16, 1836.

65. *Newark Daily Advertiser*, March 22, 24, 29, April 26, 1836; *Paterson Courier*, Aug. 13, 1835; *Lynn Record*, Jan. 8, 1834.

66. *Newark Daily Advertiser*, Jan. 24, June 1, 1835; *National Laborer*, April 2, May 7, 1836.

CHAPTER VIII

1. *Free Enquirer*, Oct. 27, 1829.

2. *Mechanics' Free Press*, June 21, 1828.

3. Stephen Simpson, *The Working Man's Manual*, pp. 202-03; *Newark Daily Advertiser*, August 10, 1835; *Working Man's Advocate*, March 6, 13, 1830; Address of Workingmen of Philadelphia, in *Mechanics' Free Press*. May 1, July 10, 1830; Commons, *op. cit.*, vol. I, p. 227.

4. *Working Man's Advocate*, Oct. 3, 31, 1829; *Mechanics' Free Press*, Jan. 2, 1830.

5. *Working Man's Advocate*, Oct. 31, 1829, Jan. 6, 30, Feb. 27, 1830; *National Laborer*, May 21, 1836; *Bulletin Business History Society*, vol. II, no. 2, pp. 11-13; *Sentinel of Freedom* (New Jersey), July 3, 1823; *Boston Post*, July 20, 1832.

6. *Working Man's Advocate*, Feb. 27, March 6, 1830, Feb. 5, 1831.

7. *Mechanics' Free Press*, Oct. 2, 1830.

8. *Working Man's Advocate*, April 24, 1830.

9. *Ibid.*, Oct. 31, 1829; *The Free Trade Advocate and Journal of Political Economy*, vol. I, May 9, 1829, p. 297; Arthur M. Schlesinger, Jr., *The Age of Jackson*, New York, 1945, pp. 119-21, 526-27.

10. *Working Man's Advocate*, Jan. 30, 1830.

11. *Sentinel of Freedom* (New Jersey), Sept. 6, 1830.

12. *New York Evening Journal*, reprinted in *Working Man's Advocate*, April 17, 1830; *Sentinel of Freedom* (New Jersey); Sept. 6, 1830.

13. Matthew Carey, *Select Excerpts*, vol. XXXI, pp. 156-60 (copy in Library Company of Philadelphia).

14. Simpson, *op. cit.*, p. 89.

15. *Mechanics' Free Press*, Oct. 31, 1829; *Working Man's Advocate*, April 20, 1830.

16. John A. Pollard, "Whittier on Labor Unions," *New England Quarterly*, vol. XII, March 1939, p. 100.

17. *Mechanics' Free Press*, May 31, 1829; Alden Whitman, *Labor Parties, 1827-1834*, New York, 1943, p. 22.

18. *Mechanics' Free Press*, Aug. 16, 1828.

19. *Ibid.*, Nov. 1, 1828.

20. *Ibid.*, Oct. 10, 1828.

21. *Philadelphia Democratic Press*, August 17, 27, 31, 1829; *Working Man's Advocate*, June 7, 1830.

22. Whitman, *op. cit.*, p. 29.

23. *Mechanics' Free Press*, Oct. 16, 1830.

24. George Henry Evans, "History of the Origin and Progress of the Working Men's Party in New York," *The Radical*, vol. II, 1842, p. 3; *New York Morning Courier and Enquirer*, April 30, 1829; Commons, *op. cit.*, vol. I, p. 236.

25. Hobart Berrian, *A Brief Sketch of the Origin and Rise of the Workingmen's Party in the City of New York*, Washington, n. d., p. 4; *Free Enquirer*, Oct. 31, Nov. 7, 1829, Nov. 27, 1830.

26. Frances Wright, "Address to the Industrious Classes," *Popular Tracts*, No. 3, p. 4.
27. *Working Man's Advocate*, Oct. 31, 1829; Evans, *op. cit.*, p. 55.
28. *New York Courier and Enquirer*, Nov. 3, 1829.
29. *Working Man's Advocate*, Nov. 14, 1829.
30. *New York Evening Post*, Nov. 5, 9, 1829; *New York Journal of Commerce*, Nov. 7, 1829.
31. *Working Man's Advocate*, Feb. 20, April 10, 17, 24, May 8, 15, 1830; *Harrisburg (Pa.) Intelligencer* quoted by *Working Man's Advocate*, May 29, 1830. *Farmers' Mechanics' and Workingmen's Advocate*, May 5, 1830; *Mechanics' Press*, May 29, 1830.
32. *New York Evening Journal*, Dec. 31, 1829, *Working Man's Advocate*, Dec. 31, 1829.
33. Amos Gilbert, "The Life of Thomas Skidmore," in *Free Enquirer*, March 30, 1834; *Working Man's Advocate*, July 29, 1830.
34. Reprinted in *Free Enquirer*, March 30, 1830.
35. *Working Man's Advocate*, March 13, 20, 1830.
36. *Ibid.*, April 3, 1830; *Young America*, March 29, 1845.
37. W. R. Lawrence, ed., *Extracts from the Diary and Correspondence of the Late Amos Lawrence*, Boston, 1855, p. 28. See also Edward Everett, *A Lecture on the Working Men's Party*, Boston, 1830. Copy in Rare Book Room, Library of Congress.
38. Reprinted in *Free Enquirer*, March 30, 1830.
39. Frances Wright, "Address to the Industrious Classes," *Popular Tracts*, No. 5, p. 4.
40. Robert Dale Owen, "Essays on Public Education," *New York Daily Sentinel*, April 13, 1830; *Working Man's Advocate*, April 17, 24, May 29, 1830; Richard W. Leopold, *Robert Dale Owen*, Cambridge, 1940, pp. 92-94, 100-102.
41. Quoted by Sidney L. Jackson, *America's Struggle for Free Schools, 1827-1842*, Washington, 1941, pp. 166-67.
42. *Working Man's Advocate*, May 29, July 10, 1829, Sept. 11, 1830. For support given by the painters' union to the State Guardianship plan, see *Free Enquirer*, Jan. 9, 1830.
43. *Ibid.*, Feb. 13, June 16, 19, 1830; *Daily Sentinel*, March 13, 1830; Commons, *op. cit.*, vol. I, p. 246.
44. *Working Man's Advocate*, May 29, June 12, Sept. 15, 1830; *Mechanics' Free Press*, June 12, 1830.
45. "Senex," in *Working Man's Advocate*, June 10, 1830.
46. *Working Man's Advocate*, July 10, 1830.
47. *Working Man's Advocate*, Sept. 4, 11, 1830. For a different version, see *The Craftsman*, Sept. 4, 1830.
48. *Ibid.*, Sept. 11, 1830; *New York Courier and Enquirer*, Oct. 8, 1830.
49. *Working Man's Advocate*, Oct. 28, Nov. 13, 1830; *New York Courier and Enquirer*, Nov. 12, 1830.
50. Arthur B. Darling, "The Workingmen's Party in Massachusetts, 1833-1834," *American Historical Review*, vol. XXIX, Oct. 1923, pp. 81-86.
51. *New York Evening Journal*, Dec. 31, 1829; *Working Man's Advocate*, Aug. 11, 1830.
52. F. T. Carlton, *op. cit.*, pp. 339-44; James Truslow Adams, *New England in the Republic, 1776-1850*, p. 369; Frank T. Carlton, *Economic Influences on Educational Progress in the United States, 1820-1850*, Madison, Wisc., 1908, p. 122.

CHAPTER IX

1. *Working Man's Advocate*, April 17, Dec. 18, 1830; *Farmers' Mechanics' and Workingmen's Advocate* (Albany), Feb. 2, 1831.
2. *Ibid.*, April 3, July 9, August 5, Oct. 30, 1830.
3. *Working Man's Advocate*, April 3, 17, 1830; *Daily Sentinel*, Aug. 4, 1830.
4. James F. Richardson, *A Compilation of the Messages and Papers of the Presidents*, Washington, D. C., 1899, vol. II, pp. 590-91.
5. Marquis James, *Andrew Jackson: Portrait of a President*, New York, 1937, p. 304.
6. *Working Man's Advocate*, Nov. 21, 1834; *New York Evening Post*, Nov. 20, Dec. 30, 1834; *Plaindealer*, Dec. 24, 1836. For a brief study of Leggett's career and political theories, see Richard Hofstader, "William Leggett, Spokesman of Jacksonian Democracy," *Political Science Quarterly*, vol. LVIII, Dec. 1943, pp. 581-94. See also Theo-

philus Fisk, *Labor the Only true source of Wealth*, Charleston, S. C., 1837, p. 4.

7. Paul Leicester Ford, ed., *The Writings of Thomas Jefferson*, New York, 1892-99, vol. X, pp. 437-39.

8. *The Man*, April 9, 1834; *Working Man's Advocate*, Aug. 13, 1834.

9. *Working Man's Advocate*, Sept.-Oct. 1832; Theodore Sedgwick, Jr., ed., *A Collection of the Political Writings of William Leggett*, New York, 1840, vol. I, p. 70, *Boston Post*, July 2, 1832.

10. *Working Man's Advocate*, Nov. 3, 10, 1832; *Contributions of the Old Residents' Historical Association*, Lowell, Mass., 1879-1904, vol. I, p. 122.

11. Reprinted in *Working Man's Advocate*, Nov. 29, 1832.

12. *Ibid.*, Sept. 12, 1833, Feb. 14, 1834.

13. *Proceedings*, 1833 Convention. Pamphlet, Library of Congress.

14. James, *op. cit.*, p. 354; Claude G. Bowers, *Party Battles of the Jacksonian Era*, New York, 1922, p. 314; R. C. McGrane, ed., *Correspondence of Nicholas Biddle*, Boston, 1919, pp. 219, 221.

15. Quoted by John McConaughy, *Who Rules America?*, New York, 1934, p. 118.

16. *Bulletin Business History Society*, vol. VII, no. 3, p. 4, vol. VIII, no. 3, p. 2.

17. *New York Courier and Enquirer*, Feb. 11, 1834. *The Man* for January and February, 1834, has many letters from workers who were discharged by employers for supporting Jackson; see also "A Unionist" in *The Man*, March 5, 1834.

18. *New York Courier and Enquirer*, Feb. 11, 1834.

19. *The Man*, April 3, May 31, 1834; *New York Evening Post*, April 14, 1834.

20. *The Man*, Feb. 20, 24, March 3, 15, 21, Aug. 2, 1834.

21. *Ibid.*, March 19, 1834.

22. *Ibid.*, May 31, 1834.

23. *Ibid.*, July 16, 1834.

24. *Ibid.*, Feb. 26, 1834; *New York Evening Post*, Feb. 10, 1834; *Working Man's Advocate*, Feb. 15, April 9, 1834.

25. *Working Man's Advocate*, April 9, 1834; *The Man*, March 25, 1834.

26. John Spencer Bassett, *The Life of Andrew Jackson*, New York, 1911, p. 701.

27. *Working Man's Advocate*, April 9, 1834.

28. *Ibid.*, May 12, Aug. 16, Oct. 10, 1834.

29 *Register of Debates in Congress*, 24th

Cong. 1st Sess, vol. II, pp. 3429-35; *National Laborer*, May 29, July 9, 1836.

30. *The Democrat*, May 14, 1835; *Working Man's Advocate*, Jan. 19, Feb. 12, April 18, 1835.

31. *New York Evening Post*, Sept. 19, 1835; *Plaindealer*, Oct. 24, 1836; Theodore Sedgwick, Jr., ed., *Political Writings of William Leggett*, vol. II, pp. 56 ff.

32. *Working Man's Advocate*, Oct. 24, 1835; F. Byrdsall, *Origin and History of the Loco-Foco Party*, New York, 1842, p. 26; *New York Courier and Enquirer*, Oct. 30, 1835.

33. Commons, ed., *Documentary History of American Industrial Society*, vol. IV, pp. 99 ff.; see also the appendix to Walter Nelles' article "Commonwealth v. Hunt," *Columbia Law Review*, vol. XXXII, pp. 1166-69.

34. People v. Fisher, N. Y., 1835, 14 Wendell, 2, 10; Commons, ed., *Documentary History of American Industrial Society*, vol. IV, p. 330.

35. Commons, ed., *Documentary History American Industrial Society*, vol. IV, pp. 315, 325, 330, 332; *The Union*, June 14, 1836; *National Laborer*, August 6, 1836.

36. *New York Evening Post*, June 13, 1836.

37. *National Laborer*, May 7, 1836.

38. *New York Evening Post*, May 31, 1836.

39. John A. Pollard, "Whittier on Labor Unions," *New England Quarterly*, vol. XII, pp. 101-02.

40. *National Laborer*, June 8, July 2, 1836.

41. *The Union*, July 11, 1836.

42. *New York Courier and Enquirer*, June 8, 1836.

43. *New York Evening Post*, June 14, 1836; *The Union*, June 15, 1836.

44. *New York Evening Post*, June 14-16, 1836.

45. *The Union*, June 15, 1836; Carl Carmer, "How Eight Poor Shoemakers of Hudson, N. Y., won Union Labor's First Victory 105 years ago," *P. M*, June 1, 1941.

46. Byrdsall, *op. cit.*, pp. 68 ff.

47. *The Union*, Nov. 7, 1836.

48. *Albany Microscope* reprinted in *The Democrat*, Nov. 8, 1836.

49. *The Democrat*, Nov. 10, 1836.

50. *National Laborer*, August 20, 1836.

51. *The Democrat*, Nov. 10, 1836.

52. *Radical Reformer and Working Man's Advocate*, August 1-5, 1835; *Democratic Review*, vol. XVI, Jan. 1845, pp.

73-75; Arthur M. Schlesinger, Jr., *op. cit.*, pp. 204-05.
53. *Boston Post*, March-Sept., 1835; Theophilus Fisk, *The Bulwark of Freedom*, Charleston, 1836, pp. 4-8; Arthur M. Schlesinger, Jr., *op. cit.*, pp. 165-76; Arthur B. Darling, "Jacksonian Democracy in Massachusetts, 1824-1848," *American Historical Review*, vol. XXIX, Jan. 1924, pp. 276 *ff*.
54. *National Laborer*, August 20, 1836.
55. *Ibid.*, August 27, 1836. For a survey of working hours in Navy Yards, see "Statement of the working hours at the different Navy Yards, taken from the correspondence of the Navy Commissioners," March 27, 1840, Van Buren Papers, Library of Congress.
56. *Ibid.*, Oct. 1, 1836.
57. *Ibid.*, Oct. 15, Nov. 10, 1836.
58. Hartz, "Seth Luther," *New England Quarterly*, vol. XIII, Sept. 1940, pp. 406-09; John B. Rae, "The Great Suffrage Parade," *Rhode Island History*, vol. I, July, 1942, pp. 90-94; *Working Man's Advocate*, August 10, 1844.
59. Arthur M. Mowry, *The Dorr's War*, Providence, 1901, pp. 241 *n*, 297-98.
60. *National Laborer*, March 10, 1837; *New York Times*, Feb. 15, 1837.
61. Henry D. Gilpin to Martin Van Buren, May 15, 22, 1837, Van Buren Papers, Library of Congress. For a similar meeting in Boston, see *Boston Weekly Reformer*, July 28, 1837.
62. Russell M. Nolen, "The Labor Movement in St. Louis prior to the Civil War," *Missouri Historical Review*, vol. XXXIV, Oct. 1939, pp. 24-25; *Boston Weekly Reformer*, July 28, 1837.
63. Orestes Brownson to Martin Van Buren, January 10, 1838, Van Buren Papers, Library of Congress.
64. *Bay State Democrat*, Dec. 26, 1840.
65. Michael Shiner, manuscript diary, Library of Congress, p. 77.
66. Dorothy B. Goebel, *William Henry Harrison*, Indianapolis, 1926, p. 352; George B. Mangold, *The Labor Argument in the American Protective Tariff Discussion*, Bulletin of the University of Wisconsin, No. 246, pp. 81-82; *Farmers and Mechanics, Look at this*, Philadelphia, 1840, pamphlet; *Bulletin Business History Society*, vol. VIII, No. 1, pp. 31-32.
67. Horatio Woodman, *Reports of the Criminal Cases Tried in the Municipal Court of the City of Boston*, Boston,

1845, pp. 610-16; Theron Metcalf, ed., *Report of Cases Argued and Determined in the Supreme Court of Massachusetts*, Boston, 1843, vol. IV, pp. 121-34; Merle E. Curti, "Robert Rantoul, Jr., The Reformer in Politics," *New England Quarterly*, vol. V, April, 1932, pp. 268-69.
68. Walter R. Nelles, "Commonwealth v. Hunt," *Columbia Law Review*, vol. XXXII, pp. 1159-60.
69. Schlesinger, Jr., *op. cit.*, p. 266.
70. *Mechanics' Free Press*, June 5, 1830; *New York Democrat*, March 9, 1836.
71. Richardson, *op. cit.*, vol. V, p. 499.
72. *Rochester Daily Union*, Oct. 5, 1844.

CHAPTER X

1. *The New Yorker*, Jan. 20, 1838.
2. Samuel Rezneck, "The Social History of an American Depression, 1837-1843," *American Historical Review*, vol. XL, July, 1935, pp. 663-67; Horace Greeley, *Recollections of a Busy Life*, New York, 1868, p. 145; F. Marryat, *A Diary in America*, Paris, 1839, p. 17.
3. Rezneck, *op. cit.*, p. 667.
4. Commons, *op. cit.*, vol. I, p. 456; Ethelbert Stewart, *op. cit.*, pp. 47-48.
5. Rezneck, *op. cit.*, p. 676.
6. Stewart, *op. cit.*, p. 76; *Bulletin of Business History Society*, vol. XV, p. 8.
7. Greeley, *op. cit.*, p. 145.
8. Rezneck, *op. cit.*, p. 672.
9. Quoted by Norman Ware, *The Industrial Worker, 1840-1860*, Boston and New York, 1924, p. 16.
10. *Working Man's Advocate*, July 6, 1844.
11. Thomas Skidmore, *The Right to Property*, p. 383.
12. *Working Man's Advocate*, Sept. 19, 1836. See also the article entitled, "Machinery—Equal Exchange of Labor," *ibid.*, August 28, 1830.
13. *Boston Quarterly Review*, vol. IV, Jan. 1841, p. 119 *ff*.
14. George D. H. Cole, *Robert Owen*, London, 1925, pp. 179-85; Thomas Kirkup, *History of Socialism*, London, 1906, pp. 60-64.
15. Arthur E. Bestor, Jr., *American Phalanxes*, unpublished Ph. D. thesis, Yale University, 1938, pp. 8-9.
16. Commons, ed., *Documentary History of American Industrial Society*, vol. VII, pp. 164-66.
17. Frederick Engels, *Socialism: Utopian*

and *Scientific*, New York, 1935, pp. 40-44.
18. Quoted by Bestor, *op. cit.*, p. 9.
19. Commons, ed., *Documentary History of American Industrial Society*, vol. VII, pp. 176-78.
20. *New York Tribune*, April 10, 1846.
21. *Ibid.*, August 6, 1842.
22. *Ibid.*, May 31, July 12, 21, 1842.
23. *Labor's Wrongs and Labor's Remedy*, copy in Columbia University Library.
24. Quoted by Bestor, *op. cit.*, p. 264.
25. *Ibid.*, pp. 45, 50-51, 174-75.
26. John Humphrey Noyes, *History of American Socialism*, Philadelphia, 1870, pp. 239-43.
27. Heinrich Stemler, *Geschichte des Socialismus und Kommunismus in Nord Amerika*, Leipzig, 1880, pp. 155-56; *The Phalanx*, August 10, 1844.
28. Bestor, *op. cit.*, pp. 74-75, 104, 225-26, 238; Noyes, *op. cit.*, pp. 279, 282-83.
29. Manning Hawthorne, "Hawthorne and Utopian Socialism," *New England Quarterly*, vol. XII, Dec. 1939, pp. 727-28.
30. Octavius Brooks Frothingham, *George Ripley*, Boston, 1882, p. 183.
31. *Voice of Industry*, Feb. 11, 1848.
32. Edwin C. Rozwenc, *Cooperatives Come to America: The History of the Protective Store Movement, 1845-1867*, Mount Vernon, Iowa, 1941, pp. 58-59, 117.
33. Frank T. Stockton, "The Molders and Productive Cooperation," *International Molders Journal*, vol. L, 1914, pp. 368-70; *New York Tribune*, Sept. 12, 1849.
34. *New York Tribune*, August 21, 1849, Jan. 14, 1850.
35. *Ibid.*, August 12, 13, 15, 1850, April 28, 1851, Jan. 9, 1852; Rozwenc, *op. cit.*, pp. 64-65.
36. Rozwenc, *op. cit.*, pp. 13, 29-33.
37. *Ibid.*, pp. 23, 43, 46-47, 54, 63.
38. *Ibid.*, p. 69.
39. *Ibid.*, pp. 43-46, 90-95.
40. Quoted by Helen Sara Zahler, *Eastern Workingmen and National Land Policy, 1829-1862*, New York, 1941, p. 45.
41. *Ibid.*, p. 35; *Radical*, vol. I, pp. 6, 36, 41.
42. *New York Tribune*, Oct. 24, 1846.
43. *Young America*, Feb. 8, 1851; see also *Working Man's Advocate*, June 22, 1844.
44. *Working Man's Advocate*, July 6, 1844. Report of the National Reform Union of New York City.

45. *Young America*, March 25, April 5, Sept. 27, 1845, Jan. 10, 1846; *Working Man's Advocate*, July 20, Sept. 28, 1844, April 5, 1845; *The Harbinger*, April 29, 1848.
46. *Young America*, Oct. 11, 1845.
47. *Ibid.*, Nov. 29, 1845, March 6, 1847; *Newark Advertiser*, May 6, 1845; *Working Man's Advocate*, Sept. 4, Nov. 9, 1844, Jan. 25, 1845.
48. *Working Man's Advocate*, Feb. 28, 1845.
49. Commons, ed., *Documentary History of American Industrial Society*, vol. VII, pp. 54-55. For a detailed analysis of the limited evidence connected with this problem, see Carter C. Goodrich and Sol Davidson, "The Wage-Earner in the Westward Movement," *Political Science Quarterly*, vol. L, 1935, pp. 168-85, vol. LI, 1936, pp. 61ff., R. S. Tucker, "The Frontier as an Outlet for Surplus Labor," *Southern Economic Journal*, October, 1940, pp. 158-86, and Murray Kane, "Some considerations of the Safety Valve Doctrine," *Mississippi Valley Historical Review*, vol. XXIII, Sept. 1936, pp. 169-88.
50. *New York Tribune*, March 23, 1857, March 28, 1860; Edgar Barclay Cale, *The Organization of Labor in Philadelphia, 1850-1870*, Philadelphia, 1940, p. 9.
51. *New York Tribune*, Oct. 24, 1846; *Newark Daily Advertiser*, Nov. 9, 1857.
52. *Voice of Industry*, Feb. 19, 1847; Commons, ed., *Documentary History of American Industrial Society*, vol. VII, p. 233; *The Harbinger*, April, 25, 1846.
53. *The Condition of Labor: Address to Members of the Labor Reform League By one of the Members*, Boston, 1847.
54. *Working Man's Advocate*, March 15, 1845; *Young America*, March 6, 1847.
55. *Working Man's Advocate*, April 6, Nov. 23, 1844.
56. Robert Dale Owen, *Labor: Its History and its Prospects*, Cincinnati, 1848.
57. V. I. Lenin, *Selected Works*, New York, 1935-38, vol. XII, p. 302.

CHAPTER XI

1. *Boston Quarterly Review*, vol. IV, Jan. 1841, pp. 122 ff.
2. *Fall River Mechanic*, May 25, July 20, 1844; *Boston Laborer*, in *ibid.*, August 3, 1844.

3. Norman J. Ware, *The Industrial Worker, 1840-1860*, p. 74.
4. *Voice of Industry*, July 3, 1845.
5. David Crockett, *A Visit to Lowell*, Philadelphia, 1837, *passim.*; Scoresby, *op. cit.*, pp. 20-26.
6. Quoted by Shlakman, *op. cit.*, pp. 135-36.
7. Charles Dickens, *American Notes*, New York, 1842, p. 77; *Old South Leaflets*, vol. III, Boston, 1885, no. 151.
8. *Working Man's Advocate*, Jan. 17, 1846.
9. *Lowell Offering*, No. III, Sept. 1843, pp. 43, 284.
10. *Ibid.*, No. I, p. 343; Lucy Larcom, *A New England Girlhood*, Boston, 1889, pp. 222-23.
11. J. Bigelow, *Corporations and Operatives: Being an Exposition of the Conditions of Factory Operatives*, Lowell, 1841, p. 28; *Voice of Industry*, Feb. 6, 1846. See also *The Awl*, July 26, 1845; *Voice of Industry*, July 17, 1845.
12. Bertha M. Stearns, "Early Factory Magazines in New England," *Journal of Economic and Business History*, vol. II, August 1930, pp. 92-98, 702.
13. *Ibid.*, p. 696.
14. *Voice of Industry*, Dec. 27, 1845; May 15, Nov. 21, 1846.
15. *Ibid.*, Jan. 2, 1846.
16. *Ibid.*, May 29, June 5, 10, 12, 1845; Andrews and Bliss, *op. cit.*, pp. 71-72.
17. *Voice of Industry*, July 31, Sept. 18, Nov. 7, 21, Dec. 27, 1845, Jan. 30, Feb. 20, April 3, 10, May 15, 1846; Andrews and Bliss, *op. cit.*, pp. 74-76. A description of one of the picnics appeared in the *Cleveland Citizen*, May 20, 1895. Labadee Collection, University of Michigan.
18. *Voice of Industry*, Jan. 9, Nov. 28, 1846; Andrews and Bliss, *op. cit.*, p. 74.
19. *Voice of Industry*, Dec. 19, 26, 1845, Jan. 9, May 5, Nov. 13, 1846; *Young America*, Nov. 15, 1845.
20. *The Labor Leaf* (Detroit, Michigan), Dec. 9, 1885. Labadee Collection, University of Michigan; Allan Mac-Donald, "Lowell: A Commercial Utopia," *New England Quarterly, vol. X*, March, 1937, p. 44; *The Awl*, July 26, 1845.
21. *Voice of Industry*, Jan. 2, 1846.
22. *Ibid.*, May 15, 1846. See *ibid.*, Jan. 9, 1846 for Miss Bagley's article inaugurating the "Female Department" of the *Voice of Industry*.
23. *Fall River Weekly News*, reprinted in *Young America*, June 14, 1845; *Voice of Industry*, June 5, 1845.
24. *Fall River Mechanic*, May 11, July 6, 1844; *Trenton Daily State Gazette*, Sept. 6, 1849.
25. *New York Evening Post*, April 5, 1847.
26. *Fall River Mechanic*, April 27, 1844.
27. *Ibid.*, Nov. 16, 1844.
28. *Fall River Mechanic*, May 18, 1844; *Rochester Daily Advertiser*, Sept. 18, 1848, quoted by Alan H. Gleason, *The History of Labor in Rochester, 1820-1880*, unpublished M. A. thesis, University of Rochester, 1941, p. 63.
29. Massachusettts Bureau of Statistics of Labor, *1st Annual Report*, 1870, pp. 221, 226; Shlakman, *op. cit.*, p. 185.
30. *New York Mechanics' Mirror*, Nov. 1846.
31. Charles E. Persons, *Labor Laws and their Enforcement*, New York, 1911, pp. 40-41.
32. *Ibid.*, pp. 22-26.
33. *Fall River Mechanic*, May 4, 25, July 6, 13, Sept. 8, Dec. 28, 1844; *The Awl*, July 17, 1844.
34. *Ibid.*, Aug. 3, 1844.
35. *Fall River Mechanic*, July 20, 1844.
36. Hewitt's Journal appeared in the *Fall River Mechanic*, Aug. 3-31, 1844.
37. *Fall River Mechanic*, Oct. 26, 1845; Ware, *op. cit.*, p. 210.
38. *Voice of Industry*, June 12, 1845.
39. *Ibid.*, Sept. 18, 1845.
40. *Ibid.*, April 3, 1846; Ware, *op. cit.*, p. 219.
41. *Pittsburgh Journal* reprinted in *Young America*, Oct. 18, 1845.
42. *New York Tribune*, Oct. 31, 1845; *Pittsburgh Spirit of Liberty*, reprinted in *Young America*, Nov. 15, 1845.
43. Andrews and Bliss, *op. cit.*, p. 70; Persons, *op. cit.*, p. 41; *Young America*, Dec. 27, 1846.
44. Persons, *op. cit.*, p. 43.
45. *Ibid.*, p. 47.
46. Massachusetts *House Document*, no. 50, 1845, pp. 8, 16.
47. James Truslow Adams, *New England in the Republic, 1776-1850*, p. 391.
48. *Voice of Industry*, July 29, 1847.
49. Ware, *op. cit.*, pp. 145-46.
50. *Voice of Industry*, Jan. 8, 1847; Andrews and Bliss, *op. cit.*, p. 77; *Young America*, June 7, 14, 1845.
51. Andrews and Bliss, *op. cit.*, p. 64;

New York Tribune, August 28, 1848; *Pittsburgh Evening Post,* July 6, 12, 17, 1848.

52. *Western Pennsylvania Magazine of History and Biography,* vol. V, April 1922, pp. 203-11.

53. *Monthly Jubilee,* vol. III, Oct. 1853, p. 401; Persons, *op. cit.,* p. 65.

54. Henry W. Farnam, *Chapters in the Social History of the United States to 1868,* Washington, 1938, p. 265.

55. Persons, *op. cit.,* p. 77.

56. *Ibid.,* p. 69; Ware, *op. cit.,* pp. 156-58.

57. Ware, *op. cit.,* pp. 159, 161.

58. Charles Cowley, *Illustrated History of Lowell,* Boston, 1868, p. 149; A. B. Darling, *Political Changes in Massachusetts, 1824-1848,* New Haven, 1925, p. 171. For a vivid contemporary account of corporation control over the ballot-box, see Amasa Walker, *The Test of Experience, or the Working of the Ballot in the United States,* E. C. Whitehurst, London, [1855].

59. *Trenton Daily State Gazette,* Sept. 6, 1847.

60. *Ibid.,* Jan. 29, 1848, Jan. 18, Sept. 5, 6, 20, Oct. 12, 1849.

61. *Ibid.,* Sept. 3, 15-17, 1850.

62. *Ibid.,* Oct. 2, 12, 21, 1850.

63. *Trenton True-American,* Nov. 5, 1850; *Trenton Daily State Gazette,* Nov. 4, 1850.

64. *Hunt's Merchants' Magazine,* vol. XLI, 1860, p. 750; Edgar W. Martin, *op. cit.,* pp. 344-45; *11th Annual Report of Massachusetts Bureau of Statistics of Labor,* 1880, pp. 9-13.

CHAPTER XII

1. G. F. Warren and F. H. Pearson, *Wholesale Prices for Two Hundred and Thirteen Years, 1720 to 1932,* Ithaca, N. Y., 1932, pp. 168, 193; Kuczynski, *op. cit.,* p. 43.

2. Kuczynski, *op. cit.,* p. 44.

3. Quoted by Helen Sumner, *op. cit.,* pp. 141-42.

4. Quoted by Martin, *op. cit.,* p. 162.

5. *New York Tribune,* June 8, 11, 15, 17, 18, 20, 1850; Ira B. Cross, *A History of the Labor Movement in California,* Berkeley, Calif., 1935, pp. 22-23.

6. *Boston Daily Transcript,* April 12, 1853.

7. *New York Tribune,* May 23, 1850.

8. Commons, *op. cit.,* vol. I, p. 587.

9. *New York Tribune,* May 23, 31, June 26, July 31, 1850.

10. *Ibid.,* Sept. 13, 1850.

11. *Ibid.,* May 20, 22, 1850.

12. *Ibid.,* Nov. 4, 1850.

13. *New York Tribune,* March 22, 1853.

14. *Native Eagle,* April 1846; George Nicholas Kramer, *A History of the Know-Nothing Movement,* unpublished Ph. D. dissertation, University of California, 1936, p. 169.

15. Ray A. Billington, *The Protestant Crusade,* New York, 1939, pp. 336-37.

16. *New York Tribune,* April 27, August 3, 1850; *New York Evening Post,* April 3, 1847.

17. *New York Tribune,* April 27, June 12, 17, 1850.

18. *Ibid.,* April 20, May 23, July 26, 1850.

19. Jesse Chickering, *Immigration into the United States,* Boston, 1848, p. 64.

20. Massachusetts Bureau of Statistics of Labor, *Eleventh Annual Report,* 1880, pp. 6-9.

21. Andrew Roy, *A History of the Coal Miners of the United States,* Columbus, 1903, pp. 72-75; *The Miner's Journal,* July 17, 1849.

22. Edward A. Wieck, *The American Miners' Association,* New York, 1940, pp. 85, 217-19.

23. Hermann Schlueter, *Die Anfänge der deutschen Arbeiterbewegung in Amerika,* Stuttgart, 1907, pp. 13-28, 83-96, 126-33.

24. *Ibid.*

25. *Die Reform,* May 1853.

26. *New York Staats-Zeitung,* March 18, 1853.

27. *Ibid.,* March 25, 1853.

28. *Ibid.,* May 9, 1853; Karl Obermann, *Joseph Weydemeyer,* Unpublished *Mss.,* Chapter V.

29. *Workingmen's National Advocate,* Apr. 16, 1853.

30. Obermann, *op. cit.,* Chapter V.

31. Commons, *op. cit.,* vol. I, pp. 550-562; Commons, ed., *Documentary History of American Industrial Society,* vol. VIII, pp. 23-25.

32. *Newark Daily Advertiser,* May 28, 1844.

33. *Proceedings of the National Convention of Journeymen Printers of the United States,* December 2, 1850, together with An Address, 1851, passim; George A. Tracy, *History of the Typographical Union,* Indianapolis, 1913, pp. 117-26.

34. Tracy, *op. cit.*, pp. 130-35.
35. *Ibid.*, p. 125.
36. Quoted by Charlotte Todes, *William H. Sylvis and the National Labor Union*, New York, 1942, p. 20.
37. Henry E. Hoagland, "The Rise of the Iron Molders' International Union," *Iron Molders Journal*, vol. XLIX, June 1913, p. 305.
38. *Philadelphia North American*, Nov. 3, 1857.
39. *Newark Daily Advertiser*, Nov. 9, 13, 1857; *Philadelphia Public Ledger*, Nov. 12, 1857.
40. *Philadelphia Public Ledger*, Oct. 26, Nov. 10, 1857; Cale, *op. cit.*, pp. 37-39.
41. Nov. 10, 1857.
42. *Philadelphia Public Ledger*, Nov. 11, 1857.
43. *Ibid.*, Nov. 12, 1857; Cale, *op. cit.*, pp. 39-41.
44. *Public Ledger*, Nov. 12, 1857.
45. *Newark Daily Advertiser*, Nov. 9, 1857.
46. *Ibid.*, Nov. 10, 1857.
47. *New York Herald*, Nov. 2, 1857.
48. *New York Times, New York Evening Post, New York Herald*, Nov. 3, 12, 1857.
49. *New York Tribune, New York Herald*, Nov. 6, 1857.
50. *Fifteenth Annual Report of the Association for the Improvement of the Condition of the Poor*, p. 22.
51. A. E. Hutchinson, "Philadelphia and the Panic of 1857," *Pennsylvania History*, vol. III, July 1936, p. 193; Samuel Rezneck, "The Influences of Depression upon American Opinion, 1857-1859," *Journal of Economic History*, vol. II, May 1942, p. 18; Leah H. Feder, *Unemployment Relief in Periods of Depression*, New York, 1936, pp. 21, 34.
52. Cale, *op. cit.*, pp. 21-22, 33-36; *Public Ledger*, April 20, 1858.
53. *Public Ledger*, March 11, May 4, 1859.
54. *Newburyport Daily Herald*, Feb. 24, 1860; *Boston Advertiser*, March 21, 1860; *Springfield Daily Republican*, Feb. 21, 1860; *Haverhill Gazette*, Feb. 24, 1860; *New York Herald*, Feb. 27, 1860; *Eleventh Annual Report Massachusetts Bureau of Statistics of Labor, 1880*, pp. 17-19.
55. *Boston Traveller*, Feb. 25, 26, 1860.
56. *Ibid.*, Feb. 25, 1860; *New York Herald*, Feb. 28, 1860.
57. *Boston Bee*, Feb. 23, 1860; *New York Herald*, Feb. 25, 1860

58. *Boston Traveller*, Feb. 15, 1860; *New York Herald*, Feb. 26, 1860.
59. *New York Tribune*, Feb. 25, 1860; *Newburyport Daily Herald*, Feb. 23, 1860.
60. "The Shoemaker's Song," in *New York Herald*, Feb. 29, 1860.
61. *Boston Bee*, Feb. 23, 27, 1860; *Newburyport Daily Herald*, Feb. 24, 29, March 2, 5, 6, 17, 1860; *Haverhill Gazette*, March 2, 1860; *Boston Traveller*, Feb. 25, 1860; *Springfield Republican*, March 1, 1860.
62. *New York Herald*, Feb. 25-March 7, 1860; *Boston Traveller*, Feb. 26-March 1, 1860.
63. *Newburyport Daily Herald*, March 7, 1860.
64. *Boston Traveller*, Feb. 28, 1860; *Newburyport Daily Herald*, Feb. 29, 1860.
65. *New York Herald*, Feb. 27, March 1, 1860.
66. *Boston Advertiser, Boston Courier*, March 8, 1860.
67. *Boston Courier, Newburyport Daily Herald*, March 17, 1860.
68. *Boston Bee*, Feb. 23, 1860; *Newburyport Daily Herald*, Feb. 29, 1860.
69. *Springfield Republican*, March 2, 1860; *Newburyport Daily Herald*, March 23, 1860.
70. *Boston Courier*, Feb. 27, 28, 1860.
71. *Boston Herald*, April 11, 1860; *Newburyport Daily Herald*, March 7, 1860; *Haverhill Gazette*, March 28, 1860.
72. See especially *Newark Daily Advertiser*, Nov. 9, 1857.
73. *Boston Courier*, Feb. 23, 1860.
74. Cross, *op. cit.*, p. 15.
75. *New York Tribune*, Oct. 30, 1856.
76. *Trenton True American*, Oct. 4, 1858.
77. *Platform and Constitution of the Workingmen's Union of the City of Trenton, New Jersey, adopted October 12, 1858*, Trenton, 1858.
78. *Trenton True-American*, Oct. 22, 1858.
79. *Ibid.*, Oct. 1, 28, 1858.
80. *Ibid.*, Oct. 27, Nov. 20, Dec. 23, 1858.
81. Edward H. Rogers, *Autobiography*, Manuscript copy in Wisconsin State Historical Society.

CHAPTER XIII

1. Quoted in Arthur R. Pearce, *The Rise and Decline of Labor in New Orleans*, unpublished Master's Thesis, Tulane University, 1938, pp. 4, 11-13.

2. *Ibid.*, pp. 10-11.
3. Thomas Anburey, *Travels Through the Interior Parts of America*, London, 1789, pp. 331-32.
4. Joseph H. Ingraham, *The Southwest by a Yankee*, New York, 1935, vol. II, pp. 284-96.
5. John S. Bassett, *The Southern Plantation Overseer*, Northampton, Mass., 1925, pp. 4-7; Frederick Law Olmsted, *A Journey in the Back Country*, New York, 1907, vol. I, pp. 58, 84-85; Charles S. Sydnor, "A Slave Owner and his Overseers," *North Carolina Historical Review*, vol. XIV, Jan. 1937, pp. 31-38.
6. Herbert Aptheker, *American Negro Slave Revolts*, pp. 128-30; James L. Watkins, "Production and price of cotton for one hundred years," *United States Department of Agriculture*, Miscellaneous Series, Bulletin No. 9, Washington, 1895, pp. 41-42.
7. F. L. Olmsted, *A Journey in the Seaboard Slave States*, New York, 1904, vol. II, p. 352. For different views on the feeding of slaves, see Charles S. Sydnor, *Slavery in Mississippi*, New York, 1933, pp. 30-39 and Ralph B. Flanders, *Plantation Slavery in Georgia*, Chapel Hill, N. C., 1933, pp. 56-59.
8. Avery Craven, *The Coming of the Civil War*, New York, 1942, pp. 78-79.
9. Ulrich B. Phillips, ed., "Plantation and Frontier Documents," *Documentary History of American Industrial Society*, vol. II, p. 31.
10. J. W. Coleman, *Slavery Times in Kentucky*, Chapel Hill, 1940, p. 130; C. G. Parsons, *Inside View of Slavery*, Boston, 1853, p. 94.
11. Ulrich B. Phillips, *American Negro Slavery*, New York, 1918, pp. 303-04.
12. Thomas Drew, *The Refugee*, Boston, 1856, p. 164.
13. Guion G. Johnson, *Ante-Bellum North Carolina*, Chapel Hill, 1937, p. 493.
14. Gilbert H. Barnes and Dwight L. Dumond, *Letters of Theodore Dwight Weld, Angelina Grimke Weld and Sarah Grimke, 1822-1844*, New York, 1934, vol. I, p. 512.
15. *Raleigh Register* (North Carolina), Feb. 20, 1818.
16. W. W. Siebert, *The Underground Railroad from Slavery to Freedom*, New York, 1899, pp. 28, 152; *The Liberator*, April 27, 1860.
17. Sarah E. Bradford, *Scenes in the Life of Harriet Tubman*, Auburn, 1869, pp. 32-33.
18. Mary T. Higginson, *Letters and Journals of Thomas Wentworth Higginson, 1846-1906*, pp. 52-53; Earl Conrad, *Harriet Tubman*, Washington, 1943, *passim.*
19. Quoted by Herbert Aptheker, "Maroons within the Present Limits of the United States," *Journal of Negro History*, vol. XXIV, April, 1939, p. 176.
20. Quoted by Harvey Wish, "American Slave Insurrections before 1860," *Journal of Negro History*, vol. XXII, July 1937, p. 306.
21. Maryville (Tenn.) *Intelligencer*, quoted by Wendell Phillips, *The Constitution, A Pro-Slavery Compact*, 3rd edition, New York, 1856, p. 208.
22. Herbert Aptheker, *Negro Slave Revolts in the United States*, p. 37.
23. Charles H. Wesley, *Negro Labor in the United States*, New York, 1927, p. 22; Aptheker, *American Negro Slave Revolts*, p. 115.
24. "Denmark Vesey," *North American Review*, vol. XCIII, June 1861, pp. 730-44.
25. George W. Williams, *History of the Negro Race in America*, New York, 1883, vol. II pp. 85-91; Herbert Aptheker, *American Negro Slave Revolts*, pp. 293-304; J. H. Esterby, *The South Carolina Rice Plantation as Revealed in the Papers of Robert F. W. Allston*, Chicago, 1945, pp. 32, 101, 136.
26. United States. *Statistical View of the United States. Being a Compendium of the Seventh Census, by J. D. De Bow, Superintendent of the U. S. Census*, Washington, 1854, Table XC, p. 94.
27. Karl Marx and Frederick Engels, *The Civil War in the United States*, New York, 1937, pp. 68-69; W. B. Hesseltine, "Some New Aspects of the Pro-Slavery Argument," *Journal of Negro History*, vol. XXI, Jan. 1936, pp. 1-14; Robert R. Russell, "The Effects of Slavery upon Non-Slaveholders in the Ante-Bellum South," *Agricultural History*, vol. XV, April 1941, p. 122; *De Bow's Review*, vol. XXIX, p. 227; William H. Seward, "Irrepressible Conflict Speech," in *Evening Journal Tracts*, Albany, No. 1.
28. Charles Nordhoff, *America for Free Working Men*, New York, 1865, p. 8.
29. *De Bow's Review*, vol. III, Feb. 1847,

p. 96; vol. VIII, p. 139; Charles S. Sydnor, *Slavery in Mississippi,* New York, 1933, p. 36; Roger W. Shugg, *Origin of Class Conflict in Louisiana,* University, La., 1939, p. 89; Andreas Dorpalen, "The German Element and the Issues of the Civil War," *Mississippi Valley Historical Review,* vol. XXIX, June 1942, p. 57.

30. Kathleen Bruce, *Virginia Iron Manufacture in the Slave Era,* New York, 1931, pp. 275-76; Kathleen Bruce in *William and Mary Quarterly,* vol. VI, Series 2, 1926, p. 298.

31. Johnson, *op. cit.,* p. 489; Robert R. Russell, *op. cit.,* pp. 124-25.

32. Johnson, *op. cit.,* p. 69; *De Bow's Review,* vol. XI, August 1851, p. 133; vol. XXIX, August 1860, p. 227.

33. United States Census Office, *Statistics of the United States,* 1860, p. 512; Olmsted, *Seaboard Slave States,* p. 542; Edgar W. Martin, *The Standard of Living in 1860,* Chicago, 1942, pp. 55-60.

34. Rosser H. Taylor, *Ante-Bellum South Carolina,* Chapel Hill, 1942, p. 81; F. Garvin Davenport, *Ante-Bellum Kentucky, A Social History, 1800-1860,* Oxford, Ohio, 1943, pp. 23-24.

35. David Rice, *Slavery Inconsistent with Justice and Good Policy,* Phila., 1792, p. 11; Daniel Webster, *Works,* Boston, 1853, vol. V, p. 310.

36. Olmsted, *Seaboard Slave States,* pp. 542-44.

37. Charles Lyell, *Second Visit to the United States,* New York, 1849, vol. II, pp. 236-37; Luther J. Jackson, *Free Negro Labor and Property Holding in Virginia, 1830-1860,* New York, 1942, pp. 59-60.

38. Kathleen Bruce in *William and Mary Quarterly,* vol. VII, Series 2, 1926, p. 299; Shugg, *op. cit.,* p. 155.

39. Shugg, *op. cit.,* pp. 126, 155.

40. J. S. Buckingham, *Slave States of America,* London, 1842, vol. II, p. 12.

41. Russell M. Nolen, "The Labor Movement in St. Louis Prior to the Civil War," *Missouri Historical Review,* vol. XXXIV, Oct. 1939, pp. 34-35.

42. "Slaves on a Federal Project," *Bulletin of the Business Historical Society,* vol.

VIII, no. 1, Jan. 1934, pp. 32-33.

43. Kathleen Bruce in *William and Mary Quarterly, vol. VI,* Series 2, pp. 279-99.

44. Ulrich B. Phillips, ed., "Plantation and Frontier Documents," *Documentary History of American Industrial Society,* vol. II, pp. 364-65; Fabien Linden, "Repercussions of Manufacturing in the Ante-Bellum South," *North Carolina Historical Review,* vol. XVI, Oct. 1940, pp. 322-23.

45. Linden, *op. cit.,* pp. 322-24.

46. Fletcher M. Green, *Constitutional Development in the South Atlantic States, 1776-1860,* Chapel Hill, 1930, pp. 160-61.

47. H. M. Wagstaff, *State Rights and Political Parties in North Carolina, 1776-1861,* Baltimore, 1906, p. 111; C. C. Norton, *The Democratic Party in Ante-Bellum North Carolina,* Chapel Hill, 1930, p. 173.

48. Norton, *op. cit.,* pp. 199-200; W. K. Boyd, "Ad Valorem Slave Taxation, 1858-1860," *Trinity College Historical Society Publications,* vol. V, 1905, pp. 31-38.

49. Boyd, *op. cit.,* p. 131.

50. Nordhoff, *op. cit.,* p. 8.

51. *Springfield Republican,* March 13, 1860; Green, *op. cit.,* p. 161.

52. *The North Star,* May 25, 1849.

53. Reprinted in *The Liberator,* Dec. 22, 1856.

54. *Montgomery Advertiser,* Dec. 13, 1860; *Mobile Mercury* reprinted in *New York Tribune,* Jan. 8, 1861.

55. *San Antonio Zeitung,* Feb. 16, 1856.

56. *Official Records of the War of the Rebellion,* Series I, vol. IX, p. 1706; vol. XV, pp. 925-26.

57. *De Bow's Review,* Jan. 1850, quoted by P. Tower, *Slavery Unmasked,* Rochester, 1856, p. 348; *New York Tribune,* Jan. 3, May 29, 1861.

58. Fabien Linden, *op. cit.,* p. 320.

59. F. L. Olmsted, *A Journey in the Seaboard Slave States,* p. 590.

60. Quoted in *The South in the Building of the Nation,* Richmond, Va., 1909, vol. V, pp. 213-14, and in Olmsted, *Seaboard Slave States,* vol. II, pp. 149-50.

61. *New York Tribune,* June 4, 1853.

CHAPTER XIV

1. *The Cooperator*, Oct. 20, 1832; Hermann Schlueter, *Lincoln, Labor and Slavery*, New York, 1913, pp. 38-39.

2. *Workingmen's Prayer, Massachusetts, 1830*, in Commons' Labor Collection, Wisconsin State Historical Society.

3. Samuel E. Morison, *The Maritime History of Massachusetts*, Boston and New York, 1930, p. 299; R. H. Luthin, "Lincoln in Massachusetts in 1848," *New England Quarterly*, vol. XIV, Dec. 1941, pp. 621-23.

4. Quoted by Philip S. Foner, *Business and Slavery*, Chapel Hill, 1941, p. 14.

5. *National Laborer*, March 26, 1836.

6. Clement Eaton, "Censorship of the Southern Mails," *American Historical Review*, vol. XLVIII, Jan. 1943, p. 274.

7. *National Laborer*, March 26, 1836.

8. *Boston Post*, August 10, 1835; *Fall River Mechanic*, Jan. 25, 1845.

9. *Ibid.*, April 27, 1844; *Virginia Herald*, reprinted in *Haverhill Gazette*, Feb. 3, 1860; "Monitor," in *National Laborer*, Nov. 19, 1836.

10. *National Laborer*, Sept. 13, 1836.

11. *Congressional Globe*, 25th Congress, 3rd Session, Appendix, pp. 237-41; *Boston Post*, Dec. 12, 1835.

12. William Drayton, *The South Vindicated*, Philadelphia, 1836, p. 241; *New York Journal of Commerce, New York Herald*, reprinted in *The Liberator*, Sept. 16, 1853.

13. *Newark Daily Advertiser*, April 26, 1836; *The Union*, March 30, 1836.

14. Cuthbert E. Allen, "The Slavery Question in Catholic Newspapers, 1850-1856," *United States Catholic Historical Society Historical Records and Studies*, vol. XXVI, 1936, pp. 120, 149-56, 167; Madeleine Hooke Rice, *American Catholic Opinion in the Slavery Controversy*, New York, 1944, pp. 86-131.

15. *Eighteenth Annual Report of the Massachusetts Anti-Slavery Society*, Boston, 1850, pp. 107-08.

16. Wendell Phillips, *Speeches, Lectures and Letters*, Second Series, Boston, 1892, pp. 22-23.

17. Allen, *op. cit.*, pp. 149-56.

18. *The Liberator*, January 29, 1831.

19. *National Anti-Slavery Standard*, August 5, Oct. 14, 1847; *The Liberator*, July 9, 1847.

20. Wendell Phillips to R. D. Webb, 1848, Phillips *Mss.*, Boston Public Library.

21. *The Liberator*, Feb. 11, 1848; Horace Greeley, *Lectures, Addresses and other Writings*, New York, 1850, p. 352.

22. *Cabotville Chronicle*, quoted in *Voice of Industry*, Jan. 2, 1846; *Fall River Mechanic*, April 27, 1844; "A Ten-Hour Woman" in *ibid.*, Oct. 5, 1844.

23. *The Man*, May 17, 1834; *National Laborer*, July 2, 1836; *Fall River Mechanic*, May 25, 1844.

24. Reprinted in *Fall River Mechanic*, Nov. 2, 1844. See also *The Awl*, July 26, 1845.

25. *Working Man's Advocate*, Jan. 25, 1845.

26. *Ibid.*, June 22, July 4, 6, August 17, 24, 1844, Sept. 27, 1845.

27. *The Pro-Slavery Argument*, Charleston, 1852, p. 31; Robert Toombs, *Lectures*, Washington, 1856, p. 11; George Fitzhugh, *Cannibals All: or Slaves Without Masters*, Richmond, 1857, pp. 29-31; William J. Grayson, *The Hireling and the Slave*, Charleston, 1854, p. 50; Harvey Wish, *George Fitzhugh*, Baton Rouge, La., 1943, pp. 174-93.

28. *Working Man's Advocate*, March 16, 1844; *True Sun* reprinted in *Young America*, Jan. 3, 1846.

29. *New York Tribune*, Feb. 16, 1850.

30. *Ibid.*, Feb. 25, 1860.

31. McNeil, *op. cit.*, p. 107.

32. *The Harbinger*, May 27, 1848.

33. *The Liberator*, Jan. 2, 1852.

34. *The Condition of Labor: Address to Members of the Labor Reform League*, p. 16.

35. Karl Marx, *Capital*, edited by Frederick Engels, New York, 1939, vol. I, p. 267.

36. Curti, *op. cit.*, p. 119.

37. McNeil, *op. cit.*, p. 122.

38. *Voice of Industry*, Nov. 26, 1847; *The New Era*, July 27, 1848; Norman Ware, *The Industrial Worker*, p. 226.

39. Quoted by Avery Craven, *The Coming of the Civil War*, p. 192.

40. *Working Man's Advocate*, April 20, 1844.

41. Quoted in Ware, *op. cit.*, p. 226.

42. *Working Man's Advocate*, May 11, 1844, Jan. 18, 1845.

43. Reprinted in *ibid.*, August 10, 1844.

44. *National Anti-Slavery Standard*, May 28, 1846.

45. McNeil, *op. cit.*, p. 107; *Condition of Labor*, pp. 13, 16.

46. Schlueter, *op. cit.*, pp. 73-74.

47. *America's Own and Fireman's Journal* (New York), July 28, Dec. 15, 1849.

48. *New York Tribune,* August 15, 1850.
49. *Ibid.,* June 13, 1850.
50. *Monthly Jubilee,* October 1853.
51. *Trenton Daily State Gazette,* Dec. 6, 1851.
52. Schlueter, *op. cit.,* pp. 75-76.
53. Bessie Louise B. Pierce, *A History of Chicago,* New York, 1940, p. 167.
54. W. G. Bean, "Anti-Jeffersonianism in the Ante-Bellum South," *North Carolina Historical Review,* vol. XII, April 1935, pp. 112 *ff; Charleston Mercury,* July 5, 1858; *De Bow's Review,* August 1860, p. 109; *Congressional Globe,* 36th Congress, 1st Session, Appendix, p. 97; Charles Nordhoff, *America for Free Workingmen,* New York, 1865, p. 18.
55. F. L. Olmsted, *A Journey in the Seaboard Slave States,* vol. I, p. 204; *New York Weekly Tribune,* Feb. 11, 1854; Wilfred Carsel, "The Slaveholders' Indictment of Northern Wage Slavery," *Journal of Southern History,* vol. VI, Nov. 1940, pp. 514-20; Laurence F. Schmecebier, *History of the Know-Nothing Party in Maryland,* Baltimore, 1897, p. 48.
56. *Fall River Mechanic,* May 11, 1844.
57. Reprinted in *The North Star,* Nov. 3, 1848.
58. *Milwaukee Free Democrat,* Aug. 21, 1857.
59. *New York Tribune,* July 3, 1856.
60. *Ibid.,* Feb. 2, 4, 14, 15, 20, March 15, 23, 1854.
61. *Ibid.,* Feb. 10, 17, 28, March 1, 6, 31 1854.
62. *New York Tribune,* June 12, 1854.
63. Commons, ed., *Documentary History of American Industrial Society,* vol. VII, p. 37; John R. Commons, "Horace Greeley and the Working Class Origins of the Republican Party," *Political Science Quarterly,* vol. XXIV, Sept. 1909, p. 488.
64. Quoted by Joseph Carlyle Sitterson, *The Secession Movement in North Carolina,* unpublished Ph. D. dissertation, University of North Carolina, 1937, p. 109; *Congressional Globe,* 34th Congress, 1st Session, Appendix, pp. 1155-56.
65. *Chicago Daily Journal,* quoted in Craven, *op. cit.,* p. 218. See also Foner, *Business and Slavery,* p. 218.
66. *New York Evening Post,* Sept. 9, 1857; T. Harry Williams, *Lincoln and the Radicals,* Madison, Wisconsin, 1941, pp. 8-9.

67. *New York Herald,* March 10, 19, 1860; George H. Martin in *Philadelphia Public Ledger,* March 13, 1860.
68. *New York Tribune,* Sept. 12, 15, 26, Oct. 20, 1856.
69. *Republican Scrap Book,* Boston, 1856, p. 34.
70. *New York Tribune, Pittsburgh Gazette,* Oct. 31, 1856.
71. *New York Tribune,* March 11, 19, 27, April 1, 1857.
72. Thomas Monroe Pitkin, *The Tariff and the Early Republican Party,* unpublished Ph. D. dissertation, Western Reserve University, 1935, pp. 262-64; James Walter, George Hoadley to Salmon P. Chase, Oct. 3, 1859, Feb. 6, 1860, Chase Papers, Library of Congress.
73. *Cincinnati Commercial,* Dec. 5, 1859.
74. Frank I. Herriot, *The Conference of German-Republicans in the Deutsches Haus, Chicago, May 14-15, 1860,* reprinted from the *Transactions of the Illinois Historical Society for 1928,* pp. 48-49, 63-64, 85-86, 93.
75. W. L. Baringer, *Lincoln's Rise to Power,* Boston, 1937, p. 274. See also J. G. Randall, *Lincoln the President,* New York, 1945, vol. I, pp. 161-63.
76. Baringer, *op. cit.,* p. 190; Nels Hokanson, *Swedish Immigrants in Lincoln's Time,* New York, 1942, p. 54.
77. Philip S. Foner. ed., *Abraham Lincoln: Selections from His Writings,* New York, 1944, pp. 15-16, 87-88; John G. Nicolay and John Hay, eds., *Complete Works of Abraham Lincoln,* New York, 1905, vol. V, pp. 247-50; Baringer, *op. cit.,* pp. 34-35; F. L. Herriot, "The Premises and Significance of Abraham Lincoln's Letter to Theodor Canisus," *Yearbook German American Historical Society of Illinois,* vol. XV, 1915, pp. 181 *ff.*
78. *New York Tribune,* Oct. 15, 16, 22, 29, 1860; *Congressional Globe,* 36th Congress, 1st Session, pp. 1872-73.
79. Pitkin, *op. cit.,* pp. 256-57; *New York Tribune,* Sept. 30, Oct. 30, 1860.
80. *Pittsburgh Gazette,* Nov. 5, 1860; Pitkin, *op. cit.,* p. 258.
81. *New York Herald,* Oct. 25, 1860.
82. Foner, *Business and Slavery,* p. 206.
83. *New York Demokrat,* Oct. 31, Nov. 2, 1860; *New York Herald,* Oct. 29, Nov. 2, 1860.
84. *Philadelphia Inquirer,* April 9, Oct. 12, 1860.

85. *Missouri Historical Review*, vol. XXXIV, p. 37; Hokanson, *op. cit.*, p. 58; *Tägliche Illinois Staats-Zeitung*, Oct. 26, 1860.
86. Max Birnbaum, *Northern Labor in the National Crisis, 1860-1861*, unpublished B. S. Thesis, University of Wisconsin, June, 1938, pp. 45-57; Jay Monaghan, "Did Abraham Lincoln Receive the Illinois German Vote?" *Journal of the Illinois Historical Society*, vol. XXXV, June, 1942, pp. 133-39.
87. Foner, *Business and Slavery*, p. 206; *New York Tribune*, Nov. 9, 1860.

CHAPTER XV

1. Reprinted in *New York Tribune*, March 15, 1861.
2. *Cincinnati Commercial*, Dec. 29, 1860.
3. *Illinois State Journal*, Dec. 29, 1860.
4. *Chicago Tribune*, Jan. 16, 18, 19, 1861; *National Intelligencer*, Jan. 15-17, 1861; *Cincinnati Commercial*, Jan. 5-8, 1861.
5. *Chicago Tribune*, Jan. 21, 1861; Carl M. Frasure, "Union Sentiment in Maryland, 1859-1861," *Maryland Historical Magazine*, vol. XXIV, 1929, pp. 214-15.
6. *New York Herald*, Jan. 14, 1861; *Philadelphia Inquirer*, Jan. 19, 1861.
7. *Cincinnati Commercial*, Jan. 5, 1861.
8. *National Intelligencer*, Jan. 17, 1861.
9. *Philadelphia Inquirer*, Jan. 18, 1861.
10. *Newark Sentinel of Freedom*, Jan. 8-10, 1861; *New York Tribune*, Jan. 10, 1861.
11. *Philadelphia Public Ledger*, Jan. 28, 1861.
12. *Philadelphia Inquirer*, Jan. 28, 1861.
13. *Philadelphia Public Ledger*, Jan. 29, 1861; Cale, *op. cit.*, pp. 44-45.
14. *New York Tribune*, Jan. 12, 1861.
15. *Ibid.*, Feb. 19, 1861; Bingham Duncan, "New Castle in 1860-1861: A Community Response to a War Crisis," *Western Pennsylvania Magazine of History and Biography*, vol. XXIV, December 1941, pp. 254-55.
16. *New York Tribune*, Jan. 7, 1861.
17. Quoted by Carl Sandburg, *Abraham Lincoln: The War Years*, New York, 1936, vol. I, p. 428.
18. *Cincinnati Commercial*, Feb. 14, 18, 1861.
19. *Philadelphia Press*, Feb 22, 25, 1861; *Philadelphia Inquirer*, Feb. 25, 1861; Cale, *op. cit.*, pp. 45-47.
20. *Philadelphia Inquirer*, Feb. 25, 1861.
21. *Ibid.*

22. Foner, *Business and Slavery*, p. 273; *Philadelphia Press*, Feb. 22, 1861; *New York Herald*, Feb. 16, 1861; *Pittsburgh Gazette*, Nov. 28, 1860; *Boston Courier*, Dec. 11, 1860, Feb. 19, 1861.
23. *Philadelphia Ledger*, Feb. 29, 1861; Cale, *op. cit.*, pp. 44-45.
24. *New York Herald*, Jan. 16, 1861.
25. *Boston Courier*, Feb. 21, 1861.
26. *Herald of Peace*, no. XXXIII, May, 1857, pp. 202-03; Curti. *op. cit.*, pp. 32-38, 122.
27. *Philadelphia Inquirer*, Jan. 18, 1861; *Cincinnati Commercial*, Feb. 14, 18, 1861; *The War of the Rebellion: A Compilation of the Official Records of the Union and Confederate Armies*, Washington, 1899, Series III, Vol. I, Serial No. 122, pp. 56-58; *New York Tribune*, Jan. 10, 15, 16, 1861.
28. Benjamin F. Butler, *Butler's Book*, Boston, 1892, p. 165.
29. *The Iron Platform*, August 1861.
30. *Lowell Vox Populi*, May 30, Nov. 15, 1861.
31. Frederick Merk, *The Economic History of Wisconsin during the Civil War Decade*, Madison, Wisc., 1916, p. 26.
32. *New York Tribune*, July 4, 1861.
33. *Ibid.*, July 9, 10, 1861; Howard R. Marraro, "Lincoln's Italian Volunteers from New York," *New York History*, vol. XXIV, January, 1943, pp. 56-57.
34. *New York Tribune*, April 24, 1861.
35. *Ibid.*, August 7, 1862.
36. *Senate Executive Documents*, 39th Congress, 2nd Session, No. 2, p. 21.
37. B. A. Gould, *Investigations in the Military and Anthropological Statistics of American Soldiers*, New York, 1869, pp. 212, 216, and especially Tables II and VIII, pp. 209 ff.
38. Saul Schindler, *Northern Labor and the American Civil War*, unpublished M. A. thesis, Brooklyn College, 1940, pp. 48, 59.
39. *Boston Daily Evening Voice*, March 17, 1865.
40. *New York Herald*, April 19, 1861.
41. Terence V. Powderly, *Thirty Years of Labor*, Columbus, 1889, p. 57; International Molders' Union of North America, Troy local, ms. records, May 2, 1861, Columbia University Library.
42. *Lowell Daily Citizen and News*, April 29, 1861; *Boston Daily Evening Voice*, Dec. 2, 1864.
43. McNeil, *op. cit.*, p. 216; J. C. Sylvis, *op. cit.*, p. 54; Merk, *op. cit.*, p. 176.

44. *Proceedings of the International Union of Machinists and Blacksmiths of North America for 1861*, Phila., 1862, p. 28.
45. Wieck, *op. cit.*, pp. 112-14.
46. Philip S. Foner, *Morale Education in the American Army*, New York, 1944, pp. 33-36; Hilquit, *op. cit.*, pp. 171-72; Schlueter, *op. cit.*, pp. 83-84; Frank Moore, *Rebellion Record*, New York, 1862, vol. I, pp. 107, 109, 235; Sceva Bright Laughlin, "Missouri Politics During the Civil War," *Missouri Historical Review*, vol. XXIII, July 1929, pp. 603-05.
47. *Fincher's Trades' Review*, Jan. 2, 1864.
48. J. C. Sylvis, *op. cit.*, p. 49; Todes, *op. cit.*, pp. 27-28. Jonathan Grossman, *William Sylvis, Pioneer of American Labor*, New York, 1945, pp. 48-49.
49. Wieck, *op. cit.*, p. 113.
50. McNeil, *op. cit.*, pp. 617-27; *Iron Molders Journal*, 1864, pp. 25, 38, 54.
51. Minutes of the Troy Iron Molders' Union, May 2, 1861, microfilm copy, Columbia University Library.
52. Mathews and Wecter, *op. cit.*, p. 146; J. C. Sylvis, *op. cit.*, pp. 232-33; E. H. Rogers, *Autobiography*, Manuscript copy in Wisconsin State Historical Society, Chapter XII.
53. Reprinted in *Boston Daily Courier*, Feb. 21, 1861.
54. *Pittsburgh Gazette*, Sept. 3, 1861; *New York Tribune*, Sept. 5, Oct. 9-15, 1861; T. Harry Williams, *op. cit.*, p. 40.
55. Sandburg, *The War Years*, vol. II, pp. 127-28; *Philadelphia Public Ledger*, Oct. 11, 1862.
56. Wood Gray, *The Hidden Civil War: The Story of the Copperheads*, New York, 1942, p. 86.
57. *The Iron Platform*, Nov. 1862.
58. J. G. Gilmore, *Personal Recollections of Abraham Lincoln and the Civil War*, Boston, 1898, p. 75; *The Liberator*, vol. XXXI, pp. 15, 122, 130, 185; vol. XXXII, pp. 21, 26, 60; *Philadelphia Press*, July 30, 1862.
59. Karl Marx and Frederick Engels, *The Civil War in the United States*, pp. 47-48.
60. Frederick Bancroft, *William H. Seward*, New York, 1900, vol. II, p. 168.
61. Bernard Schmidt, "The Influence of Wheat and Cotton in Anglo-American Relations during the Civil War," *Iowa Journal of History and Politics*, vol. XVI, April 1918, pp. 400-39; Charles

62. I. Glicksburg, "Henry Adams and the Civil War," *Americana*, vol. XXXIII, Oct., 1939, p. 462.
62. Harriet A. Weed, ed., *Autobiography of Thurlow Weed*, New York, 1883, vol. I, p. 642.
63. Schlueter, *op. cit.*, pp. 164-65.
64. Henrietta Buckmaster, *Let My People Go*, New York, 1941, p. 642; Joseph H. Park, "The English Workingmen and the American Civil War," *Political Science Quarterly*, vol. XXXIX, Sept. 1924, p. 439.
65. *London Times*, April 14, 26, 1862.
66. *Ibid.*, March 27, 1863.
67. Park, *op. cit.*, pp. 442-43; Frank J. Klingberg, "Harriet Beecher Stowe and Social Reform in England," *American Historical Review*, vol. XLIII, April, 1938, pp. 542-52.
68. Marx and Engels, *The Civil War in the United States*, pp. 131-33.
69. *Ibid.*, pp. 141-42.
70. Park, *op. cit.*, p. 443.
71. *Ibid.*, p. 439.
72. John W. Draper, *History of the American Civil War*, New York, 1867-70, vol. II, p. 591; Edward McPherson, *The Political History of the United States of America during the great rebellion from Nov. 6, 1860 to July 4, 1864*, Washington, 1864, p. 234.
73. Worthington C. Ford, ed., *A Cycle of Adams Letters, 1861-1865*, Boston, 1920, vol. I, p. 243.
74. *Ibid.*, p. 246.
75. Marx and Engels, *The Civil War in the United States*, pp. 3-4.
76. *Congressional Globe*, vol. LXIV, p. 102.
77. John W. Cromwell, *The Negro in American History*, New York, 1914, p. 242.
78. *Official Records of the War of the Rebellion*, Series I, vol. X, p. 162; Horace Greeley, *The American Conflict*, Hartford, 1873, vol. II, p. 258; *New York Tribune*, May 27, 1862.
79. *Official Records of the War of the Rebellion*, Series I, vol. XIII, p. 684, vol. IX, p. 402.
80. See also *ibid.*, Series I, vol. IX, p. 353.
81. Philip S. Foner, ed., *Frederick Douglass: Selections from his Writings*, New York, 1945, pp. 35-36, 65-74; Bell I. Wiley, *Southern Negroes, 1861-1865*, New Haven, 1938, pp. 274-75; Peter H. Clark, *The Black Brigade of Cincinnati*, Cincinnati, 1864, p. 13.
82. *New Masses*, October 20, 1942, p. 18.

83. *Official Records of the Rebellion*, Series I. vol. XXVI, pp. 688-89.
84. Herbert Aptheker, "Maroons Within the Present Limits of the United States," *Journal of Negro History*, vol. XXIV, April 1939, p. 183.
85. Philip S. Foner, *Abraham Lincoln*, pp. 71-72.

CHAPTER XVI

1. See especially Louis Hacker, *The Triumph of American Capitalism*, New York, 1940, p. 373.
2. *Fincher's Trades' Review*, June 13, 1863.
3. J. C. Sylvis, *The Life, Speeches, Labors and Essays of William H. Sylvis*, Philadelphia, 1872, p. 229.
4. August, 1863. See also *New York Times*, July 11, 1863.
5. Harvey O'Connor, *Mellon's Millions*, New York, 1933, p. 24.
6. *New York Copperhead*, May 16, 1863.
7. *Ibid.*, July 18, 1863.
8. *Ibid.*, May 30, 1863.
9. *Ibid.*, May 16, July 18, 1863; Carl Sandburg, *Abraham Lincoln: The War Years*, vol. II, pp. 361 f.
10. J. T. Headley, *The Great Riots in New York*, New York, 1873, pp. 261-68; *New York Times*, July 14-19, 1863.
11. William A. Itter, *Conscription in Pennsylvania During the Civil War*, unpublished doctoral dissertation, University of Southern California, 1941, pp. 144 f.
12. *New York Copperhead*, July 18, 1863.
13. *The Iron Platform*, Sept. 1864.
14. *New York Tribune*, July 27, 30, 1863. See also Arthur M. Schlesinger, *New Viewpoints in American History*, New York, 1922, p. 13, and J. Walter Coleman, *Labor Disturbances in Pennsylvania, 1850-1860*, Washington, 1936, pp. 42 ff.
15. *Fincher's Trades' Review*, July 25, 1863.
16. Printed in full in *The Iron Platform*, June 1864.
17. *Fincher's Trades' Review*, Oct. 24, 1863.
18. *Ibid.*, Feb. 1, 1864.
19. Quoted by George F. Milton, *Lincoln and the Fifth Column*, New York, 1942, p. 237.
20. *New York Copperhead*, May 16 and 30; June 6, 20, 1863.
21. Wood Gray, *op. cit.*, p. 159; *New York*

World, July 5, 1864; John A. Logan, *The Great Conspiracy*, New York, 1886, *passim; New York Copperhead*, July 18, 1863; Ray H. Abrams, "Copperhead Newspapers and the Negro," *Journal of Negro History*, vol. XX, April 1935, pp. 131-52.
22. *House Report*, No. 2, 37 Cong., 2nd Session, p. 35; Robert Tomes, "The Fortunes of War," *Harper's Magazine*, vol. XXIX, 1864, p. 228; Upham, "Arms and Equipment for Iowa Troops During the Civil War," *Iowa Journal of History and Politics*, vol. XVI, Jan. 1918, p. 36.
23. *United States Bureau of Labor Statistics*, Wholesale Prices, 1913, no. 114, Appendix.
24. *Merchants' and Bankers' Almanac*, 1868, pp. 138, 149; *Report of Chamber of Commerce of New York State*, 1868-1869; *New York Evening Post*, March 5, 1863, Jan. 6, 1864; Brother Basil Leo Lee, *Discontent in New York City, 1861-1865*, Washington, D. C., 1943, p. 181.
25. Quoted by James S. Allen, *Reconstruction: The Battle for Democracy*, New York, 1937, p. 116. See also *The Printer*, August, 1864, p. 116.
26. Wesley C. Mitchell, *A History of the Greenbacks*, Chicago, 1903, pp. 18-30.
27. Daniel Creamer, "Recruiting Contract Laborers for Amoskeag Mills," *Journal of Economic History*, vol. I, May, 1941, pp. 44 f.
28. *Fincher's Trades' Review*, June 20, 1863.
29. *Ibid.*, July 2, 1864.
30. *Ibid.*, Oct. 17, 1863; June 24, Sept. 24, Oct. 29, Nov. 13, 1864.
31. Wieck, *op. cit.*, p. 122.
32. *Fincher's Trades' Review*, April 29 and May 14, 1864.
33. *Fincher's Trades' Review*, July 23, 1864.
34. *Ibid.*, June 20, 1863.
35. *Ibid.*, June 11, 1864.
36. *Ibid.*, April 29, 1864.
37. E. J. Benton, "Movement for Peace without a Victory During the Civil War," *Western Reserve Historical Society*, no. 99, Dec., 1918, pp. 14-21.
38. *Fincher's Trades' Review*, June 20, 1863.
39. *Ibid.*, August 20, 1864.
40. See especially *New York Daily News*, April 22 and 23, 1864 (resolutions adopted by Carpenters' Union of Brook-

lyn) and *Boston Daily Evening Voice*, March 14, 1865 (resolutions adopted at Mass Meeting of New England Trade Unions).

41. *Fincher's Trades' Review*, July 2, Oct. 29, 1864; also Jan. 14, 1865.
42. *Ibid.*, April 29 and Dec. 31, 1864.
43. *Boston Daily Evening Voice*, Jan. 28, 1865.
44. Sandburg, *op. cit.*, vol. II, p. 621; vol. III, pp. 398 f; *Fincher's Trades' Review*, Jan. 9, 1864.
45. *Ibid.*
46. *Fincher's Trades' Review*, Nov. 18, 1863.
47. *Ibid.*, Feb. 16, 1864.
48. June 13 and 18, July 4 and 9, 1864.
49. *The Iron Platform*, Oct. 1863; Feb., March, Sept. 1864; *New York Tribune*, July 19, 1864.
50. *The Iron Platform*, Oct. 1861.
51. *Ibid.*, Sept. 1862.
52. *Ibid.*, May 1863.
53. *Ibid.*, March 1864.
54. *Ibid.*, March-April 1864.
55. *New York Tribune*, Sept. 19, 1864.
56. *Ibid.*, Nov. 7, 1864.
57. Albert Brisbane to Horace Greeley, August 2, 1864, Greeley Papers, New York Public Library.
58. H. Schlueter, *The First International*, Chicago, 1918, pp. 188-91.
59. *Fincher's Trades' Review*, Jan. 14, 1865.
60. *Boston Daily Evening Voice*, Nov. 3, 1865.

CHAPTER XVII

1. Stockton, *op. cit.*, p. 23; *Proceedings of the Machinists and Blacksmiths Convention at Pittsburgh, November, 1861*, p. 21.
2. *Fincher's Trades' Review*, Nov. 21, 1863.
3. James Andrews in *ibid.*, August 29, 1863.
4. *Ibid.*, Dec. 26, 1863.
5. San Francisco *Evening Bulletin*, Nov. 6, 1863 quoted by Cross, *op. cit.*, pp. 34-35.
6. *New York Evening Post*, July 29, 1862.
7. *Fincher's Trades' Review*, Nov. 21, 1863.
8. *Ibid.*, April 16, 1864.
9. *Ibid.*, June 6, 1863.
10. *Ibid.*, Sept. 26, 1863; see also Dec. 26, 1863; Jan. 2, April 30, 1864.

11. *Ibid.*, Nov. 21, 1863; *31st Report of the Working Women's Protective Union, 1894*, p. 8.
12. *New York Evening Post*, November 13, 1863; *31st Report of the Working Women's Protective Union, 1894*, pp. 8-9.
13. *New York Tribune*, Dec. 14, 1864, *New York Daily News*, Aug. 13, 1864; *7th Report of the Working Women's Protective Union, 1870*, p. 11.
14. U. S. Commission of Labor, *Fourth Annual Report, 1888*, p. 51; *5th Annual Report of the Working Women's Protective Union, 1868*, p. 14.
15. *New York Tribune*, Jan. 19, 1881; *Woodhull & Claflin's Weekly*, Sept. 17, 1870.
16. *Fincher's Trades' Review*, April 16, Sept. 10, 1864; Andrews and Bliss, *op. cit.*, p. 95.
17. *Fincher's Trades' Review*, June 25, 1864.
18. *Ibid.*, Feb. 4, 1865.
19. Ingree Peterson, *History of Organized Labor in Houston, Texas*, unpublished M. A. Thesis, Tulane University, 1937; Charles Philips Anson, *A History of the Labor Movement in West Virginia*, unpublished Ph. D. Thesis, University of North Carolina, 1940, p. 74.
20. *Proceedings of the Iron Molders International Union Convention*, Buffalo, 1864, pp. 7-13, Columbia University Library.
21. *Fincher's Trades' Review*, June 6, 1863; Todes, *op. cit.*, p. 37, Grossman, *op. cit.*, pp. 88-119.
22. James C. Sylvis, *op. cit.*, p. 15.
23. *Fincher's Trades' Review*, Jan. 9, 1864.
24. *William H. Sylvis Scrapbooks*, John Crerar Library, Chicago.
25. *Fincher's Trades' Review*, Mar. 11, 1866.
26. Todes, *op. cit.*, p. 38; James C. Sylvis, *op. cit.*, p. 166.
27. Commons, *op cit.*, vol. II, pp. 15-17; *Fincher's Trades' Review*, April 16, 1864; Wieck, *op. cit.*, p. 261.
28. *Fincher's Trades' Review*, July 22, Aug. 26, 1865.
29. *Ibid.*, June 6, 1863.
30. *Ibid.*, Dec. 9, 1865.
31. *Ibid.*, Oct. 10, 1863.
32. *Workingman's Advocate*, January 22, April 9, 1870.
33. Reprinted in *Fincher's Trades' Review*, July 2, Oct. 29, 1864.

34. *Ibid.*, Oct. 29, 1864.
35. *Ibid.*, Nov. 25, 1865.
36. Todes, *op. cit.*, p. 51.
37. Fite, *op. cit.*, p. 202; *Fincher's Trades' Review*, Oct. 5, 1863; *Boston Daily Evening Voice*, March 11, 1865.
38. Stockton, *op. cit.*, p. 17; *Fincher's Trades' Review*, Oct. 5, 1863.
39. *Fincher's Trades' Review*, Oct. 3, 1863.
40. Jonathan Grosman, "The Molders' Struggle Against Contract Prison Labor," *New York History*, vol. XXIII, Oct. 1942, pp. 449-57; *Fincher's Trades' Review*, Nov. 29, Dec. 3, 1864.
41. *Boston Daily Evening Voice*, Feb. 17, 1863; *Fincher's Trades' Review*, Oct. 8, 1864; April 22, May 20, 1865; Wieck, *op. cit.*, pp. 128-30.
42. Wieck, *op. cit.*, p. 258.
43. Cross, *op. cit.*, pp. 32-34; Sandburg, *The War Years*, vol. II, pp. 620-21.
44. *New York Herald*, March 25, 1863; *Fincher's Trades' Review*, Aug. 5, 1864.
45. *Fincher's Trades' Review*, Jan. 2, 1864; Cale, *op. cit.*, p. 79.
46. *Boston Daily Evening Voice*, May 20, 1865.
47. *Fincher's Trades' Review*, Dec. 19, 1863; Commons, *op. cit.*, vol. II, pp. 23-24.
48. *Fincher's Trades' Review*, Dec. 19, 1863, March 19, 1864, March 4, 1865; James C. Sylvis, *op. cit.*, p. 139.
49. James C. Sylvis, *op. cit.*, p. 139.
50. Reprinted in *Fincher's Trades' Review*, March 28, 1864.
51. *New York Herald*, April 8, 1864.
52. *Ibid.; New York Tribune*, April 8, 1864.
53. *Fincher's Trades' Review*, April 2, 1864; *New York Tribune*, April 13, 1864.
54. *Workingman's Advocate*, March 25, 1865.
55. James C. Sylvis, *op. cit.*, pp. 131-32. See also *Boston Daily Evening Voice*, Dec. 20, 24, 1864, March 13, 1865.
56. C. M. Talmadge in *Fincher's Trades' Review*, Nov. 5, 1864. See also *ibid.*, Dec. 19, 1865 and "A Mechanic," in *Boston Daily Evening Voice*, Dec. 29, 1864.
57. Commons. ed., *Documentary History of American Industrial Society*, vol. IX, p. 117; *Fincher's Trades' Review*, Jan. 2, 1864.
58. C. M. Talmadge in *ibid.*, Nov. 5, 1864.
59. *Ibid.*, Oct. 15, 1864; Commons, ed.,

Documentary History of American Industrial Society, vol. IX, p. 118.
60. *Fincher's Trades' Review*, Oct. 1, 1864; *Boston Daily Evening Voice*, Dec. 30, 1864; Commons, *op. cit.*, vol. II, p. 35.
61. Commons, ed., *Documentary History of American Industrial Society*, vol. IX, pp. 120-25; U. S. Department of Labor, *Annual Report for 1920*, Washington, 1921, p. 13.
62. *Fincher's Trades' Review*, Sept. 24, 1864.
63. Reprinted in *ibid.*, Oct. 22, 1864.
64. Marion C. Cahill, *Shorter Hours*, New York, 1932, p. 137.
65. Cale, *op. cit.*, pp. 37-38. Leaflet entitled "Systematic Labor-Reform Movement," November 17, 1863, in Wisconsin State Historical Society.
66. See especially the *New York Herald*, May 28, 1866.
67. *Labor Standard*, June 9, 1878.
68. *Ibid.*, Jan. 6, 1878; *Equity*, Apr., 1874.
69. Ira Steward, *Poverty*, a pamphlet issued by the Boston Eight Hour League, Preface.
70. *Labor Standard*, March 3, 1877.
71. Dorothy W. Douglas, "Ira Steward on Consumption and Unemployment," *Journal of Political Economy*, vol. XL, August, 1932, p. 532 ff.; Myers, *op. cit.*, pp. 85-88; Ira Steward, in *Workingman's Advocate*, March 11, 1871; *Labor Standard*, Dec. 30, 1876; William Edlin in *The Comrade*, vol. I, Dec. 1901, pp. 66 ff.
72. *American Workman* (Boston), Sept. 25, 1869.
73. Douglas, *op. cit.*, p. 532; *National Workman*, Nov. 3, 1866.
74. Commons, ed., *Documentary History of American Industrial Society*, vol. X, p. 26.
75. *Workingman's Advocate*, June 18, 1867; Jan. 14, 1870; *National Workman*, Nov. 3, 24, 1866.
76. *Fincher's Trades' Review*, Oct. 3, 31, 1863; March 26, June 4, 1864.
77. *Ibid.*, June 27, 1863.
78. Augusta E. Galston, *The Labor Movement in the Shoe Industry*, p. 138.
79. Erie correspondent in *Fincher's Trades' Review*. Sept. 9, 1865.
80. *Ibid.*, July 29, 1865; *Boston Daily Evening Voice*, May 8, 12, 1866.
81. Karl Marx, *Capital*, vol. I, p. 309.
82. *Proceedings of the Carpenters' and Joiners' National Convention, 1867*, p. 25.

CHAPTER XVIII

1. *Workingman's Advocate*, Aug. 21, 1869.
2. Commons, ed., *Documentary History of American Industrial Society*, vol. IX, pp. 126-29; *New York Tribune*, Aug. 1, 1866; *New York Times*, Aug. 22, 1866; *Workingman's Advocate*, Aug. 11, 1866.
3. Commons, ed., *Documentary History of American Industrial Society*, vol. IX, pp. 127-28.
4. James C. Sylvis, *op. cit.*, p. 67; Hilquit, *op. cit.*, p. 185.
5. *Ibid.*
6. Commons, ed., *Documentary History of American Industrial Society*, vol. IX, pp. 139-41.
7. Karl Marx and Frederick Engels, *Selected Correspondence, 1846-1895*, pp. 214-15.
8. Karl Marx, *Capital*, vol. I, p. 310.
9. Commons, ed., *Documentary History of American Industrial Society*, vol. IX, pp. 134-36.
10. James C. Sylvis, *op. cit.*, p. 7.
11. Commons, ed., *Documentary History of American Industrial Society*, vol. IX, pp. 169-71.
12. *Ibid.*
13. *Workingman's Advocate*, Dec. 28, 1868.
14. *Ibid.*, March 27, 1869.
15. *Ibid.*, Jan. 16, 1869.
16. *Ibid.*, Sept., 12, Dec. 26, 1868; Feb. 20, April 24, Sept. 4, 1869.
17. *Chicago Tribune*, Feb. 16, 1869.
18. *New York Herald*, Sept., 19, 22, 26, 1868; *Workingman's Advocate*, Sept. 4, 1869.
19. *Boston Daily Evening Voice*, Aug. 27, 1866.
20. *Workingman's Advocate*, May 29, Dec. 2, 1869; Edward McPherson, *A Handbook of Politics for 1872*, Washington, 1872, pp. 69-70.
21. James C. Sylvis, *op. cit.*, p. 324.
22. *Workingman's Advocate*, May 1, Dec. 2, 1869.
23. McPherson, *op. cit.*, p. 70; Mary Cahill, *op. cit.*, pp. 69-70; *Workingman's Advocate*, Jan. 1, 1870.
24. Reprinted in *Alabama Beacon*, August 6, 1870.
25. Cahill, *op. cit.*, pp. 69-70.
26. *Arbeiter-Union*, Sept. 12, 1868.
27. Cross, *op. cit.*, pp. 50-51; *Workingman's Advocate*, Feb. 20, 1869.

28. *Proceedings of the Convention of the National Labor Union*, Philadelphia, 1868, p. 14; *Workingman's Advocate*, Feb. 20, 1869.
29. Eaves, *op. cit.*, pp. 201-06.
30. Perlman, *op. cit.*, p. 50.
31. *National Workman*, Feb. 2, 1867; *Laws of Pennsylvania, 1867-1868*, p. 99; *Workingman's Advocate*, March 11, 1871.
32. Cahill, *op. cit.*, p. 148; Commons, *op. cit.*, vol. II, p. 147.
33. Pennsylvania Bureau of Statistics of Labor and Agriculture, *1st Annual Report*, Pt. II, pp. 232-75.
34. *New York Times*, Sept. 15, 1871.
35. *Ibid.*, June 12, 1872.
36. *Workingman's Advocate*, March 11, 1868.
37. *Woodhull & Claflin's Weekly*, May 6, 1871.
38. *Workingman's Advocate*, Oct. 10, 1868.
39. *Fincher's Trades' Review*, June 24, 1865.
40. *Workingman's Advocate*, June 26, 1869; Feb. 5, March 19, 1870; Andrews and Bliss, *op. cit.*, pp. 98-99.
41. *Proceedings of the 1869 Convention of the National Typographical Union*, p. 29; *Workingman's Advocate*, June 26, 1869.
42. *Workingman's Advocate*, May 21, Aug. 18, 1870.
43. *Proceedings of the 1872 Convention of the National Typographical Union*, pp. 50-51; Tracy, *op. cit.*, pp. 263-64.
44. *Proceedings of the Second Annual Congress of the National Labor Union.*
45. Marx and Engels, *Selected Correspondence, 1846-1895*, p. 255.
46. Commons, ed., *Documentary History of American Industrial Society*, vol. IX, p. 198; *New York Tribune*, Sept. 23, 1868; *The Revolution*, Sept. 21, 1868.
47. Commons, ed., *Documentary History of American Industrial Society*, vol. IX, p. 198.
48. *The Revolution*, July 2, Sept. 21, 1868; Todes, *op. cit.*, pp. 83-84.
49. *New York Tribune*, Aug. 19, 1869; *The Revolution*, Sept. 9, 1869; *Workingman's Advocate*, March 5, 1870.
50. James C. Sylvis, *op. cit.*, p. 222.
51. *Workingman's Advocate*, April 2, 1869.
52. *Ibid.*, June 25, Nov. 28, 1870.
53. *New York Tribune*, Aug. 19, 1869; *Workingman's Advocate*, April 23, June 25, 1870.

54. *Workingman's Advocate*, March 19, 1870.

CHAPTER XIX

1. Commons, ed., *Documentary History of American Industrial Society*, vol. IX pp. 159-60.
2. A. D. McCoy, *Thoughts on Labor in the South, Past, Present and Future*, New Orleans, 1865, p. 22; 39th Congress 1st Sess., *Senate Executive Doc.*, pp. 13, 21, 32, 35, 43, 44.
3. *Atlantic Monthly*, 1866, p. 606.
4. Quoted by James S. Allen, *op. cit.*, pp. 390-91.
5. Quoted by Manuel Gottlieb, "The Land Question in Georgia during Reconstruction," *Science and Society*, vol. III, Summer, 1939, p. 364. See also Fred A. Shannon, *The Farmer's Last Frontier, 1860-1897*, New York, 1945, pp. 83-86; *New York Tribune*, June 12, 1865; Oscar Zeichner, "The Transition from Slave to Free Agricultural Labor in the Southern States," *Agricultural History*, vol. XIII, 1939, pp. 23-27.
6. *New York Herald*, August 10, 1865.
7. W. E. B. Du Bois, *Black Reconstruction in America*, New York, 1935, pp. 230-33; Allen, *op. cit.*, pp. 73-78.
8. Howard K. Beale, "The Tariff and Reconstruction," *American Historical Review*, vol. XXXV, Jan. 1930, pp. 276-94; *The Nation*, Jan. 11, 1866; *Anti-Slavery Standard*, Oct. 19, 1867; *Congressional Globe*, 39th Congress, 1st Session, Appendix, p. 284.
9. *Workingman's Advocate*, Sept. 12, 1868; *National Workman*, Dec. 8, 1866; *Boston Daily Evening Voice*, Oct. 4, 1866; *Journal of United Labor*, August 15, 1881; *Samuel Gompers' Scrapbooks* No. I, p. 3, N. Y. Public Library.
10. *Boston Daily Evening Voice*, Dec. 28, 1865; Jan. 24, 1866.
11. *Ibid.*, April 19, 1866.
12. *Ibid.*, August 22, 1866.
13. *Ibid.*, Jan. 13, 1866.
14. *Ibid.*, Feb. 2, 1866. For other expressions on Reconstruction and unity of white and Negro workers, see *Boston Daily Evening Voice*, Dec. 13, 1865; Jan. 19, March 7, March 15, March 28, March 29, May 11, May 14, June 29, August 16, Oct. 25, Nov. 22, 1866.
15. *Fincher's Trades' Review*, May 6, 1865.

16. *National Workman*, Oct. 20, 27, 1866; Jan. 5, 1867; *New York Tribune*, April 6, 1866.
17. *Workingman's Advocate*, Aug. 11, 1866; Dec. 26, 1868; July 2, 9, 1870.
18. *Workingman's Advocate*, March-April, 1869, especially March 27, 1869; J. C. Sylvis, *op. cit.*, pp. 233-35, 333-34, 339, 342-43.
19. James C. Sylvis, *op. cit.*, p. 82.
20. Charles Wesley, *Negro Labor in the United States*, New York, 1927, pp. 135-40; W. E. B. Du Bois and A. G. Dill, eds., "The Negro American Artisan," Atlanta University *Publications*, Nov. 17, 1912, p. 36.
21. Mary M. Dodge, "Our Contraband," *Harper's Monthly Magazine*, vol. XXVII, pp. 395-403; *Workingman's Advocate*, Aug. 7, 1869.
22. *Workingman's Advocate*, Oct. 2, 1869; Jan. 28, 1871.
23. Commons, ed., *Documentary History of American Industrial Society*, vol. IX, pp. 159-60.
24. *Ibid.*, pp. 185-88.
25. *Mobile Daily Advertiser and Register*, April 2, 1867; *Charleston Daily News*, Jan. 5-9, 1867; Lawanda F. Cox, *Agricultural Labor in the United States, 1865-1900, with special reference to the South*, unpublished Ph. D. thesis, University of California, 1941, p. 112.
26. *National Anti-Slavery Standard*, Sept. 25, 1869; Du Bois, *op. cit.*, p. 361.
27. James C. Sylvis, *op. cit.*, pp. 331-48.
28. *Workingman's Advocate*, Sept. 4, 11, 1869.
29. *Ibid.*
30. *New York Times* reprinted in *Workingman's Advocate*, Oct. 2, 1869.
31. *Workingman's Advocate*, Oct. 2, 21, 1869; Feb. 5, May 7, Oct. 8, 1870; *New York Tribune*, Sept. 17, 1869.
32. *Workingman's Advocate*, June 26, 1869; *Proceedings of the International Typographical Union for 1869*, Cincinnati, 1869, pp. 16-17.
33. *Proceedings of the International Typographical Union for 1870*, Philadelphia, 1870, p. 31.
34. Reprinted in *ibid.*, p. 140.
35. *National Anti-Slavery Standard*, July 17, 1869.
36. Wesley, *op. cit.*, pp. 173-74.
37. *Charleston Daily Republican*, Nov. 26, 1869.
38. Wesley, *op. cit..* pp. 175-76; *New York Tribune*, Dec. 8-10, 1869.

39. Commons, ed., *Documentary History of American Industrial Society*, vol. IX, pp. 243-53.
40. *New York Tribune*, Dec. 8-10, 1869. See also *Proceedings of the Colored National Labor Convention*, Washington, 1870.
41. *Workingman's Advocate*, Dec. 1, 1869.
42. *National Anti-Slavery Standard*, Dec. 18, 1869; Commons, ed., *Documentary History of American Industrial Society*, vol. IX, pp. 243-53; Wesley, *op. cit.*, pp. 178-79.
43. *The New National Era*, April 21, 1870.
44. Du Bois, *op. cit.*, p. 366; *The New National Era*, April 27, 1870; *Charleston Daily Republican*, April 28, 1870.
45. *Workingman's Advocate*, Jan. 1, August 27, 1870; Wesley, *op. cit.*, pp. 164-66.
46. Commons, ed., *Documentary History of American Industrial Society*, vol. IX, p. 254.
47. *The New National Era*, Nov. 17, 1870.
48. Wesley, *op. cit.*, p. 182.
49. *Ibid.*, pp. 185 ff.
50. Du Bois, *op. cit.*, p. 367; Wesley, *op. cit.*, p. 188.

CHAPTER XX

1. *Fincher's Trades' Review*, March 18, 1865.
2. *Workingman's Advocate*, May 7, Oct. 8, 1870.
3. *National Workman*, Nov. 10, 1866.
4. *Arbeiter-Union*, March 27, 1869.
5. James C. Sylvis, *op. cit.*, pp. 186-87; *Workingman's Advocate*, Feb. 26, 1870.
6. Todes, *op. cit.*, pp. 86-87.
7. *National Workman*, Nov. 10, 1866.
8. *Workingman's Advocate*, August 24, 1867; Commons, ed., *Documentary History of American Industrial Society*, vol. IX, pp. 338-39.
9. Schlueter, *Lincoln, Labor and Slavery*, pp. 231-34; Commons, ed., *Documentary History of American Industrial Society*, vol. IX, pp. 338-39.
10. *Workingman's Advocate*, Oct. 23, Nov. 23, 1869.
11. *Ibid.* See also issue of Sept. 28, 1872.
12. Todes, *op. cit.*, p. 64.
13. F. A. Sorge, "Die Arbeiterbewegung in den Vereinigten Staaten von 1866 bis 1876," *Neue Zeit*, I Band, Stuttgart, 1891-92, pp. 391-92; *Woodhull & Claflin's Weekly*, Sept. 2, Nov. 11, 1871, Feb. 10, 1872.
14. Commons, *op. cit.*, vol. II, pp. 208-09;

Hermann Schlueter, *Die Internationale in Amerika*, Chicago, 1918, pp. 15-30; Hilquit, *op. cit.*, p. 194.
15. Commons, ed., *Documentary History of American Industrial Society*, vol. IX, pp. 356-58.
16. *Ibid.*, pp. 368-70; Hilquit, *op. cit.*, pp. 196-97; F. M. Stekloff, *History of the First International*, New York, 1926, pp. 268-72.
17. *Copy Book of the General Council of the International Workingmen's Association, Mss.*, Wisconsin State Historical Society.
18. *Workingman's Advocate*, April 13, 1872; Allen, *op. cit.*, pp. 177-80.
19. Commons, ed., *Documentary History of American Industrial Society*, vol. IX, pp. 367-78; *Workingman's Advocate*, July 30, August 6, Oct. 8, 22, Dec. 3, 1870; May 27, July 12, 1871; April 13, 1872; *Arbeiter-Union*, reprinted in *Workingman's Advocate*, June 18, 1870.
20. Jonathan Grossman, "Cooperative Foundries," *New York History*, vol. XXIV, April, 1943, pp. 196-97; Jonathan Grossman, *William Sylvis*, Chapter X; *Fincher's Trades' Review*, Sept. 3, 1864.
21. *Printer's Circular*, Nov. 1867.
22. Sylvis in *Fincher's Trades' Review*, Sept. 24, 1864; unsigned letter dated April 5, 1869 and sent from Philadelphia, in Thomas Phillips Papers, Wisconsin State Historical Society.
23. *Fincher's Trades' Review*, Oct. 22, 1864; *Workingman's Advocate*, March 19, 1870; unsigned letter dated April 5, 1869 and sent from Philadelphia, in Thomas Phillips Papers, Wisconsin State Historical Society.
24. *Charleston Daily Republican*, Dec. 2, 1869; *National Anti-Slavery Standard*, Jan. 28, 1871; J. D. Ware to Thomas Phillips, Oct. 28, 1867, Phillips Papers, Wisconsin State Historical Society.
25. Grossman, *New York History*, vol. XXIV, pp. 196-201; Frank T. Stockton, "The Molders and Productive Cooperation," *International Molders' Journal*, July 1914, p. 533.
26. Grossman, *op. cit.*, pp. 207-09; Stockton, *op. cit.*, pp. 534-35; *The Socialist*, May 6, 1876; Gleason, *op. cit.*, pp. 116, 159; undated letter dealing with the Wendell Phillips Co-operative in Thomas Phillips Papers, *Mss.*, Wisconsin State Historical Society.

27. Edward Kellogg, *Labor and Other Capital*, New York, 1849, pp. 19, 36-37, 320.
28. *Philadelphia Public Ledger*, May 9, 1868.
29. James C. Sylvis, *op. cit.*, title-page.
30. *Labor Standard*, Dec. 30, 1876.
31. James C. Sylvis, *op. cit.*, pp. 72, 82; *Workingman's Advocate*, May 15, 1869.
32. *Arbeiter-Union*, Aug. 12, 1869.
33. *Laws and Rules and Regulations of the Workingmen's Union of New York City and Vicinity*, Article 10, Section 1, New York, 1867.
34. *Workingman's Advocate*, Feb. 12, 20, 26, 1870.
35. *Boston Daily Evening Voice*, Jan. 4, 1866. See also *Proceedings of the 1867 Convention of the Carpenters and Joiners National Union*.
36. *Workingman's Advocate*, May 29, 1869.
37. *Laws of Pennsylvania*, 1872, p. 1176; Alexander Trachtenberg, *History of Legislation for the Protection of Coal Miners in Pennsylvania*, New York, 1942, pp. 32-49.
38. Eaves, *op. cit.*, p. 23.
39. *American Annual Cyclopedia, 1870*, New York, 1871, vol. X, p. 474.
40. Wendell Phillips, *Speeches, Lectures and Letters, Second Series*, p. 139.
41. *American Annual Cyclopedia, 1871*, New York, 1872, vol. XI, p. 494.
42. Wendell Phillips, "The Foundation of the Labor Movement," in *Speeches, Lectures and Letters, Second Series*, vol. II, p. 167.
43. *New York Tribune*, Dec. 7. 1871.
44. *Commonwealth*, June 29, 1872; *Equity*, June, 1874.
45. See Gen. A. M. Winn, *Valedictory Address of General A. M. Winn, President of Mechanics' State Council of California*, San Francisco, 1871, p. 55.
46. Commons, ed., *Documentary History of American Industrial Society*, vol. IX, p. 175.
47. *Workingman's Advocate*, Sept. 2, Oct. 10, 1868.
48. *The Guardian*, Nov. 11, 25, 1871; *Woodhull & Claflin's Weekly*, March 9, 1872.
49. Thomas H. McKee, *The National Conventions and Platforms of all Political Parties, 1789 to 1901*, Baltimore, 1901, pp. 154-55.
50. *New York Tribune*, Feb. 21, 1872; *Woodhull & Claflin's Weekly*, April 6, 20, 1872.

51. *New York Tribune*, Feb. 24, June 28, August 23, 1872; *The Nation*, Sept. 19, 1872.
52. *Cincinnati Daily Gazette*, Aug. 22, 1872; *Workingman's Advocate*, Sept. 14, 1872.
53. *Briefe und Auszuge aus Briefen, on Karl Marx, et al, an F. Sorge und Anders*, p. 18. Copy Book of the American General Council of the International Workingmen's Association, *August, 1871*, Mss., Wisconsin State Historical Society.
54. Commons, ed., *Documentary History of American Industrial Society*, vol. IX, pp. 228-31.
55. *New York Tribune*, Sept. 18, 1869.
56. *Proceedings of the 1871 Convention of the National Typographical Union*, p. 129.
57. *Proceedings of the Workingmen's Assembly of New York for 1871*, p. 64.
58. *Workingman's Advocate*, Feb. 18, 1871.
59. *Ibid.*, Sept. 21, 1872; May 3, 1873.

CHAPTER XXI

1. *Philadelphia Public Ledger*, May 9, 1863.
2. *Ibid.*, Feb. 4, 1869; Terence V. Powderly, *Thirty Years of Labor, 1859-1889*, p. 134.
3. *Philadelphia Public Ledger*, Dec. 30, 1869; Powderly, *op. cit.*, pp. 140-44.
4. Commons, ed., *Documentary History of American Industrial Society*, vol. IX, pp. 19-24; Terence V. Powderly, *The Path I Trod*, New York, pp. 49-53.
5. *National Labor Tribune*, Sept. 23, 1876.
6. *Quarterly Journal of Economics*, vol. I, January 1887, p. 140.
7. Hilquit, *op. cit.*, pp. 291-92.
8. Ware, *op. cit.*, p. 27; Powderly, *The Path I Trod*, p. 336.
9. Powderly, *Thirty Years of Labor*, pp. 167, 534-35.
10. Ware, *op. cit.*, p. 74.
11. *Ibid.*
12. *Proceedings of the 1879 General Assembly of the Knights of Labor*, p. 56.
13. *Decisions of the General Master Workman*, 1887, p. 23.
14. Ware, *op. cit.*, p. 156.
15. *Ibid.*, pp. 155-56.
16. Powderly, *Thirty Years of Labor*, p. 144.

CHAPTER XXII

1. *National Labor Tribune*, Nov. 13, 1875.
2. Feder, *op. cit.*, pp. 38-40; Allan Nevins, *Emergence of Modern America, 1865-1878. New York*, 1935, pp. 299-301.
3. *Labor Standard*, Aug. 19, 1876, Feb. 10, 1877.
4. *New York Tribune*, Sept. 18, 1877; *Woodhull & Claflin's Weekly*, Feb. 19, 1876.
5. Commons, *op. cit., vol. II*, pp. 175-77; *United States Industrial Commission Report for 1901*, vol. VII, p. 615; *New York Times*, Dec. 11, 1874; *The Socialist*, May 13, 1876; *Labor Standard*, Aug. 19, 1876.
6. Commons, *op. cit., vol. II*, pp. 46-48; *National Labor Tribune*, Nov. 6, 1875; *The Toiler*, Aug. 8, 1874; *Labor Standard*, Feb. 10, 24, 1877.
7. *The Socialist*, May 6, July 29, 1876; *Labor Standard*, Sept. 23, 1876.
8. The most complete reports of the movement for amalgamation appeared in the *National Labor Tribune*, August-December, 1875 and January-May, 1876.
9. Chris Evans, *History of United Mine Workers of America*, Indianapolis, 1918, vol. I, pp. 37-72.
10. *Iron Molders' Journal* reprinted in *Labor Standard*, Sept. 23, Oct. 28, 1876.
11. *The Toiler*, Aug. 8, 1874.
12. *Workingman's Advocate*, July 5, 1873.
13. *Constitution of the Industrial Brotherhood*, published by *Humanity*, the official organ, pamphlet; Commons, *op. cit.*, vol. II, p. 164.
14. Commons, *op. cit.*, vol. II, p. 167.
15. *The Toiler*, July (n.d.) 1874; *National Labor Tribune*, Oct. 2, 1875.
16. Ohio Bureau of Labor Statistics, *2nd Annual Report*, 1878, pp. 199-201; United States Bureau of Labor Statistics, *Bulletin No. 604*, Washington, 1934, p. 391; *The Socialist*, May 6, June 10, 1876; *Labor Standard*, Aug. 12, Sept. 9, 1876, Jan. 13, 1877.
17. *The Toiler*, Aug. 1, 8, 1874.
18. Feder, *op. cit.*, pp. 42, 65-66.
19. *The Nation*, Dec. 18, 1873, March 14, 1874.
20. Reprinted in *Irish World and Industrial Liberator*, Jan. 12, 1878.
21. *Workingman's Advocate*, July 2, 1870.
22. Fred A. Shannon, *The Farmer's Last Frontier*, New York, 1945, p. 54.
23. Terence V. Powderly, *Thirty Years of Labor*, pp. 183-84; *Labor Standard*, May 27, Oct. 14, 1876.
24. *National Labor Tribune*, Nov. 6, 1876; *Labor Standard*, August 26, 1876; *New York Tribune*, Feb. 7, 1878.
25. 45th Congress, 3rd Session, *H. R. Misc. Doc. No. 29*, pp. 45, 147, 202, 267, 388, 407, 470, 580, 656-64.
26. The text of the bill is printed in the *Irish World*, August 10, 1878.
27. Reprinted in *Labor Standard*, Sept. 2, 1877. See also *Scranton Republican*, August 1, 1877.
28. Printed Manifesto in International Workingmen's Association Papers, Wisconsin State Historical Society. See also "An Unemployment Manifesto During the Crisis of 1873," with Editorial Notes by Alexander Trachtenberg, *The Communist*, vol. X, June 1931, pp. 566-72.
29. *New York Times*, Nov. 16, 1873.
30. *Ibid.*, Dec. 12, 1873.
31. *Ibid.*
32. *Chicago Tribune*, Dec. 20-24, 1873; Feder, *op. cit.*, pp. 51-53.
33. *The Toiler*, Jan.-April 1874, May 23, 1874; *New York Tribune, New York Times*, Jan. 14-15, 1874.
34. *The Toiler*, August 15, Sept. 5, 1874; Sorge, in *Neue Zeit*, vol. IX, pp. 397-98; *The Socialist*, May 13, 1876; *New York Arbeiter-Zeitung*, May 19, 1874; *Copy Book of the North American Federal Council of the International Workingmen's Association*, April 1874, Ms. Wisconsin State Historical Society.
35. Commons, *op. cit.*, vol. II, pp. 226-29; Chicago *Vorbote*, June 5, 20, 1874.
36. Commons, *op. cit.*, vol. II, pp. 217-19; Sorge, in *Neue Zeit*, vol. IX, pp. 397-98; New York *Arbeiter-Zeitung*, May 26, 1874; *Records of the Philadelphia Section no. 26 of the International Workingmen's Association*, June 24, 1872, Mss., Wisconsin State Historical Society.
37. Commons, *op. cit.*, vol. II, pp. 26-29; Chicago *Vorbote*, June 5, 20, 1874.
38. Commons, ed., *Documentary History of American Industrial Society*, vol. IX, pp. 376-78; *Platform and Constitution of the Social-Democratic Workingmen's Party of North America*, New York, 1876.
39. *National Labor Tribune*, June 12, 1875.

40. Marx and Engels, *Selected Correspondence*, pp. 449-50.
41. Commons, *op. cit.*, vol. II, p. 233; *The Socialist*, May 13, 1876.
42. *Labor Standard*, August 12, 1876.
43. *Ibid.*, Jan. 6, 13, 1877.
44. *Ibid.*; J. P. McDonnell manuscript biography, J. P. McDonnell Papers, Wisconsin State Historical Society.
45. *Labor Standard*, Sept. 16, 1876, Jan. 6, 20, April 14, 1877.

CHAPTER XXIII

1. *11th Annual Report of the Massachusetts Bureau of Labor Statistics*, 1880, p. 63.
2. McNeil, *op. cit.*, pp. 223-28.
3. *Ibid.; Annual Report of the Massachusetts Bureau of Labor Statistics*, 1880, pp. 35-44.
4. Marvin W. Schlegel, "The Workingmen's Benevolent Association: First Union of Anthracite Miners," *Pennsylvania History*, vol. X, Oct. 1943, pp. 249-55.
5. Roberts, *op. cit.*, pp. 66-68; Schlegel, *op. cit.*, p. 258.
6. *Argument of Franklin B. Gowen before a Joint Committee of the Pennsylvania State Legislature*, Philadelphia, 1875, pp. 74-79.
7. *National Labor Tribune*, March 12, 1875; Schlegel, *op. cit.*, pp. 259-61.
8. *Report of the President and Managers of the Philadelphia and Reading Railroad Company to the Stockholders, 1875*, Philadelphia, 1875, pp. 16-18, *Report . . . for 1877*, Philadelphia, 1877, p. 25.
9. Anthony Bimba, *The Molly Maguires*, New York, 1932, pp. 6-61; *National Labor Tribune*, Apr. 24, Sept. 25, 1875.
10. George G. Korson, *Songs and Ballads of the Anthracite Miner*, Philadelphia, 1926, pp. 161-62.
11. *National Labor Tribune*, Sept. 4, 1875.
12. Andrew Roy, *A History of the Coal Miners of the United States*, Columbus, Ohio, 1907, p. 99.
13. *National Labor Tribune*, June 26, 1875.
14. Joseph F. Patterson, "Old W. B. A. Days," *Publications of the Historical Society of Schuylkill County, Pennsylvania*, vol. II, 1910, p. 366; *National Labor Tribune*, Sept. 4, Oct. 9, 1875; Schlegel, *op. cit.*, p. 266; George G. Korson, *Minstrels of the Mine Patch*, Philadelphia, 1938, p. 226.
15. *Miners' National Record*, April-May, 1875; *National Labor Tribune*, Oct. 9, 1875.
16. *National Labor Tribune*, May 22, 1875.
17. *Ibid.*, June 26, 1875; *New York Times*, June 16, 1875; *Miners' National Record*, October 1875.
18. *National Labor Tribune*, Sept. 11, Oct. 30, 1875; May 15, 1876; *Miners' National Record*, June, August 1875; Roy, *op. cit.*, pp. 175-78.
19. *Arguments of Franklin B. Gowen, Esq., of Counsel for the Commonwealth in the Case of the Commonwealth vs. Thomas Munley*, pp. 24, 33-36; J. Walter Coleman, *Labor Disturbances in Pennsylvania, 1850-1880*, p. 141.
20. Coleman, *op. cit.*, pp. 129-30.
21. Bimba, *op. cit.*, pp. 95-96; *Arguments of Franklin B. Gowen, Esq.*, pp. 7-8.
22. Coleman, *op. cit.*, p. 141.
23. *Ibid.*, pp. 151-52; *Bill Haywood's Book*, New York, 1929, Chapters XI-XII.
24. *Labor Standard*, Sept. 23, 1876; *Irish World*, June 16, 1877; *National Labor Tribune*, June 12, 1877.
25. *New York Tribune*, June 22, 1877; Coleman, *op. cit.*, p. 166.
26. *Irish World*, June 16, 1877.
27. Quoted by Bimba, *op. cit.*, p. 121.
28. Quoted in *Appleton's Annual Cyclopedia*, n. s., vol. II, 1877, p. 231.
29. *Scranton Republican*, July 23, 1877; *Third Annual Report of the Commissioner of Labor*, Washington, 1888, p. 1071; *Annual Report, Bureau of Labor Statistics, Ohio*, Columbus, 1883, p. 85.
30. Quoted in Samuel Yellen, *American Labor Struggles*, New York, 1936, p. 12.
31. *New York Tribune*, July 23, 1877; Philip A. Slaner, "The Railroad Strikes of 1877," *Marxist Quarterly*, vol. I, April-June 1937, p. 217.
32. Charles Phillips Anson, *History of the Labor Movement in West Virginia*, unpublished Ph. D. Thesis, University of North Carolina, 1940, pp. 190-93; Yellen, *op. cit.*, p. 10; *New York Times*, July 19, 1877; *Baltimore Gazette* reprinted in *Scranton Republican*, July 20, 1877; *Labor Standard*, August 14, 1877.
33. James McCabe, *The History of the Great Riots*, Philadelphia, 1877, p. 20; *Army Journal*, July 21, 1877.
34. *New York Times*, July 19, 1877.

35. *New York World*, July 23, 1877.
36. 57th Congress, 2nd Session, *Senate Document No. 209*, p. 191; *Scranton Republican*, July 25, 1877; Slaner, *op. cit.*, p. 221.
37. *New York Times*, July 21, 1877; O. D. Boyle, *The History of the Railroad Strikes*, Washington, D. C., 1935, p. 16.
38. *New York Times*, July 22, 1877.
39. Slaner, *op. cit.*, pp. 223-25; *Labor Standard*, July 14, 1877.
40. *Labor Standard*, July 28, 1877.
41. *New York Times*, July 22, 1877.
42. *Army Journal*, August 4, 1877; *New York Times*, July 22, 1877.
43. *Irish World*, Dec. 1, 1877.
44. *Scranton Republican*, July 23, 1877; *New York Tribune*, July 23, 1877.
45. Slaner, *op. cit.*, p. 228.
46. *New York World*, July 22-23, 1877; Slaner, *op. cit.*, pp. 28-29.
47. *New York Tribune*, July 26, 1877; *Irish World*, July 23, 1877.
48. *Labor Standard*, August 11, 1877.
49. Slaner, *op. cit.*, pp. 229-30; *Labor Standard*, July 29, 1877.
50. Cross, *op. cit.*, pp. 89-90; *Labor Standard*, Sept. 2, 1877; *Scranton Republican*, July 24, 1877.
51. Nelles, *op. cit.*, p. 517 n.; *Scranton Republican*, August 6, 1877.
52. Hermann Schlueter, *Die Internationale in Amerika*, Heft 6, p. 383.
53. *Labor Standard*, August 11, 1877; *New York Sun, New York Tribune*, July 26. 1877.
54. *Chicago Times*, July 26-27, 1877; *Scranton Republican*, July 24, 27, August 1, 1877.
55. Alan Calmer, *Labor Agitator: The Story of Albert R. Parsons*, New York, 1937, p. 28.
56. *Labor Standard*, August 11, 1877; *Chicago Times*, July 27-30, 1877; *Scranton Republican*, July 27, 1877.
57. *Chicago Times*, July 27-August 1, 1877.
58. Reprinted in *New York Sun*, July 26, 1877.
59. *Labor Standard*, August 9, 1877; *Missouri Republican*, July 23-24, 1877.
60. Russel M. Nolen, "The Labor Movement in St. Louis from 1860-1890," *Missouri Historical Review*, vol. XXIV, Jan. 1940, pp. 157 ff.
61. *Scranton Republican*, July 26, 1877.
62. Nolen, *op. cit.*, pp. 170-72; *New York World*, July 27, 1877.
63. *Scranton Republican*, July 25, 1877.

64. Nolen, *op. cit.*, pp. 171-72; Schlueter, *op. cit.*, p. 388; *New York Times*, July 27, 1877.
65. *Missouri Republican*, July 28-August 3, 1877.
66. *Labor Standard*, July 28, August 4, 1877; *New York Sun*, July 27, 1877.

CHAPTER XXIV

1. Reprinted in *National Labor Tribune*, June 19, 1875. See also *Report of the North American Central Committee of the International Workingmen's Association, 1872-1873, Mss.*, Wisconsin State Historical Society.
2. *Ibid.*, Sept. 4, 1875. See also *The Toiler*, August 1, 1874.
3. *National Labor Tribune*, Feb. 12, 1876.
4. Commons, *op. cit.*, vol. II, pp. 167-70.
5. *National Labor Tribune*, Sept. 30, 1876; *Workingman's Advocate*, Oct. 13, 1876.
6. *Labor Standard*, Oct. 28, 1876.
7. *Ibid.*, Sept. 2, 30, Oct. 7, 28, Nov. 4, 1876. See also *National Labor Tribune*, Sept. 25, 1875, and *New York Tribune*, Jan. 11, Feb. 3, 1876.
8. *New York Tribune*, Nov. 13, 1876; *National Labor Tribune*, Dec. 23, 1876.
9. *National Labor Tribune*, Dec. 23, 1876.
10. *Scranton Republican*, July 30, Aug. 8, 1877. See also *Record Book of the Cook County, Illinois, Labor Party, 1876-1877, Mss.* Wisconsin State Historical Society.
11. *New York Tribune*, July 24, 1877; "To the Laboring Interests of the United States of America, August 1, 1877," leaflet in Rare Book Room, Library of Congress.
12. *New York Tribune*, Sept. 16, 1877.
13. *Ibid.*, August 15, 28, 1877.
14. *Ibid.*, August 13-15, 1877.
15. *Ibid.*, August 13, 1877.
16. *New York Times*, Oct. 28, 1877.
17. *Ibid.*
18. *New York Tribune*, Nov. 8, 1877.
19. *New York Times, New York Tribune*, Nov. 8-15, 1877; *Rochester Union and Advertiser*, Nov. 7, 1877.
20. Commons, *op. cit.*, vol. II, p. 244; *New York Tribune*, Feb. 25, 1878.
21. *New York Tribune*, Feb. 25, 1878.
22. *Ibid.*, May 31, 1878.
23. *Scranton Republican*, Feb. 11-20, 1878.
24. *New York Tribune*, July 23, 1878.
25. *Ibid.*, May 19, 1878.
26. *Ibid.*, July 18, 25, 1878.
27. Fred E. Haynes, *Third Party Move-*

ments Since the Civil War, Iowa City, 1916, pp. 125-29.
28. *Ibid.,* p. 127.
29. *Revelations: The Epistle of Nathan the Wise,* pamphlet, 1878.
30. *New York Tribune,* Nov. 7-10, 1877.
31. *Ibid.,* Oct. 24, 1878.
32. *Atlantic Monthly,* vol. XLI, November 1878, pp. 521-30.
33. *Labor Standard,* May 5, 1878.
34. Haynes, *op. cit.,* pp. 135-40; O. G. Libby, "A Study of the Greenback Movement, 1876-1884," *Wisconsin Academy of Sciences, Arts and Letters, Transactions,* vol. XII, 1899, p. 535.
35. H. C. Nixon, *The Populist Movement in Iowa,* Iowa City, 1926, p. 23.
36. Commons, ed., *Documentary History of American Industrial Society,* vol. IX, pp. 84-85; *Philadelphia North American,* June 1, 1870; Cale, *op. cit.,* Chapter X.
37. *Workingman's Advocate,* Feb. 12, 1870; *Detroit Daily Union,* May 14, 1869; W. C. Traphage to John Samuels, July 4, 1880, Samuels Papers, Wisconsin State Historical Society.
38. *Arbeiter-Union,* May 25, 1869.
39. McKee, *op. cit.,* p. 135.
40. Cross, *op. cit.,* pp. 88-97.
41. *Ibid.;* Ralph Kauer, "The Workingmen's Party of the United States," *Pacific Historical Review,* vol. XIII, Sept. 1944, pp. 280-81.
42. *Labor Standard,* June 2, 16, 30, 1878; *Records of the Socialist Labor Party, Newark, New Jersey Section,* May 3, 1878, Mss., Wisconsin State Historical Society.
43. Cross, *op. cit.,* pp. 98-103.
44. *Ibid.,* pp. 105-06.
45. J. C. Stedman and R A. Leonard, *The Workingmen's Party of California,* San Francisco, 1878, pp. 63-64.
46. Cross, *op. cit.,* pp. 112-14.
47. *Labor Standard,* July 14, 1877; *New York Arbeiterstimme,* Sept. 2, 1877.
48. Commons, *op. cit.,* vol. II, p. 277.
49. Edward B. Mittleman, "Chicago Labor in Politics, 1877-1896," *Journal of Political Economy,* vol. XXVIIII, May 1920, pp. 412-15; J. Ehmann to Phillip Van Patten, Cincinnati, April 8, 1880, *Socialist Labor Party Correspondence,* Wisconsin State Historical Society.
50. *Bulletin of the Social Labor Movement,* vol. I, no. 2, November 1879, p. 12.
51. Mittleman, *op. cit.,* pp. 415-17; Commons, *op. cit.,* vol. II, pp. 285-90; John Shinnan to Phillip Van Patten, Cincinnati, Aug. 3, 1880, Socialist Labor Party Correspondence, Wisconsin State Historical Society.
52. Henry David, *History of the Haymarket Affair,* New York, 1936, Chapter V; A. Sartorius Freehern von Waltershausen, *Der moderne Socialismus in den Vereinigten Staaten von Amerika,* Berlin, 1890, pp. 120-43.

CHAPTER XXV

1. Reprinted in *The Toiler,* no date.
2. *Report of the Committee of the Senate upon the Relations between Labor and Capital and Testimony Taken by the Committee,* 4 vols. Washington, 1885, vol. III, pp. 6, 28, 75, vol. I, p. 450; Kucszynski, *op. cit.,* pp. 81-8.
3. *Report of the Senate upon the Relations between Labor and Capital* ... vol. III, p. 452.
4. Henry David, *History of the Haymarket Affair,* p. 18.
5. Commons, *op. cit.,* vol. II, pp. 313-14.
6. *Bulletin of the Social Labor Party,* Sept. 1880, p. 1.
7. A. Sartorius Freehern von Waltershausen, *Die Nordamerickanischen Gewerkschaften unter dem Einfluss der fortschreitenden Productionstechnik,* Berlin, 1886, pp. 134-48; F. A. Sorge, "Die Arbeiterbewegung in den Vereinigten Staaten, 1877-1885," *Neue Zeit,* 1891-1892, vol. II, pp. 242 ff.
8. *Bulletin of the Social Labor Party,* Sept. 1880, p. 1; Lucien Sanial to Robert Howard, July 31, 1879, *Socialist Labor Party Papers, New York City and County Executive Committee, Minute Book, 1879,* Wisconsin State Historical Society.
9. Sorge in *Neue Zeit,* 1891-1892, vol. II, pp. 244-45; Pearce, *op. cit.,* pp. 18-19, 23-26; Peterson, *op. cit.,* p. 22; Wesley, *op. cit.,* p. 255. Ruth A. Allen, *The Great Southwest Strike,* Austin, Texas, 1942, pp. 24-25; McNeil, *op. cit.,* p. 168.
10. Cross, *op. cit.,* p. 142.
11. *Ibid.,* pp. 325-26; *Bulletin of the Social Labor Party,* Nov. 1879, p. 10; Waltershausen, *op. cit.,* pp. 139-41.
12. Ira Steward to F. A. Sorge, Wednesday, March 14, [no date], Ira Steward Papers, Wisconsin State Historical Society.
13. *Labor Standard,* Sept. 7, Oct. 12, 1878.
14. F. A. Sorge, in *Neue Zeit,* 1891-1892, vol. II, pp. 179, 246-48.

15. *Labor Standard*, March 24, July 21, 1878, Jan. 4, 1879.
16. *Ibid.*, May 5, 1878.
17. *Ibid.*, March 27, April 10, 1880.
18. *Ibid.*, May 12, 1878.
19. Commons, *op. cit.*, vol. II, p. 306.
20. *National Labor Tribune*, April 24, June 19, 1875.
21. Commons, *op. cit.*, vol. II, pp. 199-200; Wright, *op. cit.*, pp. 146-47.
22. Powderly, *The Path I Trod*, p. 48.
23. *New York Tribune*, August 17, 1878; David J. Saposs, "The Catholic Church and the Labor Movement," *Modern Monthly*, May 1933.
24. Powderly, *Thirty Years of Labor*, pp. 225-32, 238-39.
25. *Ibid.*, pp. 218, 238.
26. *Journal of United Labor*, August 13, 1887, p. 2470; Powderly, *Thirty Years of Labor*, p. 34; "Report of the Grand Master Workman," *Proceedings of the General Assembly*, 1879, p. 55.
27. "Constitution of the General Assembly," in *Proceedings of the General Assembly*, 1878, Article I, section 2, p. 29.
28. Ware, *op. cit.*, p. 63.
29. *Proceedings of the General Assembly*, 1882, p. 278.
30. R. D. Layton to John Samuel, July 7, 1882, John Samuel Papers, Wisconsin State Historical Society.
31. *Proceedings of the General Assembly*, 1880, pp. 247-48.
32. Powderly, *Thirty Years of Labor*, pp. 255-56.
33. *Report of the Senate Committee on Education and Labor*, vol. I, pp. 7-9.
34. Powderly, *Thirty Years of Labor*, pp. 143-44; Martin Irons, "My Experience in the Labor Movement," *"Lippincott's Monthly Magazine*, June, 1886, pp. 617-18.
35. Powderly, *Thirty Years of Labor*, p. 48.
36. *Proceedings of the General Assembly*, Jan. 1879, p. 55.
37. *Ibid.*, 1879, St. Louis, p. 69.
38. *Ibid.*, 1879, Chicago, p. 129.
39. *Journal of United Labor*, July 1883; Powderly in *Pittsburgh Times*, quoted in McNeil, *op. cit.*, p. 418.
40. *Proceedings of the General Assembly*, 1882, pp. 297-98; *Journal of United Labor*, July 1883, p. 520; *Proceedings of the General Assembly*, 1882, pp. 312, 334, 347, 352, 368.
41. Samuel Gompers, *Seventy Years of Life and Labor*, New York, 1925, vol. I, p. 87.
42. *Ibid.*, pp. 38, 85.

43. *Current History*, vol. XXI, Feb. 1925, p. 671; *Atlantic Monthly*, vol. CXXXV, 1925, p. 408.
44. Gompers, *Life*, vol. I, pp. 74-75; John R. Commons, "Karl Marx and Samuel Gompers," *Political Science Quarterly*, vol. XLI, June, 1926, pp. 281-86.
45. *Labor Standard*, April 7, 1877.
46. Gompers, *Life*, vol. I, p. 96; Rowland Hill Harvey, *Samuel Gompers*, Stanford University Press, 1935, p. 17.
47. *New York Tribune*, August 13, 1878.
48. *Ibid.*, April 27, 1878.
49. *Report of the Senate Committee on Education and Labor*, vol. I, p. 460.
50. Harvey, *op. cit.*, p. 19.
51. *Labor Standard*, Oct. 21, 28, Nov. 4, 11, 18, 25, Dec. 2, 9, 16, 23, 30, 1877; Jan. 6, 13, 1878.
52. *National Labor Tribune*, Nov. 6, 1875.
53. Gompers, *Life, vol. I*, pp. 165-71.
54. *Labor Standard*, May 12, 1877.
55. Gompers, *Life*, vol. I, p. 62.
56. *Cigar Makers Official Journal*, April 1887, p. 8.
57. A. Losovsky, *Marx and the Trade Unions*, New York, 1935, *passim*.
58. Ware, *op. cit.*, pp. 263-64.
59. Gompers, *Life*, vol. I, p. 200.
60. Reprinted in *Journal of United Labor*, April 15, 1881.
61. Ware, *op. cit.*, p. 41; Harvey, *op. cit.*, p. 41; *Proceedings of the American Federation of Labor, 1881-1888*, p. 6.
62. Alfred P. James, "The First Convention of the American Federation of Labor: A Study in contemporary local Newspapers as a Source," *Western Pennsylvania Magazine of History and Biography*, vol. VII, Jan. 1924, p. 41 *n*.
63. *Proceedings*, pp. 15-16.
64. *Ibid.*, p. 3.
65. James, *op. cit.*, pp. 44-45.
66. *Proceedings*, pp. 3-4.
67. *Ibid.*, p. 18.
68. *Ibid.*, pp. 19-20.
69. *Ibid.*, p. 20; James, *op. cit.*, p. 107*n*.
70. *Proceedings*, p. 12; James, *op. cit.*, pp. 216-17, 225-26.
71. *Proceedings*, p. 18.
72. *Ibid.*, p. 23.
73. *Proceedings*, p. 14.
74. *Ibid.*, p. 17.
75. *Journal of United Labor*, November-December, 1881, p. 166.
76. Frank K. Foster to H. A. Cole, Dec. 19, 1883, Samuel Gompers Letter-Books, *Mss.*, Memorial Room, A. F. of L Building, Washington, D. C.

BIOGRAPHICAL SKETCHES

ALLEN, SAMUEL CLASSON, Congregational minister; member of Congress; candidate for governor of Massachusetts on workingmen's ticket in 1833; rallied Workingmen's Party in Massachusetts behind Jackson's hard-money policy.

ANTHONY, SUSAN BROWNELL (1820-1906), fought for abolition of slavery, Negro suffrage, and woman's rights; leader in the woman's suffrage movement; delegate to National Labor Union in 1869.

ARMSTRONG, THOMAS J., editor of the *National Labor Tribune,* published in the 1870's in Pittsburgh; nominated for governor of Pennsylvania on the Greenback-Labor ticket in 1882.

ARTHUR, PETER M. (1831-1903), associated with the Brotherhood of Locomotive Engineers from its inception in 1863; elected Grand Chief of the Brotherhood in 1874 and held that office until his death.

BAGLEY, SARAH G., Lowell factory worker; school teacher; president of the Lowell Female Labor Reform Association formed in 1845; delegate to 1845 convention of the New England Workingmen's Association.

BANCROFT, GEORGE (1800-1891), American historian; elected to the state legislature of Massachusetts in 1830 by Workingmen's Party, but declined to serve; after election of 1832 threw in his lot with the workingmen's movement and led in attack upon the Second Bank of the United States; opposed slavery; Secretary of the Navy under Polk, and in 1848 United States Minister to Great Britain.

BRISBANE, ALBERT (1809-1890), son of prominent New York landowner; went to Europe in the late 1820's and came under the influence of Charles Fourier, the great French Utopian Socialist; published in 1840 *The Social Destiny of Man,* presenting Fourier's ideas and program, after which he founded the Association movement in the United States.

BROWNSON, ORESTES AUGUSTUS (1803-1871), born in Vermont; actively connected with the workingmen's movement from 1829 to 1840; disillusioned by defeat of Van Buren in 1840 and moved over into the conservative camp.

BRYANT, WILLIAM CULLEN (1794-1878), poet and democratic publisher; editor of the *New York Evening Post* for forty years; strong supporter of Jackson during the Bank War; vigorously fought against slavery.

BUCHANAN, JOSEPH RAY (1851-1924), western labor leader and editor; sought to bring about unity between the Knights of Labor and the American Federation of Labor.

BURRITT, ELIHU (1810-1879), blacksmith, abolitionist, and strong advocate of world organization for peace; organized at Brussels in 1848 the first international peace congress.

BUTLER, BENJAMIN F. (1818-1893), championed labor's rights and a leading advocate of the ten-hour day; general in the Union Army in the Civil War; elected to Congress as an independent Greenbacker in 1878; elected governor of Massachusetts in 1882; candidate of the Anti-Monopoly Party for President of the United States in 1884.

CAMERON, ANDREW CARR (1834-1890), printer, active in Typographical Union; edited *Workingman's Advocate* of Chicago from 1864 to 1880, and was known as the greatest labor editor of his time; for six years was chairman of the Platform Committee of the National Labor Union; delegate of the National Labor Union to the Convention of the International Workingmen's Association held in 1869 at Basle.

CARL, CONRAD, editor of New York *Arbeiter-Zeitung* established by the German sections of the International Workingmen's Association in the United States in February, 1873.

CARY, MATTHEW (1760-1839), a Philadelphia businessman; writer of numerous pamphlets exposing the dreadful conditions of the laboring classes and advocating reforms; champion of universal education and internal improvements.

CHANNING, WILLIAM H. (1780-1842), famous Unitarian preacher and pacifist; lectured on the elevation of the laboring classes; hated slavery but opposed the Civil War.

COLLINS, JOHN A. (1810-1879), disciple of Robert Owen; anti-slavery organizer; founded the Skaneateles (New York) community, an anti-slavery experiment, based on Owen's principles, with *The Communist* as its organ.

COMMERFORD, JOHN, prominent in trade union movement in 1830's; secretary of the National Trades' Union; president of the General Trades' Union of New York in 1835, and editor of its official organ, *The Union;* active in the Loco-Foco movement.

COOPER, PETER (1791-1883), manufacturer and inventor who founded Cooper Union "for the advancement of science and art" in New York in 1857; supported Greenback Party and ran for president on its ticket in 1876.

CUMMINS, SAMUEL P., active in labor movement of Massachusetts in the 1860's; leader of the Knights of St. Crispin, and played a prominent role in the National Labor Union.

DANA, CHARLES ANDERSON (1819-1897), managing editor, *New York Tribune;* in 1849 met Karl Marx in Europe and arranged for him to become its European correspondent; later editor-in-chief of *New York Sun.*

DANIELS, NEWELL, one of the founders of Knights of St. Crispin.

DAVIS, JOHN M., editor of the *National Labor Tribune* of Pittsburgh; Master Workman of District Assembly 3 of the Knights of Labor.

DAY, HORACE H., wealthy Brooklyn philanthropist who was active in the National Labor Union; advocated currency reform and producers' co-operatives.

DAY, J. G., Canadian-born carpenter; president of the Workingmen's Trade and Labor Union of San Francisco formed by Dennis Kearney in 1878.

DEVYR, THOMAS A., agrarian reformer in Ireland; joined George Henry Evans land reform movement in the U. S.; edited in New York the periodicals, the *National Reformer* and the *Anti-Renter.*

DORR, THOMAS W., leader of suffrage reform movement in Rhode Island; elected governor of Rhode Island in 1842; after defeat of movement to democratize the Constitution, Dorr was sentenced to life imprisonment in 1844; released in June, 1845; in 1854 the court judgment against him was annulled; died in 1855.

DOUAI, ADOLPH, born in Germany in 1819; active in German Revolution of 1848; emigrated to Texas in 1852 and established the *San Antonio Zeitung*, an anti-slavery paper; established in Boston a three-graded school with a kindergarten, the first kindergarten attempted in America; editor of *Die Arbeiter Union* until 1870, and in 1878 became co-editor of the Socialist *New Yorker Volkszeitung*, a position he held until 1888; together with Sorge played an important role in the Marxist organizations in the U. S.

DOUGLAS, DR. CHARLES, president of the first convention of the New England Association of Farmers, Mechanics and other Workingmen; helped found in 1831 the *New England Artisan*, a weekly labor paper; helped establish a General Trades' Union in Boston in January, 1834; strong advocate of public education, and criticized factory conditions in New England.

DOUGLASS, FREDERICK (1817-1895), escaped from slavery in 1837 and became active in the anti-slavery movement as a lecturer and writer; editor of *The North Star; Frederick Douglass' Paper; Douglass' Monthly* and *The New National Era;* fought for the Emancipation Proclamation and the use of Negro troops in the Union army; president of the National Colored Labor Union; Recorder of Deeds in Washington; Minister to Haiti; active in woman's rights movements.

EARLE, WILLIAM H., organizer and president of the Sovereigns of Industry, founded in 1874 at Springfield, Massachusetts.

ENGLISH, WILLIAM, journeyman shoemaker who was a Philadelphia labor leader in the 1830's; president of the Philadelphia Trades' Union in 1835 and 1836; leader of the Workingmen's Party of Philadelphia in 1829-1831; elected to the Pennsylvania Senate on the Democratic ticket in 1835.

EVANS, CHRIS, secretary of the miners' union; secretary of the Board of Arbitration and Conciliation established by the operators and miners' union in 1894.

EVANS, GEORGE HENRY (1805-1856), born in England; editor of the New York *Working Man's Advocate* in 1829; editor of the *Man,* published in New York; in 1841 began to expound his land reform views in *The Radical* and *Young America;* organized the National Reform Association and led in campaign for a homestead act.

FARQUAHR, JOHN M., born in Scotland, April 17, 1832; printer, editor, and publisher; president of the National Typographical Union for two terms, 1860-1862; enlisted in the Union Army as private and rose to the rank of major; elected to the Forty-Ninth Congress as a Republican.

FEHRENBATCH, JOHN, president of the Machinists' and Blacksmiths' Union; favored a national federation of trade unions; was elected in 1876 to the Ohio legislature, and two years later assumed a federal post.

FERRAL, JOHN, hand-loom weaver, prominent leader of the Philadelphia labor movement in the 1830's; leader of the general strike for the ten-hour day in Philadelphia in 1835; active later in the land reform movement.

FINCH, JOHN, printer, active in the organization of the New York Trades' Union in August, 1833; author of two pamphlets, dealing with the New York labor movement.

FINCHER, JONATHAN C., machinist, elected secretary of the national union of machinists and blacksmiths in November, 1860; editor of the union's official journal; in 1863 he founded his own paper, *Fincher's Trades' Review,* one of the finest labor journals in the country; between 1863 and 1871, he started four independent labor papers; opposed independent political action; retired from the labor movement in the 1870's.

FISK, THEOPHILUS, born in 1801; radical Jacksonian leader; co-editor of the *Boston Reformer,* formerly the *New England Artisan;* delegate to the National Trades' Union convention in 1835.

FITZPATRICK, P. F., president of the iron molders' union and first vice president of the American Federation of Labor.

FOSTER, FRANK K. (1854-1909), active in the International Typographical Union, the Knights of Labor, and during the formative years of the A. F. of L.; owned and published the Haverhill, Massachusetts, *Daily Laborer* and *Weekly Laborer.*

FORAN, MARTIN A., born in Susquehanna County, Pennsylvania in 1844; cooper, organized Coopers' International Union and became its president; favored a federation of national trade unions; entered politics and became a lawyer; elected city attorney of Cleveland in 1874 and to Congress in 1884; re-elected several times.

FORD, EBENEZER, carpenter, active in the Workingmen's Party of New York; elected to the New York Assembly by the party in 1829.

GARRISON, WILLIAM LLOYD (1805-1879), journeyman printer and famous abolitionist; editor of *The Liberator* from 1831 to 1865.

GIBSON, G. W., eight-hour champion; secretary of the National Labor Union.

GOMPERS, SAMUEL (1850-1924), born in England and apprenticed to a cigar maker; came to America with his family in 1863; joined cigar makers' union; with Adolph Strasser reorganized the Cigar Makers' International Union and became president of Local 144; active in organizing the Federation of Organized Trades and Labor Unions of the United States and Canada and the American Federation of Labor; held post as president of the American Federation of Labor with the exception of one year, 1894, from its inception in 1886 until his death in 1924.

GREELEY, HORACE (1811-1872), editor and political leader; began publication of the *New York Tribune* on April 10, 1841; advocated Fourierism and worked with Albert Brisbane; attacked Negro slavery; active in the Republican Party; president of the New York Printers' Union; ran for President of the United States in 1872 as candidate of the Liberal Republican Party.

GUNTON, GEORGE (1845-1919), textile worker and editor; associated with Ira Steward in eight-hour movement; organizer for the International Labor Union in Fall River from 1878 to 1880.

HARDING, WILLIAM, president of the Coachmakers' International Union; leader of the New York Trades' Assembly; one of the founders of the National Labor Union.

HINCHCLIFFE, JOHN, publisher of the *Weekly Miner,* established at Belleville, Illinois; active in the National Labor Union and the Greenback movement.

HOWARD, ROBERT, born in 1844; secretary of the Fall Rivers' Spinners' Association in 1878; elected to the State House of Representatives in 1880 and State Senate in 1885; treasurer from 1881 to 1885 of the Federation of Organized Trades and Labor Unions of the United States and Canada.

JARRETT, JOHN, born in England in 1843; vice president of the Sons of Vulcan in 1873; president of the Amalgamated Association of Iron and Steel Workers from 1879 to 1883.

JESSUP, WILLIAM J., president of the New York State Workingmen's Association; active in the National Labor Union.

KEARNEY, DENIS (1847-1907), formed Workingmen's Trade and Labor Union of San Francisco in 1877; president of the Workingmen's Party of California.

KENNADY, ALEXANDER M. (1829-1897), printer; president of the San Francisco Trades' Assembly; active in the eight-hour movement and in the National Labor Union.

KLINGE, KARL, Lassallean Socialist; editor of the Chicago *Vorbote* in 1874; active in political labor movement of Chicago in 1877.

KRIEGE, HERMAN, active in German-American labor movement from 1845 on; ardent advocate of land reform.

LAYTON, ROBERT D., elected secretary of the Knights of Labor in 1882.

LITCHMAN, CHARLES H. (1849-1902), National Secretary of the Knights of St. Crispin, and General Secretary of the Knights of Labor for fourteen years.

LUTHER, SETH (1817-1846), carpenter and early labor organizer; secretary of Boston General Trades' Union; published several pamphlets which were very valuable in the labor movement of the 1830's.

MCBRIDE, JOHN, born in 1854; president Ohio State Miner's Union; elected to Ohio legislature in 1883 and 1885; active in the American Federation of Labor and elected president for one term in 1894.

MCDONNELL, J. P., associated with Karl Marx and the First International after 1869; came to America where he joined the Workingmen's Party of the United States; editor of its official English organ, the New York *Labor Standard;* organized the New Jersey State Federation of Trades and Labor Unions in 1883 and was its chairman for fifteen years; died in 1906.

MCGUIRE, PETER J., born in 1852; influenced by German-American Socialists and joined the Lassallean movement; later advocated pure and simple trade unionism; organized English-speaking branch of the Socialist Labor Party in 1876; organized Brotherhood of Carpenters and Joiners in 1881; drafted call for the convention that set up the Federation of Organized Trades and Labor Unions of the United States and Canada and later active in the American Federation of Labor; known as father of Labor Day.

MCNEILL, GEORGE EDWIN (1837-1906), worked with Ira Steward in the eight-hour campaign and was president of the Boston Eight-Hour League for eight years; helped establish the Massachusetts Bureau of Labor Statistics in 1869 and held post of its chief deputy until 1874; president of the International Labor Union; active in the Knights of Labor and the American Federation of Labor; published a history of the American labor movement in 1887 entitled, *The Labor Movement: The Problem of Today.*

MING, ALEXANDER, SR., printer; candidate of the New York Workingmen's party ticket for Assembly in 1829; associate of Thomas Skidmore with whom he edited the *Friends of Equal Rights.*

MING, ALEXANDER, JR., printer; leader of the Loco Foco movement; nominated for mayor of New York by Loco Focos in 1836; active in unemployed demonstrations during panic of 1837.

MOORE, ELY (1798-1860), printer; first president of the New York Trades' Union; editor of the New York *National Trades' Union,* 1834-1836; chairman of the National Trades' Union; elected labor Congressman from New York in 1834; sat in Congress until 1839.

MOST, JOHANN (1846-1906), a Socialist while in Germany, later became an anarchist and emigrated to U. S. where he edited *Die Freiheit* and was active in the anarchist movement.

MULLANEY, KATE, president of the Troy Collar Workingmen's Association; appointed officer and organizer of the National Labor Union.

MYERS, ISAAC, Baltimore caulker who became the outstanding Negro labor leader of the post-Civil War era; president of the Colored Caulkers' Union of Baltimore and of the National Colored Labor Union.

NEALL, ISAAC J., first president of the National Molders' Union; enlisted in Union army at outbreak of Civil War; wounded; re-enlisted and became a captain; active in the Molders' Union after the Civil War.

OBERKLINE, FRED, leader of German-American workingmen of Cincinnati; headed delegation which interviewed Lincoln in 1860.

OWEN, ROBERT DALE (1801-1877), eldest son of Robert Owen, the great English Utopian Socialist; came to the United States in November, 1825, with his father to set up co-operative colony in New Harmony; published the *Free Enquirer* with Frances Wright; active in the New York Working Men's Party; served in Indiana legislature three terms (1836-1838), and in Congress (1843-1847); strongly anti-slavery; helped settle Oregon dispute with Great Britain; helped found the Smithsonian Institution.

PARSONS, ALBERT RICHARD (1848-1887), printer; joined labor movement in 1874 and active in the Workingmen's Party of the United States after 1876; member of the Knights of Labor in 1876; candidate on the Socialist ticket in Chicago during 1877-1879; one of the victims in the anti-labor attack following the Haymarket affair in Chicago, May 4, 1886; condemned to death in a framed-up trial and executed in 1887.

PHELPS, ALFRED W., Connecticut labor leader active in the formation of the National Labor Union.

PHILLIPS, THOMAS (1833-1916), born in England; came to America in 1852; active in organizing shoemakers into trade unions; started in Philadelphia the first co-operative association in America based on the Rochdale plan; active in the Knights of St. Crispin and the Knights of Labor; elected president in 1889 of the Boot and Shoe Workers' International Union.

PHILLIPS, WENDELL (1811-1884), prominent abolitionist, orator, and champion of labor reform; with the emancipation of the Negro slaves he turned his attention to the relations between labor and capital; advocated independent political action of labor; active in eight-hour movement in the 1860's.

POWDERLY, TERENCE V. (1849-1924), joined Machinists' and Blacksmiths' Union in 1870; secretary of the Dictrict Assembly of Knights of Labor and elected Grand Master Workman in 1879; served as Mayor of Scranton in 1878-1882; supported Republican Party and appointed in 1897 United States Commissioner General of Immigration.

RIPLEY, GEORGE (1802-1880), active in the Boston transcendentalist movement; president of Brook Farm, literary critic for thirty-one years of the New York Tribune.

ROBINSON, FREDERICK, radical democratic leader in Massachusetts during the Jacksonian era; member of Massachusetts legislature; left Democratic Party on slavery issue to support the Republicans.

RONEY, FRANK, born in 1841; active in National Labor Reform Party; socialist and active trade unionist on the Pacific coast; organized Seamen's Union in 1880; leader of the San Francisco Assembly of Trades and Labor Unions; played an important role in the American Federation of Labor.

ROOT, GENERAL ERASTUS (1773-1846), leader of movement in New York in the 1820's to liberalize the suffrage; lieutenant governor of New York; member of Congress and of the New York State legislature.

ROY, ANDREW, prominent in Ohio coal miners' union; state inspector of mines in Ohio.

SAMUEL, JOHN (1817-1909), took part in the labor movement of the 1830's in Philadelphia; organized glass workers in 1857; chief interest in the 1860's in the co-operative movement.

SANIAL, LUCIEN, a participant in the Paris Commune; active in Socialist Labor Party and, after the split, in the Socialist Party.

SCHILLING, GEORGE A., active in the Socialist Labor Party.

SCHILLING, ROBERT, second president of the Coopers' National Union; president of Industrial Congress in 1873; one of the founders of the International Labor Union in 1878; active in Knights of Labor.

SCHLEGEL, EDWARD, Lassallean Socialist; delegate to the National Labor Union Convention in 1866; advocated formation of independent labor party.

SHEDDEN, JOHN, active in Philadelphia labor circles from 1850 to 1870; member of Philadelphia section of the First International.

SIMPSON, STEPHEN (1789-1854), note clerk in second Bank of the United States and cashier of Girard's Bank in Philadelphia; fought in Battle of New Orleans under Jackson; candidate of the Workingmen's Party of Philadelphia and the Federal Party for Congress in 1830; author of The Working Man's Manual: A New Theory of Political Economy on the Principle of Production the Source of Wealth, published in Philadelphia in 1831; at first opposed the Bank of the United States, but in an Appendix to his Manual he defended the Bank and lost his influence among the workingmen whom he had once led; in 1831 he assumed the editorship of the conservative Pennsylvania Whig.

SINEY, JOHN, outstanding figure in the early history of the coal miners' union; founded the Workingmen's Benevolent Association of Schuylkill County (a miner's organization); organized and led the Miners' National Association formed in 1873; died in 1880.

SKIDMORE, THOMAS, machinist, author of *The Rights of Man to Property*, published in 1829; advocated land reform; active in the formation of the New York Workingmen's Party in 1829; candidate of the New York Workingmen's Party for Assembly in 1829.

SLAMM, LEVI D., leader of the Journeymen Locksmiths' Union of New York during the 1830's; editor in the 1840's of the New York *Plebian*.

SORGE, FREDERICK ADOLPH (1828-1906), born in Saxony; participated in Revolution of 1848 in Germany; came to America in 1852; joined the New York Communist Club in 1858; actively corresponded with Marx and Engels; leader of the First International in America from 1869 to 1876; active in formation of the Socialist Labor Party; helped organize the International Labor Union; wrote a series of articles from 1891 to 1895 for *Neue Zeit* in Germany on the labor movement in the United States.

SOVEREIGN, JAMES R., Iowa editor who supplanted Powderly as Grand Master Workman of the Knights of Labor in 1894.

SPEYER, J. G., member of the American section of the First International; active in reorganizing the Trades and Labor Council of New York in 1876.

STANTON, ELIZABETH CADY (1815-1902), active in abolition and temperance movements; leader of woman's rights movement and one of the founders of the first Woman's Rights Convention held in Seneca Falls in 1848; delegate to the 1868 convention of the National Labor Union.

STEPHENS, URIAH SMITH (1821-1882), tailor, organized the Garment Cutters' Association of Philadelphia in 1862; in 1869 organized the Knights of Labor; Grand Master Workman until 1879.

STEWARD, IRA (1831-1883), machinist, delegate to the convention of the International Union of Machinists and Blacksmiths in 1863 where secured passage of resolution demanding the eight-hour day through legislation; thereafter labored indefatigably for the eight-hour day; president of the Boston Eight Hour League and the National Ten Hour League.

STRASSER, ADOLPH, national secretary in 1874 of the Social Democratic Party of North America, a Lassallean organization; president in 1877 of the Cigar Makers' International Union; active in formation of American Federation of Labor.

SWINTON, JOHN (1829-1901), managing editor of the *New York Times* during the Civil War; became interested in labor movement and nominated in 1874 for mayor of New York by the Industrial Political Party; met Karl Marx in Europe in 1880; published in 1883-1887 a weekly labor paper entitled, *John Swinton's Paper;* remained a champion of labor until his death.

SYLVIS, WILLIAM H. (1828-1869), member Molders' Union in 1855; treasurer of the National Molders' Union in 1859; served in the Union Army during the Civil War; president of the National Molders' Union; as outstanding labor organizer influenced the entire labor movement during the Civil War and post-Civil War era; active in founding the National Labor Union, and its president in 1868; strong advocate of independent political action for labor, co-operatives, international labor solidarity, woman's rights, etc.

TOWNSEND, ROBERT, JR., leader of the New York House Carpenters' Union during the 1830's.

TREVELLICK, RICHARD F. (1830-1895), president of the International Union of Ship Carpenters and Caulkers in 1865; president of the Detroit Trades' Assembly; president of the National Labor Union in 1869, 1871 and 1872; organized about fifty unions of laborers; helped to form the Greenback Party and active in movements for currency reform.

TROUP, ALEXANDER H., treasurer of the National Typographical Union; represented the Boston Workingmen's Assembly at the founding of the National Labor Union.

VAN PATTEN, PHILLIP, national secretary of the Workingmen's Party of the United States formed in 1876; strongly sympathized with the Lassallean Socialists; elected national secretary of the Socialist Labor Party in 1879.

BIOGRAPHICAL SKETCHES 567

WEAVER, JAMES BAIRD (1833-1912), editor of the *Iowa Tribune;* elected to the forty-sixth Congress; candidate of National Greenback-Labor Party for President in 1880 and received about 350,000 votes; later elected to Congress and active in the Populist movement.

WEITLING, WILHELM, born in Germany; came to America in 1847; and in 1850 began publication in New York of *Republik der Arbeiter* which went out of existence in 1855; leading figure in the German-American labor movement during the years 1850-1851.

WEST, WILLIAM, corresponding secretary of the New Democracy, or Political Commonwealth, founded in 1869, and its delegate to the National Labor Union; advocate of the referendum and voluntary socialism as the true method of social reform.

WEYDEMEYER, JOSEPH (1818-1866), artillery officer in Prussian Army; met Marx and Engels in 1846; came to the United States in 1851; began publication in 1852 of *Die Revolution* and later *Die Reform;* became outstanding leader of German-American labor movement; at outbreak of the Civil War enlisted as a captain in the Union Army and was retired from the army with the rank of brigadier-general; edited *Die Neue Zeit* in St. Louis after the war; regarded as pioneer American Marxist.

WEYDEMEYER, OTTO, son of Joseph Weydemeyer; continued the work of his father; after 1876 occupied a leading position in the Socialist Labor Party and on the Central Committee of the International Labor Union; in 1877 completed the first English translation of a popular edition of the first volume of Marx's *Capital.*

WHALEY, J. C. C., president of the Washington Trades' Assembly; active in the formation of the National Labor Union and first president of the organization.

WILKES, GEORGE (1817-1885), worked on New York *Subterranean;* founded the *Police Gazette* and Wilkes' *Spirit of the Times;* joined the communist movement; supported the Paris Commune and the First International.

WINDT, JOHN, journeyman printer and leader of the printers' union in New York; active in Loco-Foco and land reform movements; played a prominent part in the unemployed demonstrations during the panic of 1837; secretary of the National Reform Association; delegate to the Industrial Congresses.

WOODHULL, VICTORIA CLAFLIN (1838-1927), advocate of woman suffrage and "social freedom"; leader of section No. 12 of the American sections of the International Workingmen's Association; with her sister Tennessee Claflin began publishing in 1870 *Woodhull and Claflin's Weekly;* nominated in 1872 for the Presidency of the United States by the Equal Rights Party.

WOLLSTONECRAFT, MARY (1759-1797), English writer and feminist; literary pioneer of the emancipation of women; published in 1792 *A Vindication of the Rights of Woman,* which was widely reprinted in the United States.

WRIGHT, CARROLL DAVIDSON (1840-1909), leading social economist; chief of the Massachusetts Bureau of Statistics of Labor and for twenty years Commissioner of the United States Bureau of Labor since its inception in 1885.

WRIGHT, FRANCES (1795-1852), born in Scotland; published a book entitled, *Views of Society and Manners in America;* active in farm colonization and education of Negroes in Tennessee; editor of the New Harmony *Gazette;* with Robert Dale Owen edited the *Free Enquirer* in New York; advocated woman's rights, anti-slavery, labor reform, public education.

WRIGHT, JAMES L. (1816-1893), member of the Tailors' Benevolent Society of Philadelphia in 1837; one of the original founders of the Knights of Labor; a leading member of the Knights of Labor for over two decades.

ERRATA

P. 29, 3rd para., first line, 1676 not 1646.
P. 53, 5th para., Samuel Slater came to America in 1789 not 1798.
P. 20, line 6 should read, "hot lard" instead of "hot lead."
P. 21, 4th para., lines 6 and 7, should read, "near the Stono river."
P. 22, 1st para., lines 9 and 10, should read, "there has been the most exemplary punishment inflicted. . . ."
P. 40, 2nd para., line 7, should read, March 5, 1770.
P. 51, 4th para., line 4, should read, "the overwhelming pressure."
P. 58, 3rd para., line 1, should read, "This remarkable development was accelerated by the Civil War."
P. 64, last two lines should read, "more commensurate with their importance in society."
P. 67, 2nd line, quotation marks should be placed after "night."
P. 78, 3rd para., line 2 should read, "workers could elevate themselves."
P. 176, line 3, quotation marks should be placed before the first word in line.
P. 253, last para., line 6, should read, W. H. Siebert.
P. 256, 3rd para., next to last line, should read, thirty-seven men were executed. Add also: "Four white men, allies of the Negroes, were involved in the plot."
P. 257, 2nd para., next to last line should read, 19 were executed (16 slaves and three free Negroes). The last line should read, "and over 100 Negroes were killed. The exact number is still not known."
P. 257, 3rd para., line 7, should read, "Even before the Turner revolt the legislatures tightened the laws dealing with Negro slaves, and now they still further tightened the laws against. . . ."
P. 259, footnote, first and second lines, eliminate "on an extensive scale."
P. 265, line 2 should read, "It is this great upbearing of our masses."
P. 279, 3rd para., line 3 should read, "was indifferent."
P. 279, 4th para., last line should read, "had already become in the fields of the South."
P. 280, line 2 should read, "logic of many slave owners."
P. 317, 4th para., line 10, eliminate "white" before crew. (The officers were white, the crew was all Negro.) Line 11: Smalls was not disguised, though in physical build he is said to have resembled the ship's master.
P. 318, 4th para., add after third sentence, "Thirty-seven thousand Negroes were killed in action."
P. 318, 2nd para., line 6 should read, "Union navy."
P. 390, 3rd para., eliminate second sentence. (The Black Codes were wiped out by the state legislatures and by the first Congressional Civil Rights Act of 1866.)
P. 390, 4th para., line 3, substitute, "Many of the delegates" for "Most of the delegates."
P. 441, 3rd para., line 7, should read, "help the unions engaged in strikes."
P. 414, footnote, 2nd para., line 3 should read, "of German Workers."
P. 449, 4th para., line 6 should read, *Verbote* not *Vorbote*.
P. 475, 2nd para., line 5 should read, *National Labor Tribune*.
P. 527, transfer notes 2 to 3 in Chap. III and notes 3 to 2.
P. 529 note 15 Chap. IV should read, 61–62 instead of 6.
P. 535 note 15 Chap. VIII, New York *Evening Journal* Feb. 25, 1830 instead of Dec. 31, 1829.
P. 538 note 57 Chap. X add, "Lenin paraphrasing Marx's statement."
P. 542, note 4 should read, New York, 1835.
P. 542, note 16 should read, W. H. Siebert.
P. 547, note 64 reference to Buckmaster is to page 142 not page 642.
P. 550, note 40, should read, Grossman not Grosman.

Abolitionists, attitude towards labor movement, 270-71, 394
Adams, John Quincy, 98, 173
Adams, Samuel, 34, 35
Address to the Workingmen of New England, 106-07
Agrarianism, 135
Alien Act, 88-89
Allen, Samuel C., 146-47
Amalgamated Society, New York, 232
American Emigrant Company, 327, 410
American Federation of Labor, founding convention, 519-24
American Labor Union, 231-33
American Miners' Association, 228
American Revolution, causes of, 32-34; labor and, 32 ff., 47
Ammon, R. H., 467
Anarchists, 495-96
Ancient Order of Hibernians, 460
Anthony, Susan B., 385-87
Applegarth, R., 410-11
Apprenticeship, 20, 73-74
Articles of Confederation, 48
Associationism. *See* Fourierism
Attucks, Crispus, 40

Bacon's Rebellion, 29
Bagley, Sarah, 198-99, 271
Bancroft, George, 159
Bank of the United States, and crisis of 1834, 147-48; and Jackson, 144 ff.; labor's opposition to, 145-50; trade unions in struggle against, 148
Bank notes, labor's opposition to payment of wages in, 125
Banks, labor's opposition to, 124-25, 166
Bates, John, 227
Battle of Lexington and Concord, 37, 40-41

Beaumont, Ralph, 481, 483
Benevolent societies, 26-27
Biddle, Nicholas, 145, 146, 147
Bill of Rights, labor demands, 84
Bimba, Anthony, 463-64
Black Codes, 390-91
Blacklist, 101, 211, 353
Blanc, Louis, 179
Boston circular, for ten-hour day, 116
Boston massacre, 40
Bovay, Alvan E., 206, 282
Boycott, 111, 112, 356, 373
Breadwinners' League, New York, 479, 48
Briggs, Sam, 232-33
Brisbane, Albert, 174, 175, 176, 177, 178, 183, 272
Brisbane, Arthur, 174
Brook Farm, 177, 206, 207
Brown, John, 285, 289
Brownson, Orestes A., 162-63
Bryant, William Cullen, 155
Buchanan, James, 288, 297
Buchanan, Joseph R., 496
Burr, Aaron, 83
Burritt, Elihu, 200-01, 275-76, 305
Butler, Benjamin F., 214, 328-29, 444-45, 486

Cameron, Andrew C., 346, 351, 362, 396, 409, 412-13, 423, 429, 431, 489
Carey, Matthew, 97-100
Carl, Conrad, 413, 512
Catholic church, and Knights of Labor, 505; and slavery question, 269-70
Central Committee of the United Trades, New York, 228-29
Central Workingmen's Committee, Philadelphia, 238-39
Channing, William E., 177, 201

Chartered monopolies, labor's opposition to, 124
Chartists, 228, 418
Child labor, 65-66, 111
Chinese immigration, 425, 426, 428, 488-93
Church and state, labor demands separation of, 126
City employees, strike of, 117-18
City central labor unions, in 1820's and 1830's, 102-04, 112-13; in 1850's, 235; during Civil War, 355-57; in 1880's, 499-500
Civil War, attempts to form national labor federation during, 359-63; corruption during, 325-26; decline of trade unions during early stage of, 338; employers' offensive during, 352-55, 359-60; English workers during, 310-17; formation of national trade unions during, 344-48; industrial expansion on eve of, 55, 191; industrial growth during, 58 ff.; labor press during, 333-34; labor supports, 306-10; movement for eight-hour day during, 363-69; revival of trade unions during, 338 ff.; strikes during, 339-40; women workers during, 382
Claflin, Tennessee, 415-16
Clay, Henry, 139, 144, 146
Closed shop, 75
Coal and iron police, 354
Coffin handbill, 156
Collective bargaining, and early trade unions, 74-75; during 1850's, 223-24
Commerford, John, 130, 151, 169
Committee of Fifty, New York, 130
Committee of Fifty-One, New York, 37
Committee of Mechanics, New York, 37, 42
Commons, John R., 27, 234, 516
Common Sense, influence of, 41-42
Commonwealth v. Hunt, 163-64
Communist Clubs, 233, 308, 310, 414
Communist Manifesto, The, 435
Communists, in ante-bellum South, 264; in labor movement of the 'fifties, 230-34; in post-Civil War labor movement, 413-17; in struggle over slavery, 279, 282, 289-90. See also Marxists, Socialists
Conscription Act, 321-22, 325
Congress, defense of trade unions in, 152-53; election of trade union leaders to, 151
Conspiracy cases, in 1820's and 1830's, 154-56; and early trade unions, 78-81; origin of, 78; relation of Jeffersonians and Federalists to, 79; during strike of 1875, 459-60
Consumers' Co-operatives. See Co-operatives, consumers'
Continental Congress, 41-42
Contract Labor Law, 327

Convict labor, 125
Cook-Guyon faction, 138-39
Cooper, Peter, 478
Co-operatives, consumers, 181-83
Co-operative, producers, in 1840's, 178-81; and Knights of Labor, 436; and National Labor Union, 373; in post-Civil War period, 417-19
Copperheads, labor and, 321-37; propaganda directed towards labor, 311-12, 322-25, 329
Corporation, rise of, 56
Corruption, during Civil War, 325-26
Cost of living, during Civil War, 326; during crisis of 1837, 161; in 1790's, 66; in 1830's, 107; in 1850's, 219-20. See also Labor conditions, Wages
Crises, explanation for, 62-63; labor's answer to, 63; of 1819-1822, 97; of 1829, 98; of 1834, 147-48; of 1837, 161-62, 167-68; of 1854, 222; of 1857, 222, 237-40; of 1873, 439 ff.
Crittenden Compromise, labor supports, 299-300, 302-03
Cummings, Samuel P., 428
Currency reforms, during crisis of 1873, 476 ff.; and decline of National Labor Union, 429-30; and eight-hour advocates, 426-27

Daughters of Liberty, 36
Day, Horace H., 399, 412, 428, 477
DeBow, J. D. B., 251, 258
Democracy, effect of American Revolution on, 46-47; extension of, 95-96; struggles for, in Colonial America, 28-31
Democratic Party, labor's role in, during 1830's, 150 ff.; opposes nativist movement, 268; split in, during 1830's, 146, 154-66
Democratic-Republican Party, 87-89
Democratic-Republican Societies, 85-87
Democratic-Republican Workingmen's Association, New York, on draft riots, 323
Democratic Working Men's General Committee, New York, 151
Deutsches Haus conference, 289-90
Devyr, Thomas, 206, 274
Die Reform, 230
Die Revolution, 230
Dorr's Rebellion, 160-61
Douai, Adolph, 264, 290, 410, 452, 487, 489, 502-03
Douglas, Dr. Charles, 105, 159
Douglas, Stephen A., 295, 310
Douglass, Frederick, 271, 318, 401, 407
Draft riots, 321-24
Dred Scott decision, 277, 288

Education, labor demands public, 86, 123, 216-17, 247; state guardianship system, 137-38

Eight-hour day, law passed by Congress for, 377-78; movement for, 363-69, 381-82; and National Labor Union, 371, 374, 377-82; state laws for, 379-81

Eight-hour laws, 377-81

Eight-hour leagues, 367-68, 371, 426

Election, of 1734, 30; of 1800, 89-90; of 1808, 93; of 1828, 144; of 1832, 146; of 1834, 150-51; of 1835, 154; of 1840, 163; of 1852, 215; of 1856, 286-88; of 1860, 293-96; of 1864, 335-36; of 1869, 425; of 1870, 425; of 1871, 426; of 1872, 428-29; of 1876, 478-79; of 1877, 482, 493; of 1878, 488, 494

Emancipation Proclamation, 310-12, 315-16

Embargo, effect on manufacturing, 50; labor and the, 91-92

Emerson, Ralph Waldo, 177

Employers' offensive, during Civil War, 352-55, 359-60; during crisis of 1873, 439-40, 454-74; and early trade unions, 77 ff.

Engels, Frederick, 51-52, 228, 230, 316, 414, 435, 450, 516-17

England, economic distress in, during American Civil War, 313-14; labor conditions in, during 16th century, 14 ff.

English, William, 159, 160

English workers, demand Emancipation Proclamation, 315; and labor movement of the 'fifties, 227; role of, in Civil War, 310-17

Equal pay, 243, 384, 385, 388, 441

"Equal Rights Democracy," 153

Equal Rights Party, 157-59, 160-62, 165

Evans, George Henry, 130, 133, 141, 148-49, 151, 183-88, 206, 228, 234, 273, 275, 277, 296, 326

Evarts, William M., 284, 378

Factory system, rise of, before Civil War, 53 ff.

Factory workers, composition of, 215; conditions during 1820's and 1830's, 100-01; conditions in post-revolutionary America, 65-66; co-operation between skilled mechanics and, 111; formation of unions among, 192 ff.; strikes of, 108-10

Farmers, unity with labor, 104, 134, 475-88

Farquahr, John M., 309

Federal Constitution, effect of, on industry, 49; labor supports ratification of, 83-84

Federalists, and conspiracy cases, 79; on democracy, 84; denounce Irish, 88; oppose labor, 79

Federation of Organized Trades and Labor Unions of the United States and Canada, founding convention, 519-24

Female Labor Reform Associations, 196-99, 211-12

Ferral, John, 117, 160, 187

Fincher, Jonathan, 300, 338, 341, 344, 345, 350-51, 352, 362, 371

Fincher's Trades' Review, 350-51

First International. See International Workingmen's Association

Fisk, Theophilus, 159

Foran, Martin A., 431

Ford, Ebenezer, 130, 134-35, 151

Fourier, Charles, 170-72

Fourierism, 171-72, 174-78

Freedman's Bureau, 390

Free labor, 22-24

Fremont, John C., 286, 311, 435

French Revolution, of 1789, 85-86; of 1830, 107; of 1848, 179

Fugitive slaves, 253-54

Fuller, Margaret, 177

Gadsden, Christopher, 34, 41

Gage, Thomas, 36, 37, 40

Garrison, William Lloyd, 270, 271

General strike, for ten-hour day, 115-18, 202, 209

General Trades' Union of New York, 112-13, 151, 156, 165, 169

German-Americans, in election of 1860, 294-96; in labor movement of the 'fifties, 228-34; in secession crisis, 301, 305; in struggle against slavery, 278-79, 281-82, 289-90

German General Working Men's Union, 414

German Workingmen's Society, Cincinnati, 301

Gilchrist, Robert, 361

Gilpin, Henry D., 161-62

Gompers, Samuel, 440, 497, 512-18, 520, 521, 523, 524

Gouge, William M., 103-04

Gowen, Franklin B., 456-57, 460, 461

Greeley, Horace, 174-75, 180, 220, 265, 272, 374, 428-29

Greenbacks. See Currency Reform

Greenback-Labor Party, 479-88

Greenback Party, 476-88

Guilds in Colonial America, 26

Gunton, George, 501, 503

Hamilton, Alexander, 49, 84, 91

Harding, William, 343-44, 371

Hastings-Folger Bill, 357-59

Hawthorne, Nathaniel, 177, 178

Hayes, John W., 510

Haywood, William D., 462

Helper, Hinton Rowan, 295

Hewitt, S. C., 204-05

Hinchcliffe, John, 349, 350, 375, 377, 477
Homestead Act, 393
Hume, R. W., 386-87, 388

Immigration, during 1840's and 1850's, 224-25; and labor's attitude towards, 225-26, 425, 426, 428, 488-93
Imprisonment for debt, 124
Independent political action, in 1820's and 1830's, 121 ff.; in 1873-78, 475-96; and Lassalleans, 493-95; and National Labor Union, 423-29; in post-revolutionary America, 83
Indians, as labor supply, 13
Industrial Brotherhood, 441
Industrial Congress, 234-35, 278-79, 282, 441, 457
Industry, concentration of, 168; on eve of Civil War, 191; growth during War of 1812, 50-51; obstacles to growth of, 48 ff.; opposition to, in ante-bellum South, 263-65; use of slaves in, 259-61
International Industrial Assembly of North America, 361-63
International labor unity, during American Revolution, 36-37; in 1830's, 107-08, 149; in 1840's, 207; in 1850's, 233; during Civil War, 310-17; in post-Civil War period, 409-17
International Labor Union, 500-04
Indentured servants, conditions of, 17-18, 19-21; effect of American Revolution on system, 46; in Revolutionary army, 43
International Workingmen's Association, American sections of, 413-17; during Civil War, 317, 336; during crisis of 1873, 445-48; dissolution of, 451-52; and National Colored Labor Union, 405; and National Labor Union, 374, 411-13
Ireland, labor supports independence in, 522-23; Sons of Liberty in, 36
Irish workers, in ante-bellum South, 250; conditions of, 99; in election of 1860, 295; Federalists denounce, 88; and labor movement of the 'fifties, 226; and slavery question, 269-70
Iron industry, 55-56

Jackson, Andrew, 95, 142, 143-44, 145-46, 147, 148, 149, 150, 160, 166
Jacksonian democracy, labor and, 143-66
Jaques, Moses, 158
Jarrett, John, 519-20, 522
Jay, John, 66, 84
Jefferson, Thomas, 17, 42, 49, 89, 96
Jeffersonian democracy, labor's desire to return to, 176; sources of, 82-85
Jeffersonians, attitude towards industry, 49;

and conspiracy cases, 79, 90; defend labor, 70
Jessup, William J., 400, 410-11, 430
Johnson, Andrew, 377, 390, 391, 392, 393
Johnson, Richard M., 144, 158
July Fourth, 47
Junio, John J., 481, 485

Kansas-Nebraska Act, labor opposes, 279, 281-82
Kearney, Denis, 490-92
Kellogg, Edward, 421-22, 426
Kennady, Alexander M., 379, 381
Knights of Industry, 518
Knights of Labor, birth of, 433-38; and Catholic church, 505; constitution of, 506-09; and co-operatives, 436; early structure, 437-38; education in, 436; and Greenback Party, 477, 480, 484; growth of, 438, 504-05, 509-10; membership in, 510; nationalization, 505-08; and Negro workers, 510-11; purposes of, 435-37; rituals of, 434-35, 504; and strikes, 507-09; and trade unions, 511-12
Know-Nothing Party, 225, 283
Kriege, Herman, 228, 278
Ku Klux Klan, 478

Labor conditions, in Colonial America, 19-21, 24-26; during Civil War, 341; during crisis of 1873, 442-45; in 1820's and 1830's, 97-101; in 1840's and 1850's, 219-20; in 1880's, 497-98; in Europe, 14 ff.; in post-revolutionary America, 65-68
Labor exchange bank, 229
Labor legislation, 424-25. See also Eight-hour laws, Independent political action, Political action, Ten-hour laws
Labor organizers, 204-05, 240, 346-48, 357, 376
Labor parties. See Independent Political Action
Labor press, in 1790's, 86-87; in 1820's and 1830's, 103, 112-13, 122; in 1840's, 192-96; during Civil War, 349-52; endorsed by National Labor Union, 373; reports activities of European labor movement, 409-10; role of, during Civil War, 333-34
Labor Reform Association, 367
Labor Reform Party, Massachusetts, 425-26
Labor solidarity, 36, 76-77, 81, 435-36, 502-03, 510-11
Labor songs, 82, 94-95, 110, 150, 187, 191, 241, 344, 365, 379, 458, 459, 460
Labor Standard, 453
Labor's Wrongs and Labor's Remedy, 176
Land Reform, 183-88, 247, 273
Land Reformers, and slavery question, 273
Lassalle, Ferdinand, 414, 420

Lassalleans, 414, 420, 429, 448-49, 493-94
Lawrence, Cornelius, 150, 154
Laurrell, Ferdinand, 512, 513, 515, 516
Layton, Richard D., 508, 510
League of Universal Brotherhood, 305
Leggett, William, 145, 153, 267
Lenin, V. I., 414
Libraries, public, 115
Liberal Republican Party, 428-29
Lincoln, Abraham, 64, 291-96, 297, 301, 310, 312, 316, 320, 324, 331-33, 335-36, 354, 435
Livingston, Edward, 88, 97
Loco-Focos, advocate separation of state and bank, 161-62; during crisis of 1837, 161-62; in Dorr's Rebellion, 160-61; lead labor movement, 157, 160-66; in New York, 153-59; rise of, 153 ff.; spread of, 159-61
Long Strike of 1875, 455-60
L'Ouverture, Toussaint, 255
Lowell Female Labor Reform Association, 196-99, 211-12
Luther, Seth, 105-07, 111, 116, 159

Machinery, introduction of, 54, 59, 168-69; labor's attitude towards, 169-70, 340, 345
Machinists' and Blacksmiths' National Union, 240
Madison, James, 85, 93
Man, The, 148-49
Marx, Karl, 58, 60, 228, 230, 275, 279, 310, 312, 313, 316, 336, 367-68, 369, 374, 385, 409, 411, 412, 414, 429, 435, 516-17
Marxists' attitude towards trade unions, 516-17; conflict with Lassalleans, 448-49, 493-94; and independent political action, 493-94; and International Labor Union, 501-04; during strike of 1875, 457-58. See also Communists, Socialists
Massachusetts Amendment, 289-90, 291
Master and Servant Acts, 15
McCormick, Cyrus H., 324
Mechanics' Association, Fall River, 203-04; Georgia, 263; Lynn, 24
Mechanics' Free Press, 103, 128
Mechanics' liens, 124
Mechanics' Society, New York, 83
Mechanics' Union of Trade Associations, 102-04, 127, 165
Merchant capitalist, 67-68
Mexican War, 278
Militia system, 123, 467-68, 473-74
Miners' Union, Illinois, 63
Ming, Alexander, Jr., 151
Missouri Compromise, repeal of, 282
Molly Maguires, 460-63, 505
Monetary reform, 420-23

Monopoly, 56-57, 60-62, 124, 247
Monroe, James, 173
Moore, Ely, 151-53, 268
Most, Johann, 496
Moyer, Charles, 462
Mullaney, Kate, 385
Mutual Aid Societies, 69
Myers, Isaac, 398, 399-400, 404, 405, 408
McClellan, George B., 312, 315, 336
McDonnell, J. P., 450, 453, 503
McGuire, Peter J., 452-53, 499
McNeill, George E., 276, 426, 502, 503
McParlan, James, 461-63

National Colored Labor Union, 403-07
National Greenback-Labor Party. See Greenback-Labor Party
National Laborer, 155-60
National Labor Federation, attempts to form, during Civil War, 359-63, 370 ff.; in 1830's, 114-15. See also Federation of Organized Trades and Labor Unions of the United States and Canada, International Industrial Assembly of North America, International Labor Union, Knights of Labor, National Labor Union, National Trades' Union
National Labor League of America, 506
National Labor Party, 373, 406, 423-29, 489
National Labor Reform Party, 489
National Labor Union, Constitution of, 376; and co-operatives, 373, 417-19; decline of, 429-31; and eight-hour day, 371, 374, 377-82; First Congress, 371-75; founding of, 370-71; and International Workingmen's Association, 374, 411-13; membership in, 377; and monetary reform, 420-23; and Negroes, 375, 396-97; and political action, 372-76, 423-29; and Reconstruction, 375; Second Congress, 375-76· significance of, 431-32; and strikes, 374-75; Third Congress, 377; and woman's rights, 382-88; and women workers, 374, 382-88
National Molders' Union, 236-37, 240
National Reform Association, 228
National Trade Unions, in 1830's, 113-14; in 1850's, 235-37; during Civil War, 344-48; revival of, after crisis of 1873, 498
National Trades' Union, 114-15, 167
National Typographical Union, 235-36
Naturalization Act, 88
Neall, Isaac J., 310
Negroes, during American Revolution, 40; attitude of white workers towards, 395-96, 398-402; conditions of, during Reconstruction, 389-90, 402; enslavement of, 18-20; and Federation of Organized Trades and Labor Unions, 520; and In-

Negroes (Cont'd)
ternational Labor Union, 502-03; and
Knights of Labor, 510-11; labor conventions held by, 402-03; and National Labor
Union, 375, 389, 396-97, 399-404, 405-
06; in Revolutionary army, 43; strikes
conducted by, 27, 397-98, 465-66, 472;
struggles against slavery, 252-58; and
trade unions, 398 ff., 499 ff.; treatment
of, in ante-bellum South, 250-51; use of,
in industry in ante-bellum South, 259-
61; during War of 1812, 95
New Amsterdam, 13
New England Association of Farmers, Mechanics and other Workingmen, 104 ff.,
146, 165
New England Industrial League, 214
New England, labor parties in, 140
New England Workingmen's Association,
199, 202-07, 209, 211-12, 278
New Jersey, political action in, 216-17
New Orleans, trade unions in, 101
"New Unionism," 512-18
New York, labor party in, 130-39; political
struggles in, during 1830's, 150 ff.; work-
ingmen's convention in, 138-39
New York Society of Journeymen Ship-
wrights, 71
New York Typographical Society, 71, 72,
73, 74, 75, 93, 94
Nine-hour day, 503-04
Non-importation agreements, 35, 38
Notes on Virginia, 49

Owen, Robert, 130, 170-74, 183
Owen, Robert Dale, 130, 131-32, 136-39,
141, 173, 272
Owenism, 170-74, 418

Pacifism, 305
Paine, Thomas, 41, 45, 87
Paper money, in colonial America, 31
Parsons, Albert R., 471, 495, 496
Patents, 53
Patriotic Society, Philadelphia, 39
Patrons of Husbandry, 475-76
Penn, William, 16
Pennsylvania Constitution, 1776, 39
Pettibone, George, 462
Phelps, A. W., 396, 401
Philadelphia, general strike in, 115-18; labor
party in, 127-29; strike of city employees
in, 117-18
Philadelphia Trades' Union, 112
Philadelphia Typographical Society, 81, 94n
Phillips, Wendell, 269, 270-71, 394, 425-26
Pinkertons, 460-64
Pittsburgh, 55
Poland Committee, 62

Political action, during American Revolution, 37-40; in ante-bellum South, 262-
63; attitude of Marxists towards, 449;
attitude of trade unions towards, 423-24;
during Civil War, 334-36, 357-59; in
Colonial America, 30-31; in 1840's and
1850's, 210-11, 213-17, 245-48; and National Labor Union, 372-73; relation of,
to trade unionism, 165-66
Population, growth of, 57
Powderly, Terence V., 437, 441, 484, 485,
506, 508, 509, 511
Price control, during American Revolution,
44
Producers Co-operatives. See Co-operatives,
producers
Proletarian League, New York, 231
Public schools. See Education

Quincy, Josiah, 28, 65-66

Radical Republicans, 391, 395
Railroads, corruption in construction of, 62;
hatred of, 465; trends towards monopoly
in, 61
Rantoul, Robert, Jr., 159, 164
Reconstruction, condition of Negroes during,
389-90, 402; labor's role during struggle
over, 391-95; National Labor Union's
stand on, 375
Republican Party, emergence of, 282-83;
German-American's role in, 289-90; in-
fluence of conservatives in, 288-89; labor
supports, 285-96; split in, 428-29; stand
on Reconstruction, 395
Revere, Paul, 34, 36, 40, 84
Revolution of 1830, France, 107
Revolution of 1848, France, influence of, on
American labor, 179; support for, in
America, 275
Revolutionary Socialistic party, 496
Right of Man to Property, 169
Rights of Man, 87
Ripley, George, 177, 178, 206
Rochdale Society, 418
Rogers, Professor Arnold T., quoted, 16
Rosecrans, William, 328, 332
Roy, Andrew, 458, 486
Ryckman, L. W., 206

Sanial, Lucien, 498-99
Savage, Chief Justice, 155, 156
Schilling, George, 471, 501
Schilling, Robert, 345, 477, 483
Schlegel, Edward, 373
Schouler, William, 194, 197
Schurz, Carl, 293, 389
Secession, labor opposes, 297-306

ⴢections, of International Workingmen's Association in America, 413-17
Sedition Act, 88-89
Seward, William H., 259, 291
Shaw, Lemuel, 163-64
Shoemakers' strike, New England, 241-45
Shorter hours. *See* Eight-hour day, Nine-hour day, Ten-hour day
Simpson, Stephen, 77-78, 126
Siney, John, 424, 428, 440-41, 455, 459, 485
Skidmore, Thomas, 130, 131, 134-35, 169
Slamm, Levi D., 130, 151
Slater, Samuel, 53, 65, 147
Slavery, effect of American Revolution on, 46; effect of, on white workers in South, 258-63; extension of, 276-77; northern labor and, 266-96; opposition of Southern white workers to, 263-65; origin of, 19-20; use of, in industry, 259-61, 261-63
Slave power, labor opposes, 247, 248; program of, 280-81; retards industrial growth, 51
Slave revolts, 255-58
Smith, Adam, 16, 23
Social-Democratic Party of North America, 449
Social Destiny of Man, 174
Socialists, and Chinese immigration, 489, 490-91; conflict among, 448-50; after crisis of 1873, 498-99; and draft riots, 324; split among, 495-96; in Union army, 308-10; unity movement among, 450-53. *See also* Communists, Marxists
Socialist Labor Party, 493-95, 498-99
Social Party, 414
Society for the Diffusion of Knowledge among the Working Classes, 115
Sons of Liberty, 34 *ff.*
Sons of Neptune, 34*n.*
Sorge, F. A., 367-368, 409, 413, 415, 416, 429, 435, 450, 452, 501, 502, 504
South, labor in ante-bellum, 249-65
Sovereigns of Industry, 475-76
Speculation, 44
Speyer, Carl, 503, 504
Stamp Act, 33
Stanton, Elizabeth Cady, 347, 385-86, 387
Stephens, Uriah Smith, 392, 433-37, 483, 508, 509, 511
Stevens, Thaddeus, 284
Steward, Ira, 345, 364-69, 380, 422-23, 426, 501, 502
Strasser, Adolph, 512, 513, 514, 515, 516, 517, 518
Strikes, during American Revolution, 45; in ante-bellum South, 249, 261; during Civil War, 327-29; in Colonial America, 27-28; during crisis of 1873, 454-60, 464-74; in

1830's, 108-10, 111, 115-18; in 1850's, 241-45, 249; for eight-hour day, 380-81; by International Labor Union, 503-04; first "all women," 102; first authentic one in America, 70; for higher wages, 221-22; Knights of Labor's attitude towards, 507-09; National Labor Union's stand on, 374-75; of Negro and white workers, 269, 397, 465-66, 472; of Negro workers, 397; by Negroes against slavery, 252-53; opposition to, 417; for ten-hour day, 102-03, 115-18, 207-09, 212-13; use of government to break, 328-29, 353-55, 466-74
Suffrage, in Colonial America, 28; liberalized, 90, 95-96; in post-revolutionary America, 82; woman's, 126
Sumner, Charles, 364
Supreme Court, decision on eight-hour law, 378
Sylvis, William H., 64, 236-37, 295, 304, 309, 310, 321, 331, 337, 345-48, 352, 357, 358, 360, 362, 371, 375, 376, 377, 378, 385, 386-87, 394-95, 396, 398-99, 410, 411, 412, 413, 417, 418, 419, 420, 423, 515-16

Tammany Hall, 151, 153, 154, 159, 165, 235, 448
Tariff, 285, 295
Tea Act, 33
Temporary labor associations, 69-70
Ten-hour day, in 1790's, 102; in 1820's and 1830's, 102-03, 115-18, 130, 160, 163; in 1840's and 1850's, 199-218; for government employees, 160, 163; philosophy of, 199-202; public support of, 117; strikes for, 104-05, 207-09, 212-13
Ten-hour laws, 210-11, 213-16
Ten-Hour Republican Association, 202-03
Texas, annexation of, labor's opposition to, 277-78
Thoreau, Henry David, 220
Tompkins Square, 239, 448, 513
Tories, labor and, 45 *ff.*
Touchstone, John, 299, 303
Townsend, Robert, Jr., 151
Trades' Assembly. *See* City Central labor unions
Transportation, effect of, on industry, 50, 52
Traveling cards, and early trade unions, 76
Trent affair, 314
Trenton, Workingmen's movement in, 216-17, 246-48
Trevellick, Richard F., 345, 376, 386, 396, 410, 411, 423, 428, 429, 431, 477, 483
Troup, Alexander C., 346, 406, 477
Tubman, Harriet, 254, 319
Turner, Nat, 255, 257

Underground railroad, 253-54
Unemployed demonstrations of, 161, 237-40, 445-48
Unemployment, during crisis of 1819-1822, 97-98; during crisis of 1837, 161, 167; during crisis of 1857, 237-40; during crisis of 1873, 439-48
Union army, role of Socialists in, 308-10
United German Trades, 498
United Labor Party, Pittsburgh, 480
United Workers of America, 450
Unskilled labor, in colonial America; during 1820's and 1830's, 99
Utica, workingmen's convention in, 157-58
Utopianism, era of, 167-90. *See also* Fourierism, Owenism, Co-operatives, Land Reform
Utopians, credo of, 170-72; and trade unions, 188-90, 205-07, 211-12

Van Buren, Martin, 158, 160, 161, 162, 163, 202
Van Patten, Phillip, 494-95, 499
Vesey, Denmark, 256

Wages, in early factories, 101; during 1820's and 1830's, 98-101; during 1850's, 219-20; during Civil War, 341; during crisis of 1873, 442; in England, 14-15; increase in, due to union activity, 118; labor's opposition to payment of, in bank notes, 125; in post-revolutionary America, 66-67, 77
Walsh, John F., 457, 459
War for Independence, effects of, on industry, 48; labor and, 43 *ff.*
War of 1812, effect on industry, 50; labor and, 93-95
Ware, Norman J., 193, 435
Washington, George, 44, 255
Weaver, Daniel, 228
Weaver, James Baird, 488, 495
Weitling, Wilhelm, 228-30, 264, 278
Weld, Thomas, 253
Westward movement, labor and, 187-88, 443-45
Weydemeyer, Joseph, 63, 190, 230-34, 279, 282, 290, 295, 310, 501
Weydemeyer, Otto, 368, 501
Whaley, J. C., 346, 375
Whig Party, attempts to win labor support, 163-64; formation of, 146

Whittier, John Greenleaf, 127, 155-56, 177
Wilkes, George, 413
Willich, August, 229, 310
Wilmot Proviso, 278-79
Wollstonecraft, Mary, 109
Woman's rights, 109, 382-88
Woman's suffrage, 126, 386-87
Women workers, in Colonial America, 26; conditions of, during 1820's and 1830's, 100-01; conditions of, during Civil War, 341, 382; in early factories, 66; and International Labor Union, 503-04; men's attitude towards, 100-01, 110-11, 204, 382-85; and National Labor Union, 374 *ff.*; in New England shoemaker's strike, 243-44; trade unions formed by, 108, 343-44, 383-84
Woodhill & Claflin's Weekly, 415
Woodhull, Victoria, 415-16
Working hours, in 1820's and 1830's, 98-101, 118; in 1840's and 1850's, 195, 215-16, 217-18
Working Man's Advocate, 121, 133-34, 141-42, 351
Workingmen's Association, England, 267
Workingmen's Benevolent Association, Schuylkill County, 381
Workingmen's Convention, New York, 138-39, 157-58
Workingmen's Council of the United States, 378
Workingmen's Democratic-Republican Association, 335-36
"Working Men's Measures," 123-27, 141
Workingmen's Party of California, 490-92
Working Men's Party, New York, 130-39
Workingmen's Party of the United States, 452-53, 469-73, 477-78, 487-88
Working Men's Protective Union, 181-83
Workingmen's Union, Trenton, 246-48
Workingmen's United Political Association, New York, 336
Working Women's Protective Union, 342-43
Wright, Carrol D., 100
Wright, Frances, 129, 130, 131-32, 136-38, 162, 267
Wright, James L., 433

Yellow dog contract, 101
Young America, 186

Zenger, John Peter, 30